What makes *AM GOV* special?
Scholarship + Pedagogy = M-Series

AM GOV offers instructors unmatched scholarship, content, and currency in a succinct magazine format that engages students.

McGraw-Hill Higher Education and Blackboard have teamed up. What does this mean for you?

1. Your life, simplified. Now you and your students can access McGraw-Hill's Connect™ and Create™ right from within your Blackboard course—all with one single sign-on. Say goodbye to the days of logging in to multiple applications.

2. Deep integration of content and tools. Not only do you get single sign-on with Connect™ and Create™, you also get deep integration of McGraw-Hill content and content engines right in Blackboard. Whether you're choosing a book for your course or building Connect™ assignments, all the tools you need are right where you want them—inside Blackboard.

3. Seamless gradebooks. Are you tired of keeping multiple gradebooks and manually synchronizing grades into Blackboard? We thought so. When a student completes an integrated Connect™ assignment, the grade for that assignment automatically (and instantly) feeds your Blackboard grade center.

4. A solution for everyone. Whether your institution is already using Blackboard or you just want to try Blackboard on your own, we have a solution for you. McGraw-Hill and Blackboard can now offer you easy access to industry leading technology and content, whether your campus hosts it, or we do. Be sure to ask your local McGraw-Hill representative for details.

Connect™ was made for you. Connect™ is an interactive course platform that was designed to help you study smarter and more efficiently outside of the classroom. With an adaptive learning tool that tells you what you don't know and helps guide you through studying that content, Connect™ can help your performance jump by a grade or more!

AM GOV 2012

VICE PRESIDENT, EDITORIAL **Michael Ryan**

PUBLISHER **Mike Sugarman**

SPONSORING EDITOR **Meredith Grant**

MARKETING MANAGER **Patrick Brown**

DIRECTOR OF DEVELOPMENT **Dawn Groundwater**

DEVELOPMENT EDITOR **Naomi Friedman**

EDITORIAL COORDINATOR **Nikki Weissman**

EDITING, DESIGN, AND PRODUCTION MANAGER **Melissa Williams**

COVER AND JACKET DESIGN **Jeanne M. Schreiber**

INTERIOR DESIGN **Pam Verros and Hassan Herz**

ART MANAGER **Robin Mouat**

ILLUSTRATION **Robin Mouat, Rennie Evans, John & Judy Waller, Ayelet Arbel**

PHOTO RESEARCH **Susan Friedman**

BUYER **Tandra Jorgensen**

MEDIA PROJECT MANAGER **Andrea Helmbolt**

SUPPLEMENTS **Southern Editorial**

COMPOSITION **TBH Typecast, Inc.**

PRINTING **Quad/Graphics**

AM GOV 2012

Published by McGraw-Hill, an imprint of The McGraw-Hill Companies, Inc., 1221 Avenue of the Americas, New York, NY 10020. Copyright © 2012 by the McGraw-Hill Companies, Inc. All rights reserved. No part of this publication may be reproduced or distributed in any form or by any means, or stored in a database or retrieval system, without the prior written consent of The McGraw-Hill Companies, Inc., including, but not limited to, in any network or other electronic storage or transmission, or broadcast for distance learning.

This book is printed on acid-free paper.

Printed in the United States of America.

1 2 3 4 5 6 7 8 9 0 QDB/QDB 0 9 8 7 6 5 4 3 2 1

ISBN 978-0-07-7352637-9

MHID 0-07-7352637-1

Front Cover Photo: © The McGraw-Hill Companies   Back cover photo: © Getty Images.

Library of Congress Control Number: 2011586441

AM GOV

BRIEF CONTENTS

What's Inside AM GOV? . . . YOU ARE

YOU STARTED AM GOV. You convinced us that there had to be a better way to get across the fundamental concepts of American democracy and what it means to be an American citizen.

Students showed us they wanted more portable texts with innovative visual appeal, interactive pedagogy, an integrated approach, and relevant content designed according to the way they learn. Instructors told us they wanted a way to engage their students without compromising on high quality content.

Ralph Baker and Joseph Losco,
Ball State University

WE LISTENED

We also did our homework. McGraw-Hill conducted in-depth ethnographic research of student learning to explore what makes their reading and learning experience more engaging, memorable, effective, lasting, and enjoyable. We then interviewed instructors to identify their biggest challenges and how a completely different kind of text could serve as a solution to those challenges.

AM GOV is new, but our approach is simple. Our approach in AM GOV marries our commitment to scholarly content with the value that currency, presentation, and reasonable price have for students. We update AM GOV every year to keep the course vital and relevant. We gave AM GOV this visually rich design because our research taught us that, in our visual culture, it makes student learning excel and American government memorable.

Our goal in AM GOV is to engage students in the story of people's relationship to government and how an active and informed citizenry is essential in making democracy meaningful. We want students to recognize how their choices about government affect their lives.

With the election of a new president, we have an opportunity for American government to take on new meaning for a new generation. More current, more portable, more captivating, plus a rigorous and innovative research foundation adds up to: more learning. When you meet students where they are, you can take them where you want them to be.

We listened . . . to you. We learned . . . from you. We created . . . for you.

CONTENTS

12 THE PRESIDENCY: POWER AND PARADOX 297

Risky Business

13 BUREAUCRACY: CITIZENS AS OWNERS AND CONSUMERS 329

Student Loans, Debt, and Bureaucracy

15 PUBLIC POLICY: RESPONDING TO CITIZENS 377

Tales from Two Cities

NEW! The Race for 2012

Analyze issues behind the 2012 presidential and Congressional campaigns.

Global Perspectives

Compare the United States to other nations by interpreting charts and graphs.

global Perspectives
An International View of Political Advertising

In an international political campaign comparison, two scholars found that the United States stands out both with its complete openness toward political advertising and the great importance that campaigns attach to political ads. Many countries do not allow candidates to purchase broadcasting time for campaign messages. In Switzerland, for instance, political advertising on television is prohibited during election time. Denmark has no official bans on such advertising but political actors have agreed not to use them for their campaigns.

Some countries allow political candidates or political parties to purchase broadcasting time for campaign messages.

Some countries allow free time on public and/or commercial TV. Some countries allow both free and paid advertisement.

1. The map below shows how several countries compare. Where do most countries stand on this issue?
2. How does the United States compare to other countries?
3. What benefits do citizens gain when political candidates or parties are allowed free air time on public and/or private television?

Sources: Christina Holtz-Bacha and Lynda Lee Kaid, *The SAGE Handbook of Political Advertising* (Thousand Oaks, CA: SAGE Publications, 2006) 10.

No free time
Austria, Bulgaria, Estonia, Finland, Japan, Mexico, South Korea, Switzerland, United States

Free time on public TV
Argentina, Australia, Belgium, Czech Republic, France, Germany, Greece, Latvia, Lithuania, Netherlands, Poland, Russia, Spain

Free time on commercial TV
Italy, United Kingdom

Free time on both public and commercial TV
Brazil, Canada, Chile, Israel, Portugal

RACE FOR 2012 ★★★★★★★★★★★★★★★★★★★★★★★

THE NETWORKED CAMPAIGN

Among the advantages Barack Obama enjoyed during the 2008 presidential campaign was a sophisticated social-networking strategy, an energetic army of foot soldiers, and a trove of more than 10 million e-mail addresses of supporters to whom he could return over and over again for financial contributions. Four years later, Republicans are matching him on every count.

Whereas Republicans were trailing in the use of social media four years ago, today they enjoy the same sophistication as their Democratic counterparts. The 2010 midterm elections proved that no one party has a lock on the use of new technology. "The notion that the Internet was owned by liberals, owned by the left in the wake of the Obama victory, has been proven false," Patrick Ruffini, a Republican political strategist, told *The Washington Post.*[*]

Today, Republican candidates and elected officials are as likely to utilize all the tools of social networking as Democrats are. Republican voters matched Democrats in their use of these tools in the 2010 campaign, with 40 percent of Republican online users turning to social media to get politically involved in a campaign, compared to 38 percent of Democratic voters. "Tea Party supporters were espe-

cially likely to use social media to connect with a political group or candidate."[†] And the Democratic edge in online fundraising is quickly disappearing as well. It did not take long for Sarah Palin's Political Action Committee fundraising site to attract 2.9 million fans.

Social networking sites present candidates with an abundance of useful information that can help them market their messages more effectively through a process known as microtargeting. E-mail addresses can be cross-referenced with consumer data to discover voter patterns and habits. This allows the candidates to target their messages to narrow audiences, for example, upscale beer drinkers who drive hybrid vehicles. It also allows them to respond to supporters almost immediately and on a time frame suited to the recipient. For example, if the voter checks his or her e-mail each day at 11 p.m., that is precisely when the candidate's daily message arrives—along with a donation request. Future campaign successes, therefore, will hinge in part on how effectively candidates build and utilize online social networks.

[*] Jennifer Preston, "Republicans Sharpening Online Tools for 2012," *The New York Times,* April 20, 2011, p. A13.

[†] Aaron Smith, "Twenty-two percent of online Americans used social networking or Twitter for politics in 2010 campaign," Pew Research Center, Jan. 27, 2011. Accessed on June 2, 2011 at http://www.pewinternet.org/~/media/Files/Reports/2011/PIP-Social-Media-and-2010-Election.pdf.

Political Social Networking Activities by 2010 Vote

2010 Congressional Vote	Rep %	Dem %	Did Not Vote %
Use a social networking site	43	44	49
Percent of SNS users who used the sites to...			
Discover which candidates your friends voted for	19	21	14
Post political content	18	16	9
Get candidate or campaign info	19	15	13
Friend a candidate or cause	17	12	8
Join a political group/cause	13	11	7
Start a new political group/cause	3	3	1

Source: The Pew Research Center's Internet & American Life Project, November 3–24, 2010 Post-Election Tracking Survey.

Voters' Use of Social Networking Sites

■ Obama/Democratic voters
■ McCain/Republican voters

	2008	2010
Obama/Democratic voters	44	58
McCain/Republican voters	29	54

Source: The Pew Research Center's Internet & American Life Project, November 3–24, 2010 Post-Election Tracking Survey, N=2,257 national adults ages 18 and older including 755 cell phone interviews were conducted in English and Spanish.

PORTRAIT
OF AN ACTIVIST

Meet Molly Kawahata

On a cold November night in 2008, Molly Kawahata took to the streets of Berkeley, California with thousands of other students. "It was the moment," she recalls, "when chills shuddered my spine and tears filled my eyes.'" It was the moment Barack Obama was declared the winner of the presidential campaign.

The moment came almost two years after Molly signed on as the National High School Director of Students for Barack Obama, helping to recruit a field army of young organizers that mobilized more than 100,000 students across the country. "Students originated the campaign model, developed the communications

strategy, created the field plans, trained the organizers, ran the schedules, and tracked the numbers," she recalls. "The Students for Barack Obama campaign started and remained in student hands. In our job, we were given one vague instruction and not much more: to create a movement and see what we could do with it."

Four years later, Molly is back on the Berkeley campus completing her psychology degree after a stint at the White House. She surveys a landscape that has changed. Many young people who were politically engaged and optimistic four years ago are facing a dismal economic climate and bitter partisan bickering.

Still, she is optimistic. "There have been a lot of accomplishments—the repeal of Don't ask don't tell, student loan reform, health insurance reform—but we still have work to do. Many young people became politically involved for the first time in the 2008 Obama campaign and have remained involved in their communities since. It will be important for us to unify behind the patriotic values that we did in the 2008 election: those of empathy, empowerment, and community."

[*] Pers. Comm.

Portrait of an Activist

Discover how citizens from all walks of life contribute to American politics through new portraits.

1

CITIZENS

MILLENNIALS RISING ❙ On the evening of May 1, 2011, thousands, most of them young adults, gathered outside the White House in Washington, D.C., near ground zero in New York, and on college campuses. Many of them had heard about the "spontaneous" gatherings via Facebook or from the barrage of Tweets that circulated at a rate of over 6,000 per second. Students from nearby colleges came to the White House by Metro or walked; others drove their cars past the revelers with their stereos blaring Bruce Springsteen's "Born in the U.S.A." and Miley Cyrus's "Party in the U.S.A."[1] At the New York site, two people standing above the crowd held a large American flag as onlookers sang "God Bless America." At Ohio State, students jumped into the water at Mirror Lake on campus, a practice ordinarily reserved for home games against University of Michigan.[2]

The occasion was the announcement that the United States had killed Osama bin Laden, the mastermind of the 9/11 attacks, who had eluded capture for nearly a decade. Few of the young people believed this would mean an end to terrorism and some questioned the cause for celebration. Brianna Musselman, a student at American University, asked: "What are we celebrating? This isn't the end of terrorism. A person is dead." But Scott Talan, a professor at AU, more nearly captured the spirit of the evening as he puffed on his cigar: "It's really just nice for the United States to accomplish something we've been trying to do," he said. "It brings closure, and a lot of people needed closure."[3]

Most of those who gathered that night had been given little to celebrate in recent years. Theirs was a generation, dubbed the ●◇

SHIP IN OUR CHANGING DEMOCRACY

As You READ >>

- What kinds of citizen involvement fuel democracies?
- What ideals fuel American democracy?
- What are some of the changes and challenges facing America today?

Millennials, who had grown up in the aftermath of the 9/11 attacks. They had not known a time before boarding a plane meant walking through security and partially disrobing. They or their friends had gone off to fight one or two wars. And their reward when they graduate is an uncertain job market in an economy struggling to rise out of the doldrums.

Yet Millennials, young people born in the 1980s and 1990s who are attending or about to attend college, are less cynical, more civic-minded, and politically more engaged than their immediate predecessors in Generation X. More ethnically and racially diverse than previous college generations, they are more tolerant of different lifestyles, more technologically connected, more supportive of equal opportunities for all, and less likely to support military solutions to international problems than their elders. They are also more likely to express their political views by their choices in the marketplace; one-third have expressly used their buying power to reward or punish companies for social policies.[4]

In 2008, an estimated 23 million young people between the ages of 18 and 29 showed up to vote on Election Day. Overall, turnout among all young people rose to approximately 52 percent, the second highest participation rate since 18-year-olds first received the right to the vote in 1972.[5] This is a generation that can make a huge difference in influencing the direction of our political system. By the presidential election of 2016, Millennials will make up nearly 30 percent of all voters.[6] They are optimistic about their own futures and the future of the nation, confident in their abilities to achieve personal goals like raising a family, and engaged with their communities. Nearly 6 in 10 said they had volunteered in the past 12 months.[7]

Still, the long war on terror and the Great Recession have taken a toll. The unemployment rate for young adults between 18 and 29 surged to a record high. Enthusiasm for politics has cooled, and about half of young adults say that President Obama has failed to bring the change he promised to Washington. Political participation has also taken a nose dive. In the 2010 midterm elections, only about 23 percent of young people ages 18 to 29 showed up at the polls. And the number of young people becoming electorally engaged for the first time sank, from 43 percent in 2008 to just 15 percent in 2010.[8]

In a **democracy,** where people rule either directly or through elected leaders, **citizenship** is a two-sided coin: it confers rights and protections on members of the political community, but in return it requires allegiance and involvement. Each of us must weigh the

More than a third of young people between the ages of 18 and 29 reported being unemployed during the recent recession. Those with the least education were hardest hit.

costs and benefits of participation. The benefits may be policies we support; the costs involve our time and attention. Often, involvement will only be achieved with the active encouragement of others.

As you will see throughout this book, citizenship today is in a precarious state. For much of the past half century, the involvement of citizens in their communities has dwindled, voter turnout has remained well below that of other advanced democracies, and the level of trust between citizens and elected national leaders has reached its lowest point in almost forty years.[9] We believe that citizenship today is at a crossroads: we can build on recent gains in voter interest and reconstruct the reciprocal bonds of trust between citizen and government, or we can watch these bonds continue to fray. We can either begin finding solutions to the pressing problems that endanger our future or watch these problems continue to worsen. There are some signs that young people are ready to open a dialogue about how to construct a more vibrant democracy that works for all citizens. That is the central hope of this book. ◆

POLITICS, POWER, AND PARTICIPATION

Politics is the process by which we choose government officials and make decisions about public policy. In a democracy, citizens play a primary role in this process, but it is a role they must choose to play. Americans are not forced to leave the pleasures and obligations of private life to engage in political or community service. Yet, the vitality of our social and political institutions depends on our willingness as citizens to step outside of our private lives and to work with others voluntarily in making our neighborhoods safe, our communities strong, and our government work effectively for all. It depends on our readiness to join the collective or **civic life** of the community.

Civic life includes institutions of **government**—the body or bodies charged with making official policies for its citizens. But it also includes **civil society**, which refers to the broad array of voluntary associations that bring citizens together to deal with community and social issues of common concern. These organizations might include the Key Club, which conducts community service activities, or your campus environmental club that promotes recycling. Voluntary associations build what is called **social capital**, bonds of trust and reciprocity between citizens that form the glue holding societies together. Citizens participate in government by acts like voting, attending political meet-

ings, and campaigning for candidates they support for office. They participate in the actions of civil society when they volunteer or contribute to a good cause.

If associations build social capital and give rise to civic and political involvement, then is it better to have more voluntary associations? Some social scientists regard the number and kind of voluntary associations sustained in society as a sign of a nation's well-being.[10] That is why some of them, like Harvard's Robert Putnam, worry about what they see as a decline in civic activities ranging from attendance at school board meetings to meeting with one's neighbors. Critics have challenged Putnam's findings, noting that participation in new forms of civic activity like soccer leagues has replaced older associations and that young people have turned to electronic networking rather than face-to-face encounters in building social capital.[11]

Even if we were to agree that social capital and membership in the kind and number of voluntary associations that help create and sustain it has declined, does it matter? The simple answer is—it depends. It depends on how one envisions a citizen's relationship to government. Democratic governments extol the virtues of citizen participation and depend on citizen involvement as a source of legitimacy. Your authors believe there is ample reason for optimism about the future of civic life in America; but, as we will see, civic

democracy Form of government in which the people rule either directly or through elected leaders.

citizenship Status conferring rights and protections to members of the political community but, in return, requiring allegiance and involvement.

politics The process by which we choose government officials and make decisions about public policy.

civic life Participation in the collective life of the community.

government The body (or bodies) charged with making official policies for citizens.

civil society The broad array of voluntary associations that bring citizens together to deal with community and social issues of common concern.

social capital Bonds of trust and reciprocity between citizens that form the glue that holds modern societies together.

Citizen Activities in a Democratic Society

PRIVATE LIFE	CIVIC LIFE	
Individual activity	**Civic engagement activities**	
	Nonpolitical activities	Political participation
Family School Work	Recycling Fellowship meetings Service activities	Voting Attending political meetings Political campaigning
Cultivates personal relationships, serves individual needs—e.g., getting an education, earning a living	Provides community services and acts as a training ground for political participation	Fulfills demands of democratic citizenship

(Functions)

direct democracy Form of government in which decisions about public policy extend to the entire citizenry.

representative democracy Form of government in which popular decision making is restricted to electing or appointing the public officials who make public policy.

majority rule The requirement that electoral majorities determine who is elected to office and that majorities in power determine our laws and how they are administered.

minority rights Protections beyond the reach of majority control guaranteed to all citizens.

political power The ability to get things done by controlling or influencing the institutions of government.

involvement is not evenly spread across the entire population. This has serious consequences for ensuring an equal voice for all citizens. There is vast room for improvement, and we will highlight some promising avenues in the chapters that follow.

Types of Government

Governments may take a variety of forms, but a key distinction between them is how widely power is shared among the citizens. In a monarchy or dictatorship, a single person exercises absolute power. By contrast, in a **direct democracy**, political decision making extends to the entire citizenry. Some ancient Greek city-states, for example, made decisions about the use of power in open-air assemblies involving thousands of citizens. Only free males, however, were counted as citizens. Few modern nations employ direct democracy; most free nations prefer instead to restrict popular decision making to electing or appointing officials who make public policy. This type of government is properly called a **representative democracy**. Citizens in a representative democracy hold public officials accountable through periodic elections and the rule of law. America's representative democracy is characterized by **majority rule** and protections for **minority rights**. Electoral majorities determine who is elected to office, and majorities in power determine our laws and how they are administered. However, certain rights, like freedom of speech and religion, are beyond the reach of majority control. We will discuss these features of our political system in more detail in Chapter 2.

The right of the president and Congress to wage war, as they did after the attacks of 9/11, is explicitly granted in the U.S. Constitution.

Political Power

The legitimate use of force and political power by a representative government rests upon either explicit contracts establishing the relationship between governors and the governed—such as the U.S. Constitution—or upon certain shared values and standards that citizens have come to accept over time. Although citizens may not agree with specific government policies, they will support as legitimate, or lawful, policies founded upon accepted contracts and standards. For example, many Americans opposed the U.S. invasion of Iraq following the terrorist attacks of September 11, 2001, but few disputed the right of the president and Congress to wage war.

Even in democratic societies, questions frequently arise about who exercises real **political power** by influencing or controlling the institutions of government. One school of thought, the **ruling elite theory**, argues that wealthy and well-educated citizens exercise a disproportionate amount of influence over political decision making, despite the existence of institutions that encourage widespread participation. These individuals are more likely to have access to government officials or to become government officials themselves. They are also more informed about political issues and more interested in the outcome of these issues. The wealthy have a vested interest, for example, in reducing the amount of taxes they pay and creating favorable political and economic conditions for their investments. Some versions of ruling elite theory, however, suggest that elites actually are an important force for social advancement.[12] Empirical studies demonstrate that wealthier and better-educated citizens show a greater commitment to values such as fair play, diversity, and respect for civil liberties than those with less income or education. They are also more alert to threats to basic democratic values and more likely to insist on enforcement of individual rights.

A competing theory called **pluralism** asserts that various groups and coalitions constantly vie for government favor and the ability to exercise political power, but none enjoys long-term dominance.[13] In this view, groups that get their way today may be on the losing end tomorrow.

For example, supporters of school vouchers for private

During the recent economic downturn, many Americans didn't support providing government assistance to failed institutions, but political and financial leaders prevailed.

religious schools may be successful in securing funding for their cause from the legislature one day, only to see the courts invalidate the measure tomorrow, as happened in 2006 when the Florida Supreme Court struck down the state's voucher program. In order to maximize their chances of success, like-minded citizens organize into interest groups that employ a wide array of tactics from supporting candidates who promise to advance their cause to developing sophisticated public relations campaigns to rally support (see Chapter 8). As long as the rules guiding interest group competition are fair and fairly enforced, no one group will dominate political decision making.

In practice, modern American government is characterized by elements of each of these theories. Elite dominance tends to prevail in decisions about foreign policy and high finance.[14] For example, during the recent economic downturn, many Americans favored a policy of letting troubled financial institutions fail. However, political and financial leaders prevailed in winning support for government assistance to these institutions, arguing that many of them were too big to fail. Pluralistic group competition, on the other hand, is more evident in matters of personal choice such as abortion. Both supporters and opponents of legalized abortion, for instance, have had notable successes in advancing their agendas in the political arena. In this book, we are most concerned about increasing participation in ways that bring us closer to achieving genuinely pluralistic outcomes. Some sectors of the American population already participate at very high levels and can be sure their voices are heard, if not always heeded. Others are barely heard at all; we will identify ways throughout the book to increase their volume.

Interest groups support politicians who they believe will advance their cause.

Participation and Democracy

Active citizens who are willing to take part in government by voicing their opinions, running for elective office, and voting have always been essential to the success of democracy. The Greek philosopher Aristotle (384–322 B.C.E.) felt that citizens should not simply sit back and enjoy the benefits of society; they must also take responsibility for its operation. Modern thinkers have generally concurred. British philosopher John Locke (1632–1704) argued that the power of the government comes from the consent of its citizens and that consent is only possible when the citizenry is informed and engaged. Political theorist John Stuart Mill (1806–1873)

ruling elite theory View positing that wealthy and well-educated citizens exercise a disproportionate amount of influence over political decision making.

pluralism View positing that various groups and coalitions constantly vie for government favor and the ability to exercise political power but none enjoys long-term dominance.

Declining Social Trust Around the World—Is This the Beginning of a New Generation of Critical Citizens?

Many factors influence the bonds of trust between citizens and governments that are vital for effective governance. The chart on the right tracks levels of trust reported by college-educated adults ages 25 to 64 in the ten nations with the largest economies.

Both Europe and America seem to have experienced "a flight from politics, or what the Germans call *Politikverdrossenheit*: a weakness about its debates, disbelief about its claims, skepticism about its results, cynicism about its practitioners."[1] Political scientist Pippa Norris believes widespread cynicism about government signals the emergence of a new type of "critical citizen, dissatisfied democrats who adhere strongly to democratic values but who find existing structures of representative government invented in the eighteenth and nineteenth centuries to be wanting. . . ."[2] But these younger, well-educated citizens are not apathetic; they are more responsive to nontraditional means of participation like demonstrations or product boycotts than more traditional methods like voting since these alternate approaches promote a greater sense of social solidarity.

Questions:

1. How do levels of public confidence among European and American citizens compare to levels among some emerging nations with growing economies?
2. Does the graph support Pippa Norris's arguments? Why or why not?
3. What factors do you believe influence declining trust in government?

[1] Pippa Norris, "Introduction: The Growth of Critical Citizens?" in Pippa Norris, ed., *Critical Citizens: Global Support for Democratic Government* (New York: Oxford University Press, 1999), p. 6. See also Ronald Inglehart, *Modernization and Postmodernization: Cultural, Economic, and Political Change in 43 Societies* (Princeton, N.J.: Princeton University Press, 1997).
[2] Norris, p. 27.

Trust in National Governments
How much do you trust government to do what is right?*

	2011	2010	Change in net ratings
China	88	74	14%
Brazil	85	39	46%
Japan	51	42	9%
France	49	43	6%
Italy	45	36	9%
India	44	43	1%
United Kingdom	43	38	5%
USA	40	46	−6%
Russia	39	38	1%
Germany	33	43	−10%

0

Percentage change

Responses 6–9 on 1–9 scale; 9=highest

Source: 2011 Edelman Trust Barometer. 2011 Annual Global Opinion Leaders Study, Accessed on April 9, 2011 at http://www.edelman.com/trust/2011/.

initiative Procedure that enables citizens to place proposals for laws and amendments directly on the ballot for voter approval.

popular referendum A device that allows citizens to approve or repeal measures already acted on by legislative bodies.

believed that even when citizens are content with their government, active participation is necessary to ensure that principles like liberty and free speech don't fade from lack of use. Thomas Jefferson (1743–1826), in his more radical moments, called for periodic citizen uprisings to reinvigorate the spirit of democracy. Much of American history confirms the importance of citizen participation. Throughout our nation's history, many Americans fought long and hard to gain the oppor-

tunity to participate in democratic practices that were previously closed to them.

Many states provide expanded opportunities for citizen participation. **Initiative**, available in twenty-four states, enables citizens to draft laws and constitutional amendments for voter approval if the sponsors of the measure gather enough signatures. Similarly, twenty-four states allow for **popular referendum**, which allows citizens to approve or repeal measures already acted upon by legislative bodies. **Legislative referendum** is another form of referendum, available in all fifty states, that requires legislative bodies to secure voter approval for some measures such as changes to a state's constitution. Finally, eighteen states

permit **recall,** in which citizens can remove and replace a public official before the end of a term. Arnold Schwarzenegger was first catapulted into the governor's mansion in California as a result of the recall of former Democratic governor, Gray Davis.

A free society relies heavily upon the voluntary activities of free individuals outside of government as well. Our nation accomplishes many of its social needs through the work of charitable organizations, religious congregations, and professional groups. Thousands of charities and foundations provide money and personnel for programs ranging from support for the arts to sheltering the homeless. Volunteers power these organizations by devoting their time and energy to improve the quality of life in our communities. As we will see, these organizations also serve as training grounds for developing the skills we need to become full and active participants in our nation's political system. Government can encourage civic voluntarism by establishing networks of volunteers like AmeriCorps, the nation's domestic community service program, which recently received increased funding from the Obama administration. Though such programs have typically received strong bipartisan support, some believe that providing government incentives for volunteering diminishes the genuine spirit of giving. Whether or not volunteer activities are sponsored by government, free democratic societies depend on the readiness of individuals to take the time to get involved. They rely on the leadership skills of citizens to help find acceptable solutions to common problems. They also require adopting a set of principles or ideals that extol the worth and contributions of citizens.

John Locke (1632–1704) argued that the power of the government comes from the consent of its citizens.

AMERICAN POLITICAL IDEALS

Ideas, values, and beliefs about how governments should operate are known as **ideologies**. **Liberal democracy**, the ideology that guided the American experience, reveres individual rights and expresses faith in popular control of government. It rests upon three essential notions: natural rights, the formation of a social contract by consent of the governed, and majority rule. Its most influential advocate was John Locke. A physician by training, Locke became involved in the politics of Whig radicals who challenged the authority of the British Stuart monarchy in the late seventeenth century. These radicals, who favored placing more power into the hands of an elected Parliament, succeeded in pulling off a bloodless revolution in 1688.

Locke speculates that humans at one time probably had little need for authority because there was little competition for resources. Resources were plentiful, and most individuals found ways to avoid conflict. Each individual, to the extent possible, guarded his or her own life, liberty, and property to which he had a God-granted natural right. Over time, however, populations grew, creating competition for diminishing resources. Conflicts over ownership of property led to the need for a neutral arbiter to settle disputes peacefully. That arbiter was government. Locke believed that free and equal persons willingly entered into social contracts to establish governments in order to avoid the "incommodities" of war and conflict with others. On our own, we have a limited capacity to protect our life, liberty, and property. If we band together in government, we come to each other's aid in the protection of these natural rights.

In his *Second Treatise of Government,* Locke articulated the underlying philosophy of liberal

Hot or Not?

Should the government be in the business of promoting civic engagement and political participation?

legislative referendum Ballot measure aimed at securing voter approval for some legislative acts, such as changes to a state's constitution.

recall Procedure whereby citizens can remove and replace a public official before the end of a term.

ideology Ideas, values, and beliefs about how governments should operate.

liberal democracy Ideology stressing individual rights and expressing faith in popular control of government.

democracy.[15] He argued that humans are born naturally free and equal; no one is born subject to another's will, and no one can control another without that person's consent. People place themselves under the control of a government because of the mutual advantages it offers its citizens. Under such an arrangement, majority rule provides a reasonable basis for making decisions. In this way, each member of the community has an equal voice in decision making, and decisions reflect the consensus of most citizens. Governments, however, derive authority from the consent of those who form them, and they hold our allegiance only if they protect our life, liberty, and property better than we could on our own. If government becomes a threat to citizens' rights, the social contract fails, and the people have the option of dissolving it and beginning anew.

political participation Taking part in activities like voting or running for office aimed at influencing the policies or leadership of government.

The authors of our Declaration of Independence drew heavily on the ideas of Locke in drafting that document and making the case for independence from British rule. Ideas alone, however, do not make history; they must be advanced by proponents with the skills and determination to see them achieved. American history offers many examples of individuals who worked tirelessly to expand opportunities for **political participation** to an increasingly diverse citizenry.

is over three hundred million, drawn from all corners of the world. Hispanic Americans are the nation's fastest-growing minority group, now making up over 13 percent of the population. African Americans are a close second at about 12 percent, and Asian Americans represent about 4 percent of the population. Despite the progress these groups have made in securing civil rights, many are still not well integrated into American civic life.

The U.S. Census Bureau estimates that minorities from all backgrounds, now roughly one-third of the U.S. population, are expected to become the majority in 2042. Combined minority population in Texas, California, Hawaii, and New Mexico already exceeds the white non-Hispanic population in these states.

Fifty years ago, just over a third of all Americans lived in the suburbs; today that figure is about 55 percent. Suburbs, however, tend to be lacking in political and ethnic diversity. As the *Report of the American Political Science Association's Standing Committee on Civic Education and Engagement* emphasized in 2004, "Across the patchwork of suburban jurisdictions, individual suburbs are likely to be characterized not by integration and diversity, but by residential segregation and homogeneity."[16]

The data presented in the chart below support this finding. Whites, Hispanic Americans, and African Americans tend to live predominantly among members of their own

THE CHANGING FACE OF THE AMERICAN CITIZENRY

As we seek ways to increase the engagement of today's citizens, we must be aware that our citizenry is rapidly becoming older and more diverse. At the same time, the gap between those with substantial resources and those with few is increasing. Forces of globalization are intensifying these divisions.

Growing Diversity

When the U.S. Constitution was ratified at the end of the eighteenth century, more than four million white Europeans and their descendants lived in the United States. (This figure does not include Native Americans, as estimates of their total population during this period vary greatly; nor does it include over a half million black slaves and an estimated sixty thousand free blacks.) Today the U.S. population

The People in Your Neighborhood Most Likely Look Like You

Composition of Neighborhoods by Racial and Ethnic Groups June 6–25, 2005			
	% of non-Hispanic whites who say there are "many" of each group in area	% of blacks who say there are "many" of each group in area	% of Hispanics who say there are "many" of each group in area
Whites	86%	45%	52%
Blacks	28%	66%	32%
Hispanics	32%	26%	61%
Asians	12%	6%	13%
Recent immigrants	14%	18%	30%

Source: *Who Are the People in Your Neighborhood?* Gallup Organization, July 12, 2005.

racial and ethnic groups. This type of segregation breeds distrust, particularly at the local level. It also breeds a lack of cooperation in addressing social problems.

The past few decades have also witnessed a greater openness about sexual preferences that has produced a more politically active gay and lesbian community. In recent years, same-sex partners have pressed for the same rights as those afforded married couples. Same-sex marriages are now legal in several states in the Northeast as well as in Iowa. Still, many states have constitutional amendments that prohibit same-sex marriages, and the federal government officially recognizes marriage as the union between a man and a woman. The battle by gays for the right to the same protections as married couples is likely to continue in a nation increasingly polarized over the role of government in personal choice. In general, young Americans are more accepting of racial, ethnic, and gender differences than are their elders.[17]

Growing Older

The elderly population is expected to double by 2050, when one in five Americans will be over age sixty-five (see "The Graying of America"). The aging of the population poses some special problems. The Social Security and Medicare Boards of Trustees project substantial shortfalls for Social Security and Medicare as fewer able-bodied working-age adults work to support the needs of the growing number of elderly Americans. How will we meet this growing need for financial support and medical services? No doubt the elderly, who vote in much higher numbers than young people, will exert political pressure to keep or even increase their benefits. How will the younger generation respond? Given the enormity of the coming elder boom, will young people still be willing to support generous government programs that provide for the needs of elderly Americans?

Growing Apart

When the U.S. Constitution was written, **social class** divisions among Americans were much more visible than they are today. They manifested themselves through distinctions in dress, social stature, and political power. For example, while workmen wore functional clothing of washable unbleached linen, gentlemen regularly sported wool coats and jackets, donning powdered wigs on special occasions. More than two centuries later, class divisions are not so ob-

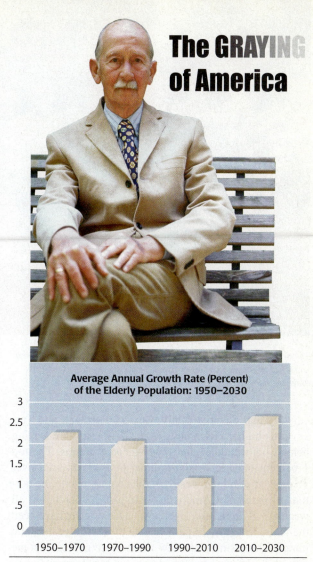

The GRAYING of America

Average Annual Growth Rate (Percent) of the Elderly Population: 1950–2030

3
2.5
2
1.5
1
.5
0

1950–1970   1970–1990   1990–2010   2010–2030

Source: U.S. Census Bureau.

vious. According to a recent inquiry into class in America, "Today the country has gone a long way toward an appearance of classlessness. . . . Americans of all sorts are awash in luxuries that would have dazzled their grandparents. Social diversity has erased many of the old markers."[18]

In a world where even the wealthy wear jeans and sweat suits, it is increasingly difficult to tell someone's status by looking at his or her clothes. During the boom years at the beginning of this century, easily available credit and the flattening of prices for technology gave many Americans access to high-end consumer items. In 2009, there were an estimated 276 million cell phone users in the United States, over 55 times the number of users in 1990. Even the vacation cruise business now caters to people of moderate income.

Yet, the gap between rich and poor is growing. According to the Organisation for Economic Cooperation and Development, the United States ranks fourth among the organization's thirty member nations in income in-

social class The perceived combination of wealth, income, education, and occupation that contribute to one's status and power in society.

The availability of cheap labor in some foreign countries has prompted many employers to transfer jobs overseas, resulting in fewer job opportunities for American workers.

equality and poverty. (Only Mexico, Portugal, and Turkey rank higher.) Rich households in America are leaving behind both middle- and lower-income groups. The top 1 percent of U.S. wealth-holding households hold over 30 percent of all the wealth in the country, while the bottom 40 percent of Americans hold just 0.2 percent of all wealth.[19] The richest 1 percent of Americans have seen their incomes grow 33 percent over the last 20 years while middle-class Americans saw much more modest income growth based in part on an increase in family work hours. Moreover, recent studies show that social mobility has stagnated over the past 40 years. A *New York Times* study reported that 40 percent of American families remained in the same income range from the 1970s to the 1990s.[20] A person born into the richest fifth of U.S. families is over five times as likely to end up at the top as someone born in the bottom fifth.[21] Among affluent Western countries, only Italy and Great Britain have lower rates of intergenerational mobility than the U.S.[22]

Throughout much of the twentieth century, many working-class Americans could count on a career in one of the nation's skilled industries like steel or auto manufacturing. Labor unions organized workers in these fields, enhancing their job security and income and propelling them into the middle classes. Over the past thirty years, however, employers have transferred many of these jobs overseas where they can employ cheaper labor. The pace of job loss in these fields seems to be quickening. Between March 1998 and May 2003, 2.9 million jobs were eliminated in U.S. manufacturing industries.[23] The recent recession has cost the nation even more manufacturing jobs, hitting America's domestic auto industry particularly hard. Increasingly, the well-paying jobs of the future for American citizens will emphasize high levels of financial

Projected Growth in Employment by Education or Training Category, 2006–2016

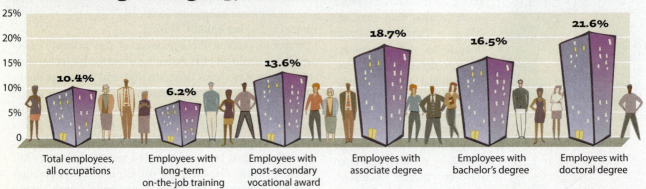

Total employees, all occupations	Employees with long-term on-the-job training	Employees with post-secondary vocational award	Employees with associate degree	Employees with bachelor's degree	Employees with doctoral degree
10.4%	6.2%	13.6%	18.7%	16.5%	21.6%

Source: U.S. Department of Labor, Bureau of Labor Statistics.

YOUTH UP FOR GRABS?

Barack Obama generated tremendous enthusiasm among young people in 2008, carrying the vote of 18–29-year-olds by a margin of 2 to 1 over his opponent, John McCain, and helping to spur youth turnout to its highest level in over 30 years. 2012, however, is a different story.

While a majority of young people approve of the overall job the president is doing, a majority disapprove of his handling of the war in Afghanistan and of the economy.* Nearly 2 in 5 consider the nation to be off on the wrong track. Although they favor the Democratic Party over Republicans, nearly as many describe themselves as Independents and 10 percent support the Tea Party. Young people remain fairly evenly divided ideologically, with 39 percent describing themselves as liberal and 34 percent as conservative. Prior to the election, 38 percent said they were likely to vote for President Obama in 2012 while 36 percent remained undecided. Equally important, only 22 percent considered themselves to be politically engaged.

Young people continue to see the relevance of politics to their daily lives. Sixty-two percent say it really does matter who is president. They care primarily about jobs, healthcare, and national security. During the 2012 campaign, this group remained an accessible constituency via Facebook, with 80 percent maintaining their own pages. While the Democrats were more adept at using social media with Mil-

lennials in 2008, Republicans made inroads in 2012. Clearly, the use of this media to engage this generation is now key to electoral success.

_____

* Information in this section comes from a national survey of youth conducted by Harvard University Institute of Politics, *Survey of Young Americans' Attitudes toward Politics and Public Service, 19th Edition: February 11–March 2, 2011.* Accessed on April 9, 2011 at http://www.iop.harvard.edu/var/ezp_site/storage/fckeditor/file/spring_poll_11_topline.pdf.

acumen, technological proficiency, and creativity. This shift places great emphasis on access to education for career advancement and financial security. At the same time, however, the cost of a college education is skyrocketing while government resources to help students cover those costs are shrinking.

Social class adds another dimension to our consideration of civic engagement. We will see in forthcoming chapters that political activity is not spread evenly across all social classes. Those who vote, run for office, contribute to political campaigns, and engage in a wide array of political and civic activities are disproportionately individuals with more wealth. As a result, the wealthy are more likely to be heard by political actors in the corridors of power.

THE FUTURE OF CITIZENSHIP

A number of ideas are surfacing about how we might alter and improve the civic engagement and political participation of American citizens today. Some states now require students to perform community service in order to graduate from high school. More colleges and universities are turning to student **service learning programs**

> **service learning programs** Agencies that help connect volunteers with organizations in need of help.

Reasons for Not Voting, 18–24-Year-Olds

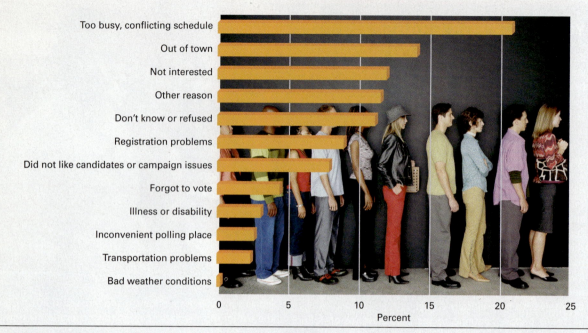

Bar chart showing reasons for not voting among 18–24-year-olds (Percent, x-axis from 0 to 25):

- Too busy, conflicting schedule — ~21
- Out of town — ~14
- Not interested — ~11
- Other reason — ~11
- Don't know or refused — ~11
- Registration problems — ~9
- Did not like candidates or campaign issues — ~8
- Forgot to vote — ~5
- Illness or disability — ~3.5
- Inconvenient polling place — ~3
- Transportation problems — ~3
- Bad weather conditions — ~1

Source: U.S. Census Bureau, Voting and Registration in the Election of November 2008.

as a legitimate educational experience. Will service learning eventually reconstruct the social capital that many believe will reinvigorate political participation? Or will it contribute to a growing sense that political solutions to social problems are futile?

Perhaps changes in our election process and voter mobilization will help. See the figure above for reasons why young people don't vote. Participation improves when government agencies become more open, when participation is made more accessible, and when a range of political and nonpolitical associations mobilize citizens to take action. For example, declaring Election Day a legal holiday might encourage more people to get to the polls. Perhaps, as voters in the state of Oregon already can, citizens will be able to vote completely by mail—or, in the future, online. The political parties are intensifying their efforts to get out the vote. Studies show that personal contact can increase participation levels. Turnout rises when voters are invited to participate by people in their communities, a technique that both major parties employed with great success in 2004 and 2008.[24] Candidates, too, are redoubling their efforts to reach out to young voters by addressing the issues they care about most, like the environment and education, and by toning down the divisive rhetoric that turns off many young people.

civic engagement Involvement in any activity aimed at influencing the collective well-being of the community.

Political communication is undergoing a sea change that promises to have a dramatic impact on **civic engagement** as well. Community groups are finding new and innovative ways to use social media to engage citizens in community efforts ranging from recycling and community beau-

tification to economic development and locating housing for those in need. Millions of dollars were raised to help victims of the Haitian earthquake in 2010 through the use of cell phones and text messaging. Political leaders have already had dramatic success using the Internet both as a

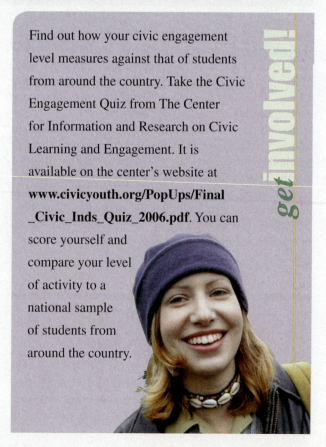

Find out how your civic engagement level measures against that of students from around the country. Take the Civic Engagement Quiz from The Center for Information and Research on Civic Learning and Engagement. It is available on the center's website at **www.civicyouth.org/PopUps/Final _Civic_Inds_Quiz_2006.pdf**. You can score yourself and compare your level of activity to a national sample of students from around the country.

get involved!

fundraising device and as a vehicle for involving citizens in political dialogue. Blogging is changing the way Americans get news about current events, although its long-term impact is uncertain. Virtually all of the 2008 presidential candidates mounted impressive websites with feedback and blogging features. Hillary Clinton solicited votes online for a campaign theme song. And Barack Obama used his website to raise record amounts of money from small contributors. In 2008, candidates employed a host of new technologies, from text messaging to web networking, to meeting young people where they live. Sustaining political involvement beyond elections is more difficult, however, as President Obama found after his election. His campaign manager, David Plouffe, directed a new organization called Organizing for America (OFA) to mobilize millions of supporters to help lobby for the President's agenda, but the impact has been minimal at best.

Political leaders have had dramatic success using the Internet and cell phone technologies to engage Americans in political and civic activism.

We will discuss many of these ideas and more throughout the course of this text. The most important ideas for improving civic engagement may not yet have been discovered. That is where you come in. As you consider your place in the social fabric of America, we hope you will share your ideas with your class, your community, and your political leaders. In the process, you will be helping to shape the way our democracy functions and fulfilling your role as citizen.

Summary

1. **What kinds of civic involvement fuel democracies?**
    *   Citizens can contribute to the civic life of democracy by participating in voluntary associations that build social capital, or bonds of trust among citizens, and by participating in the political process that fuels our form of government.
    *   Ours is a representative democracy that allows us to choose and hold accountable leaders who make our laws and policies, thereby allowing us to share in the exercise of political power. In some states individuals are given additional powers like initiative, referendum, and recall, which permit a more direct exercise of democratic control.
    *   Decisions in some areas, like how our schools are run, are likely to involve lively debate among a wide variety of interests characteristic of our pluralistic society, whereas decisions about matters like foreign policy are more likely to be dominated by the views of political, social, and economic leaders.

2. **What ideals fuel American democracy?**
    *   American democracy gets its inspiration from the liberal democratic views of John Locke and rests on three essential notions: natural rights, the formulation of a social contract by the consent of the governed, and majority rule.
    *   Natural rights include the right to life, liberty, and property. Because these rights are protected, they cannot be denied to any citizen by majority wishes.
    *   Our Constitution embodies the notion of popular consent and works best when citizens are informed and actively involved in various forms of political participation, like voting and running for office.

3. **What are some changes and challenges facing America today?**
    *   We are growing more diverse as racial and ethnic minorities constitute a larger proportion of our citizenry.
    *   We are growing older, a feature that will make it increasingly difficult to fund programs for the elderly from a smaller population of younger workers.
    *   We continue to reflect the divisions of class as those with fewer resources and education fall farther behind economically.

National Journal

COMMUNITY ORGANIZER IN CHIEF

If you are young and hungry to change the world, no place is better than Washington. Other capitals were grafted onto rivers and ports, indebted to the commerce, industry, and history that preceded them. Washington was hacked out of swamps and farms for the sole purpose of doing politics.

President Obama's political success, however, has not been purely a product of the Washington machinery. In the course of the 2008 election, Obama deployed a small army of field, regional, and state organizers to meet with local supporters. He asked them to talk to one another and to their neighbors about why they supported him, and about what they could do to help him get elected.

And that is what Obama appears to be doing with the 13 million names that remain on his mailing list. His field organizers recently began getting phone calls: Would you be interested in coming back to work? Not for Obama, exactly—the president is now responsible for the free world, two small children, and one puppy—but for what you started, an association of communities that share Obama's vision?

Obama For America 2.0 is still taking form: Funding is undecided, specifics are scarce, and focus will be shaped in part by this weekend's house parties. But the idea, apparently, is to provide paid staff support for communities organizing not just around Obama's legislative agenda but also around state and local initiatives. More important, community organizers are working out what, exactly, you do when you suddenly get your long-demanded seat at the table.

For nearly 30 years, Republicans have kept their multifaceted campaign networks alive through churches, religious groups, the National Rifle Association, and anti-abortion groups. Democrats have had no comparable infrastructure, except perhaps the shrinking labor movement. The community-organizing model was born amid the rough-and-tumble machine politics of 1930s Chicago, where getting involved in elections could only lead to corruption, and so decades passed before community organizers saw much point in pursuing electoral politics. As a result of this divide, Democrats developed a curiously fractured body of supporters, with sparse social ties among their constituent bases.

"Community organizing and electoral politics used to have one-night stands, but they'd never talk about it in the morning," says Deepak Bhargava of the Center for Community Change. "Today, they're talking they might get hitched. If we can combine the best of community-organizing relationships and commitment to issues with the scale and urgency of electoral politics, there could be a resurgence of citizen engagement in a transformative and sustained way."

Consider, for example, the Rev. Milton Wells, who made a 14-hour bus trip from Kalamazoo, Mich., to attend a recent meeting of community organizers. "We're here," he said, "just to ensure that our voices are heard and some promises that were made are kept." Wells expects Obama to fix jobs, health care, and the rights of immigrants; he, himself, will be returning to work in Kalamazoo. "I'm a firm believer that we have to participate in our miracle," he said.

If you are struck that a black pastor from Kalamazoo, where just 4 percent of the population is foreign-born, would include immigration reform among his top three priorities, then you are sensing the political change recognized and shaped by the Obama campaign and by community organizers. Democratic supporters are traditionally sorted into constituent groups, each of which is presumed to have parochial interests—the black community, the Hispanic community, labor, youth, urban college-educated whites, and so on.

From the start of his campaign, however, Obama clearly articulated a very different framework, one that transcended and unified constituent interests. "Alongside our famous individualism, there's another ingredient in the American saga, a belief that we are all connected as one people," he said in his 2004 convention speech. "It's what allows us to pursue our individual dreams yet still come together as a single American family: 'E pluribus unum'—out of many, one."

"The conservative movement was very good at talking about individualism, and there are strains there that everybody can respond to," said Gabe Gonzalez, the campaign's director. "But community values has strains that everybody can respond to, too. If you want to engage in deep structural change, it is no longer possible to engage simply at the level of issues. You have to engage in values."

Barn-raising cooperation runs every bit as deep in the American psyche as does bootstrap individualism; more than 150 years ago, Alexis de Tocqueville was astounded by Americans' propensity to join together in common causes. "Americans of all ages, all conditions, and all dispositions constantly form associations," he wrote.

By the 1960s, though, when young people by and large rejected traditional associations with broad membership and local focus, these associations tended to become issue-specific and were usually aimed at Washington. The change began with the civil-rights movement, where impatient, leadership-based groups outpaced the more sedate membership-based NAACP, and then spread into the women's movement, the environmental movement, the anti-war movement, and the citizens movements.

A few years ago, though, the pendulum began to swing back, as a new generation of young people was drawn into community and political work. "Political participation patterns for youth went down for 30 years and then suddenly, around 2001, it looks like a reverse checkmark, which has gone constantly up for the last several years," said researcher Tom Sander. "Some people think it's Obama. We think Obama was an ideal candidate to seize upon this, but the youth interest in politics was dry kindling waiting to be lit."

Andrew Virden, a field organizer for Obama, came into the campaign in the usual way: He took a look and was smitten. The Minnesota native had never done politics before, but he waited six hours in line to see Obama speak and then signed up for e-mails from the campaign. One invited supporters to apply for an organizing fellowship; he did, and in June 2008, Virden and another fellow were dropped into Marquette, Mich., a small college town on the conservative Upper Peninsula of Michigan that is not accustomed to having its own presidential campaign staff—much less two.

"Everybody thinks that by purchasing media, they can overlook the field campaign," says Jack LaSalle, former chair of the Marquette County Democrats. "Participation matters because the tools we see used in the campaign are not strictly campaign tools any more than they are labor-organizing or community-organizing tools. They are how human beings organize to work with each other."

Virden wound up spending five months in the UP, learning as he went along. When Judy Stock signed up to get an Obama yard sign at the Dickinson County Fair, Virden called to ask if she wanted to get involved in the campaign.

"No," she said. "I just want a sign."

"We're having an organizational meeting," Virden replied. "If you came to that, I could give you the sign there."

Stock didn't much want to go. She believed in Obama, having read both of his

> "Alongside our famous individualism, there's another ingredient in the American saga, a belief that we are all connected as one people. It's what allows us to pursue our individual dreams yet still come together as a single American family: 'E pluribus unum'—out of many, one."
> —Barack Obama

books and reviewed his website before asking for the sign, but she is not a joiner and is shy outside of work. On the other hand, she knew the woman hosting the meeting, and she figured that showing up might be the only way to get her yard sign.

Afterward, Virden handed her the sign and a sheet of phone numbers. Would she like to try making some calls for Obama?

She practiced the calls in her kitchen before dialing. "I made a couple of calls, which wasn't bad, so I made a couple more calls," she said. "It was interesting. I found a lot of people wanted to talk to me. If they had questions, I answered if I could; and if I couldn't, we tried to find the answers."

Then Virden asked Stock if she wanted to knock on doors. She didn't, but she agreed to walk with him as he knocked on doors one Saturday morning. "He did most of the talking at first, then he said, 'OK, you can try this,' " she said. "Once you get past the first one, it's OK. I met a lot of different people, heard a lot of good stories, and bad stories too. I lost a pants size."

At a recent forum back in Washington, analyst Juan Williams inadvertently outlined the challenge that OFA 2.0 faces. He asked a panel discussing the economic crisis for the "one thing" that community leaders in the audience could do back home.

Mishel, Johnson, Turman, and Baker all immediately identified things that Washington could do. Nobody suggested getting Judy Stock out knocking on doors again to explain universal health care, or inviting Andrew Virden to an economic-revitalization meeting.

"My personal opinion is that organizations may be overrelying on the perceived change that comes from a leadership shift," said Bill Vandenberg, director of the Open Society Institute's Democracy and Power Fund. "But I increasingly see national organizations realizing that they cannot be as useful advancing policy in D.C. if they've got nothing on the ground, and I see local groups realizing that it's not enough to work locally, because their issues intersect at the federal level as well."

The future of Obama's movement, in other words, doesn't rely on Obama, or even on whatever becomes of OFA 2.0. The future of his movement will be determined by the many people who understand what it accomplished. If you want to change the world, go to Washington; if you want to change Washington, you might want to go next door and knock.

For Discussion:

■ Were you involved in the 2008 presidential campaign? If so, how did you get involved? Was it to advance a single issue or agenda in Washington, or did one candidate simply speak to you? If you did not get involved, then why?

■ Do you agree with the author that individuals like Judy Stock, who are not part of the Washington power elite, can effect real change there? What challenges do organizers at the local level face, and what advantages do they have?

■ How would you suggest the Obama administration creatively employ its army of local volunteers and activists?

2

THE FOUNDATION OF CITIZENS' RIGHTS

CONSTITUTION CONTROVERSY ▌ Oddly enough, the historian for the House of Representatives could not recall a time it had ever been done before on the floor of the chamber. Only about a third of House members participated, and it raised controversy among politicians and the public alike. In January 2010, the eyes of the media focused on this novel 90-minute event: the reading aloud of the U.S. Constitution.

The idea for the reading came from Representative Robert W. Goodlatte, a Republican from Virginia. It drew inspiration from Tea Party supporters around the nation who complained throughout the 2010 midterm campaign that the federal government had strayed too far from its constitutional roots. "Throughout the last year there has been a great debate about the expansion of the federal government," Goodlatte told reporters, "and lots of my constituents have said that Congress has gone beyond its powers granted in the Constitution."[1]

Newly installed Republican Speaker, John Boehner (R-OH), opened the reading with the stirring words, "We the people . . ." and then handed it off to House members of both parties who took turns reading portions of the document. Although the purpose of the ➡️

TUTION

- What factors contributed to the need for a Constitutional Convention?
- What are the basic principles that inform our Constitution?
- In what ways does constitutional change occur?

reading was to inspire reverence and fidelity to the original text, members were reminded in the discussion leading up to the event that the original document was not without its flaws and that fierce debate continues about its meaning and application.

The majority party had arranged to read an altered version of the original document, one that excised those portions that were superseded by amendments. The resulting version left out mention of the three-fifths clause referencing the status of slaves at the time the document was written. The deletions angered some members like Jesse Jackson, Jr., (D-IL) who argued that the exercise "gives little deference to the long history of improving the Constitution and only seeks an interpretation of our Constitution based on the now, not the historic, broad body of law and struggle that it has taken to get there."[2]

The reading was not without drama. Representative John Lewis, a black Democrat from Georgia, received a standing ovation when he read the Thirteenth Amendment abolishing slavery. When the section in Article III was read citing the requirement that the president be a natural born citizen, a gallery protestor yelled "Except Obama" and had to be removed.[3]

In the end, the event served to reopen a perennial debate between those who see the Constitution as a repository of political wisdom requiring faithful adherence and those who see the document as a living blueprint whose meaning and application must be reinterpreted by each generation in an effort to stay true to the fundamental democratic idea that government must represent the changing values and beliefs of its people. The former view is held

Some in Congress, like Jesse Jackson, Jr. (D-IL) objected to the deletion of sections of the Constitution during the reading, arguing it gave a false impression of the document at the time it was written.

by many conservatives and Tea Party activists who claim the federal government has become too expansive and that it threatens the very freedoms the document was meant to protect. The latter view is espoused by political liberals who argue that the Framers forged a document that never envisioned a role for many citizens like the minorities and women whose interests their handiwork is now called upon to protect.

In this chapter we will examine the framework of American government embodied in the Constitution and the rights it guarantees. We will explore the odds the Framers overcame in establishing these rights for themselves—and not for some others—and how they developed an institutional framework that was flexible enough to incorporate changes that expanded those rights. We will also look at the obstacles that continue to stand in the way of full participation by all segments in our society. ✦

Jamestown, Virginia, founded in 1607, failed as a mining town but became a training ground for self-rule.

THE FOUNDATIONS OF AMERICAN DEMOCRACY

During the first 150 years of English settlement in America, the colonists gave little thought to independence. They focused on survival, which included developing and nurturing institutions of local self-government. Only when the British government looked to the colonies for financial support did relations between the Crown and the colonies sour and, aided by the agitation of radicals, deteriorate to the point of revolution.

Early Colonization

The first permanent British colony in North America was Jamestown, founded in 1607 by the Virginia Company of London for the purpose of developing trade and mining gold. In order to regulate and protect the colony, the settlers formed a government consisting of a president and seven-member council. By 1619, colonists created an assembly known as the House of Burgesses, the nation's first legislative body. Composed of representatives elected from among the settlers, it imbued the settlers with an ardor for self-rule. Unfortunately for the company, there was no gold, and harsh conditions coupled with conflicts with na-

tive populations hampered trade. The Crown took control of the failing colony in 1624, replacing the president with a royal governor. The House of Burgesses, however, survived the king's efforts to abolish it.

A year after the House of Burgesses was created, forty-one religious dissenters called Puritans established a permanent settlement in the area of modern-day Plymouth, Massachusetts. The Puritans rejected attempts by both the Catholic pope and the king of England to dictate religious doctrine or belief. Because of this stance, they found themselves barred from many professional positions that required membership in the official Church of England. Despairing of reform from within the church, they chose to establish foreign religious outposts of their own. Enroute to the New World, these dissenters entered into an agreement for self-government, known as the Mayflower Compact.

Did You Know?

...That in Puritan Massachusetts the only people allowed to vote were men who had been accepted as members of Puritan congregations—and that all residents of the colony were required to attend religious services, whether or not they had been accepted as congregation members?

Under this document, the settlers pledged to "constitute, and frame such just and equal laws, ordinances, acts, constitutions, and offices . . . as shall be thought most meet and convenient for the general good of the colony. . . ." The Compact served as a model for other colonies and gave early settlers a taste for self-government that went uncontested by the British for years.

Although they came to America to flee religious persecution, the Puritans themselves were intolerant of dissent. Soon, some settlers began to challenge Puritan orthodoxy. Faced with execution or expulsion, dissidents migrated to form their own colonies; Rhode Island, for example, grew from breakaway settlements founded by former Massachusetts residents.

By 1732, thirteen British colonies dotted the eastern coast of North America, reflecting a variety of religious and political points of view as well as a wealth of nationalities. Each colony developed its own fledgling institutions of government, which despite their differences reflected a commitment to self-rule, popular consent, and respect for law.

The Colonists Respond to Economic Pressures

British policies limited economic progress in the colonies. The Crown saw its colonies primarily as suppliers of raw materials such as cotton, tobacco, and furs to manufacturers in Britain. There these resources were made into finished goods such as clothing, tools, and furniture, many of which were then exported back to the colonies for sale. The colonists were required to trade exclusively with Britain, which meant that all finished goods exported to the colonies—regardless of their source—first passed through England. The goods were loaded on British ships and taxed before sale, making non-British products more expensive for colonists and preventing genuine competition. For years, colonists skirted these limits through tactics such as smuggling and piracy. Colonial governors, whose salaries often depended on approval by local assemblies, largely ignored these widespread practices.

The Seven Years' War (1756–1763) brought home dramatically to Britain the costs of protecting their North American colonies from France and its Native American allies, while maintaining a vast empire elsewhere in the world. The British sought to defray costs by imposing taxes on sugar and printed materials. New England merchants and distillers of rum were particularly disturbed by the sugar tax and objected that the taxes were imposed without their participation in its enactment, giving rise to the rally cry of "taxation without representation." The British responded paternalistically that colonial interests were taken into consideration by members of

Parliament even if the colonists themselves did not have a direct say. More contentious than the sugar tax, the Stamp Act impacted a far wider swath of colonists from all walks of life by requiring revenue stamps to be affixed to newspapers and pamphlets as well as all legal documents. Secret organizations known as the "Sons of Liberty" organized in several colonies to protest the Act, often by resorting to violence against customs agents representing the Crown. The Virginia House of Burgesses denounced the tax and the Massachusetts Assembly invited delegates from all the colonies to attend a meeting dubbed the Stamp Act Congress in 1765 where representatives from nine colonies adopted resolutions condemning the tax as a subversion of the rights of the colonists and asserting that no taxes could be levied on the colonies except by their own legislative bodies.

The British responded a year later by repealing the Stamp Act and easing restrictions on sugar. However, the British thirst for revenue as well as their eagerness to regain control over rebellious colonists led to a new round of taxes. In 1767, the Townsend Acts were imposed, applying duties to a wide variety of important colonial staples. As dissent grew, many colonial legislatures urged a boycott of British goods. Pamphlets like Samuel Adams's *The Rights of Colonists* stoked the flames of popular anger. The British then inadvertently helped the dissenters' cause by passing several more increasingly hated duties, including a tax on tea. In 1773, Boston radicals protested by storming East India Company ships moored in Boston Harbor, dumping their cargoes of tea into the harbor. Parliament punished the city for the "Boston Tea Party" with actions that included blockading the harbor and forcing colonists to quarter British troops in their homes.

Colonists Mobilize for Action: The Continental Congress

Tensions between Britain and her colonies were reaching a breaking point. Seeking a way to address these tensions, representatives of every colony except Georgia met in Philadelphia in September 1774 for the first Continental Congress. They approved a declaration of grievances and urged a boycott of British goods. Although hopeful of restoring good relations with Britain, the colonists strengthened their local militias and left open the possibility of another meeting should tensions not ease. It was not long before relations worsened. In an effort to disrupt the colonial military buildup, British General Thomas Gage marched toward Concord, Massachusetts, in April 1775 to confiscate munitions that were being stored there. As they marched through Lexington, the British encountered a band of Minutemen—militiamen known for their readiness to fight. A skirmish led to shots, leaving 8 dead and 10 wounded. The British moved on to Concord, destroying the munitions that remained. Much of the firepower, however, was already in the hands of militiamen who pounded the British as they moved toward Boston, killing more than 250 of them.

In the shadow of Lexington's "shot heard 'round the world," a second Continental Congress assembled in Philadelphia on May 10, 1775. This gathering produced a more radical agenda that included marshaling military forces under General George Washington and planning to finance the war effort by borrowing funds and issuing bonds. Several members, including John Dickinson, held out hope that war could be forestalled. He drafted the "Olive Branch Petition" calling upon the king to negotiate with the colonists to resolve their differences. The petition stood little chance of success, however, and the king soon declared the colonies in a state of rebellion and sent more troops to subdue local uprisings.

The convention also produced the Articles of Confederation, a constitution of sorts that consolidated the colonies loosely under a common rule. Ongoing efforts to solve the confrontation between Britain and the colonies proved futile, and in 1776, Congress appointed a committee to prepare a formal declaration asserting independence.

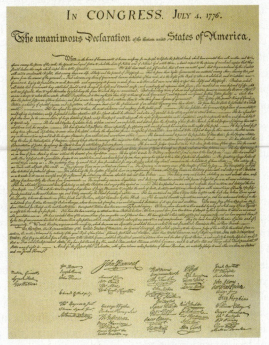

The Declaration of Independence served not only to declare war against Britain but also to assert the equality of men and the right to "life, liberty, and the pursuit of happiness."

human rights, but we need to see it in the context of the times. Notice that it reserves these rights to men. That term was not then used as a surrogate for humanity; it referred specifically to males. Only property owners of sufficient means were allowed to participate in the political process, and very few female colonists owned enough property to qualify. The signers also clearly did not agree that *all* men were created equal. Many of the signers owned slaves, and some of those who helped draft the declaration forced Jefferson to remove from the document language attacking the institution of slavery.

The Declaration of Independence served not only as a declaration of war with Britain but also as a tool to rally support from a population that lacked consensus about separation from Britain. About one-third of Americans chose to fight for independence from the Crown; another third, it is estimated, were loyal to the king and Parliament; the remainder were too busy scratching a living from the harsh frontier environment to take much interest in politics. Thomas Paine's pamphlet *Common Sense,* published the same year as the declaration, was just as significant for mustering popular support for independence. The pamphlet sold a half million copies, 120 thousand within the first three months of publication. By this time, however, the propaganda war had given way to a shooting war with the battles at Lexington and Concord the previous year.

Declaration of Independence

Although the Declaration of Independence consists mainly of a list of grievances against England's King George III, it is most important for its embodiment of John Locke's philosophy of natural rights, discussed in Chapter 1. The declaration forcefully asserts the equality of men and the inalienable rights of "life, liberty, and the pursuit of happiness," a phrase that euphemistically expresses an inherent right to own private property. It asserts that these rights are not granted by humans, but by God, and that they must be defended by government for enjoyment by each of its members. When a government can no longer defend these rights—or when it actively threatens them—the people have the right to alter or abolish that government and replace it with another that is better able to do so.

The Declaration of Independence inspires awe and respect and has been adopted by advocates of liberty the world over. It is not, however, a perfect affirmation of

THE BIRTH OF A NATION

In the prelude to the War for Independence, the colonies reconstituted themselves as states and developed governing constitutions. They had already acquired a taste for self-governance and a respect for representative democracy in which legislative bodies played a prominent role. However, no similar governing document existed for the new nation as a whole. The Second Continental Congress drafted the Articles of Confederation to serve that purpose, and it performed that function adequately during the Revolution. Shortly thereafter, however, the flaws of this document became apparent to colonial leaders, who made plans to replace it.

The Articles of Confederation: A Document Whose Time Had Come and Gone

The Articles of Confederation created a single national assembly, or Congress, in which each state possessed one vote. Congress and its various committees coordinated national affairs during the Revolution. This arrangement, however, was inadequate to address the country's myriad postwar economic and security problems. Consequently, colonial leaders began to search for a new national governing structure.

The Articles of Confederation recognized the colonies as **sovereign**, or independent, units. It created a Congress composed of delegates from every state, but its powers were quite limited. Congress was responsible for maintaining the army and navy, conducting foreign policy, and declaring war and peace. However, there was no president or judicial body and Congress's power to enforce laws was quite limited. The Articles served as the organizing document for the new nation even while disputes over its ratification dragged on during the war years with final adoption assured only with Maryland's ratification in 1781. Despite its limitations, the Articles proved useful in helping the new nation settle state claims to western territories, establish a system of governance for the Northwest Territories, and ratify the Treaty of Paris, ending the war.

In 1786, Daniel Shays led debt-ridden farmers in armed insurrection in Massachusetts, prompting the nation's new leaders to question the viability of the Articles of Confederation as a governing document.

The problems created by a central government with limited powers to respond quickly and with a single voice to collective problems became increasingly apparent as the war drew to a close. Among these were three pressing economic concerns: the lack of a common national currency, lack of control of interstate commerce, and an inability to collect federal taxes. The first two problems were closely linked. As a sovereign entity, each state issued its own currency while reserving the right to impose duties on goods imported from the others. Both of these practices hindered trade and limited the growth of interstate markets.

The government's inability to collect taxes concerned leaders who envisioned the new nation emerging as an international economic power. The Continental Congress planned to pay off the debt it amassed during the Revolution by assessing each colony a portion of the war's total cost. States would collect money to pay for the assessments by imposing taxes on their own subjects. Collection, however, proved slow and unreliable; no state fully met its obligations, and the nation's poor credit precipitated economic hardship for many. Higher interest rates prevented business expansion and increased the cost of foreign and domestic goods. Lack of financial capital also limited the national government's ability to defend its borders and to improve interstate commerce by building roads and canals. Strengthening of the powers of the central government seemed to be the solution to all three of these economic problems.

High prices for imported commodities, combined with increased taxes imposed by hard-pressed states, drove many people into debt. Small farmers were especially hard hit, and the number of people imprisoned for failure to pay debts burgeoned. In 1786, dissidents known as Regulators roamed western Massachusetts demanding debt relief for small farmers. In late summer, a group of Regulators led by Daniel Shays, himself a farmer, captured a cache of weapons from the Springfield armory. The state militia, sent to quell the disturbance, switched sides, adding fuel to the rebellion. The national government was powerless to intervene because it lacked the authority to raise or deploy a standing army. Eventually, representatives of the state's banking interests hired an army of mercenaries to attack the Regulators. It was not until February 1787 that the rebellion was quashed and Shays's followers dispersed into surrounding states. Incidents such as Shays's Rebellion convinced state leaders of their essential vulnerability and of the need for a strong central government.

The Road to Philadelphia

Although state leaders recognized the need for a stronger central government, assembling a group to reform the Articles of Confederation took some doing. In September 1786, representatives from five states (Delaware, New Jersey, New York, Pennsylvania, and Virginia) met in Annapolis, Maryland, to discuss the weaknesses of the articles. Alexander

Thomas Jefferson and the members of the Declaration Committee present the Declaration of Independence to the Second Continental Congress.

Hamilton and James Madison proposed a more inclusive meeting of delegates from every state to be held the following year in Philadelphia. Congress scheduled a meeting to commence May 14, 1787, for the "express purpose of revising the Articles of Confederation." Although calls for reform had been met by a lukewarm reception in the past, Shays's Rebellion gave the states a new sense of urgency.

It was not until May 25 that a sufficient number of delegates arrived to permit a formal discussion of reform. The fifty-five delegates represented every state except Rhode Island, which refused to send a delegation for fear that the assembly would ignore the plight of debtors who made up a substantial portion of the state's population. Judging from external appearances, Rhode Island had reason for concern. Of the fifty-five delegates, almost all were wealthy and well educated. All were white males, six owned plantations, and about a third owned slaves. More than half were lawyers and most had held leadership positions in their states. Each represented the accepted notion of a politician in an age of deference, where wealth and community standing were understood to be requirements for leadership. Nowhere was this principle of elite deference more clearly demonstrated than in the selection of

Did You Know?

. . . That the members of the Philadelphia Constitutional Convention were so concerned that they be free to discuss possible changes in the Articles of Confederation without pressure from public opinion that they nailed shut the windows of their meeting room in Independence Hall (in the middle of a very hot summer)!

George Washington, the wealthy Virginia planter and Revolutionary War hero, as the convention's president.

The delegates, however, were by no means unified in their ideas about government or about advancing the interests of any particular economic group. All understood that citizens in their home states would closely scrutinize their actions. Each county had interests and concerns that it wanted the delegate from that colony to champion. Producing a workable compromise in such a situation was an extremely difficult task, but the delegates were marked by outstanding political acumen. Grasping the sensitivity of the issues they had come to discuss, they pledged to conduct deliberations in secrecy—behind closed doors and windows—despite the sweltering heat and humidity of the Philadelphia summer. They also understood the art of compromise, and that the time had come to exercise it. The delegates were neither the demigods Jefferson called them nor a crafty elite plotting their own

> **sovereign** Independent.
>
> **bicameral** Composed of two houses.

fortunes as some historians have suggested.[4] Political scientist John P. Roche aptly describes them as a group of extremely talented democratic politicians seeking practical answers to practical problems confronting them.[5]

Constitutional Convention

Several delegates came prepared with their own plans for the shape of the national government. Edmund Randolph formally presented Virginia's plan, largely a creation of his colleague James Madison, calling for a **bicameral**, or two-house, legislature. Members of the lower house proportionate to the number of free inhabitants would be chosen by popular election, and they would in turn select the members of the upper chamber from nominees proposed by state legislatures.[6] Lawmakers would serve limited but unspecified terms and the legislative branch would have the power to nullify state laws that interfered with the powers of the national government. The plan included a single executive chosen by the legislative branch with the power to execute national laws. A judicial branch consisting of both inferior courts and a supreme body was proposed with members eligible to hold office during good behavior.

James Madison (1751–1836) came to Philadelphia with a blueprint for change and is known as the Father of the Constitution.

Talk of proportional representation in the legislative chambers made delegates from small states uncomfortable. They feared that more populous states such as Virginia, Pennsylvania, and Massachusetts would dominate the legislature. On June 15, William Paterson presented the New Jersey Plan, which was more to the liking of the small states. He proposed a **unicameral**, or a single-body, legislature, maintaining the equal state representation established under the Articles of Confederation, but granting Congress additional powers over trade and security. The plan would also establish a plural executive body chosen by Congress with the power to direct military operations, command troops, enforce national laws, and appoint federal officers. It provided that the executive was removable by the national legislature but added this could be initiated by a call of the executives of the states. A system of courts was authorized with judges of the supreme body appointed by the executive to serve for life or good behavior. Notably, the plan included a provision that national law was supreme and that states were bound to follow.

unicameral Composed of a single body.

Great Compromise Agreement at the Constitutional Convention splitting the legislature into two bodies—one apportioned by population, the other assigning each state two members.

On June 19, delegates rejected the New Jersey Plan, signaling their desire to create a completely new form of government. By June 21, they settled on support for a bicameral legislature, but the debate—like the weather—was hot. Some delegates withdrew from the convention, never to return. On July 16, Roger Sherman from Connecticut found a solution to the question of congressional representation. His committee called for seats in the lower body to be allocated based on population, while in the upper chamber each state would have an equal vote. At first, both large- and small-state delegates continued to jockey for more favorable terms. The introduction of the requirement that money bills originate in the lower house secured passage of the agreement, known as the **Great Compromise**, by a single vote.

Regional Tensions: Slavery and the Three-fifths Compromise

Thorny issues remained, the most important of which touched on the institution of slavery. While the southern economy had become extremely dependent on slaves, the northern states were developing a commercial and manufacturing economy in which slave labor was not as profitable as paid labor. Many northerners opposed slavery on economic, as well as moral and religious, grounds. Some states, such as Rhode Island, had abolished slavery completely or enfranchised free blacks who owned property.

The immediate problem that concerned delegates was the question of how to count slaves for purposes of congressional representation. Should they be treated as inhabitants or simply as property? If they were inhabitants, each would count as a person for determining a state's representation in Congress. This would give southern states a disproportionate amount of political influence relative to the North. At the same time, however, the law required states to pay federal taxes based on population. Under this formula, counting slaves as inhabitants would require southerners to pay more in taxes.

Uncomfortable with either option, southern delegates resurrected an earlier proposal to base representation on the whole number of free citizens and three-fifths of all others, excluding Indians, who did not pay taxes. "All others" clearly referred to slaves. This accommodation, called the "three-fifths compromise," won the day and secured agreement among the delegates. A related issue dividing regional delegates was the return of runaway slaves. Southern delegates demanded and received a constitutional provision directing states to return fugitive slaves to their owners.

Trade also proved to be a source of friction between states. Delegates from colonies with large trade and mercantile interests insisted that Congress must have the power to regulate commerce in ways that made their goods more competitive with foreign markets. Meanwhile, delegates from agricultural states—particularly those employing slaves—feared that such power would result in Congress taxing agricultural exports to the detriment of their own economies. They also feared that Congress would use its commerce power to halt the importation of slaves and moved to prohibit Congress from taking such action. A number of delegates raised both moral and practical objections to barring congressional regulation of slavery. Luther Martin, an attorney and planter representing Maryland, objected that slavery was inconsistent with the principles of the Revolution, while George Mason, an outspoken delegate from Virginia, argued that "the infernal traffic"

Slavery was the most divisive issue at the Philadelphia Convention, and the compromise agreed upon planted the seeds for civil war.

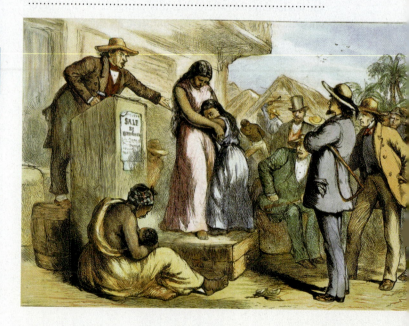

in slaves was hampering the nation's economic development.[7] Once again the delegates reached a compromise, permitting congressional regulation of commerce in principle but prohibiting taxes on exports and permitting the importation of slaves until 1808.

A number of unrelated issues that had arisen over the course of the summer had been assigned to committee for

with these precautions, delegates were reluctant to support the new agreement until Benjamin Franklin urged them to "doubt a little of their own infallibility and put their name to the instrument." Forty-two of the original fifty-five delegates remained at the closing of the convention on September 17, and thirty-nine signed the document. Three men who played prominent roles in the convention declined to

> "IN FRAMING A GOVERNMENT which is to be administered by men over men, the great difficulty lies in this: you must first enable the government to control the governed; and in the next place, oblige it to control itself."

consideration. Among these was the provision that states would set their own requirements for voting. This was a concession to the fact that qualifications differed from state to state, especially with regard to the types and amounts of property that each required. Although land was considered the standard for southern states, property in northern states assumed a variety of forms. Delegates were wary about the impact any new government might have on property use and wanted to ensure that the dominant property interests in their states at the time would control the ballot box. Committees also wrangled with issues ranging from presidential selection to the jurisdiction of the courts.

Most of the delegates had doubts about various provisions in the final document; some doubted it would survive ratification. To bolster its chances of passage, the delegates determined that the document would take effect whenever nine colonies had ratified it. This decision was taken to ensure that Rhode Island—a fiercely independent colony—could not sabotage the committee's work by itself. One of the most ingenious features of the document was the incorporation of a process for change, allowing parts of the document to be altered while preserving the structure of government as a whole. Even

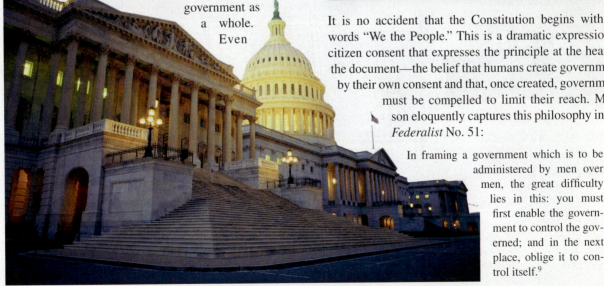

sign, fearing adverse political reaction back home: George Mason and Edmund Randolph of Virginia and Elbridge Gerry of Massachusetts. Their reluctance to sign prefigured the coming battle over ratification.

CONSTITUTIONAL PRINCIPLES

The Constitution has been called a patchwork document "sewn together under the pressure of time and events by a group of extremely talented democratic politicians,"[8] but this does not mean it lacks vision and principle. Most notably, the United States Constitution enshrines the principles of liberal democracy buttressed with protections achieved through the separation of powers, checks and balances, and federalism.

Liberal Democratic Principles

It is no accident that the Constitution begins with the words "We the People." This is a dramatic expression of citizen consent that expresses the principle at the heart of the document—the belief that humans create governments by their own consent and that, once created, governments must be compelled to limit their reach. Madison eloquently captures this philosophy in *The Federalist* No. 51:

> In framing a government which is to be administered by men over men, the great difficulty lies in this: you must first enable the government to control the governed; and in the next place, oblige it to control itself.[9]

Separation of Powers and Checks and Balances

To limit the reach of the government, the Framers incorporated into the Constitution the principles of separation of powers and checks and balances. The first principle stems from John Locke and the French philosopher Baron de Montesquieu (1689–1755). While Locke proposed separating government into a legislative branch that made law and an executive branch charged with implementing the law, Montesquieu added an independent judiciary to settle disputes that might arise between the two. Dividing the functions of government ensured that no one branch could consolidate power in its own hands. The difficulty of gaining control of all three branches also decreased the likelihood that a single group might threaten individual freedoms.

The Framers of the Constitution added a second layer of protection against excessive government power: a system of checks and balances. This involves providing each branch with overlapping powers so that no one branch could exercise complete control of any function of government. For example, the Constitution grants Congress principal responsibility for making laws, but allows the president to check this power by vetoing legislation. Congress, however, has the ability to override the veto of a president who stands in the way of needed legislative change. In turn, the courts can check the power of the other branches by challenging the constitutionality of laws passed with the consent of the legislature and the executive branch. To balance the power of the courts, the president can attempt to alter their composition through his or her power of appointment. For its part, Congress can exercise power by withholding funds from the courts or by proposing leg-

System of Checks and Balances

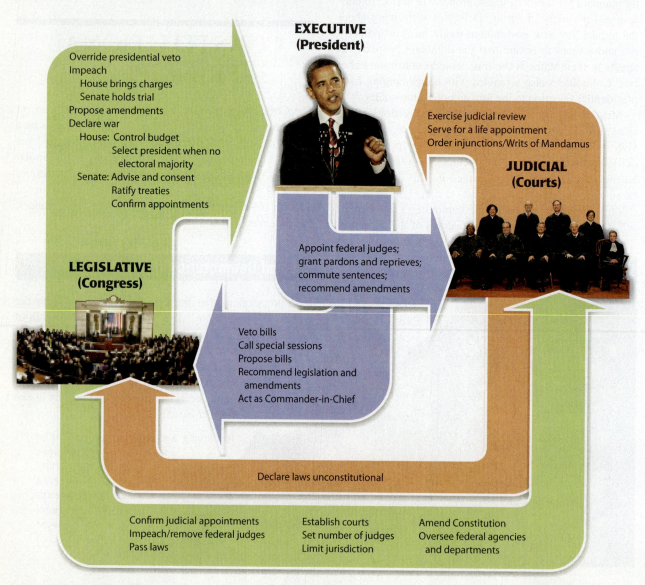

EXECUTIVE (President)

Override presidential veto
Impeach
   House brings charges
   Senate holds trial
Propose amendments
Declare war
   House: Control budget
      Select president when no
      electoral majority
   Senate: Advise and consent
      Ratify treaties
      Confirm appointments

Exercise judicial review
Serve for a life appointment
Order injunctions/Writs of Mandamus

JUDICIAL (Courts)

Appoint federal judges; grant pardons and reprieves; commute sentences; recommend amendments

LEGISLATIVE (Congress)

Veto bills
Call special sessions
Propose bills
Recommend legislation and amendments
Act as Commander-in-Chief

Declare laws unconstitutional

Confirm judicial appointments
Impeach/remove federal judges
Pass laws

Establish courts
Set number of judges
Limit jurisdiction

Amend Constitution
Oversee federal agencies and departments

While our system of checks and balances seems like a prescription for stalemate, Congress and the president can act with dispatch in times of crisis as they did in bailing out financial institutions in the wake of the home mortgage crisis.

islative changes or amendments to circumvent the court decisions.

Although this system may seem to be a prescription for stalemate, it is intended to prevent the arbitrary use of power and to give leaders sufficient time to forge consensus on divisive issues. When faced with a sense of urgency, however, the system can respond expeditiously, such as when Congress and the president (each branch controlled by different political parties) quickly approved a measure in 2008 to save troubled financial institutions involved in risky mortgages whose failure would have worsened an already faltering economy. Nevertheless, as President Obama discovered when he tried to get health-care reform passed, forging consensus on big issues across branches of government can be slow and frustrating.

Federalism

Although the Framers acknowledged the problems of governing a confederation of autonomous states, they also were aware of the people's fear of putting political power in the hands of a remote national government. To address this concern, the Framers established a form of power sharing between the states and the national government called federalism. Under a federal system, some powers—such as the power to declare war—are properly controlled by the national government whereas others—such as the ability to create cities and towns—are reserved to the states. We will see in Chapter 3 that the division of power is actually more fluid than this distinc-

tion would imply. Nevertheless, federalism was meant to protect citizens by preventing government from exercising power outside its intended sphere. According to Madison, this division of power works hand in hand with separation of powers to secure individual liberty:

> In the compound Republic of America, the power surrendered by the people is first divided between two distinct governments, and then the portion allotted to each subdivided among distinct and separate departments. Hence a double security arises to the rights of the people. The different governments will control each other; at the same time that each will be controlled by itself.[10]

CONSTITUTIONAL CONSTRUCTION

The U.S. Constitution is a relatively brief document—just 4,608 words that occupy four sheets of parchment. It consists of a preamble and seven articles, each divided into sections, prescribing the powers and limits of various units of government. The preamble expresses the liberal democratic principles upon which the nation was founded and outlines the purposes to which the new government was dedicated. Preambles have become a typical feature of national constitutions following the American example.

Article I establishes a bicameral legislature. It specifies procedures for the election of House and Senate members, their qualifications for office, apportionment of representatives among the states, filling vacancies, and selecting officers. It outlines the House's role in the impeachment of federal officials and the Senate's role in their trial. The legislative powers of Congress are established, including the authority to make those laws necessary and proper for carrying out provisions of any other laws it passes. This provision is sometimes called the **elastic clause** because of the effect it has had on expanding congressional authority. Article I specifies that revenue bills must originate in the lower House and denies to the states many powers granted to the federal legislature.

Article II establishes the executive branch, including the offices of president and vice president. It deals with issues such as qualifications for the office of president, the method of election, succession of the vice president to the office of president in case of a vacancy, the president's salary, and the oath of office. It establishes the powers of the president as commander in chief, outlines his authority in negotiating treaties, grants him the power to fill vacancies when the Senate is not in session, and specifies additional duties of the office. One section provides for impeachment as the ultimate check on the authority of federal officials.

Article III establishes the judicial branch, creating the Supreme Court and authorizing Congress to create addi-

follows). The federal government assumes responsibility for the federal debt in Article VI, which also contains the **supremacy clause** that gives federal law precedence over state law. This article also specifies that members of Congress shall swear allegiance to the U.S. Constitution without reference to religious affiliation. Article VII discusses ratification of the Constitution, a process that—as we will see—faced considerable hurdles.

THE FIGHT FOR RATIFICATION

The delegates left Philadelphia hopeful that their work would bear fruit but by no means overconfident. Even before the convention adjourned on September 17, outside observers voiced suspicions about the motives of the delegates who had shrouded themselves in secrecy for so many

THE DELEGATES LEFT PHILADELPHIA hopeful that their work would bear fruit but by no means overconfident. . . . outside observers voiced suspicions about the motives of the delegates . . .

tional federal courts. It sets the terms of appointment and removal of all federal judges. It specifies the types of cases to be heard in federal courts and how cases will come before the Supreme Court. One section also presents the legal definition of treason.

Article IV discusses the relations among the states and compels them to recognize the legitimacy of each other's duly executed laws and to grant citizens of other states equal protection under the law. It provides for extradition of persons charged with crimes and the return of runaway slaves—a provision abolished by passage of the Thirteenth Amendment ending slavery. It discusses the admission of new states and provides for federal jurisdiction over federal lands such as state parks. It guarantees that all states shall have a republican form of government that, like the national government, derives from the consent of the people. This article also promises the states federal protection from foreign invasion.

The remaining articles deal with a variety of miscellaneous issues. Article V details provisions for amending the Constitution (see discussion of the amendment process that

elastic clause Provision of Article I of the Constitution authorizing Congress to make those laws necessary and proper for carrying out the other laws it passes.

supremacy clause Provision of Article VI stipulating that the federal government, in exercising any of the powers enumerated in the Constitution, must prevail over any conflicting or inconsistent state exercise of power.

months. Even some of those who had a hand in creating the document were disgruntled. Some delegates refused to sign the document because it lacked a bill of rights. This provision, common in most state constitutions, defined individual freedoms and protections that were beyond the reach of the government. Tired and impatient to return home, most of the delegates were unwilling to tackle yet another potentially divisive issue. Supporters of the new constitution, called **Federalists**, believed the document sufficiently limited the power of federal bodies, making a bill of rights unnecessary. As it turned out, the delegates' failure to add specific protection for individual rights proved a major stumbling block to ratification.

Antifederalist Opposition

Opponents of the new document, known as **Antifederalists**, were drawn from various quarters and expressed concerns over a range of issues. Many farmers opposed creation of a new national currency, fearing that it might lower prices for their commodities or enable the very wealthy to buy up their land. Debtors saw the national government as a collection agency for wealthy lenders. Small-town residents distrusted the urban, legal, and commercial elite whose members had crafted the document. Others were angry that the delegates ignored their charge to reform the Articles of Confederation and instead created a whole new governing document. As one historian put it:

[T]he average man on the street (or farm) . . . likened [the Constitutional Convention] to an instance where a group of carpenters had been called upon to add a dormer, a walk-in closet, and a pantry, and then, without permission of the absentee owner, decided to tear down the farmhouse and build a new one from scratch.[11]

Philosophically, Antifederalists worried that the new country was so large that only a strong central government could maintain order and unity, a prospect that threatened the very existence of the states. They reminded their opponents that ancient philosophers believed democracies were only possible in small states and that large nations required the rule of a monarch or even a despot. Antifederalists argued that senators served for too long and represented excessively large territories and worried that these factors would cause senators to lose touch with the electorate. They were concerned about the role a standing army would play in enforcing federal law (and collecting federal taxes) within the states. And they worried about the lack of

the power we put in their hands. . . . I am not well versed in history, but I will submit to your recollection, whether liberty has been destroyed most often by the licentiousness of the people, or by the tyranny of rulers. I imagine, sir, you will find the balance on the side of tyranny.[12]

The Battle in the States

The Constitution found support in commercial centers, in western territories that desired protection from foreign powers and Native Americans, among land speculators and plantation owners, and in the smaller states that gained equal representation with big states in the proposed Senate. Five states quickly ratified the document by unanimous or lopsided votes, albeit at times by the use of questionable procedures. In Pennsylvania, for example, two Antifederalist delegates were forcibly removed from a local saloon and returned to the assembly hall in order to obtain a quorum, after which the convention ratified the document.

"[T]HE AVERAGE MAN on the street (or farm) . . . likened [the Constitutional Convention] to an instance where a group of carpenters had been called upon to add a dormer, a walk-in closet, and a pantry, and then, without permission of the absentee owner, decided to tear down the farmhouse and build a new one from scratch."

Trial by jury in criminal cases is guaranteed by the Sixth Amendment to the U.S. Constitution.

a written bill of rights to protect the freedoms the revolutionaries fought to achieve. Patrick Henry, whose passionate oratory had advanced the revolutionary cause, spoke with equal passion about the lack of written protections:

> How does your trial by jury stand? In civil cases gone—not sufficiently secured in criminal—this best privilege is gone. But we are told that we need not fear; because those in power, being our representatives, will not abuse

In Massachusetts, the nation's most populous state, a showdown loomed as legislators debated ratification for three weeks without resolution. When some Federalists floated the suggestion that Governor John Hancock might serve in the nation's first administration, Hancock swung his support in favor of ratification. To secure his support, however, he demanded that the final document include amendments protecting many of the individual rights guaranteed in Massachusetts's state constitution.

With Massachusetts on board, supporters of ratification turned their attention to two more large and important states: Virginia and New York. Virginia had a sizable Antifederalist contingent, but it also boasted supporters of the document who ranked among the most respected and influential figures in the nation, including Madison, Jefferson, and Washington. Despite a sometimes bitter debate, a promise to amend the document to protect certain individual rights secured ratification by a ten-vote margin on June 25, 1788.

Federalists Supporters of the Constitution and its strong central government.

Antifederalists Opponents of the ratification of the Constitution.

STATE	ORDER OF RATIFICATION	DATE OF RATIFICATION	VOTE
Delaware	1	December 7, 1787	30–0
Pennsylvania	2	December 12, 1787	46–23
New Jersey	3	December 18, 1787	38–0
Georgia	4	January 2, 1788	26–0
Connecticut	5	January 9, 1788	128–40
Massachusetts	6	February 6, 1788	187–168
Maryland	7	April 26, 1788	63–11
South Carolina	8	May 23, 1788	149–73
New Hampshire	9	June 21, 1788	57–47
Virginia	10	June 25, 1788	89–79
New York	11	July 26, 1788	30–27
North Carolina	12	November 21, 1789	194–77
Rhode Island	13	May 29, 1790	34–32

Ratification of the Constitution

Winning ratification in New York proved more difficult, and Federalists exerted great energy there to sway public opinion. In October 1787, James Madison, Alexander Hamilton, and John Jay published the first in a series of eighty-five articles, which came to be known as *The Federalist,* in the New York press extolling the virtues of the new Constitution and attempting to quell opponents' anxieties about the proposed national government. Intended primarily as a propaganda weapon in the Federalist drive to secure ratification, modern scholars hail *The Federalist* for its insightful analysis of the principles of American government.

In *The Federalist,* Madison warns that **factions**—distinct groups most often driven by economic motives—threaten the unity of the new Republic by placing their own interests above those of the nation as a whole. The cure for factionalism, Madison claims, is precisely the type of republican government found in the Constitution. He argued that the size of the new nation, rather than being a threat to citizens, actually serves to protect them. A faction that dominates a single state will find it much more difficult to dominate national politics in a large union. Even large and influential factions will have difficulty controlling large districts such as those proposed in the new republic, where elected representatives are under pressure to weigh the wishes of the diverse interests they represent. Madison also believed that "unworthy" candidates "who

faction Group—most often driven by economic motives—that places its own good above the good of the nation as a whole.

practice the vicious arts" of factionalism have more difficulty gaining electoral majorities in large republics than they do in other types of government.[13]

Despite Madison's eloquent arguments, ratification met substantial opposition that included New York governor George Clinton. Undaunted, Alexander Hamilton issued a dire warning to his fellow delegates: "Of course, you know . . . that if you refuse to ratify then New York City will secede from the state and ratify by itself, and where will the Empire State be without its crown jewel?"[14] Faced with the prospect of the state's political breakup, New York delegates ratified the Constitution by a vote of 30 to 27. Shortly thereafter, enough remaining states fell in line to ensure passage. Reluctant Rhode Island conceded the reality of the new regime by ratifying the Constitution in 1790, after the new government was already up and running.

Making Good on a Promise: The Bill of Rights

Once elected to the new Congress, Madison determined to make good on the Federalists' pledge to incorporate additional amendments. Massachusetts had proposed as many as twenty-nine amendments, but Madison moved to submit only seventeen for approval by the states; Congress approved just twelve. The first ten, which constitute our Bill of Rights, were adopted by the states by 1791.

The first three amendments emphasize political liberties including freedom of speech, freedom of religion, freedom of the press, freedom of assembly, the right to bear arms, and protection against being forced to quarter troops in peacetime. The next five outline the basic rights that constitute due process of law, designed to protect innocent citizens accused of crimes. The Ninth and Tenth Amendments deal with federal–state relations and specify that rights and powers not explicitly granted to the federal government in the Constitution remain in the hands of the people and the states.

Although the Bill of Rights protected citizens from acts of the national government, it did not restrict states from depriving their own citizens of some of these same freedoms. In 1833 (*Barrons v. Baltimore*), the Supreme Court ruled that the Bill of Rights applied only to the national government since it was fear of the powers of the national government that provoked Antifederalists to call for these additional protections. As a result, states were not constrained by government limitations imposed by the Bill of Rights or by the Supreme Court's interpretation of those rights. Citizens in many states did not enjoy protections against unreasonable government searches or the right to an attorney or to a speedy trial. Even states that did recognize these rights did not apply them equally to all citizens. In many places, minority populations lacked these basic protections. However, the ratification of the Fourteenth Amendment in 1868 provided a vehicle whereby many of the rights enumerated in the Bill of Rights could be applied to the states. You will learn more about the fight for "incorporating" these rights in Chapter 4.

Madison's Eleventh Amendment, which failed to gain approval at the time, was finally passed more than two hundred years later. It prohibits members of Congress from receiving pay raises during the same session in which they are voted. In 1982, an undergraduate at The University of Texas at Austin, Gregory Watson, discovered that no time limit had been placed on the ratification of early amendments, so Madison's proposal was still eligible for adoption. Watson mounted a one-man ratification drive targeting strategic states whose ratification was not yet secured. In May 1992, the measure received legislative approval in Alabama,

Freedoms Guaranteed by the Bill of Rights

First Amendment	Prohibits Congress from establishing religion and restricting its free exercise; also prohibits Congress from abridging freedoms of speech, press, assembly, and petition
Second Amendment	Guarantees the people the right to bear arms
Third Amendment	Prohibits enforced quartering of soldiers in times of peace and allows for the regulation of such practices in times of war
Fourth Amendment	Protects against unreasonable searches and seizures
Fifth Amendment	Prescribes the use of grand juries, protects against being tried in the same court twice for the same offense, protects against self-incrimination, prescribes due process and compensation for property taken for public use
Sixth Amendment	Guarantees speedy and public trial in criminal procedures, trial by impartial jury, the right to be informed of charges and the right to face accusers, the right to obtain witnesses and to secure counsel for defense
Seventh Amendment	Guarantees the right to a jury trial in civil cases
Eighth Amendment	Prohibits excessive bail as well as cruel and unusual punishment
Ninth Amendment	Mandates that those rights not explicitly listed are reserved for the people
Tenth Amendment	Mandates that those powers not delegated to the national government are retained by states and the people

Every year, members of Congress propose a number of amendments to the U.S. Constitution. Most of these never get a hearing. Some, like doing away with the Electoral College, are proposed repeatedly in every legislative session. Take a look at the latest proposals at the Library of Congress website, www.thomas.gov. Simply type "amendments" in the search box. You can also find out if any amendments were proposed or co-sponsored by your representative.

putting it over the top and making it the Twenty-seventh Amendment. Madison's proposed Twelfth Amendment, limiting the size of Congress, will experience no such revival, however. When Congress certified the ratification of the Twenty-seventh Amendment, it cancelled other long-standing proposed amendments, including Madison's unsuccessful twelfth proposal.

CONSTITUTIONAL CHANGE

One of the reasons the U.S. Constitution has endured for as long as it has is that the Framers made provisions for change. Although the amendment process is the most familiar way to alter the document, it is by no means the only one—in fact, it has been used sparingly. Our governmental structure—with its checks and balances, judicial review, and federalism—facilitates more subtle adaptation to accommodate changes to the social, political, and cultural landscape.

Amending the Constitution

The Framers proposed two methods for submitting amendments. Under the first method, an amendment that is in-

troduced to Congress and approved by a two-thirds vote of both houses may be submitted to the states for ratification. This method has been used to initiate every existing amendment. Alternately, if requested by two-thirds of the state legislatures, Congress may call a national convention at which amendments may be proposed. In the 1980s, supporters of an amendment requiring the federal government to balance its budget annually tried this rarely used tactic but failed to gain sufficient support to mount a convention. Some scholars worry that, like the original meeting in 1787, such a convention could wander beyond its original mandate. Presumably, the delegates could propose a whole series of changes—even a new constitution.

Amendments passed by the Congress must still be ratified by three-quarters of the states to become part of the Constitution. This can happen either by approval of the legislatures in those states or by ratifying conventions held in the states. State legislatures have ratified every amendment except the Twenty-first, which repealed the Eighteenth Amendment prohibiting the manufacture and sale of alcoholic beverages in the United States. The ratification process originally had no fixed time limit, which is why one of Madison's amendments remained viable for 203 years. In the early twentieth century, however, Congress began placing time limits on the ratification effort, usually seven years. Congress occasionally allows extensions, as it did in 1982 when it allotted an additional three years for states to consider the Equal Rights Amendment. Despite

Methods for Proposing and Ratifying Amendments

PROPOSING AMENDMENTS

1. 2/3 vote of both houses of Congress

OR

2. National Convention called by Congress at the request of 2/3 of the states

RATIFICATION

1. Approval by state legislators of 3/4 of the states

OR

2. Approval by ratifying conventions in 3/4 of the states

Recent Unsuccessful Attempts to Amend the Constitution

111th Congress (2009–2010)
- To eliminate the Electoral College
- To make decent, safe, affordable housing available for all Americans
- To define marriage as the bond between man and woman
- To fill Senate vacancies through elections
- To assure right of all citizens to quality education
- To protect rights of parents to bring up and educate their children
- To limit amount of campaign contributions to political candidates

110th Congress (2007–2008)
- To repeal the Sixteenth Amendment (permitting taxing of income)
- To prohibit flag desecration
- To ensure the right to a clean, safe, and sustainable environment
- To establish term limits for Congress
- To make English the official language of the United States

109th Congress (2005–2006)
- To specifically permit prayer at school meetings and ceremonies
- To allow non-natural-born citizens to run for president if they have been a citizen for twenty years
- To specifically allow Congress to regulate the amount of personal funds a candidate to public office can expend in a campaign
- To ensure that apportionment of representatives be set by counting only citizens
- To make the filibuster in the Senate a part of the Constitution
- To provide for continuity of government in the case of a catastrophic event

the extension, the amendment barring discrimination on the basis of sex fell three states short of ratification.

Although the Framers designed the Constitution to be adaptable to change, they did not want change to come easily. They ensured that anyone who wished to amend the Constitution would need to build broad popular support for their proposals. The track record of amendment attempts illustrates the difficulty of the task. Of the more than ten thousand amendments proposed since 1789, only 33 made it to the states for ratification and only 27 became part of the Constitution. The table above lists some recent proposed amendments that didn't make it—or at least, not so far.

Institutional Adaptation

For the Constitution to remain viable, it must be able to adapt to changing times and deal with matters that its authors could hardly have anticipated. The individuals who crafted the Fourth Amendment did not envision the government electronically monitoring the conversations of suspected terrorists, nor did they consider the need to regulate fundraising by political parties when they penned the First Amendment. Formal parties did not even exist at the time, and the Framers generally viewed them with disdain.

The president is commander in chief of the armed forces, but Congress is entrusted with the power to declare war.

The Constitution is also flexible enough to survive the recurring power struggles among competing branches of government. For example, although the Constitution grants Congress the power to declare war, presidents have repeatedly asserted broad power over the military, greatly expanding the constitutional role of commander in chief. In fact, although the United States has been involved in hundreds of armed conflicts, Congress has only formally declared war five times.[15] This reflects, in part, the changing nature of warfare. Compared to the present day, eighteenth-century weapons were crude and communications were extremely slow; national leaders had more time to respond to military threats. The pace and destructiveness of modern warfare has produced a tendency to defer to presidential authority in matters of war and peace, and presidents have not been shy about wielding such authority.

Congress, too, has expanded its powers by the way it has interpreted the language of the Constitution. For example, in the mid–twentieth century, Congress used its power to regulate interstate commerce in a way never imagined a century before to achieve a host of goals unrelated to trade or business. By prohibiting businesses that transport goods and services across state lines from practicing discrimination, Congress advanced the cause of racial integration. Prior to the Civil War, such use of this power was unthinkable.

The Constitution has also withstood substantial changes in the relationship between the states and the federal government. In 1787, the states were independent entities that jealously guarded their power from federal encroachment. Although states can still set policies for residents within their borders, the federal government often uses its budgetary power to compel them to adopt national standards. In the 1980s, for example, Congress voted to withhold federal highway funds from states that failed to adopt a minimum drinking age of twenty-one. Again, these actions reflect adaptation to changing circumstances; variations in drinking ages may have made more sense before interstate highways essentially obliterated the borders between states.

judicial review Power of the U.S. Supreme Court to review the acts of other political institutions and declare them unconstitutional.

Judicial Review

The decisions of the Supreme Court have effected greater changes to our system of government than any other actions save constitutional amendments. As cases work their way through trial and appeals courts in our state or federal judicial system (described in Chapter 14), they occasionally raise questions about the constitutionality of particular laws or acts of political institutions. When this happens, the Supreme Court renders a final verdict on whether or not these laws and actions pass constitutional muster. Most Americans take for granted the Court's role as final arbiter in interpreting the Constitution. However, the Constitution does not explicitly grant that power; instead, the Court assumed it in the 1803 case of *Marbury v. Madison.* In his opinion, Chief Justice John Marshall claimed for the Court authority for **judicial review**, the power to review the acts of other political institutions and declare them unconstitutional. Most scholars agree that the Framers assumed the Supreme Court would have this power, as did the British courts with which they were familiar. Alexander Hamilton even wrote in *The Federalist* No. 78:

> The interpretation of the laws is the proper and peculiar province of the courts. A constitution is, in fact, and must be regarded by the judges as, a fundamental law. It therefore belongs to them to ascertain its meaning as

The First Amendment protects our rights to assemble peaceably and to petition the government for redress of grievances.

well as the meaning of any particular act proceeding from the legislative body.[16]

Nevertheless, the Court sometimes endures severe criticism when it exercises this power. In its highly controversial ruling *Roe v. Wade,* the Court ruled that state laws making abortions illegal violated a woman's constitutional right to privacy. Although privacy is not explicitly mentioned in the Constitution, the Court ruled it could be inferred from the Ninth Amendment and the due process clause of the Fourteenth Amendment. Justice Harry Blackmun wrote: "The right to privacy . . . is broad enough to encompass a woman's decision whether or not to terminate her pregnancy."[17] More than three and a half decades later, the ruling still arouses heated emotional opposition and political debate. Abortion opponents have been successful in persuading state legislatures to place funding and consent restrictions on the right to obtain an abortion, and they continue to promote a constitutional amendment to reverse *Roe v. Wade.* You will learn more about this in Chapter 4.

Expanding the Franchise

At the time of its writing, the Constitution granted the vote only to propertied, white, adult males. Yet despite placing severe limits on the franchise, it offered a process for expanding individual rights and a structure that enabled citizens to effect change. Property qualifications for voting fell first in the western territories, repealed by settlers attracted by free land and eager to form new social and political networks.[18] This experience taught astute eastern politicians that they could increase their base of popular support by expanding the franchise to

Current Controversy

Should We Rethink the Great Compromise?

The Great Compromise apportioned House seats on the basis of population but gave each state equal representation in the Senate. George Washington is said to have explained the Senate's function to Thomas Jefferson as cooling the passions of House legislation much as a saucer is sometimes used to cool hot tea. Over 220 years later, some critics question the continuing relevance of the Senate's role in our democracy, noting that the body sometimes frustrates majority rule by granting members from small states the power to thwart the wishes of citizens from far larger states. The difficulty President Obama has had in getting key legislation through this body has led some to call it dysfunctional.

Alec MacGillis, a *Washington Post* reporter, suggests that changes in American society since its founding may render the Senate's current operation obsolete:

"The idea [of the Great Compromise] was to safeguard states' rights at a time when the former colonies were still trying to get used to this new country of theirs. But the big/small divide was nothing like what we have today. Virginia, the biggest of the original 13 states, had 538,000 people in 1780, or 12 times as many people as the smallest state, Delaware.

"Today, California is 70 times as large as the smallest state, Wyoming, whose population of 533,000 is smaller than that of the average congressional district, and, yes, smaller than that of Washington D.C., which has zero votes in Congress to Wyoming's three. The 10 largest states are home to more than half the people in the country, yet have only a fifth of the votes in the Senate. The 21 smallest states together hold fewer people than California's 36.7 million—which means there are 42 senators who together represent fewer constituents than [California senators] Barbara Boxer and Dianne Feinstein. And under Senate rules, of course, those 42 senators—representing barely more than a tenth of the country's population—can mount a filibuster [a powerful tactic by which a minority can put the brakes on legislative action]."*

Do the small states have too much power? Should we change the way seats are apportioned in the Senate? Or does the ability of the Senate to stall the will of legislative majorities from large states still serve an important function for our democracy?

*Alec MacGillis, "The Gangs of D.C: In the Senate, Small States Wield Outsize Power. Is This What the Founders Had in Mind?" *The Washington Post*, August 9, 2009.

those without property. By the middle of the nineteenth century, property qualifications for voting had crumbled across the nation.

Women and African Americans found voting barriers much more difficult to overcome. Prominent women such as Abigail Adams spoke for women's rights from the time of the Revolution, but women only secured the vote with passage of the Nineteenth Amendment in 1920 after decades of political protest. The nation had to endure a civil

A strong voice for equal rights, Abigail Adams (1744–1818) cautioned her husband, the second president of the United States, to "remember the ladies."

war before African Americans won their freedom with the Thirteenth Amendment and black males won the franchise with the Fifteenth Amendment. It took African Americans a further century of litigation, protest, and political campaigning to secure the full promise of the franchise through civil rights legislation in the 1960s. In 1971, the Twenty-sixth Amendment broadened the franchise even further, granting eighteen-year-olds the vote.

Although most legal barriers to voting are gone, issues of motivation, mobilization, and resources, which disproportionately affect those at the lower end of the income spectrum, remain. We will examine these in later chapters.

THE CONSTITUTION AND CIVIC ENGAGEMENT TODAY

In 2004, Congress passed legislation requiring public institutions that receive federal funds to set aside September 17, the anniversary of the signing of the Constitution, as Constitution and Citizenship Day.[19] On this day, educators are required to conduct programs designed to commemorate the legacy of our founding document. Americans, however, don't need a special day to remind them of their Constitutional heritage; millions practice it every day. We celebrate the U.S. Constitution every time we write our senators and representatives about some important issue, read press accounts of current events, attend religious services, donate money to a political cause or candidate, engage in political debate in the classroom, or make a do-

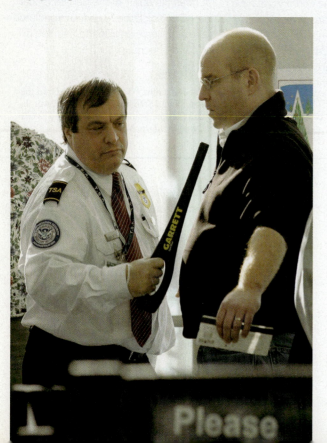

nation to an interest group. All of these activities reflect fundamental rights enshrined in our Constitution.

Yet, we should remember that rights are never totally secure. They face continuing challenges and must adapt to meet changing times. Since the 9/11 terrorist attacks, many rights have been curbed in the interest of security. In some cases, such as the baggage searches and other intrusions of personal privacy that air travelers must endure, Americans generally take these inconveniences in stride. Most feel that the need for security outweighs issues of personal privacy in such situations. Other measures the government has taken in the name of security are far more controversial. For example, Congress has given the executive branch the right to monitor international phone calls and Internet traffic without obtaining a warrant, and with less judicial oversight than was required in the past. The intelligence community can order Internet providers, phone companies, and online services like Hotmail and Skype to turn over all communications that are reasonably believed to involve a non-American who is outside the country. Agen-

Recent acts of terrorism are redefining the boundary between civil liberties and national security.

cies do not have to name their targets or get prior court approval for the surveillance. Although these measures were advanced during the Bush administration, President Obama has signaled his continued support for them, and his administration has defended them in court. Should the government assume such broad powers and make them a permanent feature of the American political system? Does government need such powers to protect its citizens—or are such powers unwarranted intrusions into our personal lives that go beyond the requirements of genuine security?

These are questions for citizens of your generation to face, just as the founding generation faced questions dealing with the right of government to quarter soldiers in their homes or to shut down town meetings held without the prior approval of royal governors. There are plenty of ways you can get involved in exploring such issues and mak-

ing your voice heard. You can join one of the many interest groups that focus their efforts on this issue and that can offer detailed information and analysis. You can hold university or community forums to solicit the views of your classmates and neighbors. You can meet with law enforcement officials and legal scholars to get their views. These are rights that your generation has inherited and are yours to keep as long as you stay involved. Thomas Jefferson's famous aphorism "the price of freedom is eternal vigilance" applies no less today than it did in his own day.

Hot or Not?

Should the government be given greater authority to access Internet records for purposes of national security?

Summary

1. What factors contributed to the need for a constitutional convention?

- After a Revolution spawned by the desire for greater economic opportunity and self-rule, the colonies were administered by a Continental Congress created by the Articles of Confederation. Colonists soon found the Articles too weak to help them pay their war debt, control interstate commerce, and put down local rebellions like the one fomented by Daniel Shays in Massachusetts.

- A call went out to convene a meeting to reform the Articles in Philadelphia, but the fifty-five delegates decided instead to create a new governing document. Disagreement over the apportionment of the legislature led to a key compromise, known as the Great Compromise, in which seats in the lower chamber were allocated on the basis of population, appeasing the larger states, whereas in the upper chamber, each state was granted equal representation (two seats), satisfying the interests of the small states. Concerns over the institution of slavery were resolved by the three-fifths compromise and by allowing the importation of slaves to continue for twenty years.

- Once the document was released, it was not met with wide acceptance. Support was generated by a series of newspaper articles that came to be known as *The Federalist,* penned by James Madison, Alexander Hamilton, and John Jay.

2. What are the basic principles that inform our Constitution?

- The basic principles of the Constitution are separation of powers, checks and balances, and a division of power between the states and the national government known as federalism.

- The Constitution establishes a bicameral legislature, a single executive, and a federal court system that includes the Supreme Court. Powers of each branch overlap in ways that make it difficult for any one branch to exercise complete control. Powers are further divided between the national and state governments, providing for what Madison called "a double security" for the rights of the people.

- Antifederalists who opposed the Constitution wanted even more individual protections and called for the adoption of a bill of rights. The Federalist supporters of the Constitution obliged by appending ten amendments during the first legislative session of Congress. The amendments, known as the Bill of Rights, guarantee free speech and freedom of religion and protect the rights of those accused of crimes.

3. In what ways does constitutional change occur?

- The Constitution can be changed through amendment; through the actions of political leaders who stretch its meaning to adapt to social, political, and economic change; and by court interpretation.

- Amending the Constitution is a two-stage process. The first stage requires either the adoption of the measure by a two-thirds vote by both houses of Congress, a procedure used for all existing amendments, or by a national convention called by two-thirds of the states. Ratification, the second stage, requires either approval by the legislatures in three-quarters of the states or approval by ratifying conventions in three-quarters of the states. The latter method was used only to repeal Prohibition.

- Political actors can also extend the meaning of the document as Congress sometimes does when it takes an expansive view of the "necessary and proper" clause.

- The Supreme Court can effect change by exercising judicial review to interpret the document over time.

The Peculiar Problem Of 'Peekaboo'

In 2002, Congress was in a hurry and in a fix. Awash in popular anger over Enron and other corporate scandals, lawmakers were working frenetically on what would become the Sarbanes-Oxley corporate accountability law. Under pressure to adopt bold reforms at top speed, Congress created a new federal agency unlike any other.

A little over three years later, in fall 2005, a handful of free-market activists and litigators met in a windowless 11th-floor conference room at the American Enterprise Institute in Washington. They included two lawyers with the Competitive Enterprise Institute, a market-oriented think tank; representatives of the Free Enterprise Fund, an activist group; former U.S. Solicitor General (and Clinton-era Special Prosecutor) Kenneth Starr; and Michael Greve, the chairman of the CEI and an AEI scholar, who brought the group together. They shared a conviction that Congress's 2002 creation was a constitutional monster.

By the time the meeting finished, the participants had decided to join forces and file suit. In February 2006, they asked the courts to strike down the Public Company Accounting Oversight Board—ubiquitously nicknamed "Peekaboo"—as unconstitutional.

A federal District Court slapped down the case on summary judgment. The D.C. Circuit Court of Appeals agreed, 2-to-1. No one paid much attention. But the yawning stopped on May 18, when the Supreme Court announced it will hear the case.

The high court is unpredictable, especially with Sonia Sotomayor, a new justice whose leanings are uncertain. But we know that at least four justices voted to review the case. We can guess that among them were most of the Court's conservatives, who take a dim view of constitutional improvisation. We can also guess that if those four votes find a fifth, the Court may agree with Judge Brett Kavanaugh, the dissenting judge on

appeal, who called Peekaboo an "unprecedented extra-constitutional stew."

What's it all about? And what should the Court do?

The Public Company Accounting Oversight Board sets and enforces standards for the accountants who audit corporations' books. Congress could have given this task to the Securities and Exchange Commission. Or it could have chartered a private overseer, on the model of the New York Stock Exchange. Or it could have set up an entirely new regulatory agency, one similar to the SEC but separate from it.

Peekaboo, however, breaks new ground. Unlike the New York Stock Exchange, it is a creation of Congress and wields powers characteristic of a government agency. Unlike the SEC, it is nominally a private, nonprofit corporation. Moreover, its five board members are not appointed by the president and cannot be removed by him. Rather, the SEC appoints them. Only the SEC can remove them, and even then only for cause (that is, for misconduct rather than, say, over a policy disagreement).

So the board is something new: an independent regulatory body nested within, and directly accountable to, another independent regulatory body. "Never before in American history," Kavanaugh wrote, "has there been an independent agency whose heads are appointed by and removable only for cause by another independent agency."

Exactly why Congress chose to create such a jackalope is not completely clear. Legislators seem to have wanted Peekaboo to have as much independence from politics as the New York Stock Exchange does, but to have as much clout as the SEC wields.

In a matter as complicated and sensitive as auditing corporate books, there is much to be said for insulation from political pressure. But it's worth mentioning that the Founders had a different idea.

Among James Madison's strokes of counterintuitive brilliance, the most counterintuitive and brilliant was that the only reliable antidote to the abuse of political power is politics itself. If you want to keep politicians out of mischief, tying their hands or placing

> The principle of keeping power accountable to elected officials sits at the very heart of the Constitution. It is too important to be weakened without a better justification than the government, in defending Peekaboo, has provided.

them under nonpolitical supervision will never work, at least not for long. Instead, pit them against each other. Force them to bid competitively for popular support. "Ambition must be made to counteract ambition," he famously wrote in Federalist 51, his argument for checks and balances. Too much insulation from politics, in Madison's view, is more dangerous than too little.

To which, Alexander Hamilton, explaining in Federalist 76 why the power to appoint should be reserved to the president, added: "The sole and undivided responsibility of one man will naturally beget a livelier sense of duty and a more exact regard to reputation." The government's coercive power to enforce laws, Hamilton was saying, is unaccountable when dispersed. It should be wielded not by a group but by an individual, the president, who answers to the people. Any other scheme invites the "multitude of new offices" and "swarms of officers" that the Declaration of Independence complains about so bitterly.

In the 1930s, the Supreme Court took a step away from the original scheme by blessing independent regulatory agencies whose policy makers were appointed by the president but could not be removed by him, except for cause. Even so, the president retains some control. He appoints SEC commissioners, for instance, and he designates the SEC's chairman at will. The accounting oversight board, by contrast, is a second step removed, accountable to the SEC, not to the White House.

Peekaboo thinks this is accountability enough. The agency argues that it is "a wholly owned subsidiary of the SEC," as Bill Gradison, a board member (and former member of Congress), said in a recent interview. "There's nothing of consequence the PCAOB can do that doesn't require advance approval by the SEC or can't be appealed to the SEC. And that's the actual way we operate around here."

The SEC approves Peekaboo's budget. The commission's signoff is necessary before any rule takes effect. The SEC can overturn any agency disciplinary action. If it wanted to, it could revoke the accounting board's powers altogether. The SEC's role is hardly a formality, Gradison says. "We don't just send something over there and they approve it. Every item that ultimately they have approved is the result of a long process."

Peekaboo thus argues that its board members are what the Constitution calls "inferior officers," meaning that they are less like agency heads ("principal officers") and more like agency staff. The District and Appeals courts agreed. Under long-standing constitutional doctrine, hirelings who take orders from agency heads don't need to be appointed by the president or confirmed by the Senate.

Hogwash, retort the challengers. "These people are running their own agency," says Michael Carvin, a lawyer with Jones Day who is representing the plaintiffs. "The notion that they're not principal officers is just silly." How can Peekaboo's board members be mere servants of the SEC when, absent a showing of wrongdoing or incompetence, the SEC can't fire them, even for point-blank disobedience?

And if Peekaboo is allowed to stand, the challengers say, what next? Imagine the possibilities: an Energy Price Enforcement Board appointed by and removable only for cause by the Federal Energy Regulatory Commission, or an Indecency Enforcement Board appointed by and removable only for cause by the Federal Communications Commission. "All are permissible under the PCAOB's theory of the case," Kavanaugh wrote in his dissent. "But in such a system, where is the president?" And what would prevent Congress from setting up third-order regulators who report to other regulators who report to still other regulators?

The Supreme Court is unlikely to put Peekaboo and its almost 500 employees out of business. What it might do is force Congress to rewrite the law—for instance, by

making the board subject to White House appointment and Senate confirmation. If so, only a few accountants and law professors would notice the difference.

Still, says Donna Nagy, a law professor at Indiana University (Bloomington), "I think it's a tremendously important case, and I think that's part of the reason the Supreme Court granted certiorari. Going forward, the question is whether Congress can and should be creating these kinds of hybrid agencies that are supervised by independent regulatory agencies."

In creating a regulator accountable only to another regulator, Congress never showed a need to abandon Mr. Madison's constitutional scheme. Nor has evidence of any such need arisen. Indeed, no one disputes that Peekaboo could perform its duties effectively with presidential appointees on its board, just as the SEC and all the other independent regulatory agencies do.

The principle of keeping power accountable to elected officials sits at the very heart of the Constitution. It is too important to be weakened without a better justification than the government, in defending Peekaboo, has provided.

For Discussion:

■ Find the Constitutional reference to "inferior officers" to which the article alludes. What impact does this reference, and its context, have on your understanding of "Peekaboo" and its Constitutional status?

■ The issue of agencies like Peekaboo doesn't garner the attention of hotter-button Constitutional issues like, say, free speech or gun control. Explain why the author considers it so important nonetheless. Do you agree?

■ What does the author propose as the possible solutions to the vague status of the "public company"? Why is a solution needed at all? Based on the facts in the piece, what solution would you favor? Does efficacy move your opinion more or less than fidelity to founding principles such as those the author cites?

3

FEDERALISM

CITIZENSHIP AND THE DISPERSAL OF POWER

IF AT FIRST YOU DON'T SECEDE . . . ❚ To shouts of "Secede!" Texas governor Rick Perry told a crowd of antitax protesters at Austin City Hall that the federal government is strangling Americans with taxation, spending, and debt. Later, he told the press, "When we came into the Union in 1845, one of the issues was that we would be able to leave if we decided to do that. My hope is that America, and Washington in particular, pay attention. We've got a great Union. There's absolutely no reason to dissolve it. But if Washington continues to thumb their nose at the American people, who knows what may come of that?"[1] Just a week before, Perry voiced support for a resolution that supports states' rights protected in the Tenth Amendment to the U.S. Constitution, telling state lawmakers the federal government had become oppressive in its size and interference with states.

Few authorities believe that Texas or any other state has the legal authority to leave the Union. That matter seems to have been settled by the Civil War. In an 1869 case involving Texas (*Texas v. White*), the U.S. Supreme Court ruled that individual states could not unilaterally secede from the Union and that the acts of the insurgent Texas legislature—even if ratified by a majority of Texans—were absolutely null. In the face of media scrutiny, Perry later backed away from his original comments.

Still, Governor Perry's dissatisfaction over the balance of power between Washington and the states reflects a sentiment shared by other governors who moved to reject federal money destined for their states as part of President Obama's 2009 stimulus package and who continue to fiercely battle his health-care reforms. Their concern is that federal money increases the national debt and comes with too many strings attached. For example, Florida Governor Rick Scott refused $2.4 billion in federal funds for high speed rail service and an additional $2 million in federal planning money for the development of health care exchanges mandated under health-care reform. Scott, like some other conservative governors, complains that the money increases government indebtedness while committing the states to using their own funds for mandates that accompany the federal legislation. Some governors like Haley Barbour of Mississippi and Bobby Jindal of Louisiana reluctantly accepted federal funds after complaining about their impact on the federal debt when their own states had difficulty meeting financial obligations without the assistance. And a legal showdown is brewing in the courts as Florida, along with more than two dozen other states, challenge the health-care law as an unconstitutional infringement on the rights of states and their citizens. The federal response is that Washington has a role to play both in propping up a sagging economy during economic downturns and in controlling health-care costs because of the industry's huge impact on interstate commerce and the national economy.

Disagreement over stimulus funding and health-care reform are just two of the more recent examples of the tensions that can arise between our national and state governments as a result of a feature of the American political landscape known as **federalism.** Federalism disperses authority among different levels of government, providing citizens with different points of access for ➥

As You READ >>

- How is power dispersed in American federalism?
- How have the powers of the national and state governments evolved over the nation's history?
- What factors influence relations between national and state governments today?

voicing their concerns, advocating policies, and engaging with political leaders. This chapter focuses primarily on government at the national and state levels, but the nation's governmental structure is much more complex. In addition to the federal and state governments, the United States is composed of 3,033 county governments, 19,492 municipal governments, 16,519 town and township governments, and over 50,000 special and school district governments.[2] Most of these governments have some taxing authority, and all conduct legal and fiscal transactions with other units of government. Relationships among these various levels of government continually evolve to reflect the changing political and financial currents of the day, potentially affecting the lives of millions of citizens. ◆

THE DIVISION OF POWER

federalism Power-sharing arrangement between the national and state governments in which some powers are granted to the national government alone, some powers are reserved to the states, some powers are held concurrently, and other powers are prohibited to either or both levels of government.

Following the American Revolution, the nation's Framers faced the problem of organizing a rapidly growing nation whose citizens cherished local rule. While history furnished ideas for power sharing within the national government—such as separation of powers and checks and balances—it offered few workable models for nation–state relations. The individuals who framed the Constitution were forced to devise their own solution—a historic innovation called federalism.

Prevailing Models for Dispersing Power

Prior to the Constitutional Convention, two models of intergovernmental relations predominated throughout the world: unitary and confederated (see the figure on the next page). Under a unitary form, all power resides in the central government, which makes the laws. State or local governments act primarily as local vehicles to implement national laws. Many of the Framers found this kind of distant government unacceptable and considered it a threat to personal liberty. This form of government characterized the British system against which the colonies rebelled and persists in many nations today, including England and France.

In a confederation, states and localities retain sovereign power, yielding to the central government only limited authority as needed. This form of government—which characterized the government under the Articles of Confederation—was also clearly unacceptable,

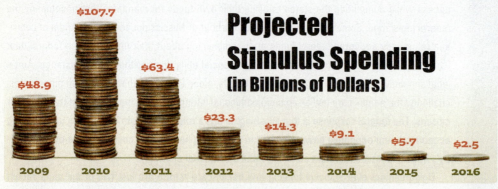

Projected Stimulus Spending (in Billions of Dollars)

$48.9 — 2009
$107.7 — 2010
$63.4 — 2011
$23.3 — 2012
$14.3 — 2013
$9.1 — 2014
$5.7 — 2015
$2.5 — 2016

Source: Christine Vestal, "Is it Time for a New Fiscal Balance between States and the Feds?" Pew Center on the States, http://www.stateline.org/live/details/story?contentId=454040Obama (accessed March 9, 2010)

leading the Framers to call a convention in Philadelphia to address its shortcomings. Confederations are, for the most part, relics of the past. Very few modern nations employ this form of government because it slows the central government's ability to act. A confederacy does, however, characterize some intergovernmental organizations that include nation-states as members, such as the United Nations.

The Federalist Solution

Even opponents of a strong national government understood that only a more "energetic" central power could remedy the defects contained in the Articles of Confederation. These included a lack of control over interstate commerce and the absence of a national currency, which seriously limited the development of national markets. Most significantly, however, the national government lacked central taxing power, making it impossible to raise money to repay the substantial debts it accumulated during the Revolution. The Continental Congress could assess each state for taxes, but it had no power to enforce col-

lection. The delegates to the Constitutional Convention faced the problem of providing the central government with enough power to function effectively but not so much that it dominated the states. Federalism was their solution.

In a federal system, four main attributes characterize power arrangements among levels of government:

1. **Enumerated powers** are specifically granted to the national government. Article I in the U.S. Constitution expressly authorizes most of these powers. Section 8 of Article I, known as the elastic clause, implies that the national government exercises additional powers by authorizing Congress to make "all laws which shall be necessary and proper for carrying into execution the foregoing powers." These powers to implement constitutionally enumerated functions are known as **implied powers**. The national government also exercises inherent powers characteristic of any sovereign nation such as the power to wage war and conduct international trade.

2. **Reserved powers** are granted specifically to the states. The Constitution places certain limits upon national power, and the Tenth Amendment reserves to the states or to the people all powers not specifically granted to the national government. Many actions states take with regard to protecting the health and welfare of their residents issue from their **police powers**.

3. **Concurrent powers** are shared jointly by the federal and state governments.

enumerated powers Powers specifically allocated to the national government alone by the Constitution.

implied powers Powers necessary to carry out constitutionally enumerated functions of government.

reserved powers Powers constitutionally allocated to the states.

police powers Authority states utilize to protect the health and welfare of their residents.

concurrent powers Powers shared by both state and national governments.

Diagrams of Unitary and Confederated Forms of Government

Unitary Government

Confederation

Arrows represent the flow of decisions and resources.

 Central   State   Local

Attributes of U.S. Federalism

Powers of National Government	Powers Reserved for State Governments	Concurrent Powers
Make war	Regulate intrastate commerce	Tax and spend
Coin money	Protect health and safety	Borrow money
	Pass laws	Establish courts
	Charter local governments	Charter banks and corporations
	Regulate voting	
	Establish schools	
Admit new states		
Regulate interstate commerce		
Establish post offices		
Raise army and navy		
Establish uniform naturalization laws		
Fix standard weights and measures		

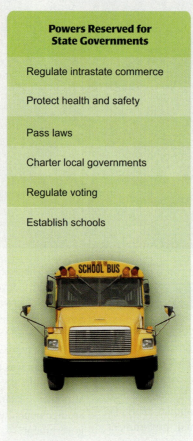
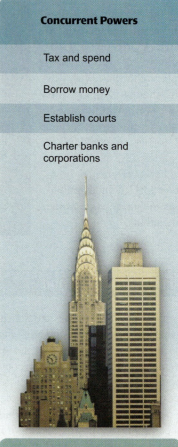
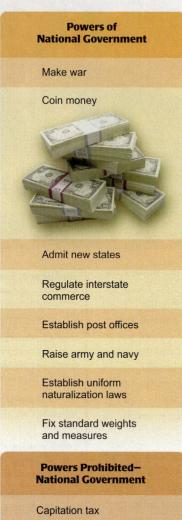

Powers Prohibited— National Government	Powers Prohibited—States	Powers Prohibited— National and State
Capitation tax	Make treaties	Ex post facto laws
Tax state exports	Impair contracts	Bills of attainder
Preferential treatment for ports	Tax exports	
Grant titles of nobility	Make war	

4. **Prohibited powers** are denied to either or both levels of government. The table above lists examples of major powers in each category.

prohibited powers Powers denied one or both levels of government.

Many supporters felt that a federal system not only was more practical but also served as an additional guarantee of individual freedoms. Madison argued that the federal system offered a dual protection of citizens' rights. In *The Federalist* No. 51, he writes:

In the compound Republic of America, the power surrendered by the people is first divided between two distinct governments, and then the portion allotted to each subdivided among separate departments. Hence a double security arises to the rights of the people. The different governments will control each other, at the same time that each will be controlled by itself.[3]

For Federalists such as Madison, federalism protected individual freedom, encouraged participation in national affairs, and enhanced public security.

Antifederalists, however, remained suspicious of the power of the national government. They found particularly worrisome the supremacy clause in Article VI, which declared federal law supreme in instances when national and state laws collided. Despite the addition of a bill of rights explicitly limiting the federal government's ability to encroach on the rights of individuals and states, Antifed-

eralists remained uncomfortable with the federal arrangement well into the formative years of the new republic. They warned that the new federal system would unravel the bonds of citizenship that they believed flourished only in small, homogeneous communities.[4] To some extent, the debate over which conditions best foster citizen participation—small, like-minded communities, or larger, more diverse ones—persists. It seems clear, however, that a federal system is well suited to a country such as the United States, where regional interests must seek accommodation with broader national goals.

THE EVOLUTION OF INTERGOVERNMENTAL RELATIONS

Although the Constitution provides ground rules for the federal allocation of power, the balance of power among various levels of government has not remained static. It has ebbed and flowed over the course of the past two and a quarter centuries, making federalism a dynamic force in our nation's history.

The National Government Asserts Itself: 1789–1832

In the early days of the new republic, former colonial allies heatedly disagreed about how much power the Constitution granted the federal government. The Constitution left all sorts of questions regarding national and state power unanswered, including the meaning of terms and phrases such as *commerce* or *necessary and proper*. Federalists in the new government, such as the treasury secretary, Alexander Hamilton, advocated exercising strong national

authority in the arena of finance and commerce, urging President Washington to support his plans for a national bank that would finance the construction of canals and roads. Secretary of State Thomas Jefferson opposed Hamilton's plan, arguing that a national bank favored northern industry over southern farming and represented unfair competition for state financial institutions. Congress authorized a twenty-year charter for the bank in 1791, setting in motion a schism between supporters of Hamilton and supporters of Jefferson that led to the growth of the nation's first political parties.

The election of Federalist candidate John Adams in 1796 increased tensions between the two groups. In 1798, Adams pushed through Congress the Alien and Sedition Laws, intended to stifle political opposition to his foreign policy. In response, Jefferson, Madison, and their allies developed the new philosophy of **nullification**, which proclaimed that states had the authority to declare national acts unenforceable within their borders. Although both the Virginia and Kentucky state legislatures passed resolutions affirming the doctrine of nullification in 1798, Jefferson ignored the doctrine after he won the presidency in 1800. Several decades later, southern secessionists resurrected his nullification philosophy as the nation moved toward civil war.[5]

> **nullification** Doctrine that asserted the right of states to disregard federal actions with which they disagreed.

Congress neglected to renew the charter of the First Bank of the United States, which expired in 1811. However, it established a Second Bank of the United States in

Alexander Hamilton (1757–1804) championed a strong federal government with the power to take the lead in the nation's economic development (left). Thomas Jefferson (1743–1826) broke with Hamilton, arguing that a national bank favored northern industry over southern farming (right).

Marshall argued that taxation by the states had the potential to destroy federal institutions and undermine the supremacy of national law.

Marshall's ruling set the stage for an expansion of national power at a time when economic production and commerce were burgeoning. Inevitably, questions soon arose regarding the national government's powers to regulate commerce. In 1824, the Marshall court heard its first case to test those powers, *Gibbons v. Ogden*. The case involved a conflict between two steamboat operators, Thomas Gibbons of New Jersey and Aaron Ogden of New York. Both men received rights to operate off the coast of New York and New Jersey: Ogden from the state of New York and Gibbons by an act of Congress. A lower court upheld Ogden's claim, ruling that the state of New York had the right to regulate commerce with neighboring states, regardless of any concurrent national power over commerce. Gibbons appealed the case to the U.S. Supreme Court.

In *Gibbons v. Ogden*, the Marshall Court upheld the supremacy of the national government in regulating commerce, not simply in intercoastal waterways but also within states when commerce between or among states was involved. Marshall also defined the term *commerce* loosely, applying it to goods as well as to passengers. This definition significantly expanded the power of Congress and the president to oversee the economic development of the new nation in areas previously considered the preserve of states. Advocates for a strong federal role in matters ranging from education to welfare would later use the same logic to support their efforts.

1816, once again raising the ire of state banking interests. Maryland reacted by enacting a tax on operations at the bank's Baltimore branch, hoping to drive it out of business. The bank's clerk, James McCulloch, refused to collect the tax, arguing that a state could not tax an institution created by the national government. After losing his battle in state court, McCulloch appealed his case to the U.S. Supreme Court, where John Marshall, a longtime Federalist supporter, presided as chief justice.

Marshall's court was asked to decide two issues: (1) Did the national government have the authority to establish a national bank, and (2) if so, could a state tax the bank's operations within its borders? In his landmark decision, *McCulloch v. Maryland* (1819), Marshall ruled against state interests on both issues. He found congressional authority to establish the bank under the "necessary and proper clause" of Article I:

> The government which has a right to do an act, and has imposed on it the duty of performing that act, must, according to the dictates of reason, be allowed to select the means. . . . To its enumeration of powers is added that of making "all laws which shall be necessary and proper for carrying into execution the foregoing powers, and all other powers vested by this constitution, in the government of the United States, or in any department thereof."[6]

dual federalism Approach to federal–state relationships that envisions each level of government as distinct and authoritative within its own sphere of action.

Marshall relied on the supremacy clause to deny states the power to tax a federal institution:

> The result is a conviction that the States have no power, by taxation or otherwise, to retard, impede, burden, or in any manner control, the operations of the constitutional laws enacted by Congress to carry into execution the powers vested in the general government. This is, we think, the unavoidable consequence of that supremacy which the constitution has declared.[7]

Dual Federalism, Disunion, and War: 1832–1865

Nation–state relations in the period preceding the Civil War were dominated by a philosophy of **dual federalism**. Dual federalism holds that the powers of the state and national governments are distinct and autonomous in their own domains. Levels of government are likened to layers in a cake that sit atop each other but do not intermingle. This viewpoint gave rise to disputes over the powers of each level of government, especially with regard to finances and the thorny issue of slavery.

Marshall's strong stance regarding the scope of federal power created resentment among southern farmers and financiers, who feared northern economic dominance. President Andrew Jackson's administration further inflamed these fears by enforcing a tariff on imported goods that protected northern manufacturers, causing some southerners to threaten secession. Jackson's vice president, South Carolinian John C. Calhoun, resigned over the matter in 1832 and justified his home state's opposition to the tariff by citing the Jeffersonian concept of nullification. Jackson adroitly solved the crisis by lowering the tariff, but talk of nullification continued as a debate over slavery took center stage in national politics.

While fear of northern dominance and support for the doctrine of nullification fueled southern passions, the Supreme Court's ruling in *Dred Scott v. Sandford* in 1857 inflamed abolitionist sentiment in the North.[8] Applying the perspective of dual federalism to bolster the power of the states, Chief Justice Roger B. Taney rejected the authority of Congress to outlaw slavery in the states and accelerated the momentum toward civil war. Republican candidate Abraham Lincoln's victory over a divided Democratic Party in the presidential election of 1860 brought the legal stalemate over slavery to an end as seven southern states seceded. Over the next four years, the United States and the Confederacy fought a bloody civil war to resolve not only the issue of slavery but also disputes over the future of our federal system that rhetoric alone could not settle.

After the Confederate surrender in 1865, Congress passed three new constitutional amendments as part of its proposed reconstruction program. The Thirteenth Amendment ended slavery. The Fourteenth Amendment guaranteed to former slaves basic rights under the U.S. Constitution. Further, it asserts that no state shall "deprive any person of life, liberty, or property, without due process of law; nor deny to any person within its jurisdiction the equal protection of the laws." The Fifteenth Amendment gave black males the vote. Of all the Civil War amendments, the Fourteenth has gen-

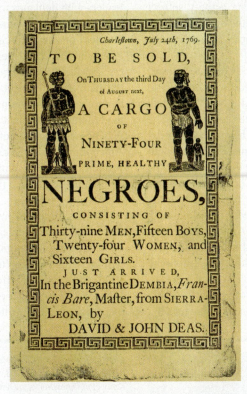

In the 1830s and 1840s, abolitionists intensified their efforts to combat the institution of slavery.

erated the most controversy and continues to define many debates surrounding federalism today.

Federalism in the Age of Commerce: 1865–1932

With the end of the Civil War and the principle of union firmly established, the nation moved into an era of unprecedented economic change and growth. Millions of rural farm workers joined large numbers of immigrants from foreign lands moving into the growing cities. The dangerous working conditions in many urban factories produced calls among reformers for government intervention to improve the lot of American workers. During this era, however, the Supreme Court consistently refused to allow the federal government to intervene in the right of states to issue licenses and to regulate commerce within their borders and rejected limits on businesses to contract for the services of employees.

In *Hammer v. Dagenhart* (1918), for example, the Supreme Court overturned federal efforts to end child labor. Associate Justice William R. Day, citing the Tenth Amendment, asserted that regulation of production was not expressly delegated to the national government and therefore was reserved to the states and to the people.[9]

The Court delivered a blow to federal efforts to restrain the growth of corporate trusts or monopolies in *U.S. v. E. C. Knight Co.* (1895).[10] The E. C. Knight Company controlled over 98 percent of the sugar refining business in the nation and sought authority for contracts to control even more. The 1890 Sherman Antitrust Act, however, sought

Failing to secure the help of the federal government, reformers during the Progressive Era turned to the states in their quest to end child labor.

to use the federal government's interstate commerce power to limit such monopolization of the market. In *U.S. v. E. C. Knight Co.,* a majority of the justices ruled that manufacturing is not commerce but an intrastate activity subject to state control. The Court argued that the activities of the company only incidentally and indirectly affected interstate commerce.

The Court was even reluctant to uphold a state's power to limit business activity within its borders. In *Lochner v. New York* (1905), the Court overturned a New York state law limiting the number of hours a baker could work. The state legislature had passed the bill on the grounds that extensive exposure to flour dust was detrimental to the health of employees and that the state had the duty to protect the health of its citizens. The Supreme Court disagreed, arguing that the law interfered with the rights of both the employee and the employer to enter freely into contract, a freedom guaranteed by the Fourteenth Amendment.[11] Justice Oliver Wendell Holmes, Jr., issued a stinging dissent that would later impact Court deliberations concerning the states' policing powers.

Progressives during this period fought unfavorable Court rulings by increasing pressure on local lawmakers.

Citizen reform groups, many headed by women such as labor rights advocate Mother Jones (See "Portrait of an Activist"), conducted marches and confronted political leaders with demands to end child labor, to improve working conditions for women, and to limit the influence of big business on the political process. The success of interest groups at the state level put pressure on federal lawmakers, producing a number of reforms that again reshaped the face of federalism. Perhaps most significant among these changes were constitutional amendments permitting the federal government to tax personal income (Sixteenth Amendment), the direct election of senators (Seventeenth Amendment), and the expansion of the voting franchise to women (Nineteenth Amendment). These amendments focused attention on the powers of the national government as an agent of change.

The Progressive Movement helped swing the pendulum in the direction of increased federal power. President Theodore Roosevelt championed mine safety and meat inspection laws, signed the Pure Food and Drug Act into law in 1906, and expanded efforts to protect the nation's forests. Woodrow Wilson later extended federal powers over commerce by pushing for the Federal Trade Commission and

Mary Harris Jones, known as Mother Jones, led a "Children's Crusade" in 1903, marching from Kensington, Pennsylvania, to Oyster Bay, New York, to confront President Theodore Roosevelt at his summer home with a demand to end child labor.

PORTRAIT
OF AN ACTIVIST

Mother Jones
and the March to Oyster Bay

It must have been a strange sight to see the sixty-six-year-old woman with a band of scrawny children, accompanied by fifes and drums, marching through the streets of New York. Mother Jones, as this Irish immigrant was known, had marched from Kensington, Pennsylvania—site

of a textile mill where the children and their parents were striking—to confront President Theodore Roosevelt at his summer home at Oyster Bay. Along the way, she stopped to make speeches in which she asked the children to show the stumps of fingers, hands, or limbs they had lost while working in the dangerous mills.

Although Roosevelt refused to see her or pursue national legislation outlawing child labor, Jones returned to Pennsylvania and continued her fight. Her efforts first bore fruit at the state level. In 1904, only fourteen states forbade employment of children under the age of fourteen in factories; by 1929, nearly every state outlawed the practice. In 1904, only two states maintained an eight-hour workday for children under age sixteen in factories; by 1929, twenty-nine states did.[*]

Change in the states led to progress at the national level. In 1936, Congress passed the Walsh-Healey act, which prevented the use of child labor by companies engaging in business with the federal government. In 1938, the Fair Labor Standards Act became law, prohibiting the interstate shipment of goods made by companies employing minors.

** Walter Trattner, *Crusade for the Children: A History of the National Child Labor Committee and Child Labor Reform in America* (Chicago: Quadrangle, 1970), p. 184.*

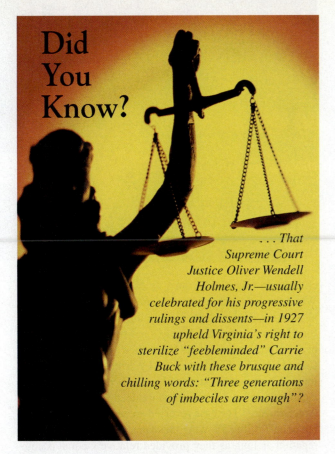
the Clayton Antitrust Act of 1914. Although subsequent Court actions weakened some of these measures, by the time of the New Deal, the tide was clearly moving in the direction of greater federal authority.

The New Deal and the Growth of National Power: 1932–1937

Economic, not political, developments triggered the most dramatic increase in federal authority, as the prosperity of the early twentieth century gave way to the Great Depression of the 1930s. In response to the national crisis, President Franklin Roosevelt's administration created programs of economic regulation and development

President Franklin D. Roosevelt (1933–1945) proposed a New Deal with numerous federal programs designed to address Depression Era insecurities.

in areas that had previously been the states' domain, including health, welfare, labor relations, and agriculture. Programs for social and employment security, a federal works project, a national program for rural electrification, and regulation of the banking and securities industries all increased federal participation in American life. Although federally operated, many of these programs required state participation involving financial and human resources. The public reacted positively to Roosevelt's so-called New Deal initiatives, providing him with a landslide re-election victory in 1936. The Supreme Court's reaction was not as enthusiastic.

In a series of cases, the Court struck down key pieces of New Deal legislation, with Chief Justice Charles Evans Hughes and his conservative allies on the bench usually prevailing by a 5 to 4 vote. In 1935, the Court invalidated the National Industry Recovery Act in the case of *Schechter v. U.S.*[12] The Court ruled that the act, which empowered the president to regulate the hours, wages, and minimum ages of industrial employees, was an unconstitutional delegation of legislative authority from Congress to the president. In *U.S. v. Butler* (1936) the Court invalidated portions of the Agricultural Adjustment Act, which rewarded some farmers for reducing production of certain commodities in order to reduce surpluses that drove down prices. The Court declared that such federal activities intruded into state and individual decisions protected by the Tenth Amendment.[13]

Anticipating more bad news from the Court, Roosevelt proposed a Court reorganization plan that would add one new judge for each sitting justice over the age of seventy. Although Roosevelt pitched the plan as a way to lighten the workload of elderly justices, he actually intended to

Linda Brown of Topeka, Kansas, asked the Supreme Court to allow her to attend a local school that only allowed white children, helping to end segregation in Brown v. Board of Education.

use it to pack the court with justices of his own choosing who would produce decisions more to his liking. The plan proved unnecessary, however, when the Court began to decide subsequent decisions in the president's favor. Many historians credit the Court's change in course to Justice Owen Roberts, who altered his previously hostile stance toward New Deal legislation. His "switch in time saved nine" prevented a confrontation over possible expansion of the Court beyond nine members. With legal opposition blunted, the federal government proceeded to remake federalism by forever changing the role of the national government in the lives of every American.

Cooperative Federalism: 1937–1960s

After 1937, Court opposition to New Deal legislation waned and **cooperative federalism** became the dominant model for state–federal relations. This approach emphasizes federal–state partnerships as the primary means for solving public policy problems. It marries the federal government's financial advantage in tax collection with the states' ability to target services to local populations. The federal government typically sets minimum standards for benefits such as welfare or medical care and funds a portion of the costs. States have some flexibility in enhancing federal benefits and delivering services, but they must also contribute to funding the program. Cooperative federalism still characterizes federal–state relations today in areas including health, welfare, the environment, education, and highway safety.

Such cooperative arrangements eased power struggles between federal and state governments and allowed the different units of government to reach mutual accommodations on a host of issues. The term *marble cake federalism* is sometimes used to describe the blending of federal guidelines with state administration and implementation that characterized much social policy from the 1930s to the early 1960s.

Creative Federalism: 1960s–1970s

Linda Brown of Topeka, Kansas, just wanted to be able to attend her local elementary school like African American children in other states such as New York or California. When the local school board denied her admission to the all-white school and shuttled Linda to a separate school for black children, her family sued for admission. When her case and several others found their way to the Supreme Court in 1954, Chief Justice Earl Warren found for a unanimous Court that the state of Kansas had denied Linda the equal protection of the law guaranteed by the Fourteenth Amendment.[14] The case reversed an earlier 1896 "separate but equal" ruling allowing the states to practice racial segregation as long as they provided relatively equal accommodations for each race. In *Brown v. Board of Education*, the Court insisted that separate "is inherently unequal" and, in subsequent cases, demanded that states tear down the barriers to equal citizenship with "all deliberate speed."

The decision sparked a revolution in citizen rights and federalism. It cast a spotlight on the sometimes parochial side of state and local politics, one that seemed to sacrifice the rights of those without a voice at the state capitols. It likewise gave hope to those who had been discriminated against by state law that the national government would insist that every state accord all of its citizens the same rights under the law. In a flurry of subsequent decisions, the Court made it clear that states must conform to national standards regarding citizen rights. It also affirmed that it would interpret the Fourteenth Amendment's "due process" and "equal protection" clauses to affect national standards in areas ranging from abortion[15] to criminal prosecution[16] to voting.[17]

The Civil Rights Movement of the 1950s and 1960s produced not only new federal programs but also a model of **creative federalism** that sought to eradicate racial and economic injustice by targeting money directly at citizen groups and local governments. Some programs offered assistance directly to local populations, completely bypassing the states. Others allowed the federal government to take over certain operations in states that failed to adopt federal standards within a specific period of time.

Some federal initiatives expanded the social safety net initiated in the New Deal by extending health and welfare benefits to millions more Americans. Many of these programs required state financial participation, and this involvement has grown substantially over time. In 1965, for example, the federal government moved to ensure health-care coverage for the poor under a program known as Medicaid, which provides partial federal funding in return for guarantees from the states that they will provide minimum coverage for all those eligible. Over time this

Although pleased with reduced regulation, states soon felt the impact of reduced federal expenditures as they had to assume a greater share of the cost of government programs. This was particularly problematic for states because most of them, unlike the national government, are required to balance their budgets every year. To the added dismay of many state officials, devolution did not stop the

IN BROWN V. BOARD OF EDUCATION, the Court insisted that separate "is inherently unequal" and demanded that states tear down the barriers to equal citizenship with "all deliberate speed."

program has expanded in scope, and together with new requirements emerging from health-care reform legislation passed in 2010, the cost of keeping people healthy will place an increasing financial burden on state coffers. In some instances, the federal government also places restrictions on who can get federal funds. To qualify for federal money to build roads and bridges, for example, states might be required to set aside funds to employ a certain percentage of minority contractors.

In 1972, Richard Nixon sought to disentangle the federal government from aid to the states. He proposed a program called **revenue sharing** that funneled money directly to states and local governments on the basis of formulas that combined population figures with levels of demonstrated need. The expansive nature of these programs and qualifications spawned a reaction that changed the nature of the federal–state partnership once again.

New Federalism and the Devolution of Power: 1980–Present

The election of Ronald Reagan in 1980 brought changes to federalism that limited the role of the federal government. Reagan favored a model of smaller government, known as **devolution**, which returned power to states and localities. To achieve this end, he called for cutting federal programs and reducing federal regulations that had made compliance with federal programs so burdensome to state officials. He also reduced federal expenditures for many existing programs and ended revenue sharing.

President Ronald Reagan (1981–1989) sought a "devolution" of political power with states playing a more active role in governing.

federal government from imposing new national standards or from denying the states authority to develop their own policies in some areas. Reagan himself fought state regulatory initiatives in the areas of commerce and traffic safety and signed into law a measure that required states to raise the minimum drinking age to twenty-one or face a reduction in federal highway funding.

The pace of devolution accelerated in the 1990s, as all three branches of government seemed willing to cede power to the states. In 1995, Congress passed legislation requiring the federal government to provide detailed justification for programs that require states to spend more than a certain amount of money. The following year, President Bill Clinton supported welfare reform legislation that expanded the options available to states for administering welfare policy. In 1995, the Supreme Court signaled its willingness to put the brakes on federal authority by refusing to interpret the commerce clause as allowing the national government to restrict the possession of handguns within a thousand feet of a school. The Court said such activity had nothing to do with commerce.[18] More recently, the Court has strengthened state immunity from federal background checks for handgun buyers[19] and relaxed standards for compliance with federal antidiscrimination laws in such areas as age[20] and disability.[21]

Some observers of these trends fear a reversal of hard-won rights guaranteed by the Fourteenth Amendment. They worry that the nation will return to an era of patchwork rights where some jurisdictions offer more protections than others or, even worse, that the states will institute a more restrictive environment for individual rights that

cooperative federalism Federal–state relationship characteristic of the post–New Deal era that stressed state and federal partnership in addressing social problems.

creative federalism Federal–state relationship that sought to involve local populations and cities directly in addressing urban problems during the 1960s and 1970s.

revenue sharing A grant program begun in 1972 and ended in 1987 that funneled money directly to states and local governments on the basis of formulas that combined population figures with levels of demonstrated need.

devolution A movement that gained momentum in the 1980s to grant states greater authority over the local operation of federal programs and local use of federal funds.

favors the wishes of legislative majorities. Even with recent devolution activities, however, the national government's financial resources allow it to retain a strong hand in steering the future course of federalism by providing states with financial incentives to adopt uniform policies.

Even supporters of devolution don't want to abandon federal leadership completely. Former president George W. Bush championed the federal government's role in setting national testing standards for the nation's public schools in his signature legislation, the No Child Left Behind Act. He also voiced support for an amendment to the U.S. Constitution prohibiting gay marriages in order to prevent states from granting marriage rights to gay couples.

Despite the trend toward devolution, the current era has witnessed presidents and Congress inclined to allow states authority and flexibility when those measures advance their own policy priorities but demand greater federal control when states move in a different direction. This is no less true for the Obama administration than it was for those in the recent past. For example, while President Obama is content to allow states to pursue their own paths when it comes to matters like gay marriage, he has taken advantage of the recent economic downturn to aggressively use federal stimulus monies to advance initiatives championed at the federal level in the areas of health care, education, and energy policy. Some of these initiatives even require the use of state financial resources to accomplish these ends. Some believe these actions border on a reversal of the traditional relationship between the states and federal government. "Rather than states being

the laboratories of democracy in and of themselves," one expert says, "some of them will become the federal government's laboratories of democracy."[22] This has created new tensions as state legislatures challenge federal authority by refusing federal cash in areas like transportation, by passing restrictive legislation in matters like immigration, and by raising legal challenges to federal initiatives like the health-care reform act.

The future of federalism is likely to be clouded by financial uncertainty, especially in the face of the recent serious recession. States are finding that some federal programs are so burdensome that much of their state budgets are devoted to matching federal expenditures. This is particularly true of Medicaid, which, in some states, consumes 20 percent or more of state funds. To cope, some states have begun cutting benefits and freezing reimbursements to doctors and hospitals. No doubt federal–state relations will continue to evolve as both levels of government tussle over funding and their respective responsibilities in a challenging economic environment.

Hot or Not?

Who should make decisions about school curriculum: the federal government, the states, or local school boards?

FEDERAL–STATE RELATIONS

We have already discussed the broad outlines of federal–state relations from a historic perspective, noting the political currents that have characterized the relative powers of each level of government. We now turn our attention to the means by which these relationships continue to be redefined fiscally, politically, and legally.

The debate over healthcare reform pit supporters of a federal mandate against states' rights activists.

THE STATES STRIKE BACK

If the 2010 midterm elections can be considered a referendum on the first two years of the Obama administration, the 2012 campaign might be considered a referendum on the policies of the newly elected Republican class that was swept into office across the nation. The 2010 election increased the number of Republican controlled state legislatures from 14 to 26 and saw the number of Republican governors grow from 23 to 29. Republican controlled state bodies have not been shy about taking on the federal government. They have taken bold action to alter state budgetary priorities, changed the rules governing public employment and school funding, and created new accountability measures for classroom teachers. Some have passed legislation aimed at blunting the impact of the new health-care reform bill passed by the Obama administration and authorized the challenge of the federal law in the courts. States such as Indiana have blocked the award of federal funds to Planned Parenthood because it is an abortion provider. And some have passed restrictive immigration laws that pose a possible clash with federal authority. In many ways, these actions are a rebuke of the Obama administration's attempt to steer state policy by using federal stimulus money to impose federal standards on the states in matters ranging from unemployment compensation to health-care and Medicaid reform to the award of education funds.

2012 is to a significant extent a reaction to these state initiatives. Some believe Republican-controlled states have over-reached. States such as Wisconsin, where Governor Scott Walker stripped public employee unions of bargaining rights, face a backlash that began with the recall of state senators. And the legal battle between the states and the federal government has drawn voter attention as challenges to immigration and health-care reform go to the courts.

Fiscal Relations

Although national and state governments have concurrent powers to tax and spend, the federal government collects far more tax revenue than do the states—nearly three-fifths of all tax revenue—and spends almost twice as much as state and local governments combined. Much spending goes directly to individuals in the form of income security through programs such as Social Security and Medicare for the elderly. Many other programs, however, are funded through grants-in-aid, which account for about 17 percent of the federal budget. Nearly 90 percent of these grants go directly to state governments, accounting for almost 30 percent of all state revenues.[23] In turn, much of the money spent by local governments comes from state grants.

Grants-in-aid are as old as the republic, but their use became more widespread during the middle of the nineteenth century. One of the most successful aid programs was the Morrill Act of 1862, which granted land to states for building public universities specializing in agriculture, mechanics, and military science. Early in the twentieth century, the federal government increased the amount it appropriated for grants to the states, as it assumed greater responsibility for interstate transportation as well as for the

health and welfare of its citizens. Grants programs further expanded during the New Deal to address state needs arising from the Great Depression and again in the 1960s as the federal government earmarked more funding for local programs to revitalize urban life and to reduce poverty.[24]

> **categorical grants** Federal programs that provide funds for specific programs such as flood assistance.

The federal government employs several types of grant programs: categorical, block, program, and formula grants. Some types of grants give the donor more authority in specifying how the money is spent. Other types provide the recipient with more choices.

Categorical Grants The largest class of federal grants consists of **categorical grants**, reserved for special purposes such as health care for the poor, highway safety, or flood assistance. These grants sometimes require the receiving government to provide matching funds and may include additional provisions to ensure the funds are spent in a manner Congress approves. Such funds, for example, cannot be allocated in a way that discriminates on the basis of the race, ethnicity, or gender of those receiving government services.

On February 17, 2009, President Obama signed into law the American Recovery and Reinvestment Act, providing $787 billion in stimulus money aimed at creating jobs to further economic recovery starting at the state level.

Medicaid is the largest categorical grant to the states, providing half or more of the funds necessary to medically insure state residents who fall below a certain income level. The states are required to pick up the remaining costs and to provide a minimum level of assistance. In recent years, presidents have used categorical funds to entice states to participate in education reform. Under President Obama's "Race to the Top" program, the Department of Education makes competitive grants to states that promise to advance more strenuous teacher evaluation and open new charter schools.

The federal government currently sponsors over 750 categorical grant programs designed to help states and local governments solve problems they cannot tackle with their own resources.[25] Critics claim that these programs impose burdensome requirements on recipients and create a bewildering array of overlapping programs that lack coordination.

Block Grants Originally devised in 1966, **block grants** combine funding purposes of several categorical grants into one broader category, allowing greater flexibility in how the money is spent.[26] A block grant for public health, for example, may combine previous grants that allocated funds for eradicating individual illnesses. Block grants allow the recipient government to decide how to spend its resources and relieve it of the need to apply for grants from several different agencies. Unlike many categorical grants, however, block grants place a cap on federal funds. Critics of block grants claim that federal policymakers often have no way of knowing how the money is spent or whether target programs meet the needs for which the money is allocated.[27]

Ronald Reagan combined seventy-seven categorical programs into just nine block grants in 1981 as part of his commitment to devolving federal power.[28] Congress slowed the move toward block funding in subsequent years

block grants Federal programs that provide funds for broad categories of assistance such as health care or law enforcement.

program grants Federal programs that provide funds for very narrow purposes and contain clear time frames for completion—e.g., construction of a portion of highway.

formula grants Federal programs that use mathematical calculations or demographic factors to allocate funds to states or localities.

but embraced it as a centerpiece of welfare reform in 1996. Prior to this time, categorical grants provided assistance to families living in poverty, guaranteeing funding to recipients as long as they were in need. The new legislation

Federal Grants to States and Localities, FY 2011 (Estimated)

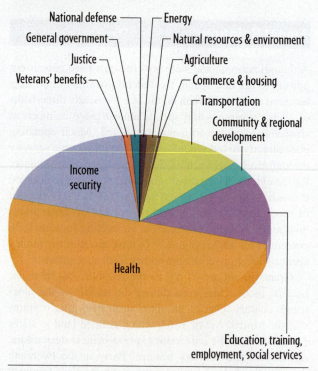

Source: Office of Management and Budget. Note: These projections were subjected to cuts during fiscal year negotiations with Congress.

Some programs, like the No Child Left Behind Act, establish federal mandates but do not supply all the money necessary to carry them out.

called for block grants that allowed the states to vary the amount and time for which recipients qualified for assistance. This new approach allows states to adjust requirements to local needs but creates a degree of variation that is sometimes confusing to recipients and difficult for policymakers to monitor.

Other Federal Grants Other grant programs exist to address a variety of needs. **Program grants** have narrow purposes like categorical grants but are limited to specific time periods. Often, they reflect congressional interest in finding novel approaches to addressing particular needs. For example, the Department of Homeland Security makes money available for protecting ports and transportation systems. **Formula grants** allocate money to state or local governments according to needs calculated in a predetermined manner. For example, the No Child Left Behind Act passed under the administration of George W. Bush targeted funding to school districts with high concentrations of poor children. While it gave states and districts some flexibility in how they spent the funds, some states complained the act did not supply enough money to carry out the extensive testing required under the law.

The 2009 American Recovery and Reinvestment Act adds a layer of complexity to many grant-in-aid programs. For example, the portion dealing with Medicaid, the health-care program for the poor, prohibits states from changing their rules about eligibility in order to qualify for increased funding; the education portion requires states to maintain funding at 2006 levels or above; and the Child Care Development block grant prohibits states from using new funding to replace current spending on these programs.[29] Similarly, the new federal health-care law makes dozens of formula and program grants available to the states for programs like community health, creation of high-risk insurance pools and health-exchange databases, HIV prevention, and quality measurement. Since many of these require matching state funds, some states have been reluctant to apply for them whereas others have refused

funding and joined court challenges against the legislation.

Political Relations

The interests of political actors at the national, state, and local levels are often at odds for a number of reasons. Policymakers at each level face a different constellation of legal, social, and political pressures that can affect their fortunes at the polls. As a result, it is not unusual for them to differ over how best to fund government programs. As noted, some types of grants—categorical grants, in particular—give the federal government more authority over the recipient government. Categorical grants that provide visible benefits, like highways and bridges, continue to be popular with Congress. They enable lawmakers to take credit for creating programs and for steering federal funds to their home districts or states. In addition, they provide strict accountability for the use of federal money. Some programs funded in this way also create grateful constituents who receive ongoing benefits that are protected by law. Lawmakers who depended on minority voters for electoral support, for example, often champion categorical grants, which can include provisions for affirmative action hiring or for minority participation.

By contrast, many state and local officials favor the decentralization, experimentation, and flexibility associated with block grants. They argue that local officials know best how to address local problems and that they should be free to experiment to find solutions that work best for their own citizens. Members of local government have a stake in maximizing the flow of federal dollars and minimizing the cost of compliance to taxpayers. With block grants, they may be able to devote more dollars to pressing needs without raising taxes. They may even be able to subsidize purely state and local functions by the infusion of federal funds with few strings attached. Congress, however, has curbed the growth of block grants, and studies show that the administration of block grants is uneven. Some states with a highly professional bureaucracy have successfully addressed social problems with block grants, while other states have lagged behind.[30]

State and local officials are also concerned about the growing use of **federal mandates**—federally imposed requirements on state and local governments ranging from election reform to water treatment. They are especially anxious about **unfunded mandates**, which are requirements that Congress passes without providing funds to carry them out. In 1995, Congress passed the Unfunded Mandates Reform Act to stem the tide of such mandates. The act requires

> **federal mandates** Federal requirements imposed on state and local governments, often as a condition for receiving grants.
>
> **unfunded mandates** Requirements imposed on state and local governments for which the federal government provides no funds for compliance.

the Congressional Budget Office to flag legislation that costs state governments or private sector bodies within the states more than $50 million for compliance. The bill's sponsors hoped that members of Congress would be unwilling to pass legislation that clearly increased the costs passed along to their home states. Although a Congressional Budget Office review found that this tactic substantially reduced the growth of unfunded mandates, such mandates persist.[31] The No Child Left Behind Act, for example, required states to adopt rigorous testing of students in a variety of subjects but failed to provide full funding for its implementation. The National Council of State Legislatures estimates that the act has cost the states more than $27 billion in unreimbursed expenditures since its inception.[32]

Debates over federal funding have spurred the growth of **intergovernmental lobbies** to advance the interests of various state and local governing bodies. The National Governors Association is perhaps the oldest of these, tracing its roots to the administration of Theodore Roosevelt. The U.S. Conference of Mayors also lobbies actively at the state and national levels for programs that address urban problems. Other lobbying groups represent professional bureaucrats and administrators responsible for the daily operation of government programs. Only a handful of such groups existed prior to 1900; by the mid-1980s, that number had mushroomed to more than one hundred.[33]

It must also be realized that some types of policies are more likely to be promoted and more likely to be successful if they are undertaken by one level of government rather than another.[34] For example, the national government is better equipped than state and local governments to address problems that spill across geographic boundaries, like air pollution, or that involve the infusion of substantial resources, like aid to the poor. State and local governments are better at addressing issues that require pinpoint targeting of resources, like economic development for cities or education reform.

Constitutional Issues

One important area of contention is the Constitution's commerce clause, which had been broadly interpreted since the New Deal to allow Congress to regulate activity within states if those activities impact interstate business or the national economy. The Court has even allowed the use of the clause in civil rights cases barring discrimination, such as *Heart of Atlanta Motel Inc. v. United States* (1964). In *Garcia v. San Antonio Metropolitan Transit Authority* (1985), the Court held that Congress has the power under the

intergovernmental lobbies
Professional advocacy groups representing various state and local governing bodies.

full faith and credit
Constitutional provision requiring each state to recognize legal transactions authorized in other states.

commerce clause to extend the Fair Labor Standards Act to state and local governments. This act requires that employers provide minimum wage and overtime pay to their employees.[35] In 1995, however, the Court, in *United States v. Lopez,* signaled its willingness to put the brakes on the expansion of powers granted under the commerce clause. The case involved Alfonzo Lopez, who was charged with violating the 1990 Gun-Free School Zones Act for carrying a concealed firearm into his Texas high school. He argued that the law was unconstitutional since it relied upon the commerce clause to regulate an activity that was not strictly economic. The Supreme Court agreed, arguing that carrying a firearm near a school was insufficiently related to commerce to justify regulation. The Court similarly limited Congress's reach in *United States v. Morrison* (2000) when it invalidated a provision of the federal Violence Against Women Act (VAWA). The case involved a Virginia Tech freshman who claimed she was raped by two members of the football team. When the state did not bring an indictment, the federal government used the VAWA to intervene. The Court invalidated portions of the act saying that the law outlawed criminal activity already regulated by the states and that it had no clear connection to commerce. The Court also said the federal government had over-reached in applying the Fourteenth Amendment in this case since the amendment applies to regulating the behavior of states and does not directly apply to individuals.

The lower courts are currently struggling with another case with far-ranging implications. Many states have challenged the new health-care law passed during the Obama administration. Among its provisions is one which requires individuals to purchase health insurance if they are not currently covered. The lower courts have delivered mixed verdicts, with some declaring the health care law unconstitutional since the interstate commerce clause does not extend the federal government's power to enforce a mandate on individual citizens. Other courts have accepted the government's argument that people who do not obtain coverage inevitably affect the pricing and availability of policies for everyone else and that controlling these costs is a justifiable reason to use the commerce power. Appeals courts have also offered their own opinions, but the Supreme Court will have the final say regarding these claims.

The Court moved again in recent years to limit congressional power over the states in a series of cases citing the Tenth Amendment. In the 1976 case *National League of Cities v. Usery,* the Supreme Court invalidated a federal law that extended the minimum wage to almost all state and local employees. The Court's majority argued that the Tenth Amendment prohibited the national government from dictating what states can pay their employees. In 1992, the Court said Congress could not require

Hot or Not?

Should states and local governments have the power to regulate handguns?

In 2008, the Supreme Court affirmed an individual citizen's Second Amendment right to bear arms, setting up future judicial challenges over the legality of gun bans in major cities across the country.

the state of New York to dispose of low-level radioactive waste at its own expense in order to meet federal mandates just because the private party that generated it could not find suitable alternate means for disposal. Citing the Tenth Amendment, Justice Sandra Day O'Connor said the law "would 'commandeer' state governments into the service of federal regulatory purposes, and would for this reason be inconsistent with the Constitution's division of authority between federal and state governments."[36] Several years later, the Court invalidated a provision of the Brady Handgun Violence Prevention Act requiring the chief law-enforcing officers in the states to run background checks on handgun purchasers. The Court once again held it unconstitutional to enlist the state in enforcing federal law.[37] However, in 2005, the Court ruled against California in striking down a state law permitting the possession and use of marijuana for medical purposes, holding that Congress's authority to control the trafficking of controlled substances trumped the state's Tenth Amendment rights.[38]

Some states have proposed or passed resolutions of state sovereignty based on the claim that the Tenth Amendment gives them the authority to nullify federal laws with which its legislature disagrees. These resolutions, however, lack the force of law.

Several cases in the late 1990s also cited the Eleventh Amendment in upholding state sovereignty. In these cases, the state was found to be immune from lawsuits brought by its own citizens whether filed in federal court or within the state's own court system. For example, in *Alden v. Maine* (1999), probation officers sued the state for failure to pay overtime in violation of federal law. Citing the Eleventh Amendment, the court ruled the states are immune from such suits. Writing for the majority, Justice Anthony Kennedy held:

> Federalism requires that Congress accord States the respect and dignity due them as residuary sovereigns and joint participants in the Nation's governance. Immunity from suit in federal courts is not enough to preserve that dignity, for the indignity of subjecting a non-consenting State to the coercive process of judicial tribunals at the instance of private parties exists regardless of the forum.[39]

More recently, the Court has issued mixed judgments on Eleventh Amendment protections for the states. While the Court upheld Florida's claim of immunity from lawsuits by rejecting a suit brought by state university employees claiming age discrimination,[40] it affirmed the right of a disabled man to sue the state of Tennessee for not complying with portions of the federal Americans with Disabilities Act by providing elevator access to a state courtroom.[41]

Clearly, the range of powers legitimately exercised by the national and state governments continues to undergo constitutional examination by the courts. Similarly, the range of powers exercised by local governments has not escaped Supreme Court scrutiny. In 2008, a divided court in *District of Columbia v. Heller* rejected a strict gun control law in the District of Columbia, arguing that the Constitution provides federal protection for an individual's right to bear arms.[42] In 2010, the Court, in *McDonald v. City of Chicago,* extended the constitutional protection of the Second Amendment's right to keep and bear arms to every jurisdiction in the nation.

INTERSTATE RELATIONS

To function well, our federal system requires coordination not simply between the national and state governments but across state boundaries and even among localities within the states. The Framers provided some guidance for interstate relations in the Constitution, but the contours of interstate cooperation and competition continue to evolve.

Cooperation and Competition

The **full faith and credit** provision of the U.S. Constitution directs states to recognize legal judgments in lawsuits that are valid in another state. An individual who owes a sum of money to a creditor in Pennsylvania cannot escape his obligation by fleeing over the border into Delaware. Delaware is required to recognize the judgment and enforce it if the creditor pursues him. Recognizing that not all interstate relations would be amicable, however, the Framers provided that states with legal disputes may take their cases directly to the Supreme Court. One current issue that touches upon this provision is gay marriage. If one state recognizes gay partners as legally married with all the rights and benefits that accrue to married couples, must a state that outlaws gay marriage grant the same recognition to the couple if they move within its borders? Does federal law recognizing marriage as between a man and woman trump same-sex partner marriages in the states?

The establishment of same-sex marriage laws in some states raises the question of whether other states must recognize these unions when gay couples move.

Section 2 of Article IV provides that the citizens of each state shall be entitled to all the same **privileges and immunities** of citizens of the several states. This wording is ambiguous, however, and litigants often have asked the courts to interpret its meaning. The Supreme Court has ruled that states may not discriminate against nonresidents when it comes to fundamental rights like freedom to make a living and access to the political and legal processes of the state. However, states can treat nonresidents differently in a number of other areas. For example, nonresident workers may pay different tax rates than residents, and nonresident students may pay higher tuition and fees at state schools.[43]

Cooperation among states is often fostered by the use of **interstate compacts**, a device that is given explicit approval "with the consent of Congress" in the Constitution (Article I, Section 10). Such compacts may involve agreements to share environmental responsibility for waterways that cross their borders or to develop transportation authorities across borders with the power to collect fares and distribute revenues. Of course, not all states see eye to eye when it comes to the use of resources that cross borders. Disagreements can result in political conflict or even litigation before the Supreme Court. In 2007, Illinois residents and political leaders forced an Indiana oil refinery to back down from its plans to release higher levels of waste products into Lake Michigan along the lakeshore both states share. Indiana had given permission for the increased waste disposal but was saved from litigation and continued political turmoil when the refinery itself decided to withdraw its request.

Recent years have witnessed increased competition among states as they vie for business investment. Despite growing burdens faced by many states as a result of economic stagnation, increased costs for education and welfare, and federal mandates, states have been reluctant to raise taxes for fear they will scare off potential investors or lose businesses already planted within their borders. Competition has grown particularly fierce over foreign investments that make up a larger portion of American business operations as globalization picks up steam. States find themselves

privileges and immunities
Constitutional phrase interpreted to refer to fundamental rights, such as freedom to make a living, and access to the political and legal processes of the state.

interstate compacts
Cooperative agreements made between states, subject to congressional approval, to address mutual problems.

in escalating bidding wars by offering companies tax breaks and other incentives. It is estimated that in 1980, "landing a new Nissan plant cost Tennessee $11,000 per job created. In 1985, recruiting the Saturn Corporation cost the state $26,000 per job. In 1992, it cost South Carolina more than $68,000 per job to bring in a BMW plant, and the estimates range from $150,000 to $200,000 per job for the Mercedes Benz plant in Alabama" that began operating in 1997.[44]

Innovation in the States

In his dissent in the case of *New State Ice Company v. Liebmann* (1932), Justice Louis Brandeis argued that the state of Oklahoma should have the authority to determine which businesses serve the public interest and therefore should be required to obtain state licenses. This was a legitimate way for them, he felt, to protect public health and safety. His dissent is most famous, however, for his faith in the power of states to innovate within our federal system:

> To stay experimentation in things social and economic is a grave responsibility. Denial of the right to experiment may be fraught with serious consequences to the Nation. It is one of the happy incidents of the federal system that a single courageous State may, if its citizens choose, serve as a laboratory; and try novel social and economic experiments without risk to the rest of the country.[45]

American history is replete with examples of public policy innovation by states that served as a catalyst for widespread change. In 1898, South Dakota passed a law granting voters the right to initiate all forms of legislation. States throughout the Midwest quickly adopted the measure, as did many western states. More recently, welfare reform initiatives that originated in Wisconsin in the early 1990s served as a model for national legislation in 1996. Health care for

States have engaged in bidding wars by offering tax breaks and other incentives to win foreign investors.

Average Time for Diffusion of Innovations (in Years)

Time Period	All Adoptions	First 20 Adoptions
1870–1899	52	23
1900–1929	40	20
1930–1966	26	18

Source: Jack L. Walker, "The Diffusion of Innovations Among the American States," *American Political Science Review* 63, September 1969, 895.

low-income populations has also improved as a result of state initiatives in recent years. Massachusetts passed a law mandating the purchase of health-care insurance in 2006, and President Obama adopted a similar approach in his effort to promote universal health-care coverage in 2009.

Just how extensive is innovation and diffusion in the American federal system? The question is hard to answer because innovation is difficult to measure. Nevertheless, several studies cast light on the matter. In a pathbreaking study published in 1969, political scientist Jack L. Walker studied the spread of innovations in eighty-eight public policy areas ranging from corrections to welfare from 1870 to the mid-1960s.[46] Walker found that larger, wealthier states whose urban populations are well represented in the state legislature are most likely to innovate and to more rapidly adopt ideas pioneered in other states. New York, Massachusetts, and California consistently scored near the top in state innovation.

Stronger competition between parties seems to have increased state innovation after 1930. Presumably, competition makes the political parties less complacent and more likely to innovate in order to bring new voters to their cause. Walker also found greater innovation in states with more professional legislatures and state bureaucracies. Regional competition also increases innovation; states adjacent to innovators are themselves more likely to innovate. Finally, he found that the changes in mass communication and technology allowed for more rapid and widespread adoption of new initiatives. More recent studies have found that innovation is related to a state's level of economic development and the availability of policy entrepreneurs—what we might call legisla-

tive risk takers—who are willing to spend considerable personal effort in advancing new ideas.[47]

Walker and others have confirmed that federal grants-in-aid significantly shorten the time of diffusion, especially among states that typically are slower to embrace innovation.[48] Some states are willing to innovate consistently, but the federal government must prod others into action.

Just as some levels of government are better equipped to handle certain functions than others, each level of government also provides a unique combination of opportunities and challenges for citizen participation. Let us turn to this topic now.

States as Innovators in Same-Sex Partner Laws

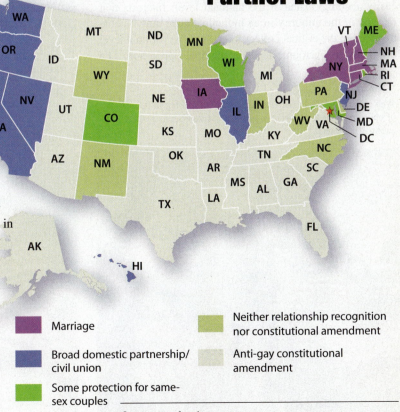

Marriage

Broad domestic partnership/civil union

Some protection for same-sex couples

Neither relationship recognition nor constitutional amendment

Anti-gay constitutional amendment

Source: www.freedomtomarry.org

FEDERALISM AND CIVIC ENGAGEMENT TODAY

Because federalism diffuses power across many competing power centers, it multiplies the number of opportunities for citizen political participation. Few of us may have the opportunity to shape national policies directly as members of the U.S. House or Senate, but many opportunities exist for citizen political involvement at the state and local level as elected officials or as volunteer members of boards, associations, and neighborhood councils. These positions afford citizens the opportunity for intensive, direct participation in policymaking and implementation and serve as training grounds for those who wish to take the national political stage.

Participation at each level of government is also laden with its own pitfalls and challenges. It may be easier to devise solutions for states and localities, since local populations are more homogeneous and share some of the same regional values and traditions.[49] Of course, entrenched traditions that are difficult to overcome may also hinder progress. For example, many states have passed referenda to ban gay marriages and to bar social services for illegal immigrants.

Although participation in the national political arena requires patience in negotiating among competing interests and respect for a wide diversity of values and traditions, measures calling for the expansion of rights are often more easily accommodated at the national level. Interests that may be in the minority in an individual state may be able to generate the critical collective mass at the national level necessary to overcome local or regional opposition. The

civil rights movement demonstrated the strength numerical minorities can amass at the national level.

A group of political scientists studying the opportunities and challenges of federalism for civic engagement summarized the matter as follows:

> Active citizenship seems to flourish most naturally at the local level and in smaller communities. This does not mean that those who favor civic engagement should abandon wider and more inclusive goals or that those who favor diversity and inclusion should abandon local institutions. It does mean, however, that these two dilemmas—of scale and diversity—pose difficult political challenges.[50]

Our discussion in this section echoes the debate that raged between Federalists and Antifederalists during the ratifica-

With over a half-million elective offices in the United States, 96 percent of which are at the local level of government, opportunities for political involvement abound.

Ballot initiatives have become increasingly popular devices for ensuring popular participation in setting the legislative agendas in many states. You can check on the most recent ballot initiatives in your state by examining the list maintained by Project Vote Smart at http://votesmart.org/index.htm. If you are interested in placing an item on the ballot, you can contact your state's secretary of state for information about the requirements. Most states require a certain number of signatures on a petition and sometimes charge a nominal filing fee.

get involved!

tion of the U.S. Constitution. Federalists argued for the benefits of combining local and regional interests in a national policy, whereas Antifederalists were concerned that national politics would lack the unity of purpose and intensity of citizen involvement present at the state and local levels. U.S. history shows that federalism is flexible enough to accommodate both perspectives, and both viewpoints often have been useful in charting our nation's course.

While a federal system such as ours—with many layers of government—provides added security for citizen rights, it requires that we participate in governmental decisions at multiple levels and understand the challenges of participating at each level. Alexis de Tocqueville took note of this when he toured America in the 1830s:

But when one examines the Constitution of the United States, the best of all known federal constitutions, it is frightening to see how much diverse knowledge and discernment it assumes on the part of the governed. The government of the Union rests almost entirely on legal fictions. The Union is an ideal notion which exists, so to say, only in men's minds and whose extent and limits can only be discerned by the understanding.[51]

How much more daunting must it be for busy citizens to fulfill the obligations of citizenship in our federal republic today!

Summary

1. **How is power dispersed in American federalism?**
- The Constitution grants some powers, called enumerated, to the national government. The power to declare war is one example.
- It reserves other powers for the states. For example, state governments are empowered to create cities and towns.
- It allows some powers, like taxing and spending, to be shared jointly.
- It prohibits both levels of government from taking certain actions like passing ex post facto laws.

2. **How have the powers of the national and state governments evolved over the nation's history?**
- Federalism has produced periodic shifts in the relative strength of the national and state governments, sometimes strengthening the national government and sometimes weakening it.
- From our founding until about 1832, the national government asserted broad powers, particularly through court decisions that affirmed the supremacy of national law.
- From 1832 until the Civil War, a period of dual federalism dominated in which national and state powers were kept fairly distinct, like the layers of a cake.
- After the war, the courts granted more powers to the states, particularly in the arena of economic regulation.
- The New Deal produced dramatic growth in the powers of the national government despite resistance by the courts.
- From about 1937 until the 1960s, the national and state governments forged cooperative partnerships in addressing social problems, with each partner contributing something to a mix sometimes described as a marble cake.
- The 1960s and 1970s witnessed a period of creative federalism as the national government, in particular, experimented with new ways of addressing local problems directly.

- Ronald Reagan initiated an era of devolution in which the national government turned more power and responsibility for programs over to the states and local governments.

3. **What factors influence relations between national and state governments today?**
- National–state relations are influenced by fiscal and political relations as well as by constitutional and legal controls.
- The national government shares resources with the states by making available various types of grants.
  - Categorical grants provide funds for very specific programs and may come with a wide variety of strings attached.
  - Block grants fold money for programs into broader categories and provide for more local discretion in spending.
  - Program grants are often provided for a limited time period.
  - Formula grants distribute money according to calculations based on local needs.
- Members of Congress often prefer to provide categorical grants over which they retain some control. State and local officials often prefer block grants that provide more local discretion. State and local officials often complain about mandates that require states to provide services but do not provide necessary resources.
- Conflicts over the powers of the state and national governments often revolve around legal issues raised by the Tenth Amendment, which reserves to the states powers not granted to the federal government, and the Eleventh Amendment, which limits the legal liability of state governments.
- Larger, wealthier states with substantial urban populations and policy entrepreneurs are more likely to innovate with the resources provided by the federal government.

National Journal

DEPENDENT STATES USHER IN A NEW FEDERALISM

Education Secretary Arne Duncan had some harsh words for Wisconsin's education laws during a November visit to Madison. He complained that the state's policies, particularly its cap on charter schools and its refusal to use test data in evaluating teachers, were antiquated, unacceptable, and even "ridiculous."

Rather than take offense, his hosts acted quickly to appease him.

The very next day, Wisconsin's Assembly and Senate passed a package of four bills designed to bring the state in line with Duncan's vision. In so doing, Wisconsin became the 10th state in 2009 to alter its education laws to please the Education secretary.

The reason is money. Last year's economic stimulus law provided Duncan with $4.35 billion to give to states that pursue innovations in education. The so-called Race to the Top fund is competitive: All the states want a share of the money, and the Education secretary can give out the aid largely as he sees fit, without having to rely on any set formula.

But there is not enough money to go around, which is why the states are doing everything they can to satisfy Duncan. No other Education secretary has ever had that much cash at his disposal. "There's no question those of us in Wisconsin want to have as strong an application as we can to get at the $4.35 billion," said John Lehman, who chairs the state Senate Education Committee. "It is true that there is a big carrot that got people thinking."

The Obama administration has been using a lot of carrots to elicit support for its policy goals, from forcing states to accept new Medicaid recipients to cracking down on distracted drivers. With states facing their worst financial outlook in decades, they are becoming increasingly reliant on money from Washington. "It wouldn't surprise me if federal funding ends up being 40 percent of state budgets during the current fiscal year," said Marcia Howard, executive director of Federal Funds Information for States, which on behalf of state legislators and governors tracks federal grant money. Federal dollars—dominated by Medicaid funds—made up just over 25 percent of state spending as recently as 2008 before jumping to 30 percent for the fiscal year that ended in most states last June.

With so much money being transferred from Washington to state capitals, the administration is practicing what might be called golden-rule federalism: Whoever has the gold makes the rules. "The fact that states are so broke offers unprecedented opportunities for the federal government to intrude into areas that were strictly the purview of states," said Sujit CanagaRetna, a senior fiscal analyst with the Council of State Governments.

President Obama thus presents a paradox when it comes to federalism. Barely five years out of the Illinois Legislature, he has expressed more genuine interest in collaborating with the lower levels of government than perhaps any other president since Jimmy Carter. Several Cabinet secretaries have been working together to craft joint programs to find a more coherent approach to matching federal efforts with local programs. Obama's Office of Management and Budget and the newly created White House Office of Urban Affairs are pushing all federal departments and agencies to do likewise.

But at the same time, Obama is clearly presiding over a greater centralization of power and policy-making in Washington. It was inevitable that states would have to cede ground that they had been able to hold for themselves in recent years, given a president determined to set his own mark in a swath of domestic policy areas, such as education and health care. But the states' growing dependence on Washington for aid has greatly accelerated the shift.

And their ability to set their own courses as independent actors is diminishing. "This is an administration that doesn't take the states and locals as it finds them—it has an agenda," says Paul Posner, a federalism expert at George Mason University. "The agenda they have is not framed in terms of helping state and local governments with their problems, but in pushing their own goals."

It has always been the case that when states and local governments cut spending, they try to spare federal programs. After all, if the federal government is paying 50 percent of a program's cost, they would have to cut $2 in spending just to save $1 for their own treasury. Not surprisingly, state budgets have long been subject to federal whims, both through the creation of programs that impose new mandates and the simple expansion of the federal government.

If state spending tended to increase during federal expansions under Democratic administrations, Republican presidents took a different tack. Under the Nixon and Reagan models, block grants meant offering states less money but more flexibility. Their proposals had the dual purpose of reining in spending and giving states more authority.

It's the opposite of Obama's approach, which is more in line with Lyndon Johnson's during the Great Society—finding innovative ways to use grants to get states and localities to pursue federal policy goals. "In the absence of reauthorization of some of the grant programs, the Obama administration is using regulations to impose their agenda," said Marcia Howard of Federal Funds Information for States, a joint project of the NCSL and the governors association. "You could call it a heavy federal hand, but it's more inducements, using more carrots than sticks to get states to do what they'd like them to do."

In response, many state officials complain that federal priorities are starting to crowd out their own. This may sound a little ungrateful. The influx of federal dollars may be edging out other parts of state budgets on a percentage basis, but it's not as if their absence would allow states to spend more in areas such as corrections or parks. As things now stand, states would simply have less to spend.

Some states have heatedly invoked the 10th Amendment in stressing supposed limits on federal policy-making. Legislative chambers in Texas and North Dakota approved resolutions last year proclaiming state sovereignty and demanding an immediate end to federal mandates not enumerated in the U.S. Constitution.

But it looks increasingly as if the Republican governors who opposed the stimulus—and appeared at the time merely to be seeking to score partisan points—had a valid argument. South Carolina's Mark Sanford, Mississippi's Haley Barbour, and others noted that it would be a mistake to accept federal money that obligates them to continue the spending when the federal pipeline runs dry a year or two later. As that time draws nearer on such programs as unemployment insurance and energy-efficiency block grants, more of their colleagues are worried about what they'll do when the funding drops off.

Obama's instincts are not those of a centralizer, however. Nearly every state and local government lobbying group readily concedes that outreach and access are much improved on his watch. They say that his administration attempts to take a collaborative approach whenever it can, with a

> "The fact that states are so broke offers unprecedented opportunities for the federal government to intrude into areas that were strictly the purview of states."
> —Sujit CanagaRetna

special interest in reshaping the interaction between the federal government and metropolitan regions.

Obama's administration has deferred to lower levels of government in areas where it was conducive to constituency politics. In October, the Justice Department announced that it would (in most cases) not prosecute suppliers of medical marijuana who were in compliance with state laws.

Like every administration—and more quickly than most—Obama's White House may have recognized that it needs state and local governments to carry out much of its program. But despite its care in consulting with them and in seeking ways to foster regional economic growth, this administration mostly treats state and local governments in just that way—as a means for carrying out its own agenda.

The Obama administration approach may be most evident when it comes to education. The administration is spending record amounts on education, and it clearly expects states to get with its program when it comes to ideas such as lifting caps on the number of charter schools and using standardized test data in evaluating teachers. "States were

complaining under Bush because they had all these education mandates with no funding," said David Wyss, chief economist for Standard & Poor's. "At least with Obama they're getting the funding to match the mandates, but the mandates are increasing."

In certain ways, education-reform activists are glad that Duncan is showing states a firm hand. Recent experience, they note, suggests that the federal government can require states to do certain things—but it can't make states do them well. Bush's 2002 No Child Left Behind law required states to use standardized tests to ensure that a rising share of their student populations were proficient in language arts and math. But the law left it up to the states to determine what "proficiency" meant, and it's clear that many of them have gamed the system to guarantee that more of their students can pass.

The question remains whether education—a classic example of a state and local responsibility that the federal government has been involved in for only 50 years—is best run by an agenda driven out of Washington. "It's absolutely the case that the administration is taking enormous liberties with its ability to use emergency funds, especially the stimulus, to push states into policy adoption," said Frederick Hess, director of education policy studies at the American Enterprise Institute.

"If one believes that there's sufficient expertise and farsightedness in Washington, that the key is to cudgel these recalcitrant states into behaving, then I'm sure this is encouraging," Hess said. "It so happens that I actually like what they're pushing states to do, but my concern is that this model of federal leadership is problematic. The question of federalism depends on whether one actually believes there is value in the checks and balances, and the states as the laboratories of democracy."

For Discussion:

■ Do you agree with the Texas and North Dakota legislatures that Washington's extension of grant money contingent on cooperation with its agenda violates the Constitutional separation of state and federal powers? Why or why not?

■ When do you think it is appropriate for Washington to help shape the state agenda, and when do you think the federal government should stay out? What are the critical differences?

■ Using examples from this article, explain how the Obama administration differs from previous administrations in its handling of the federalism issues surrounding distribution of funds.

4

CIVIL LI

EXPANDING CITIZENS' RIGHTS

ACTIVISTS FOR JUSTICE ▌ On the morning of March 25, 2010, Hank Skinner was transferred to the site of the Texas death chamber for a 6:00 P.M. execution. For years, Skinner had insisted upon his innocence, claiming that DNA testing of crime-scene evidence would prove he had not committed the multiple murders. All the leading state newspapers called for the stopping of his execution. Protestors in Paris, France, marched in front of the American Embassy to plead for his life. The Pope opposed his execution. Skinner has just met with his wife and two daughters, telling them, "If I die tonight, you've got to move on with your life—you've got to accept it and move on."[1] The day passed quickly with final phone calls to the family and conversations with the prison chaplain and warden. At 5:00 P.M. he sat down to his final meal of Popeyes chicken, fried catfish, a salad with ranch dressing and bacon bits, onion rings, and a chocolate milkshake. At this moment, less than an hour before his execution, the prisoner learned that the Supreme Court of the ➡️

BERTIES

As You READ >>

- Why was the incorporation of the Bill of Rights by the Supreme Court important?
- What are the First Amendment rights?
- What are some of the other important civil liberties guaranteed by the Constitution?

United States had granted him an indefinite stay. He would not be given the lethal injection on this day. His good fortune was due in large part to a group of undergraduate journalism students and their professor, who were affiliated with the Innocence Network.

The Innocence Network is a litigation and public policy organization that is dedicated to exonerating wrongfully convicted individuals through DNA testing. The organization today is composed of nonprofit legal organizations in the United States, Canada, the United Kingdom, Australia, and New Zealand. Since the organization's inception in 1992, the number of postconviction exonerations in the United States has increased dramatically. (The photo on the previous pages shows Professor Protess and members of the Innocence Network celebrating as an innocent man that they helped exonerate is released from prison). Seventy percent of the prisoners who were freed after DNA testing were members of minority groups, and in 40 percent of the cases, the DNA testing led to the actual perpetrator being identified. Of the 272 persons that have been exonerated, 17 had been sentenced to death before DNA evidence proved their innocence and led to their release.

American death penalty cases receive much attention abroad because the United States finds itself in the minority of countries that still have the death penalty. Only 21 percent of all nations maintain the death penalty. The United States is joined by, among others, Egypt, Libya, Afghanistan, China, and Iran. The latter two countries lead the world in the number of executions. Ninety-five nation states that represent 49 percent of the world's independent countries have abolished the execution sanction. They include almost every European nation as well as Mexico and Canada. An additional 25 percent including Chile and Russia have had a moratorium on executions for at least ten years. A few others just retain the death penalty for wartime crimes.

One of the best-known of the organizations that comprise the Innocence Network is the Medill Innocence Project at Northwestern University. Project director Professor David Protess and his students have uncovered evidence that has freed eleven innocent persons including five who had been on death row. Their findings led ex-Governor George Ryan of Illinois to issue a moratorium on the death penalty. The moratorium eventually led to Illinois's permanent ban.

During the 1999–2000 academic year, Professor Protess and eight of his undergraduate journalism students reinvestigated the case of Hank Skinner, who had been sentenced to death by a Texas jury for murdering his girlfriend and her two grown sons on New Year's Eve 1993. Skinner had always maintained that he was too impaired from the consumption of alcohol and drugs to have committed the violent crimes. He also indicated that his girlfriend's uncle, who was known to be violent and had threatened the victim that evening, was the likely perpetrator. After his conviction, Skinner kept asking for DNA testing of physical evidence that included vaginal swabs and fingernail clippings from his late girlfriend, hairs found in her hand and two knives found at the scene, a dish towel, and a windbreaker jacket that Skinner claimed belonged to the victim's uncle. When the students questioned the major trial witness against Skinner, she recanted her story and claimed the prosecutor forced her to lie.[2] The Medill Innocence Project went on to recruit 8,000 members and supporters to write protest letters to the governor of Texas. The professor even offered to pay for the DNA testing.

The result of the activism was the 2010 stay of execution from the U.S. Supreme Court and later the Court's acceptance of Skinner's case. In 2011, Skinner won another victory from the Court in his case of *Skinner v. Switzer*. The 6–3 majority held that he could use a federal civil rights law to seek DNA testing on evidence that was not performed before his conviction. However, Hank Skinner's case is still far from resolved. First, Skinner has to gain access to the evidence in another trial. The state will argue that Skinner's trial lawyers did not initially pursue the issue and now it is too late. Further, if testing is allowed, it is not clear whether it will prove his innocence or guilt or be inconclusive.

The example of students working to help correct an injustice is indicative of the focus on rights today. Americans often turn to the courts to protect their rights, and the U.S. Supreme Court looms large in the lives of citizens due to its role as interpreter of our basic rights. Court decisions have protected citizens from the actions of all governments at every level of American politics and defined the extent of citizens' rights in a wide variety of areas. The Court's decisions are not always consistent or predictable, however, because the cases often involve the conflict of basic rights, and the members of the Court and the political climate change over time. In this chapter, we will study the nature of those basic rights and freedoms, known as **civil liberties**. ◆◆

HERITAGE OF RIGHTS AND LIBERTIES

Some of the first settlers in North America declared their dedication to individuality and freedom by setting forth their rights in public documents.[3] As early as 1641, the Massachusetts General Court adopted the "Body of Liberties," which defined the rights of citizens in the Massachusetts Colony. By the time of the American Revolution some 125 years later, each state had its own constitution containing a **bill of rights** that protected a variety of civil liberties. The delegates who met in Philadelphia in 1787 to create a new governing structure saw no need to add a bill of rights to the new constitution.

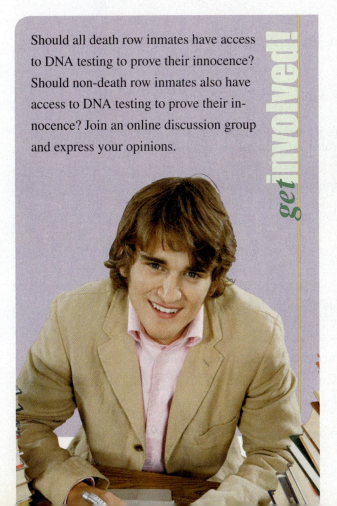

get **involved!**

Should all death row inmates have access to DNA testing to prove their innocence? Should non-death row inmates also have access to DNA testing to prove their innocence? Join an online discussion group and express your opinions.

The Constitution and Rights

Records of the 1787 deliberations show that the delegates soundly rejected a bill of rights on at least four separate occasions.[4] They did not, however, ignore the subject of individual freedoms. The new constitution forbade the legislature from passing ex post facto laws and bills of attainder. An ex post facto law creates a criminal law and then applies it retroactively to convict persons who committed the behavior before it was a crime. Bills of attainder are legislative pronouncements of guilt that should be left for a court to decide. The delegates also made it difficult for government to deny writs of habeas corpus to accused or convicted persons. Writs of habeas corpus allow individuals to petition judges to assess whether there is sufficient cause to hold an accused person for trial or to imprison a convicted person who may have received an unfair trial. The Federalists opposed adding a bill of rights, however, because they believed that a government founded on the principles of separation of powers and checks and balances would produce a political system free from tyranny. In addition, since the Constitution granted the national government only certain specific powers, the Federalists felt that the states would wield enough power to safeguard the civil liberties of their citizens. Hamilton argued in *The Federalist* No. 84 that a bill of rights was not only unnecessary but also dangerous, because it was foolhardy to list things that the national government had no power to do.[5]

The Federalists successfully prevented the convention from adding a bill of rights to the proposed constitution, but

> **civil liberties** The personal freedoms of individuals that are protected from government intrusion.
>
> **Bill of Rights** The freedoms listed in the first ten amendments to the U.S. Constitution.

> **Did You Know ?**
>
> *. . . That a bill of attainder is a law passed by a legislature that simply declares a person or group of people guilty—usually of treason—without any trial? Bills of attainder were sometimes enacted by the British Parliament and the colonial legislatures.*

they found public opinion against them when the document went to the states for ratification. After the first five states ratified the document, momentum for a constitution that lacked a bill of rights slowed considerably. Swayed by Antifederalist rhetoric championing personal freedom, seven of the last eight states approved the document only on the condition that Congress add amendments protecting individual liberties as soon as possible.

selective incorporation The process of applying some of the rights in the Bill of Rights to the states through the due process clause of the Fourteenth Amendment.

The Bill of Rights

After winning a seat in the First Congress, Federalist leader James Madison fulfilled his faction's promise by drafting seventeen new amendments. The Senate rejected five of the proposed amendments, and the states rati-

fied ten of the twelve that Congress sent to them; these amendments became known as the Bill of Rights.[6]

Incorporation

From its adoption, the Bill of Rights stirred controversy concerning how widely it protected the rights it set forth. Did the Constitution protect these rights only from violation by the national government, or did they also protect citizens from the unjust actions of state governments? The Supreme Court first addressed this issue in 1833 in the case of *Barron v. Baltimore*.

John Barron had sued the city of Baltimore for damaging his wharf by dumping sand in the water during road construction. His lawyers argued that the Fifth Amendment's guarantee that "private property cannot be taken for public use, without just compensation" should apply to the states as well as to the national government. Writing the opinion for a unanimous Court, Chief Justice John Marshall limited the application of the Bill of Rights to

The Bill of Rights

1 First: Free exercise of religion, establishment of religion, free press, free speech, peaceful assembly, right to petition government

2 Second: Right to keep and bear arms

3 Third: No quartering of soldiers without owner's consent

4 Fourth: No unreasonable searches or seizures

5 Fifth: Grand jury indictment, double jeopardy prohibition, no self-incrimination, due process protection, no seizure of property without just compensation

6 Sixth: Jury trial in criminal cases, right to speedy and public trial, notice of the nature of the accusation, right to confront witnesses against and call witnesses in favor, right to counsel

7 Seventh: Jury trial in civil cases

8 Eighth: No excessive bail, no cruel and unusual punishment

9 Ninth: Rights not limited by the list of rights in the first eight amendments

10 Tenth: Powers not delegated to the national government are reserved to the states and the people

America's Response— What Are Your Constitutional Rights?

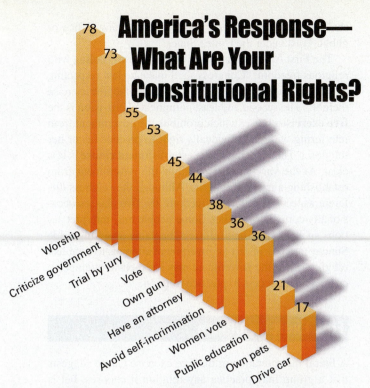

- Worship — 78
- Criticize government — 73
- Trial by jury — 55
- Vote — 53
- Own gun — 45
- Have an attorney — 44
- Avoid self-incrimination — 38
- Women vote — 36
- Public education — 36
- Own pets — 21
- Drive car — 17

America's answers to "Which of the following rights are guaranteed by the First Amendment of the U.S. Constitution?" (in percentages)

Source: McCormick Tribune Freedom Museum, "Americans' Awareness of First Amendment Freedoms," March 1, 2006.

actions of the national government only.[7] He argued that the Antifederalists explicitly called for a bill of rights to protect citizens in their relations with the new national government. He also reasoned that Congress would have clearly stated its desire to have the amendments apply to the states if that had been the goal.

Passage of the Fourteenth Amendment after the Civil War reopened the question of the applicability of the Bill of Rights. That amendment includes the due process clause: "*No state . . . shall deprive a person of life, liberty, or property without due process of law.*"[8] Lawyers argued that if the rights enumerated in the due process clause— life, liberty, and property—were equivalent to the rights in the Bill of Rights, then the states would be bound by the first ten amendments to the U.S. Constitution. At first, proponents of this view met with little success. Ultimately, however, the Court used a process known as **selective incorporation** to conclude that most of the Bill of Rights should apply to the states. Only two of the first ten amendments remain unincorporated: the Third and Seventh. In addition, the Fifth Amendment right to a grand jury hearing and the Eighth Amendment freedom from excessive bail and fines do not apply to the states.

Selective incorporation greatly enhanced the expansion of rights in the United States because the vast majority of individual actions occur in the states. Most people who exercise their rights of free speech and assembly, for instance, do so in one of the states, unless they carry their

protests to Washington, D.C. The process of selective incorporation also created a uniform definition of our basic rights that is independent of geography. A criminal defendant has the same basic constitutional rights whether he or she lives in Iowa or New York.

The Modern Emphasis on Rights

Selective incorporation helped to usher in an era of greater emphasis on individual rights in which even the most humble citizens claim fundamental protections from government violation. Even so, many citizens today are only dimly aware of their constitutional rights. When asked to name their First Amendment rights besides freedom of speech, a significant number of Americans incorrectly listed the right to vote, to own a gun, to obtain a public education, and even the right to own pets and drive a car. Sadly, more respondents correctly named multiple characters on *The Simpsons* television program than multiple rights in the First Amendment.

Knowledge of First Amendment Rights vs. the Simpsons Characters

- 1 or more correct: Simpsons characters 72, First Amendment rights 65
- 2 or more correct: Simpsons characters 52, First Amendment rights 28
- 3 or more correct: Simpsons characters 43, First Amendment rights 8
- 4 or more correct: Simpsons characters 34, First Amendment rights 2
- 5 correct: Simpsons characters 22, First Amendment rights 0

■ Simpsons characters   ■ First Amendment rights

Cumulative answers correct (in percentages)

Source: McCormick Tribune Freedom Museum, "Americans' Awareness of First Amendment Freedoms," March 1, 2006.

FREEDOM OF RELIGION

The first two freedoms listed in the Bill of Rights pertain to the exercise of religion. This is unsurprising; many of the early settlers left Europe to escape religious persecution and to establish communities where they could freely practice their own religions. Although many states placed the guarantee of religious freedom in their state constitutions, the delegates who met in Philadelphia to consider a new constitution had differing ideas about the role of religion in the new country. At a particularly difficult point in the deliberations, Benjamin Franklin proposed that the delegates should pray "for the assistance of Heaven, and its blessings on our deliberations."[9] Nearly all the other delegates attacked Franklin's motion, arguing that a prayer session might offend some of the delegates. The original text of the Constitution reflects this reluctance to address the issue of religion, which is mentioned only once in the document. Article VI requires all government officials to take an oath to "support this Constitution; but no religious Test

The free exercise of religion clause of the First Amendment protects religious beliefs but not all religious activities, such as the handling of poisonous snakes.

shall ever be required as a Qualification to any Office or public Trust under the United States."

The First Amendment contains two clauses dealing with religious freedom: "Congress shall make no law respecting an establishment of religion, or prohibiting the free exercise thereof." The second and least complicated provision is the **free exercise clause**, which prohibits the government from interfering with an individual's right to practice his or her religion.[10] The meaning of the **establishment clause** is less clear. At the very least, it prohibits the government from establishing a national religion. Although they address different aspects of religious freedom, the two clauses occasionally come into conflict. Some people may interpret actions such as providing military chaplains or setting aside Sunday as a day of rest as government attempts to establish religion, while the government may see them as attempts to create greater access to practice religion.

Free Exercise Clause

A literal interpretation of the free exercise clause suggests that a group may practice any religion it chooses, but is such an interpretation reasonable? What if the members engage in dangerous practices such as handling poisonous snakes or illegal ones such as taking hallucinogenic drugs? Should the government prohibit religious activities that are dangerous or offensive to a majority of the community?

Historically, American lawmakers and judges have adhered to the so-called belief–action distinction, articulated by President Thomas Jefferson in an 1802 letter to the Danbury Baptist Association: "Religion is a matter which lies solely between man and his God; that he owes account to none other for his faith or his worship; that the legislative powers of the Government reach actions only, and not opinion."[11] Jefferson believed that free exercise of religion is not absolute; government may regulate religious actions. The Supreme Court has supported this position, upholding the constitutionality of laws affecting religious practices as

Which Should Have More Influence on U.S. Law?

According to...	The will of the American people (%)	The Bible (%)	Don't know (%)
White Evangelical	34	60	6
White Mainline	78	16	6
Catholic	72	23	5
Secular	91	7	2
Average	63	32	5

Source: The Pew Forum on Religion and Public Life, "Many Americans Uneasy With Mix of Religion and Politics," 2.

long as the legislation serves the nonreligious goal of safeguarding the peace, order, and comfort of the community and is not directed at any particular religion.[12] As a result, the Court has sustained laws prohibiting religiously sanctioned polygamy (the practice of taking multiple wives) and use of the drug peyote during religious services.[13] By contrast, the Court invalidated a law that forced a Seventh-day Adventist to work on Saturday—her faith's Sabbath—in order to receive unemployment benefits.[14] The Court also upheld the right of the Amish to withdraw their children from public school before the age of sixteen.[15] The Amish believe the materialism, competition, and peer pressure that characterize secondary education would have a negative effect on their children's religious beliefs, Bible reading, and appreciation of a simple, spiritual life.

Congress and Religious Freedom

Congress does not always agree with the way the Court interprets the free exercise clause. In recent years, the legislative branch has shown greater support for freedom of religious expression than has its judicial counterpart. In 1986, for example, the Court ruled that an ordained rabbi, who was a captain in the U.S. Air Force, could not wear his yarmulke (skullcap) while in or out of uniform. Congress reacted by passing a 1987 law that allowed members of the armed forces to "wear an item of religious apparel while in uniform so long as the item is neat and conservative" and does not "interfere with the performance" of military duties.[16]

After the Court outlawed the use of peyote in religious ceremonies, Congress expressed renewed concern over the Court's reasoning in free exercise cases. In 1993, Demo-

cratic senator Ted Kennedy, a Catholic, and Republican senator Orrin Hatch, a Mormon, led congressional passage of the Religious Freedom and Restoration Act (RFRA). Normally staunch ideological opponents, Kennedy and Hatch joined up to champion a law urging the Court to use a more liberal judicial test to interpret the free exercise clause that would result in less interference with an individual's ability to practice his or her religion. The Court, however, ruled the law unconstitutional, arguing that Congress had no power to tell the Court how to interpret the Constitution.[17]

free exercise clause The First Amendment provision intended to protect the practice of one's religion free from government interference.

establishment clause The First Amendment prohibition against the government's establishment of a national religion.

Establishment Clause

While free exercise cases involve government intrusion into the practice of religion, establishment clause cases deal with the formal relationship between religion and government. We will see that the United States has usually followed a tradition of attempting to separate church from state, yet there has also been a strong inclination to mix politics and religion. This is not surprising because Americans are a very religious people. A recent poll has shown that 88 percent of the population believe in God, a majority responded that religion is important in their lives and that they pray on a daily basis, and 39 percent attend church at least once a week.[18] As a result, questions like "Should the Bible or the will of the people have more influence on the passage of laws?" become pertinent. (See the table above.)

Majority Say Churches Should Keep out of Politics

On social and political matters, churches should…

Express views   Keep out

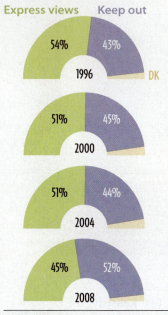

54%   43%
1996   DK

51%   45%
2000

51%   44%
2004

45%   52%
2008

Source: Pew Forum, "More Americans Question Religion's Role in Politics," August 21, 2008, 1.

Should Churches Endorse Candidates?

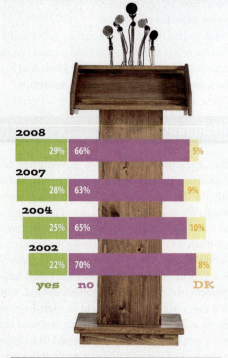

2008
29%   66%   5%
2007
28%   63%   9%
2004
25%   65%   10%
2002
22%   70%   8%

yes   no   DK

Source: Should Churches Endorse One Candidate Over Another?, Pew Forum, October 1, 2008, 1.

The trend recently has been that Americans are reluctant to mix religion and politics, as these figures show.

Polls of church-attending Americans reveal that the clergy discuss a variety of issues such as poverty, abortion, war, laws regarding homosexuals, and stem cell research. Even the Founding Fathers disagreed about the relationship between church and state. Jefferson wrote that the First Amendment built "a wall of separation between Church and State." This is known as the separationist position because it prohibits most if not all forms of government support for religion.

Most scholars contend that a majority of the Founding Fathers disagreed with Jefferson and instead held accommodationist views. Accommodationists argue that the establishment clause forbids the government from showing preference to one religion with respect to another and prohibits the government from establishing a national religion.[19] However, they believe that government may constitutionally support religion as long as it does not discriminate against any particular faith.

The ambiguity of the establishment clause led the Supreme Court to develop a test for resolving establishment cases. According to the ***Lemon*** test, a law must meet three conditions in order not to violate the establishment clause:

1. The law must have a secular (nonreligious) purpose.
2. The primary effect of the law must be one that neither advances nor inhibits religion.
3. The law must not foster an excessive government entanglement with religion.

Using the test, the Court struck down a Pennsylvania law that provided direct state financial aid to pay teachers at a religiously affiliated school. The majority ruled that the law created an excessive entanglement between the state government and religion by requiring close government oversight of church matters.[20] Using similar reasoning, the Court upheld a state law granting property tax exemptions to religious organizations. The majority in that case argued that taxing the churches would create an extensive government entanglement.[21]

Most of the establishment clause cases that have reached the Supreme Court in recent years have involved issues such as the teaching of religion in public schools; religious use of public school facilities and funds; recitation of prayers in public schools; government aid to religiously affiliated schools; and official endorsement of religious displays such as a nativity scene or the Ten Commandments. Some observers see these disputes as examples of conservative Christians imposing their religious views on others. However, many of the nearly 70 percent of Americans who consider themselves to be Christians see them as a reaction to perceived government hostility toward religion, reflected in attempts to remove prayer from schools or religious displays from public buildings.

Who Has Gone Too Far?

Respondents:	Conservative Christians in imposing their religious values %	Liberals in keeping religion out of government %
Republican	31	87
Conservative	24	90
Moderate/Liberal	46	82
Democrat	59	60
Moderate/Conservative	51	70
Liberal	80	38
Independent	56	65
Total	49	69

Source: The Pew Forum on Religion and Public Life, "Many Americans Uneasy with Mix of Religion and Politics," 1. August 24, 2006.

Religion and Public Schools

Since the Supreme Court ruled government-sponsored school prayer unconstitutional in the early 1960s, the nation's schools have been a leading battleground in the issue of establishment. Battles frequently have erupted over state laws that attempt to force the curriculum of secular subjects to reflect particular religious beliefs. Such laws often target subjects that discuss the origins of human life. In 1968, the Court struck down a 1928 Arkansas law that made it a crime for any university or public school instructor to "teach the theory or doctrine that mankind ascended or descended from a lower order of animals" or to "adopt or use . . . a textbook that teaches" evolutionary theory.[22] It has also invalidated a Louisiana law that prohibited public schools from teaching evolutionary principles unless theories of "creation science" were also taught.[23]

Today, opponents of evolution are advancing the same argument under the term *intelligent design*. This theory claims that some biological structures such as DNA codes are so complex that they could not have occurred because of evolution but must be the work of an intelligent designer. Proponents argue that intelligent design should be taught in schools alongside other scientific theories. Public leaders such as former president George W. Bush and former Senate majority leader Bill Frist have endorsed the idea. Opponents and the lower courts, however, have failed to see any differences from the earlier attempts to ban evolutionary theory from the schools.

Religious Use of Public School Facilities and Funds

As a matter of fairness and constitutional protection, do religious groups have the same right to use public school build-

ings as other groups? The Supreme Court answered the question "yes" with respect to public universities and later also ruled that religious groups should have access to secondary schools.[24] The Court also ruled that the establishment clause does not require schools to refuse religious groups the same right to free expression as secular groups. In the case of *Rosenberger v. University of Virginia* (1995), the Court struck down the University of Virginia's refusal to allow student religious groups access to funds collected by a mandatory fee of $14 from all full-time students. The university had established a student activities fund to which only nonreligious student organizations could apply for money to pay for the costs associated with the printing of their publications. The Court held that the establishment clause did not mandate discrimination against religious expression.

Prayer in School

School prayer is probably the most controversial of the establishment clause issues. Reciting prayers and reading Bible passages have been commonplace practices in public schools throughout our nation's history. Separationists believed such practices violated the establishment clause and embarked upon a plan to have the Supreme Court abolish them. In the case of *Engel v. Vitale* in 1962, the Court declared that compelling students to recite a twenty-two-word prayer written by the New York State Board of Regents violated the First Amendment.[25] Writing for the majority, Justice Hugo Black stated that "a union of government and religion tends to destroy government and degrade religion." The next year, the Court overturned a Pennsylvania law that required school officials to read at least ten verses from the Bible and the Lord's Prayer each day over the loudspeaker.[26]

The Pennsylvania decision was met with public disapproval; only 24 percent of those surveyed at the time agreed with the ruling, and by 2000, that figure still stood at just 38.8 percent.[27] Despite the decision, many school districts in the South continued the practice of reading the Bible in class.

> **Lemon test** The three-part test for establishment clause cases that a law must pass before it is declared constitutional: it must have a secular purpose; it must neither advance nor inhibit religion; and it must not cause excessive entanglement with religion.

In response to public opinion, Congress members have made over one hundred fifty unsuccessful attempts to introduce constitutional amendments to return prayer to public classrooms. Supporters of school prayer have also continued to appeal cases to the Supreme Court, with no more success. Since 1992, the Court has struck down a silent prayer law,[28] the participation of clergy at high school graduation ceremonies,[29] and the traditional Texas practice of delivering a public prayer over a public address system before a high school football game.[30] The silent prayer issue may again become a salient one because a 2005 Gallup poll indicated that American adults prefer silent prayers in public schools to spoken prayers by a margin of 69 to 23 percent, and 84 percent of teens between the ages of 13 and 17 preferred a moment of silence to allow students an opportunity to pray.[31]

Aid to Religious Schools

The Supreme Court has also wrestled with the question of whether government may provide financial aid to religious schools, and if so, how much. In recent years, the Court has moved in an accommodationist direction on this question. Beginning in 1993, it held that a state may pay to provide a sign-language interpreter for a disabled student at a Roman Catholic high school without violating the establishment clause.[32] Four years later, the Court reversed two earlier cases and ruled that public school teachers may give remedial instruction to at-risk students who attend religious schools.[33] In *Mitchell v. Helms* (2000), the Court found federal aid to religious schools for computer resources, educational materials, and library holdings constitutional, again overruling two earlier cases.

In a landmark 2002 case, the Court upheld the constitutionality of providing government vouchers to attend religious schools. The Cleveland school system, reputedly one of the nation's worst, offered parents up to $2,250 in vouchers to attend private schools, either religious or nonreligious. Over 95 percent of the students who used vouchers to attend private schools enrolled in religious schools. In a 5 to 4 decision, the Court ruled that the program did not violate the establishment clause.[34] The majority argued that the program was neutral in nature and based on private choice rather than government endorsement of a religious school. In 2011, the Court continued to support the private school option by prohibiting Arizona taxpayers from challenging a state tax-credit system that permitted tax credits to be used for religious-school tuition scholarships. The five-member majority in *Arizona Christian School Tuition Organization v. Winn* ruled that the policy did not violate the establishment clause because the tax credits are donations of private money and not state money redirected to religious institutions.

Government Endorsement of Religion

How does placing the words "In God We Trust" on our coins and Federal Reserve notes square with the separation between government and religion mandated by the establishment clause? When does government tolerance of religious expression constitute active endorsement of religion? The Court recently has attempted to establish guidelines to determine what kinds of displays are permissible on government property. For example, it has revised the second part of the *Lemon* test to hold that public display of a nativity scene on government property is unconstitutional if its effect is to endorse religion. Using such a test, they found a nativity scene located in a government building with the words "Glory to God in the Highest" to be a Christian religious display that violated the establishment clause,[35] but not a government-sponsored nativity scene in a private park with a Santa Claus and a banner displaying the number of shopping days until Christmas.[36]

Similarly, in a 2005 decision, the Court ruled a monument of the Ten Commandments on the grounds of the Texas Capitol permissible because it was part of a historical exhibit including forty other monuments such as tributes to the Alamo, Confederate veterans, and Korean War veterans.[37] The same year, however, it found the posting of the Ten Commandments inside two Kentucky courthouses an unconstitutional endorsement of religion.[38] In 2010, the Court ruled in *Salazar v. Buono* that Congress did not promote religion when it attempted to avoid an establishment clause issue by trading an acre of federal land containing a white, wooden cross approximately five feet tall with the Veterans of Foreign Wars for five privately owned acres elsewhere in the same Mojave Desert preserve.

Hot or Not?

When you go to a place of worship, do you want your pastor, priest, rabbi, or imam discussing political issues?

" . . . a union of government and religion tends to destroy government and degrade religion."

FREEDOM OF SPEECH

Freedom of speech is essential to a democratic political system. Without the ability to speak about politics, citizens cannot make intelligent judgments about candidates, political parties, and public policies. Freedom of expression is also essential for the intellectual enlightenment of a society and the human race. John Stuart Mill wrote that freedom of speech was the only way to discover the truth. Mill saw a free society as one that traded in a "marketplace of ideas" that would either confirm previous beliefs or provide new perceptions of the truth.[39]

Speech takes several different forms, which are subject to different levels of protection. Sometimes speech consists not of spoken words, but rather an act such as burning a flag or wearing a sign. As with freedom of religion, freedom of speech is not absolute in the United States. The Supreme Court has established boundaries for permissible speech by refusing to protect utterances that are obscene, defamatory, or that constitute what it calls "hate speech."

Political Speech

Political leaders often believe that freedom of speech is less important than considerations such as national security, public order, the right to a fair trial, and public decency. This sometimes produces legislation limiting freedom of speech to serve goals perceived as vital to the nation's interest. Popular opposition to U.S. participation in World War I led Congress to pass the 1917 Espionage Act, which made it a federal crime to obstruct military recruiting, to circulate false statements intending to interfere with the military, or to attempt to cause disloyalty in the military. The government later prosecuted Charles Schenck, the general secretary of

Even hate groups like the Ku Klux Klan enjoy the protection of free speech as interpreted by the clear and present danger test.

the Socialist Party of Philadelphia, under the act for printing and mailing fifteen thousand pamphlets urging draftees to resist conscription. The Supreme Court upheld his conviction but, in doing so, left a broad scope for permissible speech.

In articulating the **clear and present danger test** to determine free speech cases, Justice Oliver Wendell Holmes ruled that Schenck's writings would be constitutionally protected in ordinary times but "the character of every act depends upon the circumstances in which it is done." He compared writing such a pamphlet during wartime to falsely shouting fire in a crowded theater, stating that the context of a speech determines its permissibility. Only words that produce both a clear (obvious) and a present (immediate) danger are prohibited.[40] Justice Louis Brandeis supported Holmes, reasoning that prohibition is an appropriate remedy only for speech that threatens immediate harm. Given time to discover the facts through discussion and education, more speech serves the public interest better than enforced silence.[41]

Following World War I, fear of the new Communist government in Russia and the spread of Communism led to new limits on freedom of speech. At this time, the Supreme Court replaced the clear and present danger test with more restrictive tests such as the **bad tendency test**, which asked, "Do the words have a tendency to bring about something bad or evil?"[42] In 1969, however, the Court returned to the clear and present danger test to protect the right of a Ku Klux Klan leader to make a speech in Ohio.[43] Since that

> **clear and present danger test** Free speech test that only prohibits speech that produces a clear and immediate danger.
>
> **bad tendency test** Free speech test that prohibits speech that could produce a bad outcome, such as violence, no matter how unlikely the possibility the speech could be the cause of such an outcome.

time, the Court has continued to use this more liberal test despite security concerns related to international terrorism and U.S. overseas military actions.

Campaign Speech

Robust protection for political speech is necessary to maintain the open and public nature of our electoral system, but legitimate questions exist about what constitutes political speech, and the extent to which it is protected. Perhaps the most contentious of these is the question of whether money—in the form of campaign contributions—can be considered speech. Campaign contributions allow citizens and interest groups to express their views by supporting and influencing political candidates and parties. They also enable campaigns, candidates, political parties, and their supporters to present views to the electorate. However, are they equivalent to speech and thus deserving of constitutional protection?

Legal challenges to the 1974 Federal Election Campaign Act gave the U.S. Supreme Court the opportunity to answer those questions. Among its provisions, the act limited the amount of money that individuals and groups could contribute to federal campaigns in a calendar year. It also placed caps on total group and individual expenditures on behalf of a candidate, as well as the amount candidates could spend on their own campaigns. The Court upheld limits on contributions in order to prevent a political quid pro quo system in which government policies might be purchased by the highest bidder. On the other hand, it ruled that restrictions on expenditures violated free speech guarantees because individuals, groups, and candidates alike had the right to vigorously advocate their positions.[44]

The Court's decision led to a dramatic increase in campaign expenditures by individuals, interest groups, candidates, and political parties. Concerned about the escalating costs of campaigns, Congress passed the Bipartisan Campaign Reform Act of 2002. The law bans unlimited contributions to national political parties and places some limits on the expenditures of groups advocating the election or defeat of a particular candidate. In *McConnell v. Federal Election Commission* (2003), the Supreme Court upheld almost all of the provisions of the act, but in the 2007 case of *Federal Election Commission v. Wisconsin Right to Life/McCain et al. v. Wisconsin Right to Life*, it crafted a major exception to the limitations on broadcast ads by ruling that unless an ad could not reasonably be interpreted as anything other than an ad urging the support or defeat of a candidate, the ad would be allowed in the thirty-day period before a primary or sixty-day period before a general election.

In 2010, however, the Court further clarified its position on broadcast ads in the case of *Citizens United v. Federal Election Commission.* The case involved the attempt of a conservative nonprofit group to broadcast commercials of their scathing documentary, *Hillary: The Movie* and to run the movie on a cable video-on-demand service. In 2008, a federal district court had ruled that the attempt violated the provision of the McCain-Feingold law banning "electioneering communications" paid for by a corporation before a primary election.

In reversing that decision, the Supreme Court held that the government cannot restrict corporations from spending money to influence political campaigns. It based its decision on the argument that such censorship violated the freedom of speech guarantee of the First Amendment. The Court's opinion could soon open the door to direct contributions to candidates from corporations and unions that are still prohibited today. Conservative groups like the Center for Competitive Politics hailed the decision as a win for the political rights of small businesses and grassroots groups; whereas, liberal groups like Common Cause feared the decision would now allow corporate profits to drown out voices of the public. They believe the flow of this money could corrupt the political system.

> *The Supreme Court held that the government cannot restrict corporations from spreading money to influence political campaigns.*

Commercial Speech

On an average day, people hear far more commercial speech than political speech. Companies are trying to sell us countless goods and services on every type of media outlet. In fact, studies show that Americans are more familiar with many advertising slogans than with First Amendment rights.

The courts traditionally have viewed commercial speech as being less worthy of free speech protection than political speech because the government has a legitimate interest in protecting consumers from deceptive advertising. If the advertising is not deceptive, however, the Court will protect it. The Supreme Court, for example, has invalidated a Virginia regulation making it unlawful for a pharmacy to advertise the prices of its prescription medications[45] and has supported the constitutional right of lawyers to advertise the prices of routine legal services.[46]

Symbolic Speech

At the time the Bill of Rights was written, political protesters expressed themselves through impassioned speeches and printed publications. Changing technology, however, has multiplied the channels for delivering and receiving political messages that go beyond the spoken or written word. Today, a protest march or a flag burning is more likely to receive media coverage than a forty-five-minute speech or a twenty-page pamphlet. When such activities convey a political message or viewpoint, courts may consider them to be **symbolic speech** worthy of First Amendment protection.

The Supreme Court has ruled that governments may suppress symbolic views if doing so serves an important purpose other than the suppression of unpopular speech. Using that reasoning, it has supported the federal government's authority to ban the burning of draft cards because the cards contain information necessary for the implementation of a military conscription system.[47] On the other hand, it struck down a school ban on the wearing of black armbands to protest the Vietnam War, ruling that the symbolic speech did not negatively affect the school's educational mission.[48] The Court has even held that desecration of the American flag may be considered a form of protected speech. In 1989, the Court invalidated a Texas law that prohibited burning the American flag, arguing that the law's sole purpose was to suppress speech.[49] The decision motivated Congress to pass the Flag Protection Act of 1989, which penalizes anyone who "knowingly mutilates, defaces, physically defiles, burns, maintains on the floor or ground, or tramples upon any flag of the United States." Applying the same reasoning as the Texas case, the Court found that the federal law violated the guarantee of free speech.[50]

Boundaries of Free Speech

The Supreme Court traditionally has given less consideration to speech that is not necessary to stimulate the marketplace of ideas and to preserve the workings of a democratic political system. For example, the Court has declined to grant First Amendment protection to utterances and writings that are obscene or de-famatory. More recently, the Court has added hate speech to the category of unprotected expression.

Obscenity

While the Supreme Court has consistently held that obscenity falls outside the boundaries of free speech, it has struggled to define the meaning of *obscene*. Justice Potter Stewart expressed the difficulty in his famous utterance: "I shall not today attempt to further define [obscenity]. . . . But I know it when I see it."[51] If Justice Stewart were alive today, would he view *Playboy* or Howard Stern's radio program as obscene? The answer depends on the judicial test he used to determine obscenity. Today, the Supreme Court uses the ***Miller* test**, which asks three questions:

1. Does the average person, applying contemporary community standards, believe that the dominant theme of the material, taken as a whole, appeals to a prurient interest?

> **symbolic speech** Actions meant to convey a political message.
>
> ***Miller* test** The current judicial test for obscenity cases that considers community standards, whether the material is patently offensive, and whether the material taken as a whole lacks serious literary, artistic, political, or scientific value.

The Supreme Court has ruled that flag burning may be protected as symbolic free speech.

2. Is the material patently offensive?

3. Does the work, taken as a whole, lack serious literary, artistic, political, or scientific value?[52]

If the answer to any of the three questions is no, the Court considers the work not to be obscene.

Trying to regulate obscenity on the Internet has been difficult for Congress. In 1996 it passed the Communications Decency Act (CDA) that prohibited transmission of any obscene or indecent material over the Internet to anyone under the age of eighteen. In *Reno v. American Civil Liberties Union* (1997), the Supreme Court ruled the term *indecent* was too vague to prohibit speech.

slander Oral statements that are false and injure another's reputation.

In 1998 Congress tried again to limit the transmission of obscene materials in cyberspace with the Child Online Protection Act (COPA). Rather than prohibiting "obscene and indecent" materials, the statute banned any material "harmful to minors." The Supreme Court rejected this law as well with its argument that the "community standards" principle has no application to the Internet because of the unlimited geographic scope of online communications (*Ashcroft v. American Civil Liberties Union,* 2004). In 2011, the Court refused to create a new category of speech beyond the protection of the First Amendment. In *Brown v. Entertainment Merchants Association,* it struck down a California law that barred the sale of violent games to children.

Defamation

Free speech allows a vigorous exchange of ideas and criticisms that are sometimes hurtful and even mean-spirited. Legislative bodies have placed limits on such comments by allowing a person to sue anyone who makes false statements that injure his or her reputation. **Slander** is a false oral statement that causes injury, whereas **libel** is a written statement that has the same effect. Truth is an absolute defense in a slander or libel suit; a true statement cannot injure or defame.

The Court made it much more difficult for public figures to win defamation suits against their critics with its opinion in *New York Times Company v. Sullivan* (1964). In this case, the Court introduced the new *Sullivan* **rule**, which required that a public official in a libel or slander case not only prove the statements in question are false but also that the defendants wrote or spoke the words with malice. The Court defined *malice* as (1) knowledge the statements were false or (2) reckless disregard for whether the statements were false or not. The Court felt that this higher standard of proof was necessary to avoid self-censorship by critics of public officials, who may not have the ability to guarantee the truth of all their assertions.

Hate Speech

Hate speech involves prejudicial and hostile statements concerning characteristics such as race, ethnicity, sex, sexual orientation, or religion. Many communities and college campuses have adopted laws and policies banning hate speech. Advocates argue that these policies help minorities and women gain equal opportunity to jobs and education by creating less hostile public environments. Opponents of hate speech laws argue that preserving freedom of expression is a more important goal than ensuring civil discourse. Many contend that allowing greater freedom of speech will enhance racial and sexual equality more effectively than placing limits on free speech.[53]

FREEDOM OF THE PRESS

Because both freedom of speech and freedom of the press deal with expression, similar principles underlie each. Both forms of communication are essential to democracy due to their role in transmitting information. As we learned, the Founders knew and stressed the importance of an informed public in creating a successful democracy. The press protections they incorporated into the Constitution reflect those beliefs.

Prior Restraint

The authors of the Constitution and the Bill of Rights agreed with the famous English jurist William Blackstone, who wrote that authors and publishers may only be tried for legitimate criminal violations once their article is published and their words have entered into the marketplace of ideas. He rejected the notion that government had the right to exercise **prior restraint**, the ability to prevent publication of material to which it objected.[54] The U.S. Supreme Court embraced this position in the 1931 case of *Near v. Minnesota*, in which it invalidated a Minnesota law intended to prevent publication of material deemed to be malicious, scandalous, and defamatory.

The Court did note, however, that the government's interest in protecting national security, regulating obscenity, or preventing the incitement of violence may justify prior restraint in the most exceptional cases. The Nixon administration cited national security considerations in 1971, when it attempted to restrain *The New York Times* and *The Washington Post* from publishing the "Pentagon Papers," a series of articles about U.S. involvement in Vietnam based on government documents. The Court rejected the administration's argument, ruling that government may not prevent the press from exercising its right to criticize public officials and its duty to inform readers.

The "Pentagon Papers" case seems to have settled the matter of prior restraint, as the Court has heard no further cases of significance in this area. After the terrorist attacks on September 11, 2001, however, the Department of Defense requested that journalists refrain from publishing information that could harm the country's national security. The department also hinted that the government might demand to review stories before publication or broadcast. As of this time, however, the government has censored no articles.

Government Control of Media Content

The government need not exercise prior restraint to exert control over the media. It can instead exercise control over content by prohibiting the publication of certain information. For example, states often pass laws prohibiting the publication of certain criminal matters in order to protect the victim, the offender, or the fairness of the trial. In *Cox Broadcasting Corporation v. Cohn* (1975), however, the Court ruled that the press has a First Amendment right to report the names of rape victims obtained from judicial records that are open to the public. The Court has also invalidated a state law that prohibits the publication of the identity of juvenile offenders[55] and it has struck down a trial judge's gag order that prohibited the press from covering a pretrial hearing for fear of prejudicial pretrial publicity.[56]

The government can also influence the media by mandating the publication of certain information, but only with certain limits. In one case, the Court struck down a Florida statute that required newspapers under certain circumstances to print articles written by candidates for political office. In a unanimous decision, the Court ruled that the government has no constitutional authority to order the newspaper to publish an article. To allow such a law would limit the editorial decision-making power of the paper, increase its costs, and perhaps discourage political and electoral coverage.[57]

Traditionally, radio and television have not been as free from government control as the print media. As discussed in Chapter 10, the government decided to license radio and television stations and place more restrictions upon them because of the scarcity of bandwidth. There simply were more persons who wanted to broadcast than there were frequencies to allocate. This scarcity led to the creation of the Federal Communications Commission (FCC) and imposition of such regulations as the fairness doctrine, which required broadcasters to discuss both sides of controversial public issues.

libel Written statements that are false and injure another's reputation.

Sullivan rule Standard requiring public officials and public figures in defamation suits to prove that allegedly libelous or slanderous statements are both false and made with malice.

hate speech Prejudicial and hostile statements toward another person's innate characteristics such as race and ethnicity.

prior restraint A practice that would allow the government to censor a publication before anyone could read or view it.

Special Rights

The media historically have argued for special legal rights to allow them to perform the important function of gathering and reporting the news. In most instances, the U.S. Supreme Court has looked unfavorably on these claims for special rights. It has not allowed reporters to maintain the confidentiality of their sources if the government can show compelling reasons for requesting their names, such as to advance a criminal investigation.[58] In 2005, the Court refused to review a lower court's decision to im-

Under the guarantee of freedom of the press, the media may disclose the names of juvenile offenders although they usually choose not to do so.

prison *New York Times* reporter Judith Miller for failing to cooperate with a federal investigation. Miller, who wrote an article leaking the name of a CIA operative, refused to tell federal prosecutor Patrick Fitzgerald the name of the person who gave her that information. Miller spent eighty-five days in jail until her source released her from the promise of confidentiality.

Although the media frequently assert a special right of access, the Court has placed a variety of limits on reporters' ability to gather the news. It has found that reporters enjoy no access to county jail inmates that is denied to other individuals.[59] They also have no right to enter a home when police are executing a warrant.[60] The justices also failed to recognize a First Amendment right of the media to attend a closed pretrial hearing in a highly publicized case.[61] The Court ruled differently, however, with respect to a judge's attempt to close a trial to the media and the public. It held in *Richmond Newspapers v. Virginia* (1980) that the media's right to attend trials is implicit in the freedom of the press guarantee.

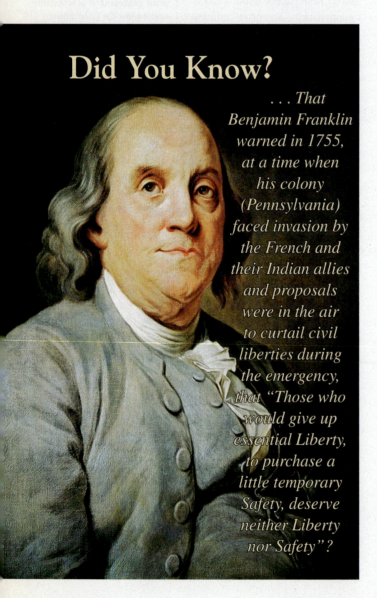

Did You Know?

. . . That Benjamin Franklin warned in 1755, at a time when his colony (Pennsylvania) faced invasion by the French and their Indian allies and proposals were in the air to curtail civil liberties during the emergency, that "Those who would give up essential Liberty, to purchase a little temporary Safety, deserve neither Liberty nor Safety"?

FREEDOM OF ASSEMBLY AND ASSOCIATION

The First Amendment freedom of assembly is one of the cornerstones of American democracy, granting citizens the right to gather and engage in politics. It is the basis for the formation of interest groups and political parties that attempt to forge public policy and determine who will hold public office. Implied in the freedom of assembly is the right to associate by joining with like-minded individuals to pursue common goals. The freedoms of speech, press, and assembly would be nearly meaningless if one had to do them alone.

Freedom of Assembly

Freedom to assemble is critical for the survival of a democratic political system. Yet this does not mean that people can assemble to advance their own political agenda whenever and wherever they please. The government may have competing interests that override such freedoms, such as keeping the peace, maintaining order, and protecting the flow of commerce. As a result, governments have the authority to impose "time, place, and manner restrictions" on the conditions of a political gathering.

The freedom of assembly cases that come before the Court typically reflect debate about the significant controversies of the day. During the 1960s, such cases arose from the often emotionally charged civil rights demonstrations in southern cities. In one case, police arrested nearly two hundred African American student demonstrators in South Carolina for refusing orders to disperse after an hour of peaceful protest at the state capitol building. The Supreme Court reversed the conviction, holding that a peaceful demonstration at the seat of state government was the proper way "to petition government for a redress of grievances."[62] In later cases, however, the Court ruled that political assemblies in front of courthouses and jails were not constitutionally protected. The justices feared that protests in front of a courthouse to advocate a certain outcome for a trial could adversely affect the administration of justice and perceptions of the judicial system.[63] The Court ruled out peaceful demonstrations at a jail because jails, unlike state capitol buildings, are not typically open to the public because of security concerns.[64]

In the 1980s, the Court dealt with several cases stemming from confrontations between antiabortion protesters and supporters of a woman's constitutional right to have an abortion. Many states and communities have passed laws to regulate demonstrations outside abortion clinics. The Court upheld the enforcement of noise restrictions and buffer zones around the clinics' entrances and driveways, but not restrictions on signs or buffer zones to the backs and sides of the clinics.[65] The Court has also upheld a Colorado statute in 2000 that prohibited any person from

Right to assembly protects protesters, as long as the assembly is peaceable. This protest in front of the U.S. Marine Corps Recruiting Center in Berkeley reflects anti-Iraq war sentiments.

approaching closer than eight feet to a clinic patient for the purpose of distributing literature, displaying a sign, or engaging in oral protest, without the patient's consent.[66]

Freedom of Association

The U.S. Supreme Court first recognized the implied right of freedom of association when southern states began to restrict the associational rights of civil rights groups. In the 1958 case of *NAACP v. Alabama*, the civil rights group appealed an Alabama law that mandated that the group turn its membership list over to a state agency. The Court struck down the law, arguing that disclosure of the group's membership list in Alabama could lead to economic reprisal, loss of employment, physical coercion, and public hostility against the individual members. Later, the Court recognized the right of the NAACP to use litigation to further its goals by stressing that the First Amendment supports the vigorous advocacy of a group's views.[67]

More recently, private organizations such as business clubs, fraternal organizations, and civic groups have tested their freedom to restrict membership on the basis of race, sex, or sexual orientation. Does freedom of association allow private groups to discriminate? Yes and no. In *Roberts v. United States Jaycees* (1984), the Court found that freedom of association is not an absolute right, nor does it pertain equally to all private organizations. It afforded smaller and more intimate groups—such as a married couple and families—as well as organizations espousing clear political and ideological views, the most protection. It ruled that the First Amendment's protection of larger national organizations such as the Jaycees, which do not express strong ideological views and do not have highly selective membership guidelines, is inferior to the state's interest in combating arbitrary discrimination. The Court reached similar decisions in cases involving the Rotary Club[68] and a private New York men's club.[69] It ruled that the right of a woman to belong and establish informal business contacts outweighs the right of the organization to associate with whomever they want.

By contrast, the Court upheld the right of a private association to prevent gay rights groups from marching in a Saint Patrick's Day parade the association was organizing in Boston.[70] The Court also upheld the right of the Boy Scouts of America to revoke the adult membership of an assistant scoutmaster who at college announced to others that he was gay. The five-person majority agreed with the organization that the retention of a gay member was inconsistent with the values represented by the phrase "morally straight and clean."[71]

RIGHT TO KEEP AND BEAR ARMS

The text of the Second Amendment—"*A well regulated Militia, being necessary to the security of a free State*, the right of the people to keep and bear Arms, shall not be infringed"—has generated significant disagreement and controversy among gun owners and those who favor limits on firearm ownership.[72] Gun control opponents such as the National Rifle Association emphasize the words that are not italicized. They stress that the government owes citizens the right to own guns in order to secure their freedom. Those who favor restrictions on gun ownership stress the italicized words that imply that only persons who are members of a government militia have the right to own firearms. They believe the Second Amendment confers a collective right that only conveys the right to possess a gun to members of a military unit.

For years the meaning of the Second Amendment drew little attention from American courts. In 1939, the Supreme Court agreed with the collective right position when it decided a case that upheld the right of the federal government to require the registration of firearms.[73] By not incorporating the amendment, however, the Court left the states with a great deal of authority to restrict or protect gun ownership. In recent years, states have tended to protect the rights of gun ownership: Forty-four state constitutions now include language that recognizes the right to keep and bear arms.

Then in 2008, the Court dramatically changed the meaning of the amendment with its decision in *District of Columbia v. Heller*. Heller, an armed security guard, sued the District after it rejected his application to keep a handgun at home for protection. His application violated a strict 1976 D.C. ordinance that banned the private ownership of all handguns. Rifles and shotguns were allowed if they were kept disassembled or in a trigger lock or some similar device. By a 5 to 4 majority, the Court ruled that the Second Amendment confers an individual right for citizens to keep and bear arms to protect themselves.[74] The Court's decision has spurred a great deal of controversy as well as questions about its policy implications. The Court expanded its earlier decision in 2010 by ruling that an individual's right to bear arms applies also to state and local gun control laws (*McDonald v. Chicago*). The opinion emphasized, however, that the Court was not saying that the Second Amendment provided a right to "carry any weapon whatsoever in any manner whatsoever and for whatever purpose."

In January of 2011, in Tucson, Arizona, a disturbed young man with a Glock semi-automatic pistol gravely wounded Representative Gabrielle Giffords (D-AZ) and then turned to fire upon the crowd attending her outdoor political event. By the time he was subdued, six people were dead and many others were wounded. Despite the shock that ran through the nation, the incident failed to provoke a meaningful conversation about gun violence in the United States.

their British rulers, the Framers of the Bill of Rights were determined to provide procedural guarantees throughout the criminal justice system to ensure fairness and justice for the accused. Such protections are embodied in the Fourth, Fifth, Sixth, and Eighth Amendments.

Recent history has shown that not all accused persons are afforded the constitutional protections of the Bill of Rights that are discussed below. Chapter 12 details how President George W. Bush used presidential emergency powers after the attack of September 11, 2001, to curtail the rights of persons suspected of being enemy combatants in a war of terrorism against the United States. Detainees at the Guantanamo Bay prison were not allowed to know the charges against them, to have access to attorneys, to have evidence presented that was not hearsay or the fruits of coercion, nor to have access to federal courts to challenge their detention. Such rules were not only controversial but led many to become concerned about the preservation of civil liberties in the United States. In *Boumediene v. Bush* (2008), the Supreme Court continued to reject most of these procedures, writing that the Constitution was meant to survive in extraordinary times, and therefore, detainees have a right of habeas corpus in federal courts unless Congress explicitly exercises its constitutional authority to suspend the right.

The Fourth Amendment: Searches and Seizures

The Fourth Amendment guarantees freedom from "unreasonable searches and seizures," but the only type of search the Constitution mentions is one authorized by a search warrant. To obtain a warrant, police must present a neutral judge with an affidavit swearing there is reason to believe that a crime has been committed and that evidence can be found in a specific place. The judge then must determine whether **probable cause** exists to issue the search warrant. Judges usually require the probable cause standard for wiretaps and electronic surveillance as well. Since the passage of the USA Patriot Act in 2001, however, federal agents investigating terrorism can trace e-mail messages with less than probable cause. In late 2005, it came to

RIGHTS OF THE ACCUSED

The early Americans showed their unhappiness with the British criminal justice system by devoting four of the first eight amendments almost exclusively to rights granted to accused persons.[75] Remembering the treatment of colonial leaders by

"Don't tase me bro!" What are the rights of a student to interrupt a speech, and do the police have the right to use a taser gun to subdue him?

Lock 'em Up

Rate of incarceration in selected nations (per 100,000 people)

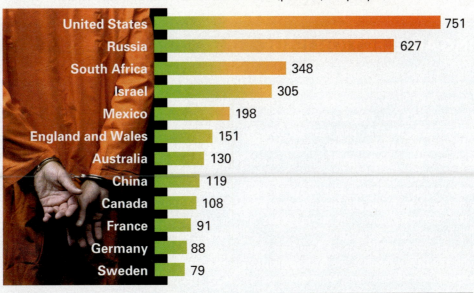

United States	751
Russia	627
South Africa	348
Israel	305
Mexico	198
England and Wales	151
Australia	130
China	119
Canada	108
France	91
Germany	88
Sweden	79

Source: International Center for Prison Studies at King's College London; Marc Maner, The Sentencing Project; Bureau of Justice Statistics; Anthony N. Doob, Center for Criminology, University of Toronto, April 22, 2008.

light that the National Security Agency had been operating a special collections program that allowed it to intercept the communications of about fifty-five Americans without a court order. The Bush administration initiated the program by executive order, without congressional authorization.

The Constitution does not preclude the possibility of warrantless searches, it only requires that such searches be reasonable. But what is reasonable? The Supreme Court has recognized several categories of warrantless searches as reasonable:

1. The police may conduct a search at the time of a valid arrest. They may search any area within the suspect's immediate control where he or she might obtain a weapon or conceal evidence.[76]

2. The courts also recognize a search as valid if the police receive permission voluntarily from a person with the authority to give it. In 2001, the Supreme Court ruled that a person on probation must consent to have his or her property searched if the probation officer has a reasonable suspicion of wrongdoing.[77]

3. Searches without warrants have also been justified when conducted in hot pursuit of a criminal who has just committed a crime, is considered dangerous, and who may destroy evidence if the police must delay a search in order to obtain a warrant.[78]

4. In the case of *Terry v. Ohio* (1968), the Supreme Court approved stop-and-frisk searches in which an experienced police officer believes a suspect is about to commit a crime. The Court reasoned that the police had the power to prevent crimes and that the frisk was necessary to protect the safety of the officer. The Court held in a 2000 case that a young man running from a high-crime area when he saw uniformed police officers created sufficient suspicion to justify such a search.[79]

5. In 1973, the Supreme Court created a new category of warrantless searches known as "loss of evidence searches." In such cases, police may conduct a search if they reasonably suspect that a delay will result in the suspect destroying evidence.[80] In this instance, the Court allowed police to take fingernail scrapings of a murder suspect at the time of the interrogation and before an arrest because of the risk that the evidence could be easily destroyed at a later time.[81] This ruling also forms the legal basis for drug-testing programs such as the one discussed at the beginning of the chapter. However, the Court struck down a hospital-instituted drug-screening program for patients that gave results to the police as a requirement for receiving medical care.[82]

6. In considering the constitutionality of warrantless searches, the Court also has taken into consideration the place being searched and the means of the search. For example, it has ruled that the police may search a field for marijuana plants, even though the area is marked with No Trespassing signs.[83] Police may conduct an aerial search for marijuana plants growing in a greenhouse that is missing some of its roof panels.[84] They may not point a thermal imager at a home, however, to detect heat emanating from bulbs used to grow marijuana indoors.[85] The Court has generally given the police greater authority to search automobiles because of their ability to leave the jurisdic-

probable cause A practical and nontechnical calculation of probabilities that is the basis for securing search warrants.

REMOVING AN ELECTION ISSUE

On Monday, April 4, 2011, the Obama administration announced that Khalid Sheikh Mohammed, the self-proclaimed mastermind of the 2001 terrorist attacks on the United States, would be tried with four alleged co-conspirators by a military commission at the U.S. naval base on Guantanamo Bay, Cuba. This announcement was remarkable for three reasons. First, it reversed President Obama's executive order to close the terrorist prison at Guantanamo Bay. Second, it altered the administration's plan to try Mr. Mohammed in a civilian court. Finally, the announcement was made on the same day that Obama sent his supporters an e-mail launching his reelection campaign.

During his inaugural address, President Obama had committed to closing the facility, rebuking the Bush administration when he stated, "As for our common defense, we reject as false the choice between our safety and our ideals." Two days later he began to act on his rhetoric by issuing an executive order to close the Guantanamo Bay prison within a year and to prohibit extreme interrogation practices. The president's promise proved difficult to keep, however. Problems arose over where to move the detainees. Initial proposals to move the prisoners to Kansas, Michigan, and South Carolina were rejected by local political leaders. In December of 2009 the federal government acquired a prison in Thomson, Illinois, as a possible location to house the Guantanamo detainees.

All of the speculation regarding the prisoner movement led to criticism of Obama's plan from both the political right and left. Critics from the right argued that moving the terrorist suspects to American soil would place Americans in unnecessary danger. The Obama administration countered that the Guantanamo prison serves as a lightning rod for terrorists and increases chances of a domestic attack. From the left, the Amnesty International USA policy director said the move would not really be an advance in civil liberties but merely a change of the zip code of Guantanamo. Congress, in reaction to the national debate, passed legislation in December of 2010 that prohibited the use of federal money to transfer detainees from Guantanamo Bay to the United States.

From the beginning of his presidency, Obama made it clear that he preferred to try terrorist suspects in civilian rather than military courts. In 2009, his attorney general announced that Khalid Sheikh Mohammed and his four associates would be tried in a civilian court in New York City. The plan was thwarted, however, by New York City Mayor Michael Bloomberg and other city leaders. Critics of Obama's plan also argued that military tribunals should be used to try terrorists because they permit greater use of hearsay evidence and sometimes allow coerced evidence. Obama spokesmen responded at that time by arguing that civilian courts are just as effective in getting convictions as evidenced by the successful trials of Jose Padilla and Zacarias Moussaoui.

In reversing his commitments to close the prison and to try those accused of terrorism in civilian courts, the president recognized that he could not overcome the political opposition to his plan and that he now needed to get these two contentious issues behind him as he launched his campaign for reelection. His decision, however, rendered him vulnerable to attack on the campaign trail, where broken promises can haunt incumbents.

---

exclusionary rule The judicial barring of illegally seized evidence from a trial.

Miranda rights The warning police must administer to suspects so that the latter will be aware of their right not to incriminate themselves. The rights include the right to remain silent, the right to know statements will be used against them, and the right to have an attorney for the interrogation.

tion of law enforcement officials, and because of the government's interest in regulating auto traffic and safety. Recently, however, it has not allowed officers at highway checkpoints to look for ordinary criminal wrongdoing such as the possession of illegal drugs.[86] The Court also widened its protection of motorists with its 2009 ruling in *Arizona v. Gant*. The majority held that the police may not search the interior of an auto if the occupant has been arrested and cannot gain access to the car.

The Court was also concerned with how to enforce its Fourth Amendment decisions. What sanction could the Court provide to prevent the police from making unreasonable searches? It eventually adopted the **exclusionary rule** that excludes any evidence gathered illegally from consideration at trial, thus removing the incentive for the police to make illegal searches.[87] The Court has allowed some exceptions to the exclusionary rule, for example, when it believes the police are acting in good faith.[88]

The Fifth Amendment: Self-Incrimination

The Fifth Amendment protects the accused against self-incrimination, a right that places limits on police interrogation of criminal suspects. Nevertheless, law enforcement officers frequently employed physical or psychological pressure during private interrogation sessions in order to gain confessions. To remedy this problem, the Court adopted the now familiar *Miranda* **rights**, which require officials to remind suspects of their Fifth Amendment rights. In the 1966 case of *Miranda v. Arizona*, the Court ruled that "prior to any questioning, the person must be warned that he has a right to remain silent, that any statements he does make may be used against him, and that he has a right to the presence of an attorney, either retained or appointed." The warning of silence allows the suspect to make an intelligent constitutional choice concerning self-incrimination. The presence of an attorney guarantees that the right is protected under the intense pressure of a police interrogation. The Court will deny the admissibility of a confession if the police failed to notify the suspect of his or her *Miranda* rights. In 2000, the Court reaffirmed its support of the *Miranda* ruling by declaring unconstitutional a congressional statute mandating a return to a lesser confession standard.[89]

The Sixth Amendment: Right to Counsel

The Sixth Amendment guarantees the accused the right to counsel. At the time the Constitution was written, there were very few attorneys in the United States—most defendants handled their own cases—and criminal law was relatively uncomplicated. As American society became more complex, so did the laws needed to regulate and punish criminal behavior. By the twentieth century, criminal defendants increasingly began to hire attorneys to represent them. Because of the great complexity of modern criminal law, many observers now consider the right to counsel the most important of the rights possessed by the accused. Good legal advice is invaluable at every stage of the criminal justice process; it is no accident that the right to have an attorney is a key element of the *Miranda* warnings.

Although accused criminals had the right to an attorney, nearly 75 percent of them could not afford one. This put most defendants at a significant disadvantage when confronting a government prosecutor. The Supreme Court challenged the constitutionality of this situation under certain circumstances in *Powell v. Alabama* (1932). The year before, police in Alabama arrested nine African American youths, known as "the Scottsboro boys," for allegedly raping two white girls. The jury convicted eight of the nine suspects and sentenced them to death. Upon appeal, the Court ruled that in unusual situations such as these—the defendants were young and uneducated, they were facing the death penalty, and their fate was subject to intense public pressure—the accused were entitled to counsel at the government's expense.[90]

In 1963, the Court expanded the right to counsel for indigent defendants facing felony charges in response to the efforts of Clarence Gideon.[91] Tried and convicted in Florida without the aid of an attorney for the felony crime of breaking and entering, Gideon became a "jailhouse lawyer" by reading law books and filing legal briefs. After many attempts by Gideon, the Supreme Court agreed to hear his case in 1962, and voted that poor defendants did have the right to an attorney when confronting felony charges. Nine years later, the Court expanded its policy by ruling that indigent defendants facing even one day in jail are entitled to legal representation. Such cases may involve complex legal issues, and a guilty verdict leaves the defendant with the stigma of a criminal conviction.[92] Supplying attorneys for all cases can be an expensive proposition for state governments, however. Recognizing this fact, the Court ruled that the state need not supply counsel unless the defendant faces the possibility of jail time if convicted.[93] In a recent case, however, the Court struck down a lower court ruling against a defendant without counsel who received a suspended sentence and two years' probation. The justices concluded that the state should have provided the defendant with counsel because he faced a possible deprivation of his freedom.[94]

The Sixth Amendment: Trial by Jury

The Sixth Amendment guarantees criminal defendants the right to a jury trial. Although 95 percent of all criminal cases are settled out of court by an informal process known as plea bargaining, the right to a jury trial remains a cornerstone of our criminal justice system. The courts select potential jurors—known as the jury pool, or venire—from government records such as voter registration lists or property tax assessment rolls. In two separate cases, the Supreme Court ruled that jury pools may not exclude blacks or women.[95] The Court has also ruled that prosecutors and defense attorneys may not exclude potential jurors on the basis of race or gender.[96]

At the time the Sixth Amendment was written, the United States employed English trial procedure, in which a twelve-member jury had to reach a unanimous verdict to convict a defendant. By the 1960s, however, many states had reduced the size of juries and made it easier to obtain a conviction. They reasoned that smaller juries and nonunanimous verdicts would save time and money, and result in fewer hung juries. In 1970, the Court upheld the constitutionality of smaller juries in noncapital (not involving the death penalty) cases.[97] Two years later, it held that nonunanimous verdicts in noncapital cases also were constitutional. The Court rejected the assertion that the disagreement of a minority of jurors raised questions of "reasonable doubt" about the verdict.[98]

The Eighth Amendment: Cruel and Unusual Punishment

The Eighth Amendment's ban on cruel and unusual punishment was probably the Framers' reaction to the barbarous methods of torture and execution practiced in medieval England, such as being stretched on the rack and/or disemboweled. Most of the debate over cruel and unusual

Executions in the U.S.

In the U.S., executions are down 53% since 1999

Source: Death Penalty Information Center.

punishment in the United States, however, has focused on the death penalty.

The issue received little attention from the Supreme Court until the 1970s. Then, in 1972, a deeply divided Court ruled that the Georgia death penalty was unconstitutional because it led to unacceptable disparities in executions. African Americans who murdered whites were much more likely to receive the death penalty than whites convicted of the same crime.[99] Only two of the justices, however, said the death penalty was unconstitutional in all circumstances.

Four years later, the Court clarified its position by upholding a new Georgia death penalty statute in *Gregg v. Georgia*.[100] The Court found the law constitutional because it contained adequate safeguards for the defendant. The law prescribed separate phases for trial and sentencing. The trial phase would determine the defendant's guilt or innocence; a verdict of guilty triggered a second phase to consider punishment. The law required jury or judge to consider both aggravating factors and mitigating factors in making a sentencing decision. An aggravating factor is any factor that makes the crime worse, such as murder for hire or felony murder. A mitigating factor is any factor that might excuse the crime to some extent, such as reduced mental capacity on the part of the defendant. The law also provided for an automatic appeal to the state's highest court.

Opponents of the death penalty have been encouraged by recent events. Public support for the death penalty has declined since 1992, as has the number of executions

and death penalty sentences (see graph at left), with the revelation that many innocent persons have been sentenced to death. The declining murder rate has also contributed to a decrease in executions.

In 2000, former governor George Ryan (R-IL) ordered a moratorium on all executions in his state after DNA tests led to the release of thirteen men on death row. Other states are now offering free DNA testing for death row inmates. In 2002, the Supreme Court ruled that the execution of mentally retarded defendants is cruel and unusual punishment; at the time, such executions were legal in twenty states.[101] Three years later, the Court prohibited the death penalty for any defendant who was under the age of eighteen when he or she committed murder.[102] Before the decision, the United States was one of a handful of countries, including China, Pakistan, Iran, and Saudi Arabia, that executed juveniles. Despite these rulings, however, the national government and three-fourths of the states still have the death penalty, and the United States is now the only Western democracy that uses it.

Opponents of the death penalty were cheered again when the Supreme Court agreed to hear a Kentucky case that challenged the state's administration of the lethal injection method of execution: which chemicals were administered, the training of the personnel, the adequacy of the medical supervision, and the risk of error. The prisoner's contention was that if the first drug, the barbiturate, was an insufficient anesthetic, the next two drugs that paralyzed the prisoner and stopped the heart could cause excruciating pain without the prisoner being able to move or cry out. Such pain, it was contended, would constitute cruel and unusual punishment. While the Court considered the case, it stayed the execution of the prisoners from states with the le-

States Without the Death Penalty

Source: Death Penalty Information Center.

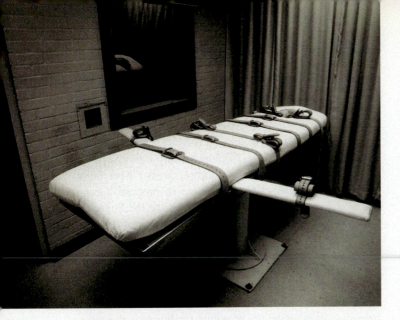

The Supreme Court has ruled that the death penalty is not the type of cruel and unusual punishment that is prohibited by the Eighth Amendment of the Constitution.

thal injection procedure, and some states voluntarily halted their executions until the Supreme Court rendered its decisions. As a result, only forty-two executions were carried out in 2007 and none in the early part of 2008 until the Court rendered its decision. (See the graph on page 86.)

In April 2008, the Court upheld the Kentucky law.[103] For a 7–2 majority, Chief Justice John Roberts wrote: "Simply because an execution method may result in pain, either by accident or as an inescapable consequence of death, does not establish the sort of 'objectively intolerable risk of harm' that qualifies as cruel and unusual" punishment. Within days of the opinion, states began lifting their execution bans and went on to execute 37 persons in 2008 and 52 in 2009.

The Court ended its term in 2008 by rejecting the death penalty for those convicted of raping a child.[104] A closely divided Court held that with the exception of treason and espionage cases, the death penalty should not be applied when the life of the victim was not taken. Prior to the decision, only five states allowed for the execution of rapists whose victims were children, and the others except for Louisiana applied the penalty only in cases where the defendant had previously been convicted of raping a child. The fact that only five states had such laws and that no prisoner had been executed for the crime for a period of 44 years led the Court to conclude that a national consensus had been formed on the issue. The following year the Supreme Court made it easier for death row inmates to sue for access to DNA evidence that could prove their innocence. In *Skinner v. Switzer,* the prosecutors in Texas had tested some but not all of the evidence from the crime scene. The justices ruled that the defendant could sue the prosecutor under a civil rights law for refusing to allow testing of all the DNA evidence.

> **Gregg v. Georgia** The Supreme Court decision that upheld the death penalty in the United States.

In 2010, the Court extended the concept of cruel and unusual punishment to apply to sentences of life in prison without the possibility of parole for juveniles. It held in *Graham v. Florida* that such a sentence leaves a young defendant without hope and thus violates the Eighth Amendment provision.

THE RIGHT TO PRIVACY

Although the Constitution does not explicitly mention a right to privacy, the Supreme Court has found an implied constitutional right to privacy and has declared that right to be fundamental.[105] Asserting a claim of privacy, however, does not guarantee success before a court. In *National Aeronautics and Space Administration v. Nelson,* the Supreme Court upheld in 2011 the use of background checks by the government on scientists and other workers at NASA Jet Propulsion Laboratory. The employees had argued that the background checks that included questions pertaining to drug use, counseling, and "trustworthiness" were too intrusive. The most controversial applications of the right to privacy have been in cases dealing with the beginning and end of life.

Abortion

Until the 1970s, abortion was not a major political issue. Most states considered it a crime, while including exceptions such as a pregnancy that threatened the health of the mother or one that resulted from rape or incest. That changed after an itinerant circus worker named Norma McCorvey challenged a Texas state law that criminalized abortion. The pregnant McCorvey already had a child

The Death Penalty and Public Opinion

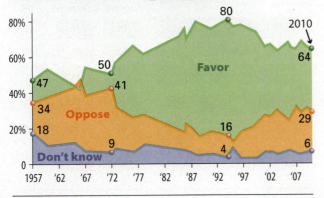

Source: Gallup Poll, 1957–2010.

PRIVATE ABORTION CARE

We promise to support and respect you.

- Abortion by pill or surgery
- Free pregnancy testing
- We accept Medicaid and insurance
- We offer financial aid

WHOLE WOMAN'S HEALTH

512-973-8002

www.wholewomanshealth.com

A woman's right to an abortion stems from the 1973 case of Roe v. Wade.

in the care of her mother and did not want to have another; nor did she want to submit to an illegal back-alley abortion. Under the pseudonym Jane Roe, McCorvey ultimately appealed her case to the Supreme Court.[106] In *Roe v. Wade* (1973), the Court concluded that the constitutional right to privacy was broad enough to include the termination of a pregnancy. According to the majority ruling, a woman's right to privacy gives her an absolute right to terminate her pregnancy during the first trimester. In the second trimester, the government can regulate

abortions only to protect the health of the mother. It is only in the third trimester that the government's interest in potential life outweighs the privacy interests of the mother, because at that point the fetus is viable and can live outside the womb. Since the passage of *Roe v. Wade*, an estimated one million abortions have been performed every year in the United States.

The *Roe* decision intensified the country's division over the issue of abortion.[107] Antiabortion groups have been unsuccessful in persuading Congress to propose a constitutional amendment banning abortions or the Supreme Court to overturn *Roe*. They have been successful, however, in getting state legislatures (and Congress, to a lesser extent) to adopt abortion restrictions. The Supreme Court has upheld state provisions requiring parental consent for abortions performed on minors, informed consent provisions, and a twenty-four-hour waiting period.[108] It also upheld state bans on the use of public facilities for abortions and has required viability testing at twenty weeks.[109] The justices have also validated the Hyde Amendment, which banned the use of Medicaid funds for poor women who wanted to secure abortions.[110] In the case of *Planned Parenthood of Southeastern Pennsylvania v. Casey* (1992), the Court declared it would not abandon a woman's right to an abortion first articulated in *Roe*, but the Court did dismantle the trimester system, since viability testing can be conducted in the second trimester. In 2007, the Court outlawed a later-term abortion method called intact dilation and extraction, which abortion opponents refer to as "partial birth abortion."[111]

The Right to Die

Longer life expectancies, and modern medicine's ability to prolong the life of terminally ill or comatose patients, have increased Americans' concern with issues regarding the right to die. The Court has ruled that individuals have a constitutional right to die that is derived from their

Support for right to die laws

79% Total 1990

84% Total 2005 +5%

Age	Percentage in favor 1990	Percentage in favor 2005	Change %
Under 50	84	85	+1
50 or older	72	83	+11
White Protestant	80	84	+4
Evangelical	81	81	0
Non-evangelical	79	87	+8
Catholic	79	84	+5
White Catholic	80	91	+11
Secular	84	88	+4

Physician-assisted suicide

Approve 46% Disapprove 45% Don't know 9% Total

	Percentage Approve	Disapprove	DK
White Protestant	46	48	6
Evangelical	30	61	9
Non-evangelical	65	31	4
Catholic	40	50	10
White Catholic	48	42	10
Secular	62	28	10

Source: The Pew Research Center For The People & The Press, "Strong Public Support for Right to Die," January 5, 2006.

constitutional right to privacy.[112] The problem occurs when patients have not made clear their wishes in a living will. In such situations, family members may disagree as to the patient's wishes, and, in the most unusual of situations, politicians may get involved for a variety of altruistic and self-serving reasons. Such was the case in 2005 of Terri Schiavo, a Florida woman who had been in a vegetative state for over a decade when her husband went to court to have her feeding tube removed. Her parents opposed this decision and asked for custody. Before doctors eventually removed the feeding tube, the Florida state legislature, the Florida governor, Congress, and the president of the United States all attempted to intervene in this most private family issue.

Although the Court defends the right to die, it has not given its approval to assisted suicide. The Supreme Court ruled unanimously in *Washington v. Glucksberg* (1997) that no right to assisted suicide exists in the Constitution. Michigan physician Jack Kevorkian brought sympathetic national attention to the issue by helping terminally ill patients kill themselves quickly and painlessly. The Court, however, has upheld state laws criminalizing assisted suicide, citing the state's interest in preserving human life and protecting the vulnerable group of ill and predominantly elderly patients.

CIVIC ENGAGEMENT AND CONSTITUTIONAL LIBERTIES

Because so many of the political issues facing the nation are settled in the courts, organized interest groups inevitably have fought legal battles and sought judicial support for their views. Lawsuits are especially attractive political instruments for individuals or small groups whose size, limited financial resources, and lack of prestige reduce their influence in the electoral process. Although they may lack the ability to influence the outcome of elections, individuals and smaller groups can make persuasive constitutional and moral arguments to courts. The Jehovah's Witnesses, for instance, have won over 70 percent of their cases before the nation's highest court.

As recently as 2002, their legal corporation, the Watchtower Bible and Tract Society, was successful in overturning a city permit requirement for door-to-door religious solicitation.[113]

The Jehovah's Witnesses traditionally go to court to defend the rights of their own members, but some groups sponsor cases on behalf of others. The American Civil Liberties Union (ACLU), for example, waits for a case to arise within its field of concern and then assumes all or part of the function of representing the litigant in court. Founded during the Progressive Era to combat growing militarism, the ACLU is the symbol of a new era of citizenship. It represents those people who believe one or more government policies violate their constitutional rights and takes on cases representing significant constitutional principles.

In some instances, a group may file a **test case** to challenge the constitutionality of a law. This involves deliberately bringing a case to court to secure a judicial ruling on a constitutional issue. In Chapter 5, we will see how the NAACP used this strategy to advance the cause of civil rights in the courts. The Supreme Court ruling in *Griswold v. Connecticut* (1965), regarding a state ban on advertising or selling contraceptives, was the result of a series of test cases. After a series of unsuccessful test cases, the director of the Connecticut Planned Parenthood League and a physician openly challenged the law by publicly advising married couples on how to use various contraceptive devices. After being arrested and convicted, they appealed the decision to the Supreme Court.

> **Roe v. Wade** The Supreme Court case that legalized abortions in the United States during the first two trimesters of a pregnancy.
>
> **test case** Practice by which a group deliberately brings a case to court in order to secure a judicial ruling on a constitutional issue.

get involved!

Using a service like LexisNexis, Westlaw, or www.law.cornell.edu, examine the amicus curiae briefs that were submitted for different civil liberties cases. Summarize your arguments for the class and analyze why those particular groups are interested in that particular issue.

Too Fat to Fly: Civil Liberties or Civil Rights?

A news story in 2010 reignited a controversy that may have a much deeper meaning for our society than it would first appear. Kevin Smith, the director of the Bruce Willis movie *Cop Out* as well as *Clerks,* and *Chasing Amy,* was thrown off a Southwest Airlines flight for being too fat. He had actually booked and paid for two seats on a later flight but moved as a standby passenger to an earlier flight that had only one available seat. The airline has a policy that requires travelers to be able to fit safely and comfortably in one seat. It uses the armrest test that requires customers who cannot lower both armrests to buy an extra seat. After he had taken his seat, Smith was told he was a safety risk because the cramped conditions could jeopardize a quick exit from the plane in case of an emergency.

On his Twitter account, Smith wrote: "I broke no regulation, offered no safety risk (what, was I gonna roll on a fellow passenger?). I was wrongly ejected from the flight." He later tweeted, "The @ Southwest Air Diet. How it works: you're publicly shamed into a slimmer figure. Crying the weight off has never been easier."

Other airlines such as Continental, Air France, and United have similar policies. United invoked its policy in 2008 after receiving complaints from seven hundred passengers whose seatmates did not fit into a single seat. Passengers like Mark Sweeting, a frequent flier from Portland, Oregon, said: "I fly coast to coast several times a year, and I cannot tell you how many times I have been pinned in by a morbidly obese human."*

The space problem is exacerbated today because all airline passengers, including Mr. Smith and Mr. Sweeting, are forced into smaller areas on most carriers so the companies can sell more seats. In the case of Kevin Smith, Southwest Airline did place him on a subsequent flight and offered him a $100 voucher.

It is unclear whether this air travel situation raises civil liberties concerns (the subject of this chapter) or civil rights concerns (the subject of the next chapter). The rights of passengers have to be balanced and all sides have the right to express their views, whether it be to promote comfort or to prevent humiliation (civil liberties). There is also an issue of fairness concerning whether obese persons are the object of discrimination (civil rights). The fairness of airline policies requiring large persons to buy two tickets is complicated by the fact that the policies are not always enforced. When they are enforced, however, the result is often humiliation suffered by the large passenger who is singled out in front of a plane full of passengers and forced to deplane. Advocates for the obese argue that charging large persons for an extra seat is not the solution. Peggy Howell, the public relations director at the National Association to Advance Fat Acceptance (NAAFA), says such policies "add yet another way to discriminate against already marginalized fat people. We see this more as an attempt at getting money out of the consumer's pocket than any concern for our well-being as some have claimed."†

The NAAFA is a nonprofit civil rights organization. Its existence suggests that the prevalence of obesity in the United States is a more complex issue than many believe. Without a doubt, the United States leads the world in the highest percentage of obese citizens. Yet as Americans are getting steadily heavier, the ideal societal body type is getting steadily thinner. This paradox creates discriminatory behavior in society. The pervasive cultural prejudice directed toward fat people in the United States is called "fatphobia," "sizeism," or "weightism." Whatever its name, such discriminatory behavior can have real consequences in people's lives.

Two scholars have concluded that there is a "pound penalty" for heavy employees, who make less money than their thinner peers.‡ Even if a pound penalty can be proven by an employee, however, Michigan is the only state that bans discrimination based on weight. The problem, however, is that simply being overweight does not qualify as a disability. Given such realities, someday weight discrimination may become more widely accepted as a form of prejudice just like racial, gender, ethnic, age, and sexual orientation prejudice. If that acceptance occurs, then weight discrimination may begin to receive legal protection. You will note in the next chapter that obese persons are not yet a group that is traditionally thought of in terms of civil rights protections.

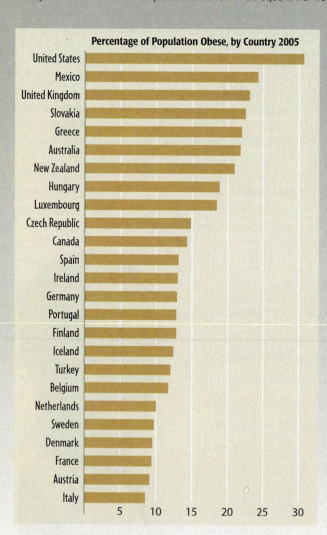

Percentage of Population Obese, by Country 2005

Country	Percentage
United States	
Mexico	
United Kingdom	
Slovakia	
Greece	
Australia	
New Zealand	
Hungary	
Luxembourg	
Czech Republic	
Canada	
Spain	
Ireland	
Germany	
Portugal	
Finland	
Iceland	
Turkey	
Belgium	
Netherlands	
Sweden	
Denmark	
France	
Austria	
Italy	

Source: Obesity Estimates Clinical Data (OECD), "Health Data," 2005.

*Michelle Higgins, "Excuse Me, Is This Seat Taken?" *The New York Times,* February 28, 2010.

† Ibid.

‡ Charles Baum and William Ford, "The Obesity Wage Penalty," *Health Economics* Vol. 13-9, September, 2004; Kelly D. Brownell and Rebecca Puhl, "Stigma and Discrimination in Weight Management and Obesity," *The Permanente Journal,* Vol. 7, No 3, Summer 2003.

The Court found the law unconstitutional, because it violated a right to privacy.

Organized groups also try to influence the outcome of constitutional liberties cases by filing **amicus curiae**, or "friend of the court," **briefs**. These are legal arguments that provide additional support to the arguments supplied by each side in the case. When a plaintiff challenges the constitutionality of a state policy before the U.S. Supreme Court, the state attorney general customarily seeks support from his or her counterparts in other states by asking them to file friend of the court briefs. This strategy backfired in the *Gideon* case, when the Florida attorney general received support from only two states but opposition from twenty-three others. In most constitutional liberties cases, groups from both sides of the issue submit amicus curiae briefs. The more such briefs are filed with the Supreme Court, the more likely it is to accept a case.[114]

In 1963, the Supreme Court recognized that the activities of interest groups in advancing civil liberties issues before the Court were themselves protected by the Bill of Rights. In *NAACP v. Button,* the Court rejected the state of Virginia's attempt to stop the NAACP and other groups from sponsoring lawsuits. The Court ruled that the First Amendment does more than protect abstract discussion; it also protects vigorous advocacy. The justices went on to recognize that the freedoms of speech and association encompass the right to advance issues through the legal system.

> **amicus curiae brief** Legal briefs filed by organized groups to influence the decision in a Supreme Court case.

Summary

1. **Why was the incorporation of the Bill of Rights by the Supreme Court so important?**

- The addition of the Bill of Rights to the Constitution changed the landscape of civil liberties in the United States, but it only protected citizens from abuses by the national government.

- Through the use of the incorporation doctrine, the Supreme Court interpreted the due process clause of the Fourteenth Amendment in such a way to apply most of the Bill of Rights to abuses by state and local governments as well.

- The policy of selective incorporation helped usher in an era of greater emphasis on individual rights.

- Through use of the incorporation doctrine, the Supreme Court has become the key institution for interpreting citizens' basic rights.

2. **What are the First Amendment rights?**

- The First Amendment rights include the establishment and freedom of religion clauses, freedom of speech, freedom of the press, freedom of assembly, freedom of association, and the right to petition the government.

- The Court has developed the *Lemon* test to determine whether government policies violate the establishment clause.

- To determine whether one's freedom of religion rights have been violated, the Court balances the importance of a government policy with the amount of burden placed on one's religious beliefs.

- Today the Court uses the clear and present danger test to decide free speech cases, but in the past they used more restrictive tests.

- The concept of prior restraint is the guiding principle in freedom of press cases.

- The Court has balanced the freedom of assembly protection against the government's interest in preserving the peace, regulating the flow of traffic, jail security, and the administration of justice.

- In freedom of association cases, the Court has recognized the implied privacy right inherent in an association with the competing right to be free from discrimination.

3. **What are some of the other important civil liberties guaranteed by the Constitution?**

- The Second Amendment guarantees the right to keep and bear arms, and the Court is now interpreting this to be an important individual right that makes some laws banning guns unconstitutional.

- The Constitution also provides rights for accused persons, such as only reasonable searches and seizures, no self-incrimination, the right to counsel, the right to a jury trial, and protection from cruel and unusual punishment.

- In deciding rights of the accused cases, the Court has established categories for which searches are legal, has produced guidelines for a constitutional death penalty law, and has constructed the *Miranda* rules to deter self-incrimination questions.

- The Court has also recognized an implied right to privacy that has produced important decisions in abortion and right to die cases.

READING A TORTURE MEMO

Abu Zubaydah wasn't giving up the goods. In the four months since March 2002, when U.S. agents captured and detained the man they believed was Al Qaeda's logistics chief, Zubaydah had said nothing that would lead investigators to other possible terrorist networks inside the United States. He was chatty. Even cordial at times. But in the estimation of CIA officials interrogating him, he had handed over no "actionable intelligence," hard facts that could lead investigators to other Qaeda plotters. And that was a problem, because counter-terrorism officials were becoming more and more convinced that a follow-up to the 9/11 attacks was in the offing.

Zubaydah's captors strongly suspected that he possessed information that could help disrupt a new terrorist assault. "There was a lot of concern that there would be multiple attacks, almost in sequence," a former senior CIA official who was directly involved in the agency's interrogation program for terrorist suspects told *National Journal*. "Things were moving rapidly. . . . It was, 'We know this guy's got more information.'"

The CIA passed its assessment along to lawyers at the Justice Department. "Specifically, [Zubaydah] is withholding information regarding terrorist networks in the United States or in Saudi Arabia and information regarding plans to conduct attacks within the United States or against our interests overseas," lawyers from Justice's Office of Legal Counsel wrote in a memo to the CIA's top lawyer, affirming for the record what they said CIA officials had told them. The memo was signed by then Assistant Attorney General Jay Bybee. "Moreover, your intelligence indicates that there is currently a level of 'chatter' equal to that which preceded the September 11 attacks."

The Justice Department's memo, titled "Interrogation of Al Qaeda operative" and dated August 1, 2002, describes a high-level and secretive dialogue about whether the CIA should try to get more information from Zubaydah through aggressive and violent means, including suffocation by water, face slapping, and sleep deprivation. The lawyers based their analysis on whether these methods constituted torture entirely upon "facts" about Zubaydah's previous interrogations that they said had come from the CIA.

The memo was one of four documents declassified by President Obama in April, 2009. Collectively, the memos helped form the now-discarded legal rationale for using what the Bush administration, the International Committee of the Red Cross, and a host of military and intelligence officers say is torture. And yet, if the Justice lawyers can be believed to have acted in good faith, the documents are also illustrative of the mood hanging over the CIA officials who were interrogating Zubaydah as the first anniversary of the September 11 attacks approached. Both CIA and Justice officials seemed to be gripped by competing impulses: the urgent need to disrupt any other possible attacks and the belief that Zubaydah might know about them versus their personal desire to avoid the threat of indictment for torturing an unarmed prisoner.

Throughout the intelligence community in the summer of 2002, information about Al Qaeda was coming in quickly, but the spy agencies weren't well positioned to make sense of it.

"It was hard to differentiate whether this was reactionary chatter," tough talk from terrorists with little to back it up, "or planning," the former official said. The intelligence agencies had intercepted terrorists' phone calls and e-mails, and scoured purloined laptop computers and journals; they were also getting leads passed back through human sources in the field. The Qaeda refrain amounted to, "We need to follow up on this," the former official said, referring to 9/11.

Zubaydah's interrogators "tried the psychological routine, befriending him," the former official said. They didn't think it worked. The Justice Department memo states at the outset that the CIA believed that "Zubaydah has become accustomed to a certain level of treatment and displays no signs of willingness to disclose further information." The agency wanted to move to what it called "the increased pressure phase."

The August 2002 memo describes the application of said pressure in precise detail. The lawyers gave interrogators specific instructions on how to rough Zubaydah up without, in their view, legally torturing him. The interrogation techniques are largely based on those developed by the Pentagon as part of a training program for combat pilots and Special Forces troops on how to withstand harsh interrogation if they were ever captured in battle.

"The amount of restraint [the interrogators] used was phenomenal," the former CIA official said. Arguing that many Americans would have been filled with rage at the mere sight of the self-confessed Qaeda planner, who told his captors he would kill again if released, the former official said that CIA interrogators stayed within the lines. "They followed the rules."

The CIA's inspector general has found, however, that Zubaydah and another prisoner captured later were subjected to waterboarding a total of 266 times, and that the application of the waterboard exceeded the limits spelled out in the August 2002 memo. The former CIA official interviewed by *National Journal* questioned whether the number was accurate, but he acknowledged that he had no evidence to refute it.

John Kiriakou, a CIA officer who was with the team that captured Zubaydah in Pakistan, later told ABC News that his personal rage led him to support harsh treatment of the prisoner. "I was so angry," he said. "And

I wanted so much to help disrupt future attacks on the United States that I felt it was the only thing we could do." Kiriakou characterized waterboarding as torture, but he argued that it was necessary to get information from Zubaydah. After the waterboard was applied, "he answered every question," Kiriakou said. "The threat information he provided disrupted a number of attacks, maybe dozens of attacks."

The former senior CIA official said that information extracted from Zubaydah "prevented multiple attacks." On that point, he said, he was "certain." He elaborated, "We got some extremely useful tactical and strategic information." The first category included "names of individuals actively planning attacks," and the latter consisted of countries where the United States should focus its counter-terrorism efforts, as well as the names of "targets" within those countries, the former official said.

The New York Times recently reported National Intelligence Director Dennis Blair's claim that that Zubaydah's interrogation got results. "High-value information came from interrogations in which those methods were used and provided a deeper understanding of the Al Qaeda organization that was attacking this country," Blair wrote in a memo to his staff, after the Justice Department memos were released.

Just how useful Zubaydah's information was and whether his brutal interrogation was necessary have been intensely debated since the first details of his interrogation were revealed.

Among others, FBI officials who were involved in his interrogation have played down Zubaydah's contribution. Agent Daniel Coleman, who helped the FBI analyze some of Zubaydah's diaries, told *New Yorker* writer Jane Mayer that the prisoner was a "schizophrenic personality" and that Qaeda chief Osama bin Laden would not have entrusted Zubaydah with secrets like those the CIA thought he possessed.

But this much is certain. In August 2002,

prosecutions of the Justice Department lawyers who wrote the interrogation memos.

An extensive investigation of interrogation policy and practice, written by the Senate Armed Services Committee, has put those lawyers in the crosshairs. The report concludes that the principal authors of the August 2002 memo, John Yoo and Bybee, sought to "redefine torture." Before drafting the memo, Yoo met with Alberto Gonzales, who was then top counsel to President

> Both CIA and Justice officials seemed to be gripped by competing impulses: the urgent need to disrupt any other possible attacks and the belief that Zubaydah might know about them versus their personal desire to avoid the threat of indictment for torturing an unarmed prisoner.

with the chatter level and nerves running high, the interrogators had no way of knowing precisely what Zubaydah knew or didn't know. They believed he knew more than he was telling. They wanted to press him. "Frankly, there were lives at stake," Kiriakou told ABC News. "He had information, and we wanted to get it."

Obama has vowed that CIA employees who carried out interrogations and the agency officials who oversaw them will not face prosecution. But in comments to a reporter this week, he left the door open to

Bush, and David Addington, Vice President Cheney's counsel, "to discuss the subjects he intended to address" in the memo, the report found.

Obama has said that as far as he is concerned, the CIA interrogators acted in good faith. Now the question is whether the same can be said of the lawyers who gave them the legal cover to act and the senior Bush administration officials who knew in advance what the lawyers planned to say.

For Discussion:

■ Do you believe Justice Department lawyers should face criminal consequences if found to have authorized torture? Why might President Obama reason that their behavior is more actionable than that of the interrogators themselves? What defense might those lawyers offer?

■ Is there ever, in your opinion, an argument for torture? Are harsh methods of interrogation ever justifiable in curbing imminent danger? Do you believe the agents and officials quoted in the article when they claim that the repeated waterboarding of Zubaydah saved lives? Why or why not?

■ What other complications has the War on Terror raised in our concept of civil liberties? Do any of the methods for information gathering mentioned in the article give you pause? What level of protection should suspected terrorists—who are often foreign nationals like Zubaydah and rarely citizens—expect from our Constitution and courts? Can civil liberties be maintained without compromise during wartime?

5

CIVIL RIG

GHTS

TOWARD A MORE EQUAL CITIZENRY

THE LITIGIOUS CHEERLEADER ▌ Jennifer Gratz, a senior at Anderson High School in Southgate, Michigan, was the very picture of an all-American girl—blond, pretty, athletic, and socially active. She was a cheerleader, a student government representative, and homecoming queen. Jennifer had always dreamed of attending the University of Michigan as a premed student. Although neither of her parents had attended college, both stressed the importance of hard work, a message Jennifer took to heart. Besides her extracurricular activities, she was a National Honor Society member with a 3.79 grade point average that placed her twelfth in her class of 299 students. She was so confident of being admitted to the Ann Arbor campus that she applied to no other colleges.

Like any other high school senior, Jennifer waited anxiously for her letter of acceptance. One spring day after coming back from cheerleading practice, she saw the envelope from the University of Michigan. Her stomach churned when she realized the envelope was thin. Thin envelopes from universities typically mean rejection or placement on a waiting list. When she found out that the university had not accepted her, Jennifer could hardly believe her fate. She discovered that she had been rejected because of the University of Michigan's affirmative action program for undergraduate admission, which awarded 20 points to every applicant from a designated underrepresented group. Those groups included African Americans, Hispanic Americans, and Native Americans. In order to gain admission, an applicant had to receive 100 of a possible 150 points. The automatic awarding of 20 points to members of certain groups was meant to ensure greater diversity among the student population. By receiving those 20 extra points, minority applicants with grades and extracurricular activities similar to Jennifer's were admitted, and she herself would have been accepted if she had been a member of an underrepresented group. Jennifer's first reaction was "I was discriminated against because of my race."[1] She then turned to her father and asked, "Can we sue them?"[2] ◆➤

- How has the Supreme Court's attitude toward the civil rights of African Americans evolved?
- How have other minority groups benefited from the civil rights struggles of African Americans?
- What was unique in women's struggles for civil rights in the United States?

Jennifer's first reaction was, "I was discriminated against because of my race." She then turned to her father and asked, "Can we sue them?"

Conservative interest groups had long believed that affirmative action produces reverse discrimination that punishes qualified white applicants, and their lawyers were looking for cases to advance their claim. One such group, the Center for Individual Rights (CIR), interviewed Jennifer and considered her the ideal litigant. She had no other agenda than to be treated fairly. She was attractive, poised, and confident in her beliefs. Most important, she was female. As one CIR spokesperson put it, "The perception of a man bringing a lawsuit like this is that he's an angry white male and he's bitter. I think the perception of Gratz is that she got a bad break. She doesn't have an ax to grind. She's appealing in a way that maybe not all white males would be."[3]

In 2003, Jennifer's case reached the U.S. Supreme Court, which found the university's undergraduate admissions program unconstitutional with respect to the equal protection clause of the Fourteenth Amendment. The 6 to 3 majority determined that by automatically awarding 20 points for minority status, the university failed to give the individual consideration to each applicant that equal protection demands. Jennifer won her case, but the wheels of justice turned too slowly for her to live her dream. After being denied admission to the university's Ann Arbor campus, she ended up going to a branch campus in Dearborn and living at home. She still wonders how different her life might have been if she had been able to go away to school on the university's main campus. Jennifer claims that the initial rejection affected her confidence and led her to conclude that she must not be smart enough to be a premed student. She became a mathematics major instead and now works for a vending machine company in California.

Jennifer Gratz challenged the undergraduate admissions program at the University of Michigan after being denied admission to the Ann Arbor campus.

Jennifer's case is instructive with respect to civil rights in the United States. Minority groups historically have faced great obstacles to achieving equality in the United States and have turned to the Supreme Court seeking justice. African Americans endured the degradation of slavery, segregation, and poverty in their quest for equality. The Supreme Court ultimately responded positively to their legal arguments by the way it reinterpreted equality. This interpretation, in turn, mobilized civil rights advocates who fought for other disadvantaged groups, such as Native Americans, Hispanic Americans, Asian Americans, the disabled, seniors, gay and lesbian groups, and women. Jennifer believed that earlier decisions made to protect the equality rights of these minority groups made her a victim of reverse discrimination. The story of disadvantaged groups' struggle for equality, and the impact it has had on the nation, is the subject of this chapter. ◆◆

AFRICAN AMERICANS AND CIVIL RIGHTS

Whereas civil liberties focus on the personal freedoms guaranteed individuals in the Bill of Rights, **civil rights** concern the protection of persons in historically disadvantaged groups from discriminatory actions. Civil rights constitute a positive action by government to guarantee that every person, regardless of his or her group identity, is treated as an equal member of society.[4] Yet despite espousing equality as one of the nation's core values, the United States has often failed to make that value a reality for millions of Americans. Many groups of Americans have had to struggle for equal rights.

Most people associate the quest for civil rights in the United States with the struggles of African Americans. American blacks were among the first groups to agitate for civil rights, and no other group has had to overcome comparable obstacles to equality: slavery, segregation, and discrimination in voting, housing, and employment. Their battle for equality has served as a road map for other mistreated groups in terms of both inspiration and tactics.

Slavery

When the delegates to the Constitutional Convention met in Philadelphia in 1787, slavery had existed in North America for nearly 170 years. By this time, the owners of large southern plantations relied heavily on slave labor to produce their cash crops. As a result, the southern delegates to the convention made it clear that they would never sacrifice slavery in order to achieve a new constitution. Although some northern delegates, such as Gouverneur Morris, denounced slavery, powerful southern opposition prevented any attempt to abolish slavery via the new constitution. In the end, each state was left to decide for itself whether to permit slavery.

> **civil rights** Protection of historically disadvantaged groups from infringement of their equality rights by discriminatory action.

The attempts by the nation's early leaders to prevent the issue of slavery from dividing the country were short-lived. As the nation's population moved westward in the early 1800s, northern and southern representatives faced a dilemma regarding the admission of new states to the Union. Would such states have free or slave status? The issue came to a head in 1820, when Missouri applied for admission to

Division of Free and Slave States After the Missouri Compromise

- Free states and territories in 1820
- Slave states and territories in 1820
- Closed to slavery by the Missouri Compromise
- Missouri Compromise Line (36°30')
- *Except for Missouri, new territories and states closed to slavery north of this line*

Source: Alan Brinkley: *American History,* 2007, McGraw-Hill.

Thirteenth Amendment
Civil War amendment that specifically prohibited slavery in the United States.

Fourteenth Amendment
Civil War amendment that provided all persons with the privileges and immunities of national citizenship; the guarantee of equal protection of the laws by any state; and the safeguard of due process to protect one's life, liberty, and property from state government interference.

the Union as a slave state. Northern senators opposed Missouri's admission, which would give the states with slavery a majority of seats in the Senate. The Missouri Compromise temporarily settled this divisive issue by granting Missouri admission as a slave state and allowing Maine to enter the Union at the same time as a free state. The compromise also banned the admission of any slave states from the Northwest Territory above 36 degrees, 30 minutes north latitude, with the exception of Missouri. Unfortunately, the issue of slavery became even more volatile with the continued westward migration of settlers.

Dred Scott

At this explosive point in American history, the Supreme Court heard the *Dred Scott* case in 1857.[5] Scott was a slave whose owner held him in bondage while in the free state of Illinois and the free federal territory of Minnesota. Scott sued for his freedom, arguing that he was emancipated as soon as his owner took him into free territory. The Court, however, rejected Scott's argument, noting that African Americans had long been treated as an inferior race that was unfit to associate with whites in either social or political relations. As a result, they had no rights and thus could justly be reduced to slavery to be bought and sold as ordinary articles of merchandise. Hence, slaves could never be citizens and bring lawsuits to the courts. Chief Justice Roger Taney interpreted the Constitution to be consistent with this view. Taney's opinion went further, arguing that Congress lacked the authority to ban slavery in the western territories because doing so violated the due process rights of slave owners to own property under the Fifth Amendment. The decision dealt a swift blow to Scott's freedom and the country's antislavery forces. It invali-

Dred Scott was a slave who asked for his freedom in the federal courts and lost when the Supreme Court in 1857 ruled that slaves had no constitutional rights.

dated the Missouri Compromise and helped set the stage for the Civil War by removing any possibility for Congress to resolve the divisive issue of slavery in a manner that satisfied all Americans.

The Civil War and Reconstruction

The Civil War and the Reconstruction Period marked the end of slavery and the first great advance of civil rights in the United States. In 1862, at the height of the war, President Lincoln issued the Emancipation Proclamation. This executive order freed all the slaves in states that were still in rebellion as of January 1, 1863. Since the Emancipation Proclamation freed only those slaves living in the South, the complete abolition of slavery did not occur until the adoption of the **Thirteenth Amendment** in 1865. It provided that "neither slavery nor involuntary servitude" shall exist within the United States except as a punishment for the commission of a crime.

However, the passage of the Thirteenth Amendment did not ensure equality for African Americans. The 11 states of the former confederacy failed to ratify the **Fourteenth Amendment**, which provided all persons with the privileges and immunities of national citizenship, guaranteed equal protection under the laws of any state, and safeguarded due process to protect one's life, liberty, and property from state government interference. This led Congress to institute the Reconstruction Program, which was designed to prevent the mistreatment of former slaves in the South. Reconstruction legislation dissolved the state governments in the South and partitioned them into five military districts. These new governments enfranchised blacks and disqualified many white voters who had fought against the Union in the Civil War. Under such pressure, southern legislators ratified the Fourteenth Amendment in 1868. Two years later, the **Fifteenth Amendment** gave former slaves the right to vote.

Soon afterward, however, a partisan political deal at the highest levels of government dashed the hopes and aspirations of the former slaves. In the presidential election of 1876, electoral votes in three states were in dispute, making the election too close to call. Both Republican Rutherford B.

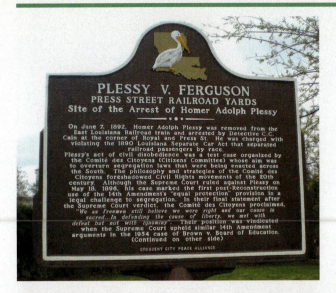

PORTRAIT
OF AN ACTIVIST

Homer Plessy

Homer Plessy was born on St. Patrick's Day in 1863, less than three months after the issuance of Abraham Lincoln's Emancipation Proclamation. He grew up in a racially enlightened New Orleans where blacks could attend integrated schools, sit in any streetcar seat, and marry whomever they wanted.

Jim Crow laws were introduced in his state during his early adult years, however, and Plessy, who worked as a shoemaker, became the vice president of a group dedicated to reforming public education in New Orleans. Five years later in 1892, he volunteered for the mission to ride in the white railroad car and get arrested for violating the state's new segregation law. State Judge John Howard Ferguson found Plessy guilty, ruling that the law was constitutional because the train traveled only within the state. After the United States Supreme Court upheld the state's decision, Plessy fell into relative obscurity working as an insurance collector. He died on March 1, 1925, and no verifiable photograph of him is available for viewing.

On February 10, 2009, Keith Plessy and Phoebe Ferguson, descendants of the two principals, appeared together to announce the formation of the Plessy and Ferguson Foundation that will create new ways to teach the history of civil rights through film, art, and public programs. Two days later the foundation placed a historical marker at the corner of Press Street and Royal Street, the site of Homer Plessy's famous arrest in 1892.

Hayes and Democrat Samuel Tilden claimed victory. Congress established a bipartisan commission to determine the victor, but behind the scenes, the Republican Party forged a plan to retain control of the White House. It promised Democratic representatives from southern states that a Republican administration would withdraw federal troops from the South and provide funds to rebuild the area. The Democrats accepted the deal and the commission declared Hayes the winner, bringing the Reconstruction period to an end. The former slaves were once again at the mercy of their former oppressors.

Segregation

The constitutional amendments and the various civil rights laws of the Civil War era were of little value unless the federal government enforced them. Sadly, once federal troops pulled out of the South, most northern whites lost interest in civil rights, and the former slave states went back to business as usual. This included segregated living, enforced by **Jim Crow laws** that required whites and African Americans to use separate hotels, separate restrooms, sep-

arate drinking fountains, and even separate cemeteries.[6] The laws also prohibited interracial marriage. Any violation of the segregation code could lead to violent reprisals by the Ku Klux Klan.

On June 7, 1892, Homer Plessy bought a ticket in New Orleans and boarded a train headed for Covington, Louisiana. He took a seat in the white coach, even though he later described himself as "seven-eights Caucasian and one-eighth African blood."[7] When Plessy refused to comply with the conductor's order to move, he was arrested for violating the state of Louisiana's new segregation law requiring railroads to carry blacks in separate cars. Plessy's arrest, however, was no accident, but the result of months of planning by the black community in New Orleans in cooperation with railroad officials (who otherwise would not have known Plessy's race). That event on a warm Louisiana day would culminate in a U.S. Supreme Court ruling that defined the status of civil rights in the country for decades to come.

Fifteenth Amendment Civil War amendment that extended suffrage to former male slaves.

Jim Crow laws Legislation in the South that mandated racial segregation in public facilities such as restaurants and restrooms.

Segregation in the South included separate restrooms for both races.

Plessy appealed his conviction to the Supreme Court, where his attorney argued that racial segregation on train cars perpetuated the notion of black inferiority that accompanied the institution of slavery. Since the law did not apply to "nurses attending the children of the other race," he reasoned that this legal exception was made because whites were willing to endure blacks who had a clearly dependent status. As a result, he concluded, the law violated the spirit and intent of the Thirteenth Amendment that ended slavery and the Fourteenth Amendment that promised equal protection under the law.

In May 1896, the Supreme Court handed down its decision supporting the Louisiana law and Plessy's conviction. This case established the "separate but equal" doctrine that would dominate U.S. Supreme Court decisions for another 58 years. Under this doctrine, the government considered segregated facilities legal as long as they were equal. In reality, the Court tolerated segregation even when the facilities were clearly unequal. The Plessy decision ushered in the worst period of civil rights violations since the abolition of slavery.

Voting Barriers

The end of Reconstruction, and subsequent Supreme Court decisions, provided southerners with an incentive to discriminate against African Americans and led to a pervasive attempt to deny blacks their rights under the Fifteenth Amendment. Southern officials argued that the amendment did not guarantee African Americans the right to vote but, rather, prohibited states from denying the right to vote on the basis of race or color. This led them to construct so-called "racially neutral" laws to prevent African Americans from voting. Poll taxes, literacy tests, property qualifications, and even the notorious grandfather clause—a rule that an African American could not vote if his grandfather slave had not voted—could be used to exclude any voter who failed to meet the specific requirement.[8] In practice, these devices were used by white election officials to keep African Americans from voting; most African Americans were too poor to pay poll taxes or to own property and were not educated enough to pass a literacy test, and none of them had grandfathers who had been allowed to vote.

NAACP

African Americans watched with despair as the walls of segregation rose around them. Their hopes for equality that had been based on the Civil War amendments and civil rights laws were nearly gone. In 1909, the publisher of the *New York Evening Post,* who was the grandson of the famous abolitionist William Lloyd Garrison, called a conference to discuss the problem of "the Negro." The group soon evolved into the National Association for the Advancement of Colored People (NAACP).

By the 1930s, the leaders of the NAACP decided to test the constitutionality of *Plessy v. Ferguson* in the federal courts. Lacking the political clout to accomplish legislative change, they believed the federal courts in time might rule that the separate but equal doctrine was a barrier to any hope of equality for African Americans. The NAACP sponsored test cases as forums in which to present sociological data and statistics that provided the courts with evidence of discrimination. The organization decided to concentrate on the field of education, beginning with cases of segregation in graduate and professional schools. Because so few African Americans had attained such advanced educational levels, the NAACP reasoned that whites would be less threatened by such minor changes. They also reasoned that the courts would be more inclined to rule in their favor, because there was little chance that the government would have to implement the decision. Only later did they challenge the segregation of elementary and high schools, which would affect millions of students and the social mores of the country.[9]

The NAACP enjoyed several victories following this strategy, including successfully challenging the exclusion of an African American student from a state law school. The group later paved the way for the Court to declare unconstitutional the establishment of a segregated Texas law school for African Americans only.[10] The NAACP successfully argued that an African American student who was isolated in a segregated state graduate school was denied an equal education.[11]

Modern Era of Civil Rights

The success of the NAACP before the Supreme Court ushered in an era of a more equal citizenry. In each of the higher education cases mentioned, the Court decided that the plaintiffs had been denied the opportunity for an equal education. In other words, the facilities were separate but they were not equal. After 1950, the NAACP concluded it was time to change the plan of attack. It decided to pressure the Court to overrule the *Plessy* decision on the grounds that separate facilities, even if equal, were unconstitutional because segregation *itself* was unconstitutional under the equal protection clause of the Fourteenth Amendment.

Did You Know?

. . . That the NAACP (National Association for the Advancement of Colored People) was formed by a group of black and white progressives at a meeting at Niagara Falls—on the Canadian side of the border, because on the U.S. side no hotel would rent rooms to blacks?

The organization was now ready to challenge legal segregation in the nation's primary and secondary public schools.

Brown v. Board of Education The 1954 *Brown* case actually related to five separate cases brought against local school districts in Delaware, South Carolina, Virginia, the District of Columbia, and Kansas. The plaintiffs in each case challenged the legality of their districts' separate but equal laws. The new chief justice, Earl Warren, wrote the opinion for the unanimous Court striking down the separate but equal laws. Warren acknowledged that the original intent of the Framers of the Fourteenth Amendment was unclear but argued, "We must consider public education in the light of its full development and its present place in American life throughout the Nation." He reasoned that modern public education was essential for full political participation because it opens up life opportunities and provides the basis for intelligent citizenship. Warren's opinion also confirmed the wisdom of the NAACP's tactic of relying on psychological and sociological studies in its brief, given the lack of legal precedents to support its cause. The unanimous Court held that to separate children from others because of their race generates within them a feeling of inferiority "that may affect their hearts and minds in a way very unlikely ever to be undone."

Because the *Brown* case dealt only with **de jure segregation**—discrimination by law—it primarily affected the southern states that had passed Jim Crow laws. It did not address **de facto segregation**—racial separation based on factual realities such as segregated housing patterns—which existed throughout the United States. In 1955, the following year, the Court ruled in *Brown II* that the racially segregated school systems must be abandoned "with all deliberate speed."[12] They also determined that federal district judges would enforce the decision, instead of state court judges who were more susceptible to local political pressure. Unfortunately, the phrase *with all deliberate speed* gave the southern states the opportunity to delay desegregation and ultimately to engage in massive resistance to the change.

de jure segregation
Segregation mandated by law or decreed by government officials.

de facto segregation
Segregation that occurs because of past economic and social conditions such as residential racial patterns.

Federal troops were needed to support the Supreme Court's school integration decision in Brown v. Board of Education.

Southern resistance to public school integration led to federal action on several occasions. In 1957, President Dwight D. Eisenhower sent federal troops to enforce the integration of the school system in Little Rock, Arkansas. Throughout the 1960s, Congress drafted major civil rights legislation to advance the cause of desegregation. Some federal judges ordered students bused to schools in other neighborhoods to achieve racially balanced school districts.[13] By 1995, however, support for direct federal intervention had declined, and the Court announced that it would not look favorably on continued federal control of districts like one in Kansas City that had spent millions of dollars under federal direction to attract white students from the suburbs.[14]

Civil Rights Mobilization

The *Brown* decisions sparked not only southern resistance but also a popular civil rights movement exemplified by people such as Rosa Parks. Parks was a petite woman who worked as a seamstress and served as the NAACP youth council adviser in Montgomery, Alabama. She had been active in NAACP activities such as voter registration drives, but she did not intend to launch a civil rights crusade on the Decem-ber afternoon in 1955 when she refused to leave her seat in the front of the bus to make room for a white passenger. Her act of defiance was not only illegal but also dangerous. Montgomery's buses were segregated by law, and African Americans had been beaten and even killed for not obeying bus drivers. Parks later said she did not move because she thought she had the right to be treated the same way as any other passenger on the bus.

Police arrested Parks, who was later convicted of violating the state's segregation law and fined ten dollars. The NAACP responded by distributing handbills urging African Americans to boycott the Montgomery bus system to protest Parks's arrest. Martin Luther King, Jr., a recently arrived minister, emerged as a leader in the yearlong boycott effort. When a lower federal court finally ordered the buses to integrate, the tactic of nonviolent protest had proved its value. Parks received the Congressional Gold Medal in 1999, and upon her death in 2005 political leaders across the nation praised her efforts and character.

The civil rights movement spawned new groups in addition to the NAACP that pursued different strategies to secure equality for African Americans. King formed the Southern Christian Leadership Conference (SCLC), which spurned litigation as a major tactic and instead used nonviolent protest to achieve equality. Whereas the SCLC drew heavily on its base in the southern black community, other groups such as the Student Nonviolent Coordinating Committee

Martin Luther King, Jr., drew national attention to the civil rights movement with his "I Have a Dream" speech in 1963.

The 1964 Civil Rights Act bars discrimination by public accommodations engaged in interstate commerce. For instance, a hotel that has customers from other states or orders any products from other states cannot refuse to serve customers based on their race.[16] The act also prohibits discrimination in employment on the grounds of race, religion, national origin, or sex. The law established the Equal Employment Opportunity Commission (EEOC) to enforce and monitor bans on employment discrimination and to withhold federal funds from state and local government programs that discriminate against providers or consumers. A year later, Congress passed the **Voting Rights Act of 1965**, which increased voter protections by outlawing literacy tests and by allowing federal officials to enter southern states to register African American voters. This provision enabled hundreds of thousands of African Americans to register to vote in southern states. The provision, Section 5 of the law, survived a constitutional challenge in 2009 in the case of *Northwest Austin Municipal Utility District Number One v. Holder.* The Supreme Court made it clear, however, that such remedies may no longer be necessary in today's improving racial climate.

(SNCC) were more grassroots in orientation and recruited young people of all races. These new groups organized events (such as boycotts, sit-ins at segregated restaurants, and "freedom rides" pairing civil rights activists with college students) that were designed to draw attention to segregation of public accommodations. Martin Luther King, Jr., became the most famous civil rights leader in the country with his eloquence and courage. He grabbed national attention in August 1963 when he organized a massive march on Washington, D.C., and delivered his famous "I Have a Dream" speech: "I have a dream that my four little children will one day live in a nation where they will not be judged by the color of their skin but by the content of their character. I have a dream today." The march was intended to demonstrate widespread support for President John F. Kennedy's proposal to ban all discrimination in public accommodations and to argue for an end to discrimination against African Americans in all aspects of life.

Civil Rights Legislation

Senior southern Democrats in Congress, supported by conservative Republicans, opposed Kennedy's proposal. Because of their long tenure in Congress, these Democrats held key committee positions that allowed them to dominate both houses of Congress and frustrate the president's plans. Kennedy's assassination on November 22, 1963, changed the political landscape. His successor, Lyndon Johnson, was a Texan who had been a powerful majority leader in the Senate. He knew how to get legislation passed and he knew how to talk to the southern members of Congress. This knowledge, added to the wave of sympathy that accompanied the death of the young president, led Congress to pass the historic **Civil Rights Act of 1964**.[15]

Retrospective

The efforts of those who participated in the civil rights movement dramatically changed the lives of African Americans and their role in civic life. The passage and enforcement of voting laws have resulted in substantial numbers of African Americans winning election to public office since the 1960s. Although still underrepresented at the national level, even considering the election of Barack Obama, blacks have made considerable advances in state and local government. Today, it is not surprising to find an African American serving as a sheriff in Mississippi or as a mayor in Alabama. Blacks still have a long way to go, however, to achieve full equal-

Civil Rights Act of 1964
Historic legislation that prohibited racial segregation in public accommodations and racial discrimination in employment, education, and voting.

Voting Rights Act of 1965
Federal legislation that outlawed literacy tests and empowered federal officials to enter southern states to register African American voters; the act dismantled the most significant barriers to African Americans' suffrage rights.

RACE RELATIONS

For Barack Obama the 2012 campaign began with one of the same hurdles he confronted in his run for the presidency four years earlier. The "birther" movement had begun in 2008 when some of his critics, without offering proof, claimed that Obama was born in Kenya and thus not eligible to be president. At that time the Obama campaign had responded by issuing a "certification of live birth" which was an official document from the Hawaii Department of Health. Two fact-checking groups, FactCheck.com and PolitiFact, confirmed that the "certificate of live birth" was authentic.

When real estate mogul, Donald Trump, began to flirt with idea of running for president in early 2011, he used the "birther" issue as his primary talking point and people were listening. A poll taken in April of 2011 showed that the issue was gaining velocity. The poll revealed that nearly half of Republican voters believed Obama had been born in a country other than the United States and almost a quarter of them did not know where he was born.

It was at this point that Obama decided to respond. He wrote a letter to officials in Hawaii seeking a waiver for release of his long-form birth certificate. Then his personal attorney, Judy Corley, flew to Hawaii to pick up two copies of the certificate. The next day the president made a dramatic appearance at a White House press briefing with the document. Making the document public, the president firmly stated that the "silliness" must end so that important issues like the 2012 budget could be thoroughly debated. The examination of the long-form birth certificate showed that the only difference between it and the commonly issued short form was the name of the hospital and the signature of the attending physician. Trump responded by saying he hoped the certificate was authentic and then pivoted quickly by demanding that the president release his academic records because Trump had heard that the president was not a very good student and questioned his admission to Columbia University and the Harvard Law School.

The focus on the "birther" issue was a clear attempt to brand Obama, in the minds of voters, as an "other," putting him in a class with Muslims and other unfamiliar groups. And at different times, political figures and the media have raised the question as to whether Obama's political opponents are peddling racism in raising the "birther" issue and questioning the president's academic qualifications. Such charges beg the question, "Would a white candidate and president be treated the same way?" Certainly, mudslinging and attempts to paint opponents in the most unfavorable light possible is not new to the campaign trail. Yet, it is not the tactic, so much as the potential effectiveness of the tactic among the voters, that raises the question of whether Republican opponents are using the "race card" against Obama. These opponents are applying basic principles of political psychology: strong prior attitudes can powerfully influence responses to an unfamiliar issue, especially if authoritative sources, such as conservative talk radio hosts, respected political leaders, and like-minded social networks fan the flames of uncertainty. Uninformed assumptions about members of an unfamiliar group can and have influenced political decisions in the past that many citizens of the United States today would regard as racist. One group may all too readily make incorrect assumptions about a person's work ethics, integrity, or academic potential based on their race, ethnicity, religion, or gender. Hence, it is not so much the accusations from political opponents, but the willingness of voters to believe the accusation that raises the question of whether theses opponents are making use of pre-existing racist attitudes. Two scholars' analysis of the 2008 campaign concluded that Obama was associated with Kenya, Indonesia, and a multi-racial heritage and that many viewed Obama as "other."*

Throughout the 2008 campaign, Republicans often claimed that Obama used the "race card" to his benefit, and certainly, many felt that the election of an African American president was a significant achievement for the United States. But the reemergence of the "birther" issue suggests that perhaps Obama's 2008 election did not herald, as many optimists hope, an end to racism in the United States.

---

* See David Sears and Michael Tesler, *Obama's Race: The 2008 Election and The Dream of a Post-Racial America* (Chicago: University of Chicago Press, 2010.)

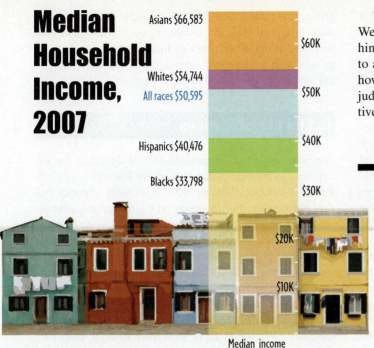

Median Household Income, 2007

Asians $66,583
Whites $54,744
All races $50,595
Hispanics $40,476
Blacks $33,798

$60K
$50K
$40K
$30K
$20K
$10K

Median income

Source: Pew Hispanic Center tabulations of 2007 American Community Survey (1% IPUMS).

ity in America. The income of the average African American family today is barely two-thirds that of the average white family. African Americans are more likely to be convicted of crimes than whites and are more likely to receive harsher punishments, including the death penalty. Many African Americans still live in segregated neighborhoods, and for them and others, the struggle for civil rights continues. The election of Barack Obama, however, is being viewed as a positive development in the advancement of civil rights. For many, it has improved racial relations in the United States. See the table below.

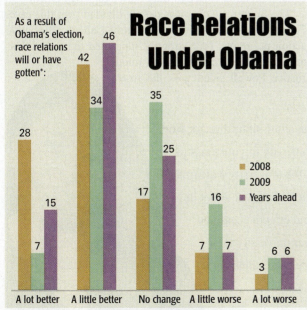

Race Relations Under Obama

As a result of Obama's election, race relations will or have gotten*:

- 2008
- 2009
- Years ahead

	A lot better	A little better	No change	A little worse	A lot worse
2008	28	42	17	7	3
2009	7	34	35	16	6
Years ahead	15	46	25	7	6

Source: Gallup Polls, November 5, 2008 and October 22, 2009.

The struggle for civil rights is the struggle for equality. We have seen how Supreme Court decisions have both hindered and advanced the efforts of African Americans to achieve equality. In the next section we will examine how the Supreme Court interprets equality by creating judicial tests and by determining how to evaluate affirmative action programs.

INTERPRETING EQUALITY

When a disadvantaged group takes a discrimination case to the U.S. Supreme Court, its success depends on how the Court interprets the word *equality*. The word *equality*, however, appears nowhere in the original Constitution or the Bill of Rights. The Court must, therefore, interpret the concept in the context of the Fourteenth Amendment, which guarantees that no state shall deny any person the "equal protection of the laws." In order to interpret equality, the Court has created judicial tests and responded to affirmative action programs.

Judicial Tests

The Court has stated that it prohibits only "invidious discrimination"—that is, discriminatory acts that have no rational basis. But who decides what is rational or reasonable? To answer that question, the Supreme Court constructs judicial tests, specific standards that a government policy must meet in order to be ruled constitutionally permissible. These tests specify which party has the burden of proof. That is, must the party challenging the policy prove that the policy is unconstitutional, or must the government prove that the policy is constitutional? Since judicial tests are not part of the Constitution, the Supreme Court has great latitude to decide how and when to use them.

> **rational basis test** Equal protection test used by the Supreme Court that requires a complainant to prove that the use of a classification such as age, gender, or race is not a reasonable means of achieving a legitimate government objective.

The Supreme Court has constructed three tests for cases arising under the equal protection clause of the Fourteenth Amendment. The oldest of these is known as the **rational basis test**. It considers whether a law that gives preference to one group over another is a reasonable means to achieve a legitimate governmental purpose. The rational basis test sets a high bar by compelling the litigant to prove that the legislature passed an unreasonable law. With this in mind, Justices Douglas and Marshall began to ask for additional tests to protect litigants.[17] In 1976, Justice Brennan authored a new test known as the

intermediate scrutiny test Equal protection test used by the Supreme Court that requires the government to prove that the use of classifications such as age, gender, or race is substantially related to an important government objective.

strict scrutiny test Equal protection test used by the Supreme Court that places the greatest burden of proof on the government to prove that classifications such as age, gender, or race are the least restrictive means to achieve a compelling government goal.

affirmative action Programs that attempt to provide members of disadvantaged groups with enhanced opportunities to secure jobs, promotions, and admission to educational institutions.

intermediate scrutiny test. It places the burden of proof on the government, and its standards are considered more exacting than the means and ends requirements of the rational basis test. Even before Justice Brennan formulated the intermediate scrutiny test, the Supreme Court adopted the **strict scrutiny test** for racial discrimination cases. This test places the burden of proof on the government to prove that the law serves a compelling government end and that the racial classification law is the "least restrictive means" of achieving that end. Today, the Court uses the rational basis test for discrimination allegations based on economic status, sexual preference, or age; the intermediate scrutiny test for gender discrimination cases; and the strict scrutiny test for racial and ethnic discrimination cases.

Affirmative Action

The quest for civil rights has come to mean more than the elimination of biased behavior toward certain groups. It has also come to mean that government should provide remedies to promote equality. As early as the 1940s, presidents issued executive orders to attempt to expand federal government employment opportunities for African Americans. Since that time, both the government and the private sector have sponsored **affirmative action** programs to ensure equality for historically disadvantaged groups and to eliminate the effects of past discrimination. Affirmative action programs attempt to clear a path to the good life for those whose progress was blocked in the past. Their goals include helping members of disadvantaged groups gain admission to universities, secure employment in all occupational fields, and win promotions once hired.

Affirmative action programs move beyond the traditional notion of equality of opportunity to promote the goal of equality of outcome. Instead of aiming to ensure that everyone has the same chance to receive a good education or good job, they strive to ensure that every group in society has the same rate of success in attaining a good education and a good job. In order to secure equal results, affirmative action promotes preferential treatment for members of

groups that have suffered from "invidious discrimination." Such programs typically create separate racial classifications and provide members of historically disadvantaged groups with preferential consideration for admission to universities or promotion in the workplace.

Racial Classifications

The Supreme Court responded to this approach for the first time in the case of ***Regents of the University of California v. Bakke*** (1978). In order to increase minority student enrollment, the University of California at Davis developed two admissions programs to fill the one hundred seats in its freshman medical school class. The regular admissions program evaluated candidates on the basis of undergraduate grades, standardized test scores, extracurricular activities, letters of recommendation, and an interview. The special admissions program was reserved for applicants who indicated they were economically or educationally disadvantaged or who were African American, Chicano, Asian, or Native American. Those in the special admissions program were judged on the same factors as the other applicants, but they competed only against each other. Sixteen of the 100 seats for the entering class were filled from the special admissions program.

In 1973, Allan Bakke, at the age of 33, applied for admission to the University of California at Davis medical school. Bakke is a white male who had graduated with honors from the engineering program at the University of Minnesota, had received a master's degree in engineering from Stanford, had worked for the National Aeronautics and Space Administration, and was a Vietnam veteran. He was denied admission in both 1973 and 1974. Arguing that his qualifications were higher than those admitted under the special admissions program, Bakke sued. He claimed that the university's dual admissions program violated the equal protection clause of the Fourteenth Amendment.

The Supreme Court was deeply divided over this case. Four justices had serious reservations about affirmative action programs, four strongly supported them, and Justice Powell was caught in the middle. Justice Powell sided with the first

get involved!

Invite an admissions director from your university to your class to discuss the university's affirmative action plan. Ask about its goals and effectiveness and how your university interprets court decisions on the issue.

group in holding that the university had used race to discriminate against Bakke, who should be admitted to the medical school. Powell applied the strict scrutiny test to the university's admission program, concluding that even though a diverse student body is a compelling governmental interest, the use of racial quotas was an impermissible means of achieving that interest. However, he did align with the affirmative action supporters by stating that such programs were permissible if they did not include quotas and used race as just one of many factors in considering admission.

The *Bakke* case left many questions unanswered. Exactly how could racial classifications be used in university admissions programs? Could racial quotas be used to increase employment opportunities for racial minorities? Could gender classifications be used in affirmative action programs?

The Supreme Court has answered these questions over the past few decades. In 1979, the Court held that an apprenticeship training program at a Kaiser Aluminum and Chemical plant in Louisiana was legal, even though it contained racial quotas.[18] The Court stressed that the company and the United Steelworkers union voluntarily agreed to implement the program and that the plan was temporary in nature. Eight years later, it upheld the use of racial quotas to reverse the effects of long-standing discrimination in the Alabama Department of Public Safety.[19] The Court has also ordered quotas for minority union memberships and added gender as a category to be included in private affirmative action programs.[20] In 2009 in the case of *Ricci v. DeStefano,* however, the Supreme Court held that the city of New Haven, Connecticut, was wrong in throwing out a firefighters promotion exam because white applicants scored higher than African American or Hispanic American applicants. The ruling has the potential of changing employment practices nationwide and potentially limiting the liability of employers when there is no evidence of intentional discrimination.

Hot or Not?

Do you think that affirmative action programs for school admissions should be eliminated?

Current Impact on Education

The Supreme Court reconsidered the constitutionality of affirmative action programs in the 1990s. The court held that federal laws classifying people by race were unconstitutional, even if they were designed to achieve well-meaning ends.[21] As a result, several states enacted legislation that banned the use of racial preferences in education. In *Hopwood v. Texas* (1996), the Fifth Circuit Court of Appeals held that preferential policies affecting admission to the state universities in Texas, Mississippi, and Louisiana violated the Fourteenth Amendment. The state of California dropped its affirmative action program in light of this ruling. The elimination of these affirmative action programs significantly decreased the proportion of African American and Hispanic American students in the California university system. The greatest benefactors of the new race-blind admissions policy were Asian American students. The same pattern was evident at the University of Texas, where Asian Americans made up 18 percent of the entry class by the end of the century but only 3 percent of the state's population.[22]

Many believed the Supreme Court would clarify its position on affirmative action when it agreed to hear two appeals challenging affirmative action programs at the University of Michigan. *Gratz v. Bollinger* (2003) challenged the university's undergraduate admissions policies, and *Grutter v. Bollinger* (2003) questioned the admissions policies for the University of Michigan law school. The *Gratz* case overturned the undergraduate admissions program, but the Court reached a different result in the law school case.

Regents of the University of California v. Bakke The 1978 Supreme Court case that declared unconstitutional the use of racial quotas to achieve a diverse student body but allowed the use of race as one of many factors in admissions decisions.

The University of Michigan Law School's admissions policy looked beyond test scores and grade point averages in order to admit a diverse student body. Its goal was to achieve a critical mass of minority students so that they would not feel isolated or feel the need to be spokespersons for their race. The policy did not set quotas for members of underrepresented groups, nor did it award points for minority status. The Court ruled that this admissions policy was narrowly tailored and permitted the individual review of applicants in a nonmechanical way.

The policy of affirmative action has led to protests of reverse discrimination.

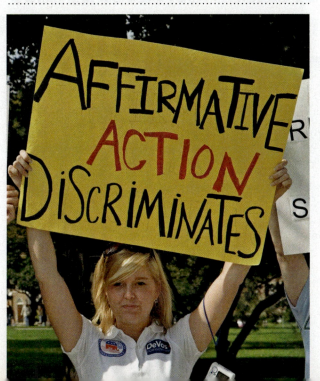

The Court clarified its position in 2007 when it held that public school systems could not use voluntary programs designed to integrate schools that take explicit account of a student's race. In outlawing the programs of Louisville, Kentucky, and Seattle, Washington, Chief Justice Roberts wrote for the five-person majority that "the way to stop discrimination on the basis of race is to stop discriminating on the basis of race."[23] The dissenting justices angrily denounced the decision—one that will affect the assignment of students to schools in hundreds of school districts across the United States—as a break from the famous *Brown* decision of 1954.

Continuing Controversy

The constitutionality of affirmative action programs is still uncertain in many areas, and the debate about the wisdom of these policies continues. Opponents of affirmative action programs believe that merit is the only fair way to distribute the benefits of society.[24] They claim that such programs amount to unfair **reverse discrimination** and argue that both the Fourteenth Amendment and the 1964 Civil Rights Act prohibit the use of racial discrimination. They feel that keeping Allan Bakke out of medical school is an example of racial discrimination. Supporters, on the other hand, argue that merit is not always self-evident and may include subjective considerations. They assert not only that affirmative action is necessary to compensate for the effects of past discrimination but also that it benefits the entire community by taking advantage of the talents of all citizens participating in a diverse social, economic, and political environment. Finally, they point to research that indicates that gains for disadvantaged groups come with only small costs to white males.[25] As we will see, these groups include not only African Americans but also a wide range of other minorities, and even the largest single segment of the U.S. population—women.

reverse discrimination Argument that the use of race as a factor in affirmative action programs constitutes unconstitutional discrimination against the majority population.

OTHER MINORITY GROUPS

African Americans no longer represent the largest ethnic minority in the United States. The nation's Hispanic and Asian populations, in particular, have grown substantially since 1990. Many of these other minority groups have benefited to varying degrees from the African American struggle to secure equal rights. The victories won by the black civil rights movement gave hope to other minorities that they, too, could work successfully to overcome historical discrimination.

Native Americans

Government policy toward Native Americans has gone from genocide and isolation to assimilation, and finally to citizenship. Congress and the federal courts initially promoted westward expansion at the expense of Native American rights. One author has referred to Native American policy as "genocide-at-law" because it encouraged both the land confiscation and cultural extermination of the native population.[26] The government forcibly resettled the displaced Native Americans onto isolated reservations. In the 1880s, Congress adopted a new strategy of assimilating Native Americans into the mainstream of cultural life. Legislation banned native languages and rituals and required children to attend boarding schools located off the reservation. The federal government did not grant Native Americans citizenship and the right to vote until 1924. It took another 22 years after that for Congress to settle financial claims resulting from the confiscation of native lands.

Despite their poor treatment at the hands of the government, Native Americans formed no formal social or political movements to protest their unequal status until the 1960s. At the height of the civil rights movement, however, Native Americans began to mobilize. Native American activists such as Dennis Banks and Russell Means of the American Indian Movement (AIM) drew attention to the plight of Native Americans. In 1969, Native American activists seized Alcatraz Island in San Francisco to dramatize the loss of Native American lands. Two years later, Dee Brown published the best-selling book, *Bury My Heart at Wounded Knee*,[27] which focused on the 1890 massacre of

Population Increases by Race and Ethnicity from 1990 to 2050

Racial or ethnic category	Percent of population in 1990	Percent increase by 2000	Percent increase by 2050 (projection)
White	75.1	5.9	7
Black	12.3	15.6	71
Native American	0.9	26.4	–
Asian	3.6	46.3	213
Hispanic	12.5	57.9	188

Source: www.anthro.palomar.edu.

nearly 300 Sioux by the U.S. Cavalry in Wounded Knee, South Dakota. The book helped to mobilize public opinion against the poor treatment of Native Americans in much the same way as Harriet Beecher Stowe's *Uncle Tom's Cabin* did for African Americans a century earlier. In 1973, armed members of AIM held hostages at Wounded Knee for 71 days until the national government agreed to consider Native American treaty rights.

Like the NAACP, Native Americans began to use the courts to accomplish their goals, filing hundreds of test cases and forming the Native American Rights Fund (NARF) to finance them. Their victories include the securing of land, hunting and fishing rights, and access to ancient burial grounds and other sacred locations. The 1968 Civil Rights Act included an Indian Bill of Rights, leading one author to conclude that Native Americans have now entered the self-determination phase of their history.[28] Nevertheless, Native Americans still suffer more than most Americans from ill health, poverty, and poor educational opportunities. Nearly half live on or near a reservation.

An ongoing area of controversy for Native Americans is the continued use of stereotypical and demeaning names and mascots by some professional and collegiate athletic teams. Native Americans have called upon the NFL's Washington Redskins and major league baseball's Atlanta Braves to change their team names. They have also complained about what they consider the offensive caricature of a Native American used as a mascot by baseball's Cleveland Indians. At the college level, the NCAA adopted a new restriction on the use of Native American nicknames, mascots, and logos. Thirty schools have been asked to explain their use of such items under a new appeals system. Some college teams, such as the Florida State Seminoles, the Utah Utes, and the Central Michigan Chippewas, have been allowed to keep their nicknames after deliberations with the NCAA. Other universities continue to appeal.

Hispanic Americans

Hispanic Americans are currently the largest minority group in the United States, making up more than 16 percent of the country's population. They come primarily from Puerto Rico, Mexico, Cuba, El Salvador, and Hon-

Hispanic Categories in the United States

Dominican **2.7%**
Salvadoran **3.4%**
Cuban **3.4%**
Puerto Rican **9%**
All other Hispanic **14%**
Mexican **68%**

Source: U.S. Census Bureau.

duras. Immigrants from Mexico make up the majority of Hispanics in California, Arizona, Texas, and New Mexico, while large numbers of Caribbean Hispanics populate the states of New York, New Jersey, and Florida.

As with Native Americans, the Hispanic American drive for civil rights began in earnest during the mid-1960s. Hispanic leaders carefully observed African American groups and adopted many of the same tactics. Inspired by the NAACP's Legal Defense Fund, Hispanics formed similar organizations, including the Mexican American Legal Defense and Educational Fund (MALDEF). They, too, brought test cases before the courts to realize goals such as implementing bilingual education, increased funding for schools in low-income minority districts, ending employment discrimination against Hispanic Americans, and challenging election rules that diluted Hispanic voting power.

Like other minority groups, Hispanic Americans did not depend exclusively on litigation in their struggle for civil rights. Drawing again on the experiences of African Americans, they staged sit-ins, marches, boycotts, and other related activities to draw attention to their concerns. The best-known Hispanic American protest leader, César Chávez, organized strikes by farm workers in the

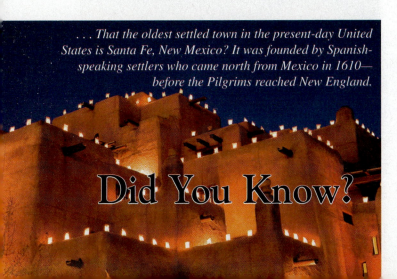

. . . That the oldest settled town in the present-day United States is Santa Fe, New Mexico? It was founded by Spanish-speaking settlers who came north from Mexico in 1610—before the Pilgrims reached New England.

Did You Know?

U.S. Hispanic Population by Growth

Hispanic population (millions)

14.6 — 1980

22.4 — 1990

35.3 — 2000

50.5 — 2010

Source: Pew Hispanic Center tabulations of 2010 American Community Survey (1% IPUMS).

late 1960s and 1970s to attain basic labor rights for migrant workers. Migrants worked long hours for little pay, lived in substandard housing that often lacked plumbing and electricity, and were unwelcome in the local schools. When farm owners refused to bargain with his group, Chávez launched a national boycott of California lettuce and grapes. The boycott was successful, as American consumers sided with the plight of migrant workers. Responding to the pressure, California passed a law giving migrant workers the right to bargain collectively.

Hispanic Americans have clearly benefited from the 1964 Civil Rights Act and other important civil rights legislation first implemented to aid African Americans. For example, a 1968 amendment to the 1964 act funded public school programs that offer English instruction in the language of children for whom English is a second language. In addition, today there are more than five thousand elected Hispanic American officials across the United States. The high-profile victory of Antonio Villaraigosa in the 2005 Los Angeles mayoral race, as well as the presidential campaign of former New Mexico governor Bill Richardson, signal that this trend is going to continue.

Asian Americans

The first Asian immigrants to this country were Chinese and Japanese laborers who came to the western United States during the late 1800s to build railroads and to work

Agricultural strikes in the 1960s and 1970s alerted the nation to the harsh economic plight of migrant workers.

Antonious Villaraigosa is the mayor of Los Angeles, California..

During World War II, more than 100,000 Japanese Americans living in the states of California, Oregon, and Washington were placed in internment camps.

in mines. When the need for railroad laborers declined, Congress passed legislation in 1882 to temporarily halt Chinese immigration. Over the next three decades, the country barred all but a few Asians through a series of informal agreements with Asian governments. In 1921, Congress began to set immigration quotas based on the country of origin. Western European nations were given large quotas and Asian countries very small ones. Only 150 persons of Japanese origin, for instance, could enter the United States annually. In 1930, Congress prohibited immigration from Japan altogether after the Japanese government protested a California law barring anyone of Japanese descent from buying property in the state. Discrimination against Asian immigration did not end until 1965, when Congress adjusted quotas to favor those groups who had previously been targets of discrimination.

World War II marked the darkest chapter in the history of Japanese American civil rights. The Japanese attack on Pearl Harbor that brought the United States into the war made Japanese Americans the objects of great fear and hatred, especially on the West Coast. Shortly after Pearl Harbor, Japanese Americans living on the West Coast were subject to nightly curfews. In February 1942, President Franklin D. Roosevelt issued an executive order removing more than 100,000 Japanese Americans from their homes in California, Oregon, and Washington and plac-

ing them in internment camps for the duration of the war. In ***Korematsu v. United States*** (1944), the U.S. Supreme Court ruled the internment was constitutional. Noting the law was based on a racial classification, the Court applied the strict scrutiny test. The Court held, however, that the security of the United States was a compelling governmental interest and that interning Japanese Americans was the least restrictive means to identify potentially disloyal members of the population. Concluding that war involved hardship, the Court ruled the treatment of Japanese Americans was not a civil rights violation. In the late 1980s, Congress expressed its disagreement with this view and granted benefits to former internees.

Asian Americans are the fastest-growing minority group in the United States today, growing from 0.5 percent to more than 4 percent of the population in the last half century. They have gained prominent positions in American society and experienced notable academic success based solely on merit. They may still be subject to discrimination, however. Asian Americans' academic success has not yet been matched by corresponding positions in business management, the professions, or political office; nor have young Asian Americans exhibited high levels of political engagement. Despite this, the 2008 election was the most racially and ethnically diverse in U.S. history. (See table below.)

> **Korematsu v. United States**
> The 1944 Supreme Court decision that upheld the constitutionality of the U.S. government's internment of more than 100,000 Americans of Japanese descent during World War II.

Demographic Composition of Voters

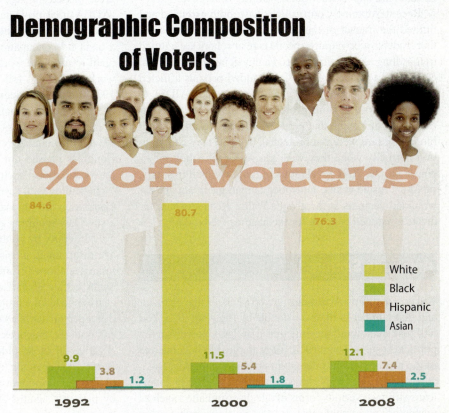

% of Voters

	1992	2000	2008
White	84.6	80.7	76.3
Black	9.9	11.5	12.1
Hispanic	3.8	5.4	7.4
Asian	1.2	1.8	2.5

Source: Pew Research Center.

Disabled Americans

After every war over the last century, disabled Americans have lobbied hard for antidiscrimination laws. World War I veterans were largely responsible for the first rehabilitation laws passed in the late 1920s. Following the civil rights campaigns of the 1960s, World War II, Korean War, and Vietnam War veterans saw the success other minority groups were having with respect to civil rights laws and began to work for greater protection for disabled Americans.[29] The 1973 Rehabilitation Act added people with disabilities to the list of Americans who were to be protected from discrimination. The 1975 Education of All Handicapped Children Act entitled all children to a free public education appropriate to their needs. Prior to the legislation, four million disabled students were receiving either no education or one that did not fit their needs.

The crowning piece of legislation for Americans with disabilities was the 1990 Americans with Disabilities Act (ADA). It guarantees access to public facilities, workplaces, and communication services. No longer can the stairs, telephones, and buses that kept this minority group out of schools, offices, theaters, and restaurants be used as excuses to deny access. The statute required schools, governments, and businesses to make existing facilities accessible. Wheelchair ramps and grab bars in restrooms have become common sights on the American landscape since 1990. Yet a 2004 survey of disabled Americans conducted by *USA Today* reveals that a majority of them do not believe the law has made a difference in their lives and that 4 in 10 do not expect their quality of life to improve.

Recent Supreme Court rulings have both extended and limited the impact of the ADA. In 1999, the Court ruled that students who require special care at school are entitled to it as long as they do not need a physician to deliver that care.[30] The year before, the Court added persons afflicted with acquired immune deficiency syndrome (AIDS) to the list of those persons protected by the ADA.[31] In contrast, the Court ruled that people with bad eyesight or high blood pressure were not protected, because they can function normally when they wear glasses or take their medicine.[32] Do the 2007 revelations of the dirty facilities, rats, mold-encrusted walls, and poor outpatient treatment for wounded veterans at the army's Walter Reed Hospital indicate a reduced concern for the handicapped today?

American Seniors

Today, 38 million Americans are 65 years of age or older, and that number is likely to double by the year 2025. You will read later about the emergence of "gray power" in the political system. The AARP, for example, has become one of the most powerful interest groups in Washington, D.C., advocating for seniors' rights. Nevertheless, elderly Americans still face various forms of age discrimination such as mandatory retirement rules and cost-cutting measures that

Older Americans continue to work for material and social reasons, but they often face discrimination in the workplace.

target older, higher-paid workers for termination or layoffs. Some professional and graduate schools reject older applicants on the grounds that they will have fewer years to work in their professions upon graduation.

At the height of the civil rights movement in 1967, Congress passed the Age Discrimination in Employment Act (ADEA) that protected workers over the age of 40 from age discrimination unless an employer proved that age was a bona fide occupational qualification. The law even applied to an older worker who was replaced by a younger worker who also fell under the protection of ADEA.[33] In 1975, civil rights legislation denied federal funds to any institution discriminating against persons over 40 because of their age. Congress amended the ADEA in 1978 to raise the age of mandatory retirement from 65 to 70. In 1986, Congress phased out mandatory retirement for all but a few occupations, such as firefighting.

In dealing with cases of age discrimination, the Supreme Court uses the rational basis test. It has, however, upheld a state law requiring police officers to retire at the age of 50.[34] In 2000, by contrast, the Court made it easier to win age discrimination cases with circumstantial evidence and inferences drawn from that evidence.[35] In the 2005 case of *Smith v. City of Jackson, Mississippi,* the Court may have also expanded the protection of the ADEA. The Court ruled that a person 40 years of age or older can sue if an employer's policies, practices, or other employment actions have a negative effect on older employees, even if unintentional. But in another ruling, the Court, on the basis of the doctrine of sovereign immunity, disallowed age discrimination suits by plaintiffs against any state and local government entities without their consent.[36] Seniors fared better in a 2008

Court decision regarding the federal government. A seven-member majority ruled that federal workers who file claims of age discrimination have the same protections from retaliation as they would in the private sector.[37]

Gay and Lesbian Americans

Some scholars argue that gay and lesbian Americans have had a more difficult time in achieving equality than other minority groups.[38] They must contend with negative stereotyping and **homophobia**. This fear and hatred of homosexuals is deeply rooted in our culture and sometimes finds violent expression. The death of political science student Matthew Shepard is a particularly poignant example. The 21-year-old University of Wyoming student was attacked after attending a meeting for Gay Awareness Week on his campus. After being hit repeatedly in the head with a pistol, and kicked repeatedly in the groin, he was left tied to a fence to die by himself.

Although exact numbers are difficult to obtain, millions of Americans identify themselves as homosexual. Homosexuals enjoy higher average incomes and educational levels than other minority groups, but until recently they were not able to convert these resources into an effective drive for equal rights. Overcoming cultural bias and the strong stance taken by many religious groups against homosexuality has proved to be a daunting task. Most Americans' attitudes about the rights of homosexuals, however, depend on whether they know a gay or lesbian person.

> **homophobia** Irrational fear and hatred directed toward persons who are homosexuals.

The triggering event of the gay and lesbian rights movement in the United States was a police raid on the Stonewall Inn in New York City on June 27, 1969. The patrons of the popular gay and lesbian bar responded by throwing beer bottles and cans to protest what they viewed as constant police harassment. Stonewall had a galvanizing effect on the gay community. "Gay Power" signs appeared in the city, and gay and lesbian groups such as the Gay Activist Alliance and the Gay Liberation Front began to organize to combat invidious discrimination. Soon hundreds, and then thousands, of state and local organizations sprang up to exert pressure on legislatures, the media, churches, and schools to change laws and public attitudes toward homosexuals.

Gay and lesbian groups have achieved some significant political results at the state and local levels of government. Presently, 12 states and more than 200 cities have statutes protecting gays and lesbians from discrimination in employment, credit, housing, and public accommodations. In 1996, the U.S. Supreme Court struck down an amendment to the Colorado state constitution that invalidated state and local laws protecting gays and lesbians. The Court held the Colorado amendment to be in violation of the equal protection clause of the U.S. Constitution.[39]

At the national level, the government lifted a ban on hiring gay men and lesbians and repealed a law that prohibited gay men and lesbians from immigrating to the United States. President Bill Clinton's attempt to lift the ban on gays in the armed services, however, met resistance from military leaders who viewed homosexuality as incompatible with military service. The resulting "Don't ask, don't tell" compromise policy prevented the military from inquiring about soldiers' sexual orientation but also barred gay and lesbian soldiers from revealing their homosexuality. The policy has not served gay and lesbian military personnel well. Since

Attitudes Toward Gay Rights Depend on Whether the Respondent Knows a Gay or Lesbian Person

Gay couples should be able to adopt — 28% / 50%

Gay partners should have social security benefits — 43% / 60%

Gay and lesbian people should serve openly in the military — 48% / 63%

Hate-crime laws should include violence committed against gay and lesbian people — 54% / 69%

Gay partners should have inheritance rights — 50% / 73%

Gay and lesbian people should have equal rights in employment — 77% / 90%

Doesn't know someone gay or lesbian
Knows someone gay or lesbian

Source: www.hrc.org. Oct. 4, 2006.

the policy went into effect in 1993, more than 7,800 gay men and women have been forced out of the military. In December of 2010, President Obama signed legislation repealing the policy, but the implementation of a new open policy was delayed until the Pentagon ascertained its effect on recruiting. The following month, the Government Accounting Office reported that the "Don't ask, don't tell" policy had cost the military $193 million from 2004 until 2009.

Privacy has been an area of particular concern for gay and lesbian civil rights activists. In the 1970s and 1980s, they were successful in reducing the number of states with antisodomy laws from 49 to 24, using both state legislative and judicial strategies. In 1986, however, the Supreme Court ruled that antisodomy legislation in the state of Georgia was constitutional. It held that homosexual sex acts were not a fundamental liberty that was protected by the right to privacy in the Fourteenth Amendment.[40] The Court reversed itself 17 years later in the case of *Lawrence v. Texas* (2003), ruling that the Fourteenth Amendment protects consenting adults engaging in homosexual behavior in the privacy of their homes. On the

Gay and lesbian couples continue to face difficulties in winning the right to enter into same-sex marriages.

PRESENTLY, 12 STATES and more than 200 cities have statutes protecting gays and lesbians from discrimination in employment, credit, housing, and public accommodations.

other hand, the same Court upheld the Boy Scouts' refusal to allow a gay man to serve as a troop leader, based on the premise that such a leader would undermine the organization's "morally straight" values.[41] In 2010, the Supreme Court ruled in favor of gay and lesbian groups in two different cases. It held that a state law school can refuse to

recognize a religious student group—with student activity funding, meeting space, and other privileges—that discriminates against gay students (*Christian Legal Society College of Law v. Martinez* (2010)).The Court also decided in *Doe v. Reed* (2010) that persons who signed a petition to have an anti-gay referendum on a state ballot did not have a general First Amendment right to keep their names secret.

One of the most sensitive and controversial issues regarding gay and lesbian rights has been the legalization of same-sex marriages. The issue gained heightened attention in 1993 when the Supreme Court of Hawaii ruled that denying marriage licenses to gay couples might violate the equal protection clause of their state constitution.[42] Other states then began to worry that under the full faith and credit clause of the U.S. Constitution, they might be forced to accept the legality of same-sex marriages performed in Hawaii—or any other state that chose to legalize same-sex marriage. Opponents advocated state laws banning same-sex marriages, and a number of states enacted such laws. In 1996, Congress passed the Defense of Marriage Act, which prohibits federal recognition of gay and lesbian couples and allows state governments to ignore same-sex marriages performed in other states.

The issue ignited again in 1999 when the Supreme Court of Vermont ruled that gay couples are entitled to the same benefits of marriage as heterosexual couples.[43] The next

Support Growing for Same-Sex Marriages

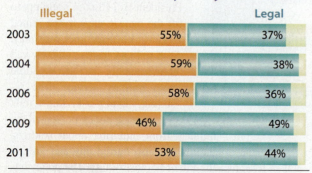

"Do you think it shoud be legal or illegal for gay and lesbian/homosexual couples to get married?"

	Illegal	Legal
2003	55%	37%
2004	59%	38%
2006	58%	36%
2009	46%	49%
2011	53%	44%

Source: ABC News/Washington Post Poll, March 10–13, 2011.

year, the Vermont legislature passed a statute permitting homosexual couples to form **civil unions**. The law entitled these couples to receive the same state benefits as married couples, including insurance benefits and inheritance rights. More public attention followed in 2004, when cities such as San Francisco began performing same-sex marriages. Media images of gay and lesbian couples waiting in line to be married spurred opponents to initiate referenda banning same-sex marriages. On the day George Bush was reelected to the presidency in 2004, ballot initiatives banning same-sex marriages passed easily in 11 states. Two years later, voters in seven states passed ballot measures amending their state constitutions to recognize marriage only between a man and a woman. Then in 2008, voters in Arizona, California, and Florida approved bans on same-sex marriage. In the 2010 case of *Perry v. Schwarzenegger*, a federal district court judge in San Francisco declared the California ban on same-sex marriages to be unconstitutional. The case likely will be heard by the United States Supreme Court in the near future. The issue will probably continue to divide the American electorate as it did in 2010, when the Iowa Supreme Court ruled that same-sex marriages could begin in the state as of April 27, and the Vermont legislature ruled in 2009 that same-sex marriage could begin in their state. The Iowa Supreme Court vote was unanimous. Three of their members faced retention elections in 2010 and they all lost. They were defeated by a grassroots, anti-same-sex marriage campaign headed by a conservative former Republican candidate for governor. Public opinion is still divided on such marriages and civil unions.

WOMEN AND CIVIL RIGHTS

The fight for civil rights by women in America differs in many respects from the struggles of the previously discussed minority groups. First, women do not represent a minority in the United States; there are more women than men in the country, and they vote in greater numbers than men. Their struggle for equal rights, therefore, is not based on their small numbers but rather on long-standing historical and cultural assumptions concerning their proper role in society. Second, women began their struggle for civil rights as early as the African American movement but were thwarted by the domi-

nant male culture. In other words, the civil rights movement for African Americans was not so much a template for the woman's movement as a parallel movement to it.

Historically there have been three high points of activity for the pursuit of women's civil rights, followed by years of little visible or public activity. This section will examine those three periods of activity and feature three issues of current concern: workplace and educational fairness, sexual harassment, and women's role in the military.

> **civil union** Legal recognition by a state of a gay or lesbian relationship; allows gay and lesbian couples to receive the same state benefits as heterosexual married couples.

Women's Mobilization Eras

Although women as early as Abigail Adams discussed the concept of political equality with their prominent husbands, the most active periods of female political mobilization occurred from 1840 to 1875, from 1890 to 1920, and from 1961 to the present.[44]

Early Women's Movement: 1840–1875

The seeds of the early women's movement were planted in 1840 when Lucretia Mott and Elizabeth Cady Stanton accompanied their husbands to London to attend a meeting of the World Anti-Slavery Society. After a long debate, the male participants denied the women the right to participate at the meeting and relegated them to sitting in the balcony as spectators. This rebuff was partially responsible for their determination to work on behalf of women's rights in the United States. Their work was delayed for eight years, however, because both women were raising young children.

The early women's movement was also an outgrowth of religious revivalism.[45] Women who were active in the abolition movement established communication networks among themselves, laying the foundation for the first

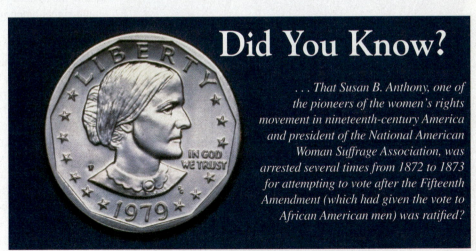

Did You Know?

. . . That Susan B. Anthony, one of the pioneers of the women's rights movement in nineteenth-century America and president of the National American Woman Suffrage Association, was arrested several times from 1872 to 1873 for attempting to vote after the Fifteenth Amendment (which had given the vote to African American men) was ratified?

women's movement in the United States. In 1848, Mott and Stanton organized the first women's rights convention in the small town of Seneca Falls, New York. Over the next 12 years, women's rights groups held seven conventions in different cities. With the outbreak of the Civil War, the movement temporarily suspended its activities to support the Union war effort. After the war, the early feminists learned a cruel political lesson. Despite the critical role they played in abolishing slavery, women were not granted the right to vote in the Fifteenth Amendment. In 1875, the U.S. Supreme Court upheld Missouri's denial of voting rights for women.[46]

The Suffrage Movement: 1890–1920

In 1890, women's rights advocates formed the National American Woman Suffrage Association (NAWSA), with Susan B. Anthony as its leader. Rather than trying to seek expanded social, legal, economic, and political rights for women, the new association concentrated primarily on securing the vote. Contemporary social trends such as the temperance movement and a concern for the working conditions of women aided the group in its efforts.[47] The tremendous growth of women's clubs in the 1880s and 1890s also invigorated the suffrage movement.[48] Enjoying more free time, white middle-class women joined self-improvement clubs such as reading societies. As women in these clubs became involved in social causes, they soon realized the inferior position shared by all women.

By 1917, the NAWSA boasted over two million members, and the suffrage movement had become a broad so-

Equal Rights Amendment
The proposed constitutional amendment that would have prohibited national and state governments from denying equal rights on the basis of sex.

The suffrage initiative became a broad social movement that led to women getting the right to vote in 1920.

cial movement, guaranteeing its success. A coalition of groups led by NAWSA secured ratification of the Nineteenth Amendment in 1920, guaranteeing women the right to vote. After this historic victory, however, the coalition that made up the suffrage movement soon disintegrated. Winning the vote was the only goal all the participating women's groups shared, and they failed to reach consensus on a postsuffrage agenda. As a result, there was little organized protest for women's rights until the 1960s.

The Second Women's Rights Movement: 1961–Present

The civil rights movement of the 1950s and 1960s attracted many female activists, just as the abolitionist movement had in the nineteenth century. Like their sisters of an earlier era, these activists encountered prejudice and were often treated as second-class citizens by their male activist counterparts. In 1961, the Supreme Court ruled that a jury selection system that virtually excluded women was constitutional because, as the center of home and family life, women should not be burdened with jury duty.[49] This case, and three events that followed in quick succession, initiated the second women's rights movement in the United States.

First, President John F. Kennedy created the President's Commission on the Status of Women in 1961. The commission's 1963 report, *American Women,* documented widespread discrimination against women in all walks of life. That same year, Betty Friedan published her bestselling book *The Feminine Mystique.* Friedan's book challenged women to assert their rights and question the traditional gender assumptions of society. Finally, the 1964 Civil Rights Act prohibited discrimination based not only on race but also on sex. It also created the Equal Employment Opportunity Commission (EEOC) to enforce the antidiscrimination measures. When the EEOC failed to enforce sex discrimination laws, female activists formed the National Organization for Women (NOW). Like the NAACP, NOW pledged to work within the system by lobbying for a constitutional equal rights amendment and by using the courts to gain equality.

NOW initially focused on the passage of the **Equal Rights Amendment** (ERA), which was first introduced in Congress in 1923 but was never given a hearing. Its wording was simple and straightforward: "Equality of rights under the law shall not be denied or abridged by the United States or by any state on account of sex." Despite intense efforts by women's rights groups, only 35 states voted for ratification, three short of the required three-quarters majority. NOW and other allied groups have been more successful in bringing equal protection cases before the U.S. Supreme Court. Using the intermediate scrutiny test,

the Court has prohibited laws that allow women but not men to receive alimony.[50] It has banned single-sex nursing schools.[51] It has also disallowed state prosecutors' use of preemptory challenges to reject either women or men in order to produce a more sympathetic jury.[52] On the other hand, the Court has upheld statutory rape laws that apply only to female victims[53] and draft registration laws that apply only to males.[54]

The modern women's movement has placed more emphasis on involving women in politics. Although women vote more than men, the number of women holding political office is still significantly lower than their share of the population. Yet this trend seems to be changing: in 2006 Nancy Pelosi became the first female speaker of the House, and Hillary Clinton emerged as the nation's first female presidential candidate to lead in national polls. Then, in August 2008, Alaska Governor Sarah Palin was chosen by John McCain as his running mate. In 2011, the secretaries of State, Health and Human Services, Homeland Security, and Labor are women, in addition to the Environmental Protection Agency administrator and the United Nations ambassador.

Current Issues

By redefining their status in American society, women entered more fully into the public lives of their communities. This move into more public arenas of society gave rise to several issues that are particularly relevant to women's groups of today: workplace equity, sexual harassment, and women's role in the military.

Young Women and Men (18–29) Voters in Presidential Elections

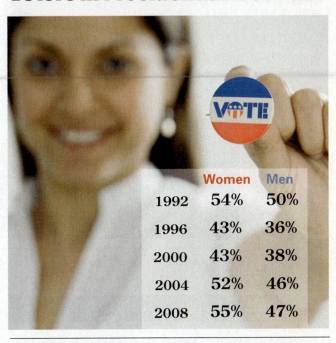

	Women	Men
1992	54%	50%
1996	43%	36%
2000	43%	38%
2004	52%	46%
2008	55%	47%

Source: www.civicyouth.org.

The initial focus of the second women's movement was the passage of the Equal Rights Amendment, which ultimately failed.

Ratio of Female to Male Earnings

Women's median weekly earnings, as a percent of men's

Women's median annual earnings, as a percent of men's

Source: Institute for Women's Policy Research, www.iwpr.org.

Workplace Equity

American life has changed dramatically since the first debates on the ERA. Very few modern women fit the traditional role of stay-at-home wife and mom. More than seventy million American women are in the workplace—

Although women continue to gain important jobs in the private and public sectors, a gap still exists between the salaries paid to women and men.

some 60 percent of all adult females in the country—and a majority of those are married. Two-thirds of American mothers who have children below school age work outside the home. Women now constitute a majority of the American civilian workforce.

Congressional legislation to promote fairness in the workplace dates back almost fifty years, to the Equal Pay Act of 1963. The legislation requires equal pay for equal work, regardless of sex. It did not address the fact that some jobs traditionally filled by women (such as nurses and secretaries) pay less than jobs traditionally held by men (such as construction workers and truck drivers). In 1972, Congress gave the EEOC the power to sue employers suspected of illegal gender discrimination. The 1991 Civil Rights and Women's Equity in Employment Act shifted the burden of proof by requiring employers to demonstrate that their hiring and promotion practices are related to job performance.

Despite these efforts, women still earn less than men earn. When the Equal Pay Act was passed, a female earned, on average, 59 cents for every dollar earned by a male. That figure has increased to 77 cents for every dollar men earn, but a significant gap still exists. Some authors suggest that wage justice can be secured only by adopting a **comparable worth** policy.[55] Such a policy attempts to compare dissimilar jobs in terms of knowledge, effort, skill, responsibility, and working conditions. Jobs that are equivalent in these terms should be compensated equally. Proponents of this approach argue that society historically has devalued jobs traditionally performed by women. They contend that the continued predominance of women in low-paid female-dominated jobs requires a compa-

Women—Working Professionals in the U.S.

	1900	1950	2005	2014 (projected)
Millions of working professionals	5.1	18.4	65.7	76

Source: AFL-CIO, Department for Professional Employees, *Fact Sheet 2006,* "Professional Women: Vital Statistics," 2006.

rable worth solution. Opponents argue that differing pay scales between jobs simply reflect free market economic forces and personal job preferences. In 2011 the Supreme Court heard a case that had the potential to clarify workplace equity for women with respect to pay and promotion decisions. Approximately 1.6 million women brought a discrimination case against Wal-Mart seeking billions of dollars in back pay. Dividing along ideological lines, the five-member Court majority, however, held that the case could not proceed as a class action suit because the female employees' claims did not have enough in common to form one lawsuit. The liberal dissenters in *Wal-Mart Stores, Inc. v. Dukes* argued that the common elements were Wal-Mart's uniform policy over pay and promotions.

Sexual Harassment

With men and women spending more time together in the workplace, **sexual harassment** has become an increasingly important issue for American women. The Supreme Court has ruled that sexual harassment qualifies as gender discrimination under Title VII of the 1964 Civil Rights Act if it is so pervasive as to create a hostile or abusive work environment.[56] In 1993, the Court reinforced its position in *Harris v. Forklift Systems.* Under that ruling, plaintiffs are not required to prove the workplace is so

hostile as to cause severe psychological injury or prevent them from performing their jobs. The Court emphasized that federal law protects a plaintiff before the harassment leads to serious psychological difficulty.

In two 1998 cases, the Court addressed the employer's responsibility for sexual harassment committed by its managers. In *Faragher v. City of Boca Raton,* the Court ruled that an employer is responsible for a supervisor's sexual harassment of an employee even if the employer is unaware of the sexual harassment. The Supreme Court thus made it easier for employees to win such cases by ruling employers need to take reasonable steps to prevent harassing behavior at the work site. The Court also ruled in 1998 that an employer can be held liable for sexual harassment caused by a supervisor's actions, even though the employee suffered no job-related harm.[57]

Most sexual harassment cases have involved the workplace, but in 1999 the Court turned its attention to sexual harassment in the public schools. The Court determined in *Davis v. Monroe County Board of Education* that a school district was liable for one stu-

comparable worth The notion that individuals performing different jobs that require the same amount of knowledge, effort, skill, responsibility, and working conditions should receive equal compensation; the proposal would elevate the pay structure of many jobs traditionally performed by women.

sexual harassment The practice of awarding jobs or job benefits in exchange for sexual favors, or the creation of a hostile work or education environment by unwarranted sexual advances or sexual conversation.

citizenshipQuiz

Can you pass the U.S. Citizenship Test? See how well you know the content in this chapter covered on the citizenship test required of foreign-born candidates for naturalization.

1. When must all men register for the Selective Service?
2. Who lived in America before the Europeans arrived?
3. What group of people was taken to America and sold as slaves?
4. What did the Emancipation Proclamation do?
5. What did Susan B. Anthony do?
6. What movement tried to end racial discrimination?

(1) At age eighteen/between eighteen and twenty-six (2) Native Americans/ American Indians (3) Africans/people from Africa (4) Freed the slaves/freed slaves in the confederate states (5) Fought for women's rights/fought for civil rights (6) Civil rights

Source: United States Citizenship and Immigration Services.

dent harassing another if the school had knowledge of the harassment or was deliberately indifferent to it. The harassment must be so severe, pervasive, and objectively offensive that it deprives the victims of access to the educational opportunities provided by the school. Sexual harassment and sexual abuse against female students at the military service academies have led to congressional and military inquiries, but the Supreme Court has yet to hear a case on the matter.

civil rights movement The litigation and mobilization activities of African Americans in the second half of the twentieth century that led to a greater realization of equality for all disadvantaged groups.

Women's Role in the Military

Until 1948, women served the military in separate units such as the Women's Army Corps (WACs) and the Nurse Corps. Since that time, the sexes have served together in regular noncombat military units, and women currently make up about 15 percent of the American armed forces. The integration of women into the regular armed forces raises a variety of controversial issues, perhaps the most contentious of which involves women's role in combat. Federal laws and military regulations prevent women from engaging in combat for a variety of reasons, including women's lack of upper body strength, the possibility of capture and rape by enemy forces, and uncertainty about

Women serving in wars face the same dangers as their male counterparts.

the behavior of men and women thrown together in a combat situation.

Should policies barring women from combat be viewed as sexual discrimination or as a sexual benefit? The realities of modern war undermine many of the traditional arguments against women serving in combat. In Iraq, for example, the lack of traditional front lines and the pervasive nature of the threat can produce casualties even among female soldiers not serving in infantry, armor, and special forces divisions. More than four times as many female soldiers have died in the Iraq War as in the Vietnam War, which suggests that noncombat policies are no longer protecting women. In 2010, the navy announced it had decided to allow women to serve on submarines.

CIVIC ENGAGEMENT AND CIVIL RIGHTS

We have seen in this chapter that the pursuit of civil rights is related to political mobilization. Political mobilization generally is the process by which candidates, parties, activists, interest groups, and social movements induce other people to engage in politics. As we discuss later in the book, people are more likely to engage in politics if they are asked. They are also more likely to participate if they possess such resources as time, skill, knowledge, and self-confidence. Mobilization for the civil rights goals of political, social, and economic equality creates a problem for activists because the people most affected

lack many of the resources related to political participation. As a result, initial civil rights activity involves leaders of interest groups and their attempts to influence judicial bodies.

Civil rights activities are often directed toward the U.S. Supreme Court because deprived groups are seeking constitutional and legal pronouncements of equality. The Supreme Court, as a result, has become known for its policy-legitimizing role in the political system.[58] The interest group leaders in New Orleans sought the intervention of courts to rule that the state's segregation laws were illegitimate. The *Plessy* case was carefully planned, even though not ultimately successful. The goal to have the Supreme Court declare the illegitimacy of racist legislation and policies remained the same for African American groups. After its formation, the NAACP pursued a plan of presenting the Court with a series of test cases concerning the segregation policies in graduate and professional schools. The Supreme Court applied the "separate but equal" doctrine of *Plessy v. Ferguson* and found the policies of those schools to be unequal. The NAACP then changed its strategy to challenge the separate but equal doctrine itself and were successful in *Brown v. Board of Education of Topeka*. After the Court ruled that segregated schools should change their policies with "all deliber-

ate speed" in the *Brown II* case, the NAACP issued a directive to all its local branches that detailed procedures for speeding the implementation of the Court decision. The directive advocated such procedures as setting timetables, familiarizing parents with the issue, and (where needed) additional lawsuits.

The success of the NAACP in the *Brown* case soon led to the civil rights movement. The **civil rights movement** was a broad coalition of political, social, and religious groups that engaged in a wide variety of activities with the general goal of securing political, economic, and social equality. A large number of national, regional, and local organizations used sit-ins, freedom rides, boycotts, and lawsuits to further their goals. Extreme pressure was placed on members of Congress to pass the 1964 Civil Rights Act and the 1965 Voting Rights Act. The movement began to build in the late 1950s, peaked in the mid-1960s, and began to wane by the late 1960s. The movement's decline was related to internal dissension within the movement and the rise of a white southern backlash. As the most important social movement of the twentieth century, however, this civil rights movement served as the model for the activities of many other groups to gain equality.

Summary

1. **How has the Supreme Court's attitude toward the civil rights of African Americans evolved?**

   - Civil rights issues concern the protection of all persons in historically disadvantaged groups from discriminatory action, but the struggle for civil rights in the United States is most often associated with African Americans.

   - The Supreme Court embraced the concept of slavery in the *Dred Scott* case.

   - The Court approved the doctrine of segregation in *Plessy v. Ferguson.*

   - The concept of de jure equality was recognized in the *Brown* decision.

   - Today, the Court struggles with the concept of affirmative action.

2. **How have other minority groups benefited from the civil rights struggles of African Americans?**

   - The civil rights struggles of African Americans have served as a road map for other groups in terms of tactics and inspiration.

   - Other disadvantaged groups such as Native Americans, Hispanic Americans, Asian Americans, disabled Americans, American seniors, and gay and lesbian Americans

   have used the civil rights tactics of litigation and social protest employed by African Americans as a template for their own struggles for equality.

   - The Court has used different interpretations of the equal protection clause of the Fourteenth Amendment to assess the unique problems faced by members of different groups, such as access for disabled persons, language and immigration issues for Hispanic groups, and homophobic attitudes faced by gays and lesbians.

3. **What was unique in women's struggles for civil rights in the United States?**

   - Women are the only other group besides African Americans whose struggles for equality led to massive social movements.

   - Their first movement led to disappointment when women were left out of the freedoms granted after the Civil War.

   - Decades later, a massive movement led to the Nineteenth Amendment granting the right to vote.

   - The most recent movement has included women under the protection of civil rights legislation and has opened up debates on workplace equity, sexual harassment, and military roles.

National Journal

Sotomayor and 'Disparate Impact'

Underlying Justice Sonia Sotomayor's most controversial decision as a circuit judge—her vote against 18 white firefighters (including one Hispanic) who were denied promotions on account of their race— is a painful conflict between two civil-rights principles that were once seen as complementary.

The first principle is the anti-discrimination ideal embodied by the original 1964 Civil Rights Act and by Dr. Martin Luther King Jr.'s dream of a nation where people "will not be judged by the color of their skin but by the content of their character." That ideal rejects intentional discrimination against—or preferences for—individuals based on race, creed, color, national origin, or sex, and calls instead for allocating opportunities based on individual ability and effort.

The second principle redefines "discrimination" to include the use by employers of any merit-based tests or other objective criteria for hiring or promotion that have a "disparate impact" on different ethnic groups—as almost all objective tests have.

Even employers who intend no discrimination can be held liable to ethnic groups that fare badly on their tests unless the employers can prove to the satisfaction of often-skeptical courts that the tests (or other selection criteria) are required by "business necessity."

The surest way for employers to avoid such disparate-impact liability has been to discard the anti-discrimination principle and allocate jobs and promotions in part on the basis of ethnicity, as detailed below.

In the firefighters' case, the city of New Haven, Conn., has defended its denial of promotions to the white firefighters, who had the highest scores on a test of job-related skills, as necessary to avoid a disparate-impact lawsuit by blacks. None of the African-Americans did well enough on the test to qualify for promotion.

Two Hispanic-American judges on the U.S. Court of Appeals for the 2nd Circuit—both appointed by President Clinton—took dramatically contrasting positions last year on the white firefighters' anti-discrimination lawsuit against the city.

A three-judge panel, which included Sotomayor, upheld, and adopted as its own, a federal District judge's ruling against the white firefighters. The panel set aside the anti-discrimination principle on the grounds that New Haven feared (among other things) that promoting the whites "would subject the city to public criticism" and would probably result in a disparate-impact lawsuit by blacks "that, for political reasons, the city did not want to defend."

So much for the anti-discrimination principle—not to mention President Obama's professed desire to find judges with "empathy" for, among others, wronged workers who sue employers and for people who invoke their "individual rights" against governments.

The other Clinton-appointed Hispanic judge, Jose Cabranes, was so disturbed when he learned of the panel's curiously "perfunctory disposition" that he sought to have it reconsidered by the full 2nd Circuit. He lost by a 7-6 vote. In a dissent for the six, Cabranes suggested that the case might involve "an unconstitutional racial quota or set-aside." He added:

"At its core, this case presents a straight-forward question: May a municipal employer disregard the results of a qualifying examination, which was carefully constructed to ensure race-neutrality, on the ground that the results of that examination yielded too many qualified applicants of one race and not enough of another?"

Back in 1971, when the Supreme Court first grafted disparate-impact rules onto the 1964 Civil Rights Act, they seemed to complement the anti-discrimination ideal.

The problems addressed by the 1971 decision were the difficulty of proving intent to discriminate and the fact that many companies—especially those employing blue-collar workers without college educations—were evading the 1964 act's ban on overt discrimination by using written tests designed less to measure job-related skills than to screen out blacks.

The Court's response was to rule that any test with a "disparate impact" on blacks—

> Indeed, the evidence in the New Haven case strongly suggests that racial politics was the city's main reason for snatching away the white firefighters' expected promotions, amid intense political pressure to give blacks a share.

meaning that disproportionate numbers had low scores—was presumed to be invalid unless required by "business necessity." Lack of intent to discriminate was no defense to such a disparate-impact suit. This remains the law today, although the Court and Congress have tinkered with the detailed rules.

Over the ensuing decades, fewer and fewer employers have engaged in intentional racial discrimination against blacks or Hispanics. Likewise, the objective tests used by employers—including the New Haven fire department's written and oral promotional exams—have been more and more carefully designed to be valid measures of job-related skills.

Two things have remained constant, however. First, blacks and, to a lesser extent, Hispanics, score markedly lower on average than whites and Asians on objective tests of job-related skills—whether for firefighter, police officer, manufacturing worker, or other blue-collar jobs.

This is what one might expect in a nation still plagued by vastly unequal educational opportunities and academic performance. Studies show, for example, that on average, the math and reading levels of black 17-year-olds are no higher than those of whites and Asians in the eighth grade. And the gap is not closing.

The second constant is the reluctance of employers either to risk the expense and bad publicity of a disparate-impact suit—no matter how unwarranted—or to gamble on their ability to prove job-relatedness and business necessity to the satisfaction of whichever judge they may draw.

Some judges seem to indulge the elitist fantasy that the knowledge measured by objective tests has little to do with non-college-educated workers' ability to perform well in positions such as fire lieutenant. Other judges stress—with more validity—that objective tests cannot measure such subjective assets as leadership ability.

For these reasons, fear of disparate-impact suits has prompted many employers either to do away with objective tests entirely or to use racial preferences insofar as necessary to hire and promote more low-scoring minorities, or both.

New Haven's decision not to promote the high-scoring white firefighters was a variation on this theme. Local civil service rules—designed to avoid the awarding of promotions based on personal or political favoritism—would not allow the city to promote low-scoring blacks. So the city decided not to promote the high-scoring whites either, even at the cost of leaving many officer positions vacant for years.

The disparate-impact dynamic has the benefit of expanding opportunities for preferred minorities. But it also has great costs. It is unjust to high-scoring white and Asian workers; it has greatly eroded the anti-discrimination principle; and it downgrades incentives for students and workers to study and learn—both in school and in rigorous test-preparation courses such as the one that helped some New Haven firefighters improve their skills and do well on the test.

That is a most unhealthy message to be sending to blue-collar families at a time when America's competitiveness is being crippled by the inferior educations of many of our high school graduates compared with those in other developed countries.

Professed fear of disparate-impact lawsuits can also provide excuses for government employers that want to discriminate against white workers. Why would they want to do that? The main reason is identity politics—for which some believe Sotomayor has expressed sympathy.

Indeed, the evidence in the New Haven case strongly suggests that racial politics was the city's main reason for snatching away the white firefighters' expected promotions, amid intense political pressure to give blacks a share.

Even the Obama Justice Department found fault, in a friend-of-the-court brief, with the failure of Sotomayor and her colleagues to question whether the city's professed concern about disparate-impact liability "may be a pretext" for racial politics. But the brief also argued that the city should prevail in any further proceedings if it can show a reasonable basis for fearing that it might lose a disparate-impact suit.

In any event, such reverse racial discrimination will persist—and perhaps become ever more pervasive—for as long as employers fear disparate-impact liability more than they fear liability for intentional discrimination against whites and Asians.

The five more conservative Supreme Court justices, who value the anti-discrimination principle more than their liberal colleagues do, are well aware of this. They seem likely to reverse the decision by Sotomayor and her panel colleagues in the New Haven case and rule for the high-scoring white firefighters. In the process, they may also make it easier for employers who intend no discrimination to fend off disparate-impact lawsuits in the future, the better to reduce the incentives for reverse discrimination against whites and Asians.

But in the long run, soon-to-be-Justice Sotomayor and other judicial nominees chosen by Obama and his successors will be the people who determine whether the anti-discrimination principle and Dr. King's dream will live on, or whether they will be swept into the dustbin of history.

For Discussion:

■ How would you decide the New Haven firefighters case if you were a Supreme Court justice? Why? What constitutional issues are at play? What competing imperatives of civil rights are involved?

■ What does the author mean by "identity politics" (paragraph 24)? Why does he view such politics or practices as inherently negative? Do you agree? Why or why not?

■ Based on this piece, do you think disparate impact has a positive or an adverse effect on civil rights? Do you agree with the author that it engenders "reverse racial discrimination"? What are some possible flaws in his argument?

6

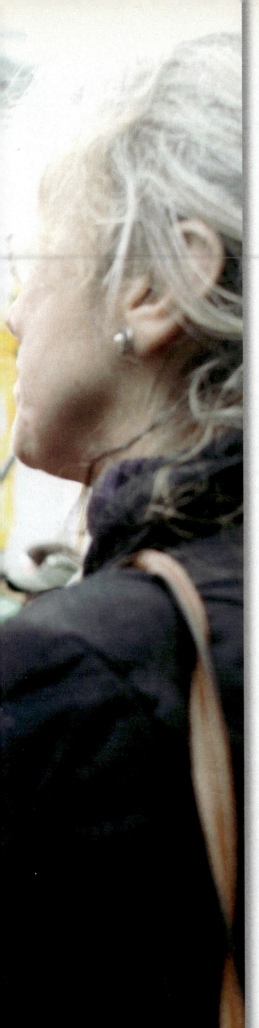

PUBLIC OPINION

DIVIDED WE STAND ▌ In 2008, voters told pollsters they wanted political leaders to overcome political gridlock and work together to solve the nation's pressing problems. Barack Obama was the beneficiary of this sentiment and he promised to bring red states and blue states together. Two years later, dissatisfied with the solutions he offered, voters handed the president a stunning defeat, replacing his Democratic majority in the House and reducing his party's strength in the Senate. On the eve of the next presidential election, Americans were more divided than ever.

One indication of this division is reflected in the emergent gap in presidential approval ratings between Democrats and Republicans.[1] But the growing partisan divide is also evident on a host of issues. Democrats support raising taxes on the wealthy to eliminate deficits; Republicans oppose it. Nearly three-quarters of Democrats worry a great deal about global warming as opposed to only a third of Republicans. Seventy percent of Democrats believe the new health-care reform law will improve health care in America; only 11 percent of Republicans feel that way. A study conducted by the Pew Center for the People & the Press reported that partisan fissures across 48 value questions on the role of government in the economy, the power of the federal government, business regulation, and the social safety net have widened, with the average difference between the opinions of Democrats and Republicans growing from 9 percent in 1997 to a new high of 16 percent by 2009.[2]

What accounts for the growing partisan gap in public opinion and what are its implications for the country? There is widespread disagreement about the answers to these questions.

Some blame the growing partisan gulf on party elites and campaign officials who promote extreme positions designed to appeal to devout followers. Modern campaigns increasingly utilize **focus groups**—small gatherings of individuals assembled by public opinion experts to test ideas prior to marketing—to frame messages designed to attract media attention and to drive their most ardent supporters to the polls. Since both major parties use these tactics to mobilize their ideological bases, independent and moderate voters often find themselves with few choices other than swinging back and forth between the seemingly extreme alternatives offered to them at election time.[3] Others believe partisan divisions reflect a geographic reassortment of the American public, with liberal Democrats and conservative Republicans living in more homogeneous communities that reinforce existing beliefs, making residents less likely to engage with voters from a different party or adapt to different viewpoints.[4] Some attribute partisan divisions ➦

As You READ >>

- What is public opinion and why is it important?
- How is opinion best measured and how do we know these measures are reliable?
- What are some of the most basic features of American public opinion today?

to the fragmentation of the media since viewers can now tune into news and opinion shows that simply fuel their own biases.[5] Still others believe the trend is actually a healthy consequence of political parties taking responsibility for sharpening their differences in order to offer voters clear choices. Each of these theories commands some empirical support, and it is likely that the state of public opinion in America today is the result of some combination of all of these factors.

Despite these sharp divisions in opinion, most Americans tell pollsters they are not satisfied with the current state of affairs. All but the most avid partisans are unhappy with the gridlock produced by the current partisan environment and overwhelmingly agree that Democrats and Republicans should work together to find common ground in solving the nation's problems. This is a paradoxical situation since many of the divisions we ask our leaders to rise above reflect real divisions among the public at large.

Public support is a valuable commodity for political leaders and one that they spend a great deal of effort and money attempting to influence. As citizens, it is important for us to filter out, as best we can, the politics from the policy and to advocate for those positions we support. In this chapter, we will explore how public opinions are formed and measured as well as the features of American public opinion today. ◆

Public opinion has become increasingly polarized in recent years on a host of issues, some of which sparked confrontations between citizenship groups throughout the country.

UNDERSTANDING PUBLIC OPINION IN THE CONTEXT OF AMERICAN POLITICS

It seems logical that a nation founded on the consent of the governed should recognize and respect the opinions of the people. However, what is less clear is exactly what opinions policymakers should pay attention to, how that opinion is to be gauged, and how political leaders should accommodate it. Should policymakers be more responsive to the opinions of a majority of their constituents, even if ill informed, or to a minority of knowledgeable and better educated civic and business leaders, or **elites**? Over the years, the ways in which opinion has been valued, measured, and utilized have changed dramatically.

The Nature of Public Opinion

Political scientist V. O. Key, Jr., once defined **public opinion** as "those opinions held by private persons which governments find it prudent to heed."[6] Key's definition points out certain essential aspects of public opinion. First, public opinion attaches itself to issues of public, rather than private, concern. Of course, the dividing line between private and public life is fluid and often contentious. Most Americans view sexual behavior as a private matter, but public debate over a woman's right to have an abortion continues unabated.

Second, public opinion sets boundaries on the type and expanse of policy proposals that citizens find acceptable. These boundaries reflect a respect for historical precedent and institutional arrangements, as well as for the political culture that informs our democratic republic.[7] A people's **political culture** is its historically rooted values and beliefs about government. Our political culture emphasizes support for the values of liberty, individualism, equality of opportunity, and private property.[8] Although policy boundaries are flexible, especially with regard to how we practice our dominant values, these values structure the types of solutions that Americans are most willing to support. For example, unlike societies such as Sweden that provide extensive "cradle-to-grave" government services, American political culture supports a far more limited government role in meeting individual needs such as health care and income security. As a result, we provide limited social support for those who demonstrate need, rather than blanket coverage for all citizens.

Third, Key's definition suggests that it might be more important for the government to heed the opinions of some citizens rather than those of others. The public is composed of various groups of individuals, some of whom are more visible to political leaders or more attentive to certain issues at particular times. When considering health-care reform, for example, political leaders are especially attentive to the views of health-care professionals, such as doctors. Physicians not only have expertise in this matter but are also likely to react intensely to changes that adversely affect their practice, and they can mount substantial opposition to measures they deem ill conceived. Similarly, the elderly, who consume more health-care dollars, are more likely to be attentive to changes in health care than young people, who are more concerned about other issues.

Finally, opinion is different from judgment. Opinions can sometimes reflect momentary feelings based on little reflection. Judgments form slowly over time with the infusion of information and thought. That is why there sometimes appears to be a difference between "overnight polls" that are taken by media outlets in response to events, such as presidential speeches, and long-term support for the policies of the chief executive. Effective leaders understand this difference and are more likely to react to settled judgments than to momentary bursts of opinion.

> **focus groups** Small gatherings of individuals used to test ideas before marketing.
>
> **elites** Individuals in a position of authority, often those with a higher level of education than the population at large.
>
> **public opinion** Opinions held by private individuals that governments find it prudent to heed.
>
> **political culture** The dominant values and beliefs of a political community.

Changes in Assessing and Using Public Opinion

The Framers felt that the opinions of common people were best limited to expression at the ballot box. In *The Federalist* No. 71, Alexander Hamilton wrote:

> The republican principle demands that the deliberative sense of the community should guide the conduct of those to whom they entrust the management of their affairs; but it does not require an unqualified complaisance to every sudden breeze of passion, or to every transient impulse which the people may receive from the arts of men, who flatter their prejudices to betray their interest. . . .[9]

Fear of faction and mob rule caused colonial leaders to be suspicious of popular attitudes. Nevertheless, political leaders were never indifferent to public attitudes. George Washington corresponded with a friend in Virginia, David Stuart, whom he relied on to mingle with ordinary people in order to find out what they thought about presidential actions.[10] And presidents have always spent time "pressing flesh" to engender support and good feelings.

Before the era of scientific polling, political leaders attempted to gauge popular support from a variety of sources. Newspaper reports and editorials provided officials with some measure of information regarding popular attitudes. In the era of the party press (see Chapter 10), however, few reports were objective. From Jackson through Lincoln, it

Public figures seldom pass up the opportunity to "press the flesh" to gain firsthand knowledge of public opinion.

was common for presidents to curry favor with journalists and editors by appointing them to government offices.[11] When the partisan press gave way to the commercial press in the second half of the nineteenth century, politicians paid close attention to opinions conveyed in newspapers printed in their home districts. They also often attempted to influence press coverage of their campaigns. Members of Congress sent newsletters to constituents extolling their skills at representation, and these were often simply reprinted verbatim in local newspapers.

Party leaders in wards and precincts could sometimes predict election results with uncanny accuracy—a result of both their proximity to average citizens and their ability to turn out those who supported their candidate. In some cases, informal polls were conducted by party leaders at political rallies among partisan supporters with predictable results duly reported to cheering crowds.

A variety of ad hoc methods of sampling also produced often surprisingly ac-

Hot or Not?

Should political leaders allow poll results to influence their decisions?

curate portraits of public opinion. Tavern owners placed "poll books" in their establishments, where townspeople could register their preferences. **Straw polls**, which sampled opinions from lists of experts, journalists, or subscribers to particular newspapers or consumer services, became popular at the turn of the twentieth century.[12] The *Literary Digest* magazine conducted perhaps the most famous of these polls, mailing millions of ballots to people from across the country from lists generated by automobile registration records and telephone directories. Despite the unscientific nature of its poll, the *Digest* accurately picked presidential winners in 1924, 1928, and 1932. In 1936, the magazine's luck ran out when it predicted an electoral victory for Alf Landon; it went out of the polling business shortly thereafter.[13]

That same year, George Gallup issued his first scientifically designed presidential election poll, based on emerging marketing research techniques. After accurately predicting Franklin D. Roosevelt's win, Gallup's newly created American Institute of Public Opinion quickly became a world leader in survey research, conducting weekly polls for a number of newspapers across the country. Gallup did not intend that politicians should slavishly follow survey results, however, and many did not. In the decades that followed, many political leaders advanced policies well beyond the mainstream of public opinion by advocating bold initiatives in areas such as race relations and civil liberties. For these public opinion leaders, polls provided not so much a road map for political success as a way of gauging how far they could advance reforms before facing serious resistance.

Today, survey research is ubiquitous. Hardly a day goes by when we do not hear about one poll or another regarding almost every aspect of life, from health care to fashion to politics. Survey research can aid in making life more enjoyable and bringing public policies more in line with public sentiment. However, it can also be used to manipulate preferences and behavior. More than ever, citizens must be able to navigate their way through polls and to understand the nature and limits of public opinion in a democracy.

HOW POLITICAL OPINIONS ARE FORMED

Individuals develop opinions about the political world from a host of sources, including family, friends, schools, and the media. We form many of the enduring attitudes, values, and beliefs that shape our opinions early in life through a process called **political socialization**. Even so, we constantly form new opinions and revise old ones as we confront new issues, new people, and new technologies.

The Process of Socialization

Pioneering studies in the 1950s and 1960s demonstrated that children begin forming impressions about the political communities in which they live as early as preschool age.[14] They embrace national symbols, such as the flag, and associate authority figures like police and firefighters with the protective functions of government. Impressions at this stage are fairly positive, although the strength of these sentiments may vary among subcultures and minority populations.[15] Children also develop an awareness of national, racial, and gender differences in early grade school, along with friendly or hostile feelings

toward specific groups. Even at this early stage, gender differences seem to appear regarding issues of war and peace, with boys more likely than girls to support military options.[16]

As children approach adolescence, they become more skeptical of political authority, begin differentiating between leaders they like and those they dislike, and learn to distinguish between the major political parties. Much of their awareness remains impressionistic at this stage. It is only with late adolescent maturity that we come to associate issue and party positions with particular ideological viewpoints, such as liberalism or conservatism. Many of the political opinions we develop in youth have sticking power. This is especially true for party identification, but less so concerning specific issues, which are more subject to reformulation over time.[17]

Civic education has a strong impact on increasing knowledge and interest in politics among young adults.[18] Young people who take courses in government, or who engage in student government opportunities in high school, are more likely to be politically active as adults.[19]

Political outlook and behavior can change as we age. Some of the age differences in politics are the result of **life cycle effects**, or changes in our life circumstances. As people age, they accumulate more property and political knowledge. They settle into community life and become

straw poll An unscientific survey of popular views.

political socialization The process by which individuals come to adopt the attitudes, values, beliefs, and opinions of their political culture.

life cycle effects The impact of age-related factors in the formation of political attitudes, opinions, and beliefs.

. . . That George Washington did not, as a little boy, chop down a cherry tree and then confess to his father that he had done it, for "I cannot tell a lie"? The story was invented by a Virginia clergyman known as Parson Mason Locke Weems, as part of a highly successful effort to enshrine Washington as a blameless hero in the American historical memory.

Did You Know?

more aware of their material self-interest. As a result, they are more likely to participate in the political system.

Other age-related differences are not as predictable. Known as **generational effects**, they result from unique issues and events confronting each **cohort**, or generation, at a time when its political identity is being forged.[20] For the generation that grew up in the 1950s and 1960s, the civil rights movement served as a catalyst for civic activism and spurred support for the expansion of individual rights and freedoms. Growing toleration is even more evident for a generation that has come of age politically during the administration of the first African American president in the nation's history. Studies show, for example, that Millennials are far are less interested than their elders in " 'identity politics' that distinguishes one group from another (by race, gender, religion, sexual orientation) and more inter-

ested in making room for everyone in a broad American middle."[21]

Agents of Political Socialization

A number of cultural and institutional forces shape and mold our opinions over a lifetime. Their relative impact on our political maturation depends on when, how long, and how strongly we are exposed to them. Families, for instance, have the greatest impact on political socialization because of our intense interactions with family members during our formative years.[22]

Family Families help to shape our interest in politics, our party affiliation, and the attitudes we hold toward others in society. Our first memories of political events often come from family members expressing their own political viewpoints. For example, many who grew up in Democratic households during the Clinton era recall hearing about economic prosperity and budget surpluses. Children of Republicans at that time are more likely to have heard about the Monica Lewinsky scandal. These early memories carry an emotional weight that we often express in adulthood by adopting the party preferences of our parents.

Parental influence is far wider than partisan affiliation alone. According to a recent study, young people whose parents discuss politics regularly in the home are more likely to exhibit trust in government, feel a greater sense of political efficacy, believe in the importance of voting, and volunteer their time.[23] Three-quarters of young people who grew up with political discussion in the home are registered to vote, compared with only 57 percent of those who grew up in households without political discussion. And children who accompany their parents to the polling place on Election Day are far more likely to develop the habit of voting themselves. It is no wonder that children of politically active families often follow in the footsteps of their parents.

Educational Institutions Early experiences in school tend to encourage support for our political system and its underlying values. Tales about George Washington and the cherry tree, and daily recitation of the Pledge of Allegiance, are intended to build positive feelings toward the government and its leaders. Middle- and high-school education fills in a little more detail of American history; but it is only in college, when most students are exposed to extensive study of our nation's

Voting, like any habit, is most enduring if developed early.

past, warts and all, that they form their own opinions about our republic. To a greater degree than many others around the world, our educational system emphasizes egalitarian themes and encourages support for equal opportunities. Unlike some European countries, such as Germany, that provide different educational tracks for the college and noncollege bound, American schools tend to provide similar educational paths for all students.

Variations in political attitudes between those who attend college and those who do not reveal important differences that higher education can make. Compared to peers who have some college experience, young adults who do not attend college—or do not intend to go to college—express less trust in government, are more likely to see politics as the business of elites rather than average citizens, are less likely to believe their votes count, and are less likely to believe that political leaders are interested in their problems. Race complicates the picture. African Americans at all levels of education express more pessimism than whites about politics in general and about their ability to bring about meaningful change.[24] This may change as more black leaders like Barack Obama overcome obstacles to seeking high office.

Religious Institutions Americans are among the most religious people in the world, as measured by expressed belief in God and attendance at church services. America's religious preferences are also more diverse than those of any other nation. Eighty-four percent of Americans claim affiliation in one of 21 major denominations or in one of the scores of minor church assemblies across the nation. In recent years, increasing numbers of Americans have described themselves as non-Christians or claimed no particular religious belief.[25] Still, the number of those who consider themselves religious and who attend services is quite high. Slightly more females than males consider themselves religious and attend services regularly.

There is little racial integration within denominations. Only 9 of the 21 largest denominations have black membership of 10 percent or higher, demonstrating the familiar refrain that "Sunday morning service is the most segregated hour in America." Hispanics, by contrast, attend services with white Catholics.

There are significant differences in party affiliation by denomination. Mormons and evangelical Protestant congregations, including Southern Baptists and Pentecostals, heavily favor the Republican Party. Mainline Protestants such as Episcopalians and Presbyterians are fairly evenly divided by party. High turnout among conservative evangelicals proved to be a powerful force for Republicans in recent elections. White evangelical Christians supported John McCain over Barack Obama in 2008 by three to one. Latino Protestants trend Democratic, while black Protestants are overwhelmingly in the Democratic camp. Although Catholics have drifted away from the Democratic Party, a plurality still call themselves Democrats. While a majority of Catholics overall supported Obama over McCain, the reverse held true for white Catholics. Support for the Democratic Party is far stronger among both black and Latino Catholics. Smaller Christian congregations skew Republican, while Jews and members of minority religions continue a long tradition of support for the Democrats. Among the growing number of those expressing no particular religious affiliations, Democrats outnumber Republicans.

Churches are important training grounds for learning civic skills, as we will see in Chapter 7. They provide opportunities to learn organizing and management skills that can be useful in the political realm. Organizing a church outing or social gathering is not much different from helping to plan a political meeting or rally. For the poor and for minorities, churches provide a venue for acquiring civic skills that is often unavail-

generational effects The impact of events experienced by a generational cohort on the formation of common political orientations.

cohort The members of one's own generation.

Party Affiliation of Various Religious Groups

% Republican / Lean Republican
% Democrat / Lean Democrat

	% Rep	% Dem
Total	35	47
Mormon	65	22
Evangelical churches	50	34
Mainline churches	41	43
Orthodox	35	50
Catholic	33	48
Jewish	24	66
Unaffiliated	23	55
Buddhist	18	66
Hindu	13	63
Muslim	11	63
Hist. black churches	10	77
Jehovah's Witness	10	15

Source: Pew Forum on Religion and Public Life, U.S. Religious Landscape Survey (Washington, DC, June 2008), 208.

able elsewhere due to limited educational and workplace opportunities.[26]

Voluntary Associations The connection between activity in voluntary associations and political engagement is less clear. For example, although college students support voluntarism in their communities, they do not regularly discuss politics and they express little interest in getting involved politically, with the possible exception of voting.[27] Often, young adults see community activism and political activism as separate domains. Those who are active politically are less likely to volunteer on a weekly basis, and those who volunteer are half as likely to be registered to vote or to take part in political activities.[28] This lack of close connection raises questions about the value of service learning for fostering political engagement. Volunteering also has little impact on increasing a general sense of trust in others, one of the elements of social capital (discussed in Chapter 1) that serves to bind members of the political community together. Instead, it increases trust only with others we perceive to be like ourselves.[29]

Media Because we hold preexisting opinions and points of view, it is difficult to disentangle the effects of media messages from the impact of other socializing agents. Although the media pervade every facet of our lives, most researchers believe the media have a minimal effect on our political views.[30] The source of one's political information, however, does seem to determine how politically informed one is. It should come as no surprise that those who get their news from newspapers (or newspaper websites) seem to be better informed than the almost two-thirds of the American public who rely on television as their major news source.[31] Newspapers provide longer, more detailed coverage of events and issues. Nevertheless, a recent study found that a large percentage of highly knowledgeable Americans turned to *The Daily Show*, *The Colbert Report*, and *PBS NewsHour* for their news.[32] Of course, it is hard to know whether they are knowledgeable because of these sources or whether they turn to these sources because they are knowledgeable. Young people are more likely to turn to the Internet for news. With the explosion in media outlets, we also see more self-selection based on one's political point of view. Conservative viewers are more likely to tune to FOX, liberals to CNN and PBS. Conservatives log on to WorldNetDaily, liberals to Daily Kos.

The media may impact our beliefs and attitudes in subtle ways. News and entertainment shows alike, for example, often communicate negative stereotypes about the political process, making it seem inherently corrupt and portraying political leaders as untrustworthy. News programs afford political scandals an inordinate amount of coverage, and late-night comics incessantly poke fun at national leaders. Our views about other races may be influenced by the way television news portrays them. For example, one study found that white viewers exposed to local news coverage of crime on television had more negative attitudes toward African Americans and expressed greater support for punitive measures against those convicted of crime.[33]

News and entertainment shows frequently poke fun at national leaders. Does this impact the way we think about politics?

GROUP DIFFERENCES IN POLITICAL OPINIONS

We all go through life assembling a variety of group identifications that make a difference in the views we hold. While we can decide to join a fraternity or sorority or play on a softball team, we cannot make choices regarding other aspects of our identity, including race, ethnic background, gender, and area of the country where we are born. The life experiences associated with given group identities generate interesting political differences across America's diverse population.

Racial and Ethnic Identity

African Americans, who make up about 12 percent of the U.S. population, generally are more liberal on domestic political issues than whites. They express much stronger support for government enforcement of civil rights and government action to aid the poor. They favor educational quotas and preferences for blacks in hiring and promotion by a four-to-one margin over white respondents.[34] They also express greater support than whites for a national health-care system and for a more progressive tax system that would redistribute the wealth more equitably among individuals.

Most Hispanic Americans are Catholics and are strongly opposed to abortion. They also desire to preserve their cultural heritage, which is reflected in their support of bilingual education in the public schools. The Hispanic American population is itself quite diverse, however, with each subgroup reflecting the strong influence of its country of origin. Cuban Americans have long expressed distrust of the communist regime in Cuba because many families fled to the United States after Fidel Castro assumed power in 1959. However, this attitude is changing somewhat among younger Cuban Americans. Puerto Ricans and Mexican Americans hold opinions similar to African Americans, especially in support of social welfare and antidiscrimination policies.

Asian Americans also display a wide variety of national origins, yet very little research is available about variation of political opinions among these groups.[35] The same is true regarding the views of Native Americans, who are in many ways the least visible ethnic group in America because nearly half live in enclaves known as reservations. A long history of displacement, discrimination, and broken promises by federal authorities has produced high levels of cynicism and distrust of government among Native Americans.

Gender

For many years, social scientists claimed that there were few differences in political attitudes and opinions between males and females. That viewpoint changed when researchers discovered a significant **gender gap** in the 1980 presidential election. Women voted about equally for Ronald Reagan and Jimmy Carter, but men favored Reagan by 19 percentage points. As discussed in other chapters, this gender gap has persisted nearly unabated in both voting behavior and party preference ever since.

Gender differences characterize opinions on specific issues as well. As the table below indicates, women are much less likely than men to support policies involving force, violence, and aggression. They are much less likely to support the death penalty, more likely to favor stricter gun control laws, and somewhat less likely to support an increase in military spending. Gender differences also exist concerning attitudes toward health care, good jobs, and helping the poor. Women express more support for government programs in

> **gender gap** Systematic variation in political opinions that exists between males and females.

Gender Differences in Political Opinions

Opinion Force, Violence, and Aggression	Men	Women Percent	Difference
Want stricter gun control laws*	42	60	18
Favor death penalty for those convicted of murder*	76	62	14
Spend too much on national defense**	30	39	9
Compassion			
Government should see to good jobs/standard of living***	23	31	8
Government should provide more services***	37	45	8
Government should provide health care for sick**	40	49	9
Government definitely or probably should help reduce differences between rich and poor**	19	23	4

* Gallup 2007 (See Lydia Said, "Shrunken Majority Now Favors Stricter Gun Laws," October 11, 2007. www.gallup.com/poll/101731 accessed April 27, 2008. Frank Newport, "Sixty-nine-Percent of Americans Support Death Penalty," www.gallup.com/poll/101863 accessed April 27, 2011.
** GSS 2006.
***ANES 2008.

all of these areas than do men. These attitudes may well stem from differences in early socialization. Studies reveal that adults accept or even encourage aggression as part of the socialization of young boys, whereas they discourage such behavior in young girls.[36]

Women also exhibit less interest in and engagement with politics than their male counterparts.[37] A recent study by Verba, Burns, and Schlozman found that these differences persisted even after controlling for occupation, education, and access to political resources.[38] There is one interesting exception to this pattern: political engagement among women is higher in states having a female U.S. senator or a female governor than in states where women do not hold these visible elective offices. Some observers conclude that the lack of political interest among women may be tied to the scarcity of role models.

Variation in Political Culture Among the States

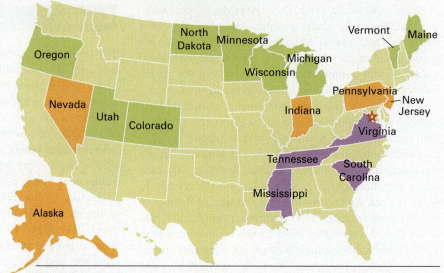

Moralistic Dominant **I**ndividualistic Dominant **T**raditionalistic Dominant

Source: Compiled from Daniel Elazar, *American Federalism: A View from the States,* 3rd Ed. (New York: Harper Collins, 1984).

Geography

Geography also plays a part in explaining differences in political opinions. Southerners, for example, tend to be somewhat more conservative, are more supportive of our military, and—along with Midwesterners—express greater pride in being an American than those who live in the Northeast or on the West Coast.[39] Some political scientists, such as Daniel Elazar, believe that these differences can be traced to regional or even state-by-state variations in political culture. According to Elazar, three strains of American political culture characterize most states: individualistic, moralistic, and traditionalistic. The remainder of the states are considered hybrids, although scholars believe one of the three major political cultures dominates each.

The *individualistic political culture* emphasizes the concept of limited government instituted primarily for the purposes of safety and security. Government should protect the marketplace but not attempt to impose its own definition of a so-called good society and the costs associated with achieving it. A *moralistic political culture* envisions an active and committed citizenry working in partnership with government to achieve the collective goals of the community. It sees government service as a noble calling demanding the high-est level of personal conduct. A *traditionalistic political culture* values established moral principles and accepts a limited role for government in protecting them. It supports a hierarchical view of society in which established elites play a dominant role.[40]

One can argue that changes in communications and transportation have created a more uniform national culture today. We all tend to watch the same TV shows, listen to the same music, and eat at the same fast-food outlets, no matter where we live. Millions of Americans move from one state or region to another each year. Nevertheless, regional variation, as evidenced by differences in ideology and party identification, is very real. As we will see in coming chapters, southern states have become increasingly conservative and Republican, while the Northeast has become more liberal and Democratic. And there are many states undergoing continuing change.

MEASURING PUBLIC OPINION

Making meaningful assessments about public opinion requires an understanding of the dimensions around which opinions form as well as accurate ways of measuring them. Simply knowing that an individual prefers one candidate over another tells us little about the individual's probable behavior in an upcoming election or the person's reasons for holding that view. Only when pollsters apply system-

direction The attribute of an individual's opinion that indicates a preference for or against a particular issue.

salience The attribute of an individual's opinion that indicates how central it is to her or his daily concerns.

intensity The attribute of an individual's opinion that measures how strongly it is held.

atic methods to measure and sample opinions can the results of a poll give us some measure of confidence about what the public is thinking.

Dimensions of Public Opinion

When legitimate pollsters ask for our views, they usually attempt to peer beneath the surface of our opinions. They seek to know not only what we believe but also how strongly we believe it, how long we have held that view, the grounds on which we base that belief, how important that belief is to us, and what we might be prepared to do about it. Together, these elements make up the various dimensions of public opinion.

The term **direction** refers to an individual's preference with respect to a particular issue. Does the respondent favor the Democrat or the Republican for president? Does he favor or oppose gay marriage? This is the dimension of an opinion that the sponsor of the poll reports most often. **Salience** is the importance we attach to an issue or topic about which we are asked. Conservation may be an issue we are prepared actively to lobby and work to promote, or we may think about the matter only when a pollster asks about it. **Intensity** consists of how strongly an individual holds a particular preference on an issue. This dimension is important because people are more likely to act on opinions they hold intensely.

The term **stability** refers to how consistently an individual maintains a particular preference over time. Americans have had stable views about the death penalty but unstable opinions about foreign policy issues. This is understandable because beliefs about crime and punishment change slowly; our views about foreign policy are tied to changing world events. The dimension of **informational support** tells us how well-informed the respondent is regarding an opinion. When a person responds to a multiple-choice question, we have no way of knowing whether he or she is reacting to the question from a basis of knowledge or ignorance. For example, many individuals incorrectly believe that it is a crime to burn the American flag. A person who has little or no information about a subject may readily change his or her opinion when supplied with accurate information.

Types of Polls

Political campaigns employ a wide variety of polls and surveys. Campaigns often conduct **benchmark surveys** at the time a candidate enters a politi-

cal race. These surveys measure the public's knowledge and assessment of the candidate at that point in time. **Trial heat surveys** pair competing candidates and ask citizens whom they would vote for in such a contest. **Tracking polls** supply the most current information on a race by polling on a daily basis. These polls allow campaigns to change their strategies on a moment's notice to respond to the latest changes in public sentiment. Such polls often interview one hundred people a day for four days and then report the totals. On the fifth day, pollsters interview an additional one hundred people whose responses become part of the total, while the one hundred responses from the first day are dropped. Respondents are subsequently added and dropped on a rotating basis for the length of the poll. *USA Today* reports tracking poll results in the presidential contest for several months before the election.

A **push poll**, the most notorious of campaign polls, is really a campaign tactic disguised as a poll. Campaign workers contact voters to provide them with negative information about their opponent and then ask the voters questions about that candidate. The goal is not to secure accurate information but to influence attitudes. Finally, **exit polls** survey voters as they leave polling places. These polls help campaign professionals analyze demographic factors that influence election outcomes. These types of polls generally are accurate but do experience occasional problems. In the

stability The attribute of an individual's opinion that measures how consistently it is held.

informational support The attribute of an individual's opinion that measures his or her amount of knowledge concerning the issue.

benchmark survey A campaign poll that measures a candidate's strength at the time of entrance into the electoral race.

trial heat survey A campaign poll that measures the popularity of competing candidates in a particular electoral race.

tracking polls Campaign polls that measure candidates' relative strength on a daily basis.

push poll Campaign tactic that attacks an opponent while pretending to be a poll.

exit poll Interviews of voters as they leave the polling place.

get involved!

Conduct an opinion poll of students in your class on an issue confronting your campus. First, try surveying a randomized selection by using a table of random numbers (found in most statistics texts). Then check the results by asking the entire class. (The larger the class, the better.) How closely does the sample track the results of the class as a whole? Before you begin, be sure to pretest the questions so that you can remove any bias or ambiguity.

One of the most embarrassing moments for election pollsters came in 1948 when they predicted Republican Thomas E. Dewey would defeat President Harry Truman. Truman won, but newspapers giving the victory to Dewey had already been printed. Here Truman holds an example.

2000 presidential election, for example, the major media networks initially cited erroneous exit poll results that awarded the state of Florida to Al Gore.

POLLING TECHNIQUES

To be informed consumers of polls, we need to understand what makes a poll scientific and which techniques differentiate good polls from bad. What makes a poll reliable? What are some of the most common flaws and how can we spot them? What information should we be looking for in order to evaluate poll results? To avoid being misled, we need to know how the poll was conducted, who was surveyed, and what questions respondents were asked.

scientific polls Any poll using proper sampling designs.

sample The individuals whose opinions are actually measured.

population The people whose opinions are being estimated through interviews with samples of group members.

probability sampling A sample design showing that each individual in the population has a known probability of being included in the sample.

Who Is Asked? Selecting the Sample

Scientific polls use the mathematical laws of probability to ensure accuracy. These laws specify that we don't need to count every member of a population as long as we count a representative group within that population in a manner that isn't biased. For example, we don't need to count every green and red marble in a large container to know their relative proportions. So long as we select marbles in a random manner, a small sample can yield a very close approximation of the proportions in the entire container.

The individuals whose opinions pollsters measure constitute the **sample**. In a national presidential preference poll, the sample is likely to include between 1,000 and 1,200 respondents. The **population** consists of the larger group of people whose opinions the poll attempts to estimate by interviewing the selected sample. In the case of a presidential preference poll, for example, the population might be all citizens of voting age or likely voters throughout the United States.

In measuring our opinions, pollsters try to select samples that accurately represent the broader population from which they are drawn. All good sampling designs use **probability sampling**, in which each individual in the population has a known probability of being selected. One type of probability sampling, **simple random sampling**, gives everyone in a population an equal chance of being interviewed. In a pure random sample of Americans, each person interviewed would have roughly one chance out of three hundred million of being selected. Probability sampling avoids the kind of selection bias that affected the 1936 *Literary Digest* presidential poll. The sample for that poll included only people with automobiles or telephones at a time when a large percentage of potential voters possessed neither of these conveniences. Without using probability sampling, it is impossible for the pollster to know how closely the sample mirrors the overall population.

Simple random sampling, however, is not feasible in a country as vast as the United States. Even census data do not contain a complete and current list of all Americans. As a result, national pollsters use **systematic sampling** as a means of approximating the ideal. They begin with a universe of known telephone numbers, names, or locations. After picking the first number or name at random, they might make additional picks in a predetermined sequence. Some polls randomly select portions of the telephone number and append randomly selected digits to complete the number. As in pure random sampling, the goal is to approximate an equal chance of selection for every individual in the population.

Sampling error refers to a poll's degree of accuracy, usually expressed as a percentage. For example, in a population where every individual has the same chance of being selected, a poll of between 1,000 and 1,200 respondents yields a sampling error of only ±3 percent. That is, the results will deviate no more

Hot or Not?

Should pollsters be prohibited from making unsolicited calls to your cell phone?

Compare survey results on the same topic from a variety of sources—for example, presidential approval ratings. Select a sample of three or four national polls from such sources as *The New York Times*/CBS News, *The Washington Post*/ABC News, or *USA Today*/Gallup. Keep track of the differences in percentages reported and try to account for such differences by examining the number of persons sampled, the time period during which the poll was executed, and the wording and context of the questions asked.

Internet polling, which is extremely inexpensive and could be conducted by virtually anyone with access to the Web and some simple software. These polls, however, pose significant risks regarding accuracy. Many Internet surveys reflect the views of a highly selective portion of the population, since respondents must choose to log on to a particular site to participate.

Perhaps a more daunting challenge confronting pollsters is the growing number of people—especially young people—who no longer have landlines and do not list their cell phone numbers. Call screening technology also helps individuals avoid the sometimes prying questions of pollsters. Pollsters are currently testing new techniques to avoid systematically excluding the views of these individuals by, for example, adjusting the sample to reflect the known proportion of various groups in the general population before analyzing the results. The samples are "weighted" by region, party, age, race, religion, and gender. In other words, pollsters know the number of men and women in the population, for example, and use that information to adjust the sample if too many or too few women are in the sample. Some polling operations combine calls to landlines and cell phones along with Internet sampling, using complex formulas to approximate the makeup of the population at large.

simple random sampling Technique of drawing a sample for interview in which all members of the targeted population have the same probability of being selected for interview.

systematic sampling A sample design to ensure that each individual in the population has an equal chance of being chosen after the first name or number is chosen at random.

sampling error The measure of the degree of accuracy of a poll based on the size of the sample.

leading question A question worded to suggest a particular answer desired by the pollster.

than three percentage points in either direction from results that would be obtained if every person in the entire population were surveyed. Suppose, for example, that a poll of 1,000 people shows Candidate A leading Candidate B by a margin of 46 percent to 42 percent. This means that Candidate A's margin among the entire voting population is anywhere from 43 percent to 49 percent, and Candidate B's is anywhere from 39 percent to 45 percent. From that information, the pollster would be wise to conclude that the race is too close to call. Polls that survey fewer individuals have a higher sampling error rate. Polls of just a few hundred are sometimes used when the sponsor lacks the money or time to conduct a larger survey, or when there is an interest in the gross dimensions of opinion and the poll sponsor is willing to accept greater uncertainty about the results.

Until now, pollsters have usually conducted polls in person or on the telephone. This could change with the advent of

What Is Asked? Paying Attention to the Questions

A reliable poll must not only use good sampling techniques but also ask the kinds of questions that will accurately capture the respondent's true opinions. It should avoid asking **leading questions**, which are phrased in such a way as to produce a predetermined response. In the 1982 Democratic primary race for governor of Ohio, candidate Jerry Springer—who went on to become a television personality—was the target of a classic example of a leading question:

Leading questions skew poll results, as was the case when current TV host Jerry Springer ran for governor in Ohio.

As you may know, in 1974, Jerry Springer, who had gotten married six months earlier, was arrested on a morals charge with three women in a hotel room. He also used a bad check to pay for the women's services and subsequently resigned as mayor of his city. Does this make you much more likely, somewhat more likely, somewhat less likely, or much less likely to support Jerry Springer for governor this year?

Few persons responding to a survey want to admit that they are uninformed about an important or timely subject. As a result, they sometimes respond with **nonattitudes**, or uninformed responses to which they have given little thought. Nonattitudes are considered artificial opinions created by the poll.[41] A poll can at least partially avoid the problem of nonattitudes by screening for the respondent's level of knowledge or interest, and by making it socially acceptable for respondents to say they are unfamiliar with a particular issue or question. Question order is also important. It is easy to imagine that your initial response to a question that asks whether you favor free speech might be affected if it were preceded by a question asking whether you believe the government has a role in limiting the spread of child pornography.

nonattitudes Opinions generated by a poll that do not exist in reality.

political cynicism The view that government officials look out mostly for themselves.

THE CONTENT OF AMERICAN PUBLIC OPINION

How knowledgeable are Americans about political issues? Do Americans develop their opinions out of confidence and trust in government institutions? Do citizens believe that their opinions matter? Do Americans really believe in the implementation of democratic principles we often uncritically espouse? Let's take a closer look at the content of Americans' attitudes and beliefs.

Political Knowledge

For years, surveys have shown that Americans' political information levels have fallen short of the democratic ideal. In general, they display a lack of familiarity with political leaders and issues of the day. In a recent *Newsweek* poll, 29 percent of respondents couldn't name the vice president, 44 percent were unable to define the Bill of Rights, and 6 percent couldn't even circle Independence Day on a calendar.[42] As expected, however, this characterization does not hold for all Americans: those who are well educated, those with higher incomes, and those who are older are

quite knowledgeable about our political system and even about world politics. Young people are more knowledgeable about cultural matters and issues like education that most directly affect their lives (see chart below). Education is the strongest single predictor of political knowledge; better informed citizens "hold more opinions, have more stable opinions that are resistant to irrelevant or biased information . . . and have opinions that are more internally consistent with each other and with basic ideological alignments that define American politics."[43]

Some types of political knowledge are more widespread than others. Americans are better informed about institutions and processes of government than they are about people and players in the political arena. For example, they are more likely to know that the Speaker of the House is the individual who presides over floor debate in the House of Representatives than the name of the current House Speaker, John Boehner. This makes intuitive sense because political personnel change more frequently, and often with less fanfare, than political institutions.

Americans are generally poorly informed about global affairs. In one recent survey, Gallup found that only 2 in 10 Americans knew that the European Union (EU) is larger than the United States. Among those saying they knew a great deal or a fair amount about the EU, only 34 percent

Young People Know Founder of Facebook, That "No Child" Law Is About Education

Percent answering correctly...	18–29 %	30–49 %	50–64 %	65+ %
No Child Left Behind is about... (Education)	75	83	84	74
Founder of Facebook? (Mark Zuckerberg)	63	64	58	25
Hillary Clinton's job? (Secretary of State)	57	72	81	81
Wisconsin protests over? (Union rights)	46	59	76	67
Current unemployment rate? (9%)	38	56	65	64
Percentage of Americans who are obese? (25%)	36	36	43	44
Most U.S. elcectricity comes from... (Coal)	35	37	44	43
U.S. government spends most on... (Medicare)	29	28	27	37
Republicans have a majority in... (House)	26	36	46	42
Speaker of the House? (Boehner)	21	36	58	55
Sample size (N) =	128	246	340	260

Source: What Americans Know: 1987–2007, Public Knowledge of Current Affairs Little Changed by News and Information Revolutions (Washington, D.C.: Pew Center Research Center, March 17–20, 2011).

correctly said that the EU's population is larger than that of the United States.[44]

The pattern of limited political knowledge has been found to be quite stable over the last 50 years of survey research. The fact that educational levels have increased significantly over that period gives cause for concern since we would expect a more educated populace to be more politically sophisticated. However, Americans are able to acquire needed information when national or international crises focus their attention. For example, interest in world affairs spiked upward immediately following the September 11, 2001, terrorist attacks. A majority of Americans could identify the Muslim nations cooperating with the American war on terrorism, could name the countries sharing a border with Afghanistan, and knew the name of the new cabinet office, Homeland Security, created in the wake of the attacks. What's more, attention spurred by the attacks increased the level of interest in politics more generally for most Americans.[45] These results illustrate the fact that political learning is instrumental and reflects self-interest. Americans are able and willing to pay attention and to learn about government when they consider events important and when they are presented with a clear and steady stream of reliable information. Of course, political bias can also act as a filter that is sometimes impervious to correction by factual information. For example, many critics of President Obama continued to profess their doubts about his American citizenship even after he released his birth certificate as they had demanded.

Despite evidence to the contrary, many Americans continue to believe that Iraq played a direct role in the 9/11 attacks.

attacks. Today, only about half of all Americans express confidence in the president and Supreme Court while fewer than one in five have confidence in Congress.

Trust in Government

Trust in government, just like confidence, has fallen since the late 1960s. Trust consists of the belief that the people who run government genuinely have the best interests of the public in mind. Lack of trust is expressed as **political cynicism**, the view that government officials mostly look out for themselves. Trust in government declined significantly in the wake of the Watergate scandal, in which President Richard Nixon was accused of covering up a break-in at the Democratic Party headquarters during his 1972 reelection campaign. Nixon subsequently resigned from office rather than face possible impeachment. Public support for the congenial Ronald Reagan lifted trust briefly and modestly in the 1980s, and trust rose temporarily once again following the 9/11 terrorist attacks. Still, as the top figure on the next page demonstrates, trust in government remains low.

The decline in trust in government cuts across all demographic groups and ages. Although young people exemplified somewhat more confidence in government shortly after 9/11, by 2006, their levels of trust in government had fallen to levels comparable to their elders. Perhaps more disturb-

Confidence in Government Institutions

In 1966, a majority of the American public had a great deal of confidence in the people running major companies, the field of medicine, the military, the Supreme Court, and our educational system. More than 40 percent had a great deal of confidence in organized religion, Congress, and the executive branch of the federal government. Then, a crisis of confidence in the leadership of major American institutions took place, variously blamed on political scandals, increased partisanship, or negative media coverage of politics.[46] No matter what the cause, confidence in U.S. institutions has never returned to its pre-1966 levels, with the exception of a short-term surge after the 9/11

Confidence in U.S. Institutions

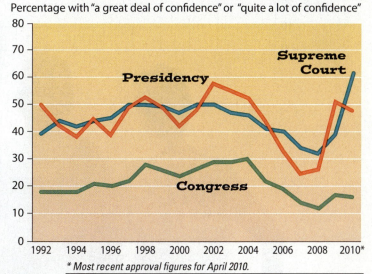

Percentage with "a great deal of confidence" or "quite a lot of confidence"

* Most recent approval figures for April 2010.

Source: Gallup Organization, *Confidence in Institutions,* June 14–17, 2009, http://www.gallup.com/poll/1597/Confidence-Institutions.aspx (accessed on April 10, 2010).

Can You Trust the Government to Do the Right Thing?

Trust in Government Index

Average score on index (percent)

80 70 60 50 40 30 20 0

1958 '62 '66 '70 '74 '78 '82 '86 '90 '94 '98 '02 '06 2010

Source: The American National Election Studies.

ing is the fact that young people are growing more distrustful of others in general. In a recent study, only 35 percent of young adults age 15 to 25 agreed that "most people can be trusted." Sixty percent believed that, as far as trust is concerned, "you can never be too careful."[47] Scholars have linked this decrease in trust to a decline in volunteerism.[48] As troublesome as this trend appears, however, we should not consider it a purely American phenomenon. Scholars have found similar declines in other industrialized countries as well.[49]

Political Efficacy

Political efficacy measures citizens' perception about their capacity to produce a desired outcome. It combines measures of a citizen's level of confidence in his or her own ability to navigate the political landscape (internal political efficacy) and the belief that individual political action does have, or can have, an impact on the political process in general (external political efficacy).[50] External political efficacy is especially important to well-functioning democracies, which are predicated on the notion of citizen self-government.

Do You Believe You Can Effect Political Change?

External political efficacy index

Source: The American National Election Studies.

The long-term trend in external political efficacy is also down, but there is much more variation in this measure over time. External efficacy seems more closely tied to political events and issues than are confidence and trust. Levels of efficacy do not substantially differ by party affiliation, but levels of trust in government do vary among partisans depending on which party is in power. Democrats express less trust when Republicans are in office and the reverse is true as well. As with other measures of attitudes and opinions, however, differences surface when we look at education and income. Those with more of both of these resources exhibit vastly higher levels of efficacy than those with less.

Support for Democratic Values

Our democracy emphasizes not only support for majority rule but also support for the rights of minorities. Tolerance for diverse viewpoints and lifestyles is necessary for the preservation of liberty and equality of opportunity. Nevertheless, pioneering studies on political toleration just following World War II suggested that general support for civil liberties was surprisingly low among average Americans.[51] Of course, this was a period characterized by fear of the threat of communism and a greater willingness to sacrifice liberties for security.[52] Toward the end of the Cold War, tolerance among the general public seems to have improved. Even today, however, Americans are not as supportive of democratic norms as one might hope, given our long tradition of liberty and diversity.

Public Tolerance for Advocates of Unpopular Positions

Many political scientists blame institutional factors for a lack of tolerance and support for political liberties. They criticize politicians for exploiting public fears to win votes, as well as the media's failure to engage citizens in a manner that encourages thoughtful consideration of often conflicting national goals.[53] Timely events also have an impact on support for basic freedoms. In 1987 and 1988, only 29 percent of Americans surveyed believed that it "will be necessary to give up civil liberties to curb terrorism." Following the terrorist attacks in 2001, that number jumped to 44 percent.[54] By 2005, however, the number had fallen again to 33 percent.[55]

Political Ideologies

A **political ideology** is an ordered set of political beliefs.[56] These beliefs usually stem from an individual's philosophy about the nature of society and the role of government. In Chapter 2, we discussed the liberal democratic ideology that informed the origins of our nation. That ideology emphasizes liberty, equal opportunity, private property, and individualism. The dominant ideologies today in America are **liberalism** and **conservatism**. Each borrows elements from our founding values.

Unlike the liberal democracy extolled by the Framers, liberalism today embraces a larger role for government in protecting and ensuring equal opportunity, such as affirmative action. Like its earlier namesake, however, liberalism places a premium on civil liberties and counsels against government intrusion in private matters of personal and moral choice. For example, liberals generally support a woman's right to obtain an abortion. Liberals have a sense of optimism about our ability to improve our lives by changing institutions and patterns of authority.

Historically, political conservatives have believed that human nature is complex, unpredictable, and often immoral. As a result, conservatives tend to be suspicious of change. They place their trust in institutions such

political efficacy The belief that an individual's actions can have an impact on the political process.

political ideology A cohesive set of beliefs that form a general philosophy about the role of government.

liberalism Political philosophy that combines a belief in personal freedoms with the belief that the government should intervene in the economy to promote greater equality.

conservatism Political philosophy that rests on belief in traditional institutions and a minimal role for government in economic activity.

	Admitted Communist		Someone against churches and religion	
	1972	2006	1972	2006
Percent who agree the advocate should be allowed to make a speech	54.7%	69.1%	67.7%	78.2%
Percent who agree the advocate should be allowed to teach in college	35.7%	62.8%	43.5%	62.7%
Percent who agree the advocate's book should remain in library	56%	69.7%	63.9%	72.8%

Source: GSS (various years).

Conservative evangelicals have made support for school prayer a cornerstone of their ideology.

as the church and the family and traditional values that have demonstrated a capacity for constraining the excesses of human conduct. Conservatives today support a limited role for government in the private economy and faith in free market mechanisms, both of which are consistent with the values of the Framers. However, conservatives today also support a more interventionist role for government in ensuring the preservation of traditional values and institutions. For example, many conservatives support prayer in public schools.

populist Political philosophy expressing support for greater economic equality and for traditional social values.

libertarianism Political philosophy that espouses strong support for individual liberty in both social and economic areas of life.

But ideology is more complex than the simple liberal-conservative dichotomy usually presented in popular culture and the media. Individuals can be liberal on some dimensions, such as support for government programs to help the poor, but conservative on other dimensions, like support for school prayer. Similarly, individuals can express liberal positions on social issues but reject government regulation in the economy, a position usually favored by conservatives.

The figure at right presents a more sophisticated model of ideological differences across two dimensions. The first dimension is economic, ranging from support for greater equality, even if government intervention is necessary to achieve it, to support for economic liberty where government plays a minor role. The other dimension deals with

our views on social issues. On this dimension views range from progressive—for example, support for gay marriage—to traditional, such as the view that marriage should take place only between a man and a woman. Those in the upper left quadrant are generally considered liberals, and those in the lower right quadrant are conservatives. Those who support greater economic equality but hold traditional views on social issues are generally known as **populists** (lower left quadrant); those who stress economic liberty and progressive social views follow a political philosophy called **libertarianism**.

The number of Americans who identify themselves as populist and libertarian is quite small.[57] About 22 percent of Americans self-identify as liberal, with a similar percentage

A Two-Dimensional View of Ideology

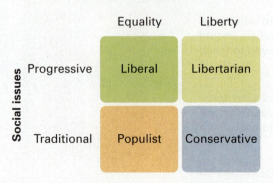

Economic issues

	Equality	Liberty
Progressive	Liberal	Libertarian
Traditional	Populist	Conservative

Social issues

Current Controversy

Are Political Ideologies Inherited?

At least since Plato, political observers have wondered if political views and orientations are inherited. Is there such a thing as a "gene for conservatism" or a "gene for liberalism"? For years, social scientists in the modern era have favored environmental factors over genetic factors. Their explanations stress "nurture" over "nature." Recently, however, studies inquiring into the genetic basis of a variety of behaviors and attitudes have increased.

In 2005, three researchers created quite a stir when they claimed to have found that one's ideology is highly inheritable—that is, traceable to one's genetic makeup. They studied the attitudes of identical twins (monozygotic twins, who share 100 percent of their genes). They analyzed responses from thousands of twins using a list of terms the researchers believed reflect basic conservative ideas (such as *women's liberation, school prayer,* and *censorship*). On the basis of positive or negative reactions to these terms, the researchers calculated a total score for conservatism and compared the results for each set of twins. The monozygotic twins they tested were much more likely to have similar responses to these items than

more genetically differentiated fraternal twins, even after environmental similarities and differences were factored in. They further hypothesized that there may be two genetically rooted types of political personalities: one conservative and the other liberal.

Conservative personalities, the researchers say, are characterized by suspicion of out-groups (for example, immigrants), a yearning for strong leadership, a desire for clear moral and behavioral codes, support for swift and severe punishment for violations of this code, and an inherently pessimistic view of human nature. Liberals, by contrast, are relatively tolerant toward out-groups, take a more content-dependent rather than rule-based approach to proper behavior, and are inherently optimistic about human nature.[*]

These findings have been attacked for methodological flaws and for over-simplifying ideological points of view.[†] The original researchers insist, however, that continued refinement of their methodology is only likely to confirm their results and that new DNA technology will improve the measurement of the genetic basis of attitudes in the future.[‡] More than 2,300 years after Plato's death, the "nature debate" is far from dead in political science.

[*] J.R. Alford, C. L. Funk, and J. R. Hibbing, "Are Political Orientations Genetically Transmitted?" *American Political Science Review*, no. 2 (2005): 164–165.

[†] See, for example, Evan Charney, "Genes and Ideologies," *Perspectives on Politics* 6, no. 2 (2008): 299–319.

[‡] J.R. Alford, C. L. Funk, and J. R. Hibbing, "Beyond Liberals and Conservatives to Political Genotypes and Phenotypes," *Perspectives in Politics* 6, no. 2 (2008): 321–328.

CUT THE OTHER GUY'S PROGRAMS

The debate over the U.S. budget deficit has raised broader questions about the role and scope of the federal government that have been center stage throughout the presidential campaign. Since the New Deal, the government has played an expansive role in regulating businesses, ensuring worker rights, managing unemployment and inflation, and providing income security through programs such as Social Security and Medicare. The sheer size of the U.S. debt, however, especially in the face of the costs of fighting two wars, supporting tax cuts, rising health-care costs and the coming retirement of the baby-boom generation has raised questions about the ability of the federal government to keep its commitment to these programs. While Americans are clear that they want to cut the deficit, there is a wide partisan gap surrounding how we achieve a balanced budget. Hence, this issue loomed large during the presidential campaign of 2012, with Republican candidates generally suggesting cuts in social programs and Democratic candidates opposing them.

Source: Washington Post, Feb. 10, 2011. Accessed on April 27, 2010 at http://voices.washingtonpost.com

Partisan Gaps Over Government Spending

Would you increase, decrease, or keep spending the same for…		Rep %	Dem %	Ind %	D–R Gap
Unemployment aid	Increase	11	47	23	+36
	Decrease	50	11	29	−39
Health care	Increase	22	56	39	+34
	Decrease	47	8	25	−39
Aid to needy in U.S.	Increase	24	57	37	+33
	Decrease	35	12	20	−23
Education	Increase	45	77	62	+32
	Decrease	15	4	13	−11
Environmental protection	Increase	16	47	41	+31
	Decrease	43	12	26	−31
Aid to world's needy	Increase	7	32	22	+25
	Decrease	70	28	45	−42
Public school systems	Increase	42	65	58	+23
	Decrease	25	4	13	−21
Roads and transportation	Increase	22	44	43	+22
	Decrease	32	18	18	−14
College and financial aid	Increase	30	51	47	+21
	Decrease	30	9	15	−21
Scientific research	Increase	28	46	35	+18
	Decrease	30	13	26	−17
Medicare	Increase	27	55	38	+18
	Decrease	20	5	14	−15
Energy	Increase	26	41	37	+15
	Decrease	28	18	22	−10
Social Security	Increase	33	45	40	+12
	Decrease	21	4	15	−17
Agriculture	Increase	29	37	31	+8
	Decrease	26	15	28	−11
Veterans' benefits	Increase	46	52	53	+6
	Decrease	8	6	5	−2
Combating crime	Increase	41	45	33	+4
	Decrease	19	13	20	−6
Terrorism defenses	Increase	38	32	30	−6
	Decrease	16	20	23	+4
Military defense	Increase	41	28	27	−13
	Decrease	18	36	33	+18

identifying themselves as moderate or middle of the road and another 32 percent calling themselves conservatives. Most Americans, however, avoid ideological extremes. In fact, nearly a quarter find it difficult to identify with any ideology at all.[58] There are very few **ideologues**, those who think about politics almost exclusively in ideological terms. For example, only about 3 percent say they are extremely liberal, with a similar percentage calling themselves extremely conservative.[59] For the most part, Americans take a pragmatic view of politics; they are more interested in finding solutions to problems than in enforcing ideological purity. This does not mean that ideological divisions do not exist. Studies show that northeastern and west coast states are growing more liberal while citizens living in the South and Midwest are more conservative; the cities and suburbs are more liberal than the rural areas; those who have not attended college are more populist and progressive on economic policy but more

ideologue One who thinks about politics almost exclusively through the prism of his or her ideological perspective.

conservative on cultural and national security policy than their college-educated counterparts. One study showed that most divisive issues were social and cultural, including the role of religion in politics, immigration, and homosexuality. However, the pollsters also found a high degree of consensus on items ranging from support for government investment in education to the need for regulation of sex and violence in popular culture, affirming the generally pragmatic nature of American public opinion.[60] A similar poll focusing on Millennials under 30 found greater tolerance on social and cultural issues and a greater likelihood to self-identify at the liberal end of the political spectrum than their elders.[61]

PUBLIC OPINION AND PUBLIC POLICY

Democratic theory posits a close relationship between public opinion and the policies generated by the political system. In a well-functioning democracy, we would expect elected leaders to act on the preferences of voters by providing policy solutions acceptable to a majority of citizens.

There are a number of uncertainties that arise in this process, however. First, voters may simply not have clear preferences on a number of issues. For example, although there is widespread support for reducing carbon emissions, there is no consensus on how best to achieve it. Should we outlaw new coal burning plants, adopt a carbon tax, or simply increase conservation? In an environment of uncertainty, public opinion is subject to influence by a variety of forces that frame issues in ways that benefit more narrow interests. In lieu of public mandates, minority interests attempting to control the agenda often subject policymakers to intense political pressure (see Chapter 8).

A second problem complicating the straightforward conversion of public opinion into policy is majority tyranny. What if majority opinion supports policies detrimental to the rights of minorities? The Framers believed that a representative government would act as a filter for public opinion, channeling it in ways that were not destructive to fundamental freedoms and rights. These concerns are not simply hypothetical; elected and appointed leaders sometimes find it necessary to act contrary to public opinion to preserve more fundamental principles. During the 1950s, for example, many southern states refused to abide by Supreme Court opinions ordering the integration of public schools. The Court was attempting to secure minority rights in an atmosphere superheated by opposing public sentiment. In this tense atmosphere, the federal government sent troops to public schools in the South to protect African American students against hostile crowds.

Despite these potential problems, studies reveal a high degree of correspondence between public opinion and public policy. Studies of policymaking from the Progressive

Era through the late twentieth century show that changes in public opinion generate responsive policies. Political scientist Eileen Lorenzi McDonagh found that when voters expressed popular support in state referenda for labor reform, women's rights, and prohibition, Congress responded by passing legislation accordingly. House members repre-

What Americans Believe

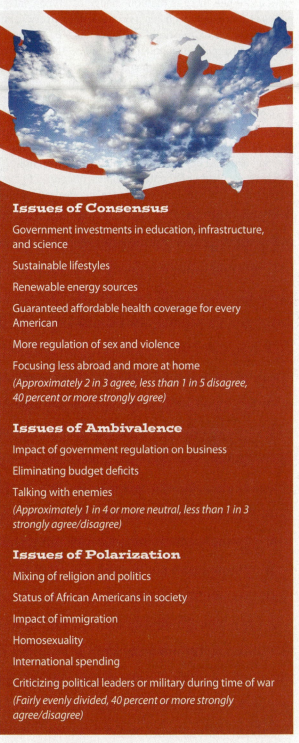

Issues of Consensus

Government investments in education, infrastructure, and science

Sustainable lifestyles

Renewable energy sources

Guaranteed affordable health coverage for every American

More regulation of sex and violence

Focusing less abroad and more at home
(Approximately 2 in 3 agree, less than 1 in 5 disagree, 40 percent or more strongly agree)

Issues of Ambivalence

Impact of government regulation on business

Eliminating budget deficits

Talking with enemies
(Approximately 1 in 4 or more neutral, less than 1 in 3 strongly agree/disagree)

Issues of Polarization

Mixing of religion and politics

Status of African Americans in society

Impact of immigration

Homosexuality

International spending

Criticizing political leaders or military during time of war
(Fairly evenly divided, 40 percent or more strongly agree/disagree)

Source: John Halpin and Karl Agne, *State of American Political Ideology 2009: A National Study of Political Values and Beliefs,* Washington, DC: Center for American Progress, March 2009.

senting areas where referenda occurred tended to cast roll call votes supporting constituents on these controversial measures.[62]

Benjamin I. Page and Robert Y. Shapiro, in a famous political science study, found similar results when they examined hundreds of national policies between 1935 and 1979. Substantial changes in opinion, they found, were almost always followed by policy change in the same direction: "When there is opinion change of 20 percentage points or more, policy change is congruent an overwhelming 90 percent of the time."[63] The finding is especially impressive when the population considers the policy in question important. Policy change is less certain when the percentage of opinion change in one direction or the other is small, and when there is a high degree of uncertainty among the public about which policy is preferable. These and other studies suggest that policymakers do heed public opinion in forging policy, even though such congruence is not, and need not be, universal in a democratic republic.[64]

There are plenty of counterexamples, of course. For example, although a majority of Americans favored waiting for United Nations approval before attacking Iraq in 2003, President Bush, with the support of Congress, proceeded with the invasion. Many Americans also opposed a bailout for major banks during the recent recession, although the government forged ahead.

PUBLIC OPINION AND CIVIC ENGAGEMENT TODAY

The role that public opinion should play in a democracy remains as highly controversial today as it was when the Framers penned our Constitution. The consent of the governed is the centerpiece of liberal democracy, but how closely should public officials track it? As we have seen, public opinion is often based on low levels of information and little understanding of the complexities of policy options. It is sometimes prone to manipulation by political consultants who seek to frame issues in self-serving ways. Some political scientists believe that public policy is best left in the hands of elites who are better informed, are more knowledgeable about government, and often are

Which Ideological Type Are You?

Recently, the Harvard Institute of Politics interviewed 3,000 young people between the ages of eighteen and twenty-nine regarding their political values and ideology. Interviews were conducted in both English and Spanish. Researchers found that young people assorted into four ideological groupings. Does one of these describe you?

New Progressives
(17 percent of the total sample)
- Agree strongly that basic health insurance and other necessities like food and shelter should be provided for those who cannot afford them;
- Agree strongly that the United States should consider the opinions of other countries when making foreign policy decisions;
- Are more likely than others to believe that the government should do more to curb climate change.

New Religious
(20 percent of the total sample)
- Believe in protecting the environment and providing health care and basic necessities to those in need;
- Believe homosexual relationships are morally wrong;
- Believe the United States should intervene militarily in other nations to protect itself from terrorists and to spread democracy.

New Conservatives
(13 percent of the total sample)
- Are very concerned about the moral direction of our country;
- Disapprove of government spending as an effective way to increase economic growth;
- Oppose universal health care and government regulation of climate change;
- Believe the military should intervene in other nations to protect itself from hostile actions.

New Passives
(40 percent of the total sample)
- Are not much interested or engaged in politics;
- Rate their views on nearly every question as "neutral";
- Largely consider themselves Independents (more than two in five, or 44 percent of this group)

Source: Esten Perez and John Della Volpe, eds. *Survey of Young Americans' Attitudes Toward Politics and Public Service:* 17th ed., Boston: Harvard Institute of Politics, 2010.

more committed to ideals of tolerance and fair play than the population at large. Some even believe that citizens themselves are more comfortable leaving policy decisions in the hands of experts.[65]

There are others, however, who believe that citizens are fully capable of making informed decisions if they are given the tools. Professors James Fishkin and Robert Lushkin have pioneered a new kind of opinion research that could yet prove an informed and engaged citizenry not only is possible but may be the essential foundation for successful and thoughtful decision making. Called *deliberative polling,* the process begins with a baseline poll of a random, representative sample of the population. Not only does this method give citizens more information, but it could also prove an effective corrective to superheated town hall meetings that sometimes degenerate into shouting matches. Carefully balanced briefing materials are sent in advance to each of the participants, who then come together to discuss the issues in small, moderated groups. At the conclusion of the discussions, the participants are surveyed again. "I think it's fair to say that the public, in aggregate if you give them a chance, is very wise," Fishkin said. "Policymakers and experts are always surprised at how smart the results are when people get together and focus on an issue. And it's usually some combination of positions that are not entirely predictable beforehand. It's not that they move left or right—they focus on the substance of the issues and come up with some way of dealing with it that often defies stereotypes. It's really inspiring."[66]

Many political scientists remain skeptical about deliberative polling and caution that such forums place citizens in an artificial environment. Nevertheless, political scientists who have studied long-term trends in public opinion reject the tendency to blame the public for inattention, apathy, and ignorance, concluding that "If society provides accurate, helpful information about public policy; if it offers moral leadership, encourages participation, and in a broad sense educates its citizenry, then there is every reason to expect that citizens will rise to the occasion and democracy will flourish."[67]

Summary

1. What is public opinion and why is it important?

- Public opinion consists of those opinions held by private persons that governments find it prudent to heed.
- In a democracy, public opinion gives elected officials a sense of what citizens want and what they are willing to accept.
- The Framers felt the opinions of common people were best expressed by voting; nevertheless, political leaders were never indifferent to public attitudes and could access them through a variety of ad hoc methods.
- Individuals develop their political opinions through a process of political socialization.
- The agents of political socialization that shape opinions include family, educational institutions, religious institutions, voluntary associations, and the media.
- The life experiences associated with racial and ethnic identity, gender, and geography generate interesting political differences across America's diverse population.

2. How is opinion best measured and how do we know these measures are reliable?

- The measurement of public opinion can be divided into the dimensions of an opinion: direction, salience, intensity, stability, and informational support.

- A variety of polls are used to measure public opinion: benchmark surveys, trial heat surveys, tracking polls, push polls, and exit polls.
- Opinion is best measured by scientific surveys using random samples in which every member of the population has about the same probability of being selected for an interview.
- The reliability of surveys depends on how well the sample is drawn and on the quality of the questions. Leading questions, for instance, can lead to nonattitudes.

3. What are some of the most basic features of American public opinion today?

- Americans are not very trusting of their government.
- Americans have lost confidence in elected leaders and institutions.
- Most consider themselves neither too liberal nor too conservative, but ideology is not evenly spread throughout the country. For example, urban areas, the Northeast, and West Coast tend to be more liberal; rural areas, the Midwest, and some western states, more conservative.
- The political knowledge of most Americans is lower than many political theorists would desire.
- Studies reveal a high degree of correspondence between public opinion and public policy decisions.

ANGER MANAGEMENT

Toward the end of 2009, about three weeks before he quit his uphill bid for a sixth term in the U.S. Senate, Democrat Christopher Dodd of Connecticut reflected on the vagaries of anger among the citizens of his state, who are worried about jobs and housing prices, the collapse of Wall Street, and America's wars in faraway lands. It was a ripe subject, for, as Dodd readily acknowledged, "people are angry, and angry at me." He provoked their wrath when Countrywide Financial gave him a VIP discount for a home mortgage—and even more when he neglected to mind the financial store as Senate Banking chairman and turned his energies to a futile quest for the 2008 Democratic presidential nomination.

National Journal shared with Dodd a sampling of the scathing things that his Connecticut constituents were saying about him. From a hair stylist: "He's worthless. I'm trying to be very, very nice." From a small-business owner: "I hope the bastard gets wiped right off the map. Whoever he's running against, I'm voting for that person."

The senator, in response, suggested that the anger was less personal than it seemed. "You and I have never seen anything like this," he said of the awful economy, in particular. "Their reflection about how they feel about people in public life," he said of his state's citizens, "is more of a reflection of how they feel about life."

That was a philosophical answer and not a bad one, even if it served to get him off the hook a bit. Anger is one of the trickiest of all political and social sentiments. Although it is easy enough to take a thermometer reading of public anger—and everyone can agree that the mercury stands at a high level right now—it is devilishly hard to predict the path that the anger will take.

This much is certain: Woe to anyone in the public arena who fails to take the anger seriously. Just look at the indelible example of Democrat Martha Coakley, beaten in the January 19 special election to fill the late Edward Kennedy's Senate seat in Massachusetts. Coakley, the commonwealth's attorney general, ran a lackadaisical campaign, allowing the insurgent Republican candidate, Scott Brown, to become the vessel for popular anger and pull off a historic upset in one of the nation's bluest states.

And one other lesson: In this incendiary environment, almost anyone can become a convenient target of blame and be singed by a sudden burst of flames. Federal Reserve Board Chairman Ben Bernanke's appointment to a new term, which at first looked like a lock, ran into trouble from senators desperate to protect their own political hides who are faulting him for reckless policies leading to 2008's financial meltdown.

Today's mad-as-hell "tea partiers" may be a full-throttle example of this personal anger. They are a prime case in point, circa 2010, of a venerable tendency for anger to find outward expression in the political culture. Although it would be nice to think that hope and optimism typically inspire political movements, in reality, movements such as these are likelier to start with raw anger, like oxygen to fire.

Furious citizens started the tea party movement as a spontaneous protest against Washington's taxpayer-financed bailouts of Wall Street banks and industrial giants such as General Motors. Although a conservative, anti-government hue tints the movement, it was not, at least in the beginning, self-consciously partisan. Tea partiers were steamed at George W. Bush's Treasury for its rescue of the banks; they are steamed at the Obama administration for what they say is Washington's effort to take over the health care system.

A primal anger, especially when it motivates a crowd acting in unison, is often associated with idiocy—so it is not surprising that the media often portray tea partiers as a gaggle of bumbling and blustery know-nothings, captive to rancid prejudices about President Obama and all other targets of their free-floating animus. This portrait, though, misses a certain canny intelligence in the tea party movement.

Chris Ford, a leader of the tea party movement in Connecticut, is without doubt an angry guy. His rage is focused on the big-spending, high-taxing, self-aggrandizing political establishment in Washington. But he is certainly not a yahoo. The folks who show up at the Connecticut tea party rallies, Ford said, are like him, "independent-contractor" types who either develop survival skills or go out of business. The group includes "carpenters, electricians, masons, restaurant owners, [and] printing company owners," he said.

Ford expresses his anger slyly, in humor and mockery. At the end of 2008, he and his tea party comrade-in-arms, Art McNally, a retired computer consultant, created the "Dump Dodd" campaign, exemplified in a button with a picture of "Joe the Voter" unloading a white-haired, money-bag-clutching Dodd from the back of a dump truck. "We're portraying Dodd as more of an incompetent buffoon," Ford explained. "He's not evil."

Ford and McNally are Republican-leaning political conservatives, but the Dump Dodd movement struck a chord with some grumpy Connecticut Democrats as well. Dodd's hasty January exit gratified the duo, naturally, but it has only boosted their appetite for more scalps. "We got Dodd to turn and run," McNally said in a phone interview the week after Dodd's retirement announcement. "We're not stopping. November 2010, we want to get rid of all incumbents. In Connecticut, it happens, they are all Democrats."

Another vulnerable Senate Democrat, Majority Leader Harry Reid of Nevada, is also high on the hit list of tea party activists. In their favor is an especially sour climate in Nevada, where unemployment exceeds the national average and nearly two-thirds of all mortgaged residential properties are under water—that is, worth less than their outstanding loan balance. Tea party activists contributed significantly to Brown's improbable victory in the Massachusetts special election as well. Sen. Barbara Boxer of California, a Democrat elected in 1992, could also prove vulnerable to the tea partiers' efforts to oust incumbents.

The latest question confronting the tea party movement is whether it can make the kind of transition that often trips up campaigns born of reflexive grassroots anger—the shift from a purely "anti" focus to a positive one, with efficient organizational machinery. The tea party folks most ardently hope for seismic change, "a revolution" that takes down the ruling political elite, as Ford said. But no such revolution appears in sight, for all the anger on the streets.

A more likely prospect is for the tea partiers to take over the Republican Party—or a least to become a weighty presence in it, much as disaffected conservative Christian evangelicals, long on the political margins, did in the 1970s and 1980s when they became a crucial bloc in Ronald Reagan's coalition. Should the tea partiers' plans not work out, they can always form a new political party, but that is a difficult route in a system stacked to favor the two established parties.

Liberal anger, too, is a live current, especially evident in attacks on Wall Street, a staple of the liberal blogosphere in sources such as The Huffington Post, whose namesake founder, Arianna Huffington, is spearheading a campaign for Americans to move their savings from large financial institutions to small, Main Street, community banks because "too-big-to-fail banks are profiting from bailout dollars and government guarantees, and growing bigger," as she wrote on her website.

Even though The Huffington Post reliably comes from the left, those words could just have easily been written by a tea party activist. For that matter, Obama's Treasury secretary, Timothy Geithner, who orchestrated the bailout of AIG, the insurance giant, while he was president of the Federal Reserve Bank of New York, is as much an object of scorn among the populist Left as among the populist Right.

And yet it is almost inconceivable that the anti-Wall Street, anti-Washington anger shared by the Left and Right in America will fuse into a joint campaign—liberals and conservatives are too invested in their ritual flogging of each other for that to happen. The future of anger-driven political movements in the United States remains captive to their imaginative limitations and their knee-jerk impulses—to the relief, no doubt, of the cowering targets at which they take common aim.

Sometimes it turns out this way. A movement begins in earnest, but not-especially-well-focused, anger and is taken over by a potentate—a particular kind of leader, unusually gifted in dealing with the masses, in seeming to channel their passions. That leader may or may not be a true representative of the flock, whose members tend to oscillate between an ingrained suspicion of any person in high authority and a yearning for the leadership that such a person might supply. Sarah Palin is the best example—she turned off some tea party activists by seeking a reported $100,000 speaking fee.

The Ross Perot movement was the most recent to display this dynamic. Perot, a little guy with jug ears and a squeaky voice, managed to take hold of a slice of an irate citizenry turned off by both parties and by Washington's profligacy. His strong performance in the 1992 presidential election set the bar for the anger candidate. He garnered nearly 20 million votes, about half as many as the losing Republican, George H.W. Bush, received, and 19 percent of the electorate.

In 2008, Obama, too, attracted a cult-like following on the campaign trail, with supporters motivated, yes, by his idealistic appeal for change but also by an intense anger at President George W. Bush personally and at Republicans generally over the Iraq invasion and other perceived evil deeds. But Obama has not really governed as a potentate; his flock is almost nowhere to be seen; his White House is as much invested in the nitty-gritty of negotiations on Capitol Hill as in bringing out the president for one of his trademark big speeches. Once a vessel for anger, Obama now risks becoming one of its prime targets, with a job-approval rating dipping below 50 percent.

Anger can be irrational, a reaction to slights that are more imagined than real. Today's public anger, though, is nothing like that. Americans have been a dealt a body blow, and their anger is righteous.

> "We're not stopping. November 2010, we want to get rid of all incumbents. In Connecticut, it happens, they are all Democrats."
>
> —Art McNally

For Discussion:

■ What do you think motivates political anger in America? Are Americans angry about particular politicians, about a political philosophy or set of policies or about something harder to track?

■ Do you think political anger is a good or a bad thing? Should an electorate strive to be cool and rational in assessing the best courses of action for its country, or can being indignant at injustice and mismanagement be good for the overall health of democracy?

■ Based either on your experience or on the portrayal of the movement in this article, how do you think tea partiers will impact upcoming elections, including the presidential race in 2012?

7

POLITICAL PA

EQUAL OPPORTUNITIES AND UNEQUAL VOICES

EVERY VOTE COUNTS ▌ It took only one vote to put Tashua Allman in the mayor's office. She beat two other contenders with her write-in candidacy to become the youngest female mayor in West Virginia history. "I didn't even realize that. I thought there were female mayors everywhere," she told a local newspaper. "But it's really cool that I've made West Virginia history."[1]

Just days before being declared the winner, Tashua graduated from Glenville State College where she majored in history with a political science concentration. Politics was not new to her, however. At Glenville State, she was student-body president for two years and headed up the College Democrats. She became interested in running for mayor of Glenville after getting involved as a volunteer in local efforts to improve and clean up the city. Tashua says she was always interested in politics and engaged in political discussions with her family.

"I just wanted the experience and to get my name out there," the 21-year-old told the Charleston *Sunday Gazette*. Despite encouragement from family and friends, she waited too long to put her name on the ballot and had to run as a write-in candidate, putting her ➡◆

RTICIPATION

- What is the nature of political participation in America?
- What are the major forms of political participation and what resources do they require?
- What is the nature of voting in the United States?

at a decided disadvantage. Nevertheless, she worked hard to get elected and, she admits, "I think I had a little luck." As part of her campaign, she created a website where she posted her ideas to improve the town and provided contact information where voters could write to get answers to their questions about her candidacy.[2]

Among her key goals for this small town of about fifteen hundred residents located near the geographic center of the state are the revitalization of the downtown district and the promotion of volunteerism among the residents of the community. Asked if she plans on making a career in politics, she responds, "Ask me again in two years."[3]

Tashua's drive might be unusual, but the story of how she became politically active is not. Like other political activists, Tashua's family and friends encouraged her political activity from an early age. Her school provided access to political organizations where she could gain experience, and she was encouraged to jump into the campaign by those close to her. Of course, it helped that she was well informed, interested, optimistic about making a difference, and ready to heed the call when the opportunity to run for office arose.

In this chapter, we will discuss the nature of political participation, the kinds of opportunities open to Americans to take part in the political process, and the factors generally associated with the likelihood that people will become involved. We will pay special attention to what motivates citizens to vote and to the reasons many choose not to do so. We will examine the economic and social backgrounds of those who are most likely to participate and how these factors affect the kinds of policies enacted by our elected leaders. Finally, we will explore potential ways to increase citizen participation in the political process. Is it important that every citizen get involved? Just ask Tashua Allman. ◄●

POLITICAL PARTICIPATION: OPPORTUNITIES, COSTS, AND BENEFITS

Free societies thrive on the active participation of citizens in the civic and political life of their communities. They also require equal access to the nation's civic and political institutions so that all who desire to contribute may do so. America, however, did not realize the promise of equal access all at once. Voting restrictions based on property ownership, race, and gender fell away only slowly, and the government did not fully enforce the voting rights of minorities until the mid-1960s.

Civic-minded reformers, working outside the formal channels of government, led the effort to remove many of these obstacles to participation. Nineteenth-century abolitionists raised political consciousness about the evils of slavery and paved the way for its eventual elimination after the Civil War. At the end of the century, civic-minded Americans who joined the suffrage movement broke down further barriers to participation, as did civil-rights groups in the twentieth century.

Opportunities for Americans to participate in government and civic life have never been greater. Political activities open to us range from voting to attending local school board meetings to running for office to campaigning for candidates to signing petitions. Outside of the arena of government, we can work for changes in our communities by joining with other residents to pressure polluters into conforming with emission-control standards or by boycotting manufacturers who don't pay their workforce a living wage or by **BUYcotting**—that is, intentionally supporting with our purchases the products of environmentally friendly companies.

Opportunities alone, however, do not guarantee participation. Personal factors such as income, age, and political socialization play a large part in determining our inclination to participate. In addition, all political and civic activities involve trade-offs between the cost of involvement and the perceived benefits. Not everyone believes they can afford the costs of participation, and many don't believe the cost is worth the effort. The perspective that choices are based on our individual assessment of costs and benefits is called the **rational actor theory**.

From the perspective of a perfectly rational actor, it is difficult to account for people taking part in some types of political participation at all—voting, for example. One vote in a national election has an infinitesimal chance of affecting the election outcome and requires the effort of registering and getting to the polls. If the candidate I vote for loses, I wasted that effort; if the candidate I prefer wins without my vote, I enjoy the

> **BUYcotting** Using purchasing decisions to support the products and policies of businesses.
>
> **rational actor theory** The theory that choices are based on our individual assessment of costs and benefits.

Civic-minded reformers can work outside government channels to bring about change. The suffragists staged protests to raise popular support for the right of women to vote.

---

get involved!

Volunteer your time for a cause you support. The possibilities are endless, from food banks for the hungry to soup kitchens for the homeless to homes for the elderly. If you need help locating an organization or identifying a cause in your area, you will find help at the Points of Light Institute's website at http://www.pointsoflight.org.

ity.[4] Still, not everyone believes political participation is worth the price. Perhaps they lack the resources to get involved, feel they are not knowledgeable enough to make an informed decision, or don't believe the candidates offer them a meaningful choice. Perhaps it's simply that no one has asked them for their vote. We will see next that the availability of resources, psychological motivation, and the invitation to get involved all play a part in our calculations of costs and benefits.

benefits without having exerted any effort. The most rational approach might be to use my time in a way that is more lucrative or enjoyable and simply hope my candidate wins. Those who enjoy the benefits from an activity without paying the costs of participation are known as **free riders**. They are a problem in a society that does not force people to participate in the political system in order to receive its benefits.

free riders Those who enjoy the benefits from activities without paying the costs of participation.

Perhaps surprisingly, large numbers of citizens defy this logic every Election Day. For them, preserving democratic opportunities for engagement outweighs the cost of gathering information about issues or candidates and going to the polls. Activists report that they receive more psychological gratification from voting than from any other political activ-

Attributes of Political Activities

Activity	Capacity for Conveying Information	Variation in Frequency and Strength of Messages Conveyed
Voting	Low	Low
Working on a Campaign	Mixed	High
Contributing to a Campaign	Mixed	High
Contacting an Official	High	Intermediate
Participating in a Protest	High	Intermediate
Performing Informal Community Work (e.g., taking part in a Neighborhood Watch)	High	High
Serving on a Local Board	High	High
Being Affiliated with a Political Organization	Mixed	High
Contributing to a Political Cause	Mixed	High

Source: Adapted from Sidney Verba, Kay Lehman Schlozman, and Henry E. Brady, *Voice and Equality: Civic Voluntarism in American Politics* (Cambridge: Harvard University Press, 1995), 48.

CHARACTERISTICS OF POLITICAL PARTICIPATION

Distinctions between political participation and other forms of civic engagement are not always clear-cut. For example, a charity walk to raise money for AIDS research may not seem like a political activity, yet it raises public awareness of the issue and may pressure political leaders to devote more public funds to the cause. The activities of religious organizations or social clubs may also seem quite removed from politics, but the skills learned in organizing events for these groups are good preparation for political action such as running for office or becoming an advocate for a cause. Alexis de Tocqueville long ago recognized the close relationship between civic and political activity, noting that civic associations pave the way for political ones.[5]

Political participation differs from civic voluntarism, however, in at least two ways. First, people undertake political activities with the intent of directly or indirectly influencing government policy.[6] This includes a wide array of actions, such as voting in elections, working for a party or candidate, or writing a letter to a congressperson in support of specific legislation. Second, political activities have broad legal consequences for the entire community, not merely for members of a private group or organization. When individuals engage in political activities to help elect a member of Congress or to change public policy regarding a military draft system, those activities affect all members of the community if the candidate is elected or the policy is adopted. The winning candidate will represent everyone in the community, and a new draft system will affect all eligible individuals as well as their families and friends.

Not all forms of political participation are identical. Some types convey more information than others, and some communicate more loudly than others. Some forms of participation give all citizens an equal voice, while others give certain members of the community more clout than others. The table on the previous page categorizes the types of political participation open to American citizens according to the amount of information they convey and the amount of variation they permit.[7]

Amount of Information Conveyed

Voting is the hallmark of democratic systems and the most-studied form of participation, yet it conveys very limited information. Voters support a political candidate for a variety of reasons, including party affiliation, agreement on issues, personal characteristics, and advertising. Their choice usually depends on a combination of these factors. With such a wide variety of potential motivations, there is no clear way to know precisely what message the voters are sending. For the same reason, voters cannot be sure how the winner will interpret the message they sent at the ballot box.

Other types of political participation convey more explicit messages. For example, working for a candidate, joining a political party, or contributing money to a campaign imparts more information about support than voting alone. Participating in a protest sends a very clear message to politicians; letters to public officials can offer even more detailed information about a constituent's concerns. At an even deeper level, community organizing or service on a local school board enables citizens to help fashion policies that express their preferences. All these activities, however, may also involve higher costs in terms of time or money.

Variation in Frequency and Strength of Messages Conveyed

Effective political communication requires citizens to convey messages frequently and loudly enough so that leaders will pay attention. Some messages can be delivered only once; their variability is low. For example, each citizen may vote once and only once in an election. Other activities permit great variation in frequency, making involve-

ment possible as often as time and resources allow. For example, serving on a school board affords an individual multiple opportunities to have his or her messages heard by other decision makers. Campaign donors can contribute at several points during a political campaign, up to the limits allowed by law.

Similarly, some acts of participation speak more loudly to political leaders than others. Conventional political wisdom suggests that candidates pay more attention to donors than to protesters, although the size and timing of the protest may have an impact on the candidacies. Not only can big donors convey their messages more frequently, but they can do so more loudly by the quantity of the dollars they contribute. We should keep in mind that the frequency and strength of the message participants convey are strongly related to the resources they possess.

INGREDIENTS FOR INVOLVEMENT

Why do some citizens become politically active while others remain on the sidelines? Three conditions are necessary for political participation. First, citizens must have the resources to participate. Some types of political activity require time; some require money; many require skill. These resources are not evenly distributed and their acquisition is tied to several factors, as we shall see. Second, participants must be interested in the political process and believe that their actions will make a difference. They must not only see political events as important to their lives but also believe that they can somehow influence the course of those events. Finally, people must be asked to participate. Much as in sports, those not recruited to play the game end up sitting on the sidelines.

Access to Resources

All acts of participation require the expenditure of resources: voting requires time; making cash contributions requires money; organizing a political rally requires time and skill. The type and amount of resources required vary according to the type of political activity. Writing to a member of Congress, for example, requires only basic literacy. For highly educated Americans, this is a relatively simple task, but many Americans lack the confidence in their communication skills to undertake it. Running for a local school board position requires more varied resources. A candidate must not only communicate effectively but also possess the ability to organize, strategize, and work with others. Conducting even a relatively small political campaign also requires time and money.

The unequal distribution of resources means that some individuals are in a better position to take political action

Resources Necessary for Various Types of Political Activities

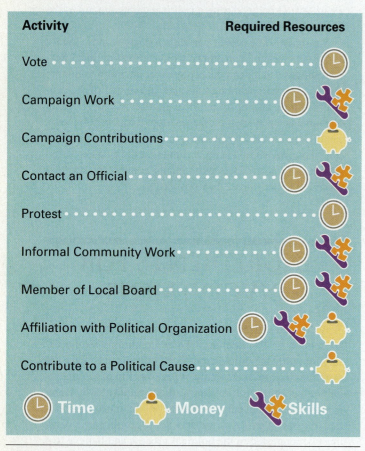

Activity	Required Resources
Vote	Time
Campaign Work	Time, Skills
Campaign Contributions	Money
Contact an Official	Time, Skills
Protest	Time
Informal Community Work	Time, Skills
Member of Local Board	Time, Skills
Affiliation with Political Organization	Time, Skills, Money
Contribute to a Political Cause	Money

Time   Money   Skills

Source: Adapted from Sidney Verba, Kay Lehman Schlozman, and Henry E. Brady, *Voice and Equality: Civic Voluntarism in American Politics* (Cambridge: Harvard University Press, 1995), 48.

than others. Politicians may not hear those with few resources as clearly or as loudly as those with more resources. Money is a prime example of a resource that is not equally distributed among citizens. Some individuals can and do donate to a large number of causes and candidates up to the limits permitted by law. Other citizens cannot afford to contribute, so this form of participation is not open to them.

Family Wealth You have probably noticed that the same family names crop up time and time again in positions of political authority. The Bush, Kennedy, and Rockefeller families are legendary not only for their wealth but also for their intergenerational commitment to public service. This is no accident; family wealth confers opportunities that make a difference in the ability to participate in political life. Wealth directly affects the ability to contribute to political fundraising, and it is indirectly related to the possession of other resources, such as the time and skill necessary to engage effectively in other types of political activity. Many upper-income professionals have flexible schedules that allow them time to take part in community and civic projects, whereas few blue-collar workers can take time out of their workday to attend such func-

tions. Family wealth often provides access to other high-status individuals who can help promote one's political aspirations.

As the figure below illustrates, the wealthy are more likely than those in low-income groups to take part in a wide range of political activities, from talking with others about political issues and candidates to voting in elections. The wealthy are more likely to engage in voluntary activities outside of politics, as well. For example, they are more likely to donate their time and money to charity. Wealth also opens doors to educational opportunities that train individuals in the skills necessary to participate in civic life. These skills include the ability to communicate effectively and to organize individuals to achieve particular goals.

Education No resource predicts political activity better than education.[8] The better educated are more likely to engage in electoral activities, including voting and working for political campaigns, and to participate in community activities such as charity fundraising. Education also has transgenerational effects; parents with high levels of education are more likely to expose their children to what Steven Rosenstone and John Hansen term "social networks that inform them about politics and reward political action."[9] Such children are more likely to hear their parents talking with acquaintances about political issues and to be encouraged to take part in political activities. As a consequence, they are more likely to develop habits of civic involvement than are children of parents with less formal education. Involvement in student government activities also enhances the likelihood of participation in politics, as does exposure to classroom teachers who encourage debate and open discussion.[10]

Religious Affiliation Many less-affluent citizens acquire civic skills from the places where they worship. Or-

Political Activity Among High- and Low-Income Groups

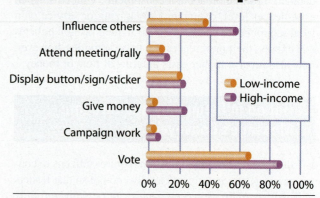

Source: Preliminary results from the *American National Election Studies, 2008 Time Series,* Ann Arbor, MI: University of Michigan Center for Political Studies, May 2009. Low-income are those with household incomes under $30,000 a year; high-income are those with household incomes of more than $100,000 a year.

Participation Rates by Race and Gender

Activity	Whites	Blacks	Hispanics† Percent	Men	Women
Vote*	66.1	65.2	49.9	61.5	65.7
Campaign work**	4.2	5.9	3.1	4.0	5.2
Campaign contribution**	11.2	7.6	5.1	10.1	9.7
Display button/sign/sticker**	15.5	33.5	16.7	19.4	20.8
Attend meeting/rally**	8.7	11.8	7.6	9.8	8.9
Try to influence others*	44.6	42.1	34.4	44.8	41.7

Sources: * Mark Hugo Lopez and Paul Taylor, *Dissecting the 2008 Electorate: Most Diverse in U.S. History,* Washington, DC: Pew Research Center, April 30, 2009.
** Preliminary results from the *American National Election Studies, 2008 Time Series,* Ann Arbor, MI: University of Michigan Center for Political Studies, May 2009.
† The term Latino is used instead of Hispanic by ANES in data collection.

ganizing activities associated with religious institutions provides useful training for political activities such as running a campaign. Religious institutions that open leadership positions to a large number of members often provide greater opportunities to learn necessary civic skills than do organizations with strongly hierarchical chains of command. This may explain why Hispanics, who generally attend highly structured Catholic congregations, are less active in civic life than are African American Protestants of similar economic means.[11] Many Protestant denominations allocate considerable authority and responsibility to local church leaders and members of the congregation. Jewish congregations are also organized in a decentralized manner, allowing members of a synagogue many opportunities for involvement and the exercise of leadership skills.

Workplace The workplace also provides opportunities to develop resources such as analytic and communication skills that are useful for political life. Upper-income jobs, however, typically provide more such opportunities than those that pay considerably less. These high-paying jobs often stress human-relations skills and provide many opportunities for exercising the organizational talent necessary to engage in politics. They also place individuals within a circle of acquaintances who are likely themselves to be politically active. Higher-income jobs also provide access to voluntary associations like Lions Club International Foundation, which help expand contacts and opportunities for political action.

By contrast, low-skill jobs that require little formal education provide fewer opportunities for making decisions or leading meetings. Labor unions, however, offer low-skill workers the opportunity to occupy leadership positions, thus providing an alternative forum for civic learning.

Union forepersons, for example, must learn to resolve disputes and to represent the rank and file to the management. Unions also promote civic activism by educating members about political issues and urging them to become active in their communities. Unfortunately, steep declines in union jobs over the last quarter century have severely undercut such opportunities for many workers.

Race and Gender Access to resources varies according to race and gender, but these variations likely reflect underlying differences in wealth and education. Whites, on average, participate in greater numbers than African Americans in political activities, and Hispanics have lower participation rates than either whites or blacks. However, participation by minority racial and ethnic groups has risen in recent years. In 2008 substantial increases in political activity among these groups occurred, especially with regard to voting. Spurred by interest in the campaign of Barack Obama, turnout among black youth and black women surged, as did other visible displays of candidate support.[12]

Women now vote at higher levels than men, whereas men contribute significantly more money to political leaders and contact political leaders more often than women.[13] Women's political contributions have increased in recent years, but a gap remains, perhaps because women receive lower pay than men with similar jobs. Women may be somewhat less likely to contact political leaders and attend rallies for candidates because far fewer leaders are female.

Political Engagement

Personal resources supply the necessary ingredients to take part in government, but they alone cannot explain

Political Inactives' Reasons for Their Inactivity

	%
I don't have enough time	39
I should take care of myself and my family before I worry about the community or nation	34
The important things of my life have nothing to do with politics	20
I never thought of being involved	19
Politics is uninteresting and boring	17
Politics can't help with my personal or family problems	17
Politics is too complicated	15
As one individual, I don't feel I can have an impact	15
For what I would get out of it, politics is not worth what I would have to put into it	14
Politics is a dirty business	13
I feel burned out	9
It is not my place	9
I don't like the people	7
It is not my responsibility	6
There are no good causes anymore	6
I might get into trouble	3

Source: Sidney Verba, Kay Lehman Schlozman, and Henry E. Brady. *Voice and Equality: Civic Voluntarism in American Politics* (Cambridge: Harvard University Press, 1995), 129.

why some people get involved while others do not. Some people become politically active because they see it as their civic duty or because politics is a vocational interest. These persons display a psychological predisposition toward political involvement called **political engagement**. Others participate only when they feel their political issues touch directly on their vital interests, such as a local ordinance that threatens to close an individual's business. Many simply feel politics has no relevance to their day-to-day lives or problems. People who hold these latter views strongly are unlikely to have the motivation to participate. Cross-cultural studies also show that political engagement is affected by the overall level of income inequality within the nation. Where greater income inequality prevails, individuals at the bottom of the income ladder are far less likely to demonstrate an interest in politics, to discuss politics, or to vote.[14] The adjacent table lists several reasons why people choose not to get involved in politics.

Political engagement involves four dimensions or elements: political interest, political efficacy, political information, and strength of party identification.[15] **Political interest** is the level of concern that a politically engaged person has about an election outcome and the candidates' positions on the issues. Politically interested individuals care which candidate will win an election and which position on an issue the government will adopt. As a result, they tend to be more politically active. Political efficacy (Chapter 6) is the sense of empowerment or satisfaction created by political involvement. This dimension has both internal and external components.[16] **Internal political efficacy** is the confidence individuals have in their ability to understand and participate in the political world. People with high levels of internal political efficacy believe they can comprehend political issues and know how to make themselves heard. **External political efficacy** is an individual's belief that the government will respond to his or her actions. Individuals with high levels of external political efficacy are confident that the government will listen when they speak and respond appropriately. People who lack a sense of political efficacy often regard political activity as intimidating and wasteful.

The third dimension of political engagement is **political information**, the amount of knowledge a person has about political issues, figures, and the workings of the political system. Citizens with more knowledge of the Constitution, political leaders, and the issues of the day are more likely to participate. That is why it is important for young people to acquire sound political education in the schools. A final dimension of political engagement is **strength of party identification**. We will see in Chapter 9 that identification with either the Democratic or Republican Party can predict not only the direction of a person's vote but also whether he or she is likely to vote at all.

It is unclear whether political engagement causes one to become active politically or whether participating in political activity increases one's sense of political engagement. The causal relationship probably runs both ways.

Personal contact is one of the most effective ways to mobilize citizens to participate in the political process.

Mobilization

Even an individual with the necessary resources, a high level of interest, and confidence in his or her ability to make a difference is unlikely to get involved unless asked to do so. Through the process of **political mobilization**, a variety of sources alert citizens to opportunities to participate and encourage them to become politically involved. These sources include political parties, elected officials, interest groups, candidates for political office, voluntary associations, friends, and neighbors.

Direct mobilization involves candidate and party organizations contacting citizens personally to invite them to take part in political activities. Examples include door-to-door canvassing, direct mail solicitation, circulation of petitions, requests for money, and letter-writing campaigns. In appealing to citizens, activists are likely to provide either inducements, such as political promises, or assistance, including transportation to the polls. Political parties traditionally played the principal role in mobilizing voters. They would inform voters about when elections were being held and which candidates were running.

Voter turnout in America peaked during the heyday of political parties at the turn of the twentieth century. During this period, turnout was as high as 80 percent or more, partly because of party efforts to touch voters directly. Political parties energized communities with parades and picnics to generate support and sought the visible loyalty of citizens by providing their constituents with jobs, government contracts, and other tangible benefits. During the twentieth century, however, the mobilizing role of parties weakened as other institutions, such as the mass media, began delivering political information without the "personal touch" of a local precinct captain or party worker.

Many scholars believe the loss of personal contact in voter mobilization contributed to a decline in voting. It is easier to ignore an admonition to vote from a television newscaster than to ignore a personal appeal from a neighbor who represents your party of choice.

Both political parties and political candidates have shown a renewed commitment to direct mobilization in recent years. George W. Bush's campaign targeted infrequent voters with repeated personal appeals and direct mailings. The Obama campaign used new technologies to reach out to millions of new voters, and his administration is trying to keep these mobilizing efforts alive during his presidency.

Indirect mobilization occurs when leaders use networks of friends and acquaintances to persuade others to participate. Political leaders know that citizens are far more likely to respond to appeals from a member of their own religious congregation, for example, than from a politician they do not know. As a result, political leaders use the power of organized groups such as professional associations, business groups like the Chamber of Commerce, labor unions, civic associations, and churches to spread enthusiasm for a candidate or a cause.

political engagement Psychological predisposition toward or interest in politics.

political interest An attribute of political participants that measures one's concern for an election outcome and the positions of the candidates on the issues.

internal political efficacy An individual's self-confidence in his or her ability to understand and participate in politics.

external political efficacy An individual's belief that his or her activities will influence what the government will do or who will win an election.

political information A measure of the amount of political knowledge an individual possesses concerning political issues, political figures, and the workings of the political system.

strength of party identification The degree of loyalty that an individual feels toward a particular political party.

political mobilization Process whereby citizens are alerted to participatory opportunities and encouraged to become involved.

direct mobilization Process by which citizens are contacted personally by candidate and party organizations to take part in political activities.

indirect mobilization Process by which political leaders use networks of friends and acquaintances to activate political participation.

Political leaders use community groups and organizations to help spread their message.

Where voluntary associations are numerous and strong, their potential impact on political participation should be great. Where such associations are few or weak, political agents have fewer organizations to utilize for recruitment. There is no doubt that the falloff in the number of Americans active in traditional types of voluntary associations has made political mobilization more difficult. Political campaigns often turn to churches or labor unions for help in mobilizing voters on Election Day. In 2004, George W. Bush employed both churchgoers and networks of community supporters who identified and mobilized infrequent voters in their neighborhoods. In 2008, Barack Obama had a sophisticated ground campaign using union members, community organizers, and college activists who knocked on doors and made phone calls to likely voters.

Several factors affect the timing, targets, and method of mobilization. First, political actors—whether through direct or indirect mobilization—are likely to target their efforts at strategic times to enhance the success of their cause. For example, political parties concentrate their activities around primary or general elections.

Second, political actors are more likely to target groups of individuals they believe will respond positively to their message and whose backgrounds make them likely targets for mobilization. Local party activists rarely try to convert supporters from the opposition party. This is also true for those who engage in indirect mobilization, such as political advocacy groups. They usually address their appeals to upper-income, highly educated individuals who have been willing in the past to write letters, to donate money, or to make phone calls in support of their cause.

Finally, the cost of the action being requested affects mobilization. Signing a petition involves little effort. Voting requires a bit more. Writing a thoughtful letter to a member of Congress can require more time, energy, and skill. People are likely to consider responding to invitations if the requests do not come too often, if there is a realistic chance of success, if they consider the outcome important, and if participation does not conflict with other important demands on their time.

VOTING

Voting is a unique political activity for a variety of reasons. As we noted earlier, a rational actor may well see very little reason to vote, based on the perceived costs and benefits. And because voting conveys little information,

Who Votes?

Total Voting*

61.7%

Percentage who reported having voted

Region**	
West	62.15
Industrial Midwest	65.36
Farm Midwest	70.23
South	60.45
Southwest	55.28
New England	66.41
Mid Atlantic	62.85
Mountain	68.49
Age***	
18 to 29 years	51
30 to 44 years	62
45 to 64 years	69
65 years and over	70
Race and Ethnicity***	
White	66.1
Black	65.2
Hispanic (of any race)	49.9
Asian	47.0
Gender	
Women	65.7
Men	61.5
Gender combined with race, ethnicity***	
Black female	68.8
White female	67.9
Hispanic female	51.8
Asian female	46.9
Black male	60.7
White male	64.2
Hispanic male	47.9
Asian male	47.1
Education****	
Less than high school diploma	39.4
High school	54.9
Some college/bachelor's degree	71.5
Postgraduate education	82.7

* Estimate of Voter Eligible Population (VEP) by Michael McDonald, *United States Elections Project.* Accessed on May 13, 2009 at http://elections .gmu.edu/CPS_2008.html.This figure is thought to be more reliable than Voting Age Population (VAP) since some voting-age citizens, like felons, are prohibited from voting. Preliminary unadjusted census figures placed turnout at 63.6%. However, both McDonald's figure and the census estimate remained preliminary at time of publication.

** (VAP) Curtis Gans and Jon Hussey, "African-Americans, Anger, Fear and Youth Propel Turnout to Highest Level Since 1960," Center for the Study of the American Electorate, American University, Washington, DC, December 17, 2008.

*** (VEP) Emily Hoban Kirby and Kei Kawashima-Ginsberg, *The Youth Vote in 2008 Factsheet,* Center for Research and Information on Civic Learning and Engagement, Tufts University, Medford, MA, April 2009.

**** (VEP) Mark Hugo Lopez and Paul Taylor, *Dissecting the 2008 Electorate: Most Diverse in U.S. History,* Washington, DC: Pew Research Center, April 30, 2009.

***** (VEP) Michael McDonald, *United States Elections Project.* Accessed on May 13, 2009 at http://elections.gmu.edu/CPS_2008.html.

even those who vote have no idea whether a candidate will respond to their needs. Nevertheless, tens of millions of Americans vote regularly in national elections. For many of them, voting confers the psychological benefit of satisfying their civic responsibilities and promotes candidates and issues important to their interests.

Who Votes? Who Doesn't?

Clearly, resources make a difference in voting. Voter turnout increases directly with employment status and wealth, level of education, and age. Regional differences also exist; both coasts have traditionally voted at higher rates than the interior of the country, although some regions, like the Midwest farm belt, are given a boost by high turnout in states such as Minnesota and Wisconsin, which recorded some of the highest participation rates in the nation in 2008 (76.1 percent and 71.3 percent, respectively).[17] As we mentioned earlier, females now vote at a higher rate than males.

Driven by interest in the Obama candidacy, black voters in 2008 reversed a long-standing trend. Turnout among black voters increased by about 5 percentage points, from 60.3 percent in 2004 to 65.3 percent in 2008, reducing the overall turnout gap between the races. Much of the gain in black turnout was driven by an increase in young and female voters. Among all racial and gender groups, black women had the highest turnout rate of all, 68.8 percent. Hispanic voters also increased their share of the electorate, turning out at a rate of nearly 50 percent of those who were eligible; the percentage of eligible Asian voters increased by nearly 3 percent. Still, white voters maintained a disproportionate share of the overall electorate (76.3 percent) relative to their share of the U.S. population (65.8 percent).[18]

Turnout generally increases with age, and 2008 was no different. However, 2008 did see an almost 2 percent increase in turnout over 2004 levels by those between the ages of 18 and 29, making 2008 the best showing for young voters since 1992 and the second highest since 18-year-olds first exercised the franchise in the 1972 presidential election. Turnout among this age group was 11 percent better than it was in 2000. Again, much of the increase was fueled by an uptick in female and minority voters. Young people with college experience turned out at a rate almost 25 percent higher than youth with no college experience.[19] It is too soon to tell if this increase reflects a long-term trend in greater youth engagement in elections. For years, young people have told pollsters they do not vote because they do not believe government is responsive to their needs. In one study, only 53 percent of young people said they felt the government and elections address the concerns of people their age; 48 percent reported that political leaders pay at least some attention to people like them.[20] The issues, the candidates, and the increased use of youth-friendly technologies employed in the 2008 campaign most certainly contributed to the resurgence of youthful voting. Time will tell if their interest in politics and elections can be sustained.

Political Engagement by Age

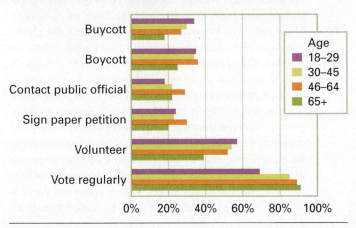

Source: Millennials: Confident. Connected. Open to Change. Pew Research Center, February 2010.

Factors Influencing Voter Turnout

There are several ways of measuring voter turnout. We can measure turnout as a percentage of all persons who are of voting age (Voting-Age Population, or VAP), or we can measure it as a percentage of those who are eligible to vote (Voter-Eligible Population, or VEP). The latter is considered the more sound measurement since it excludes those not permitted to vote, like nonresidents or felons. While the type of measure we use makes a difference in the magnitude of change in turnout from election to election, two facts stand out about turnout in presidential elections no matter how we measure it. From about 1960 to 1992, turnout in presidential elections declined, with the greatest declines occurring between 1960 and 1972. After a spike in 1992, it dipped again, only to rebound in 2004 and 2008. A second undisputed feature is that American turnout compares unfavorably with rates in other democracies, although some European countries have begun to experience turnout declines as well. Several factors help explain our poor turnout rate compared to other nations.

First, Americans must register to vote either in person or by mail, and they must reregister if they move or fail to vote in a certain number of consecutive elections. By contrast, some countries use a civil registry system that automatically registers every eligible resident. Denmark, for example, uses a computerized national civil registry to produce a voter list. The government issues each citizen a number, somewhat like our Social Security numbers, for the delivery of all government services and the payment of taxes. Voters can present the number for identification at the polls throughout the country, no matter where they live. Currently, nine states allow some form of same-day registration. 2008 voter turnout in these states was over seven percentage points higher than in other states.[21] Young people who are more mobile are more likely to turn out to

Voter Turnout Among Youth, 1972–2008

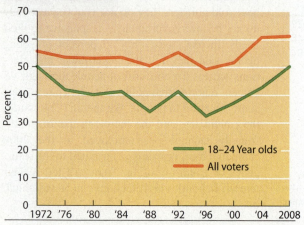

Source: Center for Information and Research on Civic Learning and Education.

Presidential Turnout Rates, 1948–2008

Percent voting

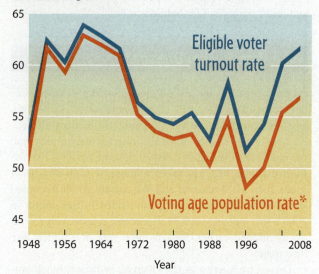

*Everyone age 18 and older living in the United States, including persons ineligible to vote, mainly noncitizens and ineligible felons, and excluding overseas eligible voters.

Source: Michael McDonald, *United States Elections Project.* Accessed on May 13, 2009, at http://elections.gmu.edu/CPS 2008.html.

vote in states with same day registration.[22] Many countries also require registration only once in a lifetime so that voters remain permanently eligible no matter where or how often they move within the country.

Secondly, the timing and scheduling of elections also affects turnout. Voting in the United States often takes place on a Tuesday, which means that most Americans must adjust their workday schedules to go to the polls. By contrast, some European countries schedule elections on a national holiday to make it easier for voters to show up at the polls. Other nations, including Norway, Japan, Switzerland, and New Zealand, hold elections on weekends. More recently, Americans have been offered the choice of voting early, in some places up to a month before the election. This option is becoming much more popular. It is estimated that as many as 30 percent of all voters in the 2008 presidential election voted early.[23] In some states, like Oregon, voting is entirely by mail. There are differences of opinion over the advisability of early voting and voting by mail, however. Some argue that it artificially cuts the campaign short for some voters and destroys the sense of shared civic responsibility that accompanies a uniform day of voting for all Americans. Others claim that the benefits in convenience and potential for increased turnout are worth the costs.

Our two-party system also helps explain low turnout in the United States. Most other Western democracies have multiparty parliamentary systems that generally represent

Average Turnout in National Elections, Western Europe and United States Since 1945

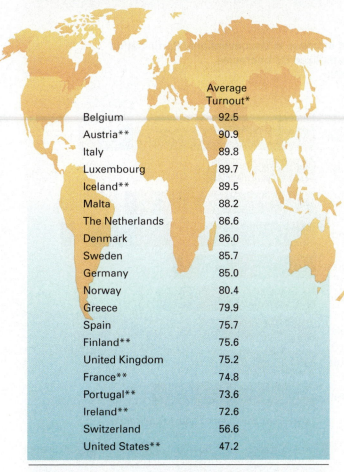

	Average Turnout*
Belgium	92.5
Austria**	90.9
Italy	89.8
Luxembourg	89.7
Iceland**	89.5
Malta	88.2
The Netherlands	86.6
Denmark	86.0
Sweden	85.7
Germany	85.0
Norway	80.4
Greece	79.9
Spain	75.7
Finland**	75.6
United Kingdom	75.2
France**	74.8
Portugal**	73.6
Ireland**	72.6
Switzerland	56.6
United States**	47.2

* Data presented are percent of registered voters, except for the United States, where percent of voting age population is given. This reduces somewhat the rate for the U.S. but does not substantially change the rank order.

** Includes results from both presidential and representational body elections.

Source: European data from International Institute of Democracy and Electoral Assistance; U.S. data from U.S. Census Bureau.

the centrist appeal of American parties is partly responsible for the poor turnout of lower-income groups because citizens in these brackets fail to hear candidates addressing their concerns.[24]

The number and frequency of elections is a fourth factor depressing turnout in the United States. The United States holds more primary and general elections at the national, state, and local levels than any other democracy. Unlike many European voters, who go to the polls once every three, four, or five years, American voters in most states are asked to vote in primary and general elections every year, and often more frequently. Special elections may be called to replace candidates who resign or are removed from office. Some states also ask citizens to vote on referenda to approve or reject particular measures ranging from tax increases to special funding for public schools. Many analysts believe the frequency with which Americans are called to vote creates **voter fatigue**, a tendency to tire of the process and refrain from going to the polls.

> **voter fatigue** A tendency to tire of the process of voting as a result of frequent elections.

Finally, the competitiveness of the race affects turnout: the more competitive the race, the more interest it draws. Voters are less likely to show up if the result is clearly predictable. Although competitive races attract more interest and participation, only about half of the presidential contests since 1952 have been close right

the interests of particular economic groups within the nation. In Great Britain, for example, the Labour Party has a long tradition of appealing to the working class; the Conservatives (popularly called the Tories), by contrast, make their appeals to the more affluent. The economic orientation of political parties can exert a powerful influence on getting out the vote by convincing voters that their economic interests are taken seriously by political leaders. In America, the major political parties rarely structure their messages primarily around economic divisions, preferring to appeal to the vast middle of the economic and ideological spectrum. (We will discuss this characteristic of American parties at greater length in Chapter 9.) Some researchers believe that

Many nations hold elections on weekends to increase turnout.

Changing Patterns of Political Participation

In today's world, where personal identity and expression are seen as more important than simply voting one's pocketbook, younger people seem less interested in traditional activities like voting or joining organizations and more interested in finding new modes of political self-expression. The table at right, based on data compiled by Ronald Inglehart and Gabriella Catterberg,[1] charts the rise in unconventional political activities in Western industrial democracies over the period from 1974 to 2000.

1. What types of unconventional political activities have increased the most?
2. Are you more likely to participate in one of these alternate forms of political engagement than more conventional forms like voting? Do you believe activities like protesting, boycotting, or BUYcotting are effective forms of participation?
3. The authors reject the notion that citizens in advanced democracies are withdrawing from civic action. Instead, they insist, citizens in today's world are increasingly critical of elite decision making and unwilling to join elite institutions, and they are increasingly ready to intervene actively to influence specific decisions. In short, "the nature of citizen politics in advanced democracies has changed."[2] Based on the data in the graph and your own experiences, would you agree or disagree with the author's assertion? Why or why not?

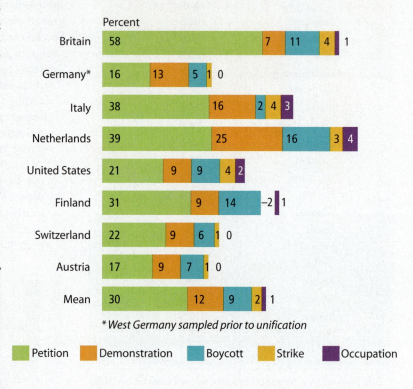

Percent Increase in Unconventional Participation in Industrialized Democracies
1974–2000

* West Germany sampled prior to unification

Legend: Petition | Demonstration | Boycott | Strike | Occupation

[1] Ronald Inglehart and Gabriella Catterberg, "Trends in Political Action: The Developmental Trend and the Post-Honeymoon Decline," *International Journal of Comparative Sociology* 43, no. 3–5 (2002): 300–316.
[2] Inglehart and Catterberg, 314.

---

up to Election Day, and congressional elections today are rarely competitive (as we will see in Chapter 11).[25]

OTHER FORMS OF POLITICAL PARTICIPATION

Many forms of political participation require citizens to spend more resources than the simple act of voting. Some,

such as volunteering to work in a political campaign or writing letters to political leaders, require additional expenditures of time. Others, such as contributing to a candidate or cause, require additional financial resources.

Beyond Voting: Activities That Require More Time

Although U.S. voter turnout compares poorly to that in other democracies, Americans show greater levels of participation in more time-consuming political activities. One study comparing the United States to Austria, the Netherlands, the United Kingdom, and Germany found that Americans ranked first in the amount of time they devoted to campaign work, contact with public officials, and community volunteering.[26] Unlike voting, there is no limit to the number of times one can perform such acts or the amount of time one can devote to them. Some stalwart activists find themselves limited only by the number of hours in the day. Activities that require more time also vary in the amount of information they convey and the level of skill necessary to perform them. Writing a thoughtful letter to a member of Congress and working a candidate's phone bank during a political campaign are two examples of time-intensive activities that convey a high level of information and require a high level of skill and knowledge.

Because time-intensive activities demand a greater level of commitment than voting, we would expect these acts to hold the potential for greater benefits. Some of the benefits may be material. A successful candidate might appoint campaign workers to advisory positions or promote policies that directly benefit them, such as a change in zoning that permits business expansion. Participation also provides psychological rewards such as the opportunity to meet and work with others who share similar views. Activists feel gratified when their work results in the implementation of policies they support.[27] Other, less conventional

forms of participation such as petitioning and demonstrating enable the individual to take some direct and personal role in promoting an idea or cause. Many times these are tools used by groups that feel they can find no other way to make their voices heard. Some people find these activities more personally rewarding than anonymous acts like voting and more relevant to their everyday lives. And Americans are not alone. The incidence of unconventional activity like protesting seems to be increasing in many developed democracies. Some researchers believe these actions represent an emerging pathway to more meaningful citizen engagement—a pathway that needs further scholarly exploration.[28]

Beyond Voting: Activities That Require More Skill

Voting is a fairly simple act. So is donating money. But some acts of political participation require more sophisticated skills. Political campaigns in America are fueled by thousands of unpaid average citizens who staff phone banks, contact donors, serve as financial consultants or liaisons with the press, coordinate activities with politi-

Meet Molly Kawahata

On a cold November night in 2008, Molly Kawahata took to the streets of Berkeley, California with thousands of other students. "It was the moment," she recalls, "when chills shuddered my spine and tears filled my eyes."* It was the moment Barack Obama was declared the winner of the presidential campaign.

The moment came almost two years after Molly signed on as the National High School Director of Students for Barack Obama, helping to recruit a field army of young organizers that mobilized more than 100,000 students across the country. "Students originated the campaign model, developed the communications

PORTRAIT
OF AN ACTIVIST

strategy, created the field plans, trained the organizers, ran the schedules, and tracked the numbers," she recalls. "The Students for Barack Obama campaign started and remained in student hands. In our job, we were given one vague instruction and not much more: to create a movement and see what we could do with it."

Four years later, Molly is back on the Berkeley campus completing her psychology degree after a stint at the White House. She surveys a landscape that has changed. Many young people who were politically engaged and optimistic four years ago are facing a dismal economic climate and bitter partisan bickering.

Still, she is optimistic. "There have been a lot of accomplishments—the repeal of Don't ask don't tell, student loan reform, health insurance reform—but we still have work to do. Many young people became politically involved for the first time in the 2008 Obama campaign and have remained involved in their communities since. It will be important for us to unify behind the patriotic values that we did in the 2008 election: those of empathy, empowerment, and community."

* Pers. Comm.

PRICE OF ADMISSION: VOTER ID LAWS

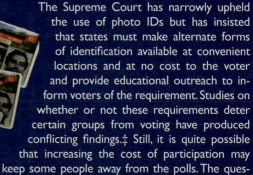

Registered voters entering the polling place in many states this year will be required to provide a photo ID. These documents are required in order to prove residency and to prevent fraud. Most of these states accept a driver's license or passport. Most states also provide free identification cards at locations where driver's licenses are issued with proof of other documentation such as a birth certificate or a utility bill listing the home address of the voter. Supporters believe proof of identification is a small price to pay in order to prevent voter fraud. Currently, nine states require photo IDs and the list is growing.*

But it is estimated that as many as 11 percent of United States citizens—mostly older, low-income, and minority citizens—do not have government-issued photo IDs.† While these individuals could receive alternative documents for free from state authorities, many claim the effort required to obtain them places an additional undue burden on otherwise eligible voters, many of whom have difficulty getting around. In some states, a college ID that does not contain a photo will not qualify as documentation needed to obtain a voter ID.

The Supreme Court has narrowly upheld the use of photo IDs but has insisted that states must make alternate forms of identification available at convenient locations and at no cost to the voter and provide educational outreach to inform voters of the requirement. Studies on whether or not these requirements deter certain groups from voting have produced conflicting findings.‡ Still, it is quite possible that increasing the cost of participation may keep some people away from the polls. The question is whether this increased cost is worth the benefit of preventing possible fraud.

* Nineteen states require some other form of identification. No states can turn voters without IDs away completely but must provide some sort of recourse for voters without IDs. See, National Conference of State Legislatures, *Voter Identification Requirements*, Updated April 19, 2011. Accessed on May 3, 2011 at http://www.ncsl.org/default.aspx?tabid=16602.
† Vishal Agraharkar, Wendy Weiser, and Adam Skaggs, *The Cost of Voter ID Laws: What the Courts Say*, Brennan Center for Justice (New York: New York University School of Law), 2011.
‡ For evidence against the adverse impact of these laws, see Jason D. Mycoff, Michael W. Wagner, David C. Wilson, *The Effect of Voter Identification Laws on Aggregate and Individual Level Turnout*, paper delivered at the Annual meeting of the American Political Science Association in Chicago, IL, August, 2007. For an example of data indicating turnout may be adversely affected, see Matt A. Barreto, Stephen A. Nuño, Gabriel R. Sanchez, *The Disproportionate Impact of Indiana Voter ID Requirements on the Electorate, Working Paper*, Washington Institute for the Study of Ethnicity and Race, November 8, 2007.

cal parties, and organize rallies. Even writing a letter to one's congressperson requires confidence in one's ability to communicate effectively. These activities put us in close contact with our elected leaders, giving us an opportunity to express our views more clearly than the act of voting alone.

Citizens who engage in these activities are not equally drawn from all segments of the political community. The more affluent are more likely to write letters, volunteer for political campaigning, make political contact with elected officials, and work on solving community problems. The affluent often have training in the skills necessary for these more demanding tasks. Nevertheless, as we have seen, religious organizations and labor unions can provide those with fewer resources opportunities to develop these same skills. Often, lower levels of participation by the poor are traceable not to lack of skill but to lower levels of interest or a lack of confidence in their political efficacy. When political activities require financial commitment, however, the discrepancy in participation

between rich and poor is not only greater, it is more difficult to overcome.[29]

Beyond Voting: Activities That Require Money

Contributing money is the political act that has the greatest capacity for variation from individual to individual. Within the limits of the law, contributors can donate as little or as much as they want. However, the

Political leaders and organizations increasingly rely on posh fundraising events to fuel their political campaigns.

clarity of the message conveyed by political donations can vary depending on the identity of the recipient. Contributing to a narrow political cause sends a clear message that one supports the goals established by the group. By comparison, contributing money to a presidential campaign may signal support for a candidate's position on Social Security reform or for his or her personal leadership abilities. The actual motivation for giving is ambiguous for the recipient.

Campaign contributions continue to come largely from those with greater resources, but the Obama campaign in 2008 demonstrated the potential of the Internet for widening the base of financial support. His campaign raised $1 million a day or more, mostly from donors contributing $250 or less.

Advocacy groups that promote a political agenda outside of the electoral arena, for example, by petitioning administrative agencies and the courts, also need money—often great sums of it. These types of activities are very expensive. As a result, political candidates and advocacy groups must turn to supporters who can afford to contribute to the cause.

Financial giving as a form of participation raises concerns about the type of citizen commitment that today's politicians and activists value most. Some scholars worry that we have entered a period of **checkbook democracy** where little is required of citizens beyond their cash.[30] Campaign strategists and advocacy group

Hot or Not?

Should BUYcotting, or selectively buying products based on a company's record of social responsibility, be considered a form of political action?

professionals in Washington offices plot political operations with little citizen input, contacting the public only for the funds necessary to keep their organizations going. Politicians rarely consult citizens about specific proposals, tactics, or campaign goals.

checkbook democracy A term that expresses the notion that little is required of citizens beyond their cash.

This deprives citizens of opportunities to develop civic skills they might acquire through face-to-face participation. The most worrisome aspect of this trend is the potential for the wealthy to dominate political participation and policy-making, shutting the less well-off out of the process.

This portrait of political participation in America is overly bleak. Many campaign organizations and advocacy groups combine citizen action with cash contributions. They alert contributors and noncontributors alike to measures that threaten their interests and mobilize them to take action by contacting elected officials by letter or phone or over the Internet. Many advocacy groups facilitate citizen communication with political leaders by providing contact in-

Many people, especially the young, are turning to consumer activism as a means of making political statements.

formation or even direct access through the association's telecommunications network.

Another type of financial activism is on the rise as well: **consumer activism**, the practice of making a political or social statement with one's buying power. Commerce today is dominated by global corporations that reach beyond single continents. Their activities often escape regulation by individual nations. Except for shareholders with major stakes in these companies, individuals have little control over their operation. Nevertheless, some consumers find it useful to make a personal statement about the behavior of these companies or their products through their buying habits. Consumers can register their disapproval for the acts of certain businesses by boycotting their products; they can reward companies they believe are exemplary by BUYcotting. Consumer activism of this sort is surprisingly widespread. Roughly half of the adult population in America reports having used their buying power to either punish or reward companies or products in the past 12 months. These activities seem to be spread across all age levels, although they are more likely to be practiced by Americans with higher incomes and among those who are most attentive to politics.[31]

consumer activism The practice of making a political or social statement with one's buying power.

THE IMPACT OF PARTICIPATION PATTERNS ON POLICY

Does it matter that those at the upper end of the socioeconomic spectrum participate more and have greater contact with political elites than the less-advantaged? If the concerns and issues that mobilize the well-off are the same as those important to the rest of the population, there should be little cause for concern. However, if the concerns of the two groups differ, then there is reason to believe that politicians are more likely to pay attention to the needs of the wealthy while ignoring those of the poor.

Voting data seem to indicate that the attitudes and preferences of voters and nonvoters are substantially similar.[32] With the possible exception of extremely close elections, like the 2000 presidential contest, increased turnout by the less advantaged would probably not affect the outcome of most elections.[33] Participation that conveys more information to leaders, however, displays a larger gap between the concerns of those who participate most and those who are least politically active. Citizens who depend on government assistance programs such as welfare, food stamps, and income support are far less likely to write letters, take part in community activities, contact political leaders, protest, or contribute time or money to a political campaign. When they do communicate with leaders, they are twice as likely as the advantaged to refer to their basic needs—food, housing, health care, and the like. By contrast, wealthier citizens—who are three times as likely as the disadvantaged to contact elected officials—are more likely to voice concerns about taxes, government spending, and the budget.[34] As a result, leaders hear more from their constituents about taxes and budgets than they hear about government programs that are vital to a large segment of the population.

Economic inequality not only affects the kind of issues political leaders are likely to take up. It also, as one researcher concludes, "stacks the deck of democracy in favor of the richest citizens and, as a result, most everyone else is more likely to conclude that politics is simply not a game worth playing."[35] Differences in access to resources, interest, and mobilization create patterns of political participation in America that result in a much louder voice for those already advantaged. In a study of Senate roll call votes, Larry Bartels found "senators appear to be considerably more responsive to the opinions of affluent constituents than to the opinions of middle-class constituents, while

> "**SOCIOECONOMIC INEQUALITY** produces inequality in political voice; this in turn fosters policies that favor the already advantaged; and these policies reinforce socioeconomic inequality."

Is electronic voting in our future?

Percent Voting in Advanced Industrialized Countries with Compulsory Voting

Country	Under 30	30–44	45–64	65 and Older
Australia (2004)	97%	98%	98%	99%
Belgium (2004)	89%	98%	97%	92%
Greece (2000)	90%	93%	95%	93%
Luxemburg (1999)	91%	93%	95%	86%

Source: Martin P. Wattenberg, *Is Voting for Young People?* (New York: Pearson Education, 2007), 168.

the opinions of constituents in the bottom third of the income distribution have *no* apparent statistical effect on their senators' roll call votes."[36] Another political scientist, Sidney Verba describes the process this way: "Socioeconomic inequality produces inequality in political voice; this in turn fosters policies that favor the already advantaged; and these policies reinforce socioeconomic inequality."[37]

Some observers might argue that this imbalance in political participation is not all bad. After all, the affluent are often better informed and more tolerant of divergent beliefs than are the less well-off. One might argue that domination of political discourse by the more affluent will result in more enlightened policies.[38] Democratic governments, however, are supposed to balance the interests of different groups. The balancing act is made more difficult when our political leaders hear disproportionately from one segment of the population.

PARTICIPATION AND CIVIC ENGAGEMENT TODAY

We have witnessed a recent resurgence in political participation, especially with regard to voting, that is encouraging. Particularly encouraging is the increase in voting by formerly underrepresented groups such as minorities and women. There is no guarantee, however, that rates of participation will continue to rise or even stabilize. If we want participation rates to improve—and if we ever hope to improve voting to rates comparable with much of the rest of the developed world—we must make participation less costly in terms of time and money, two of the biggest constraints on participation.

Hot or Not?

Should voting be made compulsory?

Several proposed reforms, such as keeping polls open longer on Election Day, could greatly reduce the inconvenience associated with the act of voting. In some states, the polls close as early as 6 P.M., disenfranchising many working people and discouraging many young adults—a group that reports the need for greater flexibility in polling hours to accommodate their work and school schedules.[39] Second, many nonvoters say they would be more likely to vote if Election Day were a national holiday or held on a weekend. Making Election Day a holiday would also heighten social awareness of the importance of the activity. The recent trend of early voting, with poll centers open for several days before the election, may be a reasonable alternative. Third, all states could adopt same-day registration. This would reduce the burden on citizens who move frequently or who want to participate but either are unaware of registration requirements or learn about them too late to comply with cutoff dates. Several states already have same-day voter registration; among these are states such as Maine, Wisconsin, and Minnesota, with some of the highest turnout rates in the nation. Other states are actually making the process of voting even more onerous by requiring the presentation of official voter identification, such as a state driver's license, at the polls. Although this may discourage voter fraud (a practice that most believe is negligible), it also has the unintended consequence of discouraging those without official IDs from voting. In 2008, the U.S. Supreme Court upheld Indiana's stringent voter ID requirement (*Crawford v. Marion County Election Board*). Finally, new methods of voting—such as Oregon's vote-by-mail experiment or pilot online-voting programs in Arizona and Washington—could complement the current procedure of casting a ballot at a polling place. These methods are proving very popular, especially among young people.

Some scholars suggest that voting rates have dipped too low for such piecemeal solutions. They recommend adopting compulsory voting as a means of reigniting the voting habit.[40] Compulsory voting laws would require eligible citizens to show up at the polls on Election Day or pay a small fine. Data show that such laws in other countries result in high turnout among every age category. However, the idea of making voting a compulsory activity seems utterly out of sync with America's reliance on volunteerism. As a result, this is one solution that may have little future in this country.

Reducing the cost of running for public office may reduce financial barriers to participation by limiting the importance of campaign fundraising. For example, to scale back the largest single cost of campaigning, networks could make free television available to political candidates. A system of partial public financing for presidential elections is already in place, and several states are experimenting with public funding of campaigns for state offices (see Chapter 9). Government could make more public funding available to those who wish to run.

Enhancing civic skills to improve participation rates is perhaps the simplest reform to achieve—at least in theory. In this area, educational institutions may be in the best position to increase their efforts and effectiveness. Over the last generation, high schools have reduced by two-thirds the median number of civics and government courses they offer. This represents an abandonment of one of the traditional functions of public schools: training students in the skills necessary to take part in their democratic heritage.[41] Schools could provide more intensive—and more interesting—courses in government. Students show more excitement and interest in politics when they are asked to get involved rather than merely to study a subject from a textbook or listen to lectures. Many schools already offer opportunities to learn by encouraging or requiring students to attend public meetings, talk to government officials, and engage in service learning activities to assist community members in solving local problems. Schools can do more to encourage voting as well. Colleges can hold voter registration drives, help students locate polling places, and assist in disseminating absentee ballots.

Current Controversy

Direct Democracy—There's an App for That

A Silicon Valley start-up company, Verafirma, has introduced new software that will make it easier to collect and verify the signatures needed to place voter initiatives on the ballot. The software allows petition supporters to gather electronic signatures on touch screen devices like the iPhone or Droid and have them directly submitted to election officials for verification.

"This can make it affordable for true grass roots efforts that don't have access to the initiative game the way it's played now because it's so costly," Verafirma co-founder Jude Barry told the *San Francisco Chronicle*.* Currently, initiative drives rely on signature gathering companies that charge up to five dollars per signature collected. In a state such as California, which requires nearly seven hundred thousand valid signatures, this can be a costly proposition. The new technology would allow supporters to gather signatures much more efficiently and at a fraction of the cost.

Research on the use of initiatives shows that voter turnout is higher in states that allow initiatives than in states that do not and that the effect is even greater as the number of initiatives on the ballot grows.† Initiatives give voters a direct say in how their leaders govern, making it clear to lawmakers what their constituents want. So the possibility that this new e-signature technology will make it easier for citizens to place initiatives on the ballot is good for democracy—right?

Not everyone agrees. In recent years, many initiatives have placed limits on government that have made it more difficult for lawmakers to govern. For example, the current financial crisis in California is traceable, in part, to initiatives that require a two-thirds vote of the General Assembly to raise taxes—a monumental hurdle. The chief justice of the California Supreme Court criticized the state's reliance on the referendum process, arguing that it has "rendered our state government dysfunctional."‡ Critics say that initiatives make it impossible for legislators to find room for compromise since avenues for resolution have been removed by the voters. Now available in 24 states and the District of Columbia, the voter initiative process has been used to bring about wide-ranging changes from increased funding for education to the abolition of affirmative action, from expanding casino gambling to the denial of educational and health benefits to the families of illegal immigrants. Making the signature collection process easier and more affordable will likely increase the number of initiatives voters see and take the process out of the hands of special interests that can afford to bankroll current petition drives.

But the question remains: Will the increased use of the initiative process improve democracy, or will it simply make it more difficult to govern?

* Torey Van Oot, "E-Signature Software Touted for Voter Drives," *San Francisco Chronicle*, April 2, 2010.

† See, for example: Daniel Smith and Caroline J. Tolbert, *Educated by Initiative: The Effects of Direct Democracy on Citizens and Political Organizations in the American States* (Ann Arbor: University of Michigan Press, 2004); Caroline J. Tolbert and Daniel A. Smith, "The Educative Effects of Ballot Initiatives on Voter Turnout," *American Politics Research* 33 (2), 2005: 283–309.

‡Jennifer Steinhauer, "Top Judge Calls California Government Dysfunctional," *The New York Times*, October 10, 2009, http://www.nytimes.com/2009/10/11/us/11calif.html?_r=3 accessed April 4, 2010.

In future chapters we will examine how institutional factors like our system of elections (Chapter 9), difficulties in establishing third-party alternatives (Chapter 9), the purposeful drawing of noncompetitive districts (Chapter 11), and the electoral college (Chapter 12) all contribute to voter disillusion and diminish interest in participation. These factors alienate many voters, making them feel that their vote is unnecessary or useless. In fact, however, Rosenstone and Hansen conclude from their comprehensive study of voting that the "blame" for the long-term decline in citizen involvement rests as much with failures of the political system as with citizens themselves. The authors state the case bluntly: "Citizens did not fail the political system; if anything, the political system failed them."[42] This need not be the case, and in subsequent chapters, we will discuss what changes can be made to reverse this situation.

Summary

1. **What is the nature of political participation in America?**
   - Americans can participate in politics in a wide variety of ways. Some activities like voting are widespread; others, like running for office, attract very few participants.
   - Many Americans are willing to pay the costs of political participation even when the benefits might seem to be minimal.
   - Different political activities vary in the amount of information conveyed, in the frequency with which they can be conducted, and in the strength of the message conveyed.
   - Political involvement requires access to resources like time, skills, and money that are the result of factors such as family wealth, education, religious affiliation, type of employment, and one's race and gender.
   - Political involvement also requires the desire to be politically engaged. Political engagement involves the dimensions of political interest, political efficacy, political information, and strength of party identification.
   - Political involvement often hinges on an invitation to take part in political activities by a process of direct or indirect mobilization.

2. **What are the major forms of political participation and what resources do they require?**
   - Voting is the most common form of political participation in a democracy, requiring time and some skill but not money.
   - Many forms of political participation require citizens to spend more resources than does the act of voting.

   - Some political activities such as writing a member of Congress or participating in a campaign are more time intensive than voting.
   - Some political activities like organizing a political meeting or making a speech require more skill than does the act of voting.
   - Other political activities such as contributing to campaigns or joining advocacy groups require money that is not a requirement for voting. Some scholars worry that we have entered an era of checkbook democracy that requires little commitment from citizens.

3. **What is the nature of voting in the United States?**
   - For many Americans, voting confers the psychological benefit of satisfying one's civic responsibility and promotes candidates and issues important to one's interests.
   - Compared to other political activities, voting conveys little information, is limited in frequency, and is low in the strength of the message conveyed.
   - Voters differ from nonvoters in resources such as wealth, employment status, and level of education. Today, one's gender, race, region of the country, and age are related to the likelihood of voting.
   - Voting turnout in the United States is affected by the registration requirement, the timing and scheduling of elections, the existence of the two-party system, and the number and frequency of elections.
   - Compared to Western European democracies, voter turnout in the United States is low.

National Journal

Anti-Tax Tea Parties Roil On

The growth and influence of the populist "tea party" movement can't be measured yet, in part because it is a grassroots movement that doesn't have a leader, a national headquarters, a central manifesto, or even a common website.

But tea party organizers and observers say that progress will be measured by their ability to win party nominations for like-minded politicians, such as Florida's conservative Marco Rubio, now competing against the more centrist Governor Charlie Crist for the Republican nomination in the 2010 Senate race.

But signs of decline may be appearing. Disagreements over social policy, currently suppressed, could split tea party backers; and the movement's grassroots leaders could be elbowed aside by those in Washington, or even be tainted by the arrival of extremists from racist groups. It's a decentralized movement, so "we cannot control who has a protest and calls it a 'tea party,'" said Phil Russo, an activist in Florida who has helped organize tea parties.

In interviews, more than 15 tea party leaders frequently traced their activism back to 2008, when they individually opposed increased spending by President Bush, and especially the bipartisan Troubled Asset Relief Program that Congress approved in October. The additional spending programs that President Obama and the Democratic Congress approved triggered more concern, which coalesced into the tea party rallies in several hundred towns on April 15.

The various organizers claimed a turnout of almost 1 million people at more than 800 events. Nate Silver, a Democratic-affiliated blogger, collated available press and police reports to produce an estimate of 311,460 participants at 346 rallies.

At an early-evening event on April 15 in Charleston, S.C., attended by 3,000 to 6,000 people, Brian Keelin, the first of three main speakers, evoked the image of a Christian nation under siege by aggressive atheists. The second speaker, Ron Parks, cited patriotic traditions going back to the American Revolution, while the third offered a libertarian small-government pitch, complete with a shout-out to President Coolidge. "We're here for our children and grandchildren. . . . We've been pushed to do this, we've been pushed to gather together," Keith Malinak, a host at local radio station WSC, said.

The audience applauded Keelin's religious imagery, but it cheered the patriotic and small-government pitches more loudly. The participants, only a few of whom were nonwhite, were polite and upbeat. Their signs declared sentiments such as "Too Much Pork; That's Our Beef"; "Our Congress Is a Toxic Asset"; and "Stop Stealing My Future." One man held a sign calling for secession, and the organizers asked another man to remove a poster that referenced Obama's parentage. The organizers ushered one speaker from the stage after he offered up a conspiratorial description of the Federal Reserve Board.

The rally attracted the state's Republican governor, Mark Sanford, and Sen. Jim DeMint, R-S.C. Neither politician tried to sell the GOP brand. "This is not about partisan politics," DeMint said. "This is about what works, what makes America exceptional, what makes us unique, what gives us the best quality of life. . . . Freedom makes America work."

Many critics dismissed the tea party protests as the work of a fringe movement spurred by Fox News or as a fake grassroots movement created by D.C. groups. But observers shouldn't pigeonhole the participants as knee-jerk critics of Obama and Democrats, said Andrew Levison, who writes for The Democratic Strategist, an online magazine run by three Democratic consultants. And once the movement's members "discover they are being used as pawns by the corporate representatives who want to get control of their movement," they will be angry, Levison predicts. These corporate interests include the D.C.-based FreedomWorks, whose chairman, former House Majority Leader Dick Armey, has lobbied on behalf of oil sheiks and the Mexican Senate, he said.

Unsurprisingly, several D.C.-based political groups are trying to extend their reach using the movement. These include the Republican Governors Association, Freedom-Works, the socially conservative American Family Association, and Americans for Progress, whose state representatives rally local voters behind a variety of advocacy causes, such as opposition to the Democrats' emerging environmental and energy-related measures.

But the tea party groups sometimes reject those outreach efforts. FreedomWorks was rebuffed in Tucson, Ariz., said organizer Trent Humphries, whose April 15 event drew perhaps 3,500 people. "We said thanks, but no thanks" and instead chose to work with SmartGirlPolitics.org, a new group that claims a membership of 10,000 conservative women, he said.

The American Family Association used its websites, radio stations, and network of local volunteers to jump-start protests in multiple locations, including the Charleston event, which AFA activist Keelin co-organized. Another AFA activist, Rita Grace, organized a rain-soaked rally of 250 people in Culpeper, Va. "I had never considered community organizing," said Grace, a mother of five who lives in Culpeper. Her anti-abortion beliefs identify her as a social conservative, but "everyone I spoke to was willing to attend," she said, including people who voted for Obama.

"We exercise no control or influence over the tea parties at all," said Michael DePrimo, a top leader for the AFA, based in Tupelo, Miss. "We were acting as a clearinghouse for information . . . the tea party movement, as far as AFA is concerned, is limited to reckless government spending and unreasonable taxation."

Libertarian-minded organizers, however, dislike the AFA's involvement. "They are poison to this movement," said Eric Odom, a leading national organizer. "They try to co-opt the grassroots brand, try to push a far-right agenda, and raise money [and] inflate numbers to push their brand," said Odom, who organized the tea party in Chicago and spurned a request from Republican National Committee Chairman Michael Steele to speak at the event. Odom is a libertarian political consultant who used grassroots supporters to help pressure the Democratic Congress last year not to extend a legislative restriction on offshore oil drilling.

To keep the disparate movement together, "we only have two rules in Orlando," Russo said. "No politicians speaking at our tea parties, and—this is more of a national rule—we don't talk about social issues." He added: "This movement is about three core values—fiscal responsibility, limited government, and free markets."

Those economic values should help to protect the movement from white-power racist groups, including Stormfront.org, that see it as a recruiting pool for their mix of positions, including racial rules and trade restrictions. "We should focus on what they care about most on the day we address them, and then connect this with a bigger vision of the struggle we face," according to a posting

> "We cannot control who has a protest and calls it a 'tea party.'"
> —Phil Russo

on the Stormfront site, signed by a racist activist, dubbed "Whites Forward."

Many, perhaps most of the tea party groups work with minimal outside aid or direction. The Charleston group's organizers first met face-to-face two days before the demonstration, and they had no contact with leaders of the tea party in Columbia, the state capital; no aid from outside groups; no outside money; and very little spare time, said Parks, who spoke to National Journal while plowing his field in Monks Corner, S.C. He gets his political news via The Drudge Report and background data from the Heritage Foundation's website, he said.

Tea party groups say they've been able to use local media outlets to spread their message. Parks said that his group's next event will be a patriotic picnic, and he hopes as many as 8,000 movement members will turn out to meet and greet other people who live in their ZIP codes. "Our intention, first and foremost, is to influence our local government," Parks said. "Once that happens, we have a voice into state and federal governments . . . [although] I anticipate it will take several years."

Tea partiers are likely to get involved in nomination battles, particularly the Crist-Rubio fight in Florida. "I'll proudly and happily . . . do whatever we can to take Crist out of the political scene," said Odom, the

national organizer. Although Crist, who appeared with Obama to promote the stimulus bill, led Rubio 53 percent to 18 percent in a mid-May poll, he has recently begun to criticize other White House-backed spending programs.

Odom is trying to build a network of tea party groups by establishing the American Liberty Alliance as an umbrella. "We have access to all of these people, but these people don't have access to each other. . . . Our goal is to provide that access to ensure that everybody is communicating with everybody," he said. Odom and others also want to identify political candidates who support their cause; tamp down ideological splits between social conservatives and libertarians; establish a political action committee; and set up a tax-exempt 501(c)(4).

GOP politicians, meanwhile, are maneuvering to win the support of tea party groups. "I'm a big-tent Republican, and the more people that come into our tent, even to browse, I say welcome," said Rep. Joe Barton of Texas, the ranking Republican on the House Energy and Commerce Committee.

And Republican activists are optimistic. "The free market for leaders will produce the people with messages that match," the AEI's Brooks said. Swing voters will turn to the GOP, he said, because "what they're getting is liberalism good and hard, and ultimately that will blow liberalism up."

Levison and others, however, see a much smaller role for the movement. "I'm not sure it can swing swing voters," he said, "or that it represents a change in the attitude of the American people."

For Discussion:

■ Based on the article, and any outside knowledge you have of the "tea party" movement, what sort of political agenda do you think it pushes?

■ Why would some tea party organizers be wary of the intrusion of the Republican Party or its aligned interest groups? Do you think they would be right to feel this way? Why or why not?

■ Recent tea parties have indeed attracted tens of thousands of members. But do you think these organized demonstrations have real potential to sway elections or make a significant impact on governance?

8

INTEREST GROUPS IN AMERICA

STUDENT PIRGs ▌ College students are not strangers to the activities of interest groups. State public interest research groups (PIRGs) emerged on college campuses across the country in the early 1970s. Today student groups are active in the states of Alaska, Arizona, California, Colorado, Connecticut, Florida, Georgia, Illinois, Indiana, Iowa, Maine, Maryland, Massachusetts, Michigan, Minnesota, Missouri, Montana, New Hampshire, New Jersey, New Mexico, New York, North Carolina, Ohio, Oregon, Pennsylvania, Rhode Island, South Carolina, Texas, Vermont, Washington, and Wisconsin.

As the California student organization touts: "We give students the skills and opportunity to practice effective citizenship. Both here on campus and out in the world, we mobilize students to investigate big social problems, come up with practical solutions, convince the media and public to pay attention, and get decision makers to act."[1]

The various state organizations provide their student members with an *Activist Toolkit* to acquire skills in recruitment, leadership development, grassroots organizing, and working with the media. Student PIRG chapters are funded by either a mandatory student fee assessed to each student at the college or university or voluntary contributions from individual students.

The accomplishments of these student interest groups have been considerable. The Student PIRGs' New Voters Project has been instrumental in registering more than 700,000 voters. It has also made more than a million personalized voting reminders since 2004, making it the nation's largest nonpartisan mobilization program targeting young voters. Student PIRGs have also worked to build support for improved mass transit including high-speed rail. By mobilizing their peers, they helped persuade Congress in 2009 to include an additional $2.5 billion for high-speed rail in their appropriations bill that more than doubled the president's original request. Their Global Warming Solutions campaign is working to educate the country about global warming solutions and working with government leaders to put those solutions into practice.

In 2008, the Massachusetts student group helped pass the Global Warming Solutions Act that requires the reduction of greenhouse gas emissions in the state to 20 percent below 1990 levels by 2020 and 80 percent by 2050. The organizations have also been a major force in efforts to protect 58 million acres of roadless areas in our national forests from road building and logging ➡

As You READ >>

- What are interest groups and what types of interests do they represent?
- Why might someone join an interest group?
- What do interest groups do?

projects. In May of 2009, Student PIRGs helped persuade Congress to pass the Credit Card Accountability, Responsibility and Disclosure (CARD) Act that will halt some of the worst abuses by the credit card industry.

These student organizations have also targeted issues of direct concern to their peers. Their Student Debt Alert campaign has a goal of raising awareness about this growing problem and recommending solutions. In 2007, they helped convince Congress to pass the College Cost Reduction and Access Act that provided both the largest increase in federal student aid in 20 years and dramatic cuts in interest rates for student loans. In 2009, these students were successful in convincing Congress to include in its economic stimulus package both more money for the work-study program and a $17 billion increase in Pell grant funding.

In addition, they are working to make textbooks more affordable. Today students spend more than $900 a year on texts, which is 20 percent of the tuition at an average university and half the tuition at a community college. In 2008, they were successful in getting an affordable textbook provision included in the federal Higher Education Opportunity Act. The provision requires that publishers provide pricing information to faculty who are considering the adoption of a particular book.

In this chapter, we will learn how interest groups like the student PIRGs organize to exert pressure on the political system to advance their collective interests. We will examine their genesis, the way they have evolved and adapted to historic change, the kinds of people who join them, the reasons why people support them, the strategies and tactics they employ, and their impact on civic engagement and public policy. ◆

Thousands of Hispanic Americans took to the streets to demonstrate support for immigration reform when Congress considered the matter during the 2007–2008 session.

ORGANIZED INTERESTS: WHO ARE THEY?

Accomplishing broad yet shared goals is always easier when a number of people pitch in to help. Both joining with neighbors to clean up a community after a storm and banding together with friends to convince your college cafeteria to purchase "free trade" coffee are examples of cooperative action. Group activity is a hallmark of America's volunteer ethic. The same is true in politics. Organized groups are nearly always more effective in attaining common goals than individuals acting alone. The term **interest group** refers to those formally organized associations that seek to influence public policy.[2] In America, it applies to a dizzying array of diverse organizations reflecting the broad spectrum of interests that make up our pluralistic society. They include corporations, labor unions, civil rights groups, professional and trade associations, and probably some of the groups with which you are associated as well.

Organized Interests

Think you don't belong to an organized interest or advocacy group? Think again. Are you a member of any of these groups?

❏ American Automobile Association (AAA)
❏ Amnesty International
❏ American Society for the Prevention of Cruelty to Animals (ASPCA)
❏ Defenders of Wildlife
❏ 4-H
❏ Future Farmers of America
❏ Interfaith Alliance
❏ Mothers Against Drunk Driving (MADD)
❏ National Audubon Society
❏ National Council of Churches of Christ in the USA
❏ National Rifle Association (NRA)
❏ National Organization for Women (NOW)
❏ Ocean Conservancy
❏ Parent Teacher Association (PTA)
❏ Sierra Club
❏ United Students Against Sweatshops (USAS)
❏ Veterans of Foreign Wars (VFW)
❏ Students Take Action Now Darfur (STAND)

Neighbors or Adversaries?

Theorists from Alexis de Tocqueville to Robert Putnam have praised voluntary associations as training grounds for citizen involvement. De Tocqueville saw collective action as evidence of democracy at work. Putnam extols organized interests for creating social capital, the glue that binds the citizenry so they can achieve collective goals. Not all political theorists, however, share these views. In *The Federalist* No. 10, James Madison warned against factions— groups of individuals, "whether amounting to a majority or minority of the whole, who are united by some common impulse of passion, or of interest, adverse to the rights of other citizens, or to the permanent and aggregate interests of the community."[3] Although opposed to factions, Madison felt that they could not be eliminated since they expressed the innately human drive for self-interest. Instead, he argued, the government must dilute their influence by filtering their views through elected officials and submerging their interests in a sea of competing interests. Only by countering the ambition of such groups with the ambition of others, he believed, could government fashion the compromises necessary to accommodate interests common to all.

Interest groups usually do not intend to work against their communities, but the benefits they seek may result in costs for others. Whether a particular group is a "good neighbor" or an adversary is often in the eye of the beholder.

> **interest group** Any formally organized association that seeks to influence public policy.
>
> **political movement** An organized constellation of groups seeking wide-ranging social change.

Distinctive Features

Like the **political movements** of the past that advanced causes such as abolition or civil rights, interest groups seek to use the power of government to protect their concerns. However, while political movements promote wide-ranging social change, interest groups are more narrowly focused on achieving success with regard to specific policies. Where the women's movement of the 1960s sought to change Americans' views about the role of women at home and in the workplace, interest groups like the National Organization for Women (NOW) focus on solving specific problems faced by women in a world that has already grown more accepting of the diverse roles women play.

Interest group causes may be purely economic, as in the case of a business seeking tax breaks or a union seeking negotiating clout; they may be ideological, as in the case of those favoring or opposing abortion rights. Some, known

Businessmen often sought favors from President Ulysses S. Grant as he indulged in brandy and cigars in the Willard Hotel lobby in Washington, D.C.

as **public interest groups**, advocate policies they believe promote the good of all Americans, not merely the economic or ideological interests of a few. Environmental groups such as the Sierra Club fall into this category. Some interest groups, such as trade associations and labor unions, have mass memberships; others represent institutions and have no individual membership at all. One example of the latter is the American Council on Education (ACE), a collection of institutions of higher education that promotes policies that benefit colleges and universities.

As with other forms of participation, those who are better educated and better off financially are more active in interest group politics. The wealthy and well-educated belong to more associations, are more likely to be active in these interest groups, and give more money to political causes than those with less education and income. Highly educated professionals are many times more likely to belong to one or more interest groups than those who lack a high school degree. It is also important to note that interest group activity has exploded over the last 40 years, even while our nation has experienced a long-term decline in voter turnout. This reflects the fact that interest groups multiply the opportunities for participation by those who are already politically active.[4]

THE ROOTS OF INTEREST GROUP POLITICS IN AMERICA

Political scientists offer a number of reasons for the growth of interest groups. First, there is the ever-present reality that Americans are joiners. Echoing de Tocqueville, historian Arthur M. Schlesinger wrote that our "instinctive resort to collective action" is "one of the strongest taproots of the nation's well-being."[5] Beyond this, interest group growth is tied to forces of change such as technological innovation, war, and the expansion of the role of government.

Interest Groups on the Rise

By the time Alexis de Tocqueville traveled across America in 1831, voluntary associations—including those with explicitly political goals—were already well established. Women, who were excluded from leadership positions in government, organized many groups that provided humanitarian relief to the poor, sick, and disabled. These "auxiliary societies," as they were sometimes called, were formed to combat perceived evils like drunkenness and prostitution.[6] Abolitionist societies were perhaps the most politically influential associations, and many of them organized across class and racial lines to advocate an end to slavery. Women also organized for the right to vote, meeting in Seneca Falls in 1848 to issue a *Declaration of Rights and Sentiments*.

By the mid-nineteenth century, economic change and advances in transportation brought rapid growth in the number of voluntary and political organizations. The development of a national railroad system led the Central Pacific Railroad to send its own representative to Washington in 1861 to protect railroad subsidies and land grants. A number of rural associations arose in reaction to these changes. For example, the Grange, an association of rural farmers, formed in opposition to high rates set by rail carriers for hauling their produce to the nation's largest markets. The origin of the term **lobbying** to describe the practice of influencing public decisions for private purposes dates back to this period. It seems that businessmen often approached President Ulysses S. Grant (1869–1877) to seek favors as he indulged in brandy and cigars while relaxing in the lobby of the Willard Hotel.

By the end of the nineteenth century, the pace of economic development displaced many rural workers, who migrated to cities to compete for dangerous, low-wage jobs in the new industrial economy. Labor organizations, charitable associations, and reform groups arose to lobby for better working conditions, an end to child labor, and safe food and medicines. As the organizing strength of political parties began to decline, interest groups emerged as the great hope for participatory democracy. They became the principal means for expressing popular views and mobilizing support for reform.[7]

World War I created a large pool of veterans who organized to petition the government for benefits in compensa-

PORTRAIT
OF AN ACTIVIST

Leonora O'Reilly,
National Consumers League Activist

Leonora O'Reilly, the daughter of Irish immigrants, was born in New York City in 1870. Since the family was poor, Leonora began working in a collar factory at the age of 11. In 1888, she made an eloquent appeal to a gathering of wealthy and educated women to do whatever they could to improve the working conditions in the city's garment district sweatshops. In response, those in attendance left their names and addresses, signaling their willingness to answer the call. Over the course of the next several years, an organization emerged to advance the cause of working women: the National Consumers League. It published a "White List" of stores that treated their workers fairly and urged women to reward these establishments with their business, even if goods were slightly more expensive. The League advocated research and dissemination of information about the manufacture and contents of all family products and urged women to shop selectively.

By 1913, the League had amassed a membership of more than 30,000 in local chapters. It later successfully defended an Oregon law limiting the workday for women to ten hours a day. The NCL's work culminated in the Fair Labor Standards Act, which created a national minimum wage in 1938. The League continues in existence today, largely as an advocacy group operating out of Washington, D.C., and is sustained by tax-free contributions (http://www.nclnet .org/).

---

tion for their service to country. In 1932, more than 30,000 World War I veterans and their families and supporters marched on Washington, D.C., and set up makeshift camps in the capital, demanding redemption of government certificates issued after the war. Although federal troops routed the so-called "Bonus Army" out of their camps, veterans eventually received the cash payments they sought. Their actions paved the way for more generous benefits for future generations of soldiers.

The New Deal spawned hundreds of groups with a stake in federal policies, as did the explosion of government regulation of business and the environment in the 1960s and 1970s. The period following World War II brought increased specialization and professionalization to the workforce at the same time as it saw increases in union affiliation. Membership in the American Bar Association quadrupled between 1945 and 1965. Union membership rose in the postwar period from about 12 percent of the nonagricultural workforce in 1930 to over 30 percent in the 1950s before cascading downward in the last quarter of the twentieth century.[8]

The Advocacy Explosion

In the 1950s and 1960s, the nation experienced a "rights revolution" that had important implications for the evolution of interest group politics in America.[9] African Americans led the way as they sought to dismantle segregationist policies in the South by lobbying the national government to enforce constitutional guarantees. Other groups followed, insisting that government help tear down the barriers of racial, ethnic, and gender exclusion that characterized associational life in earlier eras. Soon, even mainstream interests like those of consumers joined the "rights revolution." The national focus of these reform efforts made it imperative for rights advocates to establish a presence in Washington.

The period witnessed an explosion in Washington-based **advocacy groups**, associations asserting broad public goals but without local chapters and often without any formal membership.[10] Leaders of these groups, often self-appointed and aided by philanthropic organizations and think tanks that supplied financial and intellectual capital, helped forge a new relationship between citizen and leadership. Citizens no longer needed to organize locally, meet with one another, or choose neighborhood leaders. Instead, national leaders would set the agenda, formulate strategies, and lobby public officials for them. Citizens were asked to send money and write an occasional letter to a public officeholder. Political engagement, some observers believe, became more passive as citizens had their interests managed for them.[11]

public interest groups Those advocating policies they believe promote the good of all Americans and not merely the economic or ideological interests of a few.

lobbying Tactic for influencing public decisions for private purposes, usually employing personal contact with elected officials.

advocacy groups Groups organized around broad public goals but without local chapters and often without formal membership.

The impact of the explosion in advocacy has been mixed. On the one hand, these groups are instrumental in protecting individual rights and in making the products we use safer and more effective. On the other hand, they may have contributed to a more passive role for citizens. The period that witnessed a rise in Washington-based advocacy groups also witnessed an overall decline in civic voluntarism. We will return to assess these changes at the end of this chapter.

WHOSE INTERESTS ARE REPRESENTED?

The array of interest groups active in American politics is large and wide-ranging. Some groups boast large numbers, others have financial heft, and some are led by the well-connected who have access to power brokers. Each employs the resources it has at its disposal to advance its cause.

Who Has the Numbers?

The single largest sector of the interest group community is composed of trade associations, and of these, business interests predominate.[12] The U.S. Chamber of Commerce, for example, represents thousands of small and medium-sized businesses throughout the country, and the National Association of Manufacturers advances the interests of major manufacturing companies. In addition, most large corporations either maintain their own Washington offices or employ Washington-based consultants to represent them.

Professional associations such as the American Chemical Society represent the next largest sector of the Washington interest group community. Labor unions also maintain a strong presence, although union members represent a dwindling portion of the labor force. Education is a fast-growing sector, with more than a thousand individual lobbyists and organized groups such as the American Federation of Teachers practicing in the nation's capital today.

Advocacy groups represent a growing portion of the interest group community.[13] A few of these, including the Children's Defense Fund, promote the interests of those who don't have the resources to advocate for themselves. But an increasing array, such as Common Cause (dedicated to government reform) and Public Citizen (organized to safeguard consumers), cater to more wealthy contributors on whom they rely for support. Numerous single-issue groups have also organized around specific legislative concerns, such as banning handguns or outlawing abortion. The overwhelming majority of organized interests founded since 1960 have been advocacy groups,[14] but they have a high rate of attrition. Only 33 percent of advocacy organizations active in 1960 existed two decades later. The most successful of the survivors deal with environmental and consumer issues.[15]

Governments themselves also organize for representation in Washington. Virtually every nation in the world maintains a Washington office to oversee its relations with American leaders. So, too, do state and local governments, whose policies are often impacted by federal law. The

Education is a fast-growing and powerful sector of the interest group community. Together the American Federation of Teachers (AFT) and the National Education Association (NEA) boast 4.6 million members.

Which Interests Are Best Represented?

Percentage of all lobbying expenditures by organization

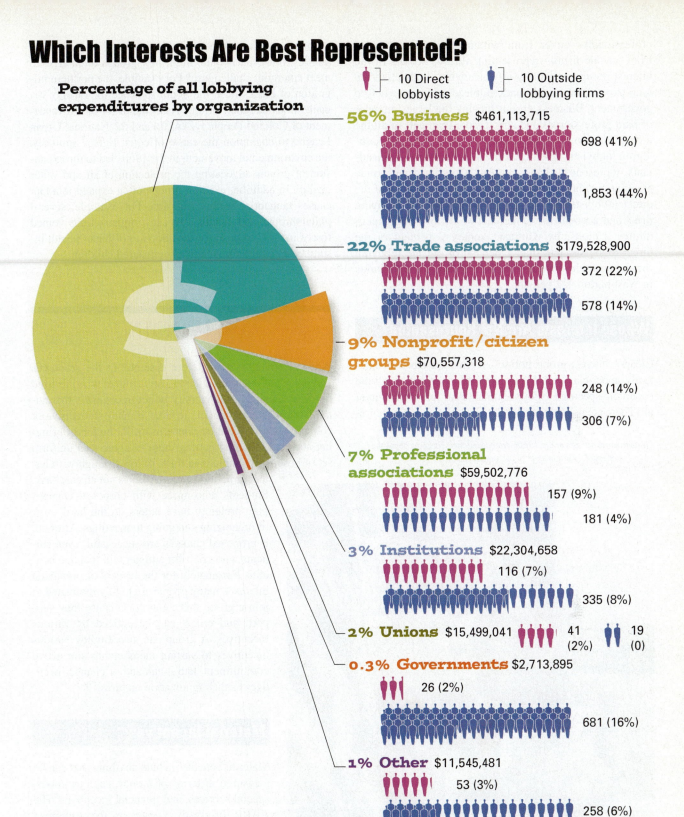

	10 Direct lobbyists		10 Outside lobbying firms

56% Business $461,113,715

698 (41%)

1,853 (44%)

22% Trade associations $179,528,900

372 (22%)

578 (14%)

9% Nonprofit/citizen groups $70,557,318

248 (14%)

306 (7%)

7% Professional associations $59,502,776

157 (9%)

181 (4%)

3% Institutions $22,304,658

116 (7%)

335 (8%)

2% Unions $15,499,041   41 (2%)   19 (0)

0.3% Governments $2,713,895   26 (2%)

681 (16%)

1% Other $11,545,481   53 (3%)

258 (6%)

Source: Compiled from Frank Baumgartner and Beth L. Leech, "Interest Niches and Policy Bandwagons: Patterns of Interest Group Involvement in National Politics," *Journal of Politics* 63, no. 4 (2001): Table 1, 1195, and Table 3, 1197.

National Association of Counties, the National League of Cities, and the U.S. Conference of Mayors are but three examples. Even executive branch agencies in the U.S. government hire legislative liaisons to communicate their needs to members of Congress.

Who Has the Money?

Another way to evaluate which interests are best represented is to examine the resources groups expend. The figure above provides information on the number of paid professionals—either from within the organization or from outside firms—representing various sectors of the interest group community in Washington. It also lists the total expenditures each made in pleading its case before government. Business groups employ the largest number of paid professionals and spend more than half of all the money spent on lobbying. Over 50 percent of all Washington lobbyists, whether in-house or working as consultants, represent business interests. Combined with trade associations, business interests employ 63 percent of the direct lobbyists and 58 percent of the outside lobbying firms and account for 78 percent of all lobbying expenditures. Unions, by contrast, employ 2 percent of the direct lobbyists, less than 1 percent of outside lobbying firms, and their share of the total lobbying expenditures in Washington is 2 percent.

Whose Interests Are Not Represented?

Clearly, interest group politics in America has a distinctively upper-class tilt. Many interests at the bottom of the economic spectrum enjoy minimal or no representation at all. There are no lobbyists for the homeless or groups representing Americans without health insurance. Interest group politics, however, is quite fluid; new groups often arise to meet emerging challenges.[16] For example, the northern migration of blacks from the South spawned the birth of organizations like the National Association for the Advancement of Colored People (NAACP) and the National Urban League to champion the cause of equal rights. Similarly, the environmental movement in the 1960s led to the expansion of groups advocating the protection of air and water quality. In addition, existing groups often expand to adopt causes tangential to their mission. For example, several philanthropic and health advocacy organizations joined forces in 2007 to push for the adoption of wider health insurance coverage for America's uninsured children.

Environmental activists in the 1960s dramatized their concerns about the nation's unhealthful air quality at public protest rallies.

WHY JOIN?

Political strength comes from assembling the resources and voices of many individuals. Any student who has tried to effect changes in university policy recognizes that administrators are more likely to listen if many students work collectively to voice their concerns. Still, the job of bringing students together, getting them to agree to a uniform set of proposals, and having them follow through with letters or petitions or marches is not an easy task. Students who agree with proposed changes may prefer to have others do the hard work of organizing and going to meetings. After all, if proposed changes are successful, even students who don't lift a finger will reap the benefits. Fortunately for the leaders of organized interests, many people are highly motivated to join a group that fights for a cause they support, and others can be enticed by various incentives. A group can also employ various incentives to sustain membership and active commitment, and it can add or change incentives as the organization matures.[17]

Material Incentives

Material benefits include anything that can be measured in terms of money, such as goods, special services, and financial incentives. The AARP, originally known as the American Association of Retired Persons, for instance, began with the goal of providing affordable health care for the elderly but now offers its members discounts in a variety of establishments, guidance in avoiding consumer fraud, organized travel opportunities, auto insurance, low-interest credit cards, and a discounted mail-order pharmacy. Offering these material benefits has helped AARP recruit more than 35 million members and become the most powerful organization in America representing the interests of the elderly. Political leaders who seek to change Social Security or Medicare policies recognize the importance of courting this organization if their proposals are to have any chance of passage.

Few organizations can match AARP's clout, but many business associations and unions offer material incentives as well. For example, the U.S. Chamber of Commerce offers member businesses access to health-care plans that are cheaper than plans they could buy on their own. Although the power of unions has waned in recent years, many can still provide members with higher negotiated wages than workers could obtain without a union card.

Solidary Incentives

Human beings are social creatures who enjoy the company of others. Membership in a group whose participants share a common interest can be very pleasurable. It provides the joiner with the likely possibility of friendship and an opportunity for "networking." Again, this is a selective benefit reserved to the members of the group that nonmembers cannot easily share. Members of professional organizations, such as the American Medical Association (AMA), look forward to annual meetings where they can renew friendships, share new ideas, and network. Often, members attending these conventions vote on resolutions outlining the political agendas the organization will pursue over the course of the coming year.

Purposive Incentives

Interest groups offer their members more than discounts and social outings. They offer the opportunity to pursue policy goals that members genuinely support. Members gain a measure of inner satisfaction from knowing that they are trying to change the world rather than just complaining about it. Despite the cynicism that sometimes pervades media reports about those engaged in public life, millions of Americans devote countless hours volunteering in big and small ways to promote causes in which they believe.

For organizations that depend heavily on purposive incentives, the role of the **political entrepreneur** is particularly important in mobilizing support among those who sympathize with the group's goals.[18] Political entrepreneurs develop support for latent causes or projects that have not yet gained widespread popularity. Even groups with passionate views, such as those on both sides of the abortion issue, rely on strong and enterprising leaders to recruit members and to sustain interest and activity.

The health insurance industry mounted a vigorous television campaign featuring a fictional couple, Harry and Louise, in a successful effort to thwart President Clinton's health-care reform program.

Assessing Motives

Economist Mancur Olson argued that it is irrational for individuals to join most groups. It is more rational, he wrote, to be a free rider who receives benefits without doing the work or paying dues. We can all enjoy clean air without being a member of an environmental group, and we can earn the latest increase in the minimum wage without carrying a union card. We can remain rationally uninvolved and spend our free time pursuing leisure activities or working at a second job to earn extra money.[19] Olson believes that providing incentives is the only way for membership in interest groups to flourish.

> **political entrepreneur** Individual who develops support for latent causes or projects that have not yet gained widespread popularity.
>
> **collective goods** Goods that are not owned privately but benefit all citizens equally, such as clean air.

Despite the seeming logic of Olson's view, people often do not make what appears to be the rational choice. Political scientist Jack Walker conducted a study in which interest group leaders ranked the benefit of each type of incentive as an inducement for attracting members. Contrary to rational choice theory, the leaders of all types of groups ranked material benefits to be the least important of all the incentives. The study also found that most groups do not even use such inducements. Instead, leaders of all kinds of groups ranked purposive incentives highest, with solidary incentives close behind.[20] Additional studies have confirmed high levels of purposeful joining, especially among interest group activists.[21] This finding should be surprising only to those who have paid insufficient attention to our history as a "nation of joiners." There is an additional consideration for free riders to ponder. If everyone acted like a free rider, **collective goods**—goods that are not owned privately but benefit all citizens equally, such as clean air—would have no champions, and all of us would suffer the consequences.

INTEREST GROUP STRATEGIES

In order to get what they want, interest groups must develop a plan and execute it with a series of specific actions. The overall plan is their **strategy**; the specific actions they undertake are **tactics**. Strategies and tactics employed by an interest group vary with the nature of the issue under consideration and the kinds of resources the group has available to it.

strategy A group's overall plan for achieving its goals.

tactics Specific actions that groups take to implement strategies.

revolving door Term referring to the back-and-forth movement of individuals between government and interest group employment.

Generally speaking, strategies can be categorized as inside or outside. Inside strategies emphasize direct personal encounters with public officials to present information or resources that might impact the course of policy. Tactics useful to implement this strategy include lobbying and contributing money to support the election of political candidates favorably disposed to the group's viewpoint. Outside strategies are activities intended to show popular support for one's cause and indirectly to create public pressure on elected officials. Outsiders usually adopt grassroots tactics that include letter writing, shaping public opinion, and orchestrating protests.

Groups adopt strategies based on the types of issues involved and the resources the group can bring to bear. Some groups have wide-ranging interests that are likely to attract the attention of a large number of Americans. For example, military intervention is an issue that affects almost everyone—from those who fight or lose family members in battle to those who simply oppose the use of their tax dollars in this manner. Both supporters and opponents of the use of military force are likely to employ outside strategies to demonstrate to lawmakers the depth and breadth of public sentiment for their position. Changes in the tax code, on the other hand, are likely to provoke the use of inside strategies by groups whose immediate but narrow interests are most directly affected. The arcane and complicated features of our tax code rarely draw widespread attention, enabling those with an immediate interest and expertise to fashion changes to their liking through direct interaction with lawmakers.

There are times when it makes sense for groups to employ both inside and outside strategies at once. For example, both proponents (for example, labor unions) and opponents (e.g., health insurers) of President Obama's health care overhaul worked closely with members of Congress and the administration to fashion changes in his reform proposals—an insider's approach. At the same time, however, they helped organize workers and employees to attend rallies and town meetings to demonstrate widespread support for their positions, and they spent lavishly on television ads to influence public opinion—outside strategies.

Resources useful in advancing a group's cause include money, numbers, prestige, and leadership. Businesses, for example, can generally count on accumulating money to communicate their message, but they cannot often count on large numbers of individuals supporting their cause. Labor unions, on the other hand, try to exert influence by the number of votes they can muster for particular candidates and parties. To be effective, however, a group's members must be dispersed geographically across areas that key lawmakers represent. Sometimes, groups with smaller numbers have an easier time organizing politically since they can maintain greater intensity and cohesiveness. Strong intensity is a characteristic of groups on both sides of the abortion issue in recent years. Prestige is also an important resource; when the American Medical Association speaks on matters of health care, for example, it can be particularly persuasive.

Rock stars like Bono have been effective in mobilizing support for increasing aid to developing nations.

Leadership from a variety of sources—scholars, celebrities, political entrepreneurs, and public officials themselves—can generate momentum around issues previously ignored by the political system. Rachel Carson's controversial 1962 book *Silent Spring* is credited with almost single-handedly launching the environmental movement. More recently, Irish rock star Bono mobilized global support to fight AIDS and to provide debt relief for poor and developing countries. Since few interest groups have sufficient quantities of all of these resources to dispense at will, each group must carefully assess how best to deploy the strengths it possesses.

byists.[22] Former members of Congress also make formidable lobbyists, sometimes maintaining virtually unlimited access to the chambers and the congressional gym. Of the 198 lawmakers who left the House of Representatives from 1998 to 2005, 43 percent became lobbyists.[23]

Some refer to the movement between government service and interest-group employment as a **revolving door**. The door swings in both directions. Not only do retiring law-

LOBBYING AND OTHER TACTICS

Interest groups have many tactics at hand to advance their positions. The table at right reveals the range of tactics many Washington groups say they employ in pleading their causes. In this section, we'll review some of the most notable.

Lobbying

In the early years of our republic, members of Congress had no offices; most lived alone in boardinghouses or hotels. The only way to contact them was to wait outside their offices, or in the lobbies of the places where they were staying, in hopes of having a word with them as they came and went. Modern-day lobbyists continue to ply their trade in the hallways of the Capitol, but interest groups have found far more sophisticated ways to increase their clout.

Who Lobbies? Average citizens lobby on behalf of issues they support by writing or calling elected leaders, but lobbying is increasingly the province of permanent and salaried professionals. Sometimes these are interest group staffers who work in Washington or a state capital directly on behalf of the group's membership. Increasingly, they are "hired guns" whose services groups purchase from professional firms specializing in government relations. An estimated fifteen thousand people work as lobbyists in Washington, D.C., and many are quite well paid.

A good lobbyist needs to be a specialist in a policy area and needs to have thorough knowledge of the political process. For this reason, former government workers are well suited for the job. Individuals who have worked as congressional staff members or in administrative agencies have the kind of policy and political knowledge useful for lobbying. One study reports that 46 former staffers from the powerful House Appropriations Committee, 36 from the Ways and Means Committee, and 34 from the House Energy and Commerce Committee have left their congressional jobs since 1998 to work as registered lob-

Exercising Influence: Interest Group Tactics

Tactic	Percent of surveyed groups employing
■ Testifying at hearings	99
■ Contacting government officials directly to present your point of view	98
■ Engaging in informal contacts with officials at conventions, over lunch, etc.	95
■ Presenting research results or technical information	92
■ Sending letters to members of your organization to inform them about activities	92
■ Entering into coalitions with other organizations	90
■ Attempting to shape the implementation of policies	89
■ Talking with people from the media	86
■ Consulting with government officials to plan legislative strategy	85
■ Helping to draft legislation	85
■ Inspiring letter-writing campaigns	84
■ Shaping the government's agenda by raising new issues and calling attention to previously ignored problems	84
■ Mounting grassroots lobbying efforts	80
■ Having influential constituents contact their representative's office	80
■ Helping to draft regulations, rules, or guidelines	78
■ Serving on advisory commissions and boards	76
■ Alerting representatives to the effects of a bill on their districts	75
■ Filing suit or otherwise engaging in litigation	72
■ Making financial contributions to electoral campaigns	58
■ Doing favors for officials who need assistance	56
■ Attempting to influence appointments to public office	53

Source: Kay Lehman Schlozman and John T. Tierney, "More of the Same: Washington Pressure Group Activity in a Decade of Change," *Journal of Politics* 45 (1983), 357.

makers and staffers join firms that lobbied them when they were in government, but government agencies often recruit issue specialists from fields that they regulate. Defenders of this practice claim that the revolving door keeps good and knowledgeable people involved in the policy process. It develops a cadre of experts, many of whom have spent their lives studying issues under government scrutiny. Critics believe the practice raises ethical concerns, especially when a person leaves a federal government position to join an interest group he or she once helped to regulate. Representative Billy Tauzin (R-LA), for example, left the House of Representatives in 2004 to become the president of the Pharmaceutical Research and Manufacturers of America shortly after writing the Medicare Drug Benefit law that is widely seen as protecting the interests of drug companies that he now represents. Former Senate Majority Leader Tom Daschle (D-SD) became a lobbyist with ties to the health-care industry once he left office, and he nearly became Secretary of Health and Human Services until his candidacy was sidetracked by the revelation that he failed to pay a portion of his back taxes. There are laws limiting the kind of access former officials may have once they leave office. President Obama recently expanded restrictions on the revolving door by curtailing executive agency hiring of individuals who have recently lobbied and by prohibiting those who leave his administration from lobbying agencies for which they have worked for a period lasting until the end of his administration or for two years after their departure.

Hot or Not?

Should the government place stricter limits on lobbying expenditures?

Lobbying Congress The Center for Responsive Politics reports that interest groups working on health-care issues spent over $263 million on lobbying members of Congress during the first six months of 2009. These groups dispatched 3,300 lobbyists to Washington to ensure their voices were heard—that's six lobbyists for every lawmaker! Despite lobbyists' sometimes unsavory reputation, most members of Congress see them as possessors of valuable resources. Two of the most valuable of those resources are information and electoral support, often in the form of campaign contributions.

Members of Congress need information, because they must vote on many highly technical pieces of legislation during the course of a legislative session. Except for the policy areas they know well because of their committee assignments, congresspersons are policy generalists who lack the kind of detailed information that lobbyists can supply. Such information is crucial to legislators because they never know which vote on a bill could become an issue in the next campaign.[24]

To maintain a good relationship with a legislator, the lobbyist must supply credible and reliable information based on accurate research. Since technical information is in short supply, overworked legislators welcome help from interest-group advocates in assessing and sometimes even drafting legislation. Lobbyists also contribute political information or cues. They communicate to legislators how a particular piece of legislation will sit with important constituencies back home. Lobbyists may communicate information by testifying at congressional committee hearings. By testifying openly, the interest group can impress its members back home with its status as a Washington player. Such visibility can increase membership and, in turn, the group's potential clout.

Lobbyists might slant information in order to "make the sale," but they dare not lie. A good lobbyist will even include information damaging to his or her cause from time to time in order to maintain credibility. As one lobbyist put it, "You can't ever afford to lie to a member of Congress because if you lose access to him, you've had it."[25]

Lobbyists need access to members of Congress in order to obtain policy results for their members. Opportunities for access in the policymaking process have increased in recent years since seniority and the powers granted committee chairs have been weakened, making individual members more important. Greater turnover, occasioned by term limits for committee chairs and self-imposed term limits by some individual legislators, has elevated the status of congressional staff members, whose cultivation can be useful in communicating a group's message to lawmakers. Staff contacts are particularly important in the smaller

Senate, whose members have greater responsibilities and time commitments.[26]

Even the White House lobbies Congress in order to secure legislation it deems important. The Office of Legislative Affairs in the White House acts as the president's liaison with Congress. This office gives the White House a very powerful means of influencing legislator behavior. For example, the White House may release information beneficial to the cause of members whose support they seek, or the president can accept an invitation to a fund-raising event for a member who is up for reelection. Some presidents pay more attention to congressional relations than others. Usually, those who work hard at nurturing support with key members are the ones most likely to gain support for their legislative agendas.

Lobbyists employ several generally recognized rules of thumb to maximize their effectiveness with Congress. They are aware that it is rarely effective to lobby opponents to one's cause in an effort to convert them. It is better to deploy one's resources working with allies in high places, especially members of key committees with jurisdiction in the area of one's interests. It is generally easier to avoid conflicts on big issues and concentrate instead on writing the details to one's advantage. It is easier to defeat a measure than to pass new ones.

Lobbying the Executive Branch Since the beginning of the twentieth century, the federal government has greatly expanded its authority over a wide range of private activities, from regulating pollutants emitted by industries to overseeing fair employment practices. This has provided interest groups with fertile ground for lobbying the cabinet departments and independent agencies of the federal bureaucracy that oversee these activities. Agency administrators and personnel are policymakers just as much as members of Congress. Their task is to write the rules that implement federal legislation. These rules involve a great deal of technical detail, take considerable time to draft, and often are the result of negotiations between bureaucrats and lobbyists for the organizations affected. Some of the rules implementing the Clean Air Act of 1991, for example, took twelve years to draft. Through the Federal Register, a daily compilation of federal regulations and legal notices, executive agencies invite public comment and reactions to proposed rules. This allows organized interests to draft written responses and appear before hearings to present their arguments.

Of course, lobbyists who have established good relationships with agency staff members can get an early start on the process by learning, in advance of public disclosure, what new rules are being considered,[27] or even helping to write these rules themselves. Sometimes members of the Executive Branch will actively court lobbyists in order to secure support for proposals they intent to initiate. President Obama actively courted members of the pharmaceutical and hospital industries in support of health-care reform, managing to secure promises from them to reduce costs.

If they fail to influence the rulemakers, interest groups can pursue a number of alternative approaches, such as challenging rules they believe to be unfair in the courts. They can also seek favorable treatment by influencing the appointment of agency officials with whom they must deal. This is generally easier if the organization has good contacts with the administration and with key senators who must confirm the appointments of top administrators. Finally, interest-group representatives can serve on advisory commissions and boards that meet with executive agencies to provide advice and guidance in areas of agency jurisdiction.[28]

Critics of executive branch lobbying worry that businesses and groups that are regulated by a particular agency often manage to "capture" the agency by exercising too much influence over the rules it writes and implements. For years, many observers believed the airline industry exercised undue influence over the Federal Aviation Administration, which resulted in overly favorable treatment regarding fee arrangements and travel routes. Research into agency capture produced no firm or universal findings, however, and the recent trend to deregulate and open business activity to market forces has weakened support for this viewpoint.[29]

Some critics also worry about what has been described as an **iron triangle**, a decision-making process dominated by interest groups, congressional committees, and executive agencies. In this arrangement, the parties cooperate by advancing each other's goals: Interest groups benefit by winning policy concessions or contracts; members of

> **iron triangle** A decision-making structure dominated by interest groups, congressional committees, and executive agency personnel who create policies that are mutually beneficial.

Iron Triangle

Interest Group

Electoral support

Friendly legislation and oversight

Lobby support for policies and budget requests

Low regulation

Funding and political support

Congress

Bureaucracy

Cooperative policy implementation

THE IMPACT OF *CITIZENS UNITED*

When the Supreme Court ruled in 2010 that the federal government cannot restrict corporations from spending money to influence the outcome of elections in *Citizens United v. Federal Election Commission,* President Obama responded immediately. He blasted the decision saying, "With its ruling today, the Supreme Court has given a green light to a new stampede of special interest money in our politics. It is a major victory for big oil, Wall Street banks, health insurance companies and other powerful interests that marshal their power every day in Washington to drown out the voices of everyday Americans."[*]

The following week the president repeated his criticism during the State of the Union address. Looking down at the six members of the Court who were present, Obama said the decision had "opened the floodgates for special interests to sway elections." The television cameras caught Justice Alito shaking his head slightly and saying "Not true."

The Republicans were first to adapt to the new political landscape. Two of their top strategists, Karl Rove and Ed Gillespie, helped to form American Crossroads and Crossroads GPS. These two conservative groups raised $71 million to influence the outcome of the 2010 midterm congressional elections. They have announced a 2012 fundraising goal of $120 million to campaign against the president.

Believing they were slow to respond to the ramifications of the *Citizens United* decision, leading Democrats, some with close ties to the White House, created Priorities USA and Priorities USA Action in 2011. These two organizations, modeled after their conservative counterparts, were set up under a section of the tax code that allows its donors to remain anonymous. Using the types of groups he once criticized has opened up the president to charges of "brazen hypocrisy" by his conservative opponents.[†] With both parties now being assisted by outside groups who can spend unlimited corporate and union money, the 2012 presidential election will be the costliest in history. Shelia Krumholz, executive director of the nonpartisan Center for Responsive Politics, predicts that $2 billion could easily be spent to win the White House.[‡] A $2 billion price tag would nearly double the monies spent in 2008.

Campaign Funds Raised by Winners in Presidential Campaigns

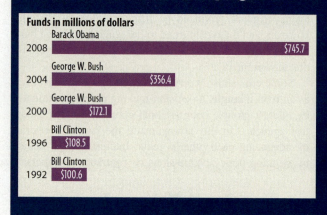

Funds in millions of dollars

2008	Barack Obama	$745.7
2004	George W. Bush	$356.4
2000	George W. Bush	$172.1
1996	Bill Clinton	$108.5
1992	Bill Clinton	$100.6

---

[*] Joan Biskupic and Fredreka Schouten, "Supreme Court rolls back campaign spending limits," USA TODAY, January 21, 2010.
[†] Jim Rutenberg, "Democrats Form Fund-Raising Groups," New York Times: The Caucus, April, 29, 2011, p.1.
[‡] Fredreka Schouten, "Deeper pockets in fashion for 2012," USA TODAY, April 5, 2011, page 1.

Congress benefit from electoral support supplied by the interest group; and federal agencies benefit from congressional approval for their administrative proposals.[30] In 1961, President Eisenhower warned about an overly cozy relationship between defense-industry lobbyists, the Pentagon, and members of congressional appropriation committees. Most policy observers today agree, however, that the threat from potential "iron triangles" is on the wane,[31] especially because of inroads made by advocacy groups in gaining access to policymakers and in opening records of meetings.[32]

Still, it is not uncommon for small groups of experts to dominate policy creation and implementation. These groups, sometimes called **issue networks**, include lobbyists, members of Congress, bureaucrats, and policy specialists from think tanks and universities. These expert groupings are more open, less formal, and less permanent than iron triangles. Actors come together around immediate issues and disband once the issue is settled. Rather than having a permanent and reciprocally beneficial relationship, their only link is shared interest and expertise in a particular policy area. Issue networks often are open to groups with opposing interests and viewpoints, unlike the iron triangles where policy interests are more uniform.

Regulating Lobbying Activity Concerns about inappropriate lobbying activity date back to the nineteenth century, when bribery in Washington was not uncommon. In 1946, Congress passed the Federal Regulation of Lobbying Act, which attempted to deter the excesses of lobbying through the concept of disclosure. The law required lobbyists to register with the clerk of the House and the secretary of the Senate if they received money used principally to influence legislation before Congress. Despite these provisions, the act did not regulate the *practices* employed by lobbyists to any great extent, and it lacked enforcement. In 1995, Congress passed a new Lobbying Disclosure Act that defined lobbyists more broadly and included those seeking access to the executive branch. It also adopted new rules on gifts and sponsored travel.

A series of high-profile scandals that erupted in 2005 raised corruption as a major issue in the congressional elections of 2006. Super-lobbyist Jack Abramoff went to prison for bilking his Native American clients out of millions of dollars while lobbying on behalf of their gaming interests. So, too, did former Congressman Bob Ney (R-OH), who was convicted of accepting illegal gifts from Abramoff. In unrelated scandals, Congressman Randy "Duke" Cunningham was forced to resign and serve jail time for accepting bribes from defense contractors who sought favors from the Defense Appropriations Subcommittee on which he served, and Representative William Jefferson (D-LA) was forced to relinquish his position on the House Ways and Means Committee amid reports of bribes after the FBI found $90,000 in cash in his freezer. Reacting to these events, the 110th Congress passed a new round of reforms, the 2007 Honest Leadership and Open Government Act, that included a ban on accepting gifts, meals, or trips from lobbyists. The bill also ended the practice of accepting free or reduced-fare trips on corporate jets, mandated greater disclosure about special pet projects (known as earmarks) that legislators insert into bills on behalf of special interests, and required greater disclosure and tracking of the source of campaign funds exceeding $15,000 that come in "bundles" from members of the same organization. It also required senators and members of the executive branch to wait two years after leaving government service before lobbying Congress; House members must wait one year.

These changes have by no means leveled the playing field for political access; lobbying Congress is a very expensive game that only the best-financed interests can play effectively. According to the Federal Election Commission (FEC), for example, assorted groups spent over $3.2 billion on lobbying in 2008. Just one organization, the U.S. Chamber of Commerce, spent more than $144 million on federal lobbying in 2009.[33] Nor are these changes likely to allay the suspicions of many Americans who perceive a culture of corruption in Washington. The reforms include loopholes that permit lobbyists to make campaign contributions that the representative or senator can then use to take the lobbyist to dinner to discuss matters of mutual interest. It is difficult to assess just what all this money buys. However, a recent 4-year study found that the most likely outcome of lobbying is to maintain status quo. Attempts to bring change are often easily defeated by sowing doubts about a new proposal's impact. Where change did occur, however, significant policy change was more likely than modest change. A variety of forces, including new leadership, a groundswell of public opinion, and events that brought attention to unresolved problems, combined to produce stable shifts in the policy environment.[34] Thus, it is vital to be at the table when events conspire to bring big change. As we have seen, however, only those groups with sufficient resources are likely to stick around for the long haul.

> **issue networks** Decision-making structure consisting of policy experts, including lobbyists, members of Congress, bureaucrats, and policy specialists from think tanks and universities.

Financing Campaigns

> The public perception out there that someone who gives a thousand dollars has influence is laughable. It really is, because that's such chump change today that it doesn't even register on the scale.
>
> *Wright Andrews, lobbyist*[35]

No one really knows when organized interests started taking over the financing of political campaigns. An early milestone was Marcus A. Hanna's success in raising more than $3.5 million for the campaign of Republican William McKinley in 1896 by assessing corporations and banks predetermined amounts to finance the campaign.[36] Since then, it seems incumbent on organizations that want an elected official's ear to "pony up." For the average individual, $1,000 is hardly "chump change," but some U.S. Senate races cost more than $30 million to run. In light of extravagant campaign costs, candidates are in a continuous search for funds, and interest groups stand ready to help.

Financing elections takes place within a web of legal restrictions that have become more complicated and contentious over time. The first regulations date to 1907, when the Tillman Act outlawed contributions directly from corporations. The act was fraught with loopholes, however, and enjoyed little genuine enforcement. It was not until the 1970s that Congress seriously revisited the issue of campaign finance regulation. The Federal Election Campaign Act of 1971 required candidates to disclose the sources of contributions but did little to reform campaign financing beyond reporting. Congress passed more sweeping legislation in 1974 in the wake of the Watergate scandal. The legislation provided for public financing for presidential elections (see Chapter 12) and the creation of the Federal Election Commission to moni-

PAC Spending Limits and Regulations

- $5,000 per candidate per election. Elections such as primaries, general elections, and special elections are counted separately.

- $15,000 per political party.

- $5,000 per PAC. PACs are allowed to give to other PACs.

- PACs are not limited in the amount they spend on advertising to support their own issues.

- PACs must register with the FEC within ten days of formation, providing name and address for the PAC, treasurer's name, and names of any connected organizations.

- Affiliated PACs (those affiliated with other organizations under the same control) are treated as one donor for the purpose of contribution limits.

Source: Federal Election Commission and www.opensecrets.org.

tor election finances and place limits on contributions by individuals, political parties, and **political action committees** (PACs). PACs are organized financial arms of interest groups that collect and distribute money to candidates for elective office.

Interest groups challenged the law's limits on political contributions by individuals and PACs as a violation of their First Amendment right to free speech. In *Buckley v. Valeo* (1976), the Supreme Court struck down some of the bill's provisions but allowed continued limits on individual and PAC contributions. With caps on the contributions allowed by any given PAC, the number of PACs increased dramatically. PAC growth represents a wide spectrum of political and economic interests, including business, labor, and citizens' groups. Even elected officials maintain so-called **leadership PACs** as a means of financing the campaigns of political allies who they believe will reciprocate with support for their own political ambitions.

Congress revisited the issue of campaign finance in 2002, passing the so-called McCain-Feingold Bill, named for its two vocal Senate sponsors, John McCain (R-AZ) and Russell Feingold (D-WI). Although interest groups challenged these reforms in 2003 and again in 2007,[37] the Supreme Court upheld most of the new law's provisions. Much of the reform had to do with limitations on money spent by political parties (see Chapter 9) and on advertising, but the bill also changed the amount of PAC contributions permitted. In 2010, however, the Supreme Court in *Citizens United v. Federal Election Commission* ruled that the portion of the McCain-Feingold law that restricted corporations from spending money to influence political campaigns violated the First Amendment (see Chapter 4).

Campaign contribution limits are shown in the adjacent figure. It shows the amount of money individuals may give to candidates and PACs, and how much PACs may contribute to candidates and other PACs. The amounts are adjusted for inflation with each election cycle. Keep in mind that interest-group members and lobbyists can contribute individually to a candidate and again to PACs that support the candidate. Lobbyists also sometimes serve as treasurers of campaign committees for candidates, thereby elevating the visibility of their group.[38]

As the figure on the next page shows, advocacy groups (nonconnected) and business interests dominate the money game. The number of issue groups like the National Rifle Association or the National Organization for Women has increased dramatically in recent years, and so have their contributions. According to one study, citizen groups constitute five of the fastest growing sources of campaign funds when individual contributions and PAC funds are combined.[39] The growth of this sector clearly suggests that civic groups, sometimes responding to requests by entrepreneurial leaders, are not shrinking from engaging in the high stakes arena of campaign finance in order to advance the interests they espouse. Corporate interests are also major players. Corporate interests may be represented by multiple PACs—once through a company PAC itself and then through several additional professional and trade PACs. Business PACs his-

PAC Expenditures by Type 1989–2010

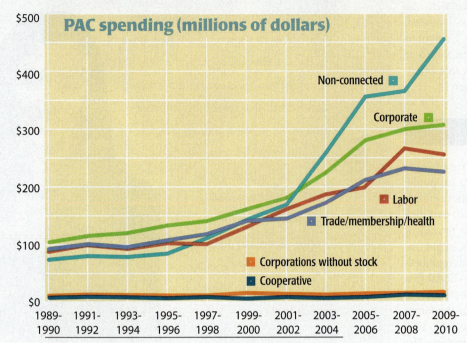

PAC spending (millions of dollars)

- Non-connected
- Corporate
- Labor
- Trade/membership/health
- Corporations without stock
- Cooperative

$500
$400
$300
$200
$100
$0

1989-1990 1991-1992 1993-1994 1995-1996 1997-1998 1999-2000 2001-2002 2003-2004 2005-2006 2007-2008 2009-2010

Source: FEC, Summary of PAC Financial Accounting, 1990–2010.

torically have given the largest proportion of their dollars to incumbents. While interests such as energy and pharmaceuticals generally favor Republicans, and others (including labor and trial lawyers) generally favor Democrats,[40] party loyalty is not the exclusive hallmark of PAC giving. All but the most ideologically committed groups commonly adjust their spending when party control changes hands.[41] For example, while the securities and investment sector gave about equal amounts to candidates from both parties in the highly competitive 2008 campaign cycle, they gave proportionately more to Republicans in 2010 when the GOP was poised to take over the House of Representatives. Labor PACs, on the other hand, give more to Democratic candidates. Although labor unions represent less than 10 percent of the total number of PACs, the amount they contribute is impressive. In the 2010 midterm election campaign, labor PACs contributed more than $63 million to federal candidates, 93 percent of it going to Democrats.[42]

Interest groups also form tax-exempt organizations, known as **527 groups**, to engage in political activities ranging from grassroots mobilization to sponsoring ads promoting or criticizing a candidate's record on an issue. They may not, however, coordinate their expenditures with political candidates. These organizations have thus far remained outside the range of government regulation. The 527 organizations spent a total of more than $600 million trying to influence voter choice in the 2010 federal and state elections.[43]

The 2010 Supreme Court ruling in *Citizens United v. Federal Election Commission* (2010) expanded the ability of special interests to spend on political campaigns. The ruling allows corporations and unions to spend unlimited amounts and may now contribute to so-called "super PACs" set up for issue advocacy, which do not require

the disclosure of donors. As a result, the amount of independent money pouring into campaigns by outside groups not directly affiliated with the candidate or political parties has quadrupled since 2006.[44]

Accessing the Courts

The courts can play a pivotal role in public policy when they affirm or reject legislative or administrative actions. However, judges cannot be lobbied in the same way that congresspersons and bureaucrats can. One of the most important tactics lobbyists can legally employ is to attempt to control the membership of the courts. Interest groups historically have played a significant role in influencing presidents and senators during the appointment process.

When a group believes that a piece of legislation will cause them harm or raises constitutional concerns, it is the group's right to litigate. Litigation is expensive, however, and groups with abundant financial resources, access to full-time staff attorneys, a wellspring of public support, and a clear issue focus are most likely to undertake it.[45] Some groups file suit in court when they are relatively certain there is little support for their cause in the court of public opinion. This is sometimes known as the **political disadvantage theory**,[46] for which the tobacco industry serves as a prime example. It is far easier to convince a court to reject an industry regulation on legal grounds than to expect sympathy from a public that is increasingly turned off by smoking. Instead of bringing suit themselves, many interest groups file *amicus curiae*, or "friend of the court," briefs outlining their support for the claims of others, especially when the case holds promise to advance their own interests.

Most of the important constitutional cases with broad policy implications decided by the Supreme Court in recent years have taken the form of test cases. These are cases brought by organized interests in an attempt to set new precedents.[47] In the 1950s, for example, the Legal Defense Fund of the National Association for the Advancement of Colored People

political action committees (PACs) Organized financial arms of interest groups used to collect and distribute money to candidates for elective office.

leadership PACs Political action committees set up by political leaders as a means to finance the campaigns of political allies whom they believe will reciprocate with support for their own political ambitions.

527 groups Tax-exempt organizations set up by interest groups to engage in political activities.

political disadvantage theory View positing that groups are likely to seek remedies in courts if they do not succeed in the electoral process.

(NAACP) won numerous court cases supporting equal rights for African Americans.[48] More recently, advocacy groups who agree with the legal claims of environmentalists, women, civil libertarians, or fundamentalist Christians have supported their cases before the Supreme Court.[49] We will return to discuss the role of advocacy groups in the courts in Chapter 14.

Grassroots Mobilization

Grassroots mobilization is the practice of organizing citizens to exert direct pressure on public officials in support of a group's policy preferences. Lawmakers want to be reelected, and they know constituents retain the power to reward or punish them at the polls. As a result, organizations with large member bases and with members spread across a broad swath of congressional districts can be especially effective.[50] The National Education Association (NEA) is one of the larger membership-based grassroots organizations, representing more than three million educators. The Christian Coalition is another, with an estimated 1.9 million members. The strength of large organizations like these comes from their ability to mobilize large numbers of citizens into action quickly. Such groups can rouse members to write or call their lawmakers, to work

on political campaigns, and to get out the vote on Election Day. Organized groups can provide workers to bring a candidate's message door-to-door, distribute campaign literature, and staff telephone banks. The electioneering efforts of the Christian Coalition helped the Republicans gain control of Congress in 1994, and the strong efforts by organized labor provided Democratic gains in both houses in 2006 and again in 2008.

Who Gives to Republicans? Who Gives to Democrats?

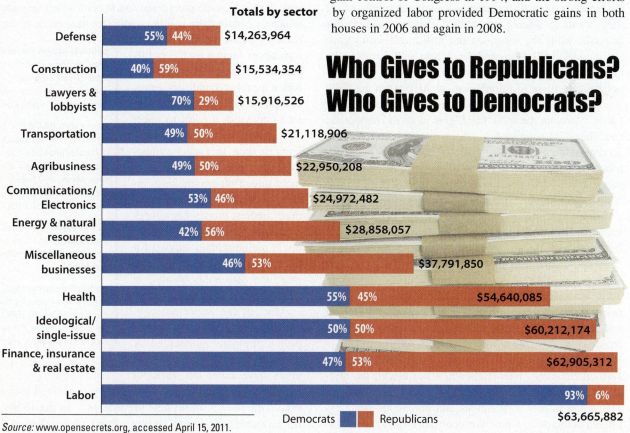

Totals by sector

Sector	Democrats	Republicans	Total
Defense	55%	44%	$14,263,964
Construction	40%	59%	$15,534,354
Lawyers & lobbyists	70%	29%	$15,916,526
Transportation	49%	50%	$21,118,906
Agribusiness	49%	50%	$22,950,208
Communications/Electronics	53%	46%	$24,972,482
Energy & natural resources	42%	56%	$28,858,057
Miscellaneous businesses	46%	53%	$37,791,850
Health	55%	45%	$54,640,085
Ideological/single-issue	50%	50%	$60,212,174
Finance, insurance & real estate	47%	53%	$62,905,312
Labor	93%	6%	$63,665,882

Democrats ■ Republicans ■

Source: www.opensecrets.org, accessed April 15, 2011.

Modern technology is making it easier than ever for interest groups to deliver constituents' messages to their elected officials. A survey by the Congressional Management Foundation, a nonpartisan group that helps train legislative staff, reported that 44 percent of Americans had been in contact with their House members or senators in the previous five years. Not unexpectedly, "84 percent of citizens contacting lawmakers had been prompted by a third party, mostly lobbying and advocacy groups."[51]

As we know from Chapter 7, those who are better educated and more affluent are more readily mobilized, and their communications are more highly prized by political leaders. Because of this, some public relations firms specialize in mining databases for high-status community leaders to contact legislators in key districts to support the sponsoring group's position. This practice, known as **mobilizing the grass tops**, earns these firms hefty fees for setting up meetings between high-profile constituents and members of Congress.[52] The National Federation of Independent Business (NFIB), for example, regularly communicates by Internet and e-mail with its members to educate and mobilize them.[53] The group maintains phone and fax numbers of its members and information about members' types of businesses, issue positions, political backgrounds, and legislative districts. This kind of data makes it easy for the NFIB to target its message to those members who are most likely to respond to calls for quick mobilization.

Another tactic, known as **astroturf lobbying**, uses deceptive practices and lack of transparency to manufacture grassroots support for an issue important to a particular set of unidentified interests. For example, in 2009 the American Coalition for Clean Coal Electricity, an organization funded by

grassroots mobilization The practice of organizing citizen support for a group's policy or candidate preferences.

mobilizing the grass tops Mining databases for high-status community leaders for purposes of contacting legislators in key districts regarding the sponsoring group's position.

astroturf lobbying Using deceptive practices and lack of transparency to manufacture grassroots support for an issue important to a particular set of unidentified interests.

Current Controversy

Waivers and Lobby Reform

President Obama's executive order designed to limit the influence of lobbyists in the executive branch included the provision that restrictions on lobbyists could be waived in cases where they might adversely affect the public interest. Such a waiver was employed when the president nominated and the Senate confirmed William J. Lynn III to be the Deputy Secretary of Defense.

Mr. Lynn has had a distinguished career and many educational attainments. A graduate of Dartmouth College, he earned a law degree from Cornell Law School and a master's degree in public affairs from the Woodrow Wilson School at Princeton University. He has served as a senior fellow at the National Defense University and was a professional staff member at the Institute for Defense Analyses. In 1987, Lynn became a member of Senator Edward Kennedy's staff as a liaison to the Armed Services Committee. During the Clinton administration, Lynn served in the Department of Defense as the Director of Pro-

gram Analysis and Evaluation and later as the Under Secretary of Defense.

When the Republicans captured the White House in 2001, Mr. Lynn entered the private sector. He became a lobbyist for the Raytheon Company. Raytheon is a defense contractor that makes $25 billion a year. They manufacture the navy's Tomahawk missile and the army's Patriot missile. The Obama administration granted a waiver and named Lynn the number two man in the Defense Department, arguing that due to his background and experience he was a critical appointment. At the time of Lynn's confirmation, Senator Kennedy wrote: "He's a proven leader in both the public and private sectors of the national security community, and his previous service in the department uniquely qualifies him to help the department run more efficiently and effectively."*

Government watchdog groups argued that this appointment was another example of the revolving door between lobbying and government. Leslie

Paige, with the Citizens Against Government Waste, said: "This town is dysfunctional . . . When it comes to commitment, and making those commitments reality, there's a huge disconnect."† "This is not the change we had hoped for," said a spokesman for the Project on Government Oversight, an organization that had asked for more details of Lynn's work.‡ Steve Ellis, with Taxpayers for Common Sense, concluded: "Certainly the revolving door is still spinning."§ Lynn defended his appointment, however, arguing that: "On coming back to the department, there are equally strict ethics procedures on what issues I can handle and which issues I can't. I will be working with the general counsel's office to ensure I follow those ethics procedures completely."** It should be noted that Raytheon sales to the government have increased 77 percent since Lynn moved back to government service.

* Drew Griffin and Scott Bronstein, "Defense Official Example of Revolving Door Between Governing, Lobbying," CNN.com, February 23, 2010.
† Ibid.
‡ Ibid.
§ Ibid.
** Ibid.

Americans for Democratic Action Ratings for Senators in 111th Congress (2009)

HEROES

100% Agreement with ADA positions

Brown (D-OH)

Klobuchar (D-MN)

Boxer (D-CA)

ZERO

Bunning (R-KY)

0% Agreement with ADA positions

Source: Americans for Democratic Action, Spring 2010 http://adaction .org/media/ votingrecords/2009.pdf accessed May 6, 2011.

Many interest groups build grassroots support for their causes by supplying voters with ratings or scorecards to guide their electoral choices. The Christian Coalition has been particularly adept at this practice, issuing ratings for candidates that have agreed with their issue positions to member churches for distribution on the Sunday prior to election. The liberal group Americans for Democratic Action (ADA) uses a similar rating scheme. The group gives each legislator a score based on the percentage of times he or she voted in favor of the group's position. In the first session of the 111th Congress (2009), the ADA found the average rating for House Republicans to be 7 percent, whereas the average score for Democrats was 85 percent. The ADA also publishes a list of House and Senate "heroes" (100 percent agreement with the group) and "zeros" (0 percent agreement with the group).

Coalition Formation

The rapid growth in the number and variety of interest groups over the last 30 years has created a strong incentive for groups to act in concert by forging coalitions. Organized groups benefit from alliances by expanding their access to resources and information, increasing their visibility, and enlarging the scope of their influence. Members of Congress and federal bureaucrats often seek out coalitions because they provide a means for reconciling intergroup differences in a way that facilitates compromise in policy formation.

Coalitions are not always easy to build because there are risks in joining. Some of the views of coalition partners may be at odds with those of other partners, and smaller groups may fear that their priorities will be submerged beneath those of larger partners. Each group must evaluate the trade-offs of joining a coalition on an issue-by-issue basis.[54] Sometimes, however, issues bring together coalitions of highly unlikely partners. For example, groups as disparate as the liberal American Civil Liberties Union (ACLU) and the conservative Rutherford Institute found common ground in opposing restrictions on civil liberties proposed in the USA Patriot Act following the 9/11 attacks. Health-care reform has also fostered coalition building. A number of organizations representing insurers, hospitals, and health-care workers—groups that had worked in opposite directions during the Clinton administration to scuttle reform—combined forces to support President Obama and ensure that each of them got a say in the Patient Protection and Affordable Care Act passed in 2010.

coal producers, allegedly hired a lobbying firm to drum up what appeared to be widespread public opposition to a proposed climate change bill in the U.S. House. The group's plans were thwarted, however, when a dozen letters supposedly written by average citizens were discovered to have been forged. Astroturf lobbying was also a popular tactic employed in the recent health-care debate by organizations representing both sides of the issue intent on demonstrating widespread support for their own positions.

Protests

Protests have always been a part of the American political landscape. They include nonviolent techniques such as picketing or marches and sit-ins like those used by the

civil rights movement under the leadership of Dr. Martin Luther King, Jr. They may also involve violence, as in Shays's Rebellion shortly after the American Revolution. Protest is the ultimate form of grassroots activity because members are asked to be willing to sacrifice their lives and their freedom for the cause. As a result, protest usually accompanies issues that are highly charged emotionally. The 1973 *Roe v. Wade* decision, for example, triggered a significant increase in protest activity that continues to surround the abortion issue to this day.

Although it is protected by the First Amendment, many observers see protest as being outside the mainstream of political activism. As a result, it is a common tactic among those with few resources and little direct access to the centers of power. Protesting might be considered the ultimate outside strategy, reserved for groups with few other visible means for making their voices heard. This does not mean, however, that protesters themselves are poor and uneducated. Some studies show that protesters disproportionately come from those with higher levels of income and education.[55] Many of the people who attended so-called tea parties in 2009 to protest the Obama administration's economic stimulus plan, for example, were well-off financially but concerned that increased government spending would result in higher taxes.

INTEREST GROUPS AND CITIZEN ENGAGEMENT TODAY

Whereas voluntary associations of earlier eras emphasized local organization and citizen training, interest group politics today is often run by professionals in Washington. This development is the result of important structural changes in the nature of our political system. As Matthew A. Crenson and Benjamin Ginsberg note, "Beginning with the development of its regulatory capacity at the start of the twentieth century, American government multiplied the mechanisms by which organized interests could achieve their ends without mobilizing their grassroots constituents."[56] Petitioning of executive-branch agencies and litigation necessitate the work of skilled professionals, not average citizens. Government and philanthropic foundations multiplied the opportunities for groups to support themselves without relying exclusively on membership contributions. As a result, interest groups increasingly seem to manage interests from above rather than fully involving the citizens they are supposed to represent.[57]

Some warn that these changes in patterns of interest group activity are transforming citizens from "participants" to "mailing lists." Today, entrepreneurial advocacy groups launch campaigns from Washington seeking direct access to lawmakers and the courts without first investing much effort in generating popular support for their positions in towns and neighborhoods.[58] The AARP, for example, has the largest membership base of any American interest group. Yet their 35 million members do not gather in conventions to determine their political agenda. Their leaders contact them by mail. Participation is limited to contributions; the leadership sets the agendas, and groups often bring their issues before courts or administrative boards without needing to demonstrate any broad support for the actions they undertake. Interest groups demand little from members but much from government.

However, interest groups have *always* depended on strong national leadership willing to employ new techniques in mobilizing popular support. Some of the largest grassroots organizations today, such as the NAACP, began as national organizations and later cultivated local chapters for support. Advocacy groups continue to play an important role in opening new avenues of expression and preserving constitutional rights for millions of previously disaffected minorities. To a large extent, interest groups have simply adapted their methods to reflect changes in the lifestyles of most Americans. Most Americans have little time to meet with neighborhood associations after a long day of work and after-dinner soccer practice with their children. They cannot monitor the fine points of legislation that may threaten their interests. Organized

Find an interest group that addresses the issues that are most important to you and communicate with that group about opportunities for working with it to advance your cause. Does the group have a local chapter? If not, find out how to start one yourself and develop plans for taking your issue to your congressional representative on behalf of the organization.

get involved!

groups recognize this reality by offering citizens a variety of participatory options; for instance, they encourage check writing and provide help in contacting local representatives. They are even developing hybrid techniques that combine national activation with local action. For example, some groups use the Internet not merely to inform citizens of legislative threats or to solicit funds but also to help local citizens organize meetings in their own communities. These "meet ups" hold the promise of reigniting community activism in the Internet age.

Finally, there is growing interest in global issues that defy national borders and traditional interest group activities. Young Americans are especially interested in global organizations like Greenpeace and Oxfam, and in expanding the frontiers of political action. Many of the organizations that address international issues, such as United Students Against Sweatshops (USAS) and the Global Fund to

Fight AIDS, Tuberculosis and Malaria, employ innovative approaches to political participation that include boycotting manufacturers who use sweatshop labor or BUYcotting—selectively purchasing from merchants who donate a portion of their receipts to a good cause.

Nevertheless, interest group politics continues to pose challenges to our voluntaristic ethic. Although citizens are indeed writing more letters and checks, boycotting, and BUYcotting, these actions continue to be taken disproportionately by those who are well off. As a result, groups reflecting the interests of the upper reaches of society are better represented when political decisions are rendered. The pluralism that thrives in a community characterized by numerous interest groups is at risk when the majority of those groups speak with what one political scientist calls "an upper class accent."[59]

United Students Against Sweatshops and other organizations have mounted effective grassroots campaigns to stop retailers from carrying clothing made by manufacturers employing unfair and unsafe labor conditions.

Summary ⌄⌄

1. What are interest groups and what types of interests do they represent?

- Interest groups are formally organized associations that seek to influence public policy.

- Unlike political movements that promote wide-ranging social change, interest groups are more narrowly focused on specific policies.

- Interest groups may organize for specific economic or ideological goals, or they may be public groups that advocate for the good of all Americans.

- There have always been interest groups in America, but they experienced their greatest growth in the 1960s and 1970s.

- Those groups representing the wealthy and the better-educated are the most numerous.

- Many interests at the bottom of the economic spectrum enjoy minimal or no representation at all.

2. Why might someone join an interest group?

- Someone might join an interest group for material incentives such as discounts for products or services or higher wages.

- Someone might join an interest group for solidary incentives, the social support from others with similar backgrounds or interests.

- Someone may join an interest group for the purposive intent to advance a cause in which they believe.

- Studies have found that material incentives are the least important for joining groups, particularly among the young.

3. What do interest groups do?

- Interest groups seek to advance the public policy interests of the people they represent.

- Groups develop an overall plan or strategy based on the type of issue involved and the resources the group can bring to bear.

- Strategies can be categorized as inside, direct personal encounters with public officials, and outside, activities showing popular support for the group's cause.

- Tactics are the specific actions taken by a group.

- Interest group tactics include lobbying, financing campaigns, filing suits in court, working to create grassroots support, protesting, and forming alliances with others to advance their cause.

National Journal

K Street Paradox

"$1.3 million per hour."

That eye-popping number doesn't refer to the salary of a Wall Street banker, a health insurance CEO, or an oil company executive. It's what K Street reported in fees in 2009, according to a recent analysis by the Center for Responsive Politics. The center derives the provocative number by dividing the amount of money lobbyists and other entities received to influence Congress and the executive branch (a record $3.47 billion, up 5 percent from 2008) by the number of hours Congress was in session (2,668). Although the figure is somewhat hyperbolic—lobbyists work many hours when Congress isn't in session—the message is clear.

"The numbers just keep going up, up, up," the center's executive director, Sheila Krumholz, said. "I was surprised, given the state of the economy last year."

Although the year on K Street started off slowly, with many lobbying firms reporting cuts in their fee income during the first few months, the downturn flattened as the year went on. Ironically, the White House's ambitious policies fueled the boom, with Obama's "change" agenda effectively making Washington the center of the country as it tackled financial services reform, energy reform, health care reform, and the $819 billion stimulus package. Even as Obama clamped down on "special interests," corporations rushed to Washington and hired lobbyists to shape legislation in their favor. According to the center, 15,712 companies or entities reported that they lobbied the federal government in 2009, 663 more than in 2008.

"It's been one of the busiest years that I have seen in a long time," said John Castellani, president of the Business Roundtable, a trade group that reported spending $13.4 million on lobbying, as its 160 corporate members engaged on almost every major piece of legislation that Congress took up this year. "Depending upon the issue, we were playing offense and defense."

Wayne Berman, a Republican and a managing director of Ogilvy Government Relations, which raked in $21.7 million in lobbying fees in 2009, said, "The president and the Democratic congressional leadership have embarked on an all-out assault on a wide range of economic interests, and those interests have sought to protect themselves by dramatically increasing their lobbying budgets."

Health care-related lobbying, in particular, drove profits on K Street. The Center for Public Integrity reported that 4,525 lobbyists were working on health care reform last year—which works out to eight for every member of Congress. According to the Center for Responsive Politics, pharmaceutical and health products companies spent a total of $266.8 million on lobbying, making it the top-spending industry for the year.

Even amid the overall K Street boom, Obama has been on a possibly quixotic quest to change Washington by reining in lobbyists' interaction with government. He began with an executive order aimed at excluding recently registered lobbyists from political appointment posts, pledging to close the revolving door between government and lobbying.

In March of 2009, Obama set restrictions on communications between lobbyists and government officials relating to stimulus funds—a regime that the administration eventually extended to everyone seeking stimulus money during the grant application process. That September, Obama banned lobbyists from government advisory boards and commissions. He also put White House

visitor logs online (which enabled anyone to see which representatives of special interests were entering the mansion), and he is pushing federal departments and agencies to develop plans for making their contacts with lobbyists more transparent to the public.

But insiders think that the rules may have had the unintended consequence of making lobbying less transparent. The administration has relied on the definition of "lobbyists" in the 1995 Lobbying Disclosure Act, which sought to impose uniform disclosure standards on the industry. The law has loopholes, however, that allow huge swaths of the influence industry—including grassroots advocacy and public-relations campaigns—to remain in the shadows.

Numerous regulations require lobbyists to register with the House and Senate; the key rule, however, applies to those who spend at least 20 percent of their time on lobbying activities and make at least two lobbying contacts during a calendar quarter. For many years, people registered "out of abundance of caution, or to show off their clients," Thomas Susman, director of government affairs at the American Bar Association, said. "There was no downside."

Now that lobbyists have become a punching bag for politicians, many people have been looking at ways to avoid registering—or to deregister from the official congressional roster.

The number of lobbyists dropped last year for the first time since 2001, to a total of 13,742, according to the Center for Responsive Politics. In 2008, 14,446 people were registered to lobby.

"Some of us are joking that the next proposal will be to put RFD tracking chips in lobbyists necks so they know where we are at all times."

—Rich Gold

"People are trying to game it so they can show on a work spreadsheet that they are spending 19.99 percent of their time lobbying, rather than the 20 percent that requires you to register," said one corporate lobbyist who didn't want to be named. As Kelly Bingel, a partner with Mehlman Vogel Castagnetti, puts it, "I think we've moved backwards in terms of disclosure. I'm seeing heads of [Washington corporate] offices on the Hill, and they aren't registering."

Stefan Passantino, a partner at McKenna Long & Aldridge, and other lawyers are doing a brisk business in advising lobbyists on the registering and deregistering strictures. "Whenever you create rules," he says, "people will try to figure out how to modify their behavior so they aren't subject to it."

Some K Streeters think that the decision banning lobbyists from boards will do the opposite of what Obama intended. Stephen Lamar, executive vice president of the American Apparel & Footwear Association, who chaired one of the trade advisory panels, said, "We think rather than increasing the diversity of voices, it will decrease them. We represented many small businesses. And those small businesses don't have the money and time to participate in these panels, so now their voices won't be heard."

Meanwhile, Obama is now focusing his attention on lobbyists and Congress. In his State of the Union address, Obama called for new limits on lobbyists' campaign contributions and bundling activities, and for new requirements under the Lobbying Disclosure Act. Lobbyists, he said, should have to report every contact with lawmakers, staff, and members of the executive branch and the substance of the interaction. The president also wants to toughen the threshold that requires lobbyists to register, below the current 20 percent time regulation in the law.

"We face a deficit of trust—deep and corrosive doubts about how Washington works that have been growing for years," Obama said in his State of the Union speech. "To close that credibility gap, we have to take action on both ends of Pennsylvania Avenue to end the outsized influence of lobbyists, to do our work openly, and to give our people the government they deserve."

This latest proposal left some lobbyists reeling. "Some of us are joking that the next proposal will be to put RFD tracking chips in lobbyists necks so they know where we are at all times," said Rich Gold, a partner at Holland & Knight. "We are either just over, or significantly over, the line on the administration's approach on these issues. I don't think this is improving people's trust in government." Bob Maloney, founder of Maloney Government Relations said, "Requiring us to report every contact would be a nightmare. What if I run into a lawmaker or their staff in the elevator or cafeteria or socially? Would I have to report that? If I did, the staff would never talk to me again."

Obama's focus on lobbyists again leaves out the many special-interest influencers—such as lawyers and CEOs—who don't have to register. Gina Mahony, policy director at Brownstein Hyatt Farber Schreck, wrote on *National Journal*'s Under the Influence blog: "Let's be honest about how lobbying really works. If you really want transparency and intellectual honesty about how this 'nefarious' industry works, then let's require 100 percent disclosure of all advocacy contacts."

Lawmakers haven't expressed much interest in embracing the lobbying reforms. Many members of Congress count lobbyists among their friends, and some even have aspirations to join the profession (witness the 318 former lawmakers who have registered to lobby since 1998, according to the Center for Responsive Politics).

Rep. Chellie Pingree, D-Maine, who formerly headed Common Cause, supports Obama's lobbying reforms but thinks that the president should put his second-year spotlight on campaign finance reform. "I would spend more time focusing on the influence of money, because I don't think it's about the time you spend with lobbyists; it's about the influence of money on the process," said Pingree, who has made passing a public financing bill, the Fair Elections Now Act, one of her top priorities. "When an interest with money comes in to lobby you, and after the meeting as they walk out the door, they say, 'Hey, I am happy to organize an event and help you with your campaign,' that is where things get confused." Pingree is a co-sponsor of the public financing proposal, which would provide matching payments for qualified small-dollar contributions; it has 140 backers in the House and 10 in the Senate.

She says, however, that Congress is missing an opportunity by not addressing public financing. "We have this level of awareness, like when you have a major scandal, everyone says, 'Oh, we have to clean this whole place up,'" she said. "I see this as an open door, and we may as well go in and try and change the whole system, not just a piece of it."

When asked whether Obama would support the Fair Elections Now Act, Eisen said, "The president supports public financing for presidential elections." Obama has not endorsed a similar system for congressional elections.

Pingree perhaps speaks for many both inside and outside the ranks of lobbyists when she concludes, "Without looking at the influence of money, there isn't really going to be change in Washington.

For Discussion:

■ Based on the article and on this chapter, what recommendations would you give President Obama on how to improve transparency in the relationship between government and lobbyists?

■ Why do you think money remains an influence in politics, despite efforts like those of the Obama administration to diminish the influence of lobbyists?

■ Do you think public financing of elections could solve the problem (if it is a problem) of the power of K Street? Why or why not?

9

PARTIES

CITIZENS AND THE ELECTORAL PROCESS

TEA'D OFF ❚ Keli Carender doesn't look like a typical conservative activist. She has a pierced nose, performs improvisational comedy on week ends, and lives in a multiethnic neighborhood. The thirty-year old's principal job is teaching math to adults in Seattle. Keli, a daughter of Democrats, only began paying attention to politics during the 2008 campaign, but none of the candidates appealed to her. When Barack Obama proposed a $787 billion stimulus to kick-start the economy shortly after his inauguration, she didn't like what she heard and started petitioning her senators to vote against the bill.[1] When she couldn't get through to them, she thought: "I can give up, go home, crawl into bed and be really depressed and let it happen. Or I can do something different, and I can find a new avenue to have my voice get out."[2]

She called some friends and wrote e-mails to prominent conservative commentators to help her organize a local rally. Although her first rally drew only a few supporters, she persevered. When the host of a financial news television program expressed similar outrage at the stimulus and called for citizens to hold protests like our forebears did at the Boston Tea Party, Keli soon found herself part of a nationwide movement with hundreds of thousands of followers.[3]

The "Tea Party" is really not a political party at all. Instead, it is a grassroots political movement (see Chapters 5 and 8) born out of frustration with government bailouts, high taxes, and the burgeoning size of the national debt.[4] It became a national force in the 2010 midterm Congressional elections when Tea Party activists helped the Republican party take control of the House of Representatives. ❧

AND POLITICAL CAMPAIGNS

As You READ

>>

- What are political parties and why do we have just two major parties?
- How are parties organized and how has our party system adapted to change?
- What is the relationship between candidates and parties in our electoral system?
- What factors do voters consider in making their election choice?

Polls show that about 18 percent of the American electorate identifies with this movement. Tea Partiers tend to be white, male, middle-class, married, older than 45, and conservative Republicans.[5]

Unlike social movements, political parties are organized to run their own candidates for elective office. The Tea Party has shied away from that option, with a few exceptions, preferring instead to endorse candidates who espouse their policy positions; but their size and energy make them especially important to the electoral process. Social movements are instrumental in building support for various policies—such as women's suffrage in the early twentieth century.[6] They also influence the growth and evolution of the major national parties, and they help tip the balance in some elections from one party to another.

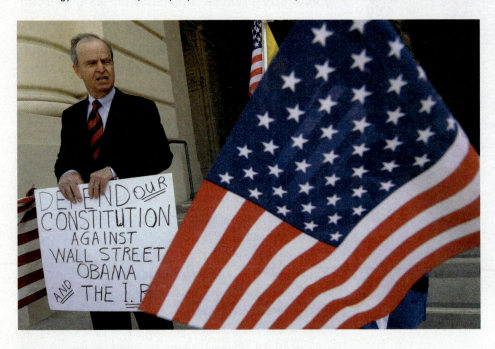

Americans vented their anger at both political parties as the recession dragged on, but Tea Party activists mostly helped energize Republican-leaning voters during the 2010 midterm elections.

The Tea Party exhibited remarkable success in the 2010 midterm elections and influence on the nation's politics during the first session of the 112th Congress. They have driven the Republican Party further to the right and forced Democrats to adopt more moderate positions than they did in the 111th Congress. Tea Party supporters continued to play an important role in the 2012 presidential campaign in mobilizing grassroots support.

In this chapter we will learn about political parties and their role in elections. We will also see how party affiliation, along with other factors such as issues and candidate personalities, influence voters in making their choices.[7] We will study the ways in which political parties have grown and developed over time as well as the ways in which they seek to represent the people who vote for them. Activists like Keli Carender may not find a comfortable place for now within either major political party, but her activism is likely to influence the future of both of them. ◆•

POLITICAL PARTIES AND ELECTORAL POLITICS

Our political system has seen a continuous extension of the right to vote. **Political parties** have played a vital role in that expansion by reaching out to new voters to increase their own strength. Political parties are organizations created for the purpose of winning elections and governing once in office.[8] Parties carry candidates' messages to voters and secure citizen loyalty to policies enacted under the party banner. They also help broker differences among groups they represent, developing policies that satisfy diverse viewpoints and encouraging compromise instead of fragmentation. They attempt to construct voting majorities that give lawmakers guidance in advancing the will of the people. Traditionally, they have also been a source of political talent, finding and grooming candidates to run for office. Finally, they have mustered voters to the polls on Election Day, calling upon citizens to fulfill their civic duties. So important have parties been in expanding the franchise, aggregating interests, recruiting candidates, and mobilizing voters, that one political scientist commented that "democracy is unthinkable save in terms of political parties."[9]

The Nature of Parties

Parties fulfill different roles for different actors. For voters, parties are useful devices for simplifying electoral choices. They signal political viewpoints or philosophies that serve as a guide in choosing candidates. Like brand names, they are both a means of personal expression and a guide to decision making. Since the New Deal, voters have typically seen the Democrats as the party of the working and middle classes and Republicans as the party of business. The Republican Party is associated with conservatism; the Democrats, with liberalism.

For candidates, parties are organizations that help them gain political power.[10] Unlike interest groups, which focus more on advancing policies than politicians, parties concentrate on getting their candidates elected to office. They are the only organizations that run candidates under their "brand" names. To do this, they must mobilize support by building coalitions among many groups to produce winning margins. As political scientist E. E. Schattschneider puts it,

they *mobilize the bias* of voters by appealing to their common interests.[11]

Finally, for elected officials, a party provides a common set of principles that help them govern. Under the party label, officials can devise, pass, and implement policies that express their common viewpoint. Voters can benefit as well by assigning to party leaders collective responsibility—for success if the party's policies succeed and for failure if they do not.[12] Since parties, unlike any other political organizations, are held accountable in elections, it is in their interest to build wide support for the positions and candidates they promote. In this chapter, our discussion will focus on the role of parties in elections, that is, the way they function as guides for individual voters and as organizations designed for winning elections. In other chapters, we will discuss their continuing and important role in governing once their members are in office.

political party Organization created for the purpose of winning elections and governing once in office.

While we have come to associate political parties with electoral and governing activities, you will search the U.S. Constitution in vain for a description of their nature or function. In fact, the Framers opposed political parties, fearing that they would split the nation into factions more focused on narrow interests than on the interests of the country as a whole. Alexis de Tocqueville captured the spirit of the Framers' sentiments when he called parties an evil—even if sometimes necessary—inherent in free governments.[13]

Of course, even as the Framers warned against factions, they were themselves dividing into factional groups that quickly assumed the function of parties. It is easy to see how disagreements over how to run the nation would generate party competition. It is more difficult to explain why the development of the American party system took the course it did. In particular, why have we developed a dual-party system instead of a system with multiple parties?

20 percent will send twenty members, and so on. Even minor parties that reach some threshold of votes are entitled to some number of seats. In Finland's 2011 election, the Finnish Social Democratic Party (SDP) received approximately one-fifth of the popular vote, which translated into 42 seats in the 200-member Parliament. However, even a small party, the Christian Democrats (KD), received enough votes to qualify for six seats in the Parliament.

By contrast, the United States employs the **single-member district** or winner-take-all system in its elections for Congress and most state legislatures. Any number of candidates may run for office in a district, but only the candidate winning a **plurality** of the vote (more than any other individual) wins the election and gets to represent the district. Minority-party or independent candidates who run without party support generally receive no seats (because they cannot win a plurality of votes). As a result, attempts to unseat a strong party candidate usually depend upon minority political forces joining together. The result over the long run is electoral contests between just two competitive parties. The principle that single-member districts generally lead to stable two-party systems is sometimes referred to as **Duverger's law**, named for the French sociologist who first proposed it.[14] The **Electoral College**, the assemblage of state electors constitutionally charged with electing the president, also limits third-party growth. With the exceptions of Maine and Nebraska, states award all their electors to the plurality winner within the state. Since victory in presidential contests requires an absolute majority of the electoral votes from all the states and the District of Columbia (270 out of 538), minor parties stand almost no chance of winning. Legislators from other states, including California, have proposed moving to a system similar to that of Maine and Nebraska. (A more detailed discussion of Electoral College politics appears in Chapter 12.)

Critics complain that our single-member district system makes it difficult for minority candidates, or anyone whose point of view varies from the mainstream, to gain a foothold in elective offices. The single-member district does discourage minority-party and independent candidates, and may reduce voter turnout by discouraging voters who do not support either major-party candidate.[15] However, it also simplifies leadership once the election is over. In the Finnish example presented earlier, what if none of the parties represented in the Diet had enough seats to control

Why Two Parties?

Many people complain that the two dominant parties in America do not give them enough choices. In fact, at least 250 candidates filed petitions with the Federal Election Commission to run for president in 2008 as either third-party or independent candidates. Of course, most had only regional or statewide appeal, and many lacked sufficient signatures to be placed on official ballots. In the face of this diverse array of potential candidates for electoral office, why do two major parties dominate American politics so thoroughly? After all, most European democracies have systems in which many parties, representing diverse points of view, compete for political power. There are several reasons why our system differs from theirs. These include election rules, the tendency of American voters to shy away from ideological extremes, state laws, and the way our elections are financed.

proportional representation
System of representation in which seats for office are apportioned according to proportion of votes received by candidates or parties.

single-member district
Electoral system in which the candidate receiving a plurality of votes wins the election to represent the district.

plurality Having more votes than any other single candidate; may not constitute a majority.

Election Rules Most multi-party systems operate within a system of **proportional representation**. In proportional systems, voters choose their leaders largely on the basis of political party rather than geography. Though there are several variations, proportional systems generally award seats in the national legislature on the basis of the percentage of the votes received by each party. For example, if one party receives 40 percent of the vote to fill a 100-member parliament, it is entitled to 40 seats. Another party winning the body? That would mean that parties needed to form coalitions to get anything done. Often, none of the parties in these coalitions are really satisfied with the results. Such coalitions are fragile and may lead either to inaction or frequent calls for new elections. By contrast, two-party systems provide more stability once the election is over. One party likely will control the legislative body and the positions of leadership within it until the next regularly scheduled election, even if its majority is slim. In any case, it should be noted that election rules have an impact on the formation of party systems.

Ideological Centrism Americans historically have downplayed differences based on class or ethnic identity. This reduces the attraction of parties that target specific groups or classes. Since most Americans are neither very liberal nor very conservative (see Chapter 6), parties that stray from a "middle of the road" position are unlikely to fare well in elections. Given these features of American life, two parties seem to be sufficient to capture the viewpoints of a majority of voters. Still, ideological differences between the parties seem to grow at times and contract at other times. The current era is one of those in which the American electorate finds itself increasingly polarized between liberal Democrats and conservative Republicans. Politics in times like this can be extremely volatile.

By contrast, Europeans find their multiparty system to be home for a wider range of viewpoints representing votes cast statewide in the last presidential election. Meeting state requirements is an expensive and time-consuming, but not impossible, operation. In 1992, billionaire H. Ross Perot, running as an independent, spent more than $60 million collecting signatures and complying with ballot access rules in all 50 states in his bid for the presidency.[16]

Financing Since the 1970s, major-party candidates in presidential campaigns have received public financing in addition to private financing of their election bids. Here, too, minor-party and independent candidates are at a disadvantage. The Federal Election Campaign Act awards matching funds to major-party candidates during the primary season and full funding during the general election campaign. (Many consider the public finance law obsolete. One major-party candidate for president in 2008 chose not to participate in the current system. We will discuss public financing for presidential elections at greater length in Chapter 12.) Third-party or independent candidates can collect their share of funds only after the election is over, and then only if they have crossed a predetermined vote threshold. Very few third-party or independent candidates can sustain the costs of a competitive campaign during the long months of the presidential contest in the hopes of

> **Duverger's law** Principle that asserts single-member district elections lead to two-party systems.
>
> **Electoral College** The assemblage of state electors constitutionally charged with electing the president.

AMERICANS HISTORICALLY have downplayed differences based on class or ethnic identity.

historic economic, regional, and ethnic cleavages. Their proportional parliamentary systems can reward even small parties that represent narrow sectarian interests by giving them a place in the legislative body. By contributing to party diversity, proportional systems may also produce higher voter turnout.

State Laws Since the U.S. Constitution does not mention political parties, regulating them is largely the job of the states. Many states make it very difficult for new parties to gain access to the ballot. Each state sets its own requirements, and the major parties that hold power in the states usually make rules that benefit themselves. For example, parties in Texas automatically qualify for ballot access if they have won 5 percent of the vote cast for any statewide office in the most recent general election, a qualification easily met by the major-party competitors. Candidates from other parties, by contrast, must collect valid signatures from citizens equaling 1 percent of the votes cast in the previous gubernatorial election. In 2008, that meant collecting more than 43,000 signatures within a 70 day period in order to qualify for a place on the state ballot. Candidates who prefer to run as independents, without benefit of any party label, have an even tougher job. In 2008, they needed the signatures of more than 74,000 citizens, or 1 percent of the

securing enough votes for reimbursement. An independent candidate or third party meeting this threshold and returning to run again in the subsequent election automatically qualifies for a portion of the public funds. Such a second run is rare, although Ross Perot ran in 1992 and again in 1996 and received public financing on his second run, this time heading the Reform Party ticket.

Candidates for lower-level offices must rely entirely on funds they raise themselves. Working with established parties in the states has a decided advantage for such candidates because the parties have cultivated long lists of dependable contributors who are extremely reluctant to support independent or third-party candidates.

GROWTH AND DEVELOPMENT OF OUR TWO-PARTY SYSTEM

Parties were born in America from the desire to produce lasting governing coalitions on issues that divided our leaders. No coalition, however, is permanent, and the history of our two-party system demonstrates that individual parties rise and fall over time for a number of reasons, including competition, failure to adapt policy or ideological positions to changing times, and internal struggles among factions.

The Evolution of American Political Parties: Five Party Eras

We saw in Chapter 2 that some, like Alexander Hamilton, envisioned a national government with broad authority in financing undertakings necessary to make the new country a commercial force in the world. Others, including Thomas Jefferson, believed Hamilton's vision took power away from states and localities. On a number of issues, these two sides fought by proxy in Congress, assembling makeshift majorities either to advance or to thwart the Hamiltonian vision. Those aligned with Jefferson and James Madison, with the help of a rudimentary campaign organization and powerful partisan press support, had won a majority of House seats by 1800. When national political figures lined up behind Hamilton's Federalists and Jefferson's Antifederalists (or Democratic-Republicans as they were known for a time), the rudiments of the first party system in America came into existence. This was mostly an elite system organized to create stable voting coalitions in the government.[17]

Andrew Jackson, aided by New York senator Martin Van Buren, later built a new organization that reached down to average voters in cities and towns across the nation; that achievement ended the first party era in America. With the use of parades, speech making, rallies, and bonfires, often fueled by monies raised in Washington or New York and funneled to local clubs across the nation, Jackson and Van Buren built the first mass political party, whose

political machine A strong party organization that maintained control by giving favors in return for votes.

patronage A practice of providing jobs in exchange for political loyalty.

civil service A merit-based system of employment and personnel management that replaced patronage.

members were by then called simply Democrats. This new party boosted popular participation substantially: Only 30 percent of those eligible voted for a presidential candidate in 1824, but voter turnout exceeded 50 percent of such voters by 1828.[18] Structural changes, such as the popular election of presidential electors (who had in earlier elections been selected by legislative leaders), sparked voter interest by giving them a larger role in the election process.

By 1836, opponents copied the pattern of organizational success pioneered by Van Buren and Jackson, ushering in the second party era. The largest opposition party, the Whigs, differed from the Democrats on a number of issues, including the use of tariffs. Internal division, and the ever-present issue of slavery, eventually combined to doom the Whig Party. From its ruins, a new Republican Party (unrelated to Jefferson's Democratic-Republicans) emerged, drawing support largely from the North and the new northwestern states. By 1860, the Democrats also had split over slavery, with northern and southern factions nominating different presidential candidates. Democratic feuding opened the way for Republican Abraham Lincoln to win the presidency in 1860 and set the stage for a showdown over slavery. It was a showdown that neither party desired—and that neither could avoid.

The parties were evenly matched during the third era of American political parties, which lasted for nearly half a century, from 1860 to 1896. During this period, Republicans controlled the presidency and Congress more often than the opposition did, but Democrats still dominated state and local politics in the South. Westward expansion and migration to the cities served to keep the politics of the era fluid, but this period also witnessed the virtually uninhibited growth of big business and the susceptibility of the nation to wild swings in economic fortune. Economic displacement, the growth of organized labor, and waves of immigrants contributed to a growing discontent, but they also provided valuable votes for the parties, which competed vigorously for Americans' allegiance. Party bosses ran **political machines**, providing services to the needy and to new immigrants in return for their votes. Votes were also exchanged for jobs, a practice known as **patronage**. The

Major Developments in the History of U.S. Political Parties

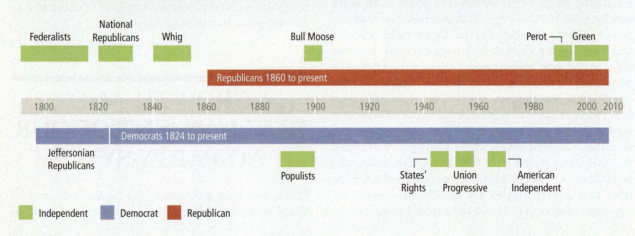

electoral politics of the time emphasized loyalty to party or faction, often inspiring violence among and against immigrant and laboring groups, who frequently viewed political success as a surrogate for personal fortune. Nevertheless, this golden age of electoral politics produced voter turnout rates higher than ever before or since.[19]

Just before the turn of the twentieth century, growing discontent with government corruption and economic depression led to a number of third-party movements. Most prominent among these parties was the Populist Party, which drew support from various politically active farmers' alliances and from displaced urban workers. Although Democrats made inroads among Populist followers, their support remained largely confined to the South and portions of the West. At the same time, Republicans experienced growth in the burgeoning metropolitan areas of the North and had strong support from industrial leaders and business interests. Republican dominance characterized the fourth party era during the first quarter of the twentieth century. This era saw a number of long-sought reforms in government, including the growth of the **civil service**, a merit-based system of employment and personnel management that replaced patronage.

The Great Depression allowed the Democrats to recapture the northern electorate. At the peak of the Depression, one worker out of four was unemployed and more than five thousand banks had failed. By 1932, the nation was poised for a major party switch as Democrats swept the White House and both houses of Congress. This signaled the beginning of the fifth party era, a time of Democratic dominance that lasted until the late 1960s. Roosevelt's political legacy was the forging of a **New Deal coalition** of Democratic supporters, including southern whites, northern industrial workers, immigrants, urban dwellers, Catholics, Jews, and blacks. This unlikely coalition proved remarkably resilient as a result of strong leadership, a willingness to ignore potentially divisive issues like race, and mobilization of voters by newly empowered groups, especially organized labor. Although Republicans were the minority party during this period, they also put together a stable coalition of upper-income whites, Protestants, growing numbers of suburbanites, and small business owners.

The Great Depression created the conditions that helped Franklin Roosevelt forge the New Deal coalition, enabling the Democrats to dominate national politics for 40 years.

1968 to Present

Democratic support for civil rights for minorities created deep fissures in the party as early as the 1940s, but these grew more serious in the 1960s. Southern whites distanced themselves from the national Democratic Party on racial issues and ran alternative candidates for president in 1948 (States' Rights Party) and 1968 (American Independent Party). By the mid-1960s, Democrats were straining to maintain the coalition that had made them the dominant party since 1932. Republicans capitalized on this disenchantment, recruiting new members in the rapidly growing South. Their "Southern strategy" appealed to social conservatives who believed the federal government had overstepped its bounds in promoting racial equality in the states and overextended its reach into the economy. From the 1960s onward, Republican gains in the once "solid Democratic South" have been dramatic, as the figure on page 208 demonstrates.

New Deal coalition
Constellation of social groups that became the core base of support for the Democratic Party after the election of Franklin D. Roosevelt.

A resurgent Republican Party regained the White House in 1968 and in subsequent years built national support as the Democratic coalition weakened. Drawing upon southern whites, conservatives, evangelical Christians, and upper-income businesspersons and professionals, Republicans gained parity with Democrats among the national electorate and achieved control of both the White House and both houses of Congress by 2002.

Since 1976, Republicans have made inroads into several formerly Democratic constituencies, including middle-income and blue-collar voters as well as union members. The Republican share of votes among southerners, housewives, and conservatives has been impressive.

Rise of the Republican South

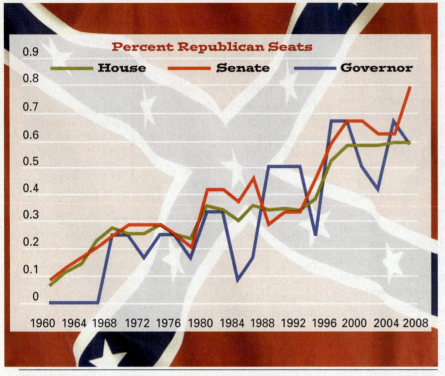

Percent Republican Seats
— House — Senate — Governor

Source: Congressional Quarterly Reports, various years. Southern states examined include Alabama, Arkansas, Florida, Georgia, Kentucky, Louisiana, Mississippi, North Carolina, South Carolina, Tennessee, Texas, and Virginia.

White Catholics have gravitated to the Republican Party in recent years, primarily because of the party's more conservative stance on social and cultural issues like abortion and homosexuality;[20] black and Hispanic Catholics continue to show strong support for Democratic Party candidates.

Meanwhile, the Democratic Party is undergoing demographic change as well. Democrats have done better in recent years among professionals with higher incomes and education—especially those with advanced degrees. Since the 1980s, a gender gap has developed between the parties, with women fairly consistently preferring Democrats over Republicans.[21] This gap hides important subgroup differences, however. For example, while single women are much more likely to vote Democratic, housewives prefer the Republicans. Democrats have increased their share of younger voters, and voters in northeastern and far western states. They do better among the rising number of Americans who seldom or never attend religious services. As a group, Democrats

realignments Periodic changes in party strength, composition, and direction.

critical elections Elections signaling realignments, often sweeping the opposition party into control of the presidency and Congress.

divided government Control of the White House by one party while the opposition party controls one or both houses of Congress.

dealignment A falloff in electoral support for both major political parties.

appear to be more consistently liberal on a number of issues ranging from abortion to gun control.

Overall, demographic and political changes have resulted in a reassortment of partisan divisions with southern and lower midwestern states growing more securely Republican, coastal states more Democratic, and the number of closely divided states shrinking. Despite fluctuations in overall levels of party support as a result of short-term events, the major parties maintained rough parity among voters until very recently. In 2001, the Gallup Organization reported about one-third of Americans considered themselves Democrats (33 percent), one-third Republicans (32 percent), and one-third Independents (34 percent). Unpopular policies pursued by the Bush administration along with a vigorous Democratic presidential campaign drove the number of self-identified Republicans down to 27 percent just after the 2008 presidential election while adding a few percentage points to the number of those identifying as Democrats and Independents. Democrats gained identifiers among the young, minorities, the middle class, the college educated, and moderates; while the GOP avoided losses only among its most loyal followers: conservatives, frequent churchgoers, and the elderly.[22] Some of this movement reflects demographic changes like the entry of more minorities and young people into the electorate. However, self-identification is volatile and driven by short-term forces as well. By 2010, the number of Americans identifying as Democrats had slipped by a few percentage points, and the number calling themselves Republicans had ticked slightly upwards.

Party Realignment

As we have said, parties undergo periodic changes in strength, composition, and direction. These changes, known as **realignments**, can come about for a variety of reasons. Sometimes major events such as the Civil War will trigger a prolonged change in party control of the institutions of government. Such events can increase voter interest and party competition, upsetting the electoral balance that defined the era before the event. Occasionally, such events give rise to significant third-party movements as well. Sometimes realignments signal a long-term change in the parties' demographic composition, as when Franklin Roosevelt forged the New Deal coalition after the Great

Depression by combining the party's traditional southern white Democratic base with northern ethnic minorities and blacks who had been loyal to the Republican Party. Sometimes realignments reflect a shift in the ideological orientation of the party or in the agenda and constellation of issues that win voters to its side. For example, at the beginning of the twentieth century, Republicans consolidated power by supporting an agenda that embraced the changes being introduced by the new industrial economy.[23]

Scholars debate the length of these cycles, some claiming that they reflect generational changes occurring every 28 to 36 years.[24] Others believe that genuine realignments occur over a 60- to 70-year period.[25] The orthodoxy in political science holds that realignments are signaled by one or more **critical elections**. In such elections, the opposition party dramatically sweeps into national power by winning the presidency and both houses of Congress, and it then begins building new voter coalitions. For example, scholars cite the elections of 1932 and 1936 as critical in transforming the political landscape in favor of the Democrats after a long period of Republican control. Some scholars, however, are skeptical of the notion of predictable cycles of party control. Instead, they prefer to rely on careful historical analysis of major transforming events such as the Civil War and individual election match-ups.[26]

Major changes have taken place in party alignment over the past few years. The once solid Democratic South is now a Republican stronghold; the once viable and strongly Democratic blue-collar vote is now splintered, more volatile, and less unified because of a drop in union membership; moderate Republicans, particularly in the northeastern states, are a disappearing breed. The Democratic Party is much more consistently liberal in orientation and membership; the Republicans, more conservative. And the nation has become more ideologically and politically divided. Still, some elements of the old alignment remain. Democrats continue to attract a disproportionate number of minorities and low-income voters; Republicans attract upper income whites and business professionals. Yet, neither party in recent years has been able to dominate the national government for a sustained period of time. In fact, much of the past forty-year period has been characterized by **divided government**, with one party controlling the White House while the other controls one or both houses of Congress. Partisan identification has been closely divided throughout much of this period, and national elections have been extremely competitive.

Some scholars believe we are undergoing a **dealignment**, in which both parties appear to be losing their relevance for the American voter.[27] More voters seem to reject both major parties, increasingly identifying as independents or nonpartisans. Many assert they are more likely to look to short-term factors such as issues or candidate characteristics rather than party when casting ballots. Many Americans split their ballots, voting Republican for national office holders but Democratic for state officials, for example.

But political parties are not dead. Party identification is still a powerful predictor of how voters will cast their ballots and whether they will vote at all.[28] Split-ticket voting has waned recently, and most independents reveal reliable partisan preferences and voting habits when pressed.

BUILT TO WIN: PARTY STRUCTURE

During the first half of the twentieth century, parties ran campaigns for candidates they selected and groomed for offices at every level of government. They relied on local party workers who could look forward to rewards for getting out the vote. Today, patronage politics has largely faded, and candidates have taken a more active role in running their own campaigns. Nevertheless, parties continue to play an important supporting role, with the national party organization assuming a larger role in coordinating campaign activities at almost every level of government. As political scientist James Q. Wilson has noted:

Parties as organizations have changed somewhat from being local associations that mobilized local electorates to being national entities that direct resources, recruit candidates and supply expertise . . . Local party organizations still exist, of course . . . but in some respects they are now overshadowed by the national organizations.[29]

In providing support, parties are organized in layers, with each layer built to win elections at its own level of operation. Each layer operates somewhat independently of the others in mapping campaign strategy, but the layers cooperate in sharing resources and mobilizing voters on Election Day.

Pyramid Structure of Party Organizations in the U.S.

National Committees

Congressional and Senatorial Campaign Committees

State Committees

Local Government Committees

Precinct Committees

National party conventions galvanize the support of partisans and help catapult the party's nominee into the general election campaign.

National Committees

Each party has a national committee made up of members from each of the state parties. The Republican National Committee (RNC) consists of more than 150 members, including one male and one female representative from each state and U.S. territory together with the chairs of the state parties. The Democratic National Committee (DNC) is larger, consisting of about 400 members. In addition to the top officers from the parties of each state and national territory, who are either elected by voters in primaries or by delegates to the states' conventions, the DNC awards a number of seats to various Democratic constituencies, including elected officials. Delegations must be equally divided between men and women. The national bodies in both parties formally elect their national party chair, although in practice each usually approves the nominee selected by the party's candidate for president. Barack Obama chose Tim Kaine, former governor of Virginia, to lead his party dur-

soft money Money that is outside the federal regulatory framework but raised and spent in a manner suggesting possible intent to affect federal elections.

ing the first two years of his administration; but, after the stinging defeat the Democrats received at the polls in the 2010 midterm elections, he replaced Kaine with Florida Congresswoman Debbie Wasserman Schultz. Schultz has concentrated her efforts on fundraising and serving as party spokesperson during the 2012 presidential cycle. John McCain's loss in 2008 led to a wide-open battle for leadership in the Republican camp. Michael Steele, former Maryland lieutenant governor, was selected on the sixth ballot by a divided Republican National Committee. But Steele had trouble healing the wounds of a divided party in the months just after the election and came under attack for some of the ways party money was spent while he was in office. He was replaced by Reince Priebus, who led the Wisconsin Republican Party to major gains in the 2010 midterm elections, after yet another drawn-out battle for the position at a meeting of the Republican National Committee in January 2011.

In addition to making policy recommendations, the national committees select sites for the presidential nominating conventions. The Democrats chose Charlotte, North Carolina, for their site in 2012, while the Republicans picked Tampa, Florida. The Democrats hoped to hang on to North Carolina after taking it away from Republicans in 2008; while the Republicans hoped to regain the important swing state of Florida with its treasure of 29 electoral votes.

The national party chair presides over everyday operations of the national headquarters, monitors electoral races throughout the nation, helps set the party agenda and rules, and acts something like a referee when there is a contested primary. Howard Dean, former Democratic National Committee chair, had to walk a fine line between Hillary Clinton and Barack Obama in the 2008 presidential contest. His job was made more difficult by an extended primary season and conflict over how to count delegates from states that had violated party rules by advancing their primaries earlier

in the year than the party had authorized. We will discuss the presidential election in more detail in Chapter 12.

In recent years, fundraising has been one of the primary functions of the national committees. Until 2002, most of these funds took the form of **soft money**, large sums, mostly from wealthy contributors, intended for "party-building" activities such as voter registration and running generic issue ads that do not mention specific candidates. In actuality, much of the money went to bolster presidential or congressional nominees in key battleground states. The

New Limits on Fundraising Following Bipartisan Campaign Reform Act, 2011–2012

	Recipients				
Donors	Candidate Committee	National Party Committee	State, District and Local Party Committee	PAC[1]	**Special Limits**
Individual	$2,500* per election	$30,800* per year	$10,000 per year combined limit	$5,000 per year[1]	$117,000* biennial limit: • $45,200* to all candidates • $79,800* to all PACs and parties[2]
National Party Committee	$5,000 per election	Unlimited transfers to other party committees		$5,000 per year	$43,100* to Senate candidate per campaign[3]
State, District & Local Party Committee	$5,000 per election combined limit	Unlimited transfers to other party committees		$5,000 per year combined limit	No limit
PAC Multicandidate[4]	$5,000 per election	$15,000 per year	$5,000 per year combined limit	$5,000 per year	No limit
PAC Not Multicandidate	$2,500* per election	$30,800* per year	$10,000 per year combined limit	$5,000 per year	No limit

* These contribution limits are increased for inflation in odd-numbered years.

1. A contribution earmarked for a candidate through a political committee counts against the original contributor's limit for that candidate. In certain circumstances, the contribution may also count against the contributor's limit to the PAC. 11 CFR 110.6. See also 11 CFR 110.1(h).

2. No more than $46,200 of this amount may be contributed to state and local party committees and PACs.

3. This limit is shared by the national committee and the Senate campaign committee.

4. A multicandidate committee is a political committee with more than 50 contributors which has been registered for at least 6 months and, with the exception of state party committees, has made contributions to 5 or more candidates for federal office. 11 CFR 100.5(e)(3).

5. A federal candidate's authorized committee(s) may contribute no more than $2,000 per election to another federal candidate's authorized committee(s). 2 U.S.C. 432(e)(3)(B).[0]

Source: Federal Election Commission.

Divergent Views: Convention Delegates and Voters in 2008

Social issue	% Democratic delegates	% Democratic voters	% All voters	% Republican voters	% Republican delegates
Abortion should be generally available	70	43	33	19	9
Illegal immigrants should be allowed to stay in current jobs and apply for citizenship	68	50	40	26	22
Gay couples should be allowed to legally marry	55	49	34	11	6
Gun control laws should be more strict	62	71	52	32	8
Political ideology					
Liberal	43	48	26	5	--
Moderate	50	34	36	30	26
Conservative	3	16	36	63	72

Source: New York Times/CBS Poll of Convention Delegates, Sept. 1, 2008.

Bipartisan Campaign Reform Act of 2002 banned parties from raising and spending soft money. However, the act increased contribution limits on **hard money**, donations that candidates or parties can use directly for electoral activities. Even with these new rules in place, the national committees have demonstrated an impressive capacity for collecting large sums of money. Many critics of the campaign reform law believed that it would divert funds from parties and into the hands of outside groups with a stake in election outcomes. This has clearly not been the case. The parties have adapted well to the ban on soft money, and today they are more significant players in financing presidential and congressional campaigns than they were before the law went into effect.[30] The Democratic National Committee, which for many years badly trailed its Republican counterpart in fundraising, has been somewhat more competitive in raising funds in recent election cycles. A controversial decision announced by the Supreme Court in January 2010 may dramatically change the role of parties in financing political campaigns.[31] The Court ruled that corporations, trade associations, unions, and nonprofit organizations may spend unlimited amounts of money advocating for or against political candidates. Parties immediately ramped up their fundraising operations in order to stay competitive with newly empowered outside groups with whom they must now compete.

hard money Campaign money received by candidates or parties that can be used for any purpose.

national convention Event held every four years by each political party to formally anoint its presidential candidate and to signal the initiation of the general election campaign.

The office of the national committee is also an important source of information and expertise. Candidates can tap national committees for the latest polling results and can secure advice from campaign consultants. The national committee also places candidates in contact with interest groups that will raise additional funds and provide volunteers and campaign workers.

A close working relationship with interest groups has transformed national parties into "networks of issue-oriented activists," as one political scientist puts it.[32] These groups have pressured the parties to adopt specific positions on divisive issues like abortion, civil rights, and gun control. Changes in party operations have also increased the role of ideological and single-issue activists. For example, beginning in the 1960s, the Democratic Party mandated greater inclusion of women and minorities at its national political conventions, diminishing its reliance on seasoned state and local party officials. Consequently, the Democratic National Committee has moved more to the left, while social conservatives have taken advantage of similar changes to move the Republican Party to the right. The result has been greater polarization of the parties at the national level.

Nowhere is the ideological divide clearer than in the makeup of delegates to the **national convention**, the quadrennial gathering of party members to nominate their party's presidential candidate (see Chapter 12 for details). The convention also approves the **platform**, or statement of issue positions, that the party will nominally espouse for the next four years. In recent years, large blocs of convention delegates have been a veritable who's who of interest group politics. Labor unions and pro-choice activists, for example, constitute a large chunk of Democratic delegates. Members of the Christian Coalition, antiabortion activists, and business groups dominate the Republican convention. Party platforms often reflect the interests of these select groups. They do not, however, necessarily reflect the views of the average voter, or even those of the average party supporter, as the table above illustrates. Candidates often run away from some planks in the party platform as they attempt to attract a wider range of voters in the general election. Still, even rank and file party supporters have become more polarized in recent years, extending the ideological gulf between the parties.

Congressional and Senatorial Campaign Committees

Each party maintains organizations to help its candidates win election or reelection to the two national legislative chambers. These committees—the National Republican Congressional Committee (NRCC), the National Republican Senatorial Committee (NRSC), and their Democratic counterparts, the Democratic Congressional Campaign Committee (DCCC) and the Democratic Senatorial Campaign Committee (DSCC)—work with other party committees and with individual candidates to raise and distribute funds, share polling data, and offer expertise about running campaigns.

Not every candidate can count on help from these committees, however. Because resources are limited, Democratic and Republican committee staffs make strategic choices about which candidates are most likely to benefit from assistance. Under the leadership of Texas Congressman Pete Sessions, the RCCC was particularly successful in raising funds to help elect a new class of freshman who entered and took control of the House in 2010. Although the DCCC outraised and outspent the RCCC, its spending came too late in the campaign to avoid the Republican tide.

The national parties can give up to $5,000 to individual House candidates and $43,100 to Senate candidates to spend directly on their campaigns. In addition, members from **safe seats**, in which the incumbent faces only limited or token opposition, often make some of their own campaign contributions available to more needy candidates. Candidates can receive additional funds through so-called leadership PACs that are affiliated with party leaders in each chamber. Like all PACs that give to multiple candidates, leadership PACs can contribute up to $5,000 per candidate per election (i.e., $5,000 for a primary election and $5,000 for the general election). Such donations may be instrumental in providing the margin of victory for recipients, and they generate a substantial amount of goodwill for the legislative donor. In the 2010 midterm campaign, House Majority Leader Eric Cantor (R-VA) contributed over $1.7 million to fellow Republicans, outspending House Speaker John Boehner (R-OH) who contributed just over $1.3 million. Not far behind were Minority Party Whip Steny Hoyer (D-MD) and former speaker Nancy Pelosi (D-CA) at $1.2 million and $825 thousand respectively.[33]

platform Statement of political principles and campaign promises generated by each party at its national convention.

safe seats Legislative districts that regularly remain in the hands of the same candidate or party.

State Committees

State parties have organizations somewhat parallel to those found at the national level. Each state organization has its own peculiarities, but most state parties are headed by state committees—sometimes known as state central committees—drawn from county, congressional district, and municipal party officials and led by a state party chair. State party officers, together with their staffs, concentrate on statewide elective offices such as governor and key state legislative positions. Members of the state committees may meet only once or twice a year to ratify policies generated by national and state leaders. Day-to-day activities remain in the hands of the chairperson.

There is quite a bit of integration of party activities between national and state organizations. For example, national and state parties may share campaign costs for joint appearances and coordinate their advertising efforts. Until soft money was banned in 2002, national parties channeled millions of dollars through state parties for party-building activities such as voter registration drives. Today, state parties often team up with independent organizations tied to national interest groups to

get involved!

Become a delegate to your party's state or national political convention. If you are 18 and registered to vote, you probably qualify. Contact your precinct leader or your party's local office. In some states, you can become a delegate by working directly for a candidate if he or she wins the primary election. In others, delegates have to file their own nominating petitions and are elected directly by the voters. In most states, you can also work closely with your local party to be considered as a delegate from your district. As a delegate, you'll attend the convention in the city selected for the event and have a voice in forging your party's platform as well as in selecting official party candidates for the general election.

Did You Know?

. . . That today's "negative campaigning" is nothing new? In 1884, Democratic presidential candidate Grover Cleveland faced accusations (which he did not deny) of having once fathered an illegitimate child, leading Republicans to shout, "Ma! Ma! Where's my Pa?" The Democrats, who ultimately prevailed in the election, responded, "Gone to the White House. Ha, ha, ha!"

Local Party Organizations

Local party units in cities, counties, and towns recruit candidates as well as organize and run campaigns for many local offices, including mayor, sheriff, and county council. They can also be influential in securing local projects and contracts from the state and national governments when their party is in power. The higher levels of party organization have an incentive to work with local parties, since the national parties ultimately rely heavily upon local personnel to get out the vote on Election Day. Nevertheless, local party units are not the powerhouses they were in the days of machine politics. Many factors contributed to this decline, including party reform, the replacement of patronage employees by a professionalized government workforce, the growth of government welfare services to replace favors once performed by local party bosses, the development of candidate-centered campaigns, and the rise of the mass media as an independent source for voter information.

Precinct Organizations

The level of organization that comes closest to the voter is usually called the **precinct**. Precincts include the population served by a polling place and can vary markedly in size, depending on population dispersion. Loyal party supporters are elected or appointed at the precinct level to act as liaisons between the voter and the party. Many precinct workers hold political jobs and have a keen interest in the outcome of elections, even though federal laws prevent hiring and firing on the basis of party allegiance. Precinct workers are our neighbors, and they can exert a powerful influence on our voting behavior. They alert us regarding local issues and inform us about voting procedures, poll locations, approaching registration deadlines, and candidates running for office. They remind us of our civic duty and even drive us to the polls on Election Day.

Recent campaigns have demonstrated how national and local party organizations can work together effectively to win elections. Parties are actively experimenting with new technologies and new methods that combine information gleaned from large national databases with canvassing provided by local party activists in order to get out the vote. Political parties are not shy about investigating consumer habits of voters and using them to identify potential supporters. Armed with this information, precinct workers, along with local candidate supporters and interest group volunteers, can design

---

organize voter registration around the state. For example, liberal groups such as America Coming Together (ACT) and conservative groups like the Club for Growth were actively involved in voter mobilization and issue-ad sponsorship at the state level during recent election cycles. The Democratic and Republican governors associations also actively participate in funding support for state candidates.

State parties have become more professionalized in recent years, with the support and encouragement of the national parties.[34] They have substantially improved their ability to raise money, and they employ some of the same high-tech communication methods used by their national counterparts. For example, state parties have developed clearly targeted mailing lists for use in both fundraising and communicating with constituents about pressing issues. The bulk of their expenditures include political contributions to candidates and local campaign committees for consultants, polling, and advertising—together with funds for administrative expenses such as salaries, rent, equipment, and travel. State committees also spend money on media for the entire ticket. Both parties have fairly consistent spending patterns; however, Republicans spend substantially more on fundraising activities.

precinct The geographic area served by a polling place and organized by local party units.

third parties Minor parties that run a slate of their own candidates in opposition to major-party organizations in an election.

Hot or Not?

Do Republican and Democratic parties do an adequate job of representing the American people, or do they do such a poor job that a third major party is needed?

Teddy Roosevelt received 27 percent of the popular vote while running under the mantle of the Bull Moose Party in 1912.

individualized messages to bring to voters' doorsteps. Text messaging, social networking, and peer-to-peer appeals are proving especially useful in mobilizing younger voters. These techniques are reinvigorating local party activity, and their use will be studied to see if they can sustain increased voter turnout. We will describe additional efforts to attract young voters later in this chapter, in the section "Parties, Political Campaigns, and Civic Engagement Today."

THIRD PARTIES AND INDEPENDENT CANDIDACIES

Minor parties are far from absent in American politics. Perennial **third parties**, as minor parties are sometimes called, include the Libertarians, the Socialist Workers, and the Green Party. Some third parties arise for a year or two and then disappear. Some social movements mobilize Americans around a set of principles or ideals but fail to run candidates on their own. The Tea Party movement ran a small number of candidates for Congress in 2010 but made much greater inroads by throwing its weight behind Republican candidates, helping the GOP recapture the House.

Our nation has witnessed important third-party challenges, even if most were short-lived. Usually, third parties and significant independent candidacies arise in periods of great change or crisis. They attract the attention of many who had not previously voted and those who perceive a lack of genuine difference between the major parties. Often they reflect a desire for change in the political direction of the nation.

Some third parties are **splinter parties**,[35] parties that break away from one of the major parties. The Republicans began as a splinter party, break-ing away from the Whigs over the issue of slavery in 1852 and eventually supplanting them as the major competitor to the Democrats. Other notable splinter parties included the Populists, who emerged as an offshoot of Democratic politics in 1892; the Bull Moose Party, which nominated former president Teddy Roosevelt in 1912 after he broke with Republicans; the States' Rights and Progressive parties, which split in different ideological directions from the Democrats in 1948; and the American Independent Party, which broke off from the Democrats over civil rights policy in 1968 by nominating Alabama governor George Wallace for president.

Some third parties are **ideological parties** that reflect a commitment to an ideological position different from that of most voters. Socialists committed to government ownership of factories and businesses gathered limited support for their cause during the early twentieth century. Libertarians, who call for smaller government and the privatization of many government services, have gathered some support, especially among younger voters.

Finally, some independent campaigns outside of the major par-

> **splinter parties** Political parties that are formed as offshoots of major political parties, usually by dissenters.
>
> **ideological parties** Minor parties organized around distinct ideological principles.

Did You Know?

. . . That the longest-running third party in American history is the Prohibition Party, founded in 1869 and still (barely) functioning? Over the course of its venerable history, several Prohibition Party members have been elected state governors and members of Congress; most recently (in 2001) someone claiming affiliation to the party was elected as a township assessor in rural Pennsylvania, and in 2004 its presidential candidate won 1,894 votes in the two states in which the party was on the ballot.

9 Parties and Political Campaigns • **215**

Third Parties and Independent Candidacies in Presidential Elections

Third party	Year	% Popular vote	Electoral votes	Fate in next elections
Anti-Masons	1832	7.8	7	Endorsed Whig candidate
Free soil	1848	10.1	0	Received 5% of vote; provided base of Republican supporters
Whig-American	1856	21.5	8	Party dissolved
Southern Democrat	1860	18.1	72	Party dissolved
Constitutional Union	1860	12.6	39	Party dissolved
Populist	1892	8.5	22	Endorsed Democratic candidate
Progressive (T. Roosevelt)	1912	27.5	88	Returned to Republican Party
Socialist	1912	6.0	0	Received 3.2% of vote
Progressive (LaFollette)	1924	16.6	13	Returned to Republican Party
States' rights Democrat	1948	2.4	39	Party dissolved
Progressive (H. Wallace)	1948	2.4	0	Received 1.4% of vote
American Independent (G. Wallace)	1968	13.5	46	Received 1.4% of vote
John B. Anderson	1980	7.1	0	Did not run in 1984
H. Ross Perot	1992	18.9	0	Formed the Reform Party and ran again in 1996
Reform Party (H. Ross Perot)	1996	8.4	0	Perot engaged in struggle for control of Reform Party
Reform/Independent (Pat Buchanan)	2000	.42	0	Little impact in 2004
Green Party (Ralph Nader)	2000	2.74	0	Denied slate to Nader in 2004

Source: Adapted from John F. Bibby, *Political Parties in the United States,* U.S. Department of State Information Programs, available online at http://usinfo.state.gov/products/pubs/archive/elect00/table.htm, accessed June 10, 2004.

In 2004 and 2008, Ralph Nader's independent presidential bids fizzled. During the 2000 election, however, his appearance on the Florida ballot helped create a virtual "tie" between Bush and Gore, throwing the contested election to the Supreme Court.

ties arise around a **single issue or candidate**. Ross Perot's impressive showing in 1992 revealed the potential strength of personal appeal coupled with a compelling issue: fiscal responsibility in the face of mushrooming budget deficits. The Green Party, which advocates environmental reform, has also fielded successful candidates in a number of state and local elections across the country.

Faced with the substantial obstacles involved in getting on the ballot and the difficulties involved with organizing supporters and amassing sufficient funds to mount a credible campaign—all the while lacking incumbent officeholders to promote programs—it is no wonder that most third-party and independent candidacies fail to persist. Many candidates emerge for one or two election cycles and then disappear because of a lack of resources. Ralph Nader's independent candidacy, for example, fizzled in 2004 after gaining almost 3 percent of the popular vote in 2000. Some independent and third parties continue on as perennial minor players (e.g., the Libertarians or the Greens). Still others are absorbed by a larger party that heeds their message, or adopts their ideology or policy prescriptions. For example, both Democrats and Republicans scurried to find ways to reduce the government's budget deficit after Perot's sizable showing in 1992.

By advancing and getting support for positions that differ from those of the established parties, third parties can signal voter discontent. Sometimes third-party and independent-candidate activity spurs an increase in voter interest and an uptick in voter turnout. By threatening the major parties, third parties can motivate them to change their policies. Occasionally, third parties act as "spoilers" by taking enough votes away from one candidate to swing the election to another. In 2000, Ralph Nader captured 97,000 votes in the crucial state of Florida. Some believe his showing helped George W. Bush win the state and the presidency.

CANDIDATES AND ELECTORAL POLITICS: CANDIDATE-CENTERED CAMPAIGNING

In the heyday of political parties, campaigns were about electing a team of candidates, for whom voters felt considerable emotional allegiance, to multiple offices. Parties groomed candidates and rewarded them for being "team players." Candidates often had worked hard and long at the lower levels of the party pyramid to demonstrate their loyalty, waiting their turn to run for office themselves. Today, campaigns are candidate-centered. Voters make judgments not solely on the basis of party loyalty, but on the positions and characteristics of the individuals seeking public office as well. Consequently, the backgrounds of those running for elective office also changed. Today's candidates need not have previous experience with political parties; they need not have worked on previous campaigns at all. Their allegiance to party creed or philosophy may be minimal. Instead, they are entrepreneurial self-starters who carry a substantial portion of the burden of campaigning themselves. We will discuss campaigns for specific offices in the chapters dealing with Congress and the presidency. Here, we will discuss the general features of today's candidate-centered campaigns for virtually all political offices.

Candidates, Money, and Expertise

One of the most important burdens for a candidate is raising money. The cost of campaigns keeps escalating at all levels of government. You may not be surprised that running for the U.S. Senate involves millions of dollars. But it is sobering to consider that running for a state legislative seat in a moderate-size state such as Indiana may cost more than $200,000 for a part-time job that pays less than

$15,000 a year. In many cases, parties look for candidates with enough personal resources to front most of the campaign expenses themselves. If the candidate cannot do so, he or she must turn to wealthy donors and organized interests for help.

Candidates devote a large part of their campaign day to raising money. In order to keep pace with the cost of campaigning for national offices, they must raise thousands of dollars a day. Personal phone calls, personal appearances, chicken dinners, and fish frys are all part of the fundraising effort, and they require both stamina and boldness. Candidates usually bear the entire cost of primary campaigns. Candidates for federal office must live by the rules of campaign finance, which limit the amount of money that individuals or PACs affiliated with interest groups may donate (see Chapter 8 for a discussion of PACs). Once the primary is over, the winning candidate can usually count on financial help from the national party. State campaign laws regulate the activities of candidates for state and local offices. Many states still allow soft-money contributions that candidates can use in a number of ways—including advertising and get-out-the-vote drives—to advance their campaigns.

single-issue or -candidate parties Minor parties arising in electoral response to important issues not addressed by major-party candidates or around a strong personality.

Hot or Not?

Should we lift restrictions on political contributions entirely?

get involved!

Volunteer with a political campaign. It doesn't matter at what level—presidential, congressional, state, even local. You are likely to learn a lot about the process and about your neighborhood. Jobs range from office work like answering the phone to canvassing neighborhoods to registering voters and delivering campaign materials or working with local press in arranging personal appearances. If you are interested in pursuing a career in politics, this kind of volunteering is essential.

THE POLITICAL LANDSCAPE

The Pew Research Center recently completed a study of partisan leanings in which they investigated the demographics and viewpoints of voters affiliated with both major political parties. They found that political parties today are composed of disparate groups that leaders may find increasingly difficult to hold together. Republican identifiers include both staunch financial and social conservatives like members of the Tea Party and main-street Republicans mostly interested in economic issues but more moderate on social issues. Democrats include not only those who hold solidly liberal views across a host of issues but also socially conservative members of the financially pressed working class as well as struggling yet optimistic young minority members known as New Coalition Democrats. While Democrats and those who lean Democratic outnumber Republicans, the GOP is more homogeneous and their members express more intense interest in politics.

A growing number of voters told Pew they are independents, not interested in either political party. Yet, members of this diverse community lean toward one party or another. Libertarians who desire a smaller government and the Disaffected who are cynical about government in general side with Republicans. Post-Moderns who are well educated and financially comfortable side with Democrats even though they express skepticism about social programs designed to help the poor and minorities. Bystanders are generally younger Americans who express the least interest in politics and are least likely to vote.

Party Affiliation and the Typology Groups

	Rep %	Dem %	Ind* %	Rep/ lean R %	Dem/ lean D %
Total	24	33	43	40	49
Staunch Conservatives	84	*	16	100	*
Main Street Republicans	76	*	24	95	2
Libertarians	28	5	67	77	11
Disaffecteds	25	0	75	60	9
Post-Moderns	7	26	67	23	58
New Coalition Dems	2	56	42	5	81
Hard-Pressed Dems	0	84	16	0	100
Solid Liberals	*	75	24	1	96
Bystanders	13	25	62	29	49

Source: Pew Research Center 2011 Political Typology. Figures may not add to 100% because of rounding.

* Independent includes those who say they have no preference, volunteered another party, said they don't know or refused to answer the party identification question.

So-called 527 groups, ideological or issue-oriented groups that get their name from the section of the IRS Code that regulates their political activity, may make unlimited independent expenditures in both federal and state campaigns. These groups can use their funds to buy issue advertisements that often attack a rival candidate on his or her positions or background, but they may not instruct you to vote for or against a specific candidate. For example, in 2004, a group called the "Swift Boat Veterans for Truth" purchased ads attacking Democrat John Kerry's military service record. The Bipartisan Campaign Act of 2002 requires disclosure of those who contribute $10,000 or more to funding such ads. In 2007, the Supreme Court struck down the portion of the law that made it illegal to run issue ads that mention any federal candidate by name within 30 days of a primary election, or within 60 days of the general election.[36] However, reformers believe many of these groups take advantage of legal loopholes that allow wealthy patrons and interest groups to boost spending

beyond the limits imposed on direct donations. In 2008, 527 organizations sponsored by the Service Employees International Union raised and spent more than $27 million on liberal-leaning candidates for federal offices. Individual donors, such as pharmaceutical executive Fred Eshelman, made contributions to conservative 527 organizations in excess of $5 million.[37]

Additional outside funding comes from nonprofit organizations, or Section 501(c)(4) and 501(c)(6) groups (which are named after sections of the tax code), that are affiliated with labor unions, trade associations, corporations, and welfare organizations. These "nonprofit" advocacy groups are not taxed and are prohibited from making direct contributions to political candidates. Nevertheless, they sponsor advertisements promoting issue positions that may directly or indirectly benefit candidates who favor their views. Section 501(c) organizations that played a prominent part in recent campaigns include conservative Republican-leaning groups like American Taxpayers Alliance, Common Sense Ohio, and CitizenLink, as well as liberal, Democratic-oriented organizations like the League of Conservation Voters and Americans United for Change. Contributions and expenditures from 501(c) organizations, unlike those from 527s, are largely undisclosed to the public.[38] In *Federal Election Commission v. Wisconsin Right to Life,* the Supreme Court in 2007 gave both 527s and 501(c)s the benefit of the doubt when it comes to distinguishing between ads that target issues and those that express advocacy for a candidate or party, opening the way for additional spending on such ads in the future.

The 2010 Supreme Court decision, *Citizens United v. Federal Election Commission,* opened the floodgates further to spending by private organizations. The case involved a conservative nonprofit advocacy group that was banned by the Federal Election Commission from airing an unflattering documentary about Hillary Clinton on cable television just days before the 2008 presidential primaries. The Supreme Court overturned the FEC ruling, holding that portions of the law they applied violated the free speech rights of corporations, nonprofit organizations, and labor unions. So long as contributions are not made directly to individual candidates or coordinated with candidate campaigns, the court ruled, such groups are free to spend as much as they like to influence election outcomes.

In the 2010 midterm elections more than two dozen such organizations exercised this newly won right. One of these groups, American Crossroads, organized by former President George W. Bush's campaign manager Karl Rove, reportedly raised and spent more than $25 million, helping the Republican Party overcome its own fundraising deficit. Currently these organizations are not required to reveal donor names, although legislation has been introduced to require such reporting. It is widely believed that the *Citizens United* case will greatly increase the cost of campaigning as candidates and political parties are forced to defend themselves from attacks made by independent groups with deep pockets.

Candidates have increasingly made use of the Internet to raise funds for their campaigns. We have already discussed the success Barack Obama had in raising millions of dollars, much of it from small donors who contributed $200 or less over the Web. On the Republican side, Ron Paul raised substantial sums from small donors using both the Internet and direct mail. Available evidence suggests that while small donors resemble large donors in some demographics such as race and income (they are more likely to be white and wealthy), a growing number of individuals of more moderate means are contributing to elections. Moreover, Internet contributors represent more diverse interests than large cash contributors, who are drawn from industry, the professions, and trade organizations.[39] These developments have spurred optimism among some that technology may provide a means for achieving a more level playing field in campaign finance. Others point out that small donations mask the influence of repeat donors and that Internet fundraising does nothing to limit the impact of independent groups like 527s.

Where does all this money go? National and statewide elections require large expenditures on mass media advertising. The amount varies with the size of the media market in which the candidate lives. A candidate campaigning for a U.S. House seat in San Francisco will spend more on television, for example, than one in Muncie, Indiana. In some campaigns, the largest advertising costs may be direct mail that targets potential supporters with the can-

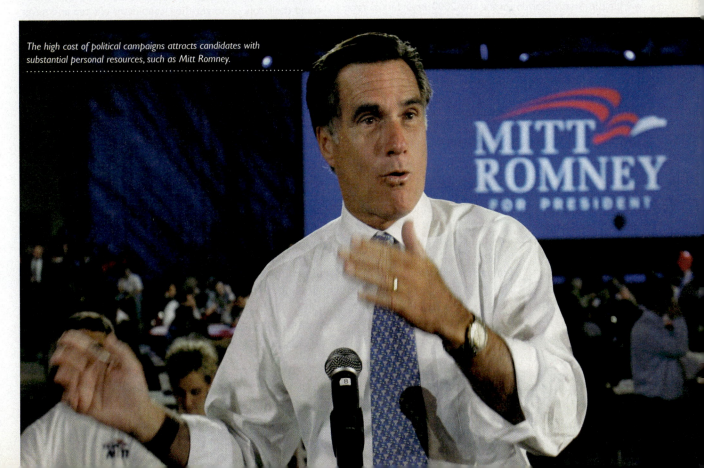

The high cost of political campaigns attracts candidates with substantial personal resources, such as Mitt Romney.

Brad Gideon with law students at Ball State University.

PORTRAIT OF AN ACTIVIST

Brad Gideon's Excellent Adventure

Working as a campaign coordinator for a presidential race was a great opportunity for Brad Gideon, but working in South Florida during the 2000 presidential race was a once-in-a-lifetime event. During his first months on the job, he was sent to coordinate Election Day activities in Palm Beach County, which became ground zero for the most contested election in U.S. history.

Because he was an attorney, Brad was asked to help when it became clear there were serious voting irregularities. "I was in the building during the first days of the recount as an observer," Brad recalls. "I helped organize an effort to collect affidavits from people who believed they voted for the wrong person or experienced other serious problems at polling locations in the state. The intense media coverage and demonstrations by people on all sides made the event seem more like a movie than real life."

By the time the Supreme Court settled the election on December 12, Brad had seen his share of disputed ballots and dangling chads, as observers dubbed the incompletely perforated tabs on the punch-card ballots. As he reflects on his experiences, Brad is not dismayed by his party's lack of success in 2000 or disheartened by the bitter political wrangling that followed the vote. "Participating in all of this gave me a greater understanding of and appreciation for the role of political parties in our system of government. Created out of pure political necessity, the political parties today still understand their role . . . to get their candidates elected and never to give up hope. There is always another election."

didate's message. Radio is also an important advertising medium, especially in rural areas.

Campaigning also requires a staff that includes a press secretary, a scheduler, and consultants. This last category may include issue experts and political strategists who analyze precinct returns to ensure that the candidate puts most of his or her effort in areas that will produce the most votes. Candidates and their strategists rely on polls that they commission to learn how they are faring among potential voters. When volunteers canvass neighborhoods, they need printed materials to leave with voters they visit. They also need some way to identify likely supporters for their candidates. Here, market research is increasingly important; even a small expenditure for mailing lists targeting products purchased by likely supporters can yield big rewards.

Candidates must also rent campaign headquarters and install phone banks so volunteers can follow up with voters as the election nears. Finally, there are costs associated with simply filing the paperwork to run, including fees and the preparation of financial statements. Candidates can share some of these expenses with the state party, especially those involving office and equipment rental and the production of printed materials that encourage voter registration and turnout. However, all of the burden for raising and spending money prior to the primaries—and most of it afterward—rests with the candidate, who acts much like an entrepreneur for a small business, one in which he or she is the product.

Candidates and the Parties

Even in the era of candidate-centered elections, candidates do rely on the resources political parties have to of-

primary election Election in which voters choose candidates to represent the political parties in the general election.

closed primary Election in which voters can choose from potential nominees only within their own party.

open primary Election in which voters can choose to vote for potential nominees from their own party or those from the other major political party.

fer. However, they usually do so only after the candidate has demonstrated electoral support in **primary elections**. This is in sharp contrast with what occurred in the heyday of party politics, when party insiders selected candidates. Today, for most offices, voters choose who will lead their parties in the general elections.

Some states employ **closed primary** elections in which voters can choose candidates only from the party for which they are registered. The idea behind the closed

In order to get elected, a candidate needs to be known. This is far easier for incumbents who have developed name recognition in earlier campaigns and who garner ongoing publicity associated with the offices they hold.

In local elections, candidates sometimes walk through neighborhoods to introduce themselves to voters and to ask for support. Something close to this occurs at the presiden-

CANDIDATES USE paid media to emphasize their good character and their stands on important issues.

primary is that only party members should be able to determine who will lead them in the general election. Most states that utilize this type of primary also exclude independent registrants from voting. **Open primaries** allow voters of both parties, and usually independents, to select candidates in whichever party's primary they choose. The **blanket primary** allows voters to choose freely from a list of every candidate regardless of party affiliation. Both major parties and some minor parties successfully challenged the California version of this system in the U.S. Supreme Court as an unconstitutional infringement on their associational rights, casting into doubt the use of similar systems in other states.[40] California voters recently approved a new primary measure that allows them to choose candidates of either party from a single ballot. The top two vote getters proceed to the general election regardless of party affiliation. In 2010, the Supreme Court upheld the constitutionality of a similar top-two primary in Washington, but opponents of the new California measure have vowed another court challenge. Some states require **runoff elections** between the top vote-getters if no one candidate receives a majority of the votes the first time around. Finally, some states employ a combination of primaries and party conventions, much like the process employed by national parties in the presidential election process, which we will discuss in Chapter 12.

Even with the volunteers, the expertise, and the money that comes with a primary victory, however, nominees cannot count on party loyalty alone to win the general election. Most decisions about strategic use of resources, such as the targeting of media, personal appearances, deployment of ground volunteers, and crafting of policy proposals, rest with the inner circle of the candidate's staff. While party and candidate may work in tandem in a well-coordinated campaign, candidates rely more heavily on their own organizations because they have more control over them. When party leaders and candidates do not see eye to eye on issues, they may go their separate ways. More than ever before, the candidates must sell their own policies and personalities to voters. Party identification alone is often not enough to carry most candidates to victory.[41]

tial level in the early caucus and primary states of Iowa and New Hampshire, where candidates sometimes show up years before the election to engage in highly personal **retail politics**. This is a time-intensive undertaking, however, and is feasible in only a limited number of campaigns, such as those in small districts or far from major media markets.

A more economical and efficient way of getting one's name and message across is by securing **earned media**, that is, free newspaper, radio, and television coverage devoted to a candidate because of some action or position he or she has taken. To encourage press coverage, candidates must demonstrate newsworthiness, which they often accomplish by calling news conferences at locations that provide interesting visual backdrops. For example, a candidate speaking about clean water policies may summon the media to a water treatment plant. Political conventions and candidate debates are also a rich source of free media coverage. Studies of voter attention to campaign activities show that, at least in presidential campaigns, voter interest in some of these events is quite high.[42]

Of course, candidates must also employ **paid media**, which include television, radio, and newspaper ads along with printed brochures. Candidates use paid media to emphasize their good character and their stands on important issues. Usually the tone of initial ads and brochures is very positive. Later in the campaign, especially if the candidate is having difficulty attracting support, he or she may resort to **negative or attack advertising**. Although today's campaigns may appear civil compared to some raucous campaigns in the nineteenth century, the reach of television magnifies the impact of negative ads on political de-

blanket primary Election in which voters can choose from among potential nominees in both parties; currently outlawed by the U.S. Supreme Court.

runoff election Second election between top two vote-getters in a race that did not produce a majority winner.

retail politics Campaign style emphasizing close personal contact between candidate and voters.

earned media Media attention for which candidates do not pay; associated with major events like debates.

paid media Media access for which candidates or party must pay a fee; advertisements.

negative or attack advertising Advertising that attacks one's opponents, usually on the basis of issue stance or character.

bate. It is always dangerous for a candidate to sponsor such ads, since they may tar the candidate as unscrupulous. It is far safer to leave the attacks to supporters. Predictably, candidates stung by such attacks often respond with their own attack ads. The result is a polarization of campaign rhetoric.

By and large, researchers have found that attack ads convey information that some voters find useful in making up their minds.[43] They disagree, however, about the long-term impact of attack ads on the political process. Some researchers have found that negative ads depress turnout, especially among independent and undecided voters.[44] Others conclude that any discouraging effect is minimal, and that negative ads may actually stimulate the interest of voters who might not otherwise have participated in an election.[45] Over the long haul, however, negative campaigning may take its toll on political interest, reducing feelings of political efficacy. Negative politics tends to wear some voters down to the point where they simply want to avoid politics completely.[46]

VOTERS IN THE ELECTORAL PROCESS: HOW AMERICANS DECIDE

Just as campaigns have changed over the course of American history, so has the way voters decide how to cast their ballots. When George Washington ran for the House of Burgesses in Virginia in 1735, voters took their cues from the voice votes of the town's most respected property holders. They were also offered material inducements. For example, Washington provided 28 gallons of rum, 50 gallons and 1 hogshead of rum punch, 34 gallons of wine, 46 gallons of strong beer, and 2 gallons of cider royal to be served to the 391 voters in his district.[47] When party strength was at its peak near the beginning of the twentieth century, voters were encouraged to cast highly visible color-coded ballots in plain view of party bosses and were entertained by parades and pageants.[48] Today, in the era of secret ballots and candidate-centered campaigns, voters are left on their own to navigate electoral decisions on the basis of party affiliation, candidate characteristics, and issue positions.

Party Choice

As we saw in Chapter 6, early socialization generally shapes party identification, which is related to characteristics including family income, level of education, parental

occupation, religion, gender, and race. These early influences are strong and have considerable staying power. For committed partisans, party affiliation is still a powerful predictor of choice of candidate.[49] The table on the next page presents a portrait of the electorate in the historic 2008 presidential election. Despite the precedent-setting election of the first African American president, an examination of election results reveals elements of both continuity and change in voting patterns.

One of the first things to notice is the strength of support among committed partisans. Democrats and Republicans overwhelmingly voted for their own party's candidate for president. We also see that the major parties drew strong support from ideologically committed voters. Liberals voted overwhelmingly for the Democratic candidate, and conservatives united to support John McCain. Independents, constituting 29 percent of the electorate, broke heavily for Obama as did the 44 percent of the national voters who call themselves moderates. Lower-income voters continued their longstanding support for the Democrats in 2008, while upper-income voters generally voted Republican. However, those at the very highest income levels gave Obama their support. The Democrats scored victories across all education levels. African Americans continued their support of Democratic candidates but did so at an even higher rate (96 percent). Obama also benefited from a 2 percent increase in black turnout, especially among black women. Hispanic American voters who were at one point thought to be up for grabs in this election voted overwhelmingly Democratic. Obama was also helped by a strong showing among young voters between the ages of 18 and 29. Though their participation rates increased only by about a point or two, they overwhelmingly voted for Obama and contributed to his margin of victory. He was the first Democrat since Jimmy Carter to win a majority of all votes (52 percent) overall. Obama won both men and women, largely as a result of the increase in black voters. Nevertheless, Obama made substantial gains over previous Democratic candidates among white voters—particularly among white men—rivaling Jimmy Carter's performance with this group in 1976. McCain performed more poorly among some groups than his Republican predecessor four years earlier. Whereas George W. Bush won rural voters by 19 points in 2004, McCain captured this group by just 6 percent. Catholics supported Obama in 2008 largely on the basis of minority and Hispanic American members, as did suburban voters.

In a nation where party identification is closely divided, independent voters are an important swing group and the 2010 elections demonstrated that this group is likely to switch preferences from election to election. Equally important is the level of voter enthusiasm. In 2008, Democrats had a clear advantage on this score, but dissatisfaction with President Obama's policies managed to draw a greater proportion of Republican voters and disgruntled independents to the polls in 2010. Midterm elections generally draw fewer and more committed voters as we will see in Chapter 11.

Portrait of the U.S. Electorate by Percentage in 2008

	Total vote 2004	Total vote 2008	Men 2004	Men 2008	Women 2004	Women 2008
Overall	100	100	47	47	53	53
Democrat	48	52	44	49	51	56
Republican	51	46	55	48	48	43
Independent	--	2	--	3	--	1

Political identification

	Republicans 2004	Republicans 2008	Independents 2004	Independents 2008	Democrats 2004	Democrats 2008
Overall	37	32	26	29	37	39
Democrat	6	9	49	52	89	89
Republican	93	90	48	44	11	10
Independent	--	1	--	4	--	1

Ideology

	Liberals 2004	Liberals 2008	Moderates 2004	Moderates 2008	Conservatives 2004	Conservatives 2008
Overall	21	22	45	44	34	20
Democrat	85	88	54	60	15	78
Republican	13	10	45	39	84	45
Independent	--	2	--	1	--	2

Region

	Northeast 2004	Northeast 2008	Midwest 2004	Midwest 2008	South 2004	South 2008	West 2004	West 2008
Overall	22	22	26	24	32	32	20	22
Democrat	56	59	48	54	42	46	50	57
Republican	43	40	51	44	58	53	49	40
Independent	--	1	--	2	--	1	--	3

Race and ethnicity

	White 2004	White 2008	Black 2004	Black 2008	Hispanic 2004	Hispanic 2008	Asian 2004	Asian 2008
Overall	79	74	12	13	6	9	2	2
Democrat	41	43	88	95	56	67	58	62
Republican	58	55	11	4	43	31	41	35
Independent	--	2	--	1	--	2	--	3

Age

	18–29 2004	18–29 2008	30–44 2004	30–44 2008	45–59 2004	45–59 2008	60 and older 2004	60 and older 2008
Overall	17	18	29	29	30	30	24	23
Democrat	54	66	46	52	48	49	46	46
Republican	45	32	53	46	51	49	54	52
Independent	--	2	--	2	--	1	--	2

Family status

	Married 2004	Married 2008	Unmarried 2004	Unmarried 2008	Have children under 18 2004	Have children under 18 2008	Gay/lesbian/bisexual 2004	Gay/lesbian/bisexual 2008
Overall	63	66	37	34	37	40	4	4
Democrat	42	47	58	65	45	53	77	70
Republican	57	51	40	33	53	45	23	27
Independent	--	2	--	2	--	2	--	3

Religion

	All Protestants 2004	All Protestants 2008	Catholics 2004	Catholics 2008	Jewish 2004	Jewish 2008	Attend church at least once a week 2004	Attend church at least once a week 2008	White Evangelical 2004	White Evangelical 2008
Overall	54	54	27	27	3	2	41	40	26	26
Democrat	40	45	47	54	74	78	39	43	21	24
Republican	59	54	52	45	25	21	61	55	78	74
Independent	--	1	--	1	--	1	--	2	--	2

Size of place

	Big cities 2004	Big cities 2008	Small cities 2004	Small cities 2008	Suburbs 2004	Suburbs 2008	Small towns 2004	Small towns 2008	Rural areas 2004	Rural areas 2008
Overall	13	11	19	19	45	50	8	7	16	14
Democrat	60	71	49	59	47	50	48	45	40	45
Republican	39	28	49	40	52	48	50	53	59	53
Independent	--	--	--	--	--	--	--	--	--	--

Education

	Not HS grad 2004	Not HS grad 2008	HS grad 2004	HS grad 2008	Some college 2004	Some college 2008	College grad 2004	College grad 2008	Postgrad 2004	Postgrad 2008
Overall	4	4	22	20	32	31	26	28	16	17
Democrat	50	63	47	52	46	51	46	49	55	58
Republican	49	35	52	46	54	47	52	48	44	40
Independent	--	2	--	2	--	2	--	3	--	2

Family income

	Under $15,000 2004	Under $15,000 2008	$15,000–$29,999 2004	$15,000–$29,999 2008	$30,000–$49,999 2004	$30,000–$49,999 2008	$50,000–$74,999 2004	$50,000–$74,999 2008	$75,000–$99,999 2004	$75,000–$99,999 2008	$200,000 and over 2004	$200,000 and over 2008
Overall	8	6	15	12	22	19	23	21	14	15	3	6
Democrat	63	73	57	60	50	55	43	48	45	51	35	52
Republican	36	25	42	37	49	43	56	49	55	48	63	46
Independent	--	2	--	3	--	2	--	3	--	1	--	2

Source: AP/Network Exit Polls.

Top Issues in the 2008 Presidential Campaign

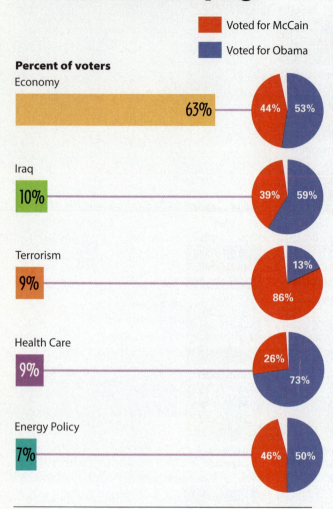

Voted for McCain

Voted for Obama

Percent of voters

Economy — 63% — 44% | 53%

Iraq — 10% — 39% | 59%

Terrorism — 9% — 13% | 86%

Health Care — 9% — 26% | 73%

Energy Policy — 7% — 46% | 50%

Source: AP/Network Exit Polls.

Not every political campaign follows a script dictated by traditional party ties. When party affiliation fails to provide reliable guidance for voters, they turn to short-term factors like issues and the personal characteristics of the candidates.

Issues

Especially for independent voters who show little attachment to party labels, issues may be an important factor in voting decisions.[50] Issue voters try to match their own views on issues they believe to be most salient with the views the candidates are presenting. Whereas issue voters seek candidates with precise views in order to evaluate their electoral choices, strong partisans may be less bothered by a candidate's

prospective voting Voting choice made on the basis of anticipated results if the candidate of choice is elected.

retrospective voting Voting on the basis of the candidate's or party's record in office.

ambiguity on the issues, because it is their partisan attachment that drives their voting choice.[51] Nevertheless, issues are not irrelevant for partisans, especially for those who are best informed and interested.

Since much attention during the campaign focuses on the candidate's promises, we would expect **prospective voting**, in which voters make their choices primarily with an eye toward what the candidate says he or she will do if elected, to be quite high. However, voters understand that many factors may prevent the candidate from fulfilling campaign pledges. As a result, **retrospective voting**, holding politicians accountable for past performance, is more often the norm.

The performance of the economy is high on the voters' list of concerns. Rightly or wrongly, voters attribute the state of the economy to elected leaders, particularly the president, and hold them accountable. But voters do not simply make choices on the basis of their own financial condition. They make judgments about the direction and strength of the economy as a whole. Does it seem that the country is experiencing growth? Is unemployment shrinking? Are prices stable?

So important are economic considerations to elections that many economists and political scientists have created models that predict outcomes on the basis of macroeconomic factors alone.[52] Though these models have impressive records of success, they are not infallible. Modelers who predicted a Democratic victory in the 2000 presidential election on the basis of a very rosy economy were proved wrong. Of course, that was an unusual election, since Al Gore did win the popular vote but lost in the Electoral College.[53] Economic modelers did a better job of predicting the outcome and margin of support for the winning candidates in subsequent presidential elections.[54]

The economy proved especially decisive in 2008, trumping all other issues in the election and helping Barack Obama overcome the resistance of some voters who considered him too inexperienced to be president. Facing an economic crisis some believed more serious than any other since the Great Depression, voters sought a change in the direction of the country. Nearly two-thirds of voters told pollsters they believed the economy was the most important issue in the election, numbers rivaling those registered back in the recessions of 1980 and 1992. Many of these voters said either their own family's economic situation had worsened—their retirement incomes and home prices plummeting—or they personally knew others who faced serious economic hardships. These voters preferred Obama by nine percentage points.[55] Social issues like stem cell research and abortion, which had worked for a number of years to the advantage of cultural and religious conservatives in the Republican Party, lacked traction in 2008. There were a handful of states that held referenda on issues like banning gay marriages; and, although the conservative position was victorious in these contests, concern among voters for these issues did not translate into votes for the Republican Party's presidential nominee.

Personal Characteristics Voters Preferred in 2008

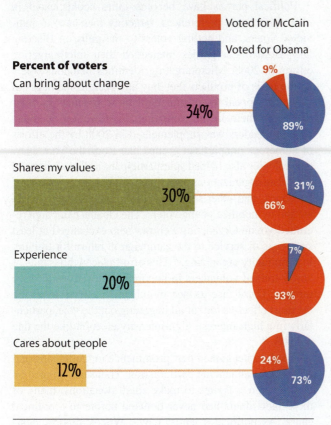

Percent of voters

Voted for McCain
Voted for Obama

Can bring about change — 34%
9%
89%

Shares my values — 30%
31%
66%

Experience — 20%
7%
93%

Cares about people — 12%
24%
73%

Source: AP/Exit Polls.

In 2008, the war in Iraq, which proved decisive for Democrats two years earlier in the midterm congressional elections, was a distant second in voters' minds. Similarly, health care and energy were less salient. However, John McCain was also battling the legacy of the sitting president, George W. Bush, whose approval ratings were among the lowest in history. Seventy-five percent of voters said they believed the country was moving in the wrong direction. Clearly, voters wanted change.

The issues that worked for the Democrats in 2008, however, worked against them in the days leading up to the midterm congressional elections in 2010. Voters took out their frustration with the lagging economy by holding Democrats accountable. They also expressed concerns over the scale of the health-care reform and growing government debt.

Candidate Characteristics

A candidate's personal characteristics have always mattered to American voters. Colonial voters saw in George Washington attributes of leadership and wealth that set him apart from others. In the glory days of party politics, however, personal characteristics took a back seat to party loyalty. In today's candidate-centered campaigns, voters once again are looking for those indefinable qualities associated with leadership.

Voters usually feel more comfortable with candidates with whom they can personally relate. Ronald Reagan was able to build a large reservoir of support among voters with his simple yet clear rhetoric and his good humor. This latter trait was on display as he joked with reporters in his hospital room shortly after he was shot by an attempted assassin. In 2004, voters told pollsters they could relate more easily with George W. Bush, who seemed more like one of them, than with John Kerry, who seemed cool and aloof.

Voters are often more likely to cast ballots for members of their own race, ethnic group, or even gender, although evidence for this is not always consistent.[56] The 2008 election demonstrated that these characteristics can be extremely powerful in generating support for a candidate. Hillary Clinton drew just over a majority of women in Democratic primaries, and Barack Obama won 96 percent of the African American vote in the general election. Of course, these characteristics can work against a candidate as well. Some observers feared that white Americans were giving pollsters erroneous yet socially acceptable responses when they said they supported the Obama candidacy. Pollsters were caught off guard by inaccurate responses in previous elections involving black candidates like the 1982 campaign of Tom Bradley for governor of California. It appears that in 2008, any racial bias voters may have felt against Obama were trumped by their desire for change and concern over the deteriorating economy. The so-called *Bradley effect* was not a widespread factor. Slightly more whites voted for the Democratic candidate in 2008 than in 2004, though white support varied widely by region and state, and Obama's candidacy was clearly helped by a surge in minority turnout. Ninety percent of all voters told exit pollsters that race was not a factor in their election choice. Instead, Obama found support among those who believed he could best bring change and who believed he cares about people. John McCain, the well-respected war hero, scored higher on attributes of experience and sharing voters' values.

Campaigns sometimes use **opposition research** to find and exploit weaknesses in opponents' backgrounds. The line between how much of this information is useful data that voters should know in evaluating the candidate (e.g., voting records) and how much is designed to smear the opposition (such as marital infidelity) is often a fine one. With party support closely divided, and candidates scrambling for just a few more votes than the opposition, the temptation to uncover and use negative information about

> **opposition research** Practice of searching for events in candidates' records or personal lives that can be used to attack them during elections.

a candidate's past can be overwhelming. The public, however, has shown some impatience with such tactics, and it is unclear how much negative campaigning they are willing to tolerate. Some observers fear that attacks on candidates' characters may further alienate voters.

PARTIES, POLITICAL CAMPAIGNS, AND CIVIC ENGAGEMENT TODAY

The 2008 presidential election witnessed one of the highest voter turnout rates in recent U.S. history. Not only was overall turnout the highest it has been in years, but turnout among 18- to 29-year-olds approached the all-time high reached in 1972. This was the third consecutive election cycle in which youth turnout increased, a string not achieved since the Twenty-sixth Amendment was adopted in 1971.[57] Scholars will comb through piles of data in the years to come to account for this performance, but a few reasons are already clear.

First, the candidates themselves generated excitement. The prospect of the first African American or the first woman leading a major party in a presidential contest electrified the electorate throughout both the primary season and the general election, spurring interest and enthusiasm. The extended primary season brought the campaign to virtually every corner of the country, and the candidates made an effort to extend the general election to all 50 states, not merely a few key battlegrounds. (We will discuss battleground states and presidential election strategy in more depth in Chapter 12.) Aided by intense voter interest and concerns over the economy, Barack Obama not only won all the Democratic states won by John Kerry in 2004 but also expanded Democratic victories to reliably Republican strongholds such as Indiana and Virginia, which had not voted for a Democrat in a presidential election since 1964. Second, the candidates offered voters a clear choice on a number of substantive issues from the war in Iraq to the economy to global warming. Divisive issues appealing to narrow constituencies took a backseat to issues that mattered to most Americans. Third, as we noted in Chapter 1, the Millennial Generation is coming of age, and its members are more attuned to politics and participation than their immediate predecessors. Finally, candidates and political parties stepped up their mobilization efforts, often using new techniques and technologies.

Political parties have become quite sophisticated in identifying voter preferences, targeting messages to individual voters, and getting voters to the polls on Election Day. Both major parties intensified their microtargeting efforts in 2008. Microtargeting identifies potential voters on the basis of products they buy and designs messages in ways that appeal to consumers of those products in order to engage them in the campaign. Mobilization of voters by party leaders was supplemented in 2008 by the efforts of numerous nonpartisan groups like Rock the Vote. New technologies also helped spur participation. The parties and candidate organizations experimented with text messaging, Facebook, and other social networking sites to spur interest and to mobilize young voters. The Obama campaign recruited young Organizing Fellows who exchanged at least six weeks of service to the campaign in return for training in community organizing.[58] This effort placed thousands of newly trained volunteers in hundreds of locations to drive turnout. These face-to-face mobilization efforts might be the most effective tool of all in getting out the vote, particularly in a high-interest, high-intensity election like the one in 2008.[59]

The Internet gained new prominence in fundraising and as a tool for enhancing participation. Thousands logged on to campaign websites to make small donations; many of these individuals had never donated before to a political cause. As political scientist Clyde Wilcox reports, campaign organizations tried to move these donors beyond merely giving and into other forms of activism. E-mail messages urged contributors to get involved in a variety of ways. "One Clinton solicitation," he notes, "provided a link to a site that would sign me up to call voters in Ohio and Pennsylvania from my home. A different Obama solicitation invited me to click on a link to call superdelegates to persuade them to support Obama. Whether the Internet can turn donors into more active citizens remains to be seen, of course. But campaigns in 2008 appeared to believe that it was possible."[60]

These developments are encouraging and may signal a reversal in the long-term decline of voter turnout. But we have also seen that political enthusiasm can quickly fade when voters are dissatisfied with public policies and economic conditions. Sustaining political engagement requires a constant dialogue between leaders and voters, one in which both parties must be willing to listen to each other.

Summary

1. What are political parties and why do we have just two major parties?

- Political parties are organizations created for the purpose of winning elections and governing once they are in office.
- For voters, parties are useful for simplifying electoral choices; for candidates, parties help them gain political power; and for elected officials, parties provide a common set of principles that help them govern.
- Constitutional election procedures like single-member districts and the Electoral College, the centrist ideology of most Americans, state laws, and the financial hurdles of mounting a campaign all help to explain why just two major parties have come to dominate our political system.
- The American political party system evolved through five eras:
  - Party formation era, which gave birth to the Federalists and Democratic-Republicans (later known simply as Democrats);
  - Democratic dominance following Jackson until Lincoln's successful Republican challenge;
  - Golden age of participation marked by high turnout, regional one-party control, and corruption;
  - Republican dominance at national level and Progressive Era reform;
  - New Deal realignment and Democratic dominance until 1960s.
- Since the 1960s, there has been relative parity among the two parties with a substantial minority not identifying with either.

2. How are parties organized and how has our party system adapted to change?

- To win elections, parties are organized into national committees, congressional and senatorial campaign committees, state committees, local government committees, and precinct committees. The national committees run the presidential nominating conventions, develop member rules, and raise significant amounts of money for electoral purposes.

- Throughout American history, parties have undergone periodic changes in strength, composition, and direction known as "realignments."
- Despite the dominance of the two-party system, there have been major third parties. These splinter parties, ideological parties, single-issue or single-candidate parties can influence the outcome of specific elections.

3. What is the relationship between candidates and parties in our electoral system?

- Candidates vie for party support through primary elections, conventions, or a combination of both.
- During the nomination period, candidates assume the bulk of the responsibilities for running their own campaigns.
- Once candidates become official party nominees, the party will provide financial and personnel support throughout the general election campaign, although individual candidates are still in charge of their own campaigns.
- Throughout the election process, candidates devote a large part of their campaign day to raising money, much of which is spent on campaign advertising.

4. What factors do voters consider in making their election choices?

- Today many voters cast their ballots on the basis of party affiliation but the strength of support among committed partisans varies.
- When party affiliation fails to provide reliable guidance for voters, they turn to other factors such as the issues. Holding politicians accountable for past performance is "retrospective voting" and voting for what candidates promise to do in the future is "prospective voting." The former is the more common type of issue voting.
- Voters also may turn to factors like the personal characteristics of the candidates as a basis for their preference in an election. Voters often feel more comfortable with candidates with whom they can personally relate or whose leadership characteristics they admire.

National Journal

Dems Find Electoral Safety Behind A Wall Of Blue

State by state, election by election, Democrats since 1992 have methodically constructed the party's largest and most durable Electoral College base in more than half a century. Call it the blue wall.

After Barack Obama's sweeping victory, 18 states and the District of Columbia have now voted for the Democratic nominee in at least the past five presidential elections. The last time Democrats won that many states so consistently was from 1932 to 1948, when Franklin Roosevelt and Harry Truman won 22 states in five consecutive presidential races.

Together, D.C. and these 18 contemporary Democratic strongholds are worth a combined 248 Electoral College votes. That's more than 90 percent of the 270 votes required to win the presidency. And the Democratic hold on all of them solidified in 2008: GOP nominee John McCain did not finish within 10 percentage points of Obama in any of them.

"McCain faced, really, the opposite of the situation the Democrats faced in the 1980s," said Earl Black, a political scientist at Rice University. "Given the states the Republicans could count on then, it was just very, very hard for the Democrats to get to 270. Now the tables have definitely turned."

Indeed, from the White House to the statehouse, Democrats now dominate these states up and down the ballot. Republicans hold just three of the 36 U.S. Senate seats in these 18 states. Democrats also control two-thirds of these 18 governorships, every state House chamber, and all but two of the state Senates. "It's like we are building a fortress," says veteran Democratic consultant Tad Devine.

Almost all of the states in the blue wall fit a common demographic profile: affluent; well-educated; ethnically and racially diverse; culturally moderate to liberal; with below-average rates of church attendance and fewer

evangelical Protestants than the national mean. In an era in which each party's electoral coalition revolves more around cultural attitudes than economic interests, the Democratic advantage in these regions represents the flip side of the Republican edge in the culturally conservative South, Plains, and Mountain West that keyed George W. Bush's victories in 2000 and 2004.

Those two triumphs demonstrated that the Democrats' hold on these states doesn't guarantee them the White House. Yet, because of Bush's inability to dent the blue wall, he won with two of the narrowest Electoral College majorities ever. And although Obama and other Democrats made substantial inroads in culturally conservative states in 2006 and 2008, the Republicans have been steadily losing ground in the culturally cosmopolitan blue states, especially since Bush first appeared on the national ballot in 2000.

That daunting trend is likely to sharpen the conflict between those in the GOP who believe that Republicans can recover only by adopting a more aggressive conservative message and those who fear that the party's current approach writes off too many voters and regions. Steve Schmidt, McCain's chief strategist, sides with the latter camp. "The party on its current trajectory is a shrinking party," Schmidt warns. "It needs to be an expanding party, and to be a national party, it needs to compete in states like New Jersey, New York, and New Hampshire, Pennsylvania and California. . . . For the party to come back and grow, it must appeal to a broader majority of people. That is now the challenge."

The Democrats' blue wall connects three distinct groups of states. It includes 10 from the Mid-Atlantic and Northeast—every state from Maryland to Maine except New Hampshire. In the Pacific West are California, Hawaii, Oregon, and Washington.

Four more come from the Midwest: Illinois, Michigan, Minnesota, and Wisconsin. And, finally, D.C.

For the GOP, the silver lining is that these states could lose as many as eight congressional seats (and, of course, Electoral College votes) in the reapportionment after the 2010 census, according to calculations by Polidata, an electoral demography firm. But even so, that would leave Democrats with a much larger base of reliable states than the GOP has. Republicans have won 13 states, worth only 93 electoral votes, over the past five elections.

Many of the foundation stones in today's blue wall were elements of the Republicans' earlier Electoral College lock; California, Illinois, New Jersey, and Vermont, for instance, each voted Republican in all six presidential elections from 1968 to 1988. Those shifts in loyalty are a reminder that there are no final victories in American politics and no permanent geographic advantages for either party. But these states also testify to the realignment of allegiances that has occurred over the past two decades as the principal glue cementing each party's coalition has evolved from class interests to cultural attitudes.

After that geographic and ideological resorting, the Democrats' blue wall is now composed almost entirely of states that combine large numbers of well-educated, affluent, and less-religious whites with substantial numbers of racial and ethnic minorities, including sizable immigrant populations. Thirteen of the 18 blue states (plus the District of Columbia) rank among the 20 states with the highest proportion of college graduates, according to 2007 Census Bureau figures. Likewise, 13 of the states (plus D.C.) rank among the 20 states with the highest median income. Counting D.C., 12 of them

rank among the 20 states with the highest percentage of foreign-born residents.

By contrast, these states are home to relatively few of the religiously devout, often evangelical, voters who are the core of the modern GOP coalition. The massive 2007 U.S. Religious Landscape survey conducted by the Pew Forum on Religion and Public Life found that the percentage of residents who described religion as very important in their life was lower than the national average in each of these 18 states, except for the survey's combined sample of Maryland and Washington, D.C.—and even that result probably represented the influence of heavily Democratic African-American voters.

At a time when social issues such as abortion divide the parties so starkly, many analysts see those cultural and religious trends as key to the Democratic grip on these states. "Basically, what they lack are the large numbers of white Protestants, especially the evangelicals, which have been the electoral base in the South and the Mountain Plains," Black says. "Outside of those regions, the groups you have to compete for are much more diverse, and since the Republicans haven't been able to expand, they are really up against it when you have increased voting by minorities."

Not so long ago, Republicans were much more competitive across this blue terrain. In 1988, George H.W. Bush won 10 of these 18 states, and held Democrat Michael Dukakis to less than 52 percent in five others. At that point, Republicans held 14 of these states' 36 Senate seats and 86 of their 219 House seats—in each case a much larger percentage than they hold today. "The Republican brand is, across the board, going bad in these states," says Schmidt, the McCain strategist.

What changed? Two factors seem most important.

One is increasing racial diversity. Since 1988, according to network exit polls, the share of the vote cast by whites has declined in almost all of these states. That trend has been especially pronounced in many of the key states that switched sides from the Republican lock to the Democratic wall. The offsetting increase has come among African-Americans, Asians, and Hispanics, all groups that are now voting overwhelmingly Democratic.

The other big change has been the growing Democratic strength among white voters with college or postgraduate degrees. Exit polls this year found that Obama won white voters with a college education in all but two of the 18 states, where he tied McCain. As these states move toward a postindustrial economy, college-educated voters constitute a larger share of the vote than they did 20 years ago in most of them, and a substantially larger share in some.

Closely related, analysts say, is the perception in many of these places that the GOP elevates religion over science (on issues such as stem-cell research or the teaching of evolution) and prizes homespun "common sense" over advanced education—an inclination symbolized by the party's frequent portrayal of small towns like Sarah Palin's Wasilla, Alaska, as the "real America."

"The anti-intellectual side of the Republican Party is offensive to people who think what makes them different is they went to school and that they are smart," says Kieran Mahoney, a veteran Republican consultant

> "For the [Republican] party to come back and grow, it must appeal to a broader majority of people. That is now the challenge."
> —Steve Schmidt

in New York. "If we are going to glory in the notion that we are not thinking this through, don't be surprised if we offend those who are thinking it through."

Republicans, Mahoney argues, will need to move away from a "moralist" definition of conservatism toward a more "libertarian" argument that links personal freedom and small government. That's the formula, he says, that allowed centrist, pro-abortion-rights Republicans such as George Pataki, William Weld, and Arnold Schwarzenegger to win governorships in these states even as Democrats dominated the federal contests.

But the Republicans may have to choose a path fast: measured on such yardsticks as income, education, and residents born abroad, Colorado and Virginia (and, to a lesser extent, North Carolina) now resemble the blue states more than they do the typical Republican bastions in the South or the Great Plains. If Republicans cannot crack the code with minority and well-educated, socially moderate white voters, states such as Colorado or Virginia that are now teetering between the parties eventually could become new bricks atop the Democrats' blue wall.

For Discussion:

■ Do you come from a "blue wall" state, a swing state, or a solid Republican state? What do you think accounts for the particular partisan character of your home state?

■ What do you think might happen if a "blue wall" (or a red wall for that matter) surpassed the 270 electoral vote count needed to win the presidency? Could one of America's two parties become electorally obsolete? How might that alter the political landscape in America?

■ Imagine you're the chairperson of the Republican Party. Faced with the blue wall problem the article describes, write a memo to your colleagues proposing a solution that involves embracing a wider spectrum of opinion on social issues without alienating your socially conservative base.

10

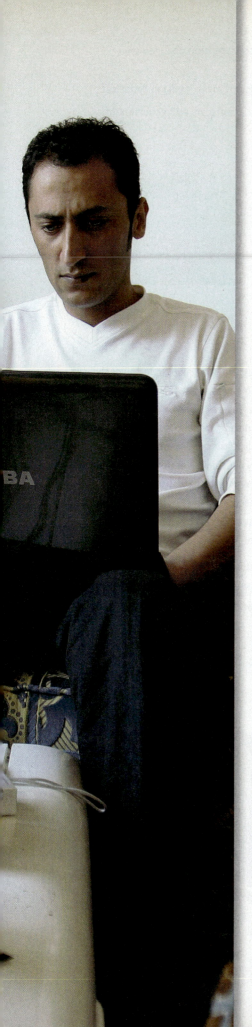

MEDIA

JOURNALISM IN THE AGE OF SOCIAL MEDIA ▌ On May 24, 2011, the burnt and tortured body of 13-year-old Hamza al-Khatib was returned to the home of his parents in Jeezah, Syria. The boy had been arrested during an antigovernment protest nearly one month before.[1] A graphic video of the mutilated body was posted to YouTube. Within a few days, the boy's posthumous Facebook page had collected almost 75,000 followers. Angry Syrians called for a "Children's Friday" protest after prayer services at mosques on Friday, June 3.[2] The Syrian government, in an apparent attempt to disrupt demonstrations and curtail media coverage, cut off most of the Internet.

On Friday at 5:30 A.M. eastern standard time, Steven J. Vaughan-Nichols was awoken by his ZDNet editor telling him to get up and start covering the events in Syria. Using Google translator and the help of their New York–based Arab–English translator, he was able to tease out the facts through careful online research. The country's Internet backbone is controlled by the state-owned Syrian Telecommunications Establishment. Several wireless data service providers, which only reach the larger cities, can be and were also shut down by the government.[3] During the course of the day, however, the Syrian government's explanation of its actions shifted, and since Internet media agencies, such as cable television, run on a 24–7 news schedule, Vaughan-Nichols wrote three successive articles on the topic over the next 11 hours.

Technological advances are leaving behind traditional journalism. Average daily newspaper circulation declined 10.6 percent from April through September 2009 compared to the same six-month span a year earlier.[4] Since March 2007, 12 papers have closed their doors. Even major newspapers are struggling. The two dailies in Chicago have declared bankruptcy and *The New York Times* has begun an online subscription plan to offset its declining revenues. The only newspapers gaining circulation are the nation's smallest ones, which tend to focus their limited resources on local news. The impact on traditional journalists has been staggering. As the careers of online journalists like Vaughan-Nichols have soared, the careers of many newspaper reporters have ended. In 2008, nearly six thousand newsroom jobs were lost, reducing the number of working journalists by 11.3 percent and putting the industry back to early-1980s employment levels.

Many newspapers, such as *The Christian Science Monitor* and the *Seattle Post-Intelligencer*, have attempted to stay afloat by changing with the times and adapting to hybrid online/print or online-only models. They have also embraced citizen journalism, showcasing photos, video ➡️

- How have the media and media consumption changed over the years?
- What are the major characteristics of mass media in America?
- How do the media cover political campaigns and government actions?

clips, or the personal accounts of people who experience an event and post these journalistic resources online or to the newspaper. Yet in an age when e-mail, texting, and social media spawn viral videos, such as the video featuring Hamza al-Khatib, news seekers are increasingly turning to new media as their primary source of news. The Internet has overtaken newspapers as a news outlet. (See figure on next page). During 2008, two percent of the population went directly to YouTube to get news of the presidential campaign.[5]

Despite dimming job prospects in traditional journalism, many universities are reporting that journalism enrollments are up. Schools are retooling a new generation of courses for new media to train online journalists. The University of California at Berkeley's Graduate School of Journalism requires incoming students to participate in a multimedia boot camp, which runs from 9 A.M. to 9 P.M. for five days where students learn Web publishing skills and how to use digital video, audio, and photo equipment. Dean Bill Grueskin of Columbia's Graduate School of Journalism believes that "Ambitious and creative young people see this as an opportunity to be part of the effort to recast and remake journalism."[6] In a similar optimistic tone, Iowa Professor Don McLeese tells his journalism class at the University of Iowa:

"This is an exciting time for journalists. It is a time for great change. Journalistically, we have more tools at our disposal than ever. We can reach more eyeballs than ever."[7] ◆

A toddler sits next to a poster depicting the brutal slaying of 13-year-old Hamza al-Khatib during a protest against the Syrian government.

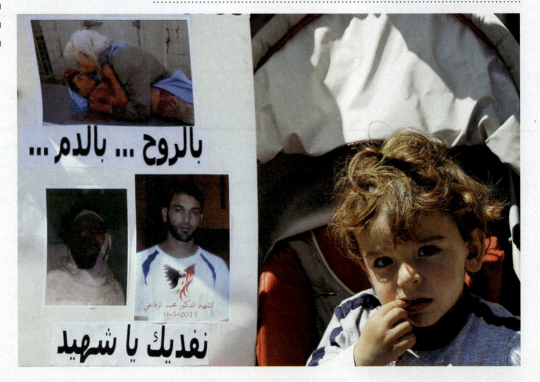

Where do you get most of your national and international news?

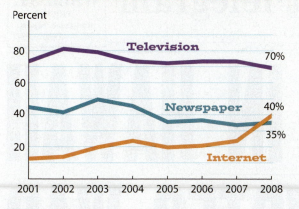

Percent

- Television — 70%
- Newspaper — 40%
- Internet — 35%

2001 2002 2003 2004 2005 2006 2007 2008

Source: Pew Research Center, "Internet Overtakes Newspapers as News Outlet," December 23, 2008, 1.

EVOLVING CIVIC LIFE AND MEDIA CHANGES

In the early days of the United States, politics was essentially an oral art conducted in taverns, boardinghouses, legislative chambers, and private parlors.[8] As the nation matured, a mass media developed—first newspapers and then the broadcast media—to keep citizens informed about local and national politics. The changes that the media have undergone over time have had an important impact on how the American people view their government and how that government connects to its citizens.

Early Days

Newspapers in colonial America did not get off to an auspicious start. The first newspaper published in America, *Publick Occurences, Both Forreign and Domestick*, appeared in Boston in 1690 and included an article on the alleged immoralities of the king of France. Offended by the article, the Massachusetts Bay Colony authorities ordered that no person could print a newspaper without first applying for a license from the government. Thus, the first American newspaper ended publication after just one edition. America's first regularly published newspaper, *The Boston News-Letter*, debuted in 1704 and appeared weekly until 1776. The paper's local and intercolonial articles included political speeches, official proclamations, crime stories, weather, and obituaries.[9]

By 1775, on the eve of the American Revolution, the colonies boasted 40 newspapers that played an important role in promoting discussion of the issues of the day. Such discussion would ultimately threaten the deferential politics that flourished in the hierarchical society of colonial America.[10]

Partisan Press

After ratification of the U.S. Constitution, political leaders such as John Adams and Thomas Jefferson quickly saw the advantage of having newspapers promote their points of view. By granting newspapers lucrative contracts to print government documents, politicians could ensure the wide dissemination of their words and deeds and secure friendly coverage of their ideas. As political

Did You Know?

. . . Nearly 1.4 billion people around the world read a daily newspaper. The United States ranks thirty-first in newspaper circulation, after countries such as Greece, the Republic of Korea, Venezuela, Singapore, Finland, Sweden, and the United Kingdom.

New York World-Telegram

Local Forecast: Light rains tonight, somewhat higher temperatures than last night; tomorrow cloudy followed by clearing, cooler than today.

VOL. 74.—NO. 135.—IN TWO SECTIONS—SECTION ONE   NEW YORK, MONDAY, DECEMBER 8, 1941.   Entered as second class matter Post Office, New York, N. Y.

LATEST WALL ST. PRICES
Real Estate, Page 31
PRICE THREE CENTS

1500 DEAD IN HAWAII
CONGRESS VOTES WAR

Tally in Senate Is 82 to 0, In House 388 to 1, with Miss Rankin Sole Objector

By LYLE C. WILSON,
United Press Staff Correspondent.

WASHINGTON, Dec. 8.—Congress today proclaimed existence of a state of war between the United States and the Japanese Empire 33 minutes after President Roosevelt stood before a joint session to ask such action and pledge that we will triumph—"so help us, God."

Democracy was proving its right to a place in the

100 to 200 Soldiers Killed in Japanese Raid On Luzon in Philippines

BULLETIN.
By the United Press.

MANILA, Dec. 8.—Press dispatches reported that 100 to 200 troops, 60 of them Americans, were killed or injured today when Japanese warplanes raided Iba, on the west coast of the island of Luzon, north of the Olangapo naval base.

BULLETIN.

Yellow journalists like Joseph Pulitzer made newspapers more sensational with bold headlines.

parties formed, this mutual relationship between printers and government officials led to the development of the partisan press. Andrew Jackson further enhanced this relationship by appointing loyal gentlemen of the press to government positions. "These appointments rewarded journalists for their role in writing positive stories."[11]

Penny Press

In the 1830s, a commercial revolution swept a segment of the country's newspapers.[12] The invention of the rotary press dramatically increased the speed and volume of printing, while driving down costs. Observers of the day coined the term *penny press* to describe the cheaper, more widely available papers. The telegraph also revolutionized newspaper journalism at this time by enabling reporters and editors to send stories instantly over immense distances. These technological advances gave publishers access to a much wider audience, making newspaper advertising more enticing to merchants eager to reach a large base of consumers. The revenues generated from advertising freed newspapers from their previous financial dependence on government contracts and political parties.

Yellow Journalism

As the nineteenth century came to an end, a new kind of journalism took hold of America's burgeoning—and increasingly immigrant—population. Known as yellow journalism, it featured sensationalized stories, pictures, and bold headlines to grab the reader's attention. The name *yellow journalism* came from "The Yellow Kid," an extremely popular comic strip, and the first to be mass published in color.

One of the leaders in the field of yellow journalism was *New York World* publisher Joseph Pulitzer. The *World* added stories concerning scandal, gossip, sex, disasters,

get involved!

Interview the news director of a local television station or the editor of your local paper. Find out what criteria he or she uses to determine what makes the headlines and what is left out. Would you make the same choices?

and sports to the usual fare of crime news. Large red or black headlines virtually "screamed excitement, often about comparatively unimportant news, thus giving a shrill falsity to the entire makeup."[13] Pulitzer's policy was to write stories that directly engaged his potential reading audience.[14] His stories often included the new technique of interviewing, or conversations between reporters and public persons that were designed to attract readers.[15] Pulitzer made his paper easy to read in order to attract immigrants, who made up 40 percent of New York City's population.[16]

By 1900, about one-third of the metropolitan papers practiced yellow journalism. Sympathy for the plight of ordinary citizens gave rise to a more aggressive form of investigative journalism known as *muckraking* in the early twentieth century. President Theodore Roosevelt was the first to use the term, comparing the process of newsgathering to using a rake specifically designed to collect manure. Journalists such as Upton Sinclair and David Graham Phillips wrote about real and apparent misdeeds by government and business in order to stimulate reform.[17] Muckraking helped to expose corruption, but it often included publishing gossip and rumor without sufficient verification.

In the early decades of the twentieth century, the press changed direction in reaction to the excesses of yellow journalism. Newspapers made a commitment to objective journalism. New schools of journalism taught that newspapers should only print statements that followed established rules, such as using at least two independent sources to corroborate any claim made in print. The growth of national news agencies, including the Associated Press, United Press International, and the International News Service, also contributed to the development of objective journalism by concentrating on reporting bare facts with little interpretation.

Journalist Edward R. Murrow had an unparalleled impact on both radio and television news, covering World War II and exposing political phonies.

Broadcast Media

The first commercial radio program in the United States, aired in November 1920, reported the results of the presidential election between Warren G. Harding and James M. Cox. By the time of the next presidential election in 1924, nearly 1,400 radio stations were operating in the United States. By the mid-1930s almost every household in America owned a radio. For the next 20 years, radio provided a popular alternative source of news and entertainment. With broadcasts

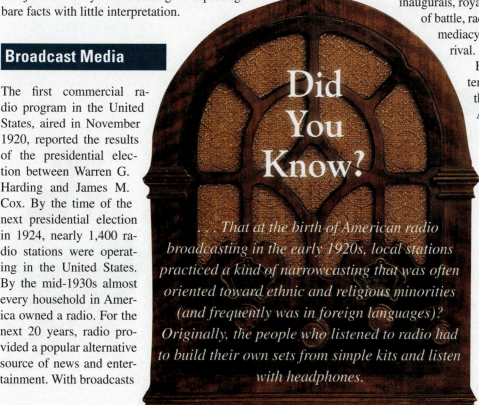

Did You Know?

... That at the birth of American radio broadcasting in the early 1920s, local stations practiced a kind of narrowcasting that was often oriented toward ethnic and religious minorities (and frequently was in foreign languages)? Originally, the people who listened to radio had to build their own sets from simple kits and listen with headphones.

from scenes of historic events such as presidential inaugurals, royal coronations, and the fields of battle, radio provided listeners an immediacy that newspapers couldn't rival.

By the 1950s, television antennas had begun to appear on the roofs of American homes. At first, television stressed entertainment and advertising; the three networks—NBC, CBS, and ABC—initially produced just one 15-minute news program apiece, five evenings a week. That changed after all three networks decided to broadcast the 1960 presidential debates between John F. Kennedy and Richard M. Nixon. When those debates garnered an audience in excess of 60 million viewers, television executives realized that news

Presidential Campaign News

First or second mentions	Oct. 2004	Oct. 2008	Change
Television	76	72	−4
Internet	10	33	+23
Newspapers	28	29	+1
Radio	15	21	+6
Magazines	2	3	+1
Other	3	2	−1

Figures add to more than 100% because mulitple responses were allowed.

Source: Pew Research Center Publications, "Internet Now Major Source of Campaign News," October 31, 2008, 1.

programming could bring profits. The networks subsequently expanded their nightly news programs to 30 minutes and competed to produce the most highly rated news shows. Television continues to be the most used medium for campaign news.

The Media Today

Citizens today have more sources for news of politics and government than ever before. Modern **mass media** includes print outlets such as newspapers and magazines, the broadcast outlets of radio and television, and computerized information services, but citizens are more likely to turn to television than any other single source. Several trends characterize media usage today: a decline in reliance on newspapers, a decline in news consumption among the young, and a growth in the consumption of narrowcasting.

Declining Reliance on Newspapers Between 1937 and 2006, the number of daily newspapers in the United States declined 29 percent, from 2,065 to 1,437. In 1880, 61 percent of the major cities in the United States had at least two competing daily papers; by 2006, that number had fallen to less than 2 percent.

We have seen that circulation numbers for daily newspapers are also declining. Total newspaper circulation reached its zenith in 1985, surpassing 62 million, but has since declined. Although it is true that the number of people reading newspapers online is growing rapidly, that growth has not offset the decline in print readership. Furthermore, declining newspaper print readership has changed the nature of newspapers. The papers are thinner and the stories shorter. There is less foreign, national, and business news. (See top figure on next page.) This finding raises questions about whether today's citizens are well enough informed to exercise the responsibilities of citizenship.

Declining Interest in News Among the Young

Americans between the ages of 18 and 29 are much less attentive to traditional news sources than are members of any other generation. Only 22 percent watch television news daily, and just 16 percent read a newspaper every day. Fully a third of young people say that they do not pay attention to the news in any form. By contrast, nearly three-fifths of those age 65 and above report reading a newspaper daily, and only 12 percent confess inattention to the news. To the extent that they get news from television, young people appear more interested in local news

Young Voters Shared Experience Digitally

The percentage of those who voted in 2008 who shared their experience at the polls in the following ways:

	All voters	18–29	30–49	50–64	65+
			Age groups		
Talked in person to people	59	68	64	58	42
Talked on the telephone to people	45	57	49	44	31
Sent e-mail	11	18	13	9	3
Sent text messages	8	23	10	–	*
Posted your experience on a social networking site	4	13	4	1	*
Wrote about your experience on a personal website or blog	2	8	2	1	–
Commented on someone else's website or blog	4	14	3	–	–

* Sample size of SNS/text messaging users is too small to analyze

Source: Pew Internet & American Life Project Post-Election Survey. November–December 2008.

Changing Focus of the News

	Decreased	Increased
Community news	8	62
State/local news	13	50
Editorial	14	17
Features/lifestyle	27	15
Business	34	17
National news	57	6
Foreign news	64	3

Percent of papers   Decreased   Increased

Source: Pew Research Center Publications, "The Changing Newsroom: Gains and Losses in Today's Papers," July 21, 2008, 1.

than in national stories available on cable TV or network news programs.

Instead of newspapers, young people report using the Internet to gather information. They report searching for news articles online at a higher rate than any other age group. They are more likely to get their news from portals like yahoo.com or msnbc.com, which stream news headlines with constant 24-hour updates. They are also more skeptical of traditional news sources and more likely to seek alternate types of reporting. One report on the use of these new media by young adults concludes, "Young people want a personal level of engagement and want those presenting the news to them to be transparent in their assumptions, biases and history."[18] Overall, the growth of campaign political news consumption online has grown dramatically over the last three presidential election cycles.

mass media The total array of mass communication, including television, radio, newspapers, magazines, and the Internet.

We have seen that young persons often bypass the traditional media by setting up social networks. In 2008, a survey found that 10 percent of all Americans have used sites such as Facebook or MySpace for some kind of political activity.[19] (See table at top of next page for leading social networking sites.) For young adults in particular, the sites are a major component of their online political experience. Sixty-seven percent of Internet users under the age of 30 have a social networking profile, and half of these profile

Media Use for 2008 Primaries Among People Ages 18–29

Internet	42%
Newspaper	25%
Television	24%
Radio	12%
Magazine	8%

Source: Pew Research Center, "Internet's Broader Role in Campaign 2008," January 11, 2008.

owners used social network sites to get or share information about the candidates and the campaign.[20] In 2008, young voters tilted toward the Democrats generally and Senator Obama specifically. Thirty-six percent of online Democrats created social networking profiles, compared to 21 percent of Republicans, and Obama supporters were more likely than the Clinton supporters to be Internet users. A 2008 study of online users revealed that those who are hungry for information are most likely to browse sites that match their views.[21] Thirty-three percent of all online political users search for news to match their own views, compared to 21 percent who seek sites that challenge their point of view. The tendency to find matching views is 10 percent greater for those that are high online users.

Increased Consumption of Narrowcasting A third trend evident today is the public's affinity for **narrowcasting**, programming that is directed to a small, specific segment of the population. In the early days of radio and television, news was broadcast to millions of Americans at the same time, which meant that most Americans shared the same news experiences; this is no longer the case. If you have access to cable or satellite television, you know about the great variety of channels available to viewers with specific and narrow interests.

Television coverage of the 2004 national party conventions provides an example of political narrowcasting.

Searching for News with a Point of View

Percent of online political users*

who typically visit political news sites that . . .

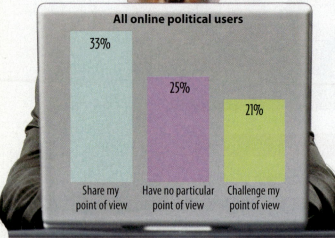

All online political users

Share my point of view	Have no particular point of view	Challenge my point of view
33%	25%	21%

*the 55 percent of the voting-age population who used the Internet for political purposes in 2008

Source: Pew Internet & American Life Project Post-Election Survey. November–December 2008. Categories based on number of online news sources visited, or number of online political activities participated in.

Top 10 Social Networking Sites for March 2011

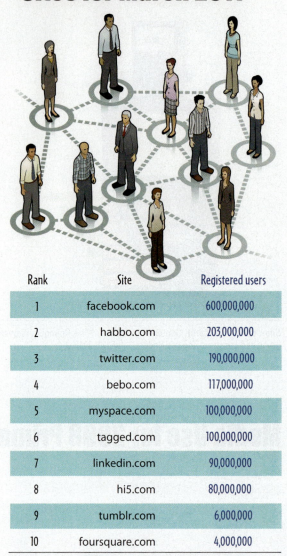

Rank	Site	Registered users
1	facebook.com	600,000,000
2	habbo.com	203,000,000
3	twitter.com	190,000,000
4	bebo.com	117,000,000
5	myspace.com	100,000,000
6	tagged.com	100,000,000
7	linkedin.com	90,000,000
8	hi5.com	80,000,000
9	tumblr.com	6,000,000
10	foursquare.com	4,000,000

Source: http://www.eripplescebu.com/2011/03/top-10-social-networking-sites-by.html.

Republicans, for instance, preferred watching Fox News because of its more conservative slant. Democrats and Independents were more likely to tune to CNN. The way these cable stations chose to present the conventions to their viewing audiences was also revealing. Fox News, CNN, and MSNBC used their primary on-air personalities Bill O'Reilly, Anderson Cooper, and Chris Matthews as hosts. Coverage of the conventions followed a talk show format as the hosts chatted with pundits, politicians, other journalists, and entertainers such as Ben Affleck and Bono. They devoted less than 10 percent of their coverage to reporting what was going on at the podium or where the candidates or the parties stood on specific issues. At least 30 percent of the coverage was spent on ranting, raving, and shouting matches.[22] At one point, Chris Matthews's aggressive style led a guest, former senator Zell Miller, to strike back, saying he was sorry we no longer lived in a

Today's media coverage of political conventions emphasizes on-air personalities such as Stephen Colbert of The Colbert Report.

world where he could challenge Matthews to a duel. The 2008 coverage continued to ignore the podium except for one or two speeches per evening.

Narrowcasting has changed the way citizens receive messages from political leaders. Commenting on the trend of narrowcasting, one author concludes that "the effect of the fragmentation in the audience will be a reduction in the commonality of Americans' political experiences."[23] Another way to look at it is that specialized programming may provide a better fit between public messages and audience needs. At the end of this chapter, we will examine how the changing media landscape affects civic engagement by allowing citizens to utilize a variety of media sources to monitor or graze for information that interests them.

THE MEDIA ENVIRONMENT IN AMERICA

Today's American mass media environment is characterized by several trends that shape the messages we receive about government and, in turn, affect the kinds of citizens

we become. These trends include private ownership that is becoming more highly concentrated; some government regulation, particularly of broadcast media outlets; an expansion of entertainment content at the expense of news content; an adversarial style of journalism that attacks politicians and their motives; and a belief by some that the media exhibit political bias.

Private Ownership

Private individuals have always owned the nation's media outlets; most modern Americans would consider any other ownership arrangement odd or even threatening. Yet, the United States is the only advanced industrial nation in the world in which virtually all the major media outlets are privately owned.[24] The only exceptions are the Public Broadcasting System, National Public Radio, and public access channels. In other Western democracies such as France and Denmark, the government owns the media.[25]

narrowcasting Programming targeted to one small sector of the population, made possible by the emergence of cable television and the Internet.

Ownership of U.S. media outlets is becoming more highly concentrated. Large chains such as J. P. Morgan and Gannett own nearly 80 percent of all daily newspapers. Gannett alone owns 99 newspapers—including *USA Today*—and 23 television stations. The concentration of ownership is even greater in the television industry. Not only are 85 percent of the commercial television stations affiliated with CBS, NBC, or ABC, but the three networks are themselves owned by large corporations with multiple media interests. In 1995, Westinghouse Electric purchased CBS; five years later, Westinghouse was bought by and later merged with Viacom, the owner of MTV and Paramount Studios. Later Viacom spun CBS off into its own separate corporation, CBS Corporation. The Walt Disney Company acquired the ABC network in 1996, and that same year Time-Warner purchased CNN. In 2011, Comcast acquired a 51 percent stake in NBC, replacing General Electric, which had owned the network since 1986.

equal time rule The rule requiring that all broadcasters provide airtime equally to all candidates if they provide it to any.

fairness doctrine The law that formerly required broadcasters to present contrasting views on important public issues.

Some media critics worry that media owners are more interested in producing good consumers than good citizens, and that this trend threatens civic engagement by fostering citizens who are politically passive.[26] They contend that an emphasis on profits has led to an excess of negative coverage, a rush to be the first to present breaking news without carefully checking for possible mistakes, and a tendency to make the news more entertaining than informative. Reporters also share this belief.

Government Regulation

As discussed in Chapter 4, the First Amendment and its interpretation by the courts provide extensive protections for newspapers. The general rule is that government can exercise no prior restraint or censorship over the press. A court may waive these restrictions if it finds that a story raises real national security concerns or violates public decency.[27] Print outlets can also be sued for stories that constitute libel, but today the print media enjoy relative protection from such suits as a result of the Supreme Court's decision in *New York Times v. Sullivan* (1964).[28]

Electronic media are subject to the same restrictions as print media, as well as several others. Because there are only a limited number of frequencies available for broadcasting, the government declared the airwaves public property. This allowed Congress to regulate use of the airwaves, both to prevent signals from interfering with each other and to ensure that no one person or group could monopolize broadcast frequencies. In 1934, Congress created the Federal Communications Commission (FCC) to regulate the electronic media of radio and television.

Ownership Limits

The FCC sets rules for private ownership of broadcast stations. Under the old "7-7-7 Rule" of the 1950s, a single owner could own no more than seven AM radio stations, seven FM radio stations, and seven television stations throughout the nation. In the 1990s, the FCC increased that number to 12 television stations and 20 of each kind of radio station. Then, in June 2003, the FCC announced new rules permitting a single company to own the leading newspaper as well as multiple television and radio outlets in a single market. This lessening of government regulation has encouraged even greater concentration of media ownership.

Content Regulation

The FCC also fashions rules affecting the content of radio and television broadcasts. In 1934, it instituted the **equal time rule** to promote equity in broadcasting. The rule requires a broadcast station to provide airtime equally to all candidates if it provides airtime to any. The rule applies to free airtime as well as to paid advertising.

In 1949, the FCC issued the controversial **fairness doctrine**, designed to ensure that broadcasters reported on news events and public issues fairly by presenting all points of view. Many broadcasters complained that the rule was difficult to define and claimed that it discouraged them from covering controversial subjects. They argued that the rule produced what courts call a "chilling effect" on political communication. In 1985, the FCC abolished the fairness doctrine, stating that the growth in the number of electronic outlets assured balance and fairness in the presentation of political topics without government oversight.

Anyone who watched the 2004 Super Bowl is probably aware of another content function of the FCC: fining sta-

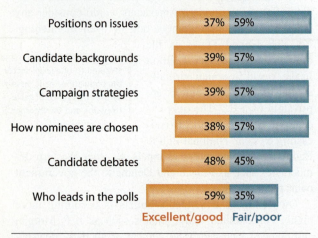

Public Criticizes Campaign Coverage

How the press has done in covering . . .

	Excellent/good	Fair/poor
Positions on issues	37%	59%
Candidate backgrounds	39%	57%
Campaign strategies	39%	57%
How nominees are chosen	38%	57%
Candidate debates	48%	45%
Who leads in the polls	59%	35%

Source: Pew Research Center, "Many Say Coverage is Biased in Favor of Obama," June 5, 2008, 3. http://pewresearch.org/pubs/862/campaign-news-interest.

tions for indecent broadcasts. In September of that year, the FCC fined CBS a record $550,000 for Janet Jackson's "wardrobe malfunction," in which the singer exposed her breast during the Super Bowl halftime show. In 2009, the Supreme Court ruled in *Federal Communications Commission v. Fox Television Stations* that the use of the f-word by Cher in 2002 and the use of the same word by Paris Hilton and Nicole Richie in 2003, both of which occurred during the telecast of the Billboard Music Awards, empowered the FCC to punish broadcasters.

Emphasis on Entertainment

As a private enterprise, the various media have always been about making money. Yellow journalism and muckraking are two prominent examples of how publishers have sought to increase the bottom line by making the news more entertaining. Today, television programs such as *48 Hours Mystery*, *Dateline*, and *20/20* blend news and entertainment programming to produce *infotainment*. The networks' evening news broadcasts feature a greater emphasis on celebrities, lifestyle issues, and human-interest stories. Some observers fear that the news has become a form of amusement rather than a public service.[29] The extensive media coverage of Charlie Sheen's personal life in 2011 fit this trend. As we will see, this aspect of the media environment has contributed to a reduction in the number of people who follow the news and an increase in those who just desire entertainment, thus widening the knowledge gap among citizens. It has also polarized those who do follow the news by encouraging them to choose the media outlet that most conforms to their beliefs.

As the news has become more of a spectacle over the past 25 years, newsreaders and reporters have become media stars. The more "face time" they garner on television, the more famous they become. Many of today's journalists make millions of dollars a year on the lecture circuit. Journalist James Fallows has written that this "gravy train" may be good for individual journalists, but detrimental for journalism.[30] Fallows believes that such "buckraking" reinforces the idea that journalists are just performers who will put on a show for a price.[31] This star

Focus on the lives of celebrities, such as Charlie Sheen, is a money-making trend in news media.

system also makes the coverage of politics more difficult: "By the 1980s, journalism's leading lights were millionaires with household names, whose fame equaled that of movie stars and sports heroes, and whose celebrity outshone the politicians they covered."[32]

Local television, whose format is increasingly oriented toward entertainment, has now become more popular than national news programming. Local news broadcasts feature a large number of crime stories (as the saying goes, in local news, "If it bleeds, it leads"), human-interest stories, weather, entertainment, and sports. Local stations place great emphasis on the appearance and personalities of the broadcasters. The anchors must be attractive, stylish, and well groomed, and the female anchor, in particular, must be young. Above all, local newscasters must engage in lively, happy banter in order to be invited back into viewers' homes; there is little emphasis on hard news. Such a trend does not encourage citizens to think deeply about important issues that confront them at the ballot box; instead, it urges them to sit back and be entertained.

> **adversarial or attack journalism** Form of interpretive journalism that adopts a hostile position toward government, politics, and political figures.

Adversarial Journalism

During the past three decades, the national media has embraced **adversarial** or **attack journalism**, which adopts a hostile position toward government, political processes, and political figures. Some scholars trace this development to growing public distrust of government in the late 1960s and early 1970s.[33] After the Vietnam War and the Watergate scandal, citizens began to believe that their political leaders had been lying to them. Young journalists, inspired by the media's role in uncovering the scheme that drove President Nixon from office, did not want to miss the next big political scandal that might catapult them to fame.

Following Watergate, the major networks poured a considerable amount of money into building investigative units that turned out stories focusing on the shortcomings of government officials, political candidates, and government programs. Reporters came to view their role as one of exposing the misstatements and misdeeds of political officials. As a result, the media inundated the American public with negative news. Citizens heard a daily drumbeat of inflammatory news about government officials, from politicians having sex with their interns to candidates misusing campaign funds.

Although some scholars worry that negative news may adversely affect the behavior of citizens, Americans are interested in negative news and eagerly tune in to hear about it. Coverage of President Bill Clinton's impeachment trial, for example, drew large audiences. In the long run, however, a steady diet of news about official wrongdoings turns citizens away from government and makes them less likely to fulfill their roles as citizens since they see the system as hopelessly corrupt. Negative news is causing citizens to tune out the political system.

More recently, some observers have complained that news reporters are now too easy on popular political leaders. When President Bush's approval ratings skyrocketed after the terrorist attacks of September 11, 2001, some media outlets relaxed their scrutiny of information coming from the White House. Few, for example, seriously questioned the president's plans to attack Iraq

because that country allegedly possessed weapons of mass destruction. When U.S. military forces discovered that no such weapons existed, *The New York Times* took the unprecedented action of publishing something of an apology to its readers for its one-sided reporting and its failure to aggressively investigate the administration's claims.[34] However, as the war in Iraq dragged on and the president suffered a series of setbacks in his handling of the hurricane-devastated South in 2005, the media provided daily coverage of the administration's missteps. Critics had a harder time sustaining the charge that the media were giving the president a "pass" on negative coverage. During the first months of the Obama administration, conservative talk show hosts like Rush Limbaugh believed the media was giving a pass to the new president.

Hot or Not?

Do celebrity scandals receive too much media coverage?

Political Bias?

Background studies have found that journalists are not representative of the general public. They are more likely to identify themselves as liberals and either Democrats or Independents; very few describe themselves as Republicans or conservatives.[35] This is particularly true of journalists who work for large newspapers and television networks. Studies indicate, however, that these background characteristics do not translate into bias against Republican and conservative candidates. A study of presidential campaigns found no evidence of significant political bias in newspapers, news magazines, and television.[36] Journalists try hard to keep political bias out of their stories because of their adherence to the professional norm of objectivity, because of their need not to offend their more conservative employers, and because they are more interested in telling a good story than espousing a particular ideology.[37]

Despite studies to the contrary, many people, especially Republicans, increasingly believe the media have a liberal bias. This has resulted in the proliferation of news and commentary shows with an admittedly conservative orientation. Talk show hosts such as Rush Limbaugh and Bill O'Reilly believe they are serving as a needed counterpoint to the liberal slant of the media establishment. Fox News, which hosts many conservative commentators, proclaims itself "fair and balanced" in order to convey the notion that it is different from other, more liberal news organizations.

The breaking of the scandal of John Edward's affair and elaborate cover-up while running for the presidency and later hoping for an Obama appointment is an example of negative news coverage that the cable stations and networks jump on to boost their ratings.

Tone of Coverage: MSNBC vs. FOX

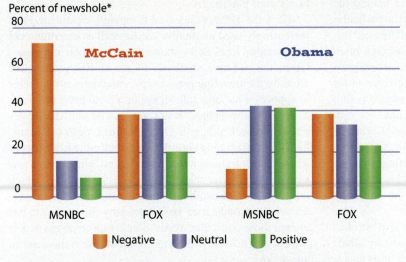

Percent of newshole*

McCain **Obama**

MSNBC FOX MSNBC FOX

🟧 Negative 🟪 Neutral 🟩 Positive

*A newshole is the amount of print-space or air-time available to report news.

Source: Pew Research Center Publications, "The Color of News: How Different Media Have Covered the General Election," October 29, 2008, 1. http://pewresearch.org/pubs/1011/color-of-news-coverage.

As we shall see, bias does turn up in almost all reports from the campaign trail and in the coverage of government. But the bias is largely commercial and sensational in nature, not political. Despite claims to the contrary, the American news media provides generally balanced coverage, while an increasing variety of specialized outlets are available for those seeking a particular point of view. It is within this environment that the various media outlets bring political campaigns to their audiences and provide the public with their competing views of the political process.

Morning Shows Emphasized Democratic Race

🟦 Stories about Democrats
🟥 Stories about Republicans

Number of stories

ABC: 167 / 83
CBS: 105 / 64
NBC: 159 / 100

Source: Media Research Center, "Slanted Morning TV Helps 2008 Democrats," November 7, 2007, 1.

A 2007 study of the presidential election showed, however, that sometimes the news is biased in a partisan way. All three of the major network morning television shows featured more stories about the Democratic candidates than the Republican candidates.[38] The former, particularly Hillary Clinton and Barack Obama, were treated like rock stars who deserved more media attention than the Republicans. Interviews with the various Democratic campaigns totaled 6 hours and 24 minutes, compared to 3 hours and 4 minutes for the Republicans. In addition, the network reporters posed issue-oriented questions to the candidates of both parties that largely reflected a liberal agenda. Of the 137 questions asked of the Democrats, 99 reflected liberal priorities and 43 of the 53 questions posed to Republicans displayed that same liberal agenda.[39] During the general election, however, the tone of the coverage often depended upon which cable news outlet was being viewed. (See adjacent figure.)

MEDIA AND POLITICAL CAMPAIGNS

Candidates and the media have different agendas that often come into conflict during political campaigns. Candidates want to talk about their positions on the issues, while the media often want to discuss campaign strategies and a candidate's standing in the polls. Although candidates and the media attempt to use each other for their own purposes, they also need each other to achieve their ends: victory for the candidate, access to the newsmakers for the media. In this section, we will examine how the media and presidential candidates interact in the course of political campaigns and the implication of those interactions for our democracy.

Free Media

Political campaigns need to be newsworthy to survive. Knowing that the media are selective about political coverage, campaign managers plan events that will attract attention and emphasize the most favorable aspects of their candidate. In the 2004 presidential race, for example, the Kerry campaign featured the candidate's Vietnam War buddies whose lives Kerry saved with his heroic actions. Broadcast of a candidate's activities or messages as news items is known as free media, or earned media, because the candidate has done something newsworthy to earn coverage. Campaign handlers carefully plan and stage these events to present candidates at maximum advantage. Putting a group of avid supporters behind the speaker suggests to television viewers that a particular candidate is attracting a widespread and enthusiastic following. In 2004, for instance, the Bush campaign often scheduled the president to speak on the issue of terrorism before supportive crowds who had been prescreened for attendance. In 2008, candidate Obama was placed before large audiences where his oratorical skills were used, whereas candidate McCain was placed in small town-hall settings that had worked for him in his 2000 and 2008 New Hampshire primary victories.

spin A campaign's favorable interpretation of their campaign and unfavorable view of their opponent's activities.

spin doctors Political campaign operatives who interpret campaign events in the most favorable light for their candidate.

A campaign can also "stroke" members of the media by granting them exclusive interviews. The campaign hopes that giving journalists a momentary competitive advantage over their rivals will earn the candidate more positive coverage. During the presidential primaries in 2000, John McCain invited journalists on his campaign bus for interviews and quickly became a favorite of many journalists.

Candidates and campaign managers also attempt to **spin** the news, that is, convince the media to apply a particular interpretation to a story. This is why members of campaign press staffs are sometimes known as **spin doctors**. They spin by placing the most favorable interpretation on their own activities, and the most negative one on their opponent's activities. In 2004, the Bush campaign extolled the virtues of the war in Iraq and questioned Ker-

ry's criticism of the war effort. In turn, Kerry interpreted every setback of the war as evidence of the administration's poor planning.

Since the 1992 presidential campaign, candidates have increasingly used alternative media such as entertainment programs or local news shows to spread their messages. Given the negative emphasis of the stories written and aired by the traveling press corps, candidates often prefer to appear on national talk shows or a local news program. There, the atmosphere is not adversarial and candidates can often speak at length. On mainstream news programs, the viewer hears only **sound bites**, small edited snippets of a candidate's statement that often last no longer than a few seconds. A reporter selects and frames a short clip, which typically shows a candidate speaking for less than an average of 10 seconds, then speculates why the candidate has uttered those particular words. Sound bite coverage makes it difficult for a candidate to communicate a message in any depth.

Presidential Debates

The presidential debates offer one of the few opportunities for the American public to compare candidates side by side. The first televised debate in 1960, between Richard M. Nixon and John F. Kennedy, demonstrated how important such events could be for changing the momentum of

Candidates often prefer appearing on news or talk show programs to get their messages out, hoping to avoid the negative coverage of traditional journalists. Here CBS's Katie Couric interviews GOP vice-presidential candidate Sarah Palin.

CBS EVENING NEWS EXCLUSIVE

global Perspectives

An International View of Political Advertising

In an international political campaign comparison, two scholars found that the United States stands out both with its complete openness toward political advertising and the great importance that campaigns attach to political ads. Many countries do not allow candidates to purchase broadcasting time for campaign messages. In Switzerland, for instance, political advertising on television is prohibited during election time. Denmark has no official bans on such advertising but political actors have agreed not to use them for their campaigns.

Some countries allow political candidates or political parties to purchase broadcasting time for campaign messages. Some countries allow free time on public and/or commercial TV. Some countries allow both free and paid advertisement.

1. The map below shows how several countries compare. Where do most countries stand on this issue?
2. How does the United States compare to other countries?
3. What benefits do citizens gain when political candidates or parties are allowed free air time on public and/or private television?

Sources: Christina Holtz-Bacha and Lynda Lee Kaid, *The SAGE Handbook of Political Advertising* (Thousand Oaks, CA: SAGE Publications, 2006) 10.

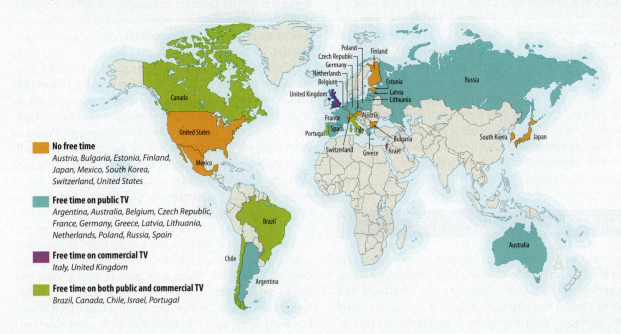

No free time
Austria, Bulgaria, Estonia, Finland, Japan, Mexico, South Korea, Switzerland, United States

Free time on public TV
Argentina, Australia, Belgium, Czech Republic, France, Germany, Greece, Latvia, Lithuania, Netherlands, Poland, Russia, Spain

Free time on commercial TV
Italy, United Kingdom

Free time on both public and commercial TV
Brazil, Canada, Chile, Israel, Portugal

---

a campaign. On television, the handsome and virile Kennedy appeared relaxed and informed; Nixon appeared pale, tired, and thin. He had spent the previous week in the hospital with a leg infection, and the shirt he wore was too large for him. That was not his only wardrobe problem, however. His staff had not investigated the debate site, so they did not realize that the gray suit he wore to the debate would blend in with the gray background of the stage. His appearance gave a whole new meaning to being "washed out." Nixon, however, was well informed on the issues and spoke with a resonant voice that sounded confident. Audiences listening on the radio believed Nixon won the debate, whereas the larger television audience saw the charismatic Kennedy as the clear winner.

Politicians and their advisors learned two important lessons from that first televised debate. First, television is a visual medium; candidates must look presidential as well as sound presidential. Second, challengers have more to gain from debating than do incumbents. Kennedy gained instant credibility just by appearing on the stage with his better-known rival, Vice President Nixon.

> **sound bites** News programs' short video clips of politicians' statements.

The 1976 debate revealed yet another characteristic of televised debates: The media will pounce on any mistake or gaffe. In response to a reporter's question, President Gerald R. Ford stated that Eastern Europe was no longer under the influence of the Soviet Union—which, of course, was not the case. At first, the public did not attach much significance to the statement. Polls taken immediately after the debate indicated that Ford won the debate over challenger Jimmy Carter by a margin of 44 to 33 percent. For the next 24 hours, however, the media stressed Ford's misstatement about Eastern Europe. After the public was inundated with this type of coverage, the next polls gave Carter the victory by a margin of 63 to 17 percent![40]

Another key to success in televised debates is passing the "living room test"—that is, coming across as someone the audience would like to invite into their homes. Michael Dukakis in 1988 and Al Gore in 2000 flunked the living room test. Media critics faulted Dukakis for appearing cold and impersonal and suggested that Gore projected the image of a know-it-all.

The 2008 debates produced no gaffes or failures to pass the "living room test," and Senator Obama's performance in all three debates was rated superior by the viewing audience. The most noteworthy aspects of the 2008 debate series was Senator McCain's threat not to participate in the first presidential debate during the financial crisis and the public's even greater interest in the vice-presidential debate. The public was curious to observe Governor Palin after her poor performance in network television interviews and after enjoying Tina Fey's impersonation of her on *Saturday Night Live*.

bloggers Citizens who create online diaries and forums for the posting of opinions and personal viewpoints.

Paid Media

Because American media are privately owned, candidates who want greater public exposure must buy advertising on the various media outlets. Campaigns see advertising as a way to capture the attention of the voters and to control their messages. Determining the effectiveness of advertising, however, is not easy. So many factors determine the outcome of an election that it is difficult to isolate the impact of any single factor, such as advertising.[41] Nevertheless, television advertising is a staple of every modern presidential campaign. In 2008, presidential candidates and the groups supporting them spent over $1.6 billion in television ads, double the amount spent in the presidential campaign in 2000.[42] Not all democracies allow political advertising; some believe that allowing candidates with greater financial resources to dominate political discourse threatens democracy. Scandinavian countries, for example, provide candidates with free access to publicly owned media.

Political advertising may be either positive or negative. Positive messages focus on a candidate's performance in office, issue positions, and character, without reference to the opposition. Negative messages focus exclusively on an opponent's weaknesses. A softer type of negative message is the comparative message, which contrasts the record of the candidate buying the ad with that of the opponent. By and large, researchers have found that attack ads can affect voter attitudes and behavior in specific elections. Voters find the information and message conveyed by the ads useful in making up their minds.[43] Scholars disagree about the long-term impact of negative ads on the political process, however. Some researchers have found that negative ads have a depressing effect on turnout, especially among independent and undecided voters.[44] Others conclude that any discouraging effect is minimal and that negative ads may actually stimulate the interest of voters who may not otherwise participate.[45]

The Internet

Since its debut as a political medium in the 1996 presidential elections, the Internet has become an increasingly important part of political campaigns. In 1996, the presidential candidates created fairly simple home pages containing their profiles, issue positions, campaign strategies, slogans, and email addresses. By 2000, the World Wide Web had become a major campaign tool for identifying potential supporters. In 2004, the campaign for Democratic contender Howard Dean used the Internet to raise millions of dollars, and the Kerry campaign later used the technology to overcome the early financial advantage President Bush enjoyed. The funds raised by the presidential candidates in 2008 dwarfed the figures from 2004. Candidates used the Internet to create virtual town meetings and to share ideas and coordinate campaign events with **bloggers**—average citizens who create online diaries and forums for the posting of opinions and personal viewpoints.

The traditional media have had to react to the emergence of the Internet. All major media outlets now have their own websites where they post breaking news stories to avoid being scooped by nontraditional journalist-bloggers like Matt Drudge. Drudge first broke the Clinton-Lewinsky story on his website after he learned *Newsweek* was considering the story. The traditional media disparage self-proclaimed journalists like Drudge as "those guys in pajamas" who lack credentials and do not follow conventional journalistic rules like requiring confirmation by independent sources.

A survey of the blogosphere by the Pew Internet & American Life Project revealed that 8 percent of all Internet users, about 12 million persons, keep a blog and that about 57 million Americans read blogs. Politics and government are the favorite topics of just over 10 percent of them.[46] The ten favorite sites for blogs in the United States are listed in the table on the next page.[47] One of them, The Huffington Post, began the $200,000 Off the Bus project in 2007. Its purpose was to send out 2,500 ordinary persons to cover the 2008 presidential campaign. Arianna Huffington, founder of the site, was quoted as saying: "At Off the Bus, because they're not part of the professional gaggle, they can come up with their own views of what's happening, which may be different from what the conventional wisdom is saying."[48] One of these ordinary persons was Mayhill Fowler, who made audiotapes of both Bill Clinton's angry tirade concerning a magazine article criticizing him and Barack Obama's comments at a closed fundraising meeting that "bitter" small-town Americans "cling to guns and religion."

Practitioners and supporters of blogging argue that it democratizes the media by allowing individuals to communicate to mass audiences. At the same time, however, it fails to provide any mechanism for distinguishing fact from fiction. It is assumed that bloggers exercise less than due diligence in researching their stories and often possess clear and stated political biases. Furthermore, unlike the traditional media, which can retract stories they get wrong, blogging often provides no formal recourse for those who have been treated unfairly. One critic points out that bloggers who attacked CBS for its faulty coverage of the president's fulfillment of National Guard obligations put out lots of inaccurate information themselves.[49] The bloggers had alleged, for example, that font and print styles used in the document secured by CBS were not available in the year the document was created. Further research by CBS revealed, however, that these options were available on some typewriter models.

As the Internet emerges as a major media outlet, many questions remain unanswered concerning its impact on political campaigns and politics in general. Will it add to further narrowcasting? Will it become the primary means for individuals to follow politics? Will the Internet increase or decrease civic engagement?

Top 10 Political Blogs, 2011

BLOG

1	The Huffington Post	Politics
2	Think Progress	Politics
3	CNN Political Ticker	Politics
4	The Note	Politics
5	Mediaite	Politics
6	Daily Kos	Politics
7	Top of the Ticket	Politics
7	Political Punch	Politics
9	Red State	Politics
10	TPMMuckraker	Politics

Source: http://technorati.com/blogs/directory/politics/ accessed July 16, 2011. The list includes a tie for seventh place.

candidate is losing ground.[51] During the presidential primaries, horse race coverage compares the candidates' standing in the polls and how much money they have raised. From those comparisons, the media predict the winners and losers. A year before the 2004 presidential election, the media declared Howard Dean the leader in the Democratic horse race because of his standing in the polls and his fundraising accomplishments. However, the anointed frontrunner—the candidate who holds the lead in a campaign by being ahead in the polls, raising more funds, and winning early primaries—quickly becomes a target not only of the other contenders but also of the media. Dean saw his campaign sputter and die a quick death when the media disparaged his overzealous reaction to his loss in Iowa as unbefitting a presidential candidate. The networks repeatedly showed Dean making what they dubbed a "scream speech," exhorting his followers not to lose faith. In 2008, neither the initial Democratic frontrunner, Hillary Clinton, nor the initial Republican frontrunner, Rudy Giuliani, was able to capture their party's nomination. Giuliani dropped out early without any victories, and Clinton finished a close second to Obama after a long and intense struggle. The Clinton candidacy seemed to be helped early on, however, when the media showed her crying at a campaign appearance in

Game Coverage

The media cover political campaigns much as they cover sports, as if campaigns were a game. They stress winning and losing, with strategy and tactics meriting more attention than a candidate's policy positions, past performance, or potential for future leadership.[50]

The favorite game reference in political coverage is the horse race. Journalists focusing on horse race coverage rely on four scripts or story ideas: the candidate is leading; the candidate is trailing; the candidate is gaining ground; the

The Clinton candidacy received a boost when the media showed her crying at a campaign appearance in New Hampshire at a time when her campaign was struggling.

New Hampshire at a time when it appeared her presidential aspirations might be dealt a quick knockout by the Obama campaign.

The game approach used by journalists in their campaign coverage fits with their cynical and negative approach to politics generally. It also supplies them with an endless series of stories. Every event can be analyzed from the perspective of strategies, motivations, winners, and losers. It is easier for reporters to use this approach. Reporting on complex issues such as nuclear proliferation and health-care reforms requires knowledge and training. The game format requires little familiarity with complex issues.

exit polls Surveys of voters taken when they leave the polling place, which are then used to project the winner of an election.

However, applying the game format to political campaigns can trivialize the process and can affect the outcome. If voters lose respect for the process, they are less likely to participate. James Fallows has written that the media have given us a view of public life that is similar to pro wrestling: "To judge by the coverage, everything is a sham. Conflicts are built up and then they blow over, and no one is sincere. . . ."[52]

Character Issues: Probing Personal Lives

Framing election campaigns as games, with players devising strategies to win at all costs, has in recent decades led the media to increase their probing of candidates' personal lives. After the decline of the partisan press in the early twentieth century, reporters tended to avoid excessive intrusion into politicians' personal affairs. For example, the media never published a photograph of President Franklin Roosevelt in a wheelchair, believing that his polio was unrelated to his performance as president. Nor did the media report on the infidelity of President John Kennedy, even though it occurred in the White House under the collective noses of the press corps. They evidently concluded that it was a personal matter. Times have changed!

In the age of adversarial reporting and "gotcha" journalism, the private lives and personal failures of candidates are now considered fair game. Scholars have cited several reasons for this trend, including media anger at political deception and wrongdoing after the Vietnam War and the Watergate scandal; Supreme Court decisions making it more difficult to sue the media for libel; and television's role in constructing new rules for political coverage. One communications scholar believes this shift in focus from substantive issues to character is the result of the shift from newspaper to television news. Television is a visual medium, and voters who get their news from this source are more likely to be interested in facial reac-

"To judge by the coverage, everything is a sham. Conflicts are built up and then they blow over, and no one is sincere."

tions and personal traits than in issue positions.[53] Still others, including journalist Cokie Roberts, believe that the addition of women to the press corps has expanded the boundaries of what the media should report.[54] As a result of all these forces coming together, sex lives, military records, divorce decrees, physical ailments, and tax returns all have become fair game for media coverage of elections.

Election Night Coverage

Election night coverage of voting results was once a relatively simple affair; newspapers waited for precincts to count the votes, then reported the results. The emergence of **exit polls** created a new dynamic for election night reporting, because the media would often know in advance which candidate the polls projected to win. Media outlets, eager to be the first to report the story, were tempted to predict the winners based on the poll numbers rather than waiting for the tabulation of actual votes. Calling a presidential election early, however, can discourage people from voting, because the outcome is already known. Thus, the media have agreed not to report any election outcome that would have an impact on races in a state where the polls are still open.

In 2000, under severe budget pressures, the broadcast networks agreed to hire a single firm, Voter News Service, to serve as a common source of exit poll data. The decision to rely on a single source of data proved disastrous. The networks first called Florida's electoral votes for Vice President Al Gore early in the evening, only to retract that call 90 minutes later when the actual vote count indicated that George W. Bush was running ahead of exit poll predictions. Fox then called Florida—and the presidency—for Bush at 2:16 A.M. eastern standard time, followed soon after by the other networks. Less than an hour later, these results came into question when votes from Florida's heavily Democratic Broward County virtually wiped away Bush's lead. By morning, all the networks announced Florida was "too close to call."

The reliance on faulty exit polls was a colossal embarrassment. NBC anchor Tom Brokaw exclaimed that NBC did not have "egg on its face" but rather an "omelet." The networks built new safeguards into their use of exit polling in 2004, but once again the exit polls were inaccurate. They showed Senator Kerry winning both Ohio and Florida, which would have given him enough electoral votes to win the presidency. This time, the networks waited for the actual votes to be counted, and the voters of Ohio and Florida provided enough votes to put President Bush over the top. The networks did not proclaim a winner until the following morning, but at least they got it right. By contrast, some

By holding frequent news conferences in the White House, President Franklin D. Roosevelt enjoyed positive media coverage longer than any modern president.

bloggers who had seen early and incomplete exit poll reports had proclaimed Kerry the winner earlier in the day.

The election night coverage in 2008 was free of mistakes. The networks were still hesitant to call races based only on exit polls and the election was not close in terms of the electoral vote totals. Obama's easy victory spared the media the embarrassment of incorrect reporting.

GOVERNMENT COVERAGE IN THE MEDIA

The dynamic that exists between the media and political candidates during campaigns also characterizes media relationships once candidates are elected leaders. Government officials need the public forum the media provides to persuade their constituents to support their policies. Journalists need information from these officials in the form of official reports, news releases, speeches, and interviews.

Interactions benefit both parties, but relationships sometimes get testy. As the media have become more cynical in their depiction of public life, officials have increased their effort to manage the news by trying to get the media to focus on the issues that portray officials in the best light. This dynamic is clearly seen in media coverage of our most visible political leader, the president.

Covering the President

The relationship between the media and the president has always contained some acrimony. During the era of the partisan press, George Washington quietly fumed at the harsh treatment from rival newspapers.[55] His successor, John Adams, became one of the great media-bashers in the nation's history. By the time Abraham Lincoln was elected president, the press had become more independent of partisan influence. Although Lincoln attempted to woo editors by giving them exclusive information and interviews, such tactics rarely worked, especially in the crisis atmosphere of the Civil War. Lincoln later censored war-related news and even had editors jailed if he believed their stories gave away military secrets or threatened Northern morale.

As the press became more independent and professional, presidents became more sophisticated in their dealings with reporters. Theodore Roosevelt added a press-room to the White House, spawning a permanent White House press corps that would become dependent on the White House as a source of news. The president treated the reporters with respect and hired a press secretary to act as a liaison between the president and the White House press corps. Press secretaries are accountable to the president, but if they lose credibility with the media for not telling the truth, the president can suffer from skeptical media coverage. Woodrow Wilson was the first president to conduct regular press conferences, at least one per week for two and a half years. He later came to detest the press corps because he did not enjoy answering all of the probing questions.[56] The presidency of Franklin Roosevelt entailed a dramatic increase in the power of the presidency as his administration responded to the dual crises of the Great Depression and World War II. Reporters now sought assignment to the White House because that was where the power resided. Once they arrived, they were flattered when the president

greeted them personally. Roosevelt held numerous press conferences and enjoyed the longest media honeymoon of any president in history.[57]

The atmosphere between the media and presidents Truman, Eisenhower, and Kennedy remained friendly, like that of a men's club. Conditions turned more adversarial with the Lyndon Johnson administration. As criticism of the Vietnam War increased, the president became more secretive. The relationship between the media and the president remained very strained during the Nixon years. As the media pursued the Watergate scandal, Nixon became surly and ordered the Internal Revenue Service to audit some of the journalists.

Ronald Reagan's skill at dealing with the media earned him the nickname "The Great Communicator." Reagan's experience as a former actor served him well in the age of television, when the smallest facial gesture or delivery of a phrase could be displayed on an evening news sound bite. His administration planned every day around a "message of the day." Reagan's staff structured his public events each day to emphasize a single theme, with the president visible in a variety of situations though not really accessible to the media. When Reagan's vice president, George H. W. Bush (father of George W. Bush), became president, he lacked his predecessor's ease with the media and was unable to communicate his vision for the country.[58] As a result, he appeared in the news less often than Reagan, even though he was personally more accessible. Bush held more press conferences in his four years as president than Reagan did in eight years.

The Clinton administration got off to a bad start with the White House press corps because of its attempts to limit journalists' access to key staff members. The media's coverage of the Clintons' Whitewater land deal, Clinton's involvement with Monica Lewinsky, and his impeachment further soured the administration's relationship with the media.

President George W. Bush ran a tight ship with respect to sharing information with the media. No member of his staff could appear on television or in print without prior approval. The president's visit to New York City in the wake of the 9/11 terrorist attacks catapulted his approval ratings and garnered positive coverage from even formerly critical outlets such as *The New York Times*. The long-running war in Iraq, and the administration's botched response to a series of hurricanes along the nation's Gulf Coast in 2005, changed the climate of coverage. The glowing coverage Bush previously enjoyed soon dissipated. Party identification plays a large role in determining whether one feels that critical coverage does more good than harm. Democrats

Changing D.C. Press Corps

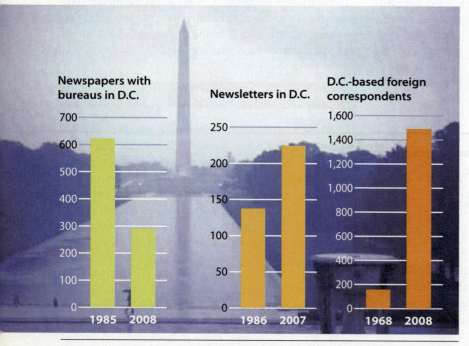

Source: Pew Research Center Publications, "The New Face of Washington's Press Corps," February 11, 2009, 1. http://pewresearch.org/pubs/1115/washington-press-corps-study.

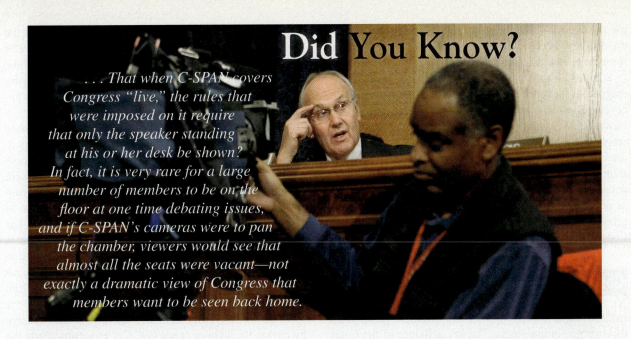

were more likely to believe criticism of Bush was good for the country; during the Clinton presidency, Republicans were more likely to see criticism of the president as beneficial.

Because favorable media coverage is vital to their success, presidents have increasingly sought to manage it in a number of ways. At press briefings, the president's press secretary exercises some control over the topics discussed and the flow of the questioning. Some members of the press can always be counted upon to throw "softball" questions that deflect criticism away from administration policies. The administration exercises even tighter control at background, or restricted, sessions between a presidential aide and the media, at which no questions are taken. Even at live TV press conferences, the president is well briefed about the questions likely to arise and has practiced set responses. Reporters may ask only one follow-up question, and the president decides which reporters to call on for questions.

The administration is especially careful when its lower-level officials speak to the media. It arms them with talking points—prepared arguments supporting administration policies and positions. Talking points are meant to ensure that officials stay "on message" by repeating the same themes the president articulates. The administration also controls its message through press releases, carefully worded official statements that reporters can cite in their articles. When the administration is unsure of the public's reaction to one of its policy options, it might send up a trial balloon—a hypothetical proposal it can back away from if public reaction is negative. The corps of journalists in Washington, D.C., at the beginning of the Obama administration is somewhat smaller and dramatically transformed from its predecessors some 20 years ago. The traditional media serving the general public have shrunk, but new niche media offering specialized and detailed informa-

tion to smaller elite audiences with targeted financial and lobbying interests have grown dramatically. The number of Washington-based foreign correspondents has also increased dramatically. (See figure on page 250.)

Covering Congress

The media cannot possibly pay as much attention to 535 members of Congress as they can to one president. Sometimes, White House pets receive more national media coverage than does the average member of Congress. In addition, Congress lacks a single leader who can speak authoritatively for the entire institution. The majority and minority leaders often have a hard time keeping their own members from breaking ranks. Nevertheless, there are more than three thousand members of the congressional media corps. The Capitol houses four separate press galleries—one each for daily publications, periodicals, photographers, and the electronic media.[59] The number of newspapers and periodicals covering Congress has declined since the 1980s.

The congressional press corps deals with the size and fragmentation of power within Congress by concentrating on three groups of members. First, they cover the Republican and Democratic Party leaders in both the House of Representatives and Senate, because these members can speak for a majority of their party colleagues. Second, they report on the House and Senate committee chairs whose work deals with an important topic of the day. The media are particularly interested in committee chairs who head up investigations into volatile topics such as the quality of American intelligence leading up to the war in Iraq or the alleged abuse of prisoners in Iraq by American soldiers. Third, local newspapers and broadcast stations like to cover their local legislators. Members of Congress have their own press secretaries and can use the Capitol's recording studios for their interviews. Individual members of Congress get considerable coverage in the local media outlets in their districts and states.

Although members of Congress often get favorable coverage from local media, the same is not true of national press coverage. As with coverage of the president, the national media treat Congress with great cynicism. Media coverage emphasizes partisan conflict, gridlock, and scandal. The media often trivialize congressional policy accomplishments, framing them as partisan victories or defeats. They portray debates over policy questions as power struggles, rather than as principled discussions of reasonable alternatives. Some scholars believe that citizens form negative perceptions of Congress based on such journalism.[60]

Covering the Supreme Court

Institutional characteristics of the Supreme Court limit its coverage in the media. The key activities of the Court are cloaked in secrecy, and most judicial decisions receive very little coverage. The public does not have access to the justices' discussions of the issues, nor their votes on the cases that take place in the conferences, until the judicial opinions are printed and distributed to the media. The justices let their formal opinions speak for themselves; they do not hold press conferences or grant interviews to explain their decisions. Although oral arguments in a case are open to the media and the public, the Court has refused to allow television to record the hearings. Only on rare occasions, such as the *Bush v. Gore* case, does it release audiotapes to the media immediately following the hearings. In addition, the language of judicial opinions is technical and difficult to summarize in a few paragraphs or in 30 seconds of broadcast time.

Despite these obstacles, the major networks and newspapers hire specialists to cover judicial proceedings, even if they give the proceedings very little coverage. The stories that the media report often deal with ideological splits on the Court and speculate on the winners and losers in a particular judicial outcome. In recent years, the media have become quite interested in judicial confirmation hearings, especially in the wake of allegations of sexual harassment against Supreme Court nominee Clarence Thomas in 1991.

In many ways, Americans are more familiar with state trial courts than they are with the U.S. Supreme Court. Crime stories permeate local news broadcasts, and some criminal trials reach national audiences. Americans were fascinated with the Michael Jackson and Scott Peterson trials, just as they were a decade earlier with the trial of O. J. Simpson. TruTV, formerly known as Court TV, has made it possible for Americans to follow such trials in depth. Court drama is a staple of late-afternoon television programming on network affiliates. More Americans are familiar with Judge Judy than they are with Justice Ruth Bader Ginsburg.

In spite of the many shortcomings of political coverage by the media, all hope is not lost. Citizens, particularly the young, are using the media as a source of information in new ways. Increasingly, they are becoming "news grazers," catching whatever bits and pieces of news they can from whatever sources are available. In addition, media outlets are expending great effort to find innovative ways to engage young people in the news.

THE MEDIA AND CIVIC ENGAGEMENT TODAY

Scholars such as Joseph Cappella and Kathleen Hall Jamieson believe modern media culture in America is increasingly fragmented, prone to emphasize negative aspects of our political system, and steeped in cynicism. They argue

Due to a lack of media coverage of the Supreme Court, more Americans know Judge Judy than know Justice Ruth Bader Ginsburg.

that it causes people to shun not only political coverage but news in general. We saw earlier that newspaper readership has declined steeply in recent decades, and the decline in network news viewership has been equally drastic. As one network news executive stated, "Network news is basically a corpse that hasn't been pronounced [dead] yet."[61]

This trend is worse among the young; only 21 percent of men under the age of thirty follow international news very closely, while 51 percent of them follow sports very closely.[62] These results prompt concern that young adults today may have turned their backs on vital news about the world in which they live.

There is some evidence that adversarial reporting and game coverage of politics cause citizens to lose confidence in our political leaders and institutions and to become increasingly cynical.[63] This cynicism extends to the media as well. Americans today are much less likely to believe the media protects democracy than they were in 1985. Only in the first few months after September 11, 2001, did views concerning the media improve temporarily.[64] Ironically, in today's information age, people have become less trusting of the information they receive.

Some observers cite the rise of alternative media, cable, and Internet news as a cause of the decline in news consumption. The wide selection of media outlets today means that many people can avoid news programming altogether. The greater choice among different media has also widened the knowledge gap between people who like news

> ## "Network news is basically a corpse that hasn't been pronounced [dead] yet."

and those who prefer entertainment. Stephen Macedo and his coauthors have concluded, "Those motivated enough to follow the news despite greater availability of other media content are more partisan. The audience that remains for the news is, therefore, more ideologically polarized than in the past."[65]

Conservative news consumers turn to Fox for their information; liberals turn to National Public Radio. With all the choices available, citizens who live side by side may have entirely different views of the political world in which they live because of the media choices they make. Former ABC reporter Ted Koppel believes that the traditional networks have added to the problem by engaging in what he calls "boutique journalism."[66] Koppel believes the traditional network news divisions today are trying to attract the demographic of 18- to 34-year-old viewers who are often just not interested.[67]

Although the trends discussed here are troublesome for a democracy that depends on informed citizens to make collective judgments on the basis of common information, there are signs that Americans—especially the young—are beginning to adapt to the new media age. Americans consume news in a completely different way than they did in previous generations; as mentioned earlier, they are becoming news grazers. Because news is available 24 hours a day, grazers set their own schedules for getting the news. They may catch a segment of news on TV or radio in the morning, scan the Internet during the day, and watch CNN or even *The Daily Show* in the evening. Today, almost half

Democracy and the News

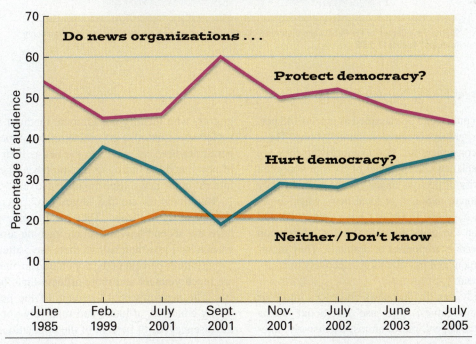

Source: Pew Research Center, "Internet News Audience Highly Critical of News Organizations," August 9, 2007.

New Patterns of News for a New Generation

Sources of News
Read · Watch · Listen to news...

News consumption "yesterday"	Total	Tradition-alists	Inte-grators	Net-Newsers	Dis-engaged
Any News	81%	83%	92%	86%	55%
Watched TV News	57%	65%	66%	47%	30%
Newspaper	34%	36%	42%	35%	14%
Paper	27%	35%	30%	8%	13%
Online	4%	*	6%	17%	1%
Both paper and online	3%	1%	6%	10%	0%
Radio News	35%	33%	46%	38%	21%
News online	29%	7%	56%	75%	13%
No Traditional News	24%	18%	12%	28%	51%
# of sources					
Two or more sources	48%	45%	70%	58%	18%
One source	33%	38%	22%	28%	36%

Source: Pew Center for the People and the Press, "Key News Audiences Now Blend Online and Traditional Sources," August 17, 2008.

of the American public can be classified as grazers (48 percent). Moreover, grazers are predominantly young. These younger news consumers are also event-driven; they are more likely to seek news during times of crisis or important events. A majority of persons under the age of thirty only follow international, national, or local news when something important happens. In today's busy, news-saturated era, grazers scan the news environment for information they deem personally important or dramatic. They monitor this environment and pay attention selectively to issues that matter to them.[68]

A recent study has divided news audiences into four categories: traditionalists, who use traditional media sources (TV, newspapers, radio) almost exclusively; inte-grators, who identify a traditional medium as their main news source but also go online several times a week for news; net-newsers, who use the net as their main source of news; and the disengaged, who have a general lack of interest in the news. (See the table above.)

Traditionalists are the largest group, comprising 46 percent of the audience. They are the oldest group, they have the second-lowest average income among the four groups, and less than half of them have attended college. Twenty-three percent of the population are integrators, who are much younger and more affluent than the traditionalists. The net-newsers, 13 percent of the population, are highly educated, affluent, and relatively young; whereas, the disengaged, 14 percent of the population, are the least

Who Tweets?

The percentage of online adults in each demographic group who use Twitter or another status update service

All online adults	Percent of U.S. adults 19
Sex	
Men	17
Women	21*
Race/ethnicity	
White (non-Hispanic)	19
African American (non-Hispanic)	26
Hispanic	18
Age	
18–29	33*
30–49	22*
50–64	9*
65+	4
Education	
Less than high school	18
High school diploma	17
Some college	21
College graduate	21
Household Income	
Less than $30,000	22
$30,000–$49,999	21
$50,000–$74,999	20
$75,000 or more	20

*Indicates a significant increase over December 2008 and April 2009.

Source: Pew Internet & American Life Project Survey conducted from August 18 to September 14, 2009. N=1,698 and margin of error is ±3% based on adult Internet users.

affluent, and the least educated. It is the integrators who are the most avid consumers of the news spending an average of 88 minutes on the news during a typical day.[69]

How will these new habits of news consumption affect our democracy? One thing that is certain is we should probably not expect media habits born of past eras to remain stagnant. What is also clear is that—like it or not—we are not going back to an era of fewer media choices and common hours for the delivery of news. What is not certain is where the new media age will take us. We are still finding our way through this information-rich age, and significant challenges lie ahead. Personalization of news websites, desktop e-mail alerts about breaking news, live and interactive news blogs, mobile phone delivery of the news, and podcasts are just some of the new approaches being pioneered to make information more accessible and

useful. By the time you graduate, there will no doubt be additional new technologies that bring personalized information to your fingertips. It is also probable that young grazers will enrich their media diet with more detailed coverage of personally important topics as they age and become better educated. At the same time, citizens may be finding alternate ways to use the media in constructive ways, and new media hold the promise of reconnecting citizens to their government.

There is no certainty, however, that all citizens will have equal access to these new ways of getting and using information. Many scholars worry about a digital divide, in which those without access to new technologies will be left behind at a time when information is the key to success. They also worry about the new digital divide between those with high-speed or broadband connections and those without. The former receive much more of their news online and participate more in the previously discussed social networking.[70] Even if access were universal, however, questions remain about the kind of democracy that is shaped by broader but shallower news consumption. Perhaps "just-in-time" systems will arise to deliver on-demand information about events and issues necessary to be an informed citizen. Perhaps new networks will put people in contact with specialists who can answer questions about issues and candidates. As the information envi-

media Quiz

Can you answer these questions? Below, see how your answers match up against those of your peers.

1. Which popular online website sponsored presidential debates on TV?

   Yahoo

   YouTube

   Google

   Facebook

2. Which U.S. newspaper did billionaire Rupert Murdoch purchase?

   Wall Street Journal

   Los Angeles Times

   New York Daily News

   USA Today

1. YouTube (44% of Americans overall, but 55% of 18–29-year-olds answered correctly.) 2. Wall Street Journal (48% of Americans overall, but only 32% of 18–29-year-olds answered correctly.)

Source: Pew Center for People and Press, "Political Knowledge Update," September 24, 2007.

Current Controversy

Is Watching *The Daily Show* Good for the Republic?

In 2007, Americans ranked comedian Jon Stewart, host of *The Daily Show* on Comedy Central as their fourth-most-admired journalist. He tied in the rankings with anchormen Brian Williams, Tom Brokaw, Dan Rather, and CNN host Anderson Cooper.[67] Yet, Stewart does not claim to be a journalist. In an interview he stated that "we feel no obligation to follow the news cycle . . . because . . . we're not journalists."[71] Are Americans confusing journalism with comedy and are they more ill-informed because of it? Not necessarily. According to a survey conducted in 2007, viewers of the show are highly informed. The regular viewers of *The Daily Show* scored in the highest percentile on knowledge of current affairs.[73] The comedy show was not their only source of news. "*The Daily Show* not only assumes, but even requires, previous and significant knowledge of the news on the part of viewers if they want to get the joke."[74]

The Pew Research Center's Project for Excellence studied the content of *The Daily Show* for the entire 2007 year in comparison to the mainstream media. The top ten topics for each are shown in the adjacent table. The top three topics for each were foreign affairs, elections and politics, and the national government. They accounted for 47 percent of the time on *The Daily Show* compared to 40 percent in the mainstream media. *The Daily Show* was less likely to spend time on subjects like crime, disease, medicine, business, and the economy that often lack a comedic element.[75] In December of 2010, however, Stewart devoted his show to advocating for legislation to award health-care benefits to 9/11 responders. The mainstream media had given the issue little coverage and the proposed bill was about to die with the adjournment of Congress. The bill did pass in the final hours of the 111th Congress, and many in the traditional media, such as *The New York Times,* credit Stewart with its success.

TOP 10 TOPICS ON *THE DAILY SHOW*

Topics (from top to bottom): Science/Technology, Crime, Race/Gender/Gay, Celebrities, Foreign (non-US), Press/Media, Lifestyle, Government, Elections/Politics, US Foreign Affairs

Percent of Newshole (x-axis: 0 to 18)

---

ronment continues to evolve, patterns of civic engagement will no doubt change as well.

The media can help their cause in creating and sustaining a market for news by working to correct some of the deficiencies cited by large numbers of news consumers. They can pay more attention to issues than personalities; make issue coverage more comprehensible to average citizens; examine the impact of policies on the lives of Ameri-

cans from diverse backgrounds; help remind citizens of their electoral duties and of the times and places they vote; spend less time covering sensational news stories and more on politics; and stop treating politics as a game or spectator sport. Educators must do better as well. They must spend more time teaching students how to be selective and critical consumers of media.

Summary ∨∨

1. How have the media and media consumption changed over the years?

- Just as civic life in America has changed, so have the media that report on that civic life.

- Early newspapers were partisan in nature, and their partisanship was rewarded with government jobs and contracts.

- Technological advances led to cheaper papers, greater circulation, and increased advertising revenues, thus allowing these papers to become politically independent.

- Near the end of the nineteenth century, many metropolitan newspapers practiced a type of sensationalist journalism known as yellow journalism, but reaction to it led to a more professional press in the twentieth century that would soon be augmented by the broadcast media of radio and television.

- Today, Americans' consumption of the news has been characterized by a steady decline in the use of newspapers, a decline in news consumption by young persons, and increased fragmentation of audiences due to narrowcasting.

2. What are the major characteristics of mass media in America?

- The mass media in America are privately owned, and that ownership is becoming more economically concentrated.

- The government regulates the electronic media by setting ownership limits and regulating content.

- The media emphasize presenting the news in an entertaining fashion.

- The media during the past three decades have adopted an adversarial approach to the news that leads many Americans to believe the coverage is biased.

3. How do the media cover political campaigns and government actions?

- The media focus on the polls, campaign strategy, and the character of the candidates rather than on the issues.

- The televised presidential debates offer the candidates an opportunity to speak to the voters in an unfiltered manner.

- National candidates spend the majority of their funds on paid media advertising that is often negative in tone.

- Once the elections are over, the media covers the winners, spending more time on the president than the more fragmented Congress and more secretive Supreme Court.

- The relationship between the media and government is both symbiotic and adversarial.

National Journal

In New Media, Image Is Still Everything

"It is unimaginable, had there been cameras in Auschwitz, that the world would have permitted the Holocaust to go forward," David Gergen, the CNN political analyst who worked in the Nixon, Ford, Reagan, and Clinton administrations, said in an interview. "We would have understood the face of evil."

Of course, by June 1942, *The New York Times* was reporting on "probably the greatest mass slaughter in history." But no one can dispute that a new age has arrived—much sooner than generally predicted and with important, if not easily discerned, geopolitical effects. The era has already spawned a student-led generation of human-rights-oriented "digi-activists," who lobby their targets, including Capitol Hill lawmakers, with homemade videos and other tools of their trade.

Some Washington policy makers, touting the freedom-spreading potential of online media networks, are pushing for U.S. funding of tools to prevent state censorship of the Internet. There is big game to be bagged here, virtual-style, advocates say—the potential to bring down the rule of the mullahs in Tehran and the autocrats in Beijing, all without a shot from a single American gun. But skeptics say that Washington's fingerprints on anti-censorship tools would taint the activists who use them.

The media world, along with eternal efforts to manipulate that world for political purposes, is moving past a time in which any professional media outlet carries much weight or authority as a conveyor of images and other components of "the news."

Not long ago, media analysts were pondering the so-called CNN effect "that continuous and instantaneous television may have on foreign policy" and "the conduct of war," as Stephen Hess of the Brookings Institution once put it. The paradigmatic example, Hess noted, was the U.S. military invasion of Somalia in 1992, prompted by the images of starving children that were beamed by satellite around the world, and not least into President George H.W. Bush's White House. "I learn more from CNN than I do from the CIA," Bush declared.

The CNN effect also played into President Clinton's hasty decision, in the fall of 1993, to withdraw troops from Somalia, announced four days after Americans were infuriated by broadcast images of a mob dragging the bodies of two dead U.S. soldiers through the streets of Mogadishu. "Television pictures brought U.S. troops to Somalia, and television pictures will pull them out," the Africa editor of The Independent, a British newspaper, correctly predicted at the time.

These days, the media era defined by the CNN effect looks like a mere interlude, a way station to the customized media milieu that is supplanting the mainstream media. For one thing, CNN now assigns a higher priority to covering global pop-culture celebrities than geopolitics.

In June, 2009, as street protests mounted in Iran against the apparently rigged re-election of President Mahmoud Ahmadinejad, CNN at first was all over the story, with star anchor Anderson Cooper's AC360 leading with the Iran upheaval for five consecutive evenings. "Tonight, as we have every night, we are piercing the firewall the Iranian government is trying to build, taking you inside" the country, Cooper declared at the top of his June 17 broadcast.

But when Michael Jackson died on June 25, CNN, like other networks, shifted to wall-to-wall "Jacko" coverage; Cooper flew to Los Angeles to anchor the story. AC360 led with Jackson for 11 straight shows, the events in Iran no longer a central focus.

CNN was demonstrating its own shrunken stature. The mainstream television media's obsession with the Jackson story did not, in fact, stop interested folks from continuing to share images of what was happening in Iran. Even when CNN was paying close attention to Iran, the iconic image that the network broadcast to viewers, the grisly street death of Neda Agha-Soltan, a young female protester, came not from the camera of some intrepid CNN videographer but from an anonymous Iranian's mobile phone, an image that was posted within minutes on YouTube and Facebook.

But is a more pluralistic media, haphazardly produced by a multiplicity of sources, a "better" media? The easy criticism is that citizen journalism and other varieties of online media production lack high standards, and so they do. For all of the mistakes that "elite" news organizations such as *The New York Times* regularly make, the errors are nothing compared with the casual misinformation and distortions that are a staple of the amateur news-gatherers and image-traffickers of the blogosphere. Indeed, one can safely predict that the number of hoaxes—"news" events staged to capture global attention—will increase with the widening availability of image-making technology.

In a widely noted testament to the power of the "social hallucinations" wrought by the age of personally generated media, Anders Colding-Jorgensen, an online media expert at the University of Copenhagen, managed to attract 10,000 Facebook group members in about a week to a fictitious cause to stop demolition of the Stork Fountain, a Copenhagen landmark, which in fact had never been slated for destruction. "We are a herd species," a blogger later commented about the experiment—with less of a need for factual, literal truth than for the need "to belong to something bigger than us."

In this sense, the new media's ability to generate propaganda images for mass consumption may prove no less potent than the film and television industry's ability to do the same thing for a litany of 20th-century dictators. Probably the new era will produce no single work to rival Leni Riefenstahl's 1934 *Triumph of the Will,* the pro-Nazi film produced by the German propaganda ministry. Such big-ticket state-commissioned projects may be a thing of the past, but the ease of online media production may offer an even more poisonous media climate.

The video-based propaganda campaigns of Al Qaeda and other stateless terrorist groups, aimed at inspiring a global community of followers and sympathizers, may prove the start of such a trend. Anti-American websites trumpeted the 2002 video of Daniel Pearl's beheading, filmed by his jihadist captors and titled, by them, "The Slaughter of the Spy-Journalist, the Jew Daniel Pearl." Age-old ethnic and religious divisions, as in the Middle East, may morph into virtual warfare between tribes of information warriors.

In the end, moreover, the images generated by citizen journalists and digi-activists may not turn the culture away from the tabloid style of presentation that has taken deep root in the mainstream media. The tabloid style is all about capturing the sensational in a condensed, raw form—as easily done in an amateur's video snippet as in a photograph displayed on the front page of the *New York Post.*

Consider how the presentation of the death of Neda, the Iranian protester, has become an object lesson within the ranks of digital activists. "Neda's transformation from a person into a symbol" is "a story of citizen media," activist Mary Joyce wrote in a blog post. "What are the lessons for activists who wish to use citizen media to frame

> "For all of the promise of the age of participatory media, the new media world could yet turn out to be a lot like the old one. As ever, the question is how much technology can alter the human equation."

a public issue? First, the media should be clear and emotional. Neda's video—the most spreadable form of media about her story—was raw and visceral. Without understanding the words of the men trying to help her or knowing much of the story, it was possible to empathize with her and feel the pain of her injustice," Joyce wrote.

In other words, Neda's story could be grasped without context—which made it uncomplicated and easy to get, but also easy to manipulate and appropriate for political purposes. Media that are this unlayered may pull heartstrings but are unlikely to clarify the muddy waters of real life.

This seems especially true because the new era appears likely to reinforce, rather than challenge, the long-standing dominance of images, as opposed to words, as the main form of media content. The supremacy of "The Image," nearly 200 years after the invention of the daguerreotype and 100 years after the invention of television—remains intact in the digital telling of stories such as Neda's. Yes, text-messaging via cellphones and word-driven technologies such as Twitter are significant features of the new media landscape, but nobody talks about "iconic" text.

The point is not that images are bad, but that they are easier to exploit for emotional

purposes and easier to strip of illuminating context. Thus, for all of the promise of the age of participatory media, the new media world could yet turn out to be a lot like the old one. As ever, the question is how much technology can alter the human equation. What are people looking for as observers and participants in the so-called "networked public square"? Do they want to be entertained, shocked, hypnotized, informed, enlightened? All of the above? Will they become inured to images of atrocity—or perhaps distrustful of them, given the potential for fakery—so that even genocide becomes no less frequent in this new age?

Now that the media is truly us, as both makers and watchers of the product, our future seems to rest on our eyeballs.

11

CONGRESS

DOING THE PEOPLE'S BUSINESS

A DREAM DEFERRED ▮ Hector Lopez came to America from Mexico with his parents when he was six weeks old. He worked hard in school and graduated from Rex Putnam High in Milwaukie, Oregon, as student body president with dreams of attending college. But in late summer 2010, Hector was arrested by Immigration and Customs Enforcement agents and deported to the border town of Matamoros, Mexico. Hector, who does not speak Spanish and has no immediate relatives in Mexico, traveled from the border to Mexico City where he looked for work. "I felt like everything was far from home, just a completely new world for me," he said. "Not knowing the language well, I wasn't ready for it all. It was almost too much to handle." Harassed by local drug dealers who forced him to flee, Hector traveled back to the U.S. border where he turned himself in to customs agents requesting asylum in the United States. Today, he sits in a detention center in Florence, Arizona, awaiting hearing.[1]

Hector is one of hundreds of thousands of young people who came to America as children of illegal immigrants but who have spent their entire lives in this country. Renewed attention to immigration and border security issues has resulted in enhanced enforcement of immigration laws and a crackdown on people like Hector who have escaped detection for years. Hispanic leaders and immigration activists have pushed for new laws that create a path toward citizenship for children of illegal immigrants. One of these proposals, the DREAM Act, gained traction when President Obama embraced it. The bill provides conditional legal status to illegal immigrant high-school graduates who came to the country before they were 16 years old, have lived in the U.S. for five years, have no criminal records, and attend college or serve in the military for two years.

Championed by numerous immigration reform groups, the bill spawned a movement driven by thousands of students without legal status who "came out" to recount their own academic achievements and the barriers they faced. A student group, United We Dream Network, began one-on-one lobbying with members of Congress and staged student demonstrations in support of the bill across the nation.[2]

In the waning days of the 111th Congress, the bill was taken up by both houses. On December 8, it passed the House of Representatives by a vote of 216 to 198. As the bill neared a Senate vote, activists kept the pressure on with rallies, hunger strikes, sit-ins, and thousands of phone calls placed to Senate offices.[3]

Senate Majority Whip Dick Durbin (D-IL), the chief sponsor of the bill, expressed optimism as the Senate vote neared but understood that the norm of majority rule doesn't always apply in the U.S. Senate. "I've known the names of most people and how they would vote for a long, long time," Durbin said. "We've been working on the fringes to try to get the five."[4] The "five" ➡

- What powers does Congress have?
- What are some factors affecting election to Congress?
- What are the keys to political power in Congress?

additional votes he sought were needed to achieve the supermajority of 60 necessary to overcome a Senate filibuster, a procedure of unlimited debate that normally spells doom for a measure.

Meanwhile, the bill's chief opponent, Jeff Sessions (R-AL), called the bill a "nightmare act" that would give amnesty to millions of illegal immigrants. He believed the bill was "a reward for illegal activity" that would cost taxpayers millions of dollars.[5] Republicans, newly emboldened by their large victories the previous month, were also reluctant to give President Obama the victory he sought.

The Senate's final tally was 55 yea, 41 nay—a majority in favor, but not enough to escape the threat of filibuster, the supermajority needed in the Senate when a determined minority stands in the way. Meanwhile, Hector Lopez remains in the Florence Detention Center.

In this chapter, we will come to understand why bills like the Dream Act face a difficult time getting through Congress. We will highlight the complex forces at work in a legislative process that is slow, deliberative, and often driven by arcane rules. It is a process that sometimes resembles a board game where a spin of the wheel can send a bill back to the start or propel a long-shot to the finish line. It is a game, however, where the stakes are high—for the political interests with a stake in the outcome; for the members who face continual electoral scrutiny; for their **constituents**, the citizens these elected officials represent; and for people like Hector Lopez whose futures are on the line. ◆

Majority Whip Dick Durbin (D-IL) expresses his optimism for the passing of the DREAM Act as he walks through the halls of Congress.

ORIGIN AND POWERS OF CONGRESS

When the Framers met in Philadelphia to devise a new system of government and draft a constitution, they turned their attention first to the body that would represent citizen interests and make laws. Ten of the 13 colonies had bicameral, or two-chamber, legislatures. The delegates' familiarity with this type of legislative arrangement led to the adoption of a two-chamber Congress despite a call by New Jersey for a unicameral, or single-body, legislature. Instead of copying Britain's parliamentary system, however, they created a new presidential form of government with multiple checks and balances.

Some delegates to the Constitutional Convention called for proportional representation in both houses of Congress. Under such an arrangement, the three most populous states—Virginia, Pennsylvania, and Massachusetts—would have commanded almost half the seats in both the upper house (the Senate) and the lower house (the House of Representatives). Luther Martin of Maryland reflected the views of many small-state delegates when he called the plan a "system of slavery which bound hand and foot ten states of the Union and placed them at the mercy of the other three."[6]

After nearly two months of deliberation, the delegates finally reached what scholars refer to as the Great Compromise. They agreed to apportion seats equally in the Senate, while apportioning seats in the House according to population. This satisfied the demands of smaller states by giving them an equal voice with larger states in at least one chamber.

The delegates carved out a number of differences between the two houses. The House of Representatives was the "people's house" with its members elected directly by the people. The Senate, however, was designed to safeguard the rights of the states and minorities against mass opinion. As a result, state legislatures elected senators until 1913, when ratification of the Seventeenth Amendment provided for the direct popular election of senators. Most of the delegates favored short terms of office and frequent elections in order to keep lawmakers on a short leash. James Madison, however, debated that members of Congress needed time to learn and ply the legislative art. A compromise fixed a two-year term for members of the House and a staggered six-year term for senators, with one-third of the Senate coming up for election every two years. In most cases, both houses jointly exercise congressional powers, but some powers reside principally with one or the other body.

> **constituents** The citizens from a state or district that an elected official represents.

In addition to power sharing between the houses, the delegates to the Constitutional Convention also debated which powers to accord to Congress and which to reserve to other branches of government. The table on page 264 lists enumerated powers, that is, powers the Constitution explicitly grants to Congress. Most notably, Congress has the power to make laws, including those that are "necessary and proper" for carrying out other duties. Over time, Congress has used this phrase, sometimes known as the elastic clause, to expand the reach of the federal government. It gives Congress the ability to adapt to changing circumstances unforeseen at the time the Constitution was written. For example, Congress today makes laws establishing agencies and procedures to protect the environment, a consideration that was hardly a worry for the Framers.

Article I of the Constitution also explicitly denies Congress certain powers, including granting of titles of nobility, imposing certain types of taxes, and suspending certain categories of individual rights. Of course, the actions of other branches also limit congressional power. The balance of power between Congress and the executive branch has changed throughout history as each has jockeyed for control over the nation's political agenda. In Chapter 14, we will also see

Major House and Senate Differences

House	Senate
House	**Senate**
Apportioned on basis of population	Equal representation (2) from each state
Fixed (since 1911) at 435 members	100 members
Two-year terms	Six-year terms (one-third elected every two years)
Members must be at least 25 years of age, 7 years a citizen, and reside in the state from which chosen	Members must be at least 30 years of age, 9 years a citizen, and reside in the state from which chosen
Power to impeach federal officeholders	Power to try federal office-holders who have been impeached
Initiate bills raising revenue	Approve treaties, cabinet-level appointments, and appointments to the Supreme Court
Choose president in case of electoral vote tie (Article II)	Choose vice president in case of tie (Article II)*

*Originally, the Constitution accorded the vice presidency to the runner-up in the presidential election, provided the presidential candidate received a majority of electoral votes. This procedure was altered by the Twelfth Amendment (1804), which provided for separate ballots in the selection of the president and vice president.

Enumerated Powers by Function*

Financial & Economic Powers

Power to levy and collect taxes and duties (expanded by the Sixteenth Amendment in 1913 to include taxing income)
Power to borrow money
Power to regulate commerce with foreign nations and among states
Power to coin money
Power to fix standards of weights and measures
Power to punish counterfeiters
Power to grant patents and copyrights
Power to establish uniform laws on bankruptcy
Power to establish post office and post roads

Defense-Related Powers

Power to declare war
Power to raise and support armies
Power to create and maintain the navy
Power to regulate the armed forces
Power to organize the militia (today's National Guard) and to call the militia into national service to defend against rebellion

Checks & Balances

Power to impeach federal officials
Power to establish lower federal courts along with specifying (with some exceptions in the case of the Supreme Court) the kinds of cases each can hear
Power to override presidential veto

Legislative Power

Power to make all laws necessary and proper for carrying out foregoing powers
Power to govern the District of Columbia

---

* Congress also has a role in the process of succession to the office of president should a vacancy occur, a procedure that was clarified and strengthened with the adoption of the Twenty-fifth Amendment in 1967.

how the judicial branch can limit the power of Congress by challenging the constitutionality of congressional actions.

CIVIC LIFE AND CONGRESSIONAL CHANGE

Congress has responded to changes in American civic life by becoming more open and hospitable to involvement by an increasingly diverse citizenry. Minorities and women, once denied a formal role, are a growing presence in the halls of Congress. Today, Americans enjoy unprecedented access to their representatives and senators through websites, e-mail, telephone, and letter. Thousands of groups representing almost every conceivable interest give citizens the opportunity to amplify their individual voices in pressuring members of Congress to respond to their concerns. Congress now does a great deal of its work in public, with floor sessions and many committee meetings broadcast live on C-SPAN, thus allowing citizens to keep watch over their lawmakers. Access and openness did not come easily or all at once, however. Powerful interests, strong and obstinate leaders in control of legislative procedures, and clashes with other branches of government have all stymied change at one time or another.

Building the Institution

When the first session of the U.S. Congress met in New York City in 1789, many of the members knew each other personally from serving together on other governing bodies, including colonial legislatures. The new Congress moved quickly to create committees, prescribe the powers of leadership, and place limits on floor debate, but most policy initiatives in these early days, including the call for a national bank and the funding of canals for commerce, came from the office of the president.

The elimination of property qualifications for voting led political leaders to mobilize newly enfranchised citizens into political parties. Control of Congress soon became a political contest with the strongest party in each chamber assuming the leadership positions. President Andrew Jackson (1829–1837) used his popularity with voters to assert authority over members of his own party in Congress by rewarding those members who supported his proposed legislation and punishing those who opposed him. Few presidents in subsequent decades would enjoy such power at the expense of Congress.

As Congress admitted additional states to the Union, new and independent Senate leaders emerged to challenge Jackson. Many represented the new Whig party, which attacked the Democrats on the issue of slavery. During this time, the Senate became the preeminent forum for debate on the issues dividing the Union, eclipsing the presidency as the hub for policy formation. Floor debates could be intense—and violent. In 1856, Congressman Preston Brooks of South Carolina assaulted Senator Charles Sumner, an antislavery advocate from Massachusetts, on the Senate floor. Brooks beat Sumner senseless with a walking stick over Sumner's opposition to admitting Kansas to the union as a slave state.[7] Debate and compromise, it seemed, could not bridge the growing divide over slavery. By the time Abraham Lincoln was elected president in 1860, hope for avoiding dissolution of the Union had all but faded. A bloody civil war ended slavery in the United States and opened the way for greater citizen participation by enfranchising all former male slaves.

After the war, southern states elected the first black members of Congress, including 13 ex-slaves. In the years that followed, Congress asserted its authority in national affairs. Party leaders such as Speaker of the House Joseph "Uncle Joe" Cannon gained enormous influence, controlling the timing and content of bills brought to the floor and effectively rewarding or punishing fellow members. Partisan power was just as strong in the Senate, which had come to dominate legislative affairs and which many Americans considered a "millionaire's club" that represented only the interests of party bosses and big business trusts.

The Era of Reform

The Progressive Era brought significant changes to Congress. A coalition of Democrats and "insurgent" Republicans wrested control of the House from Speaker Joe Cannon in 1910 and brought the chamber more in line with the growing demand for reform in government. The Seventeenth Amendment (1913) gave voters the power to elect senators directly, taking it out of the hands of local and state party bosses who had dominated the process for decades. Rule changes in both the House and Senate further curtailed the power of party leaders. The Progressive Era also produced a more professional Congress, one in which members were expected to become experts in matters under the jurisdiction of the committees on which they served. Another landmark change came in 1917, when Jeannette Rankin became the first female House member after spearheading a successful drive for women's suffrage in her home state of Montana.

The Resurgent Executive Branch

A shift in power away from Congress became increasingly apparent during the presidencies of Theodore Roosevelt and Woodrow Wilson. With the election of Franklin Delano Roosevelt in 1932, it became a central fact of American political life. With commanding Democratic majorities in both houses, FDR rushed through Congress numerous emergency measures to spur economic recovery during the Great Depression of the 1930s. The first 100 days of Roosevelt's administration were some of the most prolific in legislative history.

By 1937, however, disputes over the constitutionality of Roosevelt's New Deal legislation led conservative southern Democrats in the House to defect and form an alliance with Republicans. This conservative group created new rules designed to slow or block presidential initiatives. Cracks in Democratic solidarity also led to brief periods of Republican control of Congress after World War II. Republicans took control of the House from 1947 to 1949, and both the House and the Senate briefly in 1953.

The Rights Revolution and Congress Today

The civil rights movement of the 1950s and 1960s opened a rights revolution in which many groups sought protective legislation for various causes. Women, minority groups, environmental protection supporters, government reform advocates, as well as organized interests opposing these causes, streamed to Washington in a new wave of activism. At the same time, Congress itself became more diverse. The Senate welcomed its first Asian American, Hiram

In 1917, Jeannette Rankin became the first woman to serve in Congress even before women were granted suffrage by the Nineteenth Amendment.

MAPPING THE FUTURE?

Republican victories in 2010 state and gubernatorial races put them in a good position to hold onto the gains they made in congressional midterm elections. Their victories gave them complete control of the redistricting process in 18 states, with a total of 202 congressional seats as opposed to the Democrats who control the process in only 6 states with 47 districts. (See map.) Fear among Democrats caused some to retire and others to consider migrating to another state. Ohio Congressman Dennis Kucinich, who contemplated moving to the state of Washington, told reporters, "I intend to stay in Congress. I just don't know where my district will be."

But controlling the maps doesn't always mean controlling the outcomes. For one thing, the electorate has been quite volatile in recent years, overturning the majority party's control of Congress three times since the last redistricting. The number of partisans with only weak allegiance and a growing number of self-identified independents make safe districts harder to draw. Pennsylvania Republicans redrew their maps after a good showing in 2002. But they saw their 12 to 7 edge in 2002 dwindle to a 12 to 7 deficit after the 2008 elections, which marked the Democrats' high point over the past 10 years.[*]

Demographic shifts tend to favor the Democratic Party. States receiving the largest seat increases in 2012 (e.g., Texas, Florida) are also the states likely to see hefty gains in Hispanic American voters who trend Democratic.

Who Controls Redistricting?

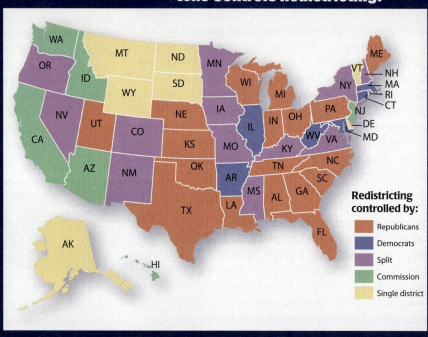

Redistricting controlled by:
- Republicans
- Democrats
- Split
- Commission
- Single district

Source: http://images.capwiz.com/file-mgr/redistricting.jpg

[*] Bob Benenson, "In Remapping, No Guarantees." Congress.org. Accessed on May 14, 2011 at http://www.congress.org/news/2011/03/11/in_remapping_no_guarantees?all=1.

---

seniority system A system that rewards those with longer service with positions of leadership.

Congressional Budget Office Nonpartisan agency created by Congress to assist in the budget process.

incumbent Current occupant of an office.

safe district Electoral district in which the candidate from the dominant party usually wins by 55 percent or more.

Fong, in 1959; its first Native American, Ben Nighthorse Campbell, in 1993; and its first African American woman, Carol Moseley Braun, in 1987.

Newly represented groups sought not only new legislation but also changes in the way Congress operated. They opened committee meetings to the public and exercised greater control over party leaders. By the mid-1970s, a new generation of legislators had weakened the **seniority system**, which awarded assignments on the most powerful committees to members with the longest continuous service. Congress adopted new procedures for legislative oversight of the federal budget, including creation of a separate **Congressional Budget Office** to provide members with an independent assessment of policy costs. In 1979, C-SPAN began publicly broadcasting House sessions.

Like the electorate, Congress today has become more polarized as each party struggles to control the legislative agenda, often with razor-thin margins. Some Congress members even complain that congressional civility has declined, making it more difficult for members to forge consensus on important matters of policy.[8] This was clearly evident in the recent debate over health-care reform. Understanding how Congress operates within this political atmosphere means knowing the roles played by party, position, and procedure—the keys to getting legislation passed. Before we examine these keys, however, we need to explore the nature of representation itself and the characteristics of those who seek to represent our interests in government.

GETTING ELECTED

The challenges facing those wishing to serve in Congress are steep. As we learned in Chapter 9, political campaigns in America are largely candidate-centered. Individuals who decide to run must muster significant resources on their own to secure their party's nomination. Even after winning a party primary, candidates continue to be largely responsible for their own campaigns. They must amass both the substantial blocks of time necessary for campaigning and the money needed to hire professional consultants and purchase advertising. Challengers face greater obstacles than **incumbents**—current officeholders—who enjoy advantages like name recognition. Candidates for the House rarely stop campaigning because they must face the voters every two years. They also face the challenge of running in districts whose geographic boundaries shift with population changes.

Resources

The average congressional district contains about 710,700 people. Imagine trying to get a message out to that many voters! Doing so requires considerable resources, among them time itself. Few people can afford to spend the countless hours necessary to greet voters, solicit funds from interest groups, and make campaign appearances while maintaining a full-time job. This is one reason the 112th Congress includes few Americans from blue-collar occupations. Wealthy individuals may be able to take enough time away from their jobs to run for office, but most Americans don't have this flexibility.

Money is another critical resource for congressional candidates, because getting a message out to voters requires lots of it. In 2010, candidates for House seats spent an average of $1,632,620 running for office. Senate candidates spent an average of $3,137,312.[9] The expenses of high profile races, however, dwarf these average figures. World Wrestling Federation promoter Linda McMahon spent more than $50 million of her own money in her losing bid for U.S. Senate from Connecticut. Michele Bachmann spent more than $11 million to hold on to her 6th District Congressional seat in Minnesota.

Candidates—especially challengers and those running in close races—must constantly solicit funds from individual contributors and PACs (political action committees—see Chapter 9). Even candidates from **safe districts**, those in which the candidate from the dominant party consistently wins 55 percent of the vote or more, are almost continuously raising large sums of money, much of which they share with party members in more competitive districts. One congressman describes the time devoted to fundraising this way:

> When I was here in Washington, I would go over to the NRCC [National Republican Congressional Committee] or the Senatorial Committee offices to make telephone calls (for) an hour, two hours every day. When I was home in Florida, which was a good portion of the time, that's the bulk of what I did. It's a very time-consuming process, on the telephone mostly, organizing fundraisers or getting individual people to contribute.[10]

Funding of political ads by outside groups not affiliated with parties or candidates climbed in 2010 to $294 million, a 327 percent increase from the $69 million spent during the last midterms in 2006.[11] Much of this came from organizations that can accept unlimited contributions from undisclosed donors as a result of the 2010 Supreme Court ruling *Citizens United v. the Federal Elections Commission.* Whereas Republican candidates were the primary beneficiaries of these groups during the 2010 elections, Democrats have vowed to match independent spending by liberal-leaning organizations in 2012. Because candidates spend so much time soliciting funds from organized interests and wealthy donors, they may be better versed in the needs of these groups than in the wishes of the average voter. Of course, Congress itself is composed largely of the wealthy and near wealthy. According to mandatory government financial disclosures, more than half of the members of the U.S. Senate have a net worth of at least one million dollars. Because disclosure forms allow senators to conceal some income, the number of senators with a net worth above the million-dollar mark is probably even higher.

. . . That the least-expensive winning campaign for the Senate in the 2008 election was run by John Barrasso (R-WY) who spent $1,981,441? The least-expensive winning campaign in the House that year was run by Marcia Fudge (D-OH) who spent $94,049.

Did You Know?

The Incumbency Factor

Even in years that witness historic electoral change, incumbents generally have a big advantage over challengers. The graph on page 268 shows

The Power of Incumbency

Percentage of House incumbents returned to office, 1994–2010

Excludes those retiring or running for other offices and incumbents running against incumbents. Data from *Congressional Quarterly,* various years, and compiled from *USA Today,* Nov. 3, 2010.

the level of success incumbents have enjoyed since 1994. In 2010, losses for incumbent Democrats contributed to a somewhat lower, but still high, incumbent retention rate.

One reason incumbents are so hard to unseat is the advantage they hold in raising money. Donors are more likely to give to candidates they believe will win; because donors know that incumbents are more likely to be successful, they give more to incumbents. This reasoning creates a self-fulfilling prophecy that reinforces and helps sustain the power of incumbency. In 2010, House incumbents raised on average nearly six times more than challengers for the general election. Senate incumbents enjoyed an even greater fundraising advantage over challengers.[12]

The party holding the majority of seats in Congress typically enjoys a fundraising advantage because of the power it exerts in formulating and passing legislation. Interest groups that want to influence legislation are more likely to direct funds to the party in power. Much depends on expectations and many donors increased their donations to Republicans in 2010 sensing

a wave of popular discontent against the Democratic majority. Of course, contributors with a particular ideological interest continue to give to candidates who support their positions, regardless of party.[13]

Incumbents, unlike challengers, also enjoy the advantage of visibility, that is, the ability to keep their names and faces in front of the public. For example, sitting members have **franking privileges** that allow them to send newsletters, questionnaires, and letters to constituents at the government's expense, except in the last days of a campaign. Challengers must finance their own mailings. Incumbents can also get free news exposure by announcing new programs for their local communities and talking with the local media about legislation before Congress. Such exposure reinforces name recognition among voters. Finally, incumbents can offer constituents help in securing assistance from government agencies, a practice known as **casework**. Voters are likely to reward a member of Congress who makes the effort to

Money and Incumbency: Senate and House Fundraising by Type of Seat

Fundraising

Senate

Type of Candidate	Total Raised	Number of Candidates	Average Raised
Incumbent	$337,324,712	30	$11,244,157
Challenger	$147,337,920	153	$962,993
Open seat	$347,455,020	122	$2,847,992
Grand total	$832,117,652	305	$2,728,255

House

Type of Candidate	Total Raised	Number of Candidates	Average Raised
Incumbent	$635,541,810	420	$1,513,195
Challenger	$295,833,642	1,115	$265,322
Open seat	$156,425,863	357	$438,168
Grand total	$1,087,801,317	1,892	$574,948

Source: Open Secrets.org. Accessed May 15, 2011 at http://www.opensecrets.org/bigpicture/incumbs.php.

help them navigate the bureaucratic maze to resolve problems with government personnel or agencies. This helps to explain why most constituents believe their representative is doing a good job despite the disdain most have for Congress as a whole.

Midterm Elections

Midterm elections—those contested in years between presidential elections—draw an average of 15 to 20 percent fewer voters than do presidential elections. The 2010 midterm was no different, drawing roughly 20 percent fewer voters than the presidential contest of 2008. Scholars have advanced many theories to explain voter drop-off in midterm elections, including election fatigue (i.e., a sense of political exhaustion after the sometimes bruising politics of presidential elections), less media coverage of politics between presidential elections, and voter apathy.

Candidates in midterm elections confront an electoral environment that is somewhat different from that of presidential election years. First, only the most committed partisans are likely to vote in midterm races. Voters with weak or no partisan ties are harder to mobilize; only the visibility and media focus of a presidential contest will draw their ac-

tive involvement. Second, the issues that motivate strong partisans often work against members of the president's party. Midterm voters sometimes use their ballots to register dissatisfaction with the president by voting against members of the same party in congressional races. In 2010, voters punished Democrats for passing a stimulus bill that failed to turn around a flagging economy and a poorly understood health-care bill that proved highly unpopular. As a rule, the president's party usually loses seats in midterm elections, as the honeymoon between voters and the president wears off. Even if a sitting president is popular, candidates from the president's party rarely benefit from their partisan ties to the president when they don't have his coattails to ride. But 2010 proved particularly painful for Democrats who lost more than 60 seats in the House and with them their majority status. The loss was the largest for a sitting president since 1938 and erased virtually all of the gains the Democrats had made in the previous two Congressional elections, particularly in the Midwest where Barack Obama helped the cause of moderate Democrats in Republican-leaning districts two years earlier.

franking privilege Free postage for members of Congress to communicate with constituents.

casework Practice of finding solutions to constituent problems, usually involving government agencies.

redistricting The practice of drawing congressional district boundaries to accord with population changes.

The table to the left illustrates wide variation in the pattern of midterm losses for the president's party in the House. The greatest losses in recent years reflect widespread voter dissatisfaction with presidential policies or performance. Often the party out of power attempts to frame the midterms as a referendum on the president's policies as the Republicans did successfully in 1994, when they seized control of Congress from the Democrats for the first time in 40 years, and again in 2010. In both cases, they pledged to end runaway spending which they blamed on the Democrats. Occasionally, however, voters reward the president's party with a bonus as they did in 1998, reflecting satisfaction with the economy under Bill Clinton's administration, and in 2002, when they signaled their support for George W. Bush's handling of the "War on Terror" following the 9/11 attacks. In the Senate, the president's party has lost seats in 13 of the last 16 midterm elections, and 2010 was no exception. Even so, President Obama's party maintained control of the Senate, but by a much smaller margin.

Gains and Losses of Congressional Seats for the Party of the President in Midterm Elections

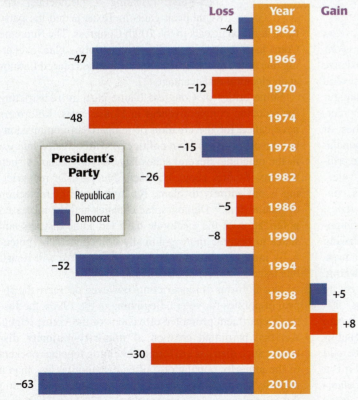

Loss	Year	Gain
−4	1962	
−47	1966	
−12	1970	
−48	1974	
−15	1978	
−26	1982	
−5	1986	
−8	1990	
−52	1994	
	1998	+5
	2002	+8
−30	2006	
−63	2010	

President's Party
- Republican
- Democrat

Source: Congressional Quarterly, various years.

Redistricting

Candidates for the House of Representatives face an additional obstacle in their quest for office: **redistricting**, the redrawing of the electoral boundaries of the districts they represent. Since people are always moving within and between states, election districts must be adjusted to reflect population changes. The Constitution prescribes **reapportionment**, or reallocation, of seats every 10 years based on the latest census data. Supreme Court rulings in the 1960s made it clear that the size of the population within each district must be relatively equal.[14] The Supreme Court also recently ruled that redistricting may take place more often.[15] Because Congress permanently fixed the total number of seats in the House at 435 in 1911, some states gain seats with reapportionment as their states grow, while others lose seats. Over the past few decades, states in the Northeast and Midwest generally have lost seats, while southern and western states have made gains.

States have adopted a variety of procedures to redraw district boundaries. Most give this power to state legislatures; some states employ advisory commissions of various sorts with the legislators having final say. Still others use backup commissions in case the legislature deadlocks. Finally, some states (e.g., Arizona and Washington) use independent commissions whose members are chosen from the public by legislative leaders. In all cases, states are expected to follow several rules of thumb: boundaries should be compact, be contiguous (i.e., adjoining or bordering), avoid splitting cities or counties, and guarantee population equality to ensure the principle of "one-person-one-vote."

Since political bodies control the process in most states, it is subject to partisan manipulation. The practice of drawing boundaries for partisan advantage is called **gerrymandering**, after the tactics employed by Massachusetts governor Elbridge Gerry in 1812 to create a district that favored Republicans over Federalists. The odd shape of the district inspired one cartoonist to depict it as a creature much like a salamander, and the term *gerrymander* has stuck ever since.

THE GERRY-MANDER.

The odd shape resulting from the partisan redrawing of this Massachusetts district in 1812—largely through the efforts of Governor Elbridge Gerry—inspired one cartoonist to depict it as a creature much like a salamander, giving rise to the term gerrymander.

reapportionment The periodic reallocation of 435 House seats among the states as population shifts from one region to another.

gerrymandering Practice of drawing congressional boundaries to the advantage of one party.

minority-majority district District in which minority members are clustered together, producing a majority of minority voters in the district.

A person can bring suit in court under the Fourteenth Amendment to prevent a redistricting plan that gives one group an unfair advantage in affecting election outcomes.[16] However, the Supreme Court has concluded that it lacks clear standards for refereeing among competing plans in such cases.[17] As a consequence, political gerrymandering continues to this day. Party leaders in control of state legislative chambers work with demographic and political consultants to fashion districts that consolidate opposition voters into as few districts as possible, while expanding the reach of their own supporters.

In 2003, Texas undertook its second redistricting in a decade, thanks to an effort by state Republicans under the leadership of former House majority leader Tom DeLay. To offset potential congressional midterm losses for his party, DeLay urged Republicans in his home state to redraw the map to corral Democrats into fewer competitive seats. The effort succeeded in electing 21 Texas Republicans—more than in any other state—and unseating 7 Democrats. The Republican gains in Texas netted the party three additional seats in the 109th Congress. The Supreme Court in 2006 upheld the Texas redistricting plan, excepting one of the districts, which it determined placed Latinos at an electoral disadvantage.[18]

Some critics of Congress blame partisan redistricting for reducing competitiveness in House races. Reformers have called for the creation of nonpartisan commissions to take over the job from politicians with a vested interest in the outcome. Several states have already adopted such reforms. Studies show, however, that partisan redistricting is not entirely to blame for high levels of reelection of incumbents.[19] Demographic changes and the increased polarization of the electorate have led some districts and states to become more politically homogeneous,[20] potentially increasing the number of safe seats. We will revisit this issue at the end of this chapter.

Not all forms of redistricting, however, decrease the appeal of politics for voters. Beginning in the 1990s, the Justice Department promoted provisions of the Voting Rights Act that permitted creation of **minority-majority districts**. Such districts are formed by fitting together pockets of the minority populations, often constituting less than a majority of the district, to enhance the chances of electing the minority population's candidate of choice. This practice faced a court challenge as being discriminatory after the North Carolina legislature created a bizarrely shaped 165-mile-long majority-minority district that snaked along Interstate 85. The Supreme Court invalidated the district on the grounds that race cannot be the sole factor used in redrawing district boundaries. It left open the door to other gerrymandered districts where race is one but not the only consideration. In 2009, however, the Supreme Court limited the creation of such districts to those in which minorities make up at least 50 percent of the voting age population.[21]

There is some evidence that minority-majority districts increase participation by African Americans and Hispanic Americans without diminishing turnout among whites. Districts where African Americans and Hispanic Americans together constitute a majority report higher turnout among both groups.[22] Nevertheless, by compressing minorities into fewer districts, this form of gerrymandering may also increase the number of districts that elect white representatives who may be less attuned to the needs of minority populations.[23] As a result, racial gerrymandering may actually work against achieving the policies that many minorities support, even as it ensures a higher number of minority members in Congress.

DOING THE JOB: RESPONSIBILITIES AND BENEFITS

Once elected, members of the House of Representatives and the Senate face a variety of tasks besides their primary function of making laws. They must deal with constituents and represent their interests in government; meet with lobbyists and interest groups; consult with fellow members; and work with policy experts on their staffs. Members receive substantial resources to help them carry out these functions.

Representing the People

One of the oldest issues facing members of Congress is how to interpret their roles as representatives. Should representatives mirror the views of their constituents on all votes, or should they exercise their own judgment on behalf of the citizens who have elected them to make such decisions? A more recent debate has arisen around the question of whether the makeup of Congress should reflect the socioeconomic, gender, and racial composition of the nation. If not so, is our national legislature truly representative?

Roles of Representatives Members of Congress typically attempt to balance several roles in representing their constituents. Some assume a **delegate role**, attempting to champion the views of their constituents on crucial issues. However, given the hundreds of votes members must cast annually, it is impossible for them to know their constituents' will on every issue. In fact, their constituents may be indifferent to or uninformed about a number of issues on which members cast ballots. This does not mean that representatives are inattentive to the wishes of their constituents. As we will see, members and their staffs spend a lot of time on constituent communications. Often representatives see themselves as **trustees**, exercising their own judgment on behalf of those they serve. For example, a member of Congress privy to classified information may vote for increased security at airport terminals despite the wishes of an impatient flying public back home.

From a practical standpoint, most members of Congress jockey back and forth between delegate and trustee roles, a practice known as the **politico** role of representation. In some matters, representatives can ill afford to stray too far from constituent wishes. For example, representatives with a substantial number of senior citizens in their districts will not likely vote for cuts in Social Security. Similarly, representatives whose constituents include

> **delegate role** Theory of representation stressing the lawmaker's role as a tribune, who reflects the people's views on issues of the day.
>
> **trustee** Theory of representation stressing the lawmaker's own judgment in legislative decision making.
>
> **politico** Approach to representation in which the lawmaker alternates between trustee and delegate roles as he or she deems appropriate.

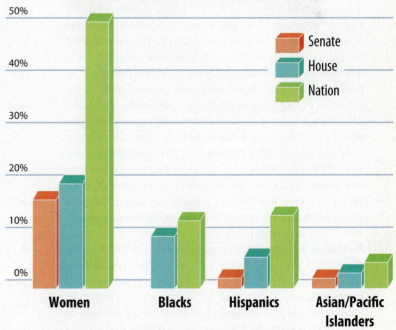

Not a Model of Diversity

Legend:
- Senate
- House
- Nation

Categories: Women, Blacks, Hispanics, Asian/Pacific Islanders

Source: CQ/Roll Call, *Guide to the New Congress,* November 4, 2010. Accessed December 12, 2010 at http://innovation.cq.com/newmember/2010elexnguide.pdf.

John Boehner (R-OH) became the new Speaker of the House in 2011 following the Republican takeover of the House in the midterm elections of 2010.

a high proportion of evangelical Christians are unlikely to vote for Medicaid coverage of abortion procedures. On issues about which their constituents are silent, most members are on their own.

How Representative Are Our Representatives? If the makeup of a "representative" political body must reflect the diversity of the population it represents, then the U.S. Congress is hardly representative. The membership is older, much better educated, more well off financially, and much less ethnically and racially diverse than the U.S. population at large. Some observers have referred to the members of Congress as primarily "pale, male, and stale." The average senator is in his or her early sixties; the average House member is in his or her late fifties. A majority of House and Senate members hold advanced degrees and come from occupations that are more prestigious and generally more lucrative than those held by the general population. Elective or appointed government office, business occupations like real estate or banking, and law predominate. They are more likely to belong to one of the many Protestant religious denominations, but Catholics make the second largest showing with more than 160 in both chambers. There are far fewer Jews or members of minority religions represented. Minorities are also generally underrepresented compared to their numerical strength in the overall population, and women are grossly underrepresented. However, Congress is becoming more diverse than it once was. More minorities and women hold leadership

positions. One of the most notable changes came in 2007 when Nancy Pelosi became the first female Speaker of the House, holding that position until Republicans recaptured the body in the 2010 midterm elections.

Although the electoral qualifications for Congress outlined in the Constitution are very broad and inclusive, the elite historically have made up the bulk of the membership. This long-standing trend reflects past patterns of discrimination, disparities in educational attainment, and difficulty in obtaining the financial resources necessary to make the long and costly run for office. Fortunately, these gaps are closing.

Pay and Perks

Benjamin Franklin proposed that elected government officials go unpaid for their service, but his views did not

Perks Aplenty: Benefits for Members of Congress

- Free office space in Washington, D.C., and in the home district

- A staff allowance (in 2007) of $831,252 for each House member and from $1,926,936 to $3,170,602 for clerical/administrative staff for Senators (depending on the population of the state and its distance from the Capitol). In addition, each Senator is authorized $472,677 to appoint up to three legislative assistants

- An expense account for telephone, stationery, and other office expenses

- Reimbursed travel to and from home district based on a formula using distance from Washington

- Routine or emergency medical health-care available on-site

- Travel allowance and free travel to foreign lands on congressional inquiries

- Extensive franking privileges

- Free access to video and film studios to record messages for constituents

- Free reserved parking at Reagan Washington National and Dulles Airports

- Discounted use of congressional gym

- Free assistance in preparation of income taxes

- Generous pension benefits

- Up to $3,000 tax deduction for living expenses while away from their districts or states

- Participation in Federal Employees Group Life Insurance Program

Source: Congressional Research Service, *Congressional Salaries and Allowances*, August 30, 2007.

carry the day. Instead, the Framers provided compensation to be paid from the federal treasury. From 1789 to 1815, members of Congress received $6 per day while Congress was in session. Members began receiving a salary in 1815, when they were paid $1,500 per year. Today, the members' annual salary is $174,000; salaries for party leaders are somewhat higher. All members receive retirement and health benefits under the same plans available to other federal employees. Additional benefits of holding office are listed in the figure on the previous page.

Home-Style Politics

Keeping in touch with constituents is vital both for members' electoral prospects and for the health of representative government. Members pursue a variety of activities to gauge the pulse of the community, such as holding town meetings in their districts, making themselves available to local press for interviews, and keeping close tabs on mail from back home. These "home-style" activities enable members to present themselves to the voters and to explain their actions in Washington.[24]

Representatives often first become aware of important issues confronting constituents through a personal communication such as a letter, fax, or phone call. These communications first pass through the hands of staff members, who sift through correspondence, tally support for issues coming up for a vote, and respond to constituents who wrote or called. They also select individual messages for the lawmaker's personal attention. Often, the letters the lawmaker sees come from high-profile constituents whose electoral support is important. Sometimes, they reflect a representative sample of opinion or simply provide a well-articulated perspective. Staff also carefully track mass mailings organized by interest groups—especially

those that are active in election-year politics—although these generally have less impact than more personalized communications. E-mail correspondence has increased the workload of staffers, and e-mail correspondence is quickly replacing mail as the primary vehicle for communication between constituents and Congress.[25]

Much of the mail a member receives involves a direct request for assistance. Staffers in the member's home district are responsible for fulfilling such requests. For example, if a veteran of the war in Iraq has difficulty obtaining a benefit to which he believes he is entitled, a call to the Department of Veterans Affairs from the office of his representative usually will resolve the problem. Such requests provide the lawmaker with the opportunity to serve as a constituent ombudsman, or personal liaison between citizens and government agencies, and filling them builds support for reelection. Constituent service can turn congressional offices into reelection machines that specialize in cultivating personal ties between constituents and representatives.[26]

Members initiate contact with constituents by mailing newsletters and questionnaires to let voters know what they are up to and solicit opinions about current issues. Increasingly, they are turning to websites to provide constituents with information about the members' legislative activities and to provide contact information for government services. Increasingly, members of Congress are reaching out to social networking sites like Facebook and Twitter to keep constituents apprised of their activities. There are even websites that track the electronic traffic of Congress members (e.g., http://legistalker.org, http://tweetcongress.org/). But lawmakers are still getting used to these modes of communicating and sometimes find themselves embarrassed by their use, as when Representative Pete Hoekstra (R-MI) found himself criticized for jeopardizing the security of House members by tweeting to constituents that he had just arrived in Baghdad with a congressional delegation. Lawmakers also use news conferences, interviews, and even one-minute speeches on the House floor to state positions on issues they believe will find favor with their constituents. Members usually reserve visits to their home districts to announce federal funding or grants they manage to secure for the region, a practice known as credit claiming.[27] Attention to home-style politics pays off for most members of Congress. Although only a minority of Americans approve of the way Congress as a whole is handling its job,[28] most believe their individual lawmaker is doing just fine—and most of the time they demonstrate their approval by returning the lawmaker to office.

Dealing with Organized Interests

Members of Congress interact frequently with lobbyists, or representatives from interest groups, to their mutual benefit. Because of the help these groups provide in cam-

Lobbyists are frequently given the opportunity to testify before congressional committees when legislation that affects their interests is debated.

The result is a cacophony that leads to an unstable legislative arena, where calm, dispassionate, and reasonable discussion is made more difficult.[30]

Lobbyists are especially interested in gaining access to committee chairs and members of committees with jurisdiction over issues important to their clients. Often this has been accomplished by performing favors like providing corporate jets for congressional travel or by raising funds for reelection campaigns. The often cozy relation between lobbyists and Congress carries with it the potential for sheer corruption. In 2005, the House forced Randy "Duke" Cunningham (R-CA) to resign after he pleaded guilty to accepting millions of dollars from defense contractors in return for using his position on the Defense Appropriations Subcommittee to steer lucrative contracts to these firms. In the face of public consternation, Congress passed a reform act in 2007 that restricts the amount and kind of gifts and travel lobbyists can provide to members of Congress, requires greater disclosure of lobbyist contributions, and lengthens the period of time for which former members of Congress, staffers, or certain members of the executive branch must refrain from lobbying their former colleagues. Additional prosecutions have accompanied this heightened scrutiny. The Office of Congressional Ethics was created to investigate ethics charges and refer misconduct charges to the House Ethics Com-

paigns and elections, they often gain favored access to Congress members and greater support for their causes. In addition to campaign contributions and voter mobilization, lobbyists and interest groups help members by supplying detailed information about the impact of legislation that only groups close to the policy may be in a position to offer. G. William Whitehurst, who represented Virginia for 18 years as a Republican member of the House, recalls "many instances when I emerged from a meeting with an industry lobbyist better informed and therefore better prepared to vote on legislation that was pending."[29] Whitehurst warned, however, about the volatile situation that results from the ever-increasing number and stridency of groups seeking access to lawmakers who, in turn, rely upon these groups for money and reelection support:

During an ethics violation investigation, Rep. Charles Rangel (D-NY) was forced to give up the chairmanship of the Ways and Means Committee. He was eventually censured by the entire House, a form of public shaming that falls short of the harshest penalty of expulsion.

mittee. One member, Charles Rangel (D-NY), was found guilty by the committee of 11 ethics violations. The Congressman was nevertheless reelected to a twenty-first term.

Working with Others

Meeting the demands of constituents, special interests, and party leadership requires legislators to rely on many other people for support. They must also learn to get along with colleagues and to adapt to the ways business is conducted in the chamber.

Personal Staff Members of Congress receive an allowance, based on the size of their districts and their role in leadership, to hire personal staff both in Washington, D.C., and in their offices back home. The Washington, D.C., staff generally tackles policy questions, whereas the district office handles much of the casework. An administrative assistant or chief of staff runs the Washington, D.C., office and monitors demands on the Congress member's time. A legislative director, or perhaps several of them, keeps the lawmaker informed about the issues coming up for a

vote and provides assessments of the merits of bills outside the lawmaker's expertise. The office likely also includes a press secretary to deal with media inquiries, an appointment secretary to schedule the lawmaker's limited time, and a number of interns and office assistants who monitor constituent requests and handle mail. Administrative assistants and caseworkers make up the bulk of the staff in home district offices. On average, about 30 people work for each senator—about half that number are employed by House members.

Staffers are an important link for citizens with their government. Members of Congress, whose time is severely limited, rarely meet directly with citizen advocates. Instead, citizens meet with staffers, who are trained to be responsive and, in most cases, diligently share the messages of constituents in meetings with the lawmaker.

Committee Staff Lawmakers also work closely with staff specialists attached to the committees or subcommittees on which the members hold assignments. Committee staffers are highly trained professionals with rich expertise in policy and procedure, who provide detailed assessments of policy problems and options for members

Allison Luczak

PORTRAIT OF AN ACTIVIST

Meet Allison Luczak, Congressional Intern

A French and political science major with an abiding interest in politics, Allison attended one of her congressman's local appearances near the midwestern town where she attends college. His discussion sparked her interest in a bill he was sponsoring, so she stayed after the meeting to

speak with him personally. "A week later, I found myself interning and had my first assignment clipping newspapers," says Allison.

Allison worked 20 hours a week in the representative's home district office. She had the opportunity to work on some exciting projects. "The main project that I worked on was the Student Leadership Forum on Faith and Values," Allison explains. "I was responsible for coordinating student nominations and arranging speakers for a weekend-long forum where college students from around the state shared stories of volunteerism and planned faith-based events in their local communities."

Allison also helped plan a ceremony where the congressman distributed the Jubilee of Liberty Medal. This medal is awarded to World War II veterans of the Normandy invasion in 1944. "I was proud to be a part of the effort to distribute the medals," says Allison. "It was especially rewarding to see the pride in the veterans' faces when they received overdue praise for the valor they displayed on behalf of the nation.

"The impact my internship has had on me is twofold," Allison says. "First, I now understand what it means to be a public servant. The best politicians are those who are empathetic, driven, and truly committed to others. Being a public official is not about oneself; it is about the common good and understanding each other, despite our ideological differences. Second, I have come to realize that sticking to whatever the party believes is illogical; my values and beliefs are firm, yet my opinions are subject to change. We cannot expect the world to adapt to us, we must adapt ourselves."

Most members of Congress hire student interns to work in their offices both in Washington, D.C., and in their home districts. To apply, contact the office of your representative or senator or log on to their websites, where internship opportunities are usually posted. Interns perform such tasks as answering telephones, running errands, helping answer mail, scheduling meetings, and researching constituent problems. Most internships are unpaid positions, so they are not for everybody. Nevertheless, they are a valuable source of knowledge and provide great contacts for career advancement.

Colleagues Of course, lawmakers also work closely with other lawmakers. Legislators meet with members of their own party to discuss legislative strategy, and with smaller groups of like-minded members to discuss common interests. These groups are known as **congressional caucuses**. Independent members, and those from third parties, must choose to caucus or meet with one or the other political party in order to have a voice in setting legislative priorities. Two Senate Independents, Bernie Sanders from Vermont and Joe Lieberman from Connecticut, choose to meet with the Democrats. Party caucuses are places where party members can work out sometimes-contentious issues that threaten party unity. Nonparty caucuses, such as the Congressional Black Caucus and the Congressional Caucus for Women's Issues, organize to discuss issues of common concern to members, but they often lack both funding and official recognition by the chamber.

to consider in drafting legislation. Committee staffers are generally older and more experienced than members of lawmakers' personal staffs. The size of a committee's staff varies according to the committee's size and jurisdiction. In the House, the average size of a committee staff is about 65; in the Senate, it is about 50. Staff composition is split between majority and minority party appointees, with the majority party always enjoying more appointments. Congress also uses professional staff to maintain specialized service agencies like the Congressional Budget Office, which provides detailed assessments of budget proposals; the Government Accountability Office, which supplies agency audits; and the Congressional Research Service, which produces specialized reports on a variety of topics at the request of members.

congressional caucuses
Party or special-interest groups formed by like-minded members of Congress to confer on issues of mutual concern.

Lawmakers' reliance on committee staff raises questions about the influence these unelected professionals have on legislation. Staffers, who often have more knowledge of the details of legislation than lawmakers, frequently assume responsibility for drafting bills, negotiating with opponents, and forging agreements. This can produce embarrassing results—or worse. After Congress passed the omnibus budget bill of 2004, it was forced to retract one provision, inserted by a staffer, which allowed members of Congress to inspect tax returns from individual citizens, a practice the courts have long held to be illegal.[31]

Getting Along Political scientists have long observed a number of norms, or practices of professional conduct, members rely upon to minimize personal conflict with colleagues. Members often demonstrate courtesy or cordiality by the ways in which they refer to one another during floor debates. Even during heated arguments, members will usually address each other as "colleagues" or "friends." For years, newcomers refrained from grandstanding to advance their personal careers. Instead, they followed the lead of more senior members to become specialists in the legislative work of their committees and cooperated with their colleagues in producing compromise legislation. The increasing partisan polarization of Congress in recent years has weakened, although not yet extinguished, many of these norms.[32]

KEYS TO POLITICAL POWER

The principal role of the legislative branch is making laws. To help it perform this function more efficiently, Congress divides its workload among smaller bodies called committees, which may be further divided into subcommittees. The process of lawmaking is complex; lawmakers who occupy key positions of authority and understand the intricacies of the legislative process can make a dramatic difference in advancing legislation or stopping it in its tracks.

The Committee System

Committees allow members of Congress to scrutinize particular types of legislation in depth, enabling committee members to develop expertise in certain topic areas. The real work of lawmaking occurs in these so-called "little legislatures." There are four basic types of committees: standing, select, joint, and conference.

Standing Committees These permanent committees, which continue from session to session, have jurisdiction in a variety of subject areas. Committee size varies depending on jurisdiction, with the House average near 40 committee members and the Senate about half that number. Standing committees typically feature subcommittees that have expertise in specific areas. For example, the Senate Committee on Foreign Relations consists of seven subcommittees that focus on different geographical regions and topic areas.

A member of the House may sit on as many as two full committees and four subcommittees, although members sitting on the most influential and time-consuming committees, like Appropriations, have fewer assignments.

Subcommittees of the Senate Committee on Foreign Relations

- Subcommittee on Western Hemisphere, Peace Corps, and Narcotics Affairs
- Subcommittee on Near Eastern and South and Central Asian Affairs
- Subcommittee on African Affairs
- Subcommittee on East Asian and Pacific Affairs
- Subcommittee on International Organizations, Human Rights, Democracy, and Global Women's Issues
- Subcommittee on European Affairs
- Subcommittee on International Development and Foreign Assistance, Economic Affairs, and International Environmental Protection

Source: U.S. Senate.

Senators may serve on even more committees, depending on the importance of the committee's role in the legislative process. Since each committee must meet at least once a month, members stay busy familiarizing themselves with bills under consideration and working with committee staff in order to stay on top of their workload.

Committees in the House and Senate in 112th Congress, 2011–2012

House Standing Committees	Senate Standing Committes
Agriculture	Agriculture, Nutrition, and Forestry
Appropriations	Appropriations
Armed Services	Armed Services
Budget	Banking, Housing, and Urban Affairs
Education and the Workforce	Budget
Energy and Commerce	Commerce, Science and Transportation
Ethics	Energy and Natural Resources
Financial Services	Environment and Public Works
Foreign Affairs	Finance
Homeland Security	Foreign Relations
House Administration	Health, Education, Labor, and Pensions
Judiciary	Homeland Security and Governmental Affairs
Natural Resources	Judiciary
Oversight and Government Reform	Rules and Administration
Rules	Small Business and Entrepreneurship
Science, Space, and Technology	Veterans' Affairs
Small Business	
Transportation and Infrastructure	
Veterans' Affairs	
Ways and Means	

Source: U.S. House of Representatives; U.S. Senate.

Top 10 States: Pork per Capita

2009 Rank	State	2009 Pork	Population
1	Alaska	$221,222,875	686,293
	Pork per Capita		$322.34
2	Hawaii	$302,678,707	1,288,198
			$234.96
3	North Dakota	$142,549,091	641,481
			$222.22
4	District of Columbia	$109,794,850	591,833
			$185.52
5	West Virginia	$257,635,000	1,814,468
			$141.99
6	New Mexico	$267,138,821	1,984,356
			$134.62
7	South Dakota	$106,070,750	804,194
			$131.90
8	Vermont	$76,944,280	621,270
			$123.85
9	Mississippi	$331,472,118	2,938,618
			$112.80
10	Delaware	$75,966,820	873,092
			$87.01

Source: Citizens Against Government Waste Pig Book 2009. Accessed on May 29, 2009 at http://membership.cagw.org/site/PageServer?pagename=reports_pigbook2009_porkpercap.

The majority party controls most of the seats on each committee, including the leadership positions. The distribution of committee seats usually reflects the party makeup of the body as a whole. Subcommittee assignments also reflect party balance and longevity, with party members bidding for available slots on the basis of seniority. Committees that deal with the ethical behavior of members, such as the Committee on Standards of Official Conduct in the House and the Senate's Select Committee on Ethics, are exceptions to these rules, containing equal numbers of Republicans and Democrats.

Both the House and the Senate employ party committees to nominate members for seats on standing committees. For Republicans, the Steering Committee performs this function in the House, and the Committee on Committees does so in the Senate. Democrats employ a Steering Committee in each chamber. Experienced members receive requested committee appointments more often than do freshman representatives, although seniority is no longer as important as it once was. A freshman's chance of attaining a desired assignment depends on a number of factors, including party, interest and expertise, the size and importance of his or her legislative district, and the member's ties to leadership. Leaders sometimes intervene to ensure that newly elected members from important districts get slots that maximize their public exposure and showcase their talents to constituents back home. Once assigned to a committee, members are expected to develop expertise on the subject of the committee's concern, usually with the aid of policy specialists on the committee staff.

Not all standing committees have equal status or power. Committees dealing with spending and taxes, such as the Appropriations and Ways and Means committees in the House and the Budget Committee in the Senate, are considered the most powerful. These committees can be crucial for serving the re-election needs of members because they approve **pork barrel projects** designed to fund popular ventures in members' districts. Sending federal dollars back to the home district allows members to show that they are making a tangible impact on the lives of constituents.

Many pork projects appear ridiculous to the casual observer. For example, the 2009 budget included $1,900,000 for the Pleasure Beach Water Taxi Service Project and $1,791,000 for swine odor and manure management research. A nonpartisan budget watchdog organization estimates that the 2009 budget included more than $29 of pork per citizen, although some states received much more than others.[33] Most of what is deemed "pork" is inserted in the form of **earmarks**, funding requests for specific projects that are added to appropriation bills by individual members, usually without oversight or public debate. Faced with mounting criticism of such spending in the media, House Republicans banned earmarks from future budgets. The Senate voted down an outright ban, but President Obama vowed to veto any legislation containing earmarks. Millions of dollars in earmarks were cut from the 2011 budget as Congress and the President worked to reduce the federal deficit. Still, the future of earmarks is uncertain. Wrangling is likely to continue about whether money narrowly targeted in appropriations bills to specific industries in specific districts constitutes an earmark since it is not a stand-alone item outside of the budgeting process. Newcomers who oppose earmarks may also find it increasingly difficult to maintain their positions when confronted by interests long accustomed to federal financing. Although controversial, pork projects mean real money for constituent groups back home and bragging rights for the members who secure them.

In the House, the Committee on Rules is of special importance because of the role it plays in fashioning the terms for debate and amendment of bills coming to the floor. Often these rules mean the difference between passage and defeat, and the majority party guards its control of procedures by assigning two-thirds of the members to this body. The Rules Committee also may initiate legislation on its own; Congress gives immediate consideration to measures the Rules Committee brings to the floor.

Select Committees The leadership of each house usually appoints select committees for a limited period to handle matters that do not routinely fit into areas of standing committee jurisdiction. For example, the House or Senate may create a committee to investigate official misconduct or inquire into unique events or problems. The activity of select committees usually culminates with official reports that the members may or may not use to generate legislation to be considered by other committees. For example, the House and Senate together created a Special Select Committee on Deficit Reduction after the 2011 debt ceiling crisis to find ways to slash $1.5 trillion from the federal budget over the next 10 years. They were to report their results to Congress for an up or down vote.

Some select committees act more like permanent standing committees. For example, the House Permanent Select Committee on Intelligence, first created in 1977, continues to hold hearings on various aspects of intelligence gathering and threats to national security. Combating global warming was an issue she and fellow California Democrats had championed but one which was resisted by Republican opponents.

Joint Committees Joint committees include members from both houses and can be either temporary or permanent. Most do not handle legislation, but monitor and report on activities of government agencies. For example, the Joint Committee on Taxation reviews tax policy and the operation of the Internal Revenue Service. Party leaders in each house appoint the members of joint committees.

Conference Committees Before sending legislation to the president for approval, the House and Senate must pass identical versions of the same law. When conflicting versions emerge, the leadership in each house selects members for a conference committee that attempts to resolve differences. Only after both the House and the Senate approve the conference reports of these committees can legislation move to the president's desk. When a single party controls both houses of Congress, conference committees concentrate mainly on accommodating the wishes of majority-party members in both chambers. In such cases, the opposition can be relied on to complain about being excluded.

Party

The majority party—the one with more elected members—controls the chamber. The majority party determines the organizational structure, the composition of internal bodies such as committees and subcommittees, positions of leadership, and the flow of the legislation itself. The minority party plays a role, but its impact is small by comparison, especially if the majority party also controls the White House. Republicans gained control of the House in the 2010 elections, spurred by voter anger with President Obama's policies, high unemployment, growing deficits, an enthusiastic Republican base in the face of dispirited Democrats, and traditional midterm voter falloff. Speaker John Boehner (R-OH) presides over a caucus which now includes a number of "tea party" supporters who helped drive out moderate establishment Republicans in 2010, moving his party farther to

pork barrel projects Term applied to spending for pet projects of individual members of Congress.

earmarks Funding for specific projects that are added by members of Congress to appropriation bills usually without oversight or public debate.

> # Did You Know?
>
> *. . . That the term* pork barrel *legislation refers to the practice of plantation owners taking salt pork from barrels to give to their slaves as a treat.*

Party Control of the 112th Congress, 2011–2013

Party Composition of the U.S. House

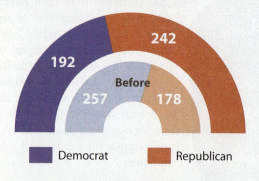

242

192

Before

257   178

Democrat   **Republican**

Party Composition of the U.S. Senate

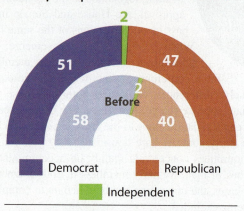

2

51   47

2
Before

58   40

Democrat   **Republican**

Independent

Source: Office of the Clerk, U.S. House of Representatives.

the right and making it more difficult for him to find common ground with Democrats.

When Congress changes hands, the new majority can be expected to alter House rules to more easily control the agenda and matters coming to the floor. In 2011, incoming Republicans reinstated a six year term limit on committee chairs that Democrats had previously removed, required sponsors of legislation to submit statements tying bills to constitutional authority, and required bills to be posted online for three calendar days before final floor consideration. In addition, they made several changes to the budgeting process including a requirement that new mandatory spending (but not tax cuts) be offset with cuts to existing programs.

Changes in party composition in both chambers since the 1980s reflect changes in the electorate. The Democrats thus have fewer members representing conservative constituencies, giving them a more liberal tilt as a group. Similarly, Republicans have tilted toward greater conservatism

Bob Turner added to the Republican majority in the House when he scored an upset victory in a heavily Democratic district in a special election to replace disgraced New York Congressman Anthony Weiner.

by picking up strength among traditionally conservative constituencies in the South.

Just as a closely divided electorate has produced divisive partisan campaigns, a closely divided Congress has produced a highly charged partisan environment in both chambers. One indicator of the intensity of partisan conflict is party unity, or the extent to which members of each party vote together and in opposition to members of the other party. Since the early 1990s, members have increasingly tended to vote along party lines, making it more difficult for moderate members of each party to reach bipartisan consensus. House Democrats voted with their party 89 percent of the time in 2010, slightly less than the 92 percent record they set in 2008. Senate Democrats voted with their party 91 percent of the time, matching their 2009 score. Party unity for Republicans was only slightly lower at 88 percent in the House and 89 percent in the Senate.[34]

With fewer moderates on both sides of the aisle, traditional civility and decorum sometimes break down, making it more difficult to forge the kind of bipartisan consensus necessary to deal with controversial problems such as health-care reform. The breakdown in civility was evident during President Obama's September 9, 2009, address to a joint session of Congress on health care. An opponent of the plan, Representative Joe Wilson (R-SC), interrupted the president's message, shouting "You lie!" which created bitterness among some members of the president's party. Partisan strife is evident in other ways as well. When the Democrats took control in 2007, they promised greater openness and flexibility in the rules of debate to allow an opportunity for the parties to work together. Although the session may have started out with good intentions, decorum broke down by midsummer, and studies showed the flexibility promised by Democrats had all but evaporated.[35] Partisan bickering in Congress turns many Americans away from politics and may reduce civic involvement. Not everyone is dissatisfied with this situation, however. Surveys show that voters whose party controls the majority

Soaring Partisanship in Congress

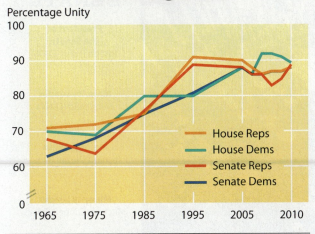

Percentage Unity

House Reps
House Dems
Senate Reps
Senate Dems

Source: Congressional Quarterly Weekly, January 3, 2011, 23.

are much more satisfied with the institution than are voters from the minority party or independents.[36]

Although the Democrats have shown great cohesion in voting recently, they by no means vote in lockstep. The overall liberal orientation of party members is blunted by a sizable number of so-called "blue dog" Democrats from southern and midwestern states whose orientation is more conservative, especially where government spending is concerned. This group argued for reductions in the president's stimulus plan and made passage of health-care reform more difficult by insisting on reducing its overall cost. It is the job of majority party leaders (discussed later) to find enough common ground among members to pass legislative items high on their agenda. Often the minority party need find only a few dissenting members of the majority to foil such plans.

Getting legislation passed is sometimes made more difficult in times of divided government when one party controls one or both houses of Congress and the other party controls the White House. Divided government has become more frequent in recent decades. We have experienced divided government during 14 of the last 20 sessions of Congress (1973–2011). Some political scientists believe that about the same amount of legislation passes under divided government as under unified government, when the same party controls both branches, and that divided government forces parties to reach across the aisle to get things done.[37] There have been some notable legislative successes in periods of divided rule. For example, President Clinton worked with Republicans after they took control of Congress in 1994 to pass landmark welfare reform. President George W. Bush worked across party lines with Senator Ted Kennedy (D-MA) to produce the No Child Left Behind Act. Voters often tell pollsters that they prefer divided government because it acts as an additional check on legislative excess. However, divided government slows down the legislative process, and may dilute legislation as a result of efforts to achieve con-

sensus.[38] It may also result in the failure to enact important legislation—especially when the legislation is initiated by Congress and opposed by the sitting president of the opposition party.[39]

Position

Parties control leadership positions in both houses, and the majority party always controls the most important offices. The majority party always has more seats on every committee than the minority party, based roughly on the proportion of seats each party controls in the chamber. Every committee chair is likewise always a member of the majority party. In addition, the majority party controls the top leadership positions responsible for the scheduling and flow of the legislative process. Just as Congress itself has adopted a more partisan outlook in recent years, so too have its leaders. Leaders are increasingly chosen for their ability to frame issues along party lines, for their skill in controlling the legislative agenda, and for their ability to raise funds for fellow party members.[40]

House Leadership The most powerful leader in the lower chamber is the **Speaker of the House**. The majority party selects one of its members to be Speaker, subject to approval by the entire House membership. The Speaker refers bills to committees for consideration and appoints members of the majority party to sit on some of the most powerful House committees, as well as all members of select and conference committees. Some of the most significant appointments are to the Committee on Rules, which sets conditions for debate. Rules can be an important source of power. Rules that extend debate can be an invitation to compromise; rules that limit debate may silence dissent. The Speaker schedules legislation for floor consideration and may choose to preside over sessions of the body, although this is frequently delegated to another member of the majority party. The Speaker helps control the flow of debate and exercises wide discretion in interpreting and applying parliamentary rules. As the one individual with a commanding view of the entire legislative process, the Speaker is in a position to know the status of all legislation at all times and has the ability to influence its course. Although the Speaker is entitled to debate and vote on all legislation, she or he normally only votes on matters of great importance or when his or her vote would be decisive.

The House has a long history of Speakers who have wielded considerable authority, such as "Uncle Joe" Cannon, who dictated House policy at the turn of the last century. Sam Rayburn (D-TX) served as Speaker three times from 1940 to 1961, with two interruptions of service when Republicans controlled the chamber. Rayburn won notoriety and respect for using his command of House rules to win passage of civil rights reform despite the opposition of southern Democrats. Newt Gingrich (R-GA), who

> **Speaker of the House** The most powerful leader of the House of Representatives.

Congressional Leadership

HOUSE

Speaker of the House
John Boehner (R-OH)

Majority Leader
Eric Cantor (R-VA)

Majority Whip
Kevin McCarthy (R-CA)

Minority Leader
Nancy Pelosi (D-CA)

Minority Whip
Steny Hoyer (D-MD)

SENATE

President of the Senate
Joseph Biden (D-DE)

Majority Leader
Harry Reid (D-NV)

Majority Whip
Richard Durbin (D-IL)

Minority Leader
Mitch McConnell (R-KY)

Minority Whip
Jon Kyl (R-AZ)

majority leader Leader of the majority party in each house, responsible for marshaling support for the party's agenda.

minority leader Leader of the minority party in each house, responsible for marshaling support for the party's agenda.

whips Assistant party leaders in each house whose jobs include ensuring that party members are present for floor votes and prepared to vote as the party prefers.

logrolling The practice of trading votes to the mutual advantage of members.

president pro tempore The second-highest-ranking official in the U.S. Senate.

served from 1995 to 1999, engineered the modern resurgence of the Republican Party in Congress. Nancy Pelosi (D-CA), the first woman to hold the office (2007–2011), lost the position to John Boehner (R-OH) when Republicans regained the House in the 2010 midterm elections.

Members of the majority party elect a **majority leader**, who assists the Speaker in setting the legislative agenda in the House. The majority leader works to generate support for the positions of party leaders, acts as a spokesperson for the party's legislative program, helps shepherd the party's legislation through the lawmaking process, and assists in scheduling floor action and the flow of debate. Majority leaders can enforce voting discipline among party members by influencing appointments to important committees, responding to staffing requests, and lending support to a member's legislation. Of course, the majority leader can also withhold favors from a member who fails to support the party's legislative agenda. Tom DeLay (R-TX), who assumed the position of majority leader in 2002, earned the nickname "The Hammer" because of his power in enforcing discipline among party members. Eric Cantor (R-VA), the current Majority Leader, has built a reservoir of personal support from his party's most conservative members that gives him political clout rivaling the Speaker's.

The minority party also selects a leader to advance its own agenda in the legislative process. This is not an easy job when the opposition holds the levers of power. Nevertheless, the **minority leader** can speak out on issues important to members, put pressure on majority-party leaders to hold hearings on controversial issues, and organize floor debate among minority-party members. The majority party may consult the minority leader on scheduling and developing procedures for floor debate, but the minority rarely has an equal voice in negotiations.

Each party also employs elected **whips**, assistant party leaders, who are responsible for building support for a party's agenda and ensuring that members are present and prepared to vote as their parties prefer. Whips also help negotiate agreements among members to trade votes so that each benefits from the actions of the other, a practice known as **logrolling**.

Senate Leadership The leadership structure in the Senate is similar to that of the House, with only a few differences at the very top. The Constitution specifies that the vice president of the United States serve as the president of the Senate, with the authority to preside over the body and to vote in case of a tie. Beyond this, the vice president exercises very little real authority in the Senate. Instead, the Senate selects a **president pro tempore**, a Latin term meaning "for a time" or temporary, to preside over meetings. Most often, the position goes to the member of the majority party who has served the longest. In actual practice, even this individual rarely carries out the duties of presiding officer. Most often, the position rotates among junior members.

The Senate majority leader is the body's most influential member, exercising responsibilities associated with both the Speaker of the House and the House majority leader. A party caucus elects the majority leader, who speaks for the party and is responsible for developing and passing the party's agenda in the Senate. As in the House, the Senate majority leader works with a minority-party leader (chosen by a minority caucus) to schedule bills for floor action and to determine limits on debate. Both majority and minority leaders work with elected whips to keep their respective parties united on roll call votes.

Senators pride themselves on their independence, making the Senate majority leader's job more difficult than that of the Speaker of the House. The Senate majority leader is considered only "first among equals." The current majority leader, Harry Reid (D-NV), faced difficulty in keeping his party united during the 110th Congress when the Republicans controlled the White House but has found his job no easier with a Democratic president and a commanding majority in the chamber. The Senate has seen its share of notable leaders. Among the most powerful was Lyndon Johnson, famous for his command of chamber rules and his ability to cajole, barter, and lecture his way into obtaining members' support for his party's agenda—even if he had to shadow them into the men's room to do so.

Committee Leadership Committee chairs enjoy substantial powers to facilitate action on the thousands of bills and resolutions introduced each session (between 8,000 and 10,000 in the House; between 3,100 and 4,500 in the Senate). Chairs can direct bills to subcommittees, appoint subcommittee chairs, set subcommittee staff and budget levels, and decide which bills get a hearing and,

consequently, which are eligible for a vote of the entire chamber.

Generally, the senior member of the majority party on a committee serves as its chairperson. Members traditionally have worked their way into leadership positions through a combination of attrition and continuous committee service. Allocating chairs by seniority preserves harmony by limiting political competition among members of the same party. Although seniority continues to be the norm, since the 1970s both parties have adopted rules that weaken the seniority system, and both parties have unseated presumptive chairs in favor of candidates considered more suitable by party leaders. For example, Democrats in 2009 ousted longtime Energy and Commerce Committee chair, John Dingell (D-MI) and replaced him with the more junior Henry Waxman (D-CA), partly because Waxman was seen as more receptive to climate-change legislation favored by the Speaker.

> **committee chairs** The leaders of congressional committees, usually members of the majority party with the most seniority on that committee.

Senate majority leader Lyndon Johnson had a reputation for "getting in your face" when he needed support for his party's legislative agenda.

In each Senate committee, members of the majority party select a chair via a secret ballot, which must be affirmed by another secret ballot of majority-party members in the entire chamber. Powers of Senate chairs are compa-

Once a bill is voted out of the authorizing committees, the House usually considers the legislation under special rules adopted by the **Committee on Rules**, which determine the procedures under which floor debate on each bill

"YOU DON'T JUST HAVE AN IDEA, draft it in bill form, and drop it in the House hopper or file it at the Senate desk. Developing the idea is very much a political process—listening to the needs and desires of people and then trying to translate it into a specific legislative proposal."

rable to those of their House counterparts and—despite the greater independence of members in this chamber—chairs have come under increasing pressure by party leaders to toe the party line. Studies of the 110th Congress showed that committee chairs were among the most liberal members of an ideologically cohesive liberal caucus. This is yet another factor that helps explain the increasingly partisan tone of the body.[41]

The highest-ranking member of the minority party on a committee is called the ranking minority member. Usually the senior minority member on the committee, he or she shares very few of the powers of the chair, but can sometimes draw attention to issues and viewpoints that differ from those of the majority party. Since they have no power to convene meetings or issue subpoenas for witnesses on their own, ranking minority members have sometimes staged "mock" hearings to air their party's positions.

Procedures

A 20-year veteran of Congress, Representative Robert S. Walker (R-PA), offered this piece of advice about Congress: "Those who understand the rules can control the process."[42] The Constitution authorizes each house to determine its own rules and procedures. Rules are especially important in the House of Representatives because of the sheer number of members and the number of bills introduced during each two-year session. House committee chairs or party leaders can bottle up legislation without releasing it to the floor for a vote. The only vehicle for freeing the legislation is a **discharge petition**, requiring the signatures of 218 members. This strategy is rarely successful, but when sufficient discontent spurs strong support for a measure that is blocked by committee, House leaders will often yield.

discharge petition Method for freeing legislation from a committee in the House that requires the signatures of 218 members.

Committee on Rules In the House of Representatives, the committee charged with determining rules for debate, amendment, and vote on bills brought to the floor.

filibuster Senate practice of continuous debate often employed to stop pending legislative action.

will occur. These include rules concerning the length of time allotted for debate and whether or not members may propose amendments. Drafted in accord with the wishes of the majority leadership, the rules frequently affect the outcome of the vote. All floor debate must be germane, that is, pertinent to the topic at hand, so that members cannot stall by diverting attention to other matters.

Senate rules are more flexible—but potentially more potent—reflecting the body's historical preference for deliberation rather than speed. As in the House, they can affect the outcome of legislative action. The Senate majority leader will schedule and bring matters to the floor for debate, sometimes in consultation with the minority leader. The majority leader can request—and usually receives—unanimous consent to waive rules that permit extensive debate. If senators object, however, debate may be unlimited. Such debate may take the form of a **filibuster** in which opponents of the legislation hold the floor for an unlimited period in the hope that the bill will be withdrawn or amended. In addition, the Senate has no rule requiring germaneness. As a result, a senator may discuss matters unrelated to the bill. Strom Thurmond (R-SC) holds the record for the longest single filibuster speech. He spoke continuously for 24 hours and 18 minutes in his successful effort to defeat a civil rights bill in 1957. Huey P. Long (D-LA) held the floor for more than 15 hours in an effort to defeat an extension of the National Industrial Recovery Act in 1935, entertaining his colleagues with a recitation of southern recipes.[43]

Members can end a filibuster through a procedure known as **cloture**. To invoke cloture, at least 16 members must sign a petition to close debate. Within two days of filing the petition, 60 senators (a three-fifths majority) must vote to end debate. If cloture succeeds, debate is limited to an additional 30 hours. In recent years, partisan divisions have caused the number of filibuster threats and cloture votes to skyrocket. Whereas there were 58 cloture votes taken during the last years of the Clinton presidency, that number swelled to 112 during the last years of the Bush White House.

Even a lone senator can use procedures to stymie action. For example, an individual senator can place a **hold** on an issue before the membership votes on it. The hold prevents any action from being taken on the issue until the leadership consults with the senator and addresses his or her concerns.

THE FUNCTIONS OF CONGRESS

Lawmaking is the preeminent function of Congress, but the body also exercises the powers to declare war, to monitor the actions of the executive agencies it creates, to impeach and try federal officials, and to fund the federal government through the budget process. In addition, the Senate ratifies treaties and confirms presidential appointments.

Lawmaking

Former congressman Lee Hamilton (D-IN) blanches when he sees diagrams illustrating how laws are made. "How boring! How sterile!" he complains. Indeed, what diagrams miss are the intricacies of interpersonal relations necessary to win support for one's cause.

You don't just have an idea, draft it in bill form, and drop it in the House hopper or file it at the Senate desk. Developing the idea is very much a political process—listening to the needs and desires of people and then

cloture The procedure that ends a filibuster with 60 votes of the Senate.

hold Action a senator may place on a bill requiring personal consultation before the matter can proceed.

Formal Procedure: How a Bill Becomes Law

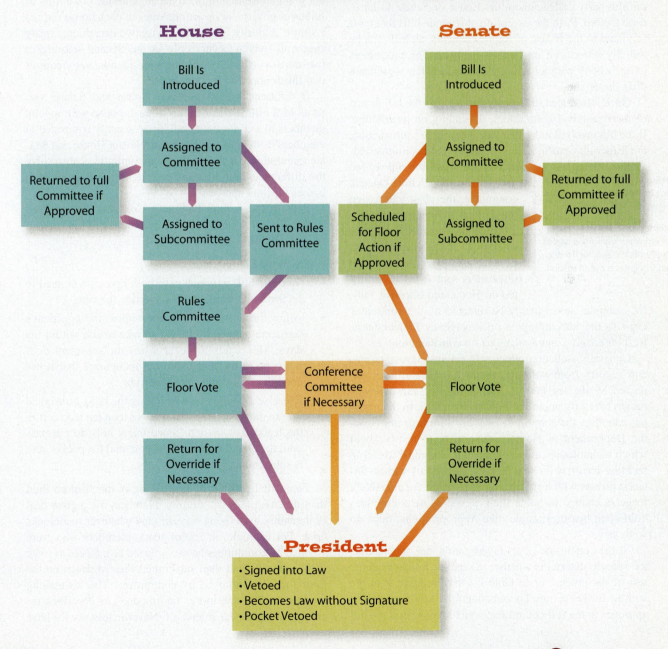

House

- Bill Is Introduced
- Assigned to Committee
- Returned to full Committee if Approved
- Assigned to Subcommittee
- Sent to Rules Committee
- Rules Committee
- Floor Vote
- Return for Override if Necessary

Senate

- Bill Is Introduced
- Assigned to Committee
- Returned to full Committee if Approved
- Assigned to Subcommittee
- Scheduled for Floor Action if Approved
- Floor Vote
- Return for Override if Necessary

Conference Committee if Necessary

President

- Signed into Law
- Vetoed
- Becomes Law without Signature
- Pocket Vetoed

trying to translate it into a specific legislative proposal. Even the earliest stages of drafting a bill involve much maneuvering. The member needs to consult with colleagues, experts, and interest groups to refine and sharpen the idea; gauge the political impact and viability of the proposal (especially with constituents); determine how to formulate the idea so it appeals to a majority of colleagues; study how it differs from and improves upon related proposals introduced in the past; decide how broadly or narrowly to draft it (to avoid it being sent to too many committees); and decide how to draft it so it gets sent to a sympathetic rather than an unsympathetic committee.[44]

With this caveat in mind, we nevertheless can sketch the formal course a bill must take in wending its way through the legislative chambers.

Bills must pass both houses to be eligible for presidential action. Much legislation today actually originates in the White House. In such cases, the president engages faithful party colleagues in the House or Senate to introduce the bill. With the exception of revenue bills that must originate in the House of Representatives, all bills can be initially introduced into either chamber. The procedures in each body parallel one another with a few significant differences.

Once introduced, the leadership assigns the bill to one or more standing committees, depending on jurisdiction. If the bill involves more than one committee's jurisdiction, the leader may partition it so that different committees address portions of the bill related to their own jurisdiction. Once in committee, the chair can assign the bill to a subcommittee for more detailed analysis and consideration. A bill dealing with new technology for use by first responders sent to the Committee on Homeland Security, may, for example, subsequently be directed by the committee chair to the Subcommittee on Emergency Preparedness, Response, and Communications for consideration.

markup Committee sessions in which members review contents of legislation line by line.

pocket veto Automatic veto achieved when a bill sits unsigned on a president's desk for 10 days when Congress is out of session.

Generally, subcommittees will request investigations and reports from various executive-branch offices impacted by the legislation. The committee can call witnesses to testify about the impact of the bill. In the previous example, the committee may call administrators from the Department of Homeland Security to testify about which technologies they believe to be the most useful in tackling terrorist threats. Representatives of various interest groups with a stake in the legislation are also likely to get a chance to voice their views. Most committees hold open hearings; some, like Appropriations, must do so by law.

At the conclusion of its investigation, the subcommittee votes to determine whether to send the bill through the rest of the process or to table it—that is, leave it to die without further action. The subcommittee sends each bill it approves to the full committee, which may amend the bill and subject it to a process known as **markup**, which involves reviewing and approving its language. The mortality rate for bills in committee is very high, approximately 90 percent, with most bills failing to gain sufficient support of party leaders to warrant further action.

In the House, bills approved by committees proceed to the Rules Committee, whose members prescribe procedures for debate and amendment on the floor. From Rules it proceeds to one of several calendars for scheduling. However, party leadership has a strong hand in determining when important bills are taken up by the entire body. The legislation is then debated on the floor where it must receive the support of a majority of members for passage. There is no parallel committee in the Senate that sets rules on a bill-by-bill basis. Instead, the Senate leadership will ask for unanimous consent regarding debate limits that the majority leader previously worked out with interested senators from both parties. If the full Senate does not grant consent, unlimited debate with the possibility of filibuster governs floor action. Votes in each house require a simple majority for passage, with two exceptions: treaty approval—which occurs only in the Senate—requires a two-thirds vote, and overriding a presidential veto requires two-thirds approval by both houses.

If differences exist between House and Senate versions of a bill, the leadership of each house will appoint members to a conference committee, usually composed of members from both parties on the relevant House and Senate committees. If the conference committee can resolve the differences, the measure returns to the floor of both bodies for final approval.

Bills that pass both houses of Congress then proceed to the White House, where the president can take one of several actions:

• Sign the bill into law.

• Veto the bill, in which case both houses will need to secure a two-thirds vote to override the veto.

• Allow the bill to become law without the president's signature simply by failing to take action within ten days. This tends to occur when the president does not support the legislation but recognizes that it has enough support for a veto override.

• Exercise a **pocket veto** by letting the bill sit unsigned for ten days when there are fewer than ten days left in the legislative session. Since many bills do not pass until the end of a session, the potential for pocket veto is substantial.

The actual process of lawmaking is much more fluid than this road map can portray. Members use a great deal of ingenuity in devising ways around whatever roadblocks arise. For example, in recent years, members who were stymied by committees have employed task forces to write their own bills and then substituted their versions on the floor for bills approved by committees. The lawmaking process has become more "unorthodox" as described recently by a political scientist.[45] Nevertheless, as we have

Declared Wars and Congressionally Authorized Military Actions

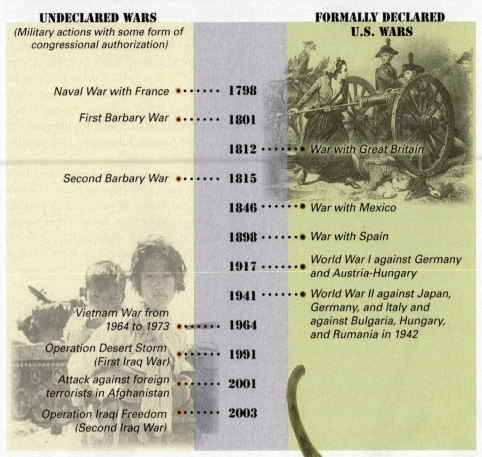

UNDECLARED WARS
(Military actions with some form of congressional authorization)

FORMALLY DECLARED U.S. WARS

Naval War with France	• • • • • • 1798	
First Barbary War	• • • • • • 1801	
	1812 • • • • • • •	War with Great Britain
Second Barbary War	• • • • • • 1815	
	1846 • • • • • • •	War with Mexico
	1898 • • • • • • •	War with Spain
	1917 • • • • • • •	World War I against Germany and Austria-Hungary
	1941 • • • • • • •	World War II against Japan, Germany, and Italy and against Bulgaria, Hungary, and Rumania in 1942
Vietnam War from 1964 to 1973	• • • • • • 1964	
Operation Desert Storm (First Iraq War)	• • • • • • 1991	
Attack against foreign terrorists in Afghanistan	• • • • • • 2001	
Operation Iraqi Freedom (Second Iraq War)	• • • • • • 2003	

stressed throughout, legislative success continues to depend on party support, access to those in top positions, and command over the procedures of the body.

Declaring War

Although the United States has formally declared war only five times in its history, it has entered into hostilities with foreign nations hundreds of times since its founding.[46] The Framers explicitly used the term *declare war* rather than *make war* in designating Congress's powers, because they wanted to leave the president free to repel a sudden attack.[47] In fact, the Framers divided the war power by granting the president the power to deploy troops as commander in chief of the armed forces (see Chapter 12), but reserving to Congress the power to declare war. Because both Congress and the president play a role in going to war, the proper role of the executive and legislative branches remains a topic of intense debate to this day.

The debate was particularly acute at the time of the Vietnam War in the late 1960s and early 1970s. Congress authorized the war by a granting of extensive power to the president, but without a formal declaration. As the war

Hot or Not?

Should Congress bring back the military draft?

dragged on and public support dwindled, members of Congress sought to reclaim congressional authority with the War Powers Resolution. The act, passed over a presidential veto in 1973, requires the president to inform Congress within 48 hours of the deployment of military forces. Unless Congress approves of the president's action or formally declares war, troops must be removed within 60 to 90 days.

Since its passage, every president—liberal and conservative, Democrat and Republican—has held the act to be an unconstitutional restraint on presidential power; in 2008, several former secretaries of state called upon Congress to rewrite the law. In situations requiring the use of force that have arisen since its passage, both Congress and the president have either ignored the act or passed additional legislation authorizing the president to use force. The wars in Iraq and Afghanistan were sanctioned by Congressional authorization after the 9/11 terrorist attacks but have dragged on for years. The authorization for interventions such as President Obama's actions to assist rebels in Libya is far less clear. Although the War Powers Resolution has never been tested in the courts, the Supreme Court has insisted that congressional support for military action does not give the president a blank check. For example, the president cannot simply create new procedures for dealing with enemy combatants that violate established law without congressional authorization.[48]

Ending a conflict once it has started is difficult, because members of Congress do not want to be seen as failing to support our

impeach To bring formal charges against a federal official, including the president.

troops. Nevertheless, Congress can effectively end combat operations by cutting the funds for a war. In 1973, Congress passed a joint resolution (H.J.Res. 636) prohibiting any further appropriation or expenditure of any funds for combat in, over, or from the shores of Vietnam and its neighbors. Repeated efforts by a Democratic majority brought to power in 2006, in large part because of public discontent over the war in Iraq, failed to bring about a similar cut in funding or an end to troop deployments when war opponents failed to muster sufficient support. President Obama ordered additional troops into Afghanistan in 2009 with little congressional opposition. When the President decided to assist NATO as it came to the aid of Libyan rebels, however, the House passed a measure rebuking the President for failing to secure congressional approval. Nevertheless, Congress did not go so far as to end funding for the campaign.

President Obama was rebuked by the House for failing to obtain Congressional authorization for his mission to aid NATO forces in support for rebels in Libya.

Impeachment

Article I of the U.S. Constitution gives the House of Representatives the sole power to **impeach**—that is, bring formal charges against—federal officials. However, it grants the Senate the power to try, and possibly remove, impeached officials from office. The House may impeach an official for three offenses: treason, bribery, or "high crimes and misdemeanors." The first two of these offenses are straightforward; the latter, however, allows Congress substantial leeway for interpretation. Congress has cited "high crimes and misdemeanors" as its reason for impeachment against two presidents: Andrew Johnson in 1868 and Bill Clinton in 1998.

Procedurally, the House Judiciary Committee drafts and votes on charges warranting impeachment. A simple majority of votes in the House is sufficient to pass the measure. Impeached officials face trial in the Senate, with senators acting as jury and members of the House appointed by that body's leadership acting as prosecutors. In cases of presidential impeachment the chief justice of

the United States presides over the trial, during which witnesses offer testimony and undergo examination and cross-examination just as in a court of law. Removal from office requires a two-thirds majority. Congress has impeached 17 federal officials, most of them federal judges. Neither of the presidents who faced impeachment was removed from office. We will discuss presidential impeachments in more detail in Chapter 12.

Oversight

Congress also provides **oversight**, or close scrutiny, of the federal agencies and programs it creates and of the actions of the other branches of government. Oversight is not an enumerated power, but it is implied by the system of checks and balances. Congress exercises its power of oversight through a wide variety of activities and mechanisms.

Congress conducts investigations to examine policy implementation or to scrutinize the activities of government personnel and officeholders. Congress has the power to subpoena witnesses to testify under oath, although witnesses can, of course, refuse to testify under rights granted by the Fifth Amendment. Live television and radio broadcasts of congressional investigations provide citizens with the opportunity to see exactly how their elected representatives protect their interests. This opportunity for civic engagement is not without its risks, however; live broadcast also allows lawmakers to exploit the hearings to gain publicity for themselves.

The executive branch often resists congressional oversight, arguing for autonomy in matters under its principal jurisdiction. The administration of President George W. Bush denied Congress access to papers and documents dealing with matters ranging from energy policy to conduct of the war in Iraq to the firing of U.S. attorneys. It also exercised "executive privilege" in refusing to permit members of the administration to testify before Congress, as when the president sought to prevent the testimony of former White House counsel Harriet Miers regarding the allegedly political firing of U.S. attorneys. President Obama has ordered a review of the use of such practices, but continued them himself during his first few months in office. Of course, the executive branch can avoid oversight more easily when the president's party controls both houses of Congress. The number of oversight hearings soared to more than 600 in the first half of 2007, when the Democrats took control of Congress. By contrast, the Republican-controlled 109th Congress held fewer than two-thirds that number during its entire two-year term.[49]

Congressional committees also exercise oversight by monitoring budgets and holding hearings on the authorization of programs run by executive agencies. The authorization of budgets is potentially Congress's most powerful tool for influencing an agency's operations. Often, however, this power is quite fragmented. For example, no fewer than 79 committees and subcommittees exercise some kind of oversight of the Department of Homeland Security and its many programs. Such fragmentation makes genuine oversight difficult, creating many opportunities for interest groups and specialists within the agencies to secure their funding objectives.

Congress can also create special commissions and task forces to evaluate policies. Such oversight activities can serve as a warning to agencies that lawmakers are displeased with their performance. They also send the message to constituents that members of Congress are doing their jobs. Until 1983, Congress could also repeal or prevent enforcement of agency rules developed by the executive branch, a provision known as the **legislative veto**. Although the Supreme Court ruled that this power was an unconstitutional infringement on the powers of the executive branch,[50] there have been examples of its continuation, and it survives so long as the president does not challenge Congress's use of the device.[51]

Similar to the legislative veto, the power of **congressional review** permits Congress to nullify agency regulations after 60 days by passage of a joint resolution by both houses and approval by

> **oversight** Congressional authority to monitor the actions and budgets of executive agencies it creates.
>
> **legislative veto** Device, declared unconstitutional in 1983, allowing Congress to rescind rules promulgated by an executive agency.
>
> **congressional review** Congressional action, requiring approval by both houses and the president, that can stop implementation of executive branch regulations.

President Bush cited executive privilege in shielding his former White House counsel, Harriet Miers, from testifying before Congress as it investigated allegations of political interference in hiring attorneys at the Justice Department. Congress responded by issuing a subpoena, one of its options in exercising oversight responsibility.

the president. In 2001, Congress used its power of congressional review to nullify a rule proposed in the waning days of the Clinton administration that would have forced employers to conduct ergonomic assessments of their workplaces to minimize worker fatigue and injury.

In our system of checks and balances, moves by either the legislative or the executive branch to control policy often spawn responses by the other branch. In order to evade oversight, or to circumvent portions of legislation that they believe infringe on presidential prerogatives, presidents have taken to issuing **signing statements**. These controversial statements explain how the president chooses to interpret the legislation he signs, and sometimes explain why he will ignore certain provisions he finds objectionable. Critics of signing statements argue that presidents who utilize them are violating the Constitution by essentially rewriting the laws that Congress has passed. We will discuss these in more detail in Chapter 12.

Budgeting

Although the president makes recommendations regarding the administration's budget priorities, the Constitution gives Congress alone the authority to decide how the money is spent. In addition, it specifies that all bills to raise revenues must originate in the House of Representatives.

The budgeting process begins when the president sends Congress a proposed budget (usually after the annual State of the Union message in January or February). A special independent agency, the Congressional Budget Office, then reviews all spending proposals and makes detailed estimates of expenditures needed to accomplish the president's policy objectives. Budget committees in both houses consult with executive agency representatives and develop a **budget resolution** that projects income and sets spending ceilings for various programs. Both houses must pass the budget resolution by April 15 of each year, but it does not require a presi-

Hot or Not?

Should Congress be forced to balance the budget every year as most state governors must do?

dential signature. The figures in the resolution guide the remainder of the budget process.

The Appropriations Committees in each house send portions of the resolution to the committees with authority over the various federal agencies requesting funds. These legislative committees authorize spending to fit within prescribed targets. Spending requests are then returned to the Appropriations Committee in each house for approval. More than two-thirds of the expenditures are nondiscretionary—that is, they go to fund ongoing commitments and operations like Medicare or Social Security. Most of the intense debates occur over the roughly 30 percent of the budget allotted for discretionary or new spending programs. If the need arises, Congress can change funding targets for various programs to stay within the budget guidelines. This amending process is known as **reconciliation**. Reconciliation has been used in recent years to effect deficit reduction, but the process can be contentious, especially since it can be used to short-circuit the use of filibusters in the Senate, where reconciliation requires only a majority vote.

Final passage of spending bills is supposed to occur just prior to the beginning of the government's fiscal year, the yearly budgeting period that begins on October 1. Often, however, Congress does not meet the deadline and must pass **continuing resolutions** that allow agencies to operate at the previous year's funding levels until the new budget is passed. If Congress fails to pass a budget on time, it can fold spending for all programs into a single bill, known as an omnibus bill. When running a deficit, Congress must also authorize the borrowing of money to meet federal obligations. This is known as raising the debt ceiling. 2011 saw a series of showdowns between Democrats and Republicans over this issue, with Republicans threatening not to allow additional borrowing without significant cuts in spending. Months of wrangling produced a compromise that included immediate budget cuts and the adoption of a "super committee" composed of members of both Houses of Congress to find ways to reduce future deficits. Given the size of the long-term federal debt and the passions of some partisans who shun raising taxes and others who recoil at the thought of slowing entitlement growth, the debt crisis is unlikely to disappear anytime soon.

Advice and Consent

The Constitution accords additional powers to the U.S. Senate under the category of "advice and consent." The first of these is the power to approve treaties negotiated by the president, which requires a two-thirds vote. The second is confirmation by simple majority of presidential appointments, ambassadors, other "public Ministers and Consuls, Judges of the Supreme Court, and all other Officers of the United States." The Framers saw the Senate's power of advice and consent as a way for Congress to check presidential power. The use of the Senate for this

Did You Know

?

. . . That when President George Washington went to the Senate to ask for its "advice and consent" regarding a treaty, the senators made it very clear that they would deliberate by themselves, without presidential participation? Since that time, no president has attempted to take part personally in any Senate proceedings.

Woodrow Wilson paid a price for his failure to include senators in negotiations for the Treaty of Versailles ending World War I. The Senate twice refused to ratify it.

purpose—rather than the House—ensured that the interests of both large and small states would be respected, because each state has equal representation in the Senate.

Ever since George Washington visited the Senate in 1789 to confer with members about a series of agreements negotiated with Native American tribes, presidents have employed a number of tactics to win Senate support for treaties. Some presidents have involved senators in the negotiation process itself, as William McKinley did in negotiating a peace treaty with Spain in 1898. Woodrow Wilson, on the other hand, paid a price for his failure to include senators in negotiations for the Treaty of Versailles, which ended World War I. The Senate twice refused to ratify the treaty. More recently, presidents have conferred with Senate leaders during the negotiating process. This approach worked particularly well for Ronald Reagan in winning approval for an arms control treaty in 1987.

The Senate generally has been reluctant to reject treaties, approving more than 15 thousand while turning down just 21.[52] Still, presidents frequently are reluctant to subject their international negotiations to Senate scrutiny. Some have circumvented the process by adopting executive agreements with other nations that carry the same force of law as treaties but do not require Senate approval. We will discuss the increasing use of these agreements in Chapter 12.

Today, the Senate is asked to confirm thousands of civilian and military nominations during each two-year session of Congress. While it confirms the vast majority of these in blocks, controversial nominees do engender significant debate. This is particularly true with respect to Supreme Court nominees, who enjoy lifetime appointments. We will discuss these at length in Chapter 14. Much of the controversy over Senate approval of presidential appointments centers around the proper meaning of "advice and consent." Some scholars and senators believe Congress should reject presidential appointees only if the nominee is deficient in competence or character. Others believe the Senate should have the discretion to deny appointment for any reason whatsoever, including disagreements over policy or political perspective.

signing statements Documents presidents append to legislation indicating their particular interpretation of its contents.

budget resolution Early step in budgeting process in which both houses of Congress set spending goals.

reconciliation Process of amending spending bills to meet budget targets.

continuing resolution Vehicle for funding government operations at the previous year's levels of support when a new budget is delayed.

CIVIC ENGAGEMENT AND CONGRESS TODAY

Although Congress today reflects the nation's changing currents of partisan affiliation, it appears poorly equipped to find broad-based solutions to problems Americans deem important, such as controlling discretionary spending, bal-

that available for presidential candidates. Of course, spending reform would also decrease the perception of corruption among the public.

A growing number of states are moving to bipartisan or nonpartisan redistricting commissions to draw congressional boundaries. In 2008, California voters passed a ballot measure placing redistricting authority in the hands of a Citizens Redistricting Commission. More than 30,000 residents applied for 14 positions on the board, which will sort through population figures and election boundaries to ensure that residents of the most-populous state are fairly represented. Shaun Bowler, a professor of political science at the University of California, Riverside told reporters, "This is just a sign of just how engaged or enraged people are by the political process."[56] The current practice of partisan gerrymandering can discourage supporters of candidates who have little chance of winning against an entrenched incumbent within a secure district.[57] To be sure, partisan redistricting is not the sole cause for noncompetitive elections; however, it contributes to a lack of confidence in the legislative process, leading some commentators to conclude that citizens no longer pick their lawmakers—instead, lawmakers pick their constituents.[58]

Finally, greater use of national forums and the creative employment of new technologies could keep constituents and lawmakers in closer communication. As expanded availability of the Internet shrinks the digital divide, legislators could host electronic town meetings to gauge their constituents' views on national problems and seek consensus-based solutions.

Ultimately, making lawmakers more attentive to long-standing problems that citizens want resolved will require greater initiative and engagement by citizens themselves. While over 90 percent of Americans believe it is their duty to communicate with their representatives in Congress, only one-fifth have actually contacted their House member or one of their senators.[59] We already know from Chapter 7 that those who do communicate are not representative of the public at large. Instead, they represent the higher social and economic tiers of the population. As a result, lawmakers hear quite a lot about the concerns of the well-to-do but very little from the poor, children, or the uninsured.

ancing the budget, reforming the tax system, and providing affordable health care for all. The skillful use of pork barrel projects and casework may ensure the loyalty of some voters, but the public expresses general dissatisfaction with the institution of Congress as a whole for its inability to solve social problems. Many citizens believe Congress is inefficient, laggard, and unresponsive, and that it has lost touch with the public.[53] Over the past decade, the number of Americans expressing trust in Congress has rarely exceeded a third of the population.[54] Fewer than half of eligible voters turn out for midterm congressional elections.

These attitudes are, in part, understandable reactions to the political dynamics of the institution today. In a closely divided Congress, bipartisan consensus takes a backseat to partisan politics as members of each party seek to please groups most important to their electoral success. Debate becomes shriller. Compromise and reconciliation of differences become more difficult to achieve. Each party pursues the politics of winning at any cost.[55] Gerrymandering, the high cost of campaigning, and incumbent privileges keep turnover low. Voters are turned off. A number of reforms could help change this picture.

First, since competitive elections tend to increase citizen interest and turnout, we could change practices that protect incumbents to level the playing field for challengers. Campaign spending reform would help to increase competition since most money flows to incumbents. Spending reform might range from allowing all candidates free media time to public financing for congressional contests much like

We also need to place more attention on civic education beyond the ballot box. Students should learn not just the value of voting but also the value of following up with elected officials to check on their political investment. Don't assume that your vote communicates any information about your issue preferences. The only sure way for lawmakers to know what you think is for you to let them hear directly from you. Members of Congress do pay attention to constituents; after all, they are doing our business.

Summary

1. What powers does Congress have?

- Our bicameral Congress has enumerated powers granted by the Constitution. These include lawmaking, budgeting, declaring war, impeachment, oversight, and advice and consent.

- Congress has implied powers granted by the elastic clause of the Constitution.

- The Senate alone has the additional powers of ratifying treaties and approving presidential appointments.

- Congressional power has developed in response to periods of national change. At first, Congress sought to build its own institutional status; it underwent reform in the Progressive era; its power waned in the twentieth century as executive power grew; and it helped expand rights for minorities during the rights revolution of the 1950s and 1960s.

- Members of Congress represent the people. There is some debate as to whether they should serve as delegates, trustees, or politicos. There is also the question of whether Congress is really a representative body reflecting the diversity of the American public.

2. What are some factors affecting election to Congress?

- Candidates must have access to resources. They need to have the time to spend countless hours campaigning, and they need access to great amounts of money.

- Incumbents have an advantage in raising funds and in name recognition because of the franking privilege, the credit they can claim for projects they bring their districts, the casework they perform for grateful constituents, and their access to the media.

- House members are faced with additional hurdles, including frequent elections, lower turnout in midterm elections, and periodic redistricting. Most incumbents are returned to office partly because they run in safe districts that have been drawn by partisans in the state legislature.

3. What are the keys to political power in Congress?

- The keys to political power in Congress are party, position, and procedure.

- Power is largely in the hands of the majority party, which controls positions of leadership and the flow of the legislative process.

- Chairpersons exercise substantial power on committees that review legislation, and they rise to the position usually on the basis of seniority and party control.

- Command of parliamentary rules and procedures like the Senate filibuster is an important element in legislative success.

- The lawmaking process is characterized by specialized committees that review and approve legislation before debate on the floor of each chamber.

National Journal

Blanche Lincoln Faces Double Jeopardy

TEXARKANA, Ark.—A stone's throw from the Texas state line, Democratic Sen. Blanche Lincoln spent a warm afternoon early last week practicing the handshake-to-handshake retail politicking her state admires. Before flying back to Washington to rejoin the Senate's efforts to clamp down on big banks, Lincoln visited the paneled boardroom of a small community bank and gingerly tried to elicit support from five influential representatives of the African-American community. She is up against a well-financed challenger, Lt. Gov. Bill Halter, in the May 18 Democratic primary.

Lincoln's Texarkana campaign representatives arranged the meeting here. And the 10 people in the room, including her campaign staff members, were well aware of the senator's re-election problems. Political analysts say that a third Senate term may well elude Lincoln in a conservative state that backed Republican John McCain for president in 2008 and has been unimpressed with the Democrats' expansion of government since Barack Obama won the White House.

Black voters in Arkansas are disenchanted with Lincoln's centrist sensibilities, particularly her reluctant, holdout voting record on the health care reform law that President Obama struggled to enact. But Lincoln needs African-American Democrats to mobilize for her in the primary and, if she gets that far, in November's general election. Organized labor and the liberal group MoveOn.org are spending millions of dollars on advertising and grassroots activities to defeat an incumbent they view as an unreliable Democrat.

"The national unions—there's no doubt there are some awful ads on TV about me

right now," Lincoln told the Texarkana group, most of whom listened quietly as the senator recounted her record of support for health care and child nutrition programs, help for Arkansas's aging population and for the state's timber and agriculture interests, and advocacy on behalf of black farmers.

"You should know that those outside groups can come in and they've spent a little over $4 million just in the last four or five weeks, just running negative ads against me," she complained in her Southern Delta twang. "They want to tell us what to do."

In a small, poor, right-to-work state where union influence is weak, Lincoln may be smart to depict herself as defending Arkansas against bullying by Big Labor, and to portray Halter as labor's puppet. In this city, Lincoln insisted that she has "a good voting record with the unions" but added, "I'm not with them 100 percent of the time." Lincoln opposed the Employee Free Choice Act, a key union goal that would make it easier to organize workplaces, after she originally supported it. Her change of heart on the "card-check" bill helped make her a target.

"With the national group, if you're not with them 100 percent of the time, they're going to get angry with you," she said, teeing up a joke that she knew would get laughs from the men gathered in the boardroom. "But you know, I don't even agree with my husband 100 percent of the time, but that doesn't mean he's going to leave me!"

After some bantering about Razorback football, local churches that she had visited, and the well-being of various children of the assembled supporters, Lincoln made a relaxed exit to catch a plane back to the nation's capital.

Watching her leave, Londell Williams, 62, a member of the elected city board of direc-

tors, told National Journal that resistance to Lincoln among some African-Americans—about 16 percent of Arkansas's population—stems from "misguided information" that he, among others here, will work hard to refute. Williams said he had distributed 442 Lincoln campaign fliers—ones showcasing a photo of the senator with Obama—at his church the previous morning. All but six of the fliers made their way out of the church, and Williams predicts that his backing for Lincoln will spread "like gangrene" within his community.

Obama and native son Bill Clinton have recorded radio ads for Lincoln. Their support, however, is not an unmixed blessing for her. When she tacks a bit left—for example, by attacking big banks and talking up her A grade from the NAACP—in hopes of winning the Democratic primary, the senator muddies her campaign boast that she votes "with Arkansas," not in lockstep with the national party. Lincoln does, in fact, side with the Senate's conservative Republicans as often as she does with her own party. In a political climate that strongly encourages party discipline, she stands out in the Senate like a party of one. This year, Lincoln is finding little refuge in the middle.

National Journal's analysis of lawmakers' 2009 voting records placed Lincoln smack in the middle of the embattled Senate centrists, elbow-to-elbow with Connecticut's independent Democrat, Joe Lieberman. Anticipating a battle for re-election but apparently not imagining a primary challenge, Lincoln voted quite a bit more conservatively in 2009 than in previous years. Her average composite liberal score in the first four years of her term was 64.8. In 2009, it was 50.3, meaning she had drifted 14.5 points to the right.

12

THE PRE

Inside Washington

Now, Lincoln's touting of Obama's endorsement ties her more closely to the liberal image of the Senate Democratic Conference. She will be battling uphill for re-election and will almost certainly try to distance herself from Obama and her party.

Wherever Lincoln speaks in her home state, she is pressed about her complicated health care reform positions, which angered liberals and conservatives alike, and which suggested to some observers that she may have more spin than spine. Lincoln ended up opposing a public insurance option she initially warmed to, and it was dropped. She maneuvered to gain attention by being among the last senators to line up to give the Democrats the filibuster-proof 60 votes needed to move their bill forward in December. But then in March she was one of only three Democrats to vote with 40 Republicans against the budget reconciliation measure that finally got the health insurance reforms to the president's desk.

Lincoln's campaign team in Little Rock accuses outside groups and opponents who are footing the bill for expensive ads around the state of distorting the senator's record on health care—by, for example, saying she was responsible for the demise of the public option. Asked whether Lincoln should have better anticipated her vulnerabilities when she made herself a holdout vote on health care, her team responded that Republicans were always going to paint her as the key 60th vote for passage and that liberals were just as determined to cast her as the villain who blocked a public option. "In any other environment in any other time, her typical M.O. works out pretty well," campaign manager Steve Patterson told *National Journal* last week.

"This is the way she rolls, and people can assign various motives to what she was do-

ing, and how it all worked out, and whether she made a mistake. But, look, that's just who she is. She works these issues," he said. "She represents a small, rural state, with four congressional districts, that routinely ranks low among the 50 states in terms of the poverty rate, the teen pregnancy rate, education. And on all these issues she's fighting to increase resources and opportunities in the state."

Lincoln, who was first elected to the Senate in 1998 and re-elected in 2004 with 56 percent of the vote, has been a familiar and popular figure in Arkansas. She talks about herself as the just-folks daughter of an east Arkansas rice farmer who instilled in her the "rock-solid" values of the state.

Lincoln's biggest challenge, Patterson said, is attempting to respond simultaneously to attacks from the Right and Left. "That's been a pretty potent combination. And not very many incumbents can withstand that," he added. "We think it will be a tough, close election, but we still think we're going to win."

In an interview at his campaign headquarters, Halter predicted that he will defeat Lincoln. "People just want change," he said.

A 73-year-old Little Rock retiree named Rosemary said as she exited the courthouse that she had voted for Halter in protest, al-

though she believes that Lincoln can win the primary and perhaps shape up to be a better candidate by November. "Both campaigns have been ghastly, full of things that are untrue and unfair, just throwing mud," she complained. "I'm sending Blanche a message."

Voting began on May 3 at designated polling places. In Texarkana, 125 people of the nearly 24,000 registered to vote in the county cast ballots that day. That number was "about average," according to a deputy clerk. About 1,000 voters showed up in the first two days at nine Little Rock polling places.

Among them were 88-year-old William Nelson, walking carefully with the aid of a crutch, and his smiling wife of eight years, Hazel Nelson, 87. The Nelsons of North Little Rock are African-Americans who proudly voted for Obama for president and decided to cast their ballots for Lincoln. "She's doing what she's supposed to be doing," William Nelson explained. "Everyone makes mistakes," he continued, referring to her handling of health care reform. "She'll do more for Arkansas than anyone else."

> "[Being attacked from both the Right and Left has] been a pretty potent combination. And not very many incumbents can withstand that. . . . We think it will be a tough, close election, but we still think we're going to win."
>
> —Steve Patterson

For Discussion:

■ What tensions does Lincoln's reelection campaign reveal that are specific to congressional races? What are the issues a congressional candidate faces in appealing to his or her state or district to which a presidential candidate or local office-seeker is more immune?

■ Do you think it's a plus or a minus to be a centrist in today's electoral climate?

■ Based on the article's presentation, do you believe Lincoln's claim that she had a robust, centrist vote on health care? Or do you imagine was politically calculated to avoid alienating either side of her state?

POWER AND PARADOX

RISKY BUSINESS ▌ It was months in the making. Backup plans were made for virtually every contingency. A full-scale mock-up had been created for trial simulations, and the training was extensive. Only the best were recruited for the operation. "At the end," the president confided, "this was only a 55/45 situation."[1]

Around noon on Sunday, May 1, 2011, President Obama, his security team, and his top military commanders assembled in the Situation Room of the White House to watch in real time as a 79-member Navy SEAL assault team descended onto the compound in Abbottabad in northwest Pakistan where it was believed Osama bin Laden was hiding. Even as the operation proceeded, the president said "we could not definitely say bin Laden was there."[2] In the days leading up to the attack, the president engaged his advisors in vigorous debate. Not all of them supported the action. Still, armed with intelligence ➤

SIDENCY

As You READ >>

- What is the path to the presidency?
- What are the major constitutional duties and nonconstitutional roles of the president?
- What agencies and personal factors help to produce a successful presidency?

collected from leads provided by 9/11 detainees and from CIA monitoring stations, the president decided the raid was worth the risk and green-lighted the operation.

As they sat in the Situation Room, "the minutes passed like days," according to John Brennan, Assistant to the President for Counterterrorism and Homeland Security. "It was clearly very tense. A lot of people were holding their breath."[3] The president and his team watched in silence as one of the choppers that was supposed to lower the SEALs into the compound encountered mechanical difficulties and had to land. An emergency backup was dispatched. The Pakistani military, unaware of the assault, reacted by summoning interceptor jets, further threatening the success of the mission.

While some of the details of what happened inside the bin Laden mansion remain unclear, word that the assault was successful and that the mastermind of the worst foreign attack on American soil was dead was communicated to the president and his aides just before 4 P.M. Applause broke out in the Situation Room and the president was reported to have reacted, "We got him." Later that evening, the president would address the nation and report:

> Today, at my direction, the United States launched a targeted operation against that compound in Abbottabad, Pakistan. A small team of Americans carried out the operation with extraordinary courage and capability. No Americans were harmed. They took care to avoid civilian casualties. After a firefight, they killed Osama bin Laden and took custody of his body.

Osama bin Laden's compound was located near a military academy in the city of Abbottabad, about 30 miles northeast of the Pakistani capital of Islamabad.

The decision to conduct the raid on bin Laden was perhaps one of the more daring a president can make. The terrorist had eluded capture and death for 10 years. A lot could have gone wrong. Years ago, President Jimmy Carter launched an assault on an Iranian compound where Americans were held hostage. The mission failed when a helicopter developed engine trouble and crashed. Certainly, President Obama had learned from bin Laden's previous evasions and from failed military rescues in the past. Yet, nothing was certain about this raid. With success, the president could bolster his own flailing presidency and regain some of the luster lost in congressional battles over the previous two years. He would receive at least a temporary boost in public approval, an opportunity to reestablish electoral **coattails** for his fellow Democrats, and a chance to breathe new life into his agenda for the nation. With failure, the president would surely be saddled with the blame and further damage to his ability to lead.

In this chapter, we will trace the growth of presidential power and the increasingly popular nature of the institution. Today, the president's power rests heavily on his ability to persuade us and take us along. His ability to persuade, in turn, rises with successes like the bin Laden raid but can easily fall, as when policies fail to bring jobs to the unemployed. In assessing the president's achievements, citizens must be attentive, realistic in their expectations, and vigilant, lest the president takes the nation somewhere it really doesn't want to go. ◆━

ORIGIN AND POWERS OF THE PRESIDENCY

The Framers were clear about what the president shouldn't be, but less certain about what exactly the office *should* be. They did not want the president to dominate the government; they had just fought a revolution to free themselves from monarchical rule. Neither, however, did they want a weak and ineffective executive; lack of central leadership had led to dissatisfaction with the Articles of Confederation. Delegates to the Constitutional Convention argued for months before agreeing on the form and powers of the office. They created a single executive with a broad scope of potential powers that were limited by checks and balances. The delegates deliberately sketched only the rough outlines of executive power, preferring to let the person they all knew would first occupy the office work out the details. George Washington did not disappoint.

Constitutional Provisions

Article II of the Constitution outlines the requirements for election to office, as well as the powers, duties, and limits on the authority of the president. It also provides for a vice president to succeed the president in case of death, resignation, or the inability to discharge the powers and duties of the office. To be eligible for the presidency, an individual must be 35 years of age, a resident of the United States for 14 years, and a natural-born citizen. This last requirement is not applicable to other federal officeholders; it reflected the Framers' desire to prevent command of the U.S. military by a foreign-born national.

The term of office is four years, and originally the Constitution placed no restriction on the number of terms a president could serve. The Twenty-second Amendment, ratified in 1951, imposed a limit of two terms. Dispute over the role the voters and the states should play in the election process led to the creation of an Electoral College (discussed later), in which state electors cast the actual ballots for a president and vice president following the popular vote by the people. The Twelfth Amendment, ratified in 1804, altered the process by requiring electors to sub-mit separate ballots for president and vice president. This change came about as a result of one presidential election that produced a president and vice president from opposing parties (1796) and another that resulted in a tie (1800).

The Constitution grants the president executive authority to take care that laws are faithfully executed; to operate executive departments; and to require written opinions from the officers of these departments. The president also enjoys the power to make appointments, including judges to the Supreme Court and all other federal courts, with the advice and consent of the Senate; to fill inferior offices and vacancies during Senate recess without Senate approval; and to grant reprieves and pardons. The office has legislative powers, including the powers to recommend legislation to Congress for its consideration, to convene both houses of Congress, and to veto legislation. In military matters, the president is the commander in chief of the armed forces. In the diplomatic arena, the chief executive can negotiate treaties and submit them to the Senate for approval upon a two-thirds vote and can appoint

> **coattails** The effect a winning candidate at the top of the ticket has in bringing success to those lower on the ballot.

ambassadors and ministers with Senate approval. As chief of state, the president receives foreign officials and dignitaries, presents information on the state of the nation, and swears an oath of allegiance to uphold the Constitution. Article II also provides for removing a president by impeachment and trial upon conviction for treason, bribery, or other high crimes and misdemeanors. These formal powers tell only part of the story of presidential power, however. In reality, the office's occupants have molded the institution in significant ways.

Crafting the Office: From Washington to Roosevelt

Well aware that his actions would guide the future course of presidents, Washington took pains not to overstep the bounds of constitutional authority and to set worthy precedents. He avoided the partisan feud between Federalists and Antifederalists; he was respectful of Congress, but still willing to assert his independence; he respected the rule of law; and he even led U.S. troops in quashing the Whiskey Rebellion of 1794. Washington also established a precedent by refusing to serve more than two terms, a practice that held informally for almost 150 years and is now enshrined in the Twenty-second Amendment. Washington fit the Framers' vision of the ideal president—a respectable gentleman with suitable wealth, experience, and connections. The notion that "any child can grow up to be president" was foreign to them.

As national parties came to dominate government and presidential politics in the early 1800s, party leaders in Congress played the leading role in choosing presidential candidates. That began to change in 1831 when the Anti-Masonic and Republican National Parties used nominating conventions composed of state party delegates to select their nominees. The following year the Democrats met in convention to nominate Andrew Jackson to a second term. Jackson built ties with the public, portraying himself as a tribune of the people and using his popularity to build support for his policies.

For a period, strong presidents such as Jackson, James Polk, and Abraham Lincoln exercised substantial author-

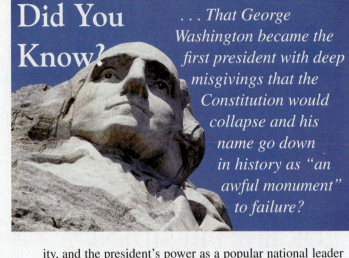

Did You Know?

. . . That George Washington became the first president with deep misgivings that the Constitution would collapse and his name go down in history as "an awful monument" to failure?

ity, and the president's power as a popular national leader grew. Lincoln, in particular, demonstrated the wide latitude a president has in responding to a crisis. Among the wartime actions he undertook were the suspension of *habeus corpus*, the confiscation of private property without due process or compensation, the blockage of Southern ports, and the trial of civilians in military courts. Lincoln even defied the orders of the federal courts. His actions demonstrate that, as one historian noted, "So long as public opinion sustains the president . . . , he has nothing to fear from the displeasure of the courts."[4]

After the Civil War, the average American looked to local politicians to address his or her problems and had few expectations of national government. Presidents acceded to this view by advancing few initiatives.

The strength of political parties began to diminish around the turn of the twentieth century as people voiced concern about the corruption of local "machine" politics. Americans looked to Washington for help in addressing labor and health concerns arising from a growing national economy and burgeoning urban life. Theodore Roosevelt gave voice to popular sentiment by using the presidency as a "bully pulpit" for effecting change and giving vent to the "view then emerging among the Progressives that chief executives were also representatives of the people."[5] Woodrow Wilson offered the most straightforward endorsement of the notion that a president is the people's representative, above parochial or partisan interest:

No one else represents the people as a whole, exercising a national choice. . . . The nation as a whole has chosen him, and he is conscious that it has no other political spokes-

Theodore Roosevelt gave voice to popular sentiment by using the presidency as a "bully pulpit" for change.

man. His is the only national voice in affairs . . . (T)here is but one national voice in the country, and that is the voice of the President.[6]

The Modern Presidency

Franklin Delano Roosevelt's presidency ushered in a new era of a powerful chief executive. Many of the policies FDR championed, including social welfare and business regulatory programs, involved the national government directly in the lives of individuals and gave the people a stake in presidential performance. The government programs he helped create further undercut the role of local parties by providing many people with direct federal aid. Business groups found it far more effective to lobby executive branch agencies than local politicians or even members of Congress. These changes increased the reach of presidential power and strengthened the bonds between individual citizens and the president. After World War II, America became a prominent world power and presidents were expected to protect our interests abroad, prevent nuclear catastrophe, and promote world trade. Today, most citizens consider the president personally accountable for the performance of government. The president is the one politician who speaks for and to the entire nation, and the one individual in government who has a commanding view of the problems faced by the nation as a whole.

Clearly, the presidency has become a more democratic institution than the Framers intended. Presidents have become custodians of the public trust and are seen by many as tribunes for common causes. The modern presidency has also given rise to an ever-increasing and complex national government that fosters an atmosphere of enlarged expectations about what presidents can accomplish. With increased expectations comes the risk of producing citizens who are cynical and more attuned to consuming government services than contributing to the political process.

Hot or Not?

Should we change the Constitution to allow naturalized foreign-born citizens to be elected president?

THE PATH TO THE PRESIDENCY

Most presidential contenders reflect the dominant characteristics of the traditional electorate: white, male, Anglo-Saxon, and Protestant. The 2008 campaign marked the first time an African American candidate was chosen as the presidential nominee from a major party and only the second time a female was chosen as a vice presidential running mate. The first female vice presidential candidate from a major party was Geraldine Ferraro in 1984. The 2008 campaign cycle also witnessed the most sustained race for the presidential nomination by a female, Hillary Clinton.

Prior government service is another characteristic that presidential candidates typically share. All but four presidents held political office before becoming chief executive; the four exceptions (George Washington, Andrew Jackson, Ulysses Grant, and Dwight Eisenhower) were military officers. Vice presidents ascended to the presidency 14 times, 9 as a result of the death or resignation of the person they served. Twelve presidents were former governors, including four of the last five. Sixteen senators have become president; three (Harding, Kennedy, and Obama) moved directly from the Senate to the White House.

GETTING ELECTED

Hurdling legal and societal barriers is only the first of many tests facing a presidential candidate. Eighteen to 24 months prior to the presidential election (and often earlier), potential candidates begin to test the waters and amass the resources necessary to mount a credible campaign. The 2008 presidential contest was the longest and most expensive in American history. Candidates began meeting with campaign advisors and consultants as early as 2006, two years before any votes were cast. All together candidates raised in excess of $1 billion in pursuit of the White House.

Fundraising

Unlike other elective offices, campaigning for the presidency is complicated by a system of public financing. Primary candidates can qualify for partial public financing of their campaign activities up until the nominating conventions. During this time, small individual donations to their campaigns are matched dollar for dollar by public funds financed by taxpayers through a $3 checkoff on the yearly income tax forms. After a party officially endorses a candidate, he or she qualifies for full public financing during the general election, provided the candidate follows certain rules and limits spending to predetermined levels. Public funding is available to minor party candidates who receive at least 5 percent of the total popular vote in the general election. If they meet this threshold, minor party candidates are allocated their share of public funds after the election.

Barack Obama became the first candidate from a major party to forgo public funding during the general election since such funding first became available in 1976. Rather than face a spending limit of $84 million by accepting public funds, Obama, buoyed by his fundraising success during the primary season, decided he would need to raise and spend more than this amount to run the 50-state campaign he planned. John McCain stuck with public funding for the general election but relied heavily on additional expenditures made on his behalf by the Republican National Committee, which was far more flush with funds than its Democratic Party counterpart, the DNC. McCain and Obama both rejected public funds during the primary season, although McCain had at first applied for such funds. In rejecting public funding during the primaries, these candidates were not pioneers. Major-party candidates have rejected primary funding for a number of years because the amounts allocated and the limits imposed have not kept up with the rising costs of campaigning. Especially when the primary campaign season is prolonged, as it was for the Democrats in 2008, those costs can be substantial. Despite early fundraising success, Hillary Clinton ended her run for the Democratic Party nomination approximately $30 million in debt.

Many observers believe we have seen the end of public financing in its current form. The cost of campaigns has forced candidates to forgo limited public funds in favor of raising virtually unlimited amounts on their own. The Internet has made this option easier by allowing candidates to raise large sums from millions of small donors to whom candidates can return for multiple contributions, up to the legal limit of $2,500 (for the 2011–2012 campaign cycle). Barack Obama obliterated previous records by raising more than $600 million, more than half from small online donations. And, of course, campaigns cannot afford to turn down checks bundled by wealthy contributors. The most important long-term change, however, may come as a result of the Supreme Court's 2010 ruling in *Citizens United v. FEC,* in which the court removed restrictions on corporate and union independent expenditures on behalf of candidates or causes. (See Chapter 8.)

caucus Voter gatherings used to select party candidates to run in the general election.

Primary Sweepstakes

The presidential nomination process today is characterized by what one political scientist has called an "invisible primary" that takes place in the years and months before the presidential election year.[7] It is a process dominated by activists, resource providers, campaign specialists, and media personnel, who together influence election outcomes by screening candidates for electability and providing some—but not others—with the resources they need to move forward in the campaign. This process has been cobbled together through a series of reforms spanning the last century but accelerating in the late 1960s and 1970s. Despite the sometimes undue influence of money and ac-

Caucus and Primary Winners in the 2008 Presidential Race

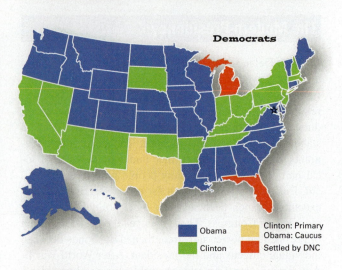

Democrats

- ■ Obama
- ■ Clinton
- ■ Clinton: Primary Obama: Caucus
- ■ Settled by DNC

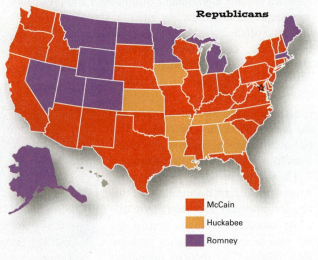

Republicans

- ■ McCain
- ■ Huckabee
- ■ Romney

tivists, however, the 2008 election demonstrated that citizens are by no means tangential to the processes of choosing our presidents.

During the pre-convention season, candidates crisscross the country, running in primary elections and electoral **caucuses**, local gatherings where townspeople meet to voice their preferences for the candidate they believe can best lead their party. Although voters in these venues express their support for specific presidential candidates, their votes actually determine the composition of pledged delegates that the states send to the party's national convention. Once they arrive at the convention, these delegates are expected to vote for the nominee they are pledged to represent.

To win nomination, a candidate must have the support of a majority of all the delegates at the convention. In 2008, Democrats sat over 4,000 delegates at their convention; the votes of 2,118 were needed to win nomination. The Republicans sat over 2,300 delegates with 1,191 needed to win. Parties allot delegates to states on the basis of population, as well as each state's performance in delivering the vote in the previous general election. Because voters select most of the delegates through this primary process, the public usually knows the identity of each party's nominee long before the conventions. However, each party also sends a number of unelected delegates whose presence, it is believed, will encourage party unity—especially in cases where no single candidate arrives at the convention with a clear majority of pledged delegates. In 2008, the Republicans sent to their convention 463 **unpledged delegates** representing members of the Republican National Committee and elected delegates from around the country. The Democrats sent to their convention 825 **superdelegates** coming from the ranks of elected party officials and state party leaders. This group emerged as a powerful, and heavily lobbied, force in the Democratic Party's nominating process because of the closeness of the race between Barack Obama and Hillary Clinton. The race remained close going into the final primaries in June; but then, superdelegates began committing their support to Obama in large numbers, giving him a lead in the total vote that Clinton could not overcome.

Not all primaries and caucuses are created equal, however. Iowa and New Hampshire, for example, are both small states that send few delegates to the party conventions (about 1 percent of the total for each party) and are not representative of the national electorate as a whole.[8] Because they traditionally host the first primaries of a campaign, however, they attract a great deal of attention and play a disproportionately large role in shaping public opinion about the candidates. Campaigning in these first states allows candidates to hone their messages before small groups of voters gathered in homes and diners throughout the states. The impact of early victories on building momentum can be substantial. In fact, one study found that voters in early primary states had up to five times the influence of voters in late primary states in winnowing the field and helping to choose their party's eventual nominee.[9] The 2008 campaign witnessed several new states entering the primary and caucus season early, including the western states of Wyoming (Republicans) and Nevada (both parties). Twenty-four states, including California, received party approval to hold their primaries on February 5, resulting in the day being called "super Tuesday" because of the wealth of delegates that date would produce. Florida and Michigan leapfrogged the parties' approved timetable in hopes of increasing their influence over the nomination process. Republican Party rules called for penalizing such states with a reduction by half of their allotted delegates; the Democrats threatened not to seat any of the delegates these states selected. Hillary Clinton won the primaries in both of these states, even though she did not actively campaign there. Barack Obama did not campaign in either state and removed his name from the Florida ballot to comply with DNC rules. Because the results from these states were contested, Obama could claim victory only after the Democratic National Committee's Rules Committee, meeting in

unpledged delegates Elected officials and party leaders chosen as delegates to the national party conventions with the ability to cast their votes for any candidate regardless of primary election results.

superdelegates Democratic Party leaders and elected officials attending the party convention who may pledge support to a candidate before the convention.

Candidates crisscrossed the country in 2008 in the longest and costliest campaign in American history.

special session on May 31, determined that it would penalize both states by allocating only half-votes to their delegates. Once Clinton conceded to Obama, however, all of the delegates from these contested states were seated.

Although it was originally believed that this onslaught of early primaries would result in party victors being crowned by early February, the process actually prolonged the contest in 2008, as competitive candidates in each party divided up the electoral map. Dogged by a very competitive Mike Huckabee, a former Arkansas governor and favorite among Christian conservatives, John McCain did not gain sufficient delegates to claim victory until his wins in Rhode Island, Texas, and Ohio on March 4. The Democrats shed many of their primary candidates by late January, but partly because of the appeal of its two leading candidates, and partly because Democratic rules give challengers an advantage by awarding delegates proportionately on the basis of the popular vote (so long as a candidate meets a certain threshold), the Democratic primary contest extended well beyond expectations. (The Republicans award delegates in a variety of ways, with some states giving the winner of the popular vote all of the state's delegates and others using a proportional allocation or some mix of both approaches.) Barack Obama, scoring big wins among young voters and African Americans, and Hillary Clinton, leading among female and lower-income voters, kept the contest competitive into the final days of the primary season. Some states saw their highest voter turnout in years, with more than 6.5 million people under the age of 30 participating nationwide.

Party Conventions

At one time, the **nominating conventions** were the sites of dramatic battles to determine the parties' platforms and nominees. Some, such as the 1860 Democratic convention, witnessed dozens of votes and extensive backroom dealmaking, eventually resulting in a split in the party. Even the nominee's choice of a running mate might offer a dramatic moment or touch off a political battle. More recently, conventions have become a place where delegates who have worked hard for their candidates unite around a nominee who has won the primary battle. Running mates are now routinely selected by the presumptive nominee even before the convention begins. Many delegates are average citizens participating in electoral politics for the first time. Changes in party rules since the 1970s ensure that they represent a diverse mix of individuals. However, elected officials and party workers are also well represented. This is a time for

nominating convention Quadrennial meeting of delegates from all states and territories for the purpose of formally choosing their party's nominee for president.

elector Member of the Electoral College.

unit rule Practice of awarding all of a state's electoral votes to the candidate who wins a plurality of the popular vote in presidential contests.

partisans to rededicate themselves to the causes the party espouses and to celebrate its historical accomplishments.

There is much truth to the claim that conventions are simply orchestrated four-day commercials for the party, where unity is enforced and genuine debate among factions is suppressed. Since the 1968 Democratic convention in Chicago, which was marked by antiwar protests and clashes between protesters and police, both parties have carefully choreographed convention proceedings and speeches to create the appearance of unity. Even debate over planks in the party platform, once conducted in open session on the convention floor, occurs in a private setting away from the convention, where the nominee's representatives exercise control. National television networks have steadily reduced their coverage of conventions in recent years, convinced that conventions offer little of substance to report. Ironically, despite the lack of inherent drama in modern conventions, voters are likely to stay tuned for long periods,[10] and interest in the 2008 campaign fueled the highest television ratings ever for both party conventions with more than 40 million viewers tuning in to hear candidates' acceptance speeches.

Each major party qualifies for public funding of the national nominating conventions. In 2008, this amounted to approximately $16.5 million. However, Federal Election Commission (FEC) rulings permit parties to receive supplemental funding from political action committees (PACs) and lobbyists well beyond this limit. This additional funding boosted expenditures for party conventions in 2008 to more than $70 million, not including the millions spent by major corporations, labor organizations, and interest groups for lavish parties meant to entertain the delegates and political leaders in attendance. Minor parties also receive partial convention funding in an amount based on their share of the popular vote in the previous presidential election.

The nomination of the first African American presidential candidate from a major national party made the Democratic convention in Denver historic. However, the closeness of the primary contest, the sometimes harsh rhetoric used by candidates on the campaign trail, and divisions within the Democratic electorate strained party unity going into the general election. Even so, Clinton endorsed Obama, and the two made a series of joint campaign stops. The Republicans, too, had internal conflicts between religious conservatives and libertarian-leaning supporters to repair, but John McCain's choice of Alaska governor Sarah Palin as his running mate electrified conservatives and energized many in the Republican base.

The General Election

Immediately following their respective conventions, the nominees mount an intense effort to connect with the public and sell themselves and their ideas to the electorate prior to Election Day. This includes making personal appearances around the country and obtaining maximum exposure in newspapers, radio, and television. Since the Kennedy-Nixon contest in 1960, televised debates have been an important feature of the general election season. All of the campaigns' efforts at this stage are guided by the quest to secure enough electoral votes to win the presidency.

The Electoral College Although a candidate's ultimate goal is to collect as many votes as possible, the candidate who receives the most popular votes does not always win the election. That is because presidential elections are won or lost in the Electoral College, a body whose members (called **electors**) cast the deciding votes in presidential elections. Representatives of large and small states at the Constitutional Convention of 1787 supported different methods for determining the outcome of presidential elections. Delegates compromised by creating an unorthodox institution that assigns to each state a number of presidential electors equal to its combined total of representatives and senators. This procedure gives delegates from large states a substantial say in the presidential elections while awarding small states two more electoral votes than their population alone would provide. The District of Columbia also has three electors in the college, bringing the total

membership to 538; a majority (270) is required for election. Electors generally consist of appointees of state party leaders, party faithful chosen at party conventions, and, in the case of independent candidates, individuals chosen for their loyalty. Electors representing the party whose candidate won the popular vote in each state assemble in their state capitals on the first Monday after the second Wednesday of December to cast official ballots.

All but two states in the Electoral College apply the **unit rule** when assigning votes to a candidate. Under this rule, the candidate who receives a plurality of popular votes (more than any competitor) in the state is entitled to all the electoral votes from that state. For instance, if Florida voters award more votes to the Republican candidate than to any other, he or she will receive all 29 of the state's electoral votes. Maine and Nebraska do not use the unit rule; instead, those states award two electors to the candidate who wins the most votes and apportion the remainder according to the popular vote in each congressional district. No elector is under a constitutional obligation, however, to cast a ballot as advertised. This produces the potential for faithless electors—electors who cast their votes for someone other than the choice expressed by the electorate. This has occurred more than 150 times in our nation's history, but it has never altered an election result.

If no candidate receives a majority of electoral votes, members of the House of Representatives choose the president from among top vote-getters, with each state receiving one vote. The Senate chooses the vice president. The Framers believed that few candidates would command a majority of the popular vote and felt that the House of Representatives would choose most presidents. They devised the Electoral College to quell political infighting but considered it unlikely to be important in most presidential contests. As it turned out, the House formally selected only two presidents—Thomas Jefferson (1800) and John Quincy Adams (1824).

Originally, each elector submitted a single ballot with two names. The candidate receiving the highest number of votes (but at least a majority of all votes) became president, and the runner-up became vice president. In 1796, this produced a president from one party and a vice president from another. Four years later, it resulted in a tie for the presidency between two candidates from the same party, Thomas Jefferson and Aaron Burr. In response to the political furor caused by these events, Congress enacted the Twelfth Amendment in 1804, requiring electors to cast separate ballots for president and vice president.

Did You Know?

. . . That four presidents won the popular vote but lost the presidency? Andrew Jackson won the popular vote but lost the election to John Quincy Adams (1824); Samuel J. Tilden won the popular vote but lost the election to Rutherford B. Hayes (1876); Grover Cleveland won the popular vote but lost the election to Benjamin Harrison (1888); Al Gore won the popular vote but lost the election to George W. Bush (2000).

Did You Know?

. . . That if a presidential election is ever thrown into the House of Representatives, the Constitution provides that members vote not as individuals but as states, with each state having a single vote? If a large state's delegation were evenly split, it might not be able to cast a vote.

The 2000 election demonstrated a potentially more troubling shortcoming with the Electoral College: One candidate can win enough electoral votes to become president while losing the popular vote. Democratic candidate Al Gore won the popular vote by over one half-million votes, but Republican George W. Bush won the presidency by a single electoral vote after a contentious showdown over ballots cast in Florida. This was not the first such occurrence; similar problems arose in the elections in 1824, 1876, and 1888. In those years, votes in the House or last-minute political negotiations between the parties settled the outcome. In 2000, a Supreme Court ruling in the case of *Bush v. Gore* ended the recount process in Florida and gave the victory to Bush.

battleground state
Competitive state where neither party holds an overwhelming edge.

express powers Powers granted to the president by the Constitution.

The 2000 election was just the most recent, and perhaps the most disturbing, example of the problems that can arise within our presidential election system. Anomalies such as these have caused some critics to wonder whether the Electoral College has outlived its usefulness and whether it has a dampening impact on political engagement today. Recent Gallup polls show that more than 60 percent of the American people would support an amendment to replace the institution with the direct election of the president.[11]

Electoral College Strategy Because the Electoral College, not the popular vote, determines the victor, candidates must devise a strategy to ensure that they gather the 270 electoral votes they need to win. This means candidates must determine which states are crucial for their success and plan their campaigns accordingly. First, each

party must secure its "base" states, those that reliably vote for that party in general elections. Candidates rarely spend significant time or other resources in their opponents' strongholds. In recent elections, political observers referred to Republican base states as "red" states and Democratic base states as "blue" states. Red states are generally less populated but more numerous and are spread across the South and Midwest. The more heavily populated blue states are concentrated along the West Coast and in the Upper Midwest and Northeast.

Second, candidates must pick and choose **battleground states**—competitive states—where neither side has a major advantage—where they feel they have the best hope of success. As campaigns carefully piece together strategies that focus on the precise combination of states necessary to reach the 270-vote mark, both candidates will be eyeing the battleground states.

In 2008, both Barack Obama and John McCain set out to change the electoral map by expanding the number of battleground states and trying to pick up states traditionally won by the opposing party. Obama campaigned hard in formerly Republican territory in Colorado, Nevada, North Carolina, and Virginia. McCain turned his attention to the Democratic-leaning states of Michigan, Minnesota, and Pennsylvania. Both candidates continued to pay close atention to Ohio and Florida, where recent presidential contests had been won or lost.

Obama had two very big advantages over McCain. First, since he did not accept public financing, he could continue to raise and spend virtually unlimited sums of money. In September, he broke all previous records by taking in more than $150 million. By contrast, McCain was limited to the publicly provided sum of $84 million for the general election campaign, although he could also count on the Republican National Committee to spend on his behalf. Nevertheless, Obama's fundraising advantage allowed him to pour millions into advertising. For example, according to the Federal Election Commission, Obama and Democratic party committees that supported his effort spent nearly $105 million from October 1 to October 15 alone. McCain and Republican party entities, by contrast, spent just over $25 million. Obama's media buys included spending in traditional Republican strongholds such as Indiana, forcing McCain to spread his scarce resources thin just to maintain visibility. In late October, Obama bought half-hour slots on prime time network TV (at a total cost of over $4 million) to present his closing arguments. Neither campaign received substantial ad support from outside groups like 527 organizations, partly because of bad publicity and fines levied in earlier campaigns, but also because both McCain and Obama discouraged such spending on their behalf.

The Shrinking Battleground

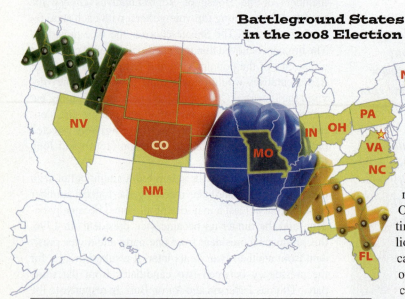

Battleground States in the 2008 Election

Source: Politico's 2008 Swing State Map. Accessed at http://www.politico.com/convention/swingstate.html

Secondly, the Obama campaign built a formidable ground operation during the long primary season that it resurrected in September and relied upon heavily in the final weeks of the campaign. More than 700 offices were opened in battleground states, operated by paid staff who organized thousands of volunteers, neighborhood by neighborhood. Unlike John Kerry, who in 2004 relied on outside groups to get out the vote, Obama utilized locally recruited citizens to canvass their own neighborhoods—an approach that has shown to be far more effective. While Republicans had employed the same techniques in 2004 and again in 2008, the Obama effort dwarfed those of their Republican counterparts. In addition, Obama made effective use of new technologies by collecting the e-mail addresses and cell phone numbers of thousands of young people who attended his campaign events, sending them periodic messages about how they could help.

Perhaps the most important advantage for Obama, however, was the financial crisis and quickly deteriorating state of the U.S. economy. Obama could point to McCain's record of support for Republican initiatives, which many believed contributed to the crisis. The Republican candidate faced an almost insurmountable hurdle being associated with the policies of a very unpopular president.

PRESIDENTIAL POWER

The American presidency has evolved into the most powerful post in the world. Effectively exercising this awesome power requires the ability to diagnose problems, assert priorities, work cooperatively with others, recruit support from other decision makers, shepherd policies through a giant bureaucracy, and communicate effectively to the public. The potential for failure is high, particularly when opponents place roadblocks in the president's path. It is no wonder that Franklin D. Roosevelt, considered to be the architect of the modern presidency, once called the presidency a lonely job. "If you are president," he once commented to an advisor, "you'll be looking at the door

Presidential powers are both real and ceremonial. The nation looks to the president for leadership in times of crisis.

over there and knowing that practically everybody that walks through it wants something out of you."[12]

As we discussed earlier, the Framers were wary of executive power. As a result, the Constitution gives presidents few **express powers**, or explicit grants of authority, and places limits on them through a system of checks and balances. Congress can also cede powers to the executive that enable the president to enforce laws. Modern presidents use these **delegated powers** to enact a great deal of legislation. When Congress authorizes a clean air law, for example, it does not specify the quantity of pollutants smokestacks may release into the atmosphere. Instead, it delegates to the executive branch the authority to make rules specifying such matters.

The president may also exercise **discretionary powers** associated with carrying out official duties. Presidents have used their discretionary power to claim extensive authority, especially during times of war or national emergency. After the September 11, 2001, terrorist attacks, President Bush issued a number of directives in the name of national security to protect the homeland. For example, he authorized the CIA to engage in political assassination of named terrorists, effectively lifting a 25-year ban on such activities. And he authorized the Treasury Department to freeze assets of alleged terrorists.[13] The president must learn how best to use this mix of express, delegated, and discretionary powers in fulfilling the various roles of the office.

delegated powers Powers ceded by Congress to the president.

discretionary powers Powers the president assumes, giving him greater authority and flexibility in performing the duties of office.

Chief Executive

As the nation's chief executive officer, the president oversees a vast bureaucracy that administers countless programs on which millions of Americans depend. Virtually every citizen has an interest in the efficient operation of the federal agencies the president oversees. Yet the scope of the federal government is so vast that a single person cannot hope to personally manage all of its affairs. The president exercises the power of appointment to hire people to run the day-to-day operations of government and to assist in broader duties, such as budgeting and law enforcement. The president may also issue executive orders to achieve policy goals in the absence of legislation, a long-standing yet controversial practice.

Appointment Even our earliest presidents appointed a substantial number of persons to government jobs. George Washington filled more than one thousand positions from customs collector to surveyor, usually on the basis of statements attesting to the candidate's good character and moral virtue.[14]

cabinet Presidential appointees to the major administrative units of the executive branch.

recess appointment Political appointment made by the president when Congress is out of session.

impoundment Presidential refusal to expend funds appropriated by Congress.

rescission Cutback of funds for particular programs that requires congressional approval.

line item veto Executive power to reject a portion of a bill, usually a budget appropriation.

The president is free to choose the leaders for top administrative posts, known as the **cabinet**, but must seek the advice and consent of the Senate for their approval (see Chapter 11). Senate committees subject nominees to extensive screening and hearing procedures before the entire body votes on confirmation. The president sometimes personally introduces nominees to senators or solicits suggestions from powerful Senate leaders. The Senate has rejected few presidential nominees in the modern era. Senators are reluctant to reject the president's preferred choice for a post unless they believe the nominee is genuinely unfit for service. Of course, lawmakers may place pressure on nominees to withdraw from consideration when background checks reveal legal or ethical lapses. This happened in the case of several Obama nominees, including Tom Daschle, the president's choice for Secretary of Health and Human Services, who was discovered not to have paid all his taxes.

When the Senate does block a nominee, the president may respond by waiting until Congress goes into recess and then appointing the nominee without Senate approval. Such **recess appointments** are effective only until the end of the next Senate session. Recess appointments are not uncommon. Bill Clinton made 139 recess appointments; George W. Bush, 171. Some can be controversial, such as President Obama's appointment of union lawyer Craig Becker to the National Labor Relations Board in 2010. The Constitution grants department heads and other government officers the power to make lower-level agency appointments.

Washington filled more than one thousand positions . . . usually on the basis of statements attesting to the candidate's good character and moral virtue.

Budgeting Although the Constitution gives Congress the power to control the purse strings, presidents have taken the initiative in proposing and implementing budgetary priorities. Before 1921, each federal agency submitted a separate budget request directly to the House of Representatives. To impose order on this chaotic process, Congress passed the Budget and Accounting Act of 1921, which required the president to coordinate the budget and submit to Congress annual estimates of program costs. The Office of Management and Budget (OMB, originally the Bureau of the Budget) assists the president in generating budget requests and monitoring expenditures. The OMB reviews agency requests, clears policy recommendations, ensures that agency expenditures and policies conform to the president's priorities, and guides the president's agenda through Washington's bureaucratic maze.[15]

The increased budgetary authority of the executive branch has given presidents immense power to control the political agenda but has also generated heated battles with Congress, which must authorize spending. Until 1974, for example, the president could rein in congressional spending by **impoundment**, or withholding of funds. Responding to what it considered the Nixon administration's overtly partisan use of this tool, Congress placed severe limits on the president's authority to withhold funds already appropriated. The president can request a **rescission**, or cutback, of funds in particular areas, but they must be approved by Congress within a specified period of time. Several presidents have sought the power to exercise a **line item veto**, the authority to slice individual programs from budgets passed by Congress. Governors in most states already have such authority. However, the Supreme Court held that enacting such a change in presidential power requires a constitutional amendment, a lengthy and politically difficult process.[16]

2011 witnessed a series of showdowns between the president and Republicans in Congress over raising the debt ceiling, a procedure that allows the government to borrow additional funds to pay bills for spending Congress has already authorized. Republicans, fueled by the enthusiasm of newly elected Tea Party members, fought any attempt to raise taxes in order to reduce the nation's growing debt. A series of potential compromises between President Obama and Speaker John Boehner fell apart. At the eleventh hour, a deal was crafted by which the debt ceiling was raised in exchange for about $1 trillion in spending cuts, and a "super committee" of members of both Houses of Congress was created to find additional ways to reduce the debt. The deal caused consternation particularly among Democrats who believed the president gave up too much in the debt crisis without getting the additional revenues he originally sought.

Law Enforcement Traditionally, law enforcement has been the province of state and local government, but as the federal government has grown and assumed greater responsibilities, the federal executive has played an ever-larger role in law enforcement. Today, executive agencies enforce not only criminal laws but also laws affecting public health, business regulation, and civil rights, among a host of other areas.

The executive branch attempted to strengthen and centralize its control over federal law enforcement in the wake of the 2001 terrorist attacks. A congressional commission investigating the attacks found that existing criminal law made it difficult, and sometimes impossible, for federal law enforcement agencies to share pertinent information regarding ongoing terrorist investigations. The commission proposed a number of steps to break down interagency barriers. These included creating a National

change decision-making procedures, or give substance and force to statutes.[18] Presidents also use them during times of crisis to carry out actions deemed essential to national security. Woodrow Wilson, for example, issued nearly two thousand such decrees during World War I.

Many of these orders are mundane, dealing with bureaucratic organization. Others are used to overturn actions of past presidents or to mollify interest groups. Barack Obama issued 74 executive orders during his first two years, many reversing the policies of his predecessor in such matters as the closing of the Guantanamo Bay detention center and expansion of stem cell research.

Some executive orders break new legal ground and are highly controversial. One of the more than 250 executive orders issued by President George W. Bush (Executive Order 13440, issued in July 2007) exempts captured Taliban, Al Qaeda, and foreign fighters in Iraq from protections of

LINCOLN REACTED to the Confederate attack on Fort Sumter by . . . suspending habeus corpus, and trying civilians in military courts. . . .

Counterterrorism Center to coordinate intelligence about potential terrorist attacks and establishing a new Office of the Director of National Intelligence to oversee intelligence from a variety of agencies.[17] More controversial were changes permitting the surveillance of domestic citizens. After the 9/11 attacks, the Bush administration sought to use wiretaps of international phone and Internet traffic without warrants in an effort to stem additional attacks. At first, Congress approved such actions—including the monitoring of conversations of U.S. citizens—so long as the targets of eavesdropping were outside the United States. In 2008, Congress placed domestic surveillance under an additional check by requiring that they be approved by a secret court.

In addition to the power to enforce the law, the president also holds the power to pardon convicted criminals. This power can be far-reaching, as demonstrated by President Gerald Ford's decision to pardon Richard Nixon after the Watergate scandal. More recently, President Bush commuted a portion of the sentence requiring prison time for vice presidential aide Lewis "Scooter" Libby, who was convicted of lying to a grand jury about a news leak regarding a CIA operative. The action drew criticism from Democrats. Despite the controversial nature of the pardon power, the Constitution does not limit it or require that the president share it with any other branch.

Executive Orders A president may issue **executive orders**, decrees with the force of law but not requiring legislative approval, for a variety of reasons. Although the Constitution does not define these orders, presidents have construed them as lawful instruments for carrying out constitutionally defined executive duties. The president issues executive orders most frequently to establish executive branch agencies, modify bureaucratic rules or actions,

the Third Geneva Convention and authorizes the CIA to use interrogation techniques like waterboarding, or simulated drowning, that are more severe than those used by military personnel. President Obama revoked this policy with his own executive order just two days into his administration. Interrogations are now limited to those authorized by the Army Field Manuals.

> **executive order** A decree with the force of law but not requiring legislative approval.

James Madison believed that executive orders threatened the separation of powers by allowing presidents to make their own laws. Nevertheless, Congress can pass laws limiting discretionary presidential action, and public opinion can limit the lengths to which a president will go before incurring the voters' wrath.

Commander in Chief

The Framers understood that the president must have the power to defend the nation and command the troops in times of conflict, but they disagreed about giving the president the power to make war. They compromised by permitting the chief executive to act to repel invasions but not to initiate war.[19] Article II, Section 2 of the Constitution reflects this compromise but has sowed confusion because of its ambiguity.

Although Congress has the constitutional power to declare war (see Chapter 11), it has done so formally only five times.[20] In most of the conflicts in which the nation has been involved, the president has asserted the authority to act in response to a perceived crisis. Abraham Lincoln, for example, reacted to the Confederate attack on Fort Sumter by raising troops, imposing naval blockades on southern ports, suspending habeas corpus, and trying

THE NETWORKED CAMPAIGN

Among the advantages Barack Obama enjoyed during the 2008 presidential campaign was a sophisticated social-networking strategy, an energetic army of foot soldiers, and a trove of more than 10 million e-mail addresses of supporters to whom he could return over and over again for financial contributions. Four years later, Republicans are matching him on every count.

Whereas Republicans were trailing in the use of social media four years ago, today they enjoy the same sophistication as their Democratic counterparts. The 2010 midterm elections proved that no one party has a lock on the use of new technology. "The notion that the Internet was owned by liberals, owned by the left in the wake of the Obama victory, has been proven false," Patrick Ruffini, a Republican political strategist, told *The Washington Post.**

Today, Republican candidates and elected officials are as likely to utilize all the tools of social networking as Democrats are. Republican voters matched Democrats in their use of these tools in the 2010 campaign, with 40 percent of Republican online users turning to social media to get politically involved in a campaign, compared to 38 percent of Democratic voters. "Tea Party supporters were espe-

Political Social Networking Activities by 2010 Vote

2010 Congressional Vote	Rep %	Dem %	Did Not Vote %
Use a social networking site	43	44	49

Percent of SNS users who used the sites to...

	Rep %	Dem %	Did Not Vote %
Discover which candidates your friends voted for	19	21	14
Post political content	18	16	9
Get candidate or campaign info	19	15	13
Friend a candidate or cause	17	12	8
Join a political group/cause	13	11	7
Start a new political group/cause	3	3	1

Source: The Pew Research Center's Internet & American Life Project, November 3–24, 2010 Post-Election Tracking Survey.

Voters' Use of Social Networking Sites

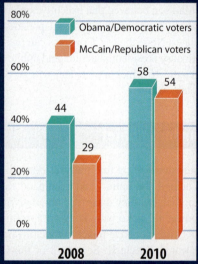

- Obama/Democratic voters
- McCain/Republican voters

2008: 44 / 29
2010: 58 / 54

Source: The Pew Research Center's Internet & American Life Project, November 3–24 2010 Post-Election Tracking Survey. N=2,257 national adults ages 18 and older including 755 cell phone interviews were conducted in English and Spanish.

cially likely to use social media to connect with a political group or candidate."† And the Democratic edge in online fundraising is quickly disappearing as well. It did not take long for Sarah Palin's Political Action Committee fundraising site to attract 2.9 million fans.

Social networking sites present candidates with an abundance of useful information that can help them market their messages more effectively through a process known as microtargeting. E-mail addresses can be cross-referenced with consumer data to discover voter patterns and habits. This allows the candidates to target their messages to narrow audiences, for example, upscale beer drinkers who drive hybrid vehicles. It also allows them to respond to supporters almost immediately and on a time frame suited to the recipient. For example, if the voter checks his or her e-mail each day at 11 p.m., that is precisely when the candidate's daily message arrives— along with a donation request. Future campaign successes, therefore, will hinge in part on how effectively candidates build and utilize online social networks.

* Jennifer Preston, "Republicans Sharpening Online Tools for 2012," *The New York Times*, April 20, 2011, p. A13.

† Aaron Smith, "Twenty-two percent of online Americans used social networking or Twitter for politics in 2010 campaign," Pew Research Center, Jan. 27, 2011. Accessed on June 2, 2011 at http://www.pewinternet.org/~/media/Files/Reports/2011/PIP-Social-Media-and-2010-Election.pdf.

civilians in military courts—acts that extend presidential power beyond constitutional limits. He failed to convene Congress for months and received support for his actions only retroactively. He agonized over the dilemma but concluded that "measures otherwise unconstitutional might become lawful by becoming indispensable to the preservation of the nation."[21]

Presidents usually can count on wide public support during times of war or when U.S. interests are attacked, a phenomenon known as **rallying around the flag**. The public is willing to give the president a free hand for only a limited time, however. For example, Americans expressed strong support for President George W. Bush's retaliatory attack on Afghanistan after the September 11, 2001, terrorist attacks. He met with more resistance, however, in the lead-up to the war in Iraq. The revelation that Iraq had no weapons of mass destruction—compounded by mounting U.S. casualties—led to a precipitous drop in public support for the operation. President Obama enjoyed widespread support for his decision to withdraw troops from Iraq, but his decision to send an additional 21,000 troops to Afghanistan to combat Taliban outposts has drawn concern from critics who warn of a protracted conflict that will test the public's patience. The president's decision to assist NATO forces in Libya also drew criticism. The president claimed that since his action did not commit U.S. ground troops but rather provided air and reconnaissance support in a humanitarian effort to protect Libyan citizens from brutal repression of their leader, Colonel Muammar Gaddafi, he did not need congressional approval. The House of

Representatives disagreed, approved a nonbinding resolution rebuking President Obama for continuing the operation without the express consent of Congress, and directed the administration to provide detailed information about its costs and objectives.

During times of crisis, the president may assume **emergency powers** to protect the nation, but their use is also controversial and has led to conflicts over the preservation of civil liberties. Following the U.S. invasion of Afghanistan in 2001, President Bush declared that military tribunals, not civilian courts, would try all **enemy combatants**—enemy fighters captured in battle—whether or not they were members of a national army. Prisoners were not allowed to hear the charges against them and had no access to attorneys. The Supreme Court in 2004 (*Hamdi v. Rumsfeld*) responded to a petition filed on behalf of a prisoner of American descent by holding that the prisoner was entitled to consult with an attorney and to contest his imprisonment before a neutral decision maker. In a companion case, *Rasul v. Bush*, the Court held that foreign-born detainees can also challenge their detention in U.S. courts.

After these decisions, the administration set up military review boards where detainees could challenge their enemy combatant status, and Congress approved the procedures with passage of the Detainee Treatment Act of 2005, which also stripped detainees of access to federal courts

rallying around the flag Sense of patriotism engendered by dramatic national events such as the September 11, 2001, terrorist attacks.

emergency powers Wide-ranging powers a president may exercise during times of crisis or those powers permitted the president by Congress for a limited time.

enemy combatant Enemy fighter captured on the field of battle whether or not a member of an army.

President Obama's pledge to close Guantanamo Bay detention center proved popular during the presidential election but difficult to implement after his inauguration as he found few takers for the prisoners either at home or abroad.

to review their cases. Once again, the Supreme Court, in *Hamdan v. Rumsfeld* (2006), ruled against administration actions, arguing that the military commissions violated international law and that the Detainee Treatment Act did not cover pending cases. The administration could not proceed without additional congressional authorization. In response to *Hamdan*, Congress quickly passed the Military Commissions Act of 2006, which stripped federal district courts of their authority to hear any detainee challenges, *including those that had already been filed.* The law also set up a process by which detainees would be tried before commissions that could consider hearsay evidence and evidence obtained through coercion. Once again, the Supreme Court, in *Boumediene v. Bush* (2008), rejected these procedures, ruling that Guantanamo detainees have a constitutional right under habeas corpus to go to court to challenge their detention. If Congress intends to suspend habeas corpus—something the Constitution does allow it to do—it must provide the accused with a more adequate substitute than the one provided in the Military Commission Act. Writing for the majority, Justice Anthony Kennedy said, "The laws and Constitution are designed to survive, and remain in force, in extraordinary times." In a stinging dissent, Justice Antonin Scalia argued that providing detainees with access to the courts "will almost certainly cause more Americans to be killed."[22] President Obama has decided to keep the system of military commissions created by President Bush to try suspected terrorists. However, he has called for the

extraordinary rendition The practice of secretly abducting terror suspects and transporting them to detention camps in undisclosed locations.

diplomatic recognition Presidential power to offer official privileges to foreign governments.

presidential doctrine Formal statement that outlines the goals and purposes of American foreign policy and the actions to take to advance these goals.

expansion of legal protections for defendants, including the banning of evidence obtained through cruel treatment and the restriction of prosecutors' use of hearsay evidence. No doubt the matter of how to treat individuals captured in the nation's war on terrorism will continue to be fought out in the courts in coming years.

Another controversial practice employed in connection with the war on terrorism was **extraordinary rendition**, or secretly abducting terrorist suspects and transporting them to detention camps in undisclosed locations. Critics assert that the United States deprives these suspects of due process and that interrogators at the camps torture them. President Obama has signed an executive order closing the CIA's foreign prisons, but he has left open the door to continued foreign rendition of prisoners. Former CIA director, Leon Panetta, told Congress the agency is likely to continue to transfer detainees to third countries and would rely on diplomatic assurances of good treatment. Critics note that these are the same assurances the Bush administration gave that proved to be ineffective.[23] The controversies these measures raise about presidential powers in wartime are unlikely to be resolved any time soon.

Chief Diplomat

The Constitution directs the president to share with the Senate responsibility for making treaties and with Congress the conduct of diplomacy. Historically, however, the president has taken the lead and Congress has then reacted to that decision. Among the tools of foreign policy at the president's disposal are diplomatic recognition, presidential doctrines, executive agreements, and summit meetings. **Diplomatic recognition** of foreign officials by a president, an extension of the Constitution's authorization to receive ambassadors and other public officials (Article II, Section 3), can elevate the world status of a nation and entitle it to certain benefits, such as expanded trade. Often, recognition is contentious, especially when it involves former enemies. The United States did not recognize the Socialist Republic of Vietnam, for example, until 1995, more than 20 years after the termination of hostilities.

Presidential doctrines are formal statements that outline the goals or purposes of American foreign policy and the actions the United States is prepared to take in advancing these goals. Presidential doctrines have a venerable history.

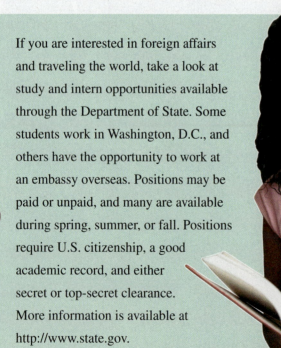

get **involved!**

If you are interested in foreign affairs and traveling the world, take a look at study and intern opportunities available through the Department of State. Some students work in Washington, D.C., and others have the opportunity to work at an embassy overseas. Positions may be paid or unpaid, and many are available during spring, summer, or fall. Positions require U.S. citizenship, a good academic record, and either secret or top-secret clearance.

More information is available at http://www.state.gov.

Perhaps the most famous is the Monroe Doctrine, issued by President James Monroe in 1823 in response to colonial expansion by European powers. The Monroe Doctrine has become a foundation on which other presidents have built to define America's interests and role in the world. It asserts the intention of the United States to resist any attempt by a European power to interfere in the affairs of any country in the Western hemisphere not already a colony. Theodore Roosevelt added the Roosevelt Corollary in 1904, announcing our nation's intention to act as this hemisphere's policeman if needed to protect neighbor nations. The Roosevelt Corollary was used to justify U.S. intervention in Latin America. President Harry Truman offered the Truman Doctrine as the foreign policy credo of the Cold War, calling for the United States to support free people who are resisting subjugation anywhere in the world. Presidents Eisenhower, Nixon, Carter, and Reagan issued similar doctrines asserting our right to defend other regions of the world, including the Middle East and the Persian Gulf.

In the wake of the September 11, 2001, terrorist attacks, George W. Bush declared a doctrine of preemptive self-defense. According to the highly controversial **Bush Doctrine**, the nation's right of self-defense entitles the United States to attack an enemy it feels presents an imminent threat to national security, even if the enemy has not attacked first. In 2003, the Bush administration utilized this doctrine to justify invading Iraq, arguing that its weapons of mass destruction constituted an imminent and grave threat to our national security. The failure to find those weapons in the war's aftermath only intensified the controversy over this doctrine. President Obama has so far avoided a doctrinal approach to foreign policy, but he has signaled important changes to the policies of his predecessor. His approach is far less ideological and more pragmatic. He has shown his willingness to use force but also an increased reliance on diplomatic and economic tools to bring about change.[24] And he is much more likely than his predecessor to seek cooperation and consensus among our allies rather than taking unilateral action.

An **executive agreement** is a pact made between the president and a foreign leader or government that does not undergo the same Senate approval process as a treaty. Many of these agreements involve the fine-tuning or interpretation of details of larger treaties. Although executive agreements, unlike treaties, do not bind future presidents, most represent long-

standing commitments to friendly nations that succeeding presidents honor, regardless of party affiliation. Modern presidents often use these agreements to conduct business once reserved for treaties, and the number of executive agreements has escalated in recent years.[25] In the final days of his administration, George W. Bush approved a status of forces agreement with Iraq that included a deadline for American troop withdrawal by the end of 2011 and additional restrictions on how and where U.S. troops conduct their missions. The United States maintains status of forces agreements, created solely by executive action, with more than one hundred nations. President Obama ended our combat mission in Iraq on August 31, 2010, by withdrawing 95,000 combat troops, some of which were dispatched to our continuing effort in Afghanistan. However, as many as 50,000 troops remain in Iraq in noncombat roles, assisting Iraqi forces to bring order to many sections of the country, an effort that may take years. In addition, the president ordered the phased withdrawal of up to 33,000 troops from Afghanistan in 2011 and 2012 with the expectation that the remaining 70,000 forces will be withdrawn by 2014 if conditions on the ground allow.

Presidents often use the power and prestige of the office to convene summit meetings, at which they meet with world leaders to influence the course of world events. Notable summits occurred in 1978, when Egyptian president Anwar al-Sadat and Israeli prime minister Menachem Begin met with President Jimmy Carter to pave the way for a peace treaty between the two nations, and in 1986, when President Ronald Reagan and Soviet general secretary Mikhail Gorbachev met in Reykjavik, Iceland, to discuss the elimination of intermediate-range nuclear missiles. This meeting produced a treaty ratified in 1988. President Obama signed a treaty with Russia aimed at making substantial cuts to their nuclear arsenal at a meeting of world leaders in Prague in the Czech Republic on April 8, 2010. The treaty was ratified by the Senate in the waning days of the 111th Congress.

> **Bush Doctrine** Foreign policy position advanced by George W. Bush asserting the U.S. government's right to authorize preemptive attacks against potential aggressors.
>
> **executive agreement** A pact that is made between the president and a foreign leader of a government that does not require Senate approval.

Chief of State

In addition to being the head of government, the president also serves as the nation's symbolic leader, or chief of state. In some nations, this duty is performed by a monarch. The Constitution attaches few official duties to this function: taking a formal oath of office, providing

The 1986 summit in Reykjavik, Iceland, between Soviet general secretary Mikhail Gorbachev and U.S. president Ronald Reagan paved the way toward concrete agreements between the two superpowers on intermediate-range nuclear forces and strategic nuclear weapons.

President Obama has traveled extensively in an effort to forge closer economic and military ties with our allies.

Congress with periodic State of the Union messages, and receiving public ministers. Nevertheless, the job of chief of state creates an emotional bond with the electorate that contributes to a president's authority; it also consumes an enormous amount of the president's time. From attending ceremonial events and state funerals, to awarding medals to war heroes, to greeting foreign dignitaries and members of championship sports teams, the president presides over countless events as symbolic leader of the nation. President Obama maintained an active foreign travel schedule, taking advantage of the mostly positive press he received abroad following his election.

As the president's public visibility has risen, the role of chief of state has assumed greater importance. Prior to the 1920s, for example, presidents fulfilled their constitutional duty to provide a message on the State of the Union by submitting their report to Congress in writing. Since that time, however, the State of the Union address has become an opportunity for the president to speak to a national audience via radio and television. This increased visibility helps the president highlight the administration's accomplishments and pressure Congress to enact presidential initiatives. Performing this duty contributes to his role as opinion leader, as discussed later in this chapter.

Lawmaker

The president plays a crucial role in the lawmaking process. In addition to the constitutional authority to recommend legislation to Congress and the power of the veto, the president exercises substantial authority through the ability to lobby members of Congress and the controversial practice of selectively interpreting congressional legislation.

Prior to the twentieth century, most presidents took a less active role in shaping legislation than their latter-day counterparts. Whereas early presidents enlisted cabinet members or aides to lobby their friends in Congress, twentieth-century presidents took more direct approaches. Teddy Roosevelt employed the bully pulpit, arguing publicly for favored legislation. Franklin D. Roosevelt's radio "fireside chats" to the nation similarly put public pressure on lawmakers to support his initiatives. FDR was also willing to enlist the help of executive agencies to advance his agenda, using the Bureau of the Budget to monitor, screen, and propose legislative action in accord with his New Deal. President Obama has invited members of Congress to the White House, held open forums with lawmakers from both parties, and used the e-mail list of millions of supporters gathered in his 2008 campaign to enlist their support in lobbying for his legislation.

The interests of the president and Congress are not necessarily congruent. The president is the one individual with a truly national constituency and vision and is responsible for the operation of the national bureaucracy that Congress funds. The president is also responsible for national security. It is through his or her legislative agenda that the president sets the course for the nation. Members of Congress, on the other hand, are more attuned to the problems and concerns of their own districts or states. Finding common ground between national and local interests can be somewhat of a challenge, and presidents exert considerable time and effort cultivating legislators to win their support.

The White House maintains an Office of Legislative Affairs, a group of policy and institutional experts that the

When the President Has Won

This graph illustrates the percentage of the times in the recent past that the president won on roll call votes on which he took a clear position. The data combines House and Senate figures.

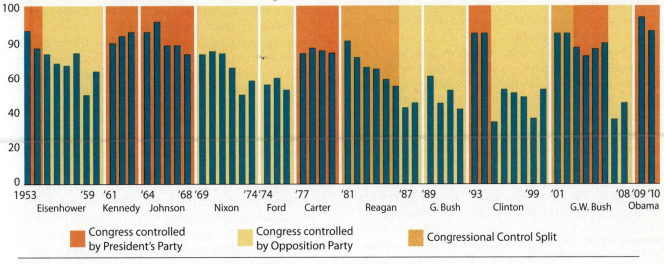

Percentage of times president won roll call votes

Legend:
- Congress controlled by President's Party
- Congress controlled by Opposition Party
- Congressional Control Split

Source: Adapted from *Congressional Quarterly Weekly*, January 3, 2011.

president can call on to write legislation, negotiate with members of Congress, and garner legislative support. In winning votes for their agenda, presidents can employ a number of tools. They can offer to direct funds to member districts for discretionary projects; they can help members from their own party raise campaign funds and make personal appearances with them; they can recommend members or their campaign contributors for political appointments. When a popular president has difficulty obtaining cooperation, he can appeal to the public and ask them to pressure Congress, a tactic that worked successfully for Ronald Reagan when he faced congressional opposition. Although the president does wield powerful weapons of personal influence in lobbying Congress, members face many pressures that the president is powerless to influence. Studies of presidential influence with Congress show that "presidents operate typically at the margins of coalition building and . . . their legislative skills are essentially limited to exploiting rather than creating opportunities for leadership."[26]

Some presidents are more successful than others in getting their agendas passed. Success depends on a number of factors, including whether Congress is in the hands of the president's own party or the opposition's, as well as on the president's popularity. Presidents generally have an easier time in their first terms when Congress is disposed to give them an opportunity to present their case, and in times of national

Hot or Not?

Should presidents be prohibited from using signing statements to interpret a law?

emergency when the president commands deference. Presidential success also depends on the number of measures on which a president takes an active stand. The chart above illustrates first-term successes and the increased likelihood of success when Congress is controlled by the president's party. President George W. Bush had a very high success rate until Congress passed into Democratic control in 2007, when he suffered one of the lowest legislative success rates in recent history. Armed with substantial majorities in both houses of Congress, President Obama enjoyed the highest level of legislative success during his first year in office of any modern president, eclipsing the success rate of Lyndon Johnson in 1965. Congress approved over 96 percent of the legislation on which he took a clearly stated position. This success, however, came at a price, as a skeptical public punished him with low approval ratings and rebuked his party with substantial losses in the 2010 midterm elections.

Even when presidents lose a legislative battle, they can still influence the course of legislation by exercising the veto. Early presidents used the veto sparingly. They generally adhered to the view that Congress should be the principal lawmaking body and tended to veto only those bills they believed violated the Constitution. Andrew Jackson was more inclined to use the veto for political reasons, but the number of presidential vetoes remained relatively small until the Reconstruction battles following the Civil War. Franklin Roosevelt pioneered the modern use of the veto as an instrument of legislative policy to thwart attacks on his priorities while advancing his own political agenda.[27] The veto is a powerful tool, because two-thirds of both houses of Congress must vote to override a presidential veto. Of the 1,492 regular presidential vetoes issued between 1789 and 2007, only 107 (about 7 percent) were overridden. George W. Bush vetoed 12 bills in his two terms and prevailed on 8, including an important troop withdrawal measure that he opposed. President Obama issued only 2 vetoes during his first two years of office.

Presidents can have an impact on how laws are interpreted by appending signing statements to legislation they approve, but to which they may have some objection or reservation. Sometimes these statements offer the president's interpretation of the act; sometimes they highlight portions that the president reserves the right not to enforce because they may be unconstitutional or infringe on legitimate presidential authority. Presidents rarely issued signing statements until the presidency of Ronald Reagan; since then, the practice has mushroomed. George H. W. Bush appended statements to 232 statutes over four years in office, and Bill Clinton utilized the device 140 times over his eight years. The practice came under public scrutiny when the number exploded to 750 during the presidency of George W. Bush. One of these was attached to a bill passed in 2006 outlawing the torture of detained enemy combatants. According to the statement, the White House reserves the right to waive portions of the bill in the interest of national security.

honeymoon period The period following an election when the public and Congress give the newly elected president the greatest latitude in decision making.

Legal scholars are divided about the use of signing statements. Some argue that the statements allow presidents flexibility in administering laws; others hold them unconstitutional, arguing that the president must either sign and enforce the entire law or veto it.[28] A 2006 report by the American Bar Association challenged the use of such statements, but presidents are unlikely to abandon the practice unless the Supreme Court acts to halt it. President Obama promised to curtail the use of signing statements but issued more than a dozen during his first two years in office, including one that reserves the right for the White House to withhold information requested by a congressional commission created to investigate the financial crisis of 2008–2009.

PRESIDENTIAL ROLES

In addition to the constitutionally mandated duties already discussed, presidents play a variety of outside roles as leaders of their political parties, economic leaders, and leaders of public opinion. These roles give the president many more opportunities for leading the nation, but they also increase citizen expectations about what the president can accomplish.

Party Leader

The president enjoys unique opportunities to advance the fortunes of fellow party members and the party's ideas through his ability to distribute patronage and to back legislative initiatives. Another way that presidents frequently demonstrate gratitude for party loyalty is to name party donors as foreign ambassadors. President Obama is no exception. Among his early appointments was Louis Susman, a former investment banker who raised millions for Democratic candidates, who received a coveted appointment as ambassador to Great Britain.

Because presidential success hinges partly on maintaining party control in Congress, presidents frequently raise funds and campaign for party members running for Congress. When the president is popular, party members seek out opportunities to share the presidential limelight at official ceremonies or campaign rallies. By contrast, lawmakers tend to avoid associating themselves with an unpopular president. As President Bush's approval ratings began to plummet and the Democrats regained control of Congress in 2006, a growing number of prominent Republicans in Congress distanced themselves from the president's Iraq War strategy. President Obama was eagerly courted by Democratic candidates seeking his assistance in raising campaign funds during the first few months after he took office. As his first year in office wore on, however, the president had a difficult time maintaining support from two factions within his party: "blue dog" Democrats who balked at the size of government deficits and health-care expenditures and liberal Democrats concerned about the president's expansion of the war in Afghanistan and his tepid support for a health-care "public option." Party support continued to be tepid after big congressional losses in 2010.

The Honeymoon: Obama's Approval Fades

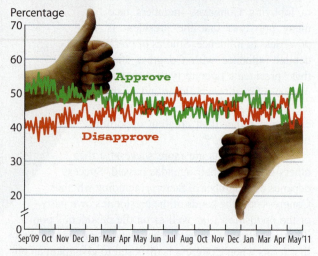

Source: Gallup Organization.

Economic Leader

Since the New Deal, presidents have amassed a vast bureaucracy to monitor economic activity and to control fiscal policy in ways that ameliorate public concerns about the economy. Although the president exerts relatively little direct power over the economy, voters typically punish presidents during times of economic hardship. Despite riding a wave of 90 percent popular approval after Operation Desert Storm in 1991, President George H. W. Bush failed in his reelection bid just a year later, thanks largely to a steep economic recession that failed to reverse course soon enough to affect the outcome. An economic crisis clearly contributed to the election of Barack Obama and set expectations high that he would turn the economy around. His inability to effect a quick recovery, however, cost him popular support and cost his party seats in Congress.

In reality, presidential power over the economy is limited more or less to making proposals about taxing and spending that change the calculations of economic actors. The results of these policies are notoriously difficult to predict with precision and take many years to work themselves through the economy. Often, their full effect is not even felt during the president's own tenure in office. Sometimes presidents are forced to improvise solutions to complex problems as in 2008 when President Bush proposed a comprehensive bailout for the financial system in response to a crisis precipitated by failures in the mortgage market. President Obama supplemented the outgoing president's bank and auto company bailouts with a $787 billion stimulus program of his own designed to jump-start the economy, and he pursued health-care reform despite concerns of growing budget deficits. The mushrooming government debt and the failure of his economic program to quickly turn around the economy caused rising opposition both within Congress and among the electorate, resulting in declining public approval and massive losses for the president's party in the 2010 midterm elections.

Presidents have a bit more flexibility over international trade. Since the 1970s, Congress has given the president fast-track authority to negotiate trade agreements with foreign governments. The president presents these agreements as comprehensive packages that Congress must approve or reject without amendment. The passage of the North American Free Trade Agreement in 1993 and the Central American Free Trade Agreement in 2005 paved the way for an increase in the use of fast-track agreements with nations in the Western hemisphere. President Obama supports free trade but campaigned on a promise to make such agreements more fair to American workers, who find themselves displaced when domestic companies outsource.

Opinion Leader

In order to be effective, a president must campaign and build public support for the administration's agenda. Following inauguration, the president usually enjoys a **honeymoon period** during which the public generally abstains from criticism of the administration and gives the president the benefit of the doubt in proposing and passing legislation. Eventually, however, attacks by opponents, the stream of world events, and legislative battles take their toll on presidential approval. President George W. Bush gained public support in the wake of 9/11 and lost it as the Iraq War dragged on. His approval hit an all-time high just after the attacks, but he left office tied for the lowest approval rating on record. President Obama began his presidency with a reservoir of good feeling and a job approval rating of nearly 70 percent. Job approval during his first one hundred days in office was on par with levels sustained by most modern presidents. However, as the economy continued to shed jobs, as projected deficits mounted, and as opponents of his health-care reform plan garnered headlines through boisterous behavior at town meetings with lawmakers during the summer months, the president's approval rating dipped to just over 50 percent, marking one of the fastest declines in recent times. The raid that killed Osama bin Laden resulted in a brief uptick in presidential approval, but his overall approval continued to hover around the 50 percent mark. Nevertheless, almost all modern presidents have been able to rebound from dips in job approval, and Barack Obama continues to enjoy high personal favorability ratings even among those who disapprove of the way he has handled certain matters such as the economy.

Presidents adopt several tactics to rally public support, such as giving speeches promoting their policies and enlisting supporters or administration officials to pitch administration proposals. It is expected that presidents face the scrutiny of the White House press corps, but modern presidents have increasingly looked for ways to communicate more directly with the public so that they may control their own message. President Obama is no exception.

Gulf Coast residents watch the president's Oval Office address during the BP oil spill crisis.

While he has logged just over the average number of press conferences for modern presidents at this stage in their administrations, he has relied more heavily on joint appearances with foreign leaders—many of these in foreign lands where his support is strong—and on interviews with journalists where he can discuss his ideas at length. He also relies heavily on e-mail, YouTube, and other social networking sites to keep in touch with his supporters.

inner cabinet Term applied to leaders from the Departments of State, Defense, Treasury, and Justice with whom the president meets more frequently than other cabinet officials.

Executive Office of the President Close presidential advisors that include the White House staff, the national security advisor, the chief of staff, and members of various policy councils.

Since the 1930s, presidents have used polls to gauge and formulate policies in tune with public opinion. Franklin Roosevelt's administration conducted trend polling that offered same-day quick responses to new issues.[29] Richard Nixon's administration used daily polling to track his support among specific demographic groups, to test his popularity against potential electoral opponents, and to explore opposition weaknesses.[30]

Skeptical of the national media's ability to faithfully communicate the president's message, Ronald Reagan's advisors gave the president and his spokespersons specific daily themes to communicate to the press. Administration spokespersons were directed to "stay on message" no matter how much reporters wished to discuss other issues. The success of this approach helped earn Reagan the moniker "the Great Communicator." When world events intervene, however, there is sometimes little a president can do to reverse the course of public opinion.

For example, President Obama was powerless to stop the spill from a BP deep-water oil rig explosion that poured millions of gallons of oil into the Gulf of Mexico, causing the worst environmental disaster in U.S. history. His inability to take charge of events cost him popular support and contributed to midterm losses for his party. He used an Oval Office address to convey the administration's resolve to contain the spill and clean up the gulf, but photos of oil spewing a mile beneath the ocean's surface demonstrated the limits of presidential power.

THE EXECUTIVE BRANCH

The president oversees a number of agencies and departments that help formulate and implement administration policies. Some, such as the departments that make up the cabinet, are legislatively created; the president has little freedom to change how they are structured. Others are part of White House operations and the president has substantially more discretion in organizing and staffing them. Over time, presidents have come to rely more heavily on staff within the White House, where the president exercises greater control.

Cabinet

The cabinet consists of political appointees chosen by the president to lead the most important government departments. Cabinet officials preside over an army of civil servants, personnel appointed for their merits or expertise regardless of political affiliation, who carry out the everyday operations of government. Ostensibly, cabinet members both advise the president and are responsible for implementing administration policies within their departments. Since George Washington's day, however, almost all presidents have relied primarily on the secretaries of defense, treasury, and state. The attorney general, who heads the Justice Department and serves as the chief counsel for the government, joins these three secretaries as part of the president's **inner cabinet**, or closest circle of top administrators.

Presidents typically look to fill cabinet positions with individuals from their own party who reflect the president's own priorities and those of valued constituent groups. Many presidents also try to balance the cabinet to reflect significant demographic groups. Presidents who win a second term often make changes in the cabinet that reflect evolving presidential priorities and as a reward for personal loyalty. Presi-

Composition of the Obama Cabinet

Department of Agriculture

Department of Defense

Department of Energy

Department of Homeland Security

Department of Interior

Department of Labor

Department of Transportation

Department of Veterans Affairs

Department of Commerce

Department of Education

Department of Health and Human Services

Department of Housing and Urban Development

Department of Justice

Department of State

Department of Treasury

Environmental Protection Agency

Vice President

Chief of Staff

Council of Economic Advisors

Office of Management and Budget

U. S. Trade Representative

U. N. Ambassador

Source: The White House.

Executive Office of the President

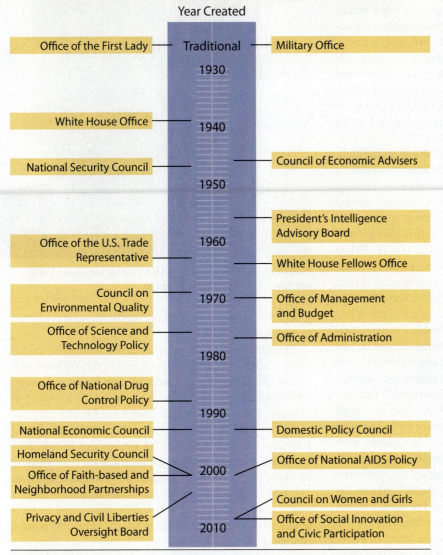

Year Created

| Traditional | |
| Office of the First Lady | Military Office |

1930

White House Office — **1940**

National Security Council — Council of Economic Advisers

1950

President's Intelligence Advisory Board

Office of the U.S. Trade Representative — **1960**

White House Fellows Office

Council on Environmental Quality — **1970** — Office of Management and Budget

Office of Science and Technology Policy — Office of Administration

1980

Office of National Drug Control Policy

1990

National Economic Council — Domestic Policy Council

Homeland Security Council — Office of National AIDS Policy

Office of Faith-based and Neighborhood Partnerships — **2000**

Council on Women and Girls

Privacy and Civil Liberties Oversight Board — Office of Social Innovation and Civic Participation

2010

Source: The White House.

dent Obama's first cabinet appointments were among the most diverse in history, with six women, four African Americans, three Hispanic Americans, and two Asian Americans. It was also moderate politically, including two Republicans and one of the most experienced with two who were sitting governors. Changes began taking place in Obama's cabinet following his party's midterm losses in 2010.

George Washington's cabinet contained just three departments: State, War, and Treasury; today that number has grown to 15.[31] This growth reflects the increased role that government has come to play in the lives of most Americans, especially since the New Deal. It also reflects presidential attention to select constituencies or government policies. President Jimmy Carter, for example, created the Department of Education to reward members of the teacher unions who were instrumental to his electoral victory. More recently, George W. Bush promoted creation of the Department of Homeland Security in response to the government's increased focus on national security threats

in the wake of the terrorist attacks on September 11, 2001. Sometimes presidents accord cabinet status to the heads of subcabinet agencies involved in key administration policies. President Obama, for instance, counts among his cabinet the vice president, the chief of staff, and the heads of the Office of Management and Budget, the Environmental Protection Agency, the Council of Economic Advisers, the United Nations ambassador, and the U.S. trade representative.

Modern presidents rarely meet with the entire cabinet except for ceremonial occasions. Dwight Eisenhower was the last president to meet regularly with his entire cabinet, and even many insiders considered those meetings unproductive.[32] Richard Nixon rarely included cabinet officials in high-level meetings; cabinet members sometimes found out about their department's new initiatives from the press. Bill Clinton did not even attend cabinet briefings, leaving that chore to the White House chief of staff. Presidents today are more likely to consult with cabinet members during meetings of policy groups created and staffed inside the White House, such as the Domestic Policy Council (discussed later in this chapter). The cabinet's role in policymaking is clearly declining. As one insider has noted, "'Cabinet government'—in which each agency manages its own affairs with the president as a general supervisor—is shibboleth, not reality."[33] Power has migrated away from cabinet agencies and become more centralized within the White House. This gives the president much more control and flexibility in meeting the demands of the office.

Executive Office of the President

In 1939, Congress created the **Executive Office of the President (EOP)** to advise the president and to help manage the growing federal bureaucracy. Over the years, the EOP has expanded through the addition of agencies created by legislative statutes as well as executive orders. Under Barack Obama, the EOP consists of more than a dozen units, one of which—the White House Office—contains over twenty entities on its own. Together, these entities employ hundreds of political appointees.

White House Office The White House Office includes political advisors, who attend to matters of daily concern for the administration: policy development, legal affairs, political affairs, press and public communications, legislative affairs, presidential travel, and the increasingly important arena of interest-group relations. These appointees and their staffs, who require no Senate confirmation, review and analyze masses of information to help the president formulate policy proposals. The White House Office of George W. Bush employed approximately four hundred people with a payroll of more than $25 million.[34]

The president's senior advisors, the White House staff, are headed by the **chief of staff**, who acts as something of a traffic cop to coordinate communication between the president and other staffers. This includes serving as a gatekeeper, deciding what information goes in and out of the Oval Office. The chief of staff is also a confidant whom the president trusts to ensure that the White House staff is carrying out its functions properly, meeting deadlines, determining priorities, maintaining cordial relations with the cabinet and Congress, and smoothly coordinating the actions of the various units of the White House. Obama's first chief of staff, Rahm Emanuel, was known for being outspoken and a shrewd party operative. The president's impressive legislative success during his first two years in office owes no small debt to Emanuel's effectiveness. Emanuel's departure to run for mayor of Chicago gave President Obama the opportunity to mend his often rocky relationship with the business community by appointing the more business-friendly Bill Daley. Daley, corporate executive and Commerce Secretary under President Clinton, brings a disciplined management style to the White House and serves as liaison to groups such as the financial sector that are vital to the president's success. A number of other senior presidential advisors such as David Axelrod also left the White House in 2011 to reprise their earlier roles as members of Obama's reelection campaign. The other members of the White House staff provide daily policy and political guidance to the president on a host of issues.

A number of bodies exist within the White House Office to help attend to the president's public image and personal relationship with key constituent groups. The Office of the Press Secretary transmits information about the president's political positions and daily activities, addresses criticism of the president's policies, and deals with questions from the White House press corps. Employees in the Speechwriting Office help the president convey ideas with clarity and rhetorical force. The Office of Political Affairs, established in 1980, is the president's bridge to the political world. These highly placed confidants walk a thin line between public employees and political consultants working outside the White House with pollsters, consultants, and the party's national committee to coordinate measures for political success. The Office of Public Engagement has become particularly important as presidents work to reward interest and constituent

chief of staff The official in charge of coordinating communication between the president and other staffers.

President Obama's first chief of staff Rahm Emanuel was instrumental in advancing the president's legislative agenda.

groups for past support and to assemble ongoing coalitions to meet new challenges.

President Obama has also created a number of policy "czars," who work as issue specialists in the White House. These specialists often coordinate new initiatives across departments and agencies to ensure policy coherence. For example, Nancy-Ann DeParle was named health czar, advising the president on health-care reform, often relegating Kathleen Sebelius, Secretary of Health and Human Services, to a secondary role.[35] Some critics are concerned by the sheer number of czars appointed by Obama (more than 25), by the confusion of roles that sometimes accompanies their power relative to cabinet-level officials, and by their ability to evade congressional oversight since few require confirmation.

National Security Council In 1947, Congress established the National Security Council (NSC) to integrate information from the nation's domestic and foreign intelligence agencies and to advise the president on matters of national security. The national security advisor, appointed by the president without Senate confirmation, heads the body and provides daily briefings to the president. Traditionally, this body has included the vice president, the secretaries of state and defense, the chairperson of the Joint Chiefs of Staff, and (since the previous administration) the Director of National Intelligence. President Obama has restructured the NSC to include other cabinet officials as needed and members of other White House agencies such as the Homeland Security Council. The restructuring is meant to expand the range of issues under the NSC's purview to include cybersecurity, energy, climate change, nationbuilding, and infrastructure. In practice, NSC membership is fluid and the group seldom meets as a whole. Instead, the national security advisor passes information to the president and formulates policy alternatives, acting much as a chief of staff for national security matters.[36]

The national security advisor oversees what has become the largest policy group in the White House, numbering around two hundred. This staff maintains a Situation Room, which collects and analyzes intelligence from around the world, handles liaison with Congress, maintains press relations, and carries on communication with security officers in other nations. The growing threat of international terrorism, however, has prompted changes in the national security organization that have reduced the power of the NSC. Most significantly, in 2002, George W. Bush appointed a new director of intelligence with wide authority over fifteen intelligence-gathering agencies. He also supplemented NSC operations with meetings of a "war cabinet" composed of the vice president; the White House chief of staff; the secretaries of state, defense, and treasury; the CIA director; and the national security advisor.[37] The "war cabinet" was instrumental in planning the Iraq invasion. President Obama plays a very "hands-on" role in national security, often chairing weekly meetings and involving himself in the details of operations from troop buildup in Afghanistan to the bin Laden raid.[38]

Office of Management and Budget Congress originally created the Bureau of the Budget as a division of the Treasury Department, but Franklin Roosevelt moved the agency to the White House in 1939 to assist him in creating an executive budget for Congress. In the 1970s, Richard Nixon changed the agency's name to the Office of Management and Budget (OMB) and altered its role. Instead of examining budget requests and monitoring spending, the OMB became a tool to help mold the president's political priorities and target areas for reduced government spending. President Reagan's OMB director, David Stockman, used the office to coordinate Reagan's tax cuts and to defend his budget policies. Reagan also mandated an OMB review of every government program to ensure that its benefits outweighed its costs. Congress reacted to this expansion of the president's role in budgeting by relying more heavily on its own budgetary analysts in the Congressional Budget Office (CBO). It is not unusual for budget figures generated by the OMB and CBO to be at odds with one another.

Policy Councils Policy councils allow the president to gather experts from both inside and outside the White House into consultative groups organized around policy areas. Among the more notable are the Domestic Policy Council and the National Economic Council. Some presidents rely on these arrangements more than others; President Clinton, for example, made extensive use of them. Barack Obama has changed the membership of some of these, including the Domestic Policy Council, to reflect priorities like climate change. He has also created a new White House Council of Women and Girls to address their dis-

tinctive concerns. President Obama often utilizes "teams" of personnel from various executive agencies and councils to address particular policy needs. Their composition is somewhat fluid and may include Cabinet Secretaries and czars. In assembling his closest advisory personnel within the White House, President Obama continues the tradition of centralizing presidential power and control dating back at least to Franklin Roosevelt.[39]

PRESIDENTIAL STYLE

Each president adopts his own management style while in office. John F. Kennedy preferred an informal arrangement, surrounding himself with experts and meeting with advisors to debate policy alternatives. Like the hub of a wheel, Kennedy was at the center of a communication and decision-making network with spokes relatively open to his most trusted advisors.[40] Richard Nixon instituted a hierarchical structure in which his chief of staff, H. R. Haldeman, tightly controlled paper flow, staffing, and access to the president. Only Nixon's national security advisor, Henry Kissinger, had unfettered access to the Oval Office.[41] President George W. Bush adopted a corporate model of leadership. A business manager by training, he behaved like a CEO who made decisions in consultation with a small cadre of managers, developing a plan for marketing, and then presenting the final product to his sales force. As one political scientist observed: "Everyone on the team is expected to 'stay on message,' reiterating with little variation arguments and rhetoric carefully vetted in advance."[42] He reportedly was not curious about the details of policy,[43] but neither was he passive. At meetings he was known to be intentionally provocative, as much to spur debate as to determine the loyalty of his

John F. Kennedy practiced a style of leadership that encouraged open debate and discussion with key advisors.

staff. He was more dependent on trusted personal advisers than committed to any formal policymaking process.[44]

Obama's style has been described as rational, rigorous, and unemotional. It is "a time consuming process in which he identifies and assembles policy experts, listens as they debate the issues, asks tough questions, and requests the opinions and recommendations of everyone in the room." While he pursues clearly progressive policy ideals, he is conciliatory and seeks compromise on the details in order to achieve pragmatic outcomes.[45]

Personality is a crucial component in presidential success, although scholars disagree about which personal traits can make or break a presidency. Studies have identified intelligence, communication skills, decisiveness, respect for democratic principles, optimism, and hope as attributes of achievers.[46] By contrast, character traits linked to failure include compulsiveness, rigidity, defensiveness, and introversion.[47] The public

imperial presidency
Perspective advanced by some scholars in the 1970s warning about excessive concentration of power in the hands of the chief executive.

clearly values a president's capacity to rise above adversity. George W. Bush, who demonstrated a lack of sure-footedness in foreign policy during his first presidential campaign, received high marks for the strength and resolution with which he responded to the September 11, 2001, terrorist attacks.

ASSESSING PRESIDENTIAL POWER AND ITS LIMITS

Following Vietnam and Watergate, scholars began to raise concerns about the rising power of the presidency and the wisdom of allowing so much power to accrue to a single office. They argued that this presented the potential for an **imperial presidency**[48]—that is, an institution shielded from

HOW DO YOU RANK THE PRESIDENTS?

Historians, political scientists, and other scholars have long debated what makes a president great. Some believe greatness lies in the individual's fidelity to values; others, in his adaptability. Still others believe a president can only be measured against the demands of his time: Trying times bring out the best. In any case, here are two snapshot views: one from scholars, the other from average citizens.

Poll of Scholars
C-SPAN, the cable service that broadcasts sessions of Congress, asked a panel of scholars from all political stripes to rate American presidents on 10 characteristics, including public persuasion, crisis leadership, economic management, and performance within the context of the times. Here are the results:

President	Overall Ranking 2009
Abraham Lincoln	1
George Washington	2
Franklin D. Roosevelt	3
Theodore Roosevelt	4
Harry S. Truman	5
John F. Kennedy	6
Thomas Jefferson	7
Dwight D. Eisenhower	8
Woodrow Wilson	9
Ronald Reagan	10

Here's the list Galllup reported when it asked a sample of 1006 respondents nationwide to rank the presidents in a February 2008 survey.

John F. Kennedy
Ronald Reagan
Bill Clinton
Abraham Lincoln
Franklin Roosevelt
George Washington
Theodore Roosevelt
Harry Truman
Jimmy Carter
Thomas Jefferson

What do you think accounts for the differences between the scholars and citizens? Does currency matter? Who do you think were the worst presidents?

Source: C-SPAN 2009 Historians Presidential Leadership Survey, accessed on June 2, 2009 at http://www.c-span.org/presidentialsurvey/overall-ranking.aspx. Source: JFK and Ronald Reagan Win Gallup's President's Day Poll, February 18, 2008. Accessed on http://www.gallup.com/poll/104380/JFK-Ronald-Reagan-Win-Gallup-Presidents-Day-Poll.aspx on July 1, 2008.

criticism and divorced from the world of average citizens. Other scholars speak approvingly of a **unitary executive**, claiming that the concentration of presidential power is both inevitable and necessary. They assert that presidents must have the flexibility to act decisively without clear legislative mandate and to enforce discipline and secrecy in dealing with subordinates.[49] President Bush followed what his advisors openly acknowledged to be a unitary perspective by regularly appending signing statements to legislation and rejecting calls for greater transparency and openness. **Executive privilege**—shielding from scrutiny documents and conversations of the president and his advisors—has a long heritage, but President Bush pushed this doctrine further than previous presidents by claiming it applied to past employees and to conversations with private citizens with whom his staff might have conferred.

President Obama has said he wants a more transparent and accountable presidency that respects the limits of the office. As a result, he has issued orders releasing more executive branch documents for public scrutiny than his predecessor (although he refused to release newly discovered photos of the alleged abuses from the Abu Ghraib prison in Iraq) and promised to limit the use of executive privilege to claims by the president. Nevertheless, President Obama has affirmed his right to withhold some information according to the **state secrets privilege**, which asserts the right of the chief executive to keep secret information from the public and from other branches of government for reasons of national security. This privilege is usually respected by courts without examining the evidence in question and can be used to dismiss claims brought by those who say they have been harmed by government action. Despite his opposition to the way the doctrine was applied in the Bush administration and his promise to seek its modification, President Obama has invoked this privilege several times in seeking to dismiss lawsuits against the government involving extraordinary rendition and warrantless wiretaps.

Nevertheless, presidents must continue to work within the framework of constitutional and political limits that make success in office quite tenuous. Ultimately, a president's power derives from the ability to skillfully persuade others, to master the tools of policymaking, and to remain faithful to the president's constitutional duties.[50] He is checked by Congress's ability to stymie his legislative initiatives and by the Court's ability to reject the constitutionality of his actions.

The most severe limit on presidential power is impeachment and removal from office, as discussed in Chapter 11. Congress has impeached two presidents—Andrew Johnson and Bill Clinton—but both survived trial in the Senate and remained in office. Richard Nixon chose to resign rather than face impeachment following revelations that he participated in covering up a break-in at the Democratic Party headquarters during the 1972 presidential campaign. Both the Johnson and Clinton impeachments reflected long-standing political animosities between the president and his opponents and paint a mixed picture of impeachment as a check on presidential power. On the one hand, they il-

lustrate the difficulties in keeping legal charges against the president free of political motivation. However, because neither president was removed from office, these examples also demonstrate that the Senate is reluctant to overturn the will of the electorate unless the charge is serious and the evidence overwhelming.

unitary executive Theory stressing the importance of giving the president greater authority in foreign policy and in enforcing discipline over members of the executive bureaucracy.

executive privilege Presidential power to shield from scrutiny White House documents and conversations among presidential advisors.

state secrets privilege Assertion of presidential right to withhold information from the public and from other branches of government for reasons of national security.

THE VICE PRESIDENCY

The vice president has few constitutional duties other than acting as president of the Senate, a position that is more ceremonial than real except when the vice president votes to break ties. The vice president is also the president's designated successor should the president be unable to fulfill the duties of the office due to death or resignation. Beyond these roles, the vice president serves in a manner dictated by the president, a situation that prompted Benjamin Franklin to recommend that the occupant of the office be called "Your Superfluous Highness."[51]

Presidential candidates choose their vice presidents for a variety of reasons. A vice presidential candidate may help balance the ticket—that is, appeal to different regions of the country or factions of a party. Liberal northeasterner John Kennedy, for example, selected Lyndon Johnson, the Texas Democratic leader of the U.S. Senate, as his running mate—although it was clear that the personalities of the two men were likely to clash. More recently, personal

Dick Cheney exercised unprecedented influence and power as vice president, particularly in the area of foreign policy.

compatibility has become more important in the selection process. George W. Bush chose Dick Cheney, former Defense Department secretary and long-time friend of the Bush family, largely based on personal factors. Cheney was low-key in comparison to Bush's folksy outgoing style; he provided expertise in foreign policy where the former Texas governor was considered weak; and he was extremely loyal, harboring no presidential ambitions of his own. It is widely believed that Barack Obama picked Joe Biden as a running mate both because of his experience in foreign affairs as chairman of the Senate Committee on Foreign Relations and because of his ability to attract white working-class voters during the election.

Recent presidents have yielded significant authority to their vice presidents. Bill Clinton gave Al Gore responsibility for making the federal bureaucracy more "customer-friendly" through his reinventing government initiative. Gore also advanced legislation to expand Internet access and led the administration's environmental initiative. Dick Cheney played an even bigger role than Gore and may well be considered the most powerful vice president in American history. Cheney played a central role in formulating George W. Bush's foreign policy. After the September 11, 2001, terrorist attacks, Cheney played a hands-on role in the planning and implementing of the war on terrorism. He was often personally involved in reviewing intelligence, dealing with foreign governments, planning military operations in Afghanistan, and building support for the invasion of Iraq. He was granted unprecedented authority by George W. Bush, including that of executive privilege. Vice President Biden has promised to restore the "balance in power" between the president and vice president.[52] Obama has assigned Biden more traditional duties, including acting as spokesperson for administration policies.

The enhancement of the powers of the office makes it much more likely that a vice president will be able to take over quickly should the president become unable to serve a complete term. The Twenty-fifth Amendment formalizes the transition process, relying on an extensive list of successors to the office first enacted in the 1947 Presidential Succession Act. It also provides for a temporary transfer of presidential power. George W. Bush used this procedure to transfer authority to Dick Cheney when the president underwent medical procedures in 2002 and 2007. A more controversial, though never yet invoked, provision of the same amendment allows the vice president, along with a majority of the cabinet, to declare a president incapacitated. In such a circumstance, the vice president would serve until the president recovered. The amendment also provides that the president can appoint a successor to the vice president with the consent of a majority of both houses of Congress should that position become vacant. President Nixon used this power to replace Spiro Agnew, who resigned amid tax-evasion charges, with Gerald Ford. Upon ascending to the presidency after Nixon's resignation, Ford used the procedure to name Nelson Rockefeller as his vice president.

CIVIC ENGAGEMENT AND THE PRESIDENCY TODAY

As the institution of the presidency has grown, our expectations of the occupants have grown as well. We look to the president for leadership in times of crisis, for solace in times of grief, for new programs to meet our needs, and for reduced taxes to suit our pocketbooks. Many of our expectations are contradictory: We want defense but not sacrifice; we want better government services but not higher taxes. A famous cartoon by artist Saul Steinberg captures the expectations many Americans have about U.S. presidents today. In the cartoon, George Washington and Abraham Lincoln are seated at a table along with the Easter Bunny, Santa Claus, and the Statue of Liberty. Political scientist Thomas Langston argues that the cartoon captures the modern idea that presidents have almost magical powers to make our wishes come true. "Like Santa Claus, the Easter Bunny, and witches, presidents are expected to give things to people which they do not have to pay for."[53]

In confronting our expectations, we face a dual challenge. First, we must be realistic in what we think government can accomplish. Because no president can deliver all we expect, it is not uncommon for us to be disappointed in presidential performance. This disappointment can easily become a rationale for abandoning our responsibilities as citizens rather than a reason for readjusting our expectations. Second, we must resist the temptation to see ourselves as mere consumers of government programs rather than as active participants in self-government.

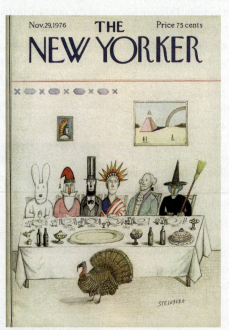

Saul Steinberg's cartoon for the cover of The New Yorker captures the exaggerated expectations many Americans have about presidential power.

As owners of the many federal agencies the president oversees, citizens must demand responsible stewardship by those we place in charge. The key to achieving both these goals is becoming an alert and informed citizen. There is simply no substitute for an electorate that examines promises and performance, attempts to separate fact from fiction, and realistically appraises what can be accomplished.

Presidents can increase their own chances of success by presenting frank appraisals of both the costs and the benefits of policies they propose and by enlisting citizens to invest themselves in policy outcomes. In doing so, the president is following in the footsteps of such presidents as Lincoln and Kennedy, who inspired sacrifice. The president must also engage in conversation with the public, recognizing that their support is crucial. With it, he can move his agenda; without it, he will be stymied.

The challenges we face as a nation are daunting—global warming, energy shortages, terrorism, health-care issues, Social Security reform, and economic uncertainty, to name a few. Most of these problems cannot be solved with quick fixes or without sacrifice.

From his first days in the White House, President Obama has shown his determination to address these challenges without delay. His record to this point is impressive, with perhaps health-care reform being his single biggest achievement. However, in advancing his ambitious agenda in short order, the president risked moving the nation more quickly than it was prepared to go. As a result, his public approval, the greatest presidential resource, has dipped and he has lost his commanding majorities in Congress. If he wishes to regain his footing, the president will have to explain more clearly to the American people where he wants us to go, why we must act now, and the consequences of inaction. He has already learned what his predecessors have discovered: Political capital is a scarce commodity that can evaporate quickly.

Summary

1. **What is the path to the presidency?**

- In the preconvention season, candidates crisscross the country, running in primary elections and caucuses to amass enough delegates to secure their party's nomination. Unpledged delegates and superdelegates are the only delegates whose support is not tied to primary and caucus results.

- Today the party conventions formalize the choice of the nominee and the platform and provide the nominee an opportunity to speak to the nation.

- The general election is decided by the tallying of electoral votes. Nominees devise strategies to ensure they gather the 270 electoral votes they need to win.

- The road to the White House requires the amassing of large sums of money, sometimes with the help of public finance laws—although the 2008 presidential election may have spelled an end to public funding.

2. **What are the major constitutional duties and nonconstitutional roles of the president?**

- The Constitution makes the president the commander in chief, the chief executive, chief of state, and the chief law enforcer. It also gives him the authority to recommend legislation and carry on diplomacy and requires that he take an oath of office and submit periodic reports on the state of the nation.

- Congress has delegated substantial powers to the president to implement the laws it makes.

- Presidents have also exercised an array of discretionary powers that can be quite far ranging in times of emergency or crisis.

- The Constitution specifies the requirements for candidates, the term of office (four years), the method of election (Electoral College), and provisions for resolving ties (House selects president and the Senate selects the vice president). The Twenty-second Amendment limits the president to two terms in office.

- Presidential power has grown over time, especially since Franklin Roosevelt. Today the president plays a number of roles not specified in the Constitution, including party leader, economic leader, and leader of public opinion.

3. **What agencies and personal factors help to produce a successful presidency?**

- The president is assisted by the cabinet and the Executive Office of the President, which includes the White House Office, the National Security Council, the Office of Management and Budget, and various policy councils. The quality of advice given to a president can help determine the success of presidential programs.

- Presidential style, which includes a president's management style and his personality, can determine the success of a presidency.

- The office of the vice president has become more important in recent years and, if skillfully managed, can contribute to the success of the sitting president.

OBAMA FINDS REALITY IS MESSY

Audacious. Barack Obama would change the way politics happens in America. Youthful. He would usher in the temperament of a new generation. Smart. He would lead the country out of the thicket it had wandered into with such distressing results.

Have hope, Obama said. Change is coming.

Yeah, well. It hasn't been the finest of first years. But nor has it been, by any means, the worst. As a candidate, Obama said that people projected onto him what they wanted to see—they invested their hopes and expectations in this unusually cool and appealing politician. And now, as 2010 gets under way, they are still projecting because there has yet to be a climactic moment, a turn in the road, a major victory, a historic accomplishment. Or, to be sure, an abject failure.

A good number of Americans are now thrusting their worries and fears onto President Obama, rather than their hopes and dreams, but what everyone is doing is waiting to see how this turns out. The health care bill—pummeled and shaken up and overhauled and practically waterboarded in Congress—will be trumpeted as a signature achievement of the new administration. But does it inspire hope? Does the final product of such a gruesome sausage-making process hold the promise of more and better change to come?

"There isn't a sense of singular accomplishment," said Lee Miringoff, director of the Marist Poll. "What Obama needs is a few big wins. He needs to put some points on the board."

Obama's approval ratings in his first year have closely tracked those of Ronald Reagan, who also held out the promise of novelty and invigoration. Support for Obama soared after his election, particularly among people who hadn't voted for him. "A lot of people were kind of kicking the tires: Maybe

this is a new day, maybe this is pretty amazing," said Ruy Teixeira, a senior fellow at the Center for American Progress. Now that support has fallen away again.

That's not a precarious situation to be in, especially when, like Reagan, Obama is personally more popular than his policies are. "This is someone who people want to succeed," Miringoff said. But Democrats, waiting for success, are growing restive. Some are dismayed by the escalation in Afghanistan, some by the compromises over health care, some by the way the administration has enabled Wall Street to flourish again.

"I think there is disappointment, particularly among young people, because things just don't seem all that different," Miringoff said. "Young people really thought they were going to get a shake-up of the system."

One possible counterargument is that real change takes time, especially if it is to include new voices. "Early on, people didn't understand the political process," Jeremy Bird, deputy national director of Organizing for America, the Obama volunteer group that now works for the Democratic National Committee, said of the rank-and-file Democrats who have been coming to meetings around the country. "People not in Washington have been shut out of that."

So part of his group's mission in 2009 was educational, he said: Here's the sausage, and this is how it got made. Bird predicted that his advocacy group will become an increasingly important player and an usher for change. "We're building a lasting infrastructure," he said, but he acknowledged that organizing to support a president's agenda is a lot harder than organizing a campaign.

The crucial turf lies in the suburbs, according to Teixeira. Obama will rise or fall depending on how he can do among America's biggest, and in many ways most skeptical, voting bloc. He won't win over the rural areas. And he has the cities locked up.

Away from the press's klieg lights, the administration has in fact been accomplishing quite a lot. Obama's team has taken dramatic steps to rewrite administrative regulations to take climate change into account. The Education Department has been promoting charter schools (not a traditional Democratic objective) and pushing a whole slew of reforms under the Race to the Top rubric. The Interior Department has been setting aside fairly vast amounts of federal land for habitat protection. The administration expanded the State Children's Health Insurance Program. It reformed student loans. It unleashed the Environmental Protection Agency to take action against greenhouse gases.

Obama made one very big move directly in the glare of the spotlight when he took over Chrysler and General Motors to rescue them from bankruptcy. Then he fired GM's chief executive, Rick Wagoner. That bailout was change, no doubt about it. But it was change that didn't sit well with a lot of Americans. Today, Obama says that if he hadn't done something dramatic the auto industry would have died, but as Teixeira points out, "You just don't get enough credit for keeping things from falling off the shelf."

Everybody knows about Franklin Roosevelt's first 100 days in office and the passage of 15 major pieces of legislation that became the foundation of the New Deal. Everybody also knows that neither Obama nor any other contemporary president could ever hope to match that record. The good news of 1933 didn't end with that first 100 days, however.

Roosevelt had the advantage of taking office just as the country's economic collapse was bottoming out. Millions of Americans earnestly believed that desperate measures were called for, and they understood how much was at stake. In spring 1933, unemployment was 25 percent; Roosevelt immediately began putting people back to

work. On October 22, William Green, the president of the American Federation of Labor, reported that 3.6 million jobs had been added since the inauguration.

Obama can only wish for such a welcome string of events.

Not only is the economy still in pretty bad shape, relatively speaking, but people are starting to lose faith in its stewards, whatever the statistics might say. A year ago there was general alarm, but as Obama took office, polls showed that a strong majority of Americans approved of his handling of the economy. In October, public disapproval outpaced approval for the first time, and the gap has continued to widen since then as unemployment remains high. These aren't desperate times, like 1933, but they're bad enough to make folks pretty cranky. At some point, the improvements already under way in the economy are bound to show. But how soon and how dramatically, no one knows.

FDR enjoyed outfoxing the Republicans. Of course, he had substantial majorities in both chambers of Congress. But in the undiluted partisanship of modern-day Washington, Obama seems less able, or less inclined, to engage in give-and-take with the other party. And this leads to a conundrum: If Obama is to change the way Washington does business, what does that mean? Steamrolling the Republicans? Or working with them?

As opposed to domestic politics, foreign policy provides presidents more leeway to act and less chance of harming their image. An administration's approach to Burma isn't going to sway too many voters on Election Day. But a cumulative impression can build—of competence, or of the reverse. Obama might be maneuvering patiently toward a resolution of the disputes with Iran or North Korea, or of the Middle East troubles. Or he might be pursuing false leads. So far,

> "These are problems that have been going on for a long time because we don't know how to solve them. . . . Obama's misfortune is that they might come to a head on his watch."
> —James Lindsay

not much to point to. The Republicans are trying to portray him as naive and outwitted by foreign adversaries, but it's a minor complaint amid joblessness, a mortgage crisis, mounting debt, and health care reform.

All but forgotten today is that Jimmy Carter began his presidency with a string of foreign-policy successes, James Lindsay of the Council on Foreign Relations said. He sponsored the Camp David Accords, concluded the Panama Canal Treaty, and opened formal ties to China. The economy, however, made him unpopular—and then came 1979, bringing the Iranian revolution and the Soviet invasion of Afghanistan, two events largely out of Carter's control, but both helping to doom his re-election effort.

Thirty years later, Iran and Afghanistan are still giant headaches for the White House, and the Middle East and China remain major concerns. Only Panama is quiet today.

"These are problems that have been going on for a long time because we don't know how to solve them," Lindsay said. "Obama's misfortune is that they might come to a head on his watch."

In a way, it's part of the usual chasm between running for office and then actually

governing, a chasm that stems from the delightful reality that candidates don't have to make hard decisions. And in Obama's case, that chasm is just a bit wider than for most, Miringoff said. "Running against a failed incumbent's policy by promising change doesn't necessarily tell you what it's going to look like," he said. Americans turn to Obama and see too much change, too little change, or perhaps the wrong kind of change. They're still looking for the definitive moment of change.

One day in December, Robert Gibbs, the White House press secretary, defended Obama's meeting with bankers and promised that it would help lead to financial reform.

"Did all the world's problems get solved today?" Gibbs asked. "I can tell you guys, no. But I can tell you this: The president is going to get financial reform."

The fact is, change is hard. A study of presidential Inaugural Addresses by the Miller Center of Public Affairs at the University of Virginia found that "hope" is Republican and "change" is Democratic. That is, William Howard Taft talked a lot about hope when he was sworn in, and so did Dwight Eisenhower and George H.W. Bush and Calvin Coolidge. Bill Clinton and Lyndon Johnson mentioned change more than any other 20th-century presidents. They got some—Johnson a lot more than Clinton—but it was a tough slog all the way. Republicans sought to inspire. Democrats sought to transform.

Obama dwelt on neither hope nor change in his Inaugural Address, judging by literal word count. His handful of scattered references to those concepts put him on a par with another Democrat—none other than Franklin Roosevelt, in that dark spring of 1933. So maybe it's not the rhetoric or the sloganeering that counts in the end. Maybe it's the results.

For Discussion:

■ How would you rate President Obama's first two years in office? What impact does his domestic and foreign policy have on this overall grade?

■ Explain the analogy the article makes between the health care bill and a sausage. What is the author saying about the legislative process?

■ Do voters expect too much from the president? Is there any way Obama could have delivered the kind of change disillusioned Democrats were expecting when they elected him?

13

BUREAU

CITIZENS AS OWNERS AND CONSUMERS

STUDENT LOANS, DEBT, AND BUREAUCRACY ■ In June of 2009 Robert Applebaum became an overnight spokesman for a generation of people burdened with student loan debt. The 35-year-old New York lawyer started a Facebook group called "Forgive Student Loan Debt to Stimulate the Economy." "I wanted to rant, so instead of sending an e-mail to a couple of my friends, I decided to start a Facebook group," Applebaum recounted. "I figured just a few of my friends would join."[1]

But, by the end of the second week 2,500 people had joined, and within two months the group had grown to 138,500 members.

Applebaum's frustration was born out of his personal experience with student loans. After graduating from Fordham law school in 1998 he took a job with the Brooklyn District Attorney's Office. His starting salary was $36,000 a year, an amount so low that he placed his student loans into forbearance for five years. When the time came to start repayment, the accumulated interest caused his student debt total to balloon to more than $100,000. In his words, "Despite having a law degree, I'm middle class and I don't have any money at all. I don't own a house or a car. My only assets are my couch and my television."[2] ❦

UCRACY

As You READ >>

- What is the federal bureaucracy?
- Who are federal bureaucrats and what do they do?
- What are the sources and limits of bureaucratic power?

Applebaum's plight is a common one. During the 2008–2009 academic year alone, students and their families took out more than $95 billion in loans, which was a 25 percent increase from the previous year. In 2010, student-loan debt, totaling more than $800 billion, surpassed credit-card debt for the first time. It is predicted that the total will surpass $1 trillion in 2011.[3] As a result, groups like Applebaum's and StudentLoanJustice.org have become part of a new movement advocating for an overhaul of the country's troubled student-loan system. Their criticism has also extended to the federal Department of Education, part of the complex national bureaucracy, which is charged with monitoring these situations.

Any student who has ever filled out a Free Application for Federal Student Aid (FAFSA) knows that the federal government is involved in the student-loan process. During the recent era of massive student debt accumulation, there were three basic types of loans available for undergraduate students. Students could acquire federal loans made by the government directly, federal loans made by banks or other lending institutions that are guaranteed by the federal government, and private loans from private lending institutions.

The most popular federal loans are the Stafford loans that are dispersed regardless of financial need and the Perkins loans that are given to students with the greatest financial need. Under the first or direct government plan, the federal Department of Education lends the student money, whether it is a Stafford, Perkins, or some other loan, which is sent directly to the college or university for tuition and fees with any remaining sums distributed to the student for living expenses. The money is eventually repaid to the Department of Education.

Under the second type of lending system that was known as the Federal Family Education Loan Program (FFEL), the government paid subsidies to banks and lenders to dole out money to borrowers and reimbursed these companies up to 97 percent of the cost of any loan that was not paid back. (See the adjacent figure.)

bureaucrats The civilian employees of the national government who are responsible for implementing federal laws.

Scandals were unearthed in 2007 involving the FFEL plan because certain lenders were giving kickbacks in money and expensive trips to college officials who steered their students to particular financial lenders. Well-known schools such as Columbia, New York University, Syracuse, Fordham, and the University of Pennsylvania were involved. Emerson College in Boston agreed to pay a total of $780,000 to students who had been forced into loans with less favorable rates.

But change in the student loan system is occurring. In his State of the Union address in 2010, President Obama cited the federal student-loan debt problem. He stressed his goal of making student loans more affordable by limiting a borrower's payments to 10 percent of his or her income above a basic living allowance. It would also keep the total cost of loan repayment manageable by forgiving all remaining debt after 10 years of payments for those in public service work and 20 years for all others. In addition, the Student Aid and Fiscal Responsibility Act (SAFRA) supported by the president included dropping the FFEL program and mandating that all colleges and universities start using only the direct loan option for federal student loans. SAFRA was passed by Congress in the spring of 2010, although critics of the bill attacked the overhaul to the system as an overreaching government takeover.

The national government's role in the student-loan process and response to the student debt problem highlights several realities about the national government's bureaucracy. First, our expectations about the national government have grown immensely. Early citizens expected the government to collect taxes, deliver the mail, and little else—certainly not support their goal of going to college.

Second, a large and complex bureaucracy provides the government services that affect the lives of many citizens. The Department of Education is just one example. Two million federal bureaucrats interact with Americans more than elected government officials do, and these interactions often lead to complaints about discourtesy, inefficiency, and even dishonesty among these workers. Finally, the president is ultimately responsible for the conduct of the bureaucracy, and he will receive the credit when the bureaucracy functions well and the blame when it does not.

Federal **bureaucrats** today exercise a great deal of power through their ability to make rules that determine how the government implements laws, as well as their authority to mediate disputes. The increased significance of the bureaucracy reflects political life in the twenty-first century. For interest groups, bureaucracy has become a target of lobbying in an effort to shape agency policies for private benefit. For public officials, bureaucracy is often a convenient scapegoat when policies go awry. For citizens, bureaucracy is increasingly treated like a business that is expected to provide reliable service even while keeping costs, and the taxes that fund them, low. Some scholars worry that we are becoming a nation that treats government like just another provider of services, rather than a nation of citizens who own the government and use it for public purposes. ◆—

Types of Student Loan Programs

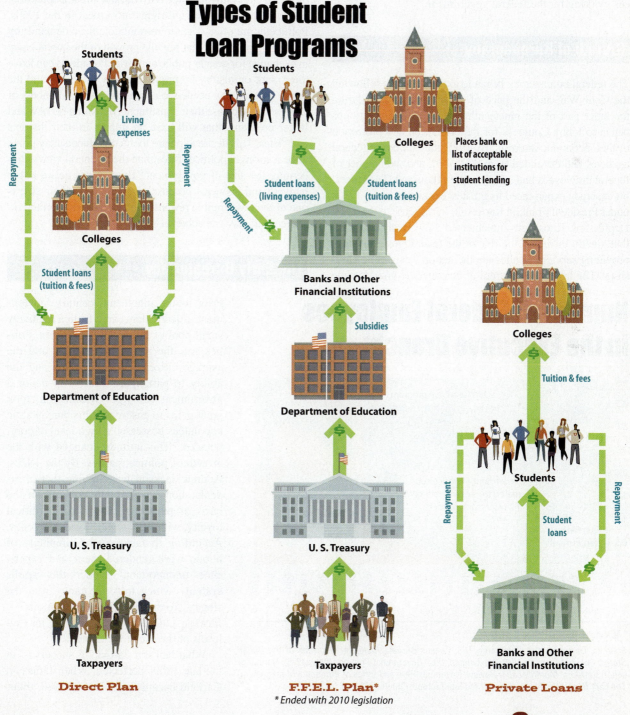

Direct Plan

F.F.E.L. Plan*
* Ended with 2010 legislation

Private Loans

BUREAUCRATIC CHANGES AND EVOLVING CIVIC LIFE

The bureaucracy has changed dramatically both in size and in the manner in which government agencies are staffed. During the 1790s, fewer people worked for the national government than worked at President Washington's Mount Vernon home.[4] The Framers presumed that the tasks of the national government would be rather limited, so they did not envision the need for a large bureaucracy. By 1800, there were still fewer than three thousand civilian employees working for the federal government.

Growth of Bureaucracy

The federal bureaucracy began to expand rapidly following the Civil War, and the pace of growth accelerated during the latter part of the nineteenth century as various groups began to lobby Congress for the promotion and protection of their economic interests. By 1925, the number of federal agencies had expanded from 90 to 170, and the number of federal employees had swollen to six thousand. The federal bureaucracy experienced its greatest expansion in the 1930s under President Franklin Roosevelt. In response to the Great Depression, Roosevelt implemented New Deal legislation that greatly increased the role of the federal government in providing services to alleviate the nation's economic hardships. The last significant era of bureaucratic growth came in the 1960s, in response to public demands that the national government do more to promote equal rights, improve working conditions, and protect the environment.

The dramatic growth of the U.S. population, and the public's increasing demand for more and better government services, have driven the expansion of the federal bureaucracy.[5] At the time of the Constitutional Convention, the United States was a small, rural nation with about five million inhabitants; it is now a postindustrial powerhouse of 300 million. As the country has become more complex and diverse, Americans have demanded improved education, better roads, cleaner air, more job training, and more protection of their rights. These demands came most often during sudden changes or crises in the political, economic, cultural, or social environment: the Civil War, the Great Depression, World War II, and the civil rights movement in the 1960s. Politicians are often eager to respond to citizen demands by expanding programs that fuel the growth of the bureaucracy in exchange for greater public approval. Presidents can leave their mark on history by promoting new programs and the larger bureaucracy needed to administer them. Members of Congress can please their constituents by voting for new and larger programs that will have an impact in their districts and states. This desire to please their constituents may prove to be a stronger political force than their general views concerning the size of government.[6] Bureaucrats desire larger budgets and agencies because an increase in their size is one of the few tangible rewards bureaucrats with limited resources and pay can achieve.

The Early Bureaucracy

Prior to the nineteenth century, government officeholders came from a relatively small pool of prominent gentlemen. Politics was the realm of the elite, and the average citizen lacked the time and the ability to participate directly in national government. George Washington took great pains to ensure that his bureaucratic appointees possessed a high level of competence.[7] This attitude changed with the growth of political parties. By the 1820s, Andrew Jackson was arguing that presidents should make appointments on the basis of patronage, or partisan political loyalty, with little regard for competency. According to Jackson, the simplicity of public work rendered merit and experience unimportant.[8] Under this **spoils system**—which took its name from the slogan "To the victor belong the spoils"— Jackson placed political cronies into all levels of the executive branch.

What Jackson started, his successors in the late 1800s perfected. When James A. Garfield became president in 1880, thou-

Number of Federal Employees in the Executive Branch*

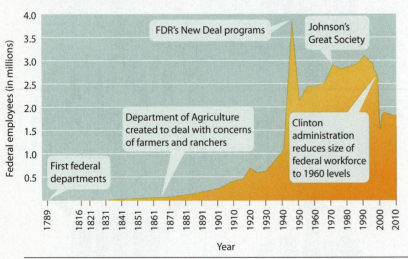

* Not including the Postal Service.

Sources: Department of Commerce, U.S. Census Bureau, *Historical Statistics of the United States: Colonial Times to 1970* (Washington, D.C.: Government Printing Office, 1975); Bureau of Labor Statistics, *Monthly Labor Review*, November 1988; and Office of Personnel Management, *The Fact Book*, http://www.opm.gov/feddata/factbook/html/fb-p08.html.

President James Garfield, who wanted to change the spoils system, was assassinated by a frustrated job seeker.

sands of job seekers besieged him, hoping to secure government positions. The crush led Garfield to write in his diary: "My day is frittered away with the personal seeking of people when it ought to be given to the great problems which concern the whole country."[9] In a cruel irony, a frustrated job seeker later assassinated Garfield.

The Reform Era

Even before Garfield's assassination, reformers had called for an end to the spoils system. They called for an honest and efficient government whose employees were competent to deliver basic services. In 1883, Congress passed the Pendleton Act, also known as the Civil Service Reform Act, which reduced the number of political appointments the president could make to the executive branch and created the Civil Service Commission. New civil service regulations produced a **merit system** that emphasized an applicant's experience, education, and job performance, as well as scores on competitive exams and performance evaluations. Initially, the merit system applied to only 10 percent of the positions in the civil service, but later legislation and executive orders increased coverage to 90 percent of all federal executive branch employees.

Bureaucracy Today

The composition of today's federal bureaucracy reflects a modern institutional emphasis on professionalism and the treatment of the public as consumers. The federal civil service adopted its current emphasis on professionalism in 1955 because of the realization that modern governments face complex problems that require more skilled civil servants. As government work has become more complex, the civil service requires employees with advanced degrees in their occupational field. As you can see from the table on page 334, today's professional bureaucracy is far removed

from Jackson's idea of government by the common man. Many highly skilled individuals look on national government service as a rewarding career.

Despite civil service reform, some political scientists argue that party patronage is not dead but has evolved to meet the conditions of modern bureaucratic life. Rather than trying to influence the outcome of elections, today's parties use the new patronage to influence the making and implementation of public policy. Rather than mobilizing the public with the promise of patronage jobs, the parties cooperate with allies both inside and outside of the government to bring about changes they desire in government policy.[10] Allies inside government include federal workers with their own views about which policies should be advanced, and outside groups include interests groups who share their policy perspectives. By mobilizing these forces, partisans can either advance their own causes or attempt to undermine the goals of their opposition. Allies of the Democratic Party include the social welfare and regulatory bureaucracies of the federal government as well as interest groups favoring government support for social welfare spending. The Republican Party is allied with the military, defense contractors, and fundamentalist Protestant churches. These institutional alignments explain why Republicans opposed President Clinton's health-care initiatives and why Democrats argued against President Bush's faith-based initiatives.

The elites of the two parties can use investigations, revelations of wrongdoing, and criminal prosecutions to disable the institutional allies of the opposition. The acronym for revelation, investigation, and prosecution (RIP) seems fitting for this new age of patronage. These are the type of disputes that are picked up by the media, and this is the type of bitter fighting that alienates citizens from engagement with the political system.

In 1993, President Bill Clinton placed Vice President Gore in charge of an effort to improve the performance of the national bureaucracy called the National Performance Review (NPR). Concerned that bureaucrats often treated

spoils system The expansion of the patronage system to a level of corruption that placed political cronies into all levels of government.

merit system The system that classifies federal civil service jobs into grades to which appointments are made on the basis of performance on competitive exams.

The Clinton-Gore "Reinventing Government" initiative viewed the public as consumers of government services.

Employment in the Federal Government* Compared to Industries

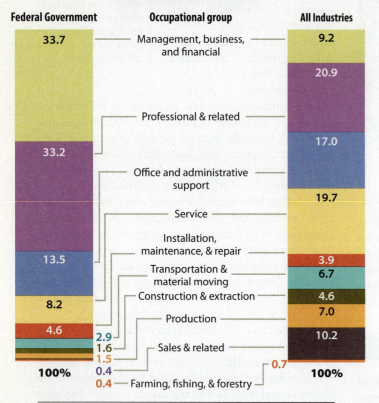

Federal Government	Occupational group	All Industries
33.7	Management, business, and financial	9.2
33.2	Professional & related	20.9
	Office and administrative support	17.0
13.5	Service	19.7
8.2	Installation, maintenance, & repair	
4.6	Transportation & material moving	3.9
2.9	Construction & extraction	6.7
1.6	Production	4.6
1.5	Sales & related	7.0
0.4		10.2
0.4	Farming, fishing, & forestry	0.7
100%		100%

* Not including the Postal Service.

Source: U.S. Department of Labor, Bureau of Labor Statistics, "Career Guide to Industries," 2010–11 Edition.

the public in a rude and uncaring manner, Clinton believed that the government should act more like a business. It should operate to curb expenses and to treat the public like consumers it values and wishes to retain. Under the rubric of reinventing government, based on the writings of David Osborne and Ted Gaebler,[11] NPR undertook policies designed to cut unnecessary spending, improve public service, treat citizens like customers, and give government employees the power to solve problems. However, viewing ourselves merely as customers of government may undermine active citizen participation.

THE NATURE OF BUREAUCRACY

A **bureaucracy** is a complex system of organization and control that incorporates the principles of hierarchical authority, division of labor, and formalized rules. The nature of bureaucracy is based on the principles of Max Weber, summarized in the figure on the adjacent page.

A hierarchy is the chain of command through which those at the top of an organization exercise authority over those below them; those with the least authority are on the bottom. A well-defined chain of command makes clear who is in charge, thus reducing conflict. The division of labor within this hierarchy is a system of job specialization that defines distinct tasks and responsibilities for each position. Division of labor leads to more efficient output of goods and services. In order to run as smoothly as possible, the organization conducts its operations according to formal rules and procedures that allow employees to make quick decisions that are free from personal bias.

Any large organization that is structured hierarchically to carry out specific tasks fits the bureaucratic model. However, there are important differences between private and public bureaucracies. First, private bureaucracies, including corporations such as Microsoft and General Motors, have a single set of bosses called a board of directors. By contrast, government bureaucracies have many bosses—the president, Congress, and the courts. Second, private corporations serve their stockholders, whereas governments are supposed to serve all their citizens. Third, private corporations exist to make a profit; government bureaucracies do not have to worry about profits, although they are supposed to deliver services efficiently and not waste taxpayers' money. Finally, the value of public goods produced by government—a quality education, safe food and water, national defense—is less tangible than the value of a new automobile or computer. As a result, citizens are likely to criticize governments for wasting money, even though private bureaucracies actually may waste much more.[12]

When carried to an extreme, the very characteristics of bureaucracy that enhance efficiency and equal treatment for government clients can also fuel the idea that bureaucrats are unresponsive and incompetent. Slavishly following "standard operating procedures" that don't take into account present conditions can lead to decisions that violate common sense and interfere with an organization's ability to respond.[13] Such failures by an organization to serve its intended purposes are called bureaucratic pathologies.[14]

A common form of bureaucratic pathology among government agencies is the drive to expand and to increase their responsibilities. When expansion becomes an end in itself, the pathology is known as bureaucratic imperialism. At other times, governmental bureaucracies fail to adapt swiftly when conditions warrant such changes. They may also focus on the task at hand to such an extent that they neglect other legitimate citizen concerns. Some observers, for example, believe that the national security bureaucracy's concentration on terrorism after the September 11, 2001, terrorist attacks led it to neglect basic civil liberties such as privacy and access to the courts. Finally, a bureau-

Weber's Model of a Bureaucracy

The concept of hierarchy The organization follows the principle of hierarchy, with each lower office under the control and supervision of a higher one.

Specialized tasks Employees are chosen based on merit to perform specialized tasks within the total operation.

Division of labor Process in which individuals are assigned specialized tasks in order to increase efficiency.

Standard operating procedures Policies are clearly enunciated so that procedures are predictable.

Record keeping Administrative acts and rules are recorded to ensure further predictable performance.

Source: John M. Pfiffner and Frank P. Sherwood, *Administrative Organization* (Englewood Cliffs, NJ: Prentice Hall, 1960), 65–67.

Federal bureaucrats may be either political appointees or career civil servants who are allowed to exercise a great deal of power in the tasks they perform. Those with authority to shape policy are generally political appointees, while those who maintain the everyday operation and services of the agencies are part of the career civil service. Political appointees, however, come and go, while career civil service employees constitute the permanent bureaucracy.

Political Appointees The most visible federal bureaucrats, who hold the most policy-sensitive positions, are political appointees chosen by the president. They include nearly 400 cabinet secretaries, undersecretaries, assistant secretaries, bureau chiefs, and approximately 2,500 lesser positions, most of whom must be confirmed by the Senate. To fill these posts, presidents seek people with managerial talents, political skills, and ideologies similar to their own. These prestigious jobs are patronage positions, awarded based on political loyalty. These powerful bureaucrats operate what some scholars call a "government of strangers," because on average they leave government work after about 22 months on the job.[16]

Once the preserve of white males, the ranks of political appointees have become substantially more diverse. In 1933, Franklin Roosevelt appointed the first woman cabinet member, Frances Perkins, to head the Department of Labor. Thirty years later, Lyndon Johnson made Robert Weaver the first African American cabinet member by appointing him secretary of Housing and Urban Development. Today, many women and minorities hold key advisory roles as political appointees. Three of the last four secretaries of state, for example, have been women, and the sole male was an African American, Colin Powell.

bureaucracy A complex system of organization and control that incorporates the principles of hierarchical authority, division of labor, and formalized rules.

cratic agency may begin to display favoritism for the interests of the groups it is supposed to oversee, rather than the interests of the public at large. When any of these pathologies come into public view, they reinforce the generally negative views that many American citizens have concerning the bureaucracy.

FEDERAL BUREAUCRATS AND THEIR WORK

Scholars often call the bureaucracy the fourth branch of the government because of the power it wields, but the Framers of the Constitution used very few words to describe it. Article II, Section 2 proclaims, "The President shall be commander in chief of the army and navy of the United States, . . . he may require the opinion, in writing, of the principal officer in each of the executive departments, upon any subject relating to the duties of their respective offices." Beyond these words, the Founders left it to Congress to establish the organization of government and the president to lead it. Nevertheless, they considered the role of the bureaucracy to be vitally important. In *The Federalist* No. 70, Alexander Hamilton wrote that ". . . a government ill executed, whatever it may be in theory, must be, in practice, a bad government."[15]

Did You Know?

. . . That the Transportation Security Administration, a federal government agency created in 2001 and moved to the Department of Homeland Security in 2003, is responsible for checking baggage at the nation's airports? Recently it has attempted to become more consumer-friendly by allowing passengers to go online to register complaints or make suggestions regarding service. The agency also provides information on wait time at security checkpoints to assist future travelers.

Frances Perkins was the first female cabinet member, serving as secretary of labor from 1933 to 1945.

Frances Perkins

The first woman to become a cabinet member in the United States, Frances Perkins learned firsthand the importance of activism. While attending Mount Holyoke College in the early 1900s, Perkins took a course in American co-

PORTRAIT
OF AN ACTIVIST

lonial history that required each student to visit a factory and survey its working conditions. Perkins's visits to several textile factories and paper mills opened her eyes to the dangerous conditions of the new industrial age. Upon graduation, she took a teaching position and met many of the most prominent social reformers of the day, including Jane Addams, Grace Abbot, and Ellen Gates Starr. She later earned a master's degree from Columbia University and soon became a social leader.

In 1911, she witnessed the infamous Triangle Shirtwaist Factory Fire that claimed the lives of 146 company employees, most of them young women. Many leapt to their deaths because the doors were locked and the stairways were too narrow to permit escape. Galvanized by the tragedy, Perkins worked on the Factory Investigating Commission and frequently testified before governmental bodies for safer working conditions. In 1919, New York Governor Al Smith appointed Perkins to the State Industrial Commission. Governor Franklin D. Roosevelt later named her to be the Industrial Commissioner of New York. When Roosevelt took office as president in 1933, he named Perkins secretary of labor.

Career Civil Service Modern federal bureaucrats are primarily white-collar workers performing a variety of professional, managerial, technical, service, and clerical tasks. In the group as a whole, there is a trend toward older employees. (See the adjacent figure.) Just under two million civil servants work for the federal government, not including the 750,000 postal employees or the millions of workers who compose the proxy administration of the national government. Only 12 percent of the recognized federal employees work in Washington, D.C.; the rest are stationed in regional offices throughout the nation. The U.S. government is divided into several bureaucratic regions, and most federal agencies have offices in each region. The term *proxy administration* applies to all the people doing work for the federal government, such as private contractors and state and local government employees who are not counted officially as part of the federal bureaucracy. The private contracting firm, formerly known as Blackwater USA, for instance, provided security personnel to guard U.S. diplomats in Iraq. The firm gained notoriety in September

2007 when it was involved in a skirmish that killed eight Iraqi civilians. The Iraqi government subsequently ordered the company to leave the country, but it is still operating in Afghanistan.

As we saw earlier, most federal bureaucrats are hired under a **civil service system** that is designed to promote a nonpartisan and specialist government service. Civil service jobs are assigned a General Schedule (GS) civil

Employment in Federal Government by Occupation, 2008–2018 (Projected)

Employment, 2008 (in thousands)	% of total	% change, 2008–2018
2,016 All occupations	100%	9.5%
680.0 Management, business, and financial occupations	33.7%	14.0%
669.3 Professional and related occupations	33.2%	9.7%
272.7 Office and administrative support occupations	13.5%	–3.9%

⬤ = 10,000 Employees

Source: Bureau of Labor Statistics, 2011, 5–6. http://www.bls.gov/oco/cg/cgs041.htm.

Base Pay Rates for Federal Employees

GS Level	Entrance level	Step increase	Maximum level
1	$17,803	varies	$22,269
2	20,017	varies	25,191
3	21,840	$728	28,392
4	24,518	817	31,871
5	27,431	914	35,657
6	30,577	1,019	39,748
7	33,979	1,133	44,176
8	37,631	1,254	48,917
9	41,563	1,385	54,028
10	45,771	1,526	59,505
11	50,287	1,676	59,505
12	60,274	2,009	65,371
13	71,674	2,389	93,175
14	84,697	2,823	110,104
15	99,628	3,321	129,517

Source: U.S. Office of Personnel Management.

service rating ranging from GS 1 (the lowest) to GS 15 (the highest). It works out that the average annual salary for General Schedule attorneys, for instance, is $111,304, whereas chemists earn $89,954 and air traffic personnel, $72,049. The nine thousand members of the Senior Executive Service occupy a higher-paying rank, using a separate rating system. These GS positions in the federal bureaucracy constitute nearly 75 percent of all the federal bureaucrats. Approximately 15 percent of all nonpostal federal employees work for agencies that have their own merit systems, such as those in the Coast Guard and career officials in the Foreign Service of the State Department.

In order to ensure a nonpartisan civil service, the Merit Systems Protection Board makes it difficult to discharge federal bureaucrats for any reason, partisan or otherwise. As a result, fewer than one-tenth of 1 percent of all federal employees have actually been fired for incompetence or misconduct in recent years. Also, most federal bureaucrats may bargain collectively through labor organizations of their choice.[17] However, when federal agencies were reorganized in the creation of the Department of Homeland Security, many federal employees of the new agency were excluded from collective bargaining protection. The Bush administration argued that it needed greater flexibility in dealing with employees involved in national security. Opponents believed this was merely a ploy to reduce the number of workers protected by employee unions.

At one time, federal bureaucrats gave up some of their political rights in exchange for job security. Today, however, the Hatch Act allows federal employees to run for office in nonpartisan elections, such as running for school board or town council, and to contribute money to campaigns in partisan elections.

What Do They Do?

The bureaucracy has the extremely important role of policy implementation, which is translating political goals imbedded in laws into specific programs.[18] Congress grants it this role through enabling legislation that gives federal agencies the legal authority to carry out congressional laws. Congress relies heavily on the specialists within the bureaucracy to formulate the specific guidelines and rules necessary to implement government policies. Some observers, however, believe that Congress has delegated too much of its legislative authority to the bureaucracy merely to avoid the political pressures of being held accountable by citizens for unpopular policies.[19]

> **civil service system** The merit-based employment system that covers most white-collar and specialist positions in the federal government.
>
> **rule making** The administrative process that creates rules that have the characteristics of a law.

Rule Making Bureaucrats play a significant policy role through the administrative process known as **rule making**. Rules are by-products of congressional legislation that

The Environmental Protection Agency writes rules to implement congressional laws regulating air pollution.

specify how to interpret or carry out a policy, and they carry the weight of law. When legislation is fairly clear-cut, it requires little bureaucratic interpretation. For instance, when Congress increases the minimum wage by 10 cents an hour over two years, the Labor Department does not need to be very creative in designing rules for employers implementing this change. However, the wording of some laws often allows administrative agencies substantial discretion.[20] For example, when Congress orders lower levels of particular pollutants in the smoke emitted by industry smokestacks, it allows the EPA to determine what levels are acceptable. This is not merely a technical matter but a political one as well, since compliance with EPA rules can cost industries millions of dollars. In such cases, agency rule makers act as policymakers as well as policy interpreters and enforcers.

Federal Register A publication of the federal government used to announce public notice of the time, place, and nature of the proceedings to be followed when new agency rules are proposed.

The figure below illustrates two important characteristics of the rule-making process. First, the Office of Management and Budget (OMB), an agency of the Executive Office of the President, controls the content of the rules issued by federal departments and agencies. Second, the process allows public participation. The agency proposing a new rule must publish the time, place, and nature of the proceedings for rule making in the *Federal Register*. At that time, it must state the purpose of the rule and give interested parties the opportunity to submit written comments. Opening up the rule-making process to citizens increases public participation, which provides bureaucrats with both the information they need to formulate the rules and a sense of popular response to the rule in the affected communities.[21] It also gives greater legitimacy to a process in which unelected bureaucrats, who are not accountable to the public at the ballot box, make the rules. A study of 180 Washington, D.C.–based interest groups revealed that a large majority of them rate work on rule making as being equal to or more important than lobbying Congress.[22] Government, trade associations, business groups, and labor unions are especially active participants in rule making.[23]

Increased public participation in the rule-making process during the 1960s and 1970s ushered in what one political scientist calls the "participation revolution."[24] During this period, social regulation expanded dramatically, extending the reach of government in such a way that "previously unorganized interests now had more than ample incentive to

The Paper Trail in Rule Making

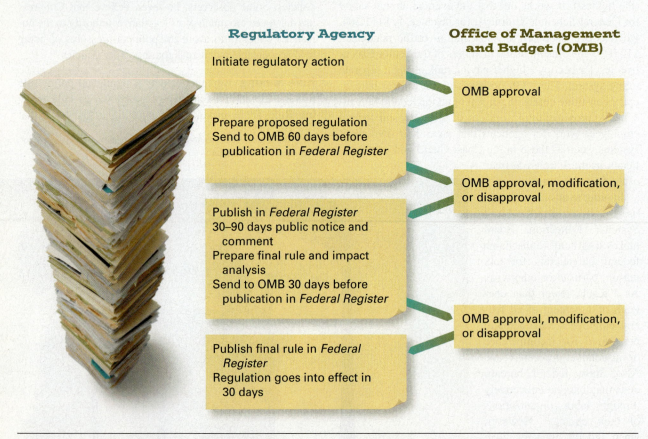

Source: From "Congress or the White House: Who Controls the Agencies?" by Kitty Dumas, *Congressional Quarterly Weekly Report*, 2002.

The Cabinet Departments

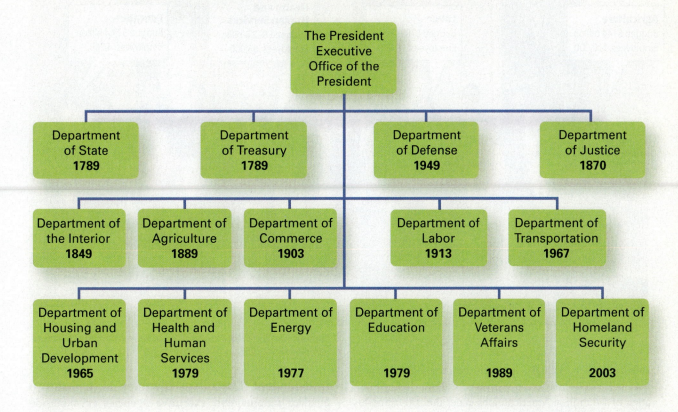

Source: Office of the Federal Register, *United States Government Manual 2002–2003* (Washington, D.C.: U.S. Government Printing Office, 2003), 21.

come together for collective action."[25] Many scholars and activists believed that direct citizen input would improve the quality of the decisions.[26] The greater public input has also produced a change in the process itself. A growing number of agencies are encouraging interest groups to become involved directly in the writing of the rules. This process, known as negotiated rule making, was formalized in the Ne-

gotiated Rulemaking Act of 1990. Groups affected by a potential new rule can now apply to have their representatives become members of a negotiating committee.

Adjudicating Disputes Bureaucrats can also make policy through the process of administrative adjudication, a quasi-judicial process for resolving disputes. Agencies use this process to bring parties into compliance with agency rules. The hearings are less formal than a trial, although many agencies use administrative law judges to conduct the hearings. The results of such procedures often set precedents for interpreting the rules in question. In the Social Security Administration alone, administrative law judges decide more than 300,000 cases annually.

Organization of the Federal Bureaucracy

In Chapter 12, we discussed federal agencies that make up the Executive Office of the President, such as the Office of Management and Budget. The remainder of the federal bureaucracy is organized into six major bureaucratic structures: (1) cabinet departments, (2) independent executive agencies, (3) independent regulatory agencies, (4) government corporations, (5) proxy administration, and (6) government-sponsored enterprises. Although the federal bureaucracy may seem like a complex maze of departments, agencies,

Agriculture
Budget: $144 billion
Employees: 100,000

Labor
Budget: $109 billion
Employees: 15,000

Health and Human Services
Budget: $892.8 billion
Employees: 65,000

Education
Budget: $77.4 billion
Employees: 4,200

President Obama and Vice President Biden, shown with members of Obama's cabinet in August 2009.

and faceless individuals, it should be remembered that it was given the primary responsibility for the saving and creation of 1.6 million American jobs under the 2009 stimulus package. It is also within the bureaucracy that decisions are made that can affect citizens in their emotional lives. After the Department of Defense lifted its media blackout for covering the return of fallen soldiers in 2009, citizens could view the somber ceremony of flag-draped coffins being carried from transport planes by soldiers in full dress uniform.

cabinet departments The 15 major administrative organizations within the federal bureaucracy that are responsible for major governmental functions such as defense, commerce, and homeland security.

line organization An administrative organization that is directly accountable to the president.

independent executive agency A governmental unit with special responsibilities that is not part of any cabinet department.

independent regulatory agency An agency existing outside the major departments that regulates a specific economic activity or interest.

Cabinet Departments The 15 **cabinet departments** are the most visible agencies in the federal government. Some agencies, such as the State Department and the Defense Department, serve broad national interests. Other agencies, including the Agriculture and Labor Departments, are known as clientele departments because many of their services are directed at particular groups. All cabinet departments are **line organizations**, meaning they are directly responsible to the president, who appoints their heads with Senate approval. Each cabinet department is composed of smaller units often known as bureaus, divisions, or offices. These subdivisions often are themselves complex organizations whose members possess a great deal of power and discretion.

Independent Executive Agencies More than two hundred **independent executive agencies** exist outside the 15 cabinet departments and the Executive Office of the President. The top table on page 341 presents a partial list of independent executive agencies. These agencies enjoy political independence by virtue of the importance of their missions. The Social Security Administration, for example, earned independent status in 1994 to ensure impartial administration of the federal old-age and disability insurance programs.

Independent Regulatory Agencies The **independent regulatory agencies** make and enforce public policy on specific economic issues. Congress created this "alphabet soup" of government (so called because we know these agencies mainly by their initials) to provide continuity and expertise in economic policy. The organization and administration of these agencies give them independence from the president, Congress, and partisan pressures. Older agencies typically feature a board of five to seven members, selected by the president and confirmed by the Senate. Board members serve longer terms than does the president—usually 12 or 15 years—that are staggered to increase the chances of a bipartisan composition. The Supreme Court further ensured these agencies' independence in 1935 when it ruled that the president could not remove appointed board members from office.[27] As a result, citizens can interact with these agencies as they do with courts, knowing that those who decide cases are independent of the other branches of government. Newer regulatory agencies such as the Equal Employment Opportunity Commission (EEOC) enjoy less independence because presidents wanted greater control over their operations.

Selected Independent Executive Agencies

Year	Date Formed	Name
1945	1947	Central Intelligence Agency (CIA)
1950	1949	General Services Administration (GSA)
1955	1950	National Science Foundation (NSF)
1960	1953	Small Business Administration (SBA)
1965	1958	National Aeronautics and Space Administration (NASA)
1970		
1975	1974	Federal Election Commission (FEC)
1980		
1985		
1990		
1995	1994	Social Security Administration
2000		

Government Corporations The most recently devised form of bureaucratic organization is the government corporation. Dating from 1933, these are businesses established and sometimes subsidized by Congress to make certain services affordable for average citizens. These corporations typically charge for their services and retain all their profits rather than distributing them as dividends to stockholders. The largest and best-known government corporation is the U.S. Postal Service.

Proxy Administration The federal government does not always carry out its administrative tasks directly; it often delegates the tasks to other parties through contracts, vouchers, grants-in-aid, and mandates. This practice, called proxy administration,[28] makes it difficult to estimate the true size of the national government because countless "shadow employees" do the government's work without officially being members of the federal bureaucracy.[29] In 1996, President Clinton announced to great public acclaim his plan to shrink the federal bureaucracy, declaring, "the era of big government is over." He neglected to mention, however, the large amount of money the government was spending to pay private firms to perform government services. One political scientist argues that presidents often use "smoke and mirrors" to disguise the real size of the national

Selected Independent Regulatory Agencies

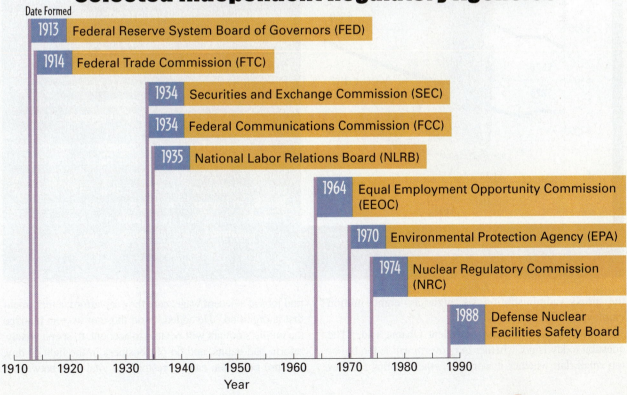

Date Formed
- 1913 Federal Reserve System Board of Governors (FED)
- 1914 Federal Trade Commission (FTC)
- 1934 Securities and Exchange Commission (SEC)
- 1934 Federal Communications Commission (FCC)
- 1935 National Labor Relations Board (NLRB)
- 1964 Equal Employment Opportunity Commission (EEOC)
- 1970 Environmental Protection Agency (EPA)
- 1974 Nuclear Regulatory Commission (NRC)
- 1988 Defense Nuclear Facilities Safety Board

Year: 1910 1920 1930 1940 1950 1960 1970 1980 1990

GOVERNMENT SHUTDOWNS

The race to the 2012 presidential election theoretically should not affect most federal bureaucrats. Except for the political appointees, they are employed under the guidelines of the civil service, making their tenure not dependent on who wins the presidency. Yet in 2011 an impasse over the budget threatened to cut off the funding to run the federal government as the parties positioned themselves for the 2012 election.

The prospect of a shutdown occurred when the parties presented far different visions for the federal budget. The Republicans, who had campaigned successfully against big government and excessive spending in the 2010 midterm elections, wanted far-reaching cuts

Most Oppose Medicare Cuts

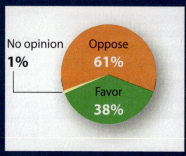

No opinion
1%

Oppose
61%

Favor
38%

Source: USA TODAY/Gallup Poll Jan. 14–16 with a random sample of 516 adults. Margin of sampling error: ± 5 percentage points.

in spending and no tax increases. They wanted to cut Medicare, which provides health insurance for 47 million seniors and people with disabilities, by turning it over to private insurers who could charge beneficiaries more or offer less. They wanted to turn Medicaid, the federal–state program covering more than 50 million low-income Americans, over to the states cutting $75 billion over 10 years by forcing lower benefits or increasing co-payments. Republican leaders, supported by the tea party deficit hawks, were concerned over the projections that the combined cost of the two health programs would nearly double by 2021. (See figure "Rising Costs of Medicare and Medicaid.") The Democrats, on the other hand, resisted. They were buoyed by the fact that a majority of Americans did not want to see reductions in spending on Medicare. (See figure "Most Oppose Medicare Cuts.")

As the president and congressional leaders failed to reach a budget compromise, the government's first shutdown since the 20-day one in 1995 appeared imminent. In a shutdown of the government, only those activities and employees that are deemed "essential" to keep the nation safe and operational continue to perform. The decision to furlough a significant number of bureaucrats during a shutdown means that some services that American citizens take for granted would be suspended. There would be no processing of income-tax returns or sending of refunds. Pay for military personnel and law-enforcement agents would be suspended. The activities at national parks and museums would close down. The space shuttle program would be halted, and citizens could not receive passports. The sending of Social Security checks, air traffic control, school lunch programs, border patrol, and military operations, however, would continue.

An eleventh-hour budget compromise was reached in April of 2011 because neither party wanted to be blamed for a cessation of government services just as their candidates were kicking off their 2012 presidential bids. Yet the threat of an impasse served as an alarming reminder of just how much political squabbles in Congress can impact the federal bureaucracy.

Rising Costs of Medicare and Medicaid

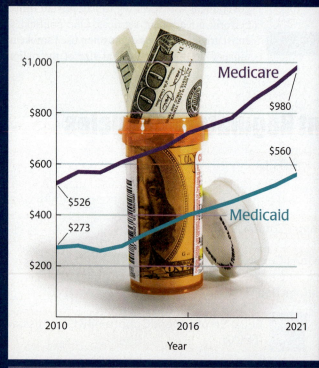

$1,000

$800

Medicare

$980

$600

$560

$526

Medicaid

$400

$273

$200

2010   2016   2021

Year

Source: Congressional Budget Office

the proxy administration as high as eight million employees.

In his inaugural address, President Obama said, "The question today is not whether our government is too big or too small, but whether it works, whether it helps families find jobs at a decent wage, care they can afford, a retirement that is dignified." He added, "And those of us who manage the public's dollars will be held to account, to spend wisely, reform bad habits, and do our business in the light of day, because only then can we restore the vital trust between a

Selected Government Corporations

Name	Date formed	Principal functions
Tennessee Valley Authority (TVA) (15,000 employees)	1933	Operates a Tennessee River control system and generates power for a seven-state region and for the U.S. aeronautics and space programs; promotes the economic development of the Tennessee Valley region; controls floods and promotes the navigability of the Tennessee River.
Federal Deposit Insurance Corporation (FDIC) (5,381 employees)	1933	Insures individuals' bank deposits up to $250,000; oversees the business activities of banks.
Export-Import Bank of the United States (EX-IM Bank) (385 employees)	1934	Promotes the sale of American-made goods abroad; grants loans to foreign purchasers of American products.
National Railroad Passenger Corporation (Amtrak) (23,000 employees)	1970	Provides a balanced national and intercity rail passenger service network; controls 23,000 miles of track with 505 stations.
U.S. Postal Service (574,000 employees)	1970	Delivers mail throughout the United States and its territories; is the largest government corporation.

people and their government." To that end, the president ordered his department heads and agency chiefs during his full cabinet meeting to come up with ways to save $100 million dollars in a 90-day period by identifying money-saving areas such as buying supplies in bulk. Critics countered that such savings were laughable because the total federal budget was $3.6 trillion.

Government-Sponsored Enterprises The federal government sets up government-sponsored enterprises (GSEs), which operate as though they were privately owned and operated. For instance, they are primarily responsible to shareholders. Over time, some of these enterprises have become fully privatized. One example is the Student Loan Marketing Association (Sallie Mae), created in 1972 to promote low-cost loans to students and privatized in 2005.

SOURCES OF BUREAUCRATIC POWER

Although federal bureaucrats are not elected, they make important decisions about the direction of public policy. Although elected policymakers derive power ultimately from the electorate, the sources of an administrative agency's power include external support, expertise and discretion, longevity and vitality, and strong leadership.

External Support

Americans' historical suspicion of intrusive government has rendered the bureaucracy vulnerable to public attack, and politicians often manipulate this mistrust during elections to gain votes. As a result, bureaucratic agencies seek external support in the form of positive attitudes toward the agency and political agreements to fund their budgets. The more external support an agency possesses, the more power it is able to wield. However, agencies can lose public support as quickly as they gain it. Prior to World War II, for example, Americans widely admired the FBI and its director, J. Edgar Hoover. However, revelations of Hoover's illegal surveillance of protest groups in the 1950s and 1960s greatly reduced the FBI's popularity. The media, with their propensity toward negative news reporting, create an environment that does not guarantee consistent public support for any agency. As a result, agencies must conduct public-relations efforts directed at both the media and the public to put their work in the best possible light.

Because both Congress and the president can curb the power of bureaucratic agencies, bureau chiefs spend considerable time cultivating good relations with members of Congress and the White House. They work primarily with congressional committees and subcommittees, congres-

Bureaucratic agencies like the FBI rely on public support for their continuing power.

far more knowledge about exotic diseases than Congress members or the president. Thus, they are in a better position to write rules regarding the prevention and treatment of disease. Likewise, during the financial crisis of 2008 and 2009, it was the executive branch leaders with Wall Street experience who developed the plans to rescue the banks and maintain a stable credit market. For bureaucratic agencies, expertise is power.

Because of their expertise, bureaucrats often enjoy great discretion in implementing public policies in the way they feel is most appropriate. In 2004, for example, the Labor Department issued new rules interpreting federal legislation concerning overtime pay. The extent of the changes in the workplace was determined at the Labor Department's discretion rather than at the discretion of Congress.

Longevity and Vitality

The rules of the civil service system make it difficult for political appointees to fire career civil servants for any reason. As a result, civil servants tend to stay in office for a long time, much longer than politicians and their political appointees. This tenure is a source of power because presidents and their appointees must rely on these career civil servants in order to accomplish their policy objectives. Bureaucrats also have an institutional memory and can view issues in a historical context. Politicians come and go, but the bureaucrats remain and provide stability for the system.[32]

The commitment of its personnel to an agency's mission is another source of bureaucratic strength as employees work together to accomplish agency goals. One way of ensuring vitality is to hire only employees with strong prior commitment to the agency. Another is to create a work environment that fosters loyalty.[33]

The National Aeronautics and Space Administration (NASA), an independent agency, is responsible for the nation's space program.

sional staff members, the Congressional Budget Office, executive department heads, presidential staff members, and the Office of Management and Budget, among others.

It is particularly important for agencies to have the support of the interests that make up their constituency. These interest groups constitute the external support necessary to blunt political opposition.[31] Hence, the Department of Agriculture needs to please farmers, and the Department of Labor needs to satisfy the demands of organized labor.

Expertise and Discretion

Bureaucrats' superior knowledge places them in a position of authority relative to other political actors, who typically lack the same depth of knowledge or understanding of specific policy issues. Researchers employed at the Centers for Disease Control and Prevention, for instance, possess

Leadership

Finally, good leaders possess the will and talent to translate an agency's resources into power. Good leaders can also enhance an agency's expertise and vitality and interact effectively with external groups.[34] Because of the fixed nature of salary schedules and the repetitive nature of some bureau work, bureau chiefs often look for innovative ways to motivate their workers. The power of bureaucratic agencies does not go unchecked, however, as we will see in the next section.

"No politician ever lost votes by denouncing the bureaucracy."

CONTROLLING BUREAUCRATIC POWER

In spite of the enormous influence and often independent nature of public bureaucracies, many actors in the political system have some tools to check bureaucratic power. The general unpopularity of bureaucracies among the American public also makes it easier for politicians to wield these tools. As James Q. Wilson wrote, "No politician ever lost votes by denouncing the bureaucracy."[35] Denouncing the bureaucracy, however, is easier than controlling it—although Congress, the White House, the courts, and even some bureaucrats have occasionally tried.

Congressional Controls

The implied powers granted under the necessary and proper clause allow Congress to create, abolish, or alter bureaucratic departments, agencies, bureaus, and commissions. Congress can exercise power over the bureaucracy by ordinary legislation. By writing a statute that is very clear and precise, Congress reduces the discretion of the bureaucratic agency to fill in the details. Congress can exercise its authority by passing sunset laws, whose provisions automatically expire at a time specified by the statute. Congress also uses legislative veto provisions in some statutes that allow it to veto future bureaucratic interpretation and implementation of a law.

Congress can employ its power of the purse to control bureaucratic authority. Passing authorization legislation sets a maximum amount that a particular agency can spend on a program. After Congress authorizes funds, it must still appropriate them, so agency heads must appear before the House Appropriations Committee to justify their monetary requests. The Appropriations Committee often serves as a budget cutter by decreasing the amount previously authorized by legislative committees.

Congress can also monitor the activities of the federal bureaucracy by exercising its oversight function. The Supreme Court has ruled that the power of Congress to legislate implies the power to conduct investigations and, if necessary, to compel the disclosure of information before legislative hearings.[36] Through such actions, Congress indicates its support for or displeasure with an agency's activities. In April 2008, for instance, the House Transportation and Infrastructure Committee directed its political wrath at the Federal Aviation Administration for creating "a culture of coziness" between the senior agency officials and the airlines they were charged with regulating. The result was a pattern of regulatory abuses and lapses that placed the flying public in danger.[37] There is no way, however, for congressional committees to monitor all the activities of the vast federal bureaucracy. Thus, Congress tends to conduct investigations of only those agencies that clearly contradict its will or those that have generated a scandal. Congress typically waits for clientele groups, lobbyists, or interest groups to report concerns about an agency and then reacts to that complaint. This suggests that citizen action can exert considerable influence on government policy.

In 1996, Congress provided itself with an additional tool to reduce the power of the bureaucracy. Congressional review gives Congress the power to strike down any newly announced agency rule if both houses pass such a resolution and the president signs it. As with other laws, Congress can override a presidential veto with a two-thirds vote in each chamber.

Presidential Controls

Without some form of control over the bureaucracy, presidents are at a major disadvantage in advancing their policies. As the national government has grown and become more complex, however, presidents have delegated in-

Did You Know?

. . . That many laws, both state and federal, have "sunset" provisions but that very rarely does the sun ever actually "set" on them? Legislators usually find it very difficult to vote against reauthorizing these laws as the deadline approaches because of the political cost involved.

creasing power to bureaucrats. As a result, presidents often have a more difficult time selling their programs to the bureaucracy than to Congress.[38]

One problem that many presidents had with the modern bureaucracy was that they had very little control over its work. They appreciated the talent and competency of the modern bureaucrat, but they wanted to choose managers of agencies who not only had managerial skills but also would understand the political goals the presidents wanted to achieve. To this end, President Jimmy Carter urged Congress to modify the civil service system. Congress complied by passing the Civil Service Reform Act of 1978, legislation that created the Senior Executive Service. The Senior Executive Service (SES) is a select group of career federal public administrators who specialize in managing public agencies. They agree to make themselves available for presidential transfers to other agencies that may require their talents in exchange for higher salaries. There are more than six thousand members of this service, and they fill most of the top managerial positions in the federal bureaucracy. The SES provides the president with greater control over the bureaucracy by making it possible to place career civil servants where he or she wants them.

Another key presidential control on the bureaucracy is the power to submit bureaucratic reorganization plans to Congress, authorized when Congress established the Executive Office of the President in 1939. President George W. Bush's administration exercised this authority to reorganize several

intelligence and law enforcement agencies with the creation of the Department of Homeland Security in 2003. On the whole, however, presidential attempts to reorganize the bureaucracy have not resulted in greater presidential control.[39]

The president exercises considerable control through his power of appointment.[40] Article II, Section 2, of the Constitution empowers the president to appoint major officials, with confirmation by a majority of the members of the Senate. It also provides that Congress shall decide the means of appointments for minor officials. Under this latter provision, Congress has empowered the president to choose some minor officials in the executive branch, such as administrative staffers, without the need for Senate approval. This has allowed presidents to build a loyal administrative base by choosing nearly three thousand political appointees who will follow his policy wishes. The president needs to be careful to avoid making loyalty the main qualification for appointment. "Loyal individuals," one insider writes, "who lack political experience can do the president more harm than good. Motivated by the best of intentions (e.g., serving the president) such officials can produce disastrous political consequences that can ultimately reduce presidential influence."[41] The president also wields the sole power to fire political appointees.

President Obama created the Council on Women and Girls by executive order in 2009 to help government agencies to respond to the challenges facing females in the twenty-first century.

This power is limited, however, because it does not extend to the vast majority of bureaucrats whose job security is protected by civil service rules, or to members of independent regulatory commissions.

Like Congress, the president can also use the budget as a tool of administrative control. Gerald Ford stated in his memoirs that "a president controls his administration through the budget. The document reflects his basic priorities."[42] Presidents can set the agenda for their administrations by calling for increases or reductions for specific social programs and by submitting larger or smaller budgets for national defense. "They can also influence the fate of a particular agency by proposing increases or reductions in funding, initiating new programs, and vetoing appropriations."[43] Today, the president depends heavily on the Office of Management and Budget to exercise control over the bureaucracy. At the beginning of the budget cycle, the OMB assigns each agency a budget limit consistent with the president's directives. After each agency sends the OMB its budgetary requests for the fiscal year, the OMB reviews the requests and makes changes before sending the budget to Congress. No agency can issue a major rule without an OMB assessment that the rule's benefits outweigh its costs. In addition, no agency can propose legislation to Congress without the approval of the OMB.

In 2009 President Obama signed an executive order that created the White House Council on Women and Girls. The mission of the council is to provide a coordinated governmental response to the challenges confronting females. To further that mission, all federal departments and bureaucratic agencies must consider how their programs and policies impact women and families in such areas as economic security, protection from violence, and health. It remains to be seen to what extent the council will be able to control bureaucratic behavior.

Judicial Controls

The courts' influence on the federal bureaucracy is much less direct than that of Congress or the president. They can intervene only if an aggrieved party files a lawsuit against an administrative agency. When that happens, the courts attempt to ascertain the legislative and presidential intent of the law to evaluate whether the administrative rules are consistent with congressional and presidential wishes. This is a difficult undertaking because, as we have noted, legislation is often purposely vague to allow the specialists in the bureaucracy to fill in the gaps in the policy and to adapt the rules to fit changing and unanticipated conditions. For that reason, the courts tend to support the actions of the bureaucrats if they are at all consistent with the politicians' wishes, and if the bureaucratic rules are consistent with the tenets of due process ensuring that all parties are treated fairly.

whistle-blowing The practice whereby individuals in the bureaucracy bring public attention to gross inefficiency or corruption in the government.

Whistle-Blowing

A more controversial method of controlling bureaucratic power originates within the bureaucracy itself. Known as **whistle-blowing**, it is the act of calling public attention to inappropriate agency behavior. To encourage whistle-blowing, Congress passed the Whistle Blower Protection Act in 1989 to protect employees from retaliation and, in some instances, provide them with a financial reward. Despite the law, many government employees are still afraid to expose corruption for fear of reprisal. Whistle-blowing has uncovered many outrageous cost overruns in government contracts, such as the Defense Department paying $600 apiece for toilet seats.

The 2008 oversight hearings of the Federal Aviation Administration referred to earlier were triggered by two whistle-blowers. One FAA plane inspector, Charalambe Boutris, contacted the congressional committee after his unsuccessful efforts to persuade his superiors to ground Southwest Airlines planes that had cracks in their fuselage. He testified that the cracks "could have resulted in sudden fracture and failure of the skin panels of the fuselage, and consequently cause a rapid decompression which would have a catastrophic impact during flight."[44] A second whistle-blower, Douglas E. Peters, testified after a superior indirectly threatened his family if he did not maintain his silence. However, the risks and uncertainty involved with whistle-blowing make it an inconsistent means of curbing bureaucratic abuses of power.

Hot or Not?

Are whistle-blowers heroes or villains?

THE BUREAUCRACY AND CIVIC ENGAGEMENT

Today, citizens have increased the nature and scope of their interactions with government. They now lobby the bureaucracy just as they do their congressional representatives, attempting to influence rules, receive favorable rulings by administrative judges, and demand greater accountability for the way their tax monies are spent. This approach to securing citizen rights has expanded civic engagement in important ways, but at a measurable cost. As citizens attend more to advancing narrow personal interests in government, they risk losing sight of their role as owners of government rather than merely consumers of its policies. Citizens belong to a political community that has a collective existence, whereas customers are people who make individual purchases. Customers are not interested in making changes that benefit citizens collectively.

Many of the changes in today's bureaucracy reflect an increasing government emphasis on privatization. The federal government contracts out a great deal of work to the private sector. Creating voucher systems for some public policy areas such as education creates competitive markets for public services. Some politicians are even advocating privatization of the Social Security system on the basis of dire forecasts that the system will have insufficient funds to pay future benefits when today's workers retire. Under the current system, workers receive a fixed amount of money each month upon retirement, which is based on the number of years worked and the amount of money earned. In a private system, the government would no longer deduct Social Security taxes, leaving workers free to invest this money as they saw fit. Such proposals of bureaucratic privatization are likely to increase in frequency in the current political environment.

Summary ∨∨

1. **What is the federal bureaucracy?**
- The federal bureaucracy is a complex organization of departments, agencies, and corporations that have the characteristics of hierarchy, specialization, and formalized rules.
- The number of civilians working in the federal bureaucracy has been influenced by the demands citizens have made for government services.
- The way federal bureaucrats have been chosen has been a reflection of the political system evolving from an elite system, to patronage, and finally to a merit system.
- Government bureaucracies produce public goods, and they are not concerned about profits but they are subject to a variety of pathologies that interfere with their ability to respond.

2. **Who are federal bureaucrats and what do they do?**
- Federal bureaucrats are the civilian employees, most of them professionals, who work for the federal government.
- Most federal bureaucrats are civil servants with job security, but the most visible ones are political appointees who hold the most policy-sensitive positions.
- Federal bureaucrats exercise much discretion when they formulate the rules for implementing laws and settling disagreements between parties through administrative adjudication.

3. **What are the sources and limits of bureaucratic power?**
- Bureaucrats draw on external support, their expertise and discretion, longevity on the job, and the vitality and leadership in the agency as sources of power.
- Congress can limit bureaucratic power by passing laws to reorganize the bureaucracy, enacting sunset laws and legislative vetoes, controlling appropriations, conducting oversight, and practicing congressional review.
- Presidents can limit bureaucratic power by submitting bureaucratic reorganization plans to Congress, proposing civil service reform, exercising the constitutional appointment and removal powers, and controlling the bureaucracy's budget.
- The courts and whistle-blowers can limit bureaucratic power on occasion.

National Journal

WHO WILL REGULATE?

Just as was the case at the birth of the United States, Barack Obama said on the campaign trail, government today must balance the dynamism of the competitive marketplace with concern for the needs of the broader community.

"The American economy does not stand still, and neither should the rules that govern it," he said. "We have overseen 21st-century innovation—including the aggressive introduction of new and complex financial instruments like hedge funds and nonbank financial companies—with outdated 20th-century regulatory tools."

Obama laid out six general principles for reforming the nation's financial sector by modernizing the regulatory system: Those who borrow from the government should expect to be regulated by it; financial actors should be governed according to their functions rather than their type of organization; the balkanized system of regulation should be rationalized; all financial firms should disclose more information about what they do; such firms should have better safeguards against running short of cash or burning through their capital reserves; and government should be able to identify threats to the stability of the overall financial system—that is, the flow of money and credit—no matter where those threats might originate.

Once Obama took office, his first two months were consumed with stabilizing a battered U.S. economy and containing a global financial conflagration. First up in Congress was his huge stimulus program, leaving him little time to think about remaking the underlying regulatory structure. It was only in late March, as the president prepared for the G-20 summit in London of the leaders of the world's major economies, that he dispatched Treasury Secretary Timothy Geithner to Congress to start fleshing out a specific plan to implement financial reform principles.

Geithner's proposal was but the first installment of Obama's promise of regulatory reform, the administration said. In the coming weeks, officials said, the White House would offer plans for protecting consumers and investors, filling gaps in the regulatory structure, and improving international coordination on matters ranging from regulating financial institutions to cracking down on tax havens and money-laundering abroad.

In this initial round of proposals, Geithner reprised Obama's call to establish a single government regulator to oversee any financial firm deemed a "systemic risk." This super-regulator would be empowered to take preventive and corrective actions.

"This crisis has made clear that certain large, interconnected firms and markets need to be under a more consistent and more conservative regulatory regime," Geithner told the House Financial Services Committee. "These standards cannot simply address the soundness of individual institutions but must also ensure the stability of the system itself."

Geithner called for more disclosure about the supervision of novel entities and products, such as derivatives, that have largely escaped regulation. Large private investment pools, known as hedge funds, would have to register with the Securities and Exchange Commission and divulge more—on a confidential basis—about their trading activities and trading partners. Complex and volatile financial instruments, such as credit default swaps (one of the major culprits in the current financial meltdown), could no longer be traded privately through ad hoc, two-party transactions. They would have to move to regulated clearinghouses, or at least be reported to so-called trade repositories on the theory that a paper trail itself is a form of safeguard.

Another Geithner proposal would have the SEC create stronger safeguards for widely used money-market funds to forestall the risk of a run on such funds—the threat of which last fall prompted Washington to step in as a temporary guarantor of Americans' money-market investments.

The Treasury secretary also called for sweeping new federal authority that Obama never mentioned during the campaign: the power to take over and liquidate any insolvent financial institution of any kind, much as the government can now do with banks.

Geithner's plan, although more specific than Obama's campaign-trail principles, nonetheless is a blueprint missing a host of critical details—from what the systemic-risk regulatory organization should look like to what exactly it would oversee to who should run it. "It's somewhere between a statement of objectives and an actual line-by-line description of legislation," said Robert Litan of the Kauffman Foundation.

The secretary's comments hinted at other corrective measures that his proposal didn't specifically address. Among these are reforming executive pay to avoid incentives for taking outsized risks and encouraging banks in good times to amass a larger cushion of reserves that could be drawn upon in bad times.

Although Geithner made it clear that the systemic-risk regulator could have jurisdiction over certain insurance firms, which are now overseen by the states, he did not resolve the ongoing debate about whether insurers should have the option to choose between state and federal regulation.

Until they get the fine print on Geithner's plan, most financial-industry interests have decided to keep their powder dry. Hedge funds, for example, can't be happy about the prospect of new rules, but their spokesman, Managed Funds Association President Richard Baker (a former House member from Louisiana), issued a neutral statement that the industry shared government leaders' "commitment to a course of action that seeks to restore financial stability and investor confidence." The association, he said, would "carefully examine recently proposed measures" to assess their "benefits and challenges."

Some of the proposals, such as moving "over-the-counter" derivatives trading to clearinghouses, have long been expected and, in some quarters, welcomed: Two private entities have recently announced plans to set up such operations.

Turning Geithner's sketch into legislation, however, will be a complicated and contentious process. The administration proposal used "all the right words," said James Barth, a finance professor at Auburn University and a former federal financial regulator. "But how exactly does one go about doing all that? How do you measure systemic risk, or tell when different types of firms have become interconnected to a [worrying] degree, as opposed to having a normal level of interconnectedness?"

Basic questions about the systemic regulator have already sparked debate. House Financial Services Committee Chairman Barney Frank, D-Mass., contends that the Federal Reserve Board is best equipped to take on the task of such regulation quickly. But dissenters, including Senate Banking Committee Chairman Christopher Dodd, D-Conn., and ranking member Richard Shelby, R-Ala., have a range of worries about expanding the Fed's role. They and others fear that it would conflict with the Fed's responsibilities for setting monetary policy; still others think that the board has done a poor job with the regulatory responsibilities

> "This crisis has made clear that certain large, interconnected firms and markets need to be under a more consistent and more conservative regulatory regime."
>
> —Timothy Geithner

it has, including overseeing bank holding companies and state-chartered banks.

There's also the threat of turf wars between congressional committees and between financial regulators. The House Agriculture Committee has long claimed jurisdiction over financial derivatives, because these products evolved from the futures market for agricultural commodities. In February, Agriculture Committee Chairman Collin Peterson, D-Minn., moved legislation through his panel that would give the Commodity Futures Trading Commission more power to oversee derivative trading. Peterson's move was an apparent bid to get the jump on the Financial Services Committee.

But Congress also faces pressure to move quickly on reforms, or at the very least to give the government resolution authority over failing nonbank financial institutions. "There's tremendous urgency to this," Litan said. "We don't know what shoes out there haven't dropped, so it would be nice to have this in place because it sends an important signal" to the markets that government has the tools it needs to restore order.

Whether Obama's regulatory blueprint can forestall meltdowns is another matter.

Barth pointed out that government has a habit of beefing up protections after a crisis without actually doing what's necessary to prevent the next one. The real problem, he argued, is not a lack of tools but a lack of resolve to use them effectively.

"After every major piece of reform legislation the same words are said: 'Never again.' But guess what?" he asked.

It's a question he doesn't have to answer: Recent headlines say it all.

For Discussion:

■ List the agencies—both those mentioned and not mentioned in this article—that have a hand in regulating big financial companies and their activities. What tensions between these agencies does the piece illuminate?

■ What do you think of Obama's plan for 21st-century regulation of the financial industry? Does it go too far in involving government in the private sector?

■ Explain the potential problem the piece mentions about the possible conflict of interest in expanding the Fed's role in regulating banks. Is the concern a legitimate one?

14

THE COURTS

JUDICIAL POWER IN A DEMOCRATIC SETTING

ANATOMY OF A SUPREME COURT CASE ▮ Pastor Fred Phelps founded the Westboro Baptist Church in Topeka, Kansas, in 1955. Today the 70-member church espouses his belief that God is punishing the United States for its tolerance of homosexuality in the military. For more than 20 years, the church has picketed nearly 600 military funerals. On March 10, 2006, Phelps, along with two of his daughters and four of his grandchildren, flew more than a thousand miles to Westminster, Maryland, to demonstrate at yet another military funeral. Outside the church, the picketers carried signs that read, "God Hates the USA/Thank God for 9/11," "America is Doomed," "Fag Troops," "Thank God for Dead Soldiers," "You're Going to Hell," and "God Hates You."

On that March day, Albert Snyder attended the funeral of his only son, Marine Lance Corporal Matthew Snyder, who had been killed in Anbar province in Iraq. The distraught father felt as "if they had taken a gun and shot me."[1]

Snyder decided to sue the church on the grounds of personal injuries of emotional distress and a type of invasion of privacy known as "intrusion upon seclusion." His hope was to stop these protests and protect other families the church might target in the future.

After a four-year legal battle, the case reached the United States Supreme Court. Although sympathetic to the grieving father, eight members of the Court held that the church's actions were protected by the freedom of speech guaranteed by the Constitution's First Amendment.[2] After winning the case, members of the Phelps family vowed to quadruple their funeral protests because "the nation's destruction is imminent."[3]

Since the early twentieth century, the Court has played an increasingly important role in the interpretation of citizens' civil liberties and civil rights. Yet the Court makes their determinations in ways quite different from the more familiar trial courts that are often the subject of television and movie dramas.

Most cases that are ultimately decided by the Supreme Court originate in other courts. Mr. Snyder filed his case against the Westboro church in a federal trial court. He was the plaintiff in the case. The jury found for him in the amount of nearly $11 million. The defendants filed ➡️

- What is the nature of the judicial process?
- How are Supreme Court justices selected?
- What is the nature of Supreme Court decision making?

Albert Snyder (center), father of slain soldier Marine Lance Corporal Matthew Snyder, spoke at a press conference in front of the United States Supreme Court.

posttrial motions with the trial judge contending that the jury award was excessive. The judge agreed but still awarded the plaintiff an amount of $5 million. The church then appealed to a federal appeals court. The Court of Appeals reversed the trial court decision. The panel of three appeals judges reviewed the picket signs and concluded that the statements were entitled to First Amendment protection because they pertained to matters of public concern. This would have ended the case if the Supreme Court had not granted a writ of certiorari to hear the case. They hear a very small percentage of cases from either federal appeals courts or state supreme courts, but they believed that this case raised sufficiently important issues to merit an appeal.

Snyder was represented by his counsel, Sean Summers, and Pastor Fred Phelps was represented by his daughter, Margie Phelps. The Supreme Court recognizes, however, that their cases raise issues that are of great concern to many more citizens and interests than just the parties to the lawsuit. As a result, they allow interested parties to submit legal arguments in the form of "friend of the court" briefs. Submitting briefs for Snyder were the Attorneys General of 48 states and the District of Columbia, 42 senators, the Veterans of Foreign Wars, and the American Legion. Among those submitting briefs for the Phelps were the American Civil Liberties Union, Scholars of First Amendment Law, Reporters Committee for Freedom of the Press, 21 news organizations, and the Liberty Counsel, a conservative group specializing in issues of religious freedom.

Unlike trials that last several hours, days, or even weeks, the Supreme Court reserves only one hour for the hearing of a case. The justices are already familiar with the case to be heard. As a result, the attorneys for Snyder and Phelps had only thirty minutes to present their legal arguments. However, the procedures of the Court allow the Justices to interrupt the lawyers at any time to ask questions. Justice Ginsburg quizzed Summers as to why the church was liable because their picketing behavior was in conformity with the state law that was passed after the incident. Justice Alito suggested that statements on the church's website suggested that the speech was of a personal or private nature and so unprotected by the First Amendment:[4] Justice Alito voiced the one dissenting opinion in the case.

Today the Supreme Court has become the institution most likely to determine the extent of personal rights that have become the focus of modern American democracy. Members of the Supreme Court exercise considerable power, but they do so in a different manner than members of Congress, the president, and bureaucrats. Their methods differ even from those of trial judges. Their ability to affect the lives of citizens has heightened public interest in their selection and in the ways they make decisions. Their prominence has also created new opportunities for citizens to interact with the Court. ❖

NATIONAL COURT STRUCTURE

The national court structure first began to take on its present look with the passage of the Judiciary Act of 1789. The Constitution provided for just the Supreme Court and "such inferior courts as the Congress may from time to time ordain and establish." Once the Constitution was ratified, the Congress moved quickly to establish a complete national judiciary, including trial courts and other appellate courts. At this time, each state government already had its own system of courts. The existence of one national court system and separate court systems in each of the states is known as a **dual court system**. Citizens of any state are subject to the jurisdiction of both state courts and national courts.

The first bill introduced in the Senate dealt with the unresolved issue of national inferior courts. After considerable debate, Congress passed the law that led to the foundation of the current judicial system. It created a three-tier system of national courts. At the base were 13 district courts, each presided over by a single district judge. In the middle were circuit courts located in every district. Each circuit court was composed of two Supreme Court justices and one district judge. The country was divided into an Eastern, a Middle, and a Southern Circuit. Two justices were assigned to each circuit and traveled to the various courts located within that circuit. At the top of the national structure was the Supreme Court, consisting of a chief justice and five associate justices.

Currently there is a division of responsibilities between the national court system and the state court systems. Most cases that begin in a state court system are resolved in that system. The only way a case can move from a state court system to the national system is by an appeal from the state's highest court to the U.S. Supreme Court. Appeals may not move in the opposite direction. A case that begins in the national court system will be resolved in that system. For the most part, state and national courts have separate jurisdiction. A few cases, such as diversity suits (civil cases that involve parties from different states) brought for amounts greater than $75,000, may be initiated in either system. Once the case is initiated, however, it must stay in that system except for a possible appeal from the state system to the Supreme Court. See the figure below showing the American dual court structure.

> **dual court system** System under which U.S. citizens are subject to the jurisdiction of both national and state courts.

District Courts

Today, the national court system includes 94 U.S. district courts. Each state contains at least one district court, and no district court crosses state lines. U.S. district courts are trial courts; they represent the entryway to the national court system. District courts typically deal with cases involving the violation of federal labor, civil rights, Social Security, truth-in-lending, federal crimes, and antitrust

Diagram of the U.S. Court System

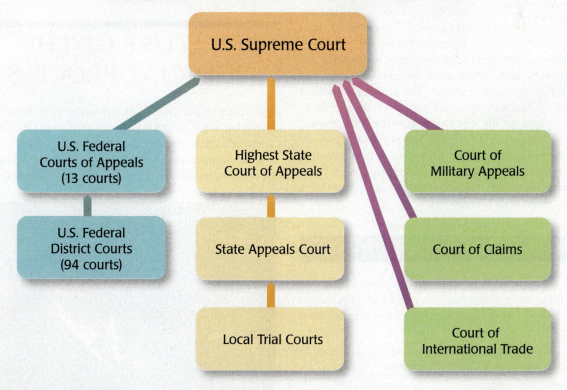

U.S. Supreme Court

U.S. Federal Courts of Appeals (13 courts)

U.S. Federal District Courts (94 courts)

Highest State Court of Appeals

State Appeals Court

Local Trial Courts

Court of Military Appeals

Court of Claims

Court of International Trade

Federal Judicial Circuits

[Map of the United States showing federal judicial circuits numbered 1–11, with D.C. Circuit and Federal Circuit labeled in Washington, D.C. State abbreviations shown: WA, MT, ND, MN, VT, NH, ME, 1, OR, ID, WY, SD, WI, MI, 2, NY, MA, RI, CT, 9, UT, 10, CO, NE, 8, IA, 7, IN, OH, 3, PA, NJ, DE, MD, CA, NV, IL, 6, WV, VA, D.C. Circuit, Federal Circuit, AZ, NM, KS, MO, KY, 4, NC, TN, AL, GA, SC, TX, 5, LA, MS, 11, FL, AK, HI, GU, MP, VI, PR]

making process and its role in the American political system.

laws. A single judge presides over the trial, which may or may not have a jury. District courts resolve disputes following the precedents of the U.S. Supreme Court and the appropriate Court of Appeals in their geographical area; they make few policy innovations themselves.

United States Courts of Appeals

In 1891, Congress passed the Court of Appeals Act creating separate appeals judges serving on nine appellate courts. Today, there are 13 U.S. courts of appeals; 11 are located in numbered circuits throughout the United States and two—the D.C. Court of Appeals and the Court of Appeals for the Federal Circuit—are in Washington, D.C. (See the figure above.) Losing parties in federal trial courts have an automatic right to appeal to these intermediate appellate courts. In resolving cases, appeals courts normally use rotating three-judge panels. The winning litigant in the original case must secure at least two votes in order to prevail; otherwise, the appeals court overturns the original decision. For particularly difficult or important cases, all the judges in a circuit may sit together to hear a case or rehear a case already decided by a three-judge panel. These *en banc* hearings are relatively rare and occur less than a hundred times in an average year.

precedent A former case that was supported by a majority on an appellate court and provides guidance for the determination of a present case.

United States Supreme Court

In many ways, the Supreme Court is the most visible and powerful court in the world. Because of its importance, we will later describe in detail the Court's decision-

The American judicial process is based on the adversary process, in which lawyers for all parties present evidence in a trial setting.

Specialized Courts

Congress also creates specialized national courts to help administer specific congressional statutes. Such courts as the Court of Appeals for the Armed Forces, the Court of Claims, and the Court of International Trade hear a limited range of cases, their judges serve varying terms, and some have no permanent judges, borrowing justices from other courts. Two courts with borrowed judges that have gained recent attention are the Foreign Intelligence Surveillance Court and the Foreign Intelligence Surveillance Court of Review. The former is a secret court formed in 1978 to hear government requests for warrants to conduct surveillance on suspected spies. The borrowed judge hears the request in a secret proceeding conducted in an office in the Justice Department building. In the proceeding, counsel represents the government, but not the person for whom the wiretap is intended. If the district judge denies the application for the warrant, the government may appeal to the Foreign Intelligence Surveillance Court of Review, which consists of three judges borrowed from the courts of appeals. However, this court seldom meets because the government has almost never failed to obtain a warrant. After the terrorist attacks on September 11, 2001, Congress expanded the powers of these courts to grant warrants to obtain evidence that can be used in criminal trials. The Bush administration has maintained, however, that federal agents do not need these warrants when conducting surveillance on suspected terrorists.

NATURE OF THE JUDICIAL PROCESS

The American judicial process is based on a number of basic principles, many of which were inherited from English law. These principles establish the ground rules for our current system of justice and outline the role of judges, the various types of law, and the types of cases different courts may hear.

Significant Supreme Court Cases

Case	Significance
Marbury v. Madison (1803)	Established the principle of judicial review.
McColloch v. Maryland (1819)	Enlarged the powers of the national government by recognizing its implied constitutional powers.
Gibbons v. Ogden (1824)	Provided a broad interpretation of the federal commerce power.
Schenck v. United States (1919)	Created the clear and present danger test for the free speech cases.
Palko v. Connecticut (1937)	Opened the door for the nationalization of the Bill of Rights.
Brown v. Board of Education (1954)	Ended the separate but equal doctrine for race relations by declaring legally segregated schools unconstitutional.
Baker v. Carr (1962)	Allowed courts to hear cases on legislative apportionment leading ultimately to the one person, one vote rule.
Gideon v. Wainwright (1963)	Recognized the right of poor criminal defendants to have counsel.
Miranda v. Arizona (1966)	Provided criminal suspects with a series of police warnings regarding their constitutional rights.
Roe v. Wade (1973)	Ruled that women's constitutional right to privacy allows abortions.

Common Law

American colonists brought with them to the new world a system of law that had developed in England over several centuries. It consisted of a national judge-made law that was common to the entire country. In time, courts published annual *Yearbooks* that summarized portions of the most important decisions. Under the common law system, judicial decisions in cases served the dual function of settling controversies and establishing **precedents**—previous decisions that have a bearing on current legal cases.[5] Since no two cases are identical, however, judges exercise a great deal of discretion when deciding whether to follow a precedent.

The common law tradition not only enhanced the role of judges but also allowed them to use the law to prevent abuse from other political leaders. When a conflict between an act of Parliament and the common law developed in 1610, an English court held that a judge could overturn the act if he determined it violated the basic principles of common law.[6] The common law tradition provided the basis for judicial review in the United States.

Did You Know?

. . . That John Marshall and Thomas Jefferson were cousins and that they detested each other, both personally and politically? Marshall, referring to Jefferson's love of abstract political theory and to his book-filled hilltop abode on Monticello, called him "the great lama of the mountain."

Judicial Review

The principle of **judicial review** states that the Supreme Court has the power to strike down acts of Congress the Court rules unconstitutional. The 1803 case of *Marbury v. Madison* formally enshrined this principle in American law. Near the end of his term as president in 1801, John Adams made a number of last-minute appointments. Among them was William Marbury, whom Adams named justice of the peace for the District of Columbia. John Marshall, the secretary of state, did not have time, however, to deliver the written commissions to Marbury and many of the other appointees before Adams's term expired. When Thomas Jefferson assumed the presidency in 1801, he ordered the new secretary of state, James Madison, to void Marbury's commission and that of many of the other late-term appointees whose commissions were undelivered. Marbury sued Madison, arguing that the Judiciary Act of 1789 gave the Supreme Court power to force the president to honor the appointment.

judicial review The power of the U.S. Supreme Court to review the acts of other political institutions and declare them unconstitutional.

John Marshall, now serving as chief justice, wrote the opinion for the Court's unanimous decision. He concluded that the portion of the Judiciary Act under which Marbury sued for his commission was at odds with the Constitution. Since the Court could not honor a law that was contrary to the Constitution, it had no power to force Jefferson to honor the appointment. Marshall ruled that the Court had a duty to declare laws null and void if they conflicted with the Constitution, establishing the precedent of Court oversight on congressional statutes.

Civil and Criminal Law

The two basic types of law under the American judicial system are civil law and criminal law. Civil law involves disputes between private parties over such matters as contracts, personal injuries, family law, and the buying and selling of property. The parties may be individuals, business corporations, or governments acting in a private capacity. Criminal law involves the prosecution of individuals who commit acts that are prohibited by the government.

The party who initiates a civil case is the *plaintiff*. The person against whom the lawsuit is brought is the *defendant*. Some types of civil law use the terms *petitioner* and *respondent* instead. Some civil cases may have multiple plaintiffs, multiple defendants, or both. In some situations, plaintiffs may bring a case known as a **class action suit**, in which one or more persons sue on behalf of a larger set of people who share the same situation. The Supreme Court writes the rules that determine how easy or how difficult it is to qualify for a class action suit. The party that initiates criminal cases is the government. The government is the plaintiff in criminal cases, because the government considers crime to be a violation of the interests of society as a whole, not just those of an individual or group.

Judicial Requirements

The judicial requirements of **jurisdiction** and **justiciability** limit the types of cases that a particular court can hear. Jurisdiction is the power of the court to hear and decide cases. The Constitution grants the U.S. Supreme Court **original jurisdiction** in cases involving ambassadors or states suing other states; and **appellate jurisdiction** in cases involving federal law, cases involving citizens from one state suing citizens from another state (diversity suits), or cases in which the federal government is a litigant.

Justiciability is a less precise term than *jurisdiction*. Chief Justice Earl Warren once referred to [justiciability] as one of "the most amorphous [concepts] in the entire domain of public law."[7]

class action suit Lawsuit in which one or more persons sue on behalf of a larger set of people claiming the same injury.

jurisdiction The power of a court to hear and decide cases.

justiciability The doctrine that excludes certain cases from judicial consideration because of the party bringing the lawsuit or the nature of the subject matter.

original jurisdiction The power of a court to hear and decide a case first.

appellate jurisdiction The power of a court to receive cases from trial courts for the purpose of reviewing whether the legal procedures were properly followed.

standing Proof that a party has suffered harm or been threatened with harm by the circumstances surrounding a lawsuit.

political questions Issues determined by the Supreme Court to be better resolved by Congress or the president.

Julia Roberts's movie role as Erin Brockovich demonstrated how courts encourage civic engagement through litigation by allowing class action suits.

May It Please the Court

Access to the U. S. Supreme Court

Jurisdiction	The power of the U.S. Supreme Court to hear the particular types of cases.
Federal questions	A lawsuit that involves a federal statute, treaty, or the U.S. Constitution.
Federal party	A lawsuit in which the federal government is either the plaintiff or defendant.
Diversity of citizenship	A civil lawsuit that involves parties from different states in which the dollar amount exceeds $75,000.

Justiciability	The exclusion of certain lawsuits to the party bringing the case or the subject of the lawsuit.
Standing	The party bringing the lawsuit must have suffered real harm.
Mootness	The controversy is no longer alive by the time it reaches the Court.
Political question	The Court will not resolve cases more properly resolved by Congress or the president.

Class Action Suits	The ability of a litigant to bring a lawsuit on behalf of a larger set of people who share the same situation.

***Amicus curiae* briefs**	Interest groups can submit their views to the Court even though they are not parties to the lawsuit.

Basically, it means that a court can exclude certain cases from judicial consideration because of the identity of the party bringing the lawsuit or the subject of the lawsuit. For a lawsuit to meet the standard of justiciability, the party bringing the case must have **standing**. That is, the defendant's actions must either harm the plaintiff or threaten the plaintiff with harm. In other words, a litigant must demonstrate a personal stake in the outcome of the case. The Court can make litigation more available to citizens by relaxing the standards of standing. The Supreme Court has ruled, for instance, that federal taxpayers have standing to challenge the constitutionality of federal programs if they can show that a specific expenditure of tax monies violates the Constitution.[8]

The federal courts also will not hear cases that involve **political questions**. The Supreme Court has acknowledged that other branches of the federal government are better equipped to address this class of constitutional issues. The concept, however, is flexible; at one time, the Court said the issue of political reapportionment was a political question,[9] but it later reversed itself in *Baker v. Carr* (1962).[10] A summary of the principles that permit access to the Supreme Court are presented in the table above.

CHANGING NATURE OF THE SUPREME COURT

The United States had no national judiciary under the Articles of Confederation.[13] It was not until the nation adopted the Constitution in 1787 that the Supreme Court came into existence as an independent and permanent court.[14] At the time, it was the object of much popular suspicion from citizens who feared the power of a national court. Alexander Hamilton was quick to assure readers, in the *The Federalist* No. 78, that the new Supreme Court would be the "least dangerous branch" of the new national government. Without the power of the purse to appropriate money, or the power of the sword to enforce the law, the Court would prove no threat to the other branches of government, Hamilton reasoned.[15]

Real Cases and Controversies

When trial judges confront legal questions in the context of a case, they or a jury must first determine the facts of the case, which are not always self-evident. The judicial process in the United States uses the adversary system, in which two opposing parties both present their own interpretation of the facts to ascertain the truth. An impartial third party, a judge or jury, has the responsibility of choosing between the two alternative versions of the facts. When Supreme Court justices receive a case, lower courts have already determined the facts. The job of the Supreme Court justices is to match the facts with the relevant law. When determining the law, the Court may interpret the meaning of a constitutional provision or a statutory provision. Either process allows the justices more discretion than might be imagined, because the meaning of these provisions is often subject to a variety of interpretations.

litigious Marked by a tendency to file lawsuits.

America is a **litigious** society that increasingly looks to the courts to resolve its disputes.[11] Americans file more lawsuits per capita than the citizens of Japan, Italy, Spain, Germany, and Sweden, but about the same as counterparts in England and Denmark.[12] As more cases are filed in the courts, the Supreme Court has more opportunity to choose which cases to hear on appeal. Congress also has made the courts more accessible to Americans with the passage of legislation that makes it easier to pay for litigation. The 1964 Civil Rights Act allows private citizens who file discrimination claims to collect their attorney's fees from the defendant if they win. Other legislation makes it easier for victims of gender bias and consumer fraud to press their claims in court. Ultimately, however, lower court decisions may be subject to Supreme Court review, and they must clear this hurdle to remain in force.

The Early Court

The Supreme Court first met on Tuesday, February 2, 1790, in the Royal Exchange Building located in what is today New York City's Wall Street district. Things began slowly for the justices, elegantly clad in the black and scarlet robes of English tradition: They had no cases to hear that first year.[16] Due to its perceived weakness in the new national government and its small workload, the early Court lacked status. Many men turned down presidential nominations to the Court, and others, including inaugural Chief Justice John Jay, soon left for positions they thought carried more respect.

Marbury v. Madison marked a watershed in the history of the Supreme Court. By establishing the principle of judicial review, the Marshall Court placed the Court squarely in the mainstream of American government and made it a force to reckon with. The Marshall Court's rulings, however, tended to affirm policies that supported the aims of the national government, contributing to a generally congenial relationship among the three branches of government.

Marshall's successor, Roger Taney, used the Court's power in quite a different fashion. Under Taney, the Court tilted much more dramatically toward protecting state power from incursion by the federal government. The Taney Court often found itself at odds with the other branches of the federal government. When the Taney Court decided to hear the *Dred Scott* case (discussed at length in Chapter 5), it caused nearly irreparable damage to the institution. By declaring the Missouri Compromise unconstitutional, the Court provided slave owners with a major political victory and incurred the wrath of abolitionists and the Republican Party. When Republican president Abraham Lincoln took office in 1861, his first inaugural address criticized the Supreme Court in some of the most scathing language ever uttered by a president about another branch of government. Congressional Republicans followed these remarks by attempting to weaken the Court through manipulating the number of justices for political advantage.[17] They also removed some of the Court's appellate jurisdiction.[18]

President Eisenhower called the nomination of liberal Chief Justice Earl Warren one of his two biggest mistakes as president.

The Court, Business, and Social Welfare

The Court would face peril again some 80 years later when the laissez-faire economic philosophy of most of its members conflicted with Franklin Roosevelt's activist program to combat the Great Depression. When the Court declared 8 of the 10 legislative proposals of the New Deal unconstitutional in 1935 and 1936, the president introduced his "Court-Packing Plan." He proposed that for every Supreme Court justice who had reached the age of 70 and chose not to retire, the president could nominate an additional judge to help with the workload. The real purpose of the proposal had nothing to do with helping elderly justices. The Court was typically voting 6 to 3 to invalidate New Deal programs. Five of the six justices voting against the president were at least 70 years of age. If Roosevelt were able to appoint new justices for all those who did not retire, he could turn a 6-to-3 deficit into a 9-to-6 victory. Believing the bill violated the judicial independence of the Supreme Court, however, Congress narrowly defeated its passage. Two members of the Supreme Court understood the politics of the moment and the long-term implications for the Court as an institution. Chief Justice Charles Evans Hughes and Justice Owen Roberts changed their positions and began consistently to uphold New Deal attempts to regulate the economy. Statutes were now surviving on 5-to-4 votes. The two justices understood how close their beloved institution had come to losing its independence.

The Court and Personal Rights

Since its retreat during the New Deal, the Court has fundamentally changed its emphasis regarding the nature of the cases it hears. Today the Court's emphasis in the area of constitutional law is civil liberties and civil rights. This modern era of support for rights is most identified with the leadership of Earl Warren, who became chief justice in 1953. The Court's direction, however, did not change dramatically under the leadership of Warren Burger or William Rehnquist. Whether the Roberts Court will continue this trend supporting civil liberties and civil rights issues remains to be seen.

SUPREME COURT DECISION MAKING

The modern Supreme Court bears little resemblance to the institution that first convened in 1790. Today, the Court meets on a regular basis and turns away work. Its annual term begins on the first Monday in October and continues until late June or early July of the following year. Through-

This court artist rendering depicts one of the first Supreme Court cases including Justice Sotomayor, the first Hispanic American woman to serve on the Supreme Court, on the bench.

out the term, the schedule alternates between two weeks of sittings and two weeks of recess. During the *sittings*, the justices hear case arguments and announce decisions. During the *recess*, they have time to think, research, and write opinions.

The Supreme Court now functions as nine small and independent law firms, each with a justice as the senior partner aided by three to four law clerks.[19] The justices spend little time interacting with each other, and such interactions are almost impersonal. As one law clerk observed, "Justices don't think that much about what other justices are doing. They spend little time with them and rarely see each other. They often come in and sit by themselves day after day without really talking to any of the other justices."[20] Most of the communication among them takes the form of a written Memorandum to the Conference (MTTC), and much of it is done by the law clerks. Clerks also provide valuable service to the justices they serve by reviewing petitions from potential appellants and writing the legal opinions explaining the outcomes of cases. All Supreme Court clerks come from top law schools, and many of them clerk in a lower federal court for a year or two before coming to the Supreme Court.

writ of certiorari Order issued by a superior court to one of inferior jurisdiction demanding the record of a particular case.

Rule of Four Requirement that a minimum of four justices must vote to review a lower court case by issuing a writ of certiorari.

In this section, we will examine how the Supreme Court chooses which cases it will hear, how it decides these cases, and then how it justifies its decisions. Once the Court makes and justifies its decisions, others must implement them. We will explore how the Court can help in this process. Finally, we will analyze what factors best explain why Supreme Court justices behave as they do.

Agenda Decisions

The Supreme Court has almost complete discretion in deciding what cases to review. Since 1988, nearly all cases that have made it to the nation's highest court arrived there on a petition for a **writ of certiorari**. *Certiorari* is a legal term that means literally "to be informed." If the Court grants such a writ, the lower court will send a record of the case to the Court for purposes of review. In a typical year, the court receives more than nine thousand petitions for writs of certiorari but accepts fewer than one hundred for full hearing and decision. Each office takes one-eighth of the petitions at random to summarize and share with the other chambers in a pool memo. Clerks perform the initial substantive review of these petitions, "marking up" the memo based on the interests and values of the individual justices and concluding with a recommendation to grant or deny.

The chief justice plays a special role in the agenda-setting process. Several times during the term, the chief justice prepares a "discuss list" consisting of the 40 to 50 cases he believes the Court should consider at the next meeting of the justices. On Friday afternoons during the sittings, the justices gather in conference to review the discuss list. At these private meetings, the justices decide whether to grant or deny certiorari. According to the **Rule of Four**, if at least four of the justices vote to grant certiorari, the Court will hear the case and notify the parties. Under Chief Justice Roberts's leadership, the Court has been accepting more cases in recent years.

One scholar asserts that the Court will deny certiorari when (1) the case is frivolous; (2) the case is too fact-bound; (3) insufficient evidence is presented in the briefs; (4) the case involves an issue the justices want to avoid; (5) the legal issue has not percolated enough in the lower courts; (6) the briefs contain disputed facts; (7) a better case is in the pipeline; or (8) the case will fragment the Court.[21] The question still remains as to which cases the justices will vote to hear. The Court itself wrote Rule 10 to govern the process. It specifies that the Court will accept cases that have been decided differently by the various federal circuits, cases that conflict with Supreme Court precedents, and state cases that conflict with federal decisions. Based on interviews with justices and law clerks, one author concluded that the justices follow Rule 10, stating that conflict in the federal circuits is "without a doubt, one of the most important things to all the justices. All of them are disposed to resolve conflicts when they exist and want to know if a particular case poses a conflict."[22]

The Court, however, does not accept all such cases with conflicts, because there are too many of them.[23] The subject of the case often determines whether it gets a hearing. During the Vinson and Warren Court eras (1946–1969), the Court was more likely to accept cases dealing with labor relations, civil rights and civil liberties, and federalism.[24] As we saw in Chapter 4, the Court is also more likely to hear a case for which supporters have submitted *amicus curiae*, or "friend of the court," briefs. The solicitor general, who is responsible for handling most Supreme Court appeals on behalf of the federal government, appears as a party or a friend of the court in more than 50 percent of the cases the Court hears each term. The influence of the office is so great that it has a suite of offices within the Supreme Court building and its occu-

pant is referred to as the "tenth justice."[25] Because of this special relationship, the Court accepts some 70 to 80 percent of cases the solicitor general's office brings before it, compared to less than 5 percent for all other petitioners.[26]

Voting Decisions

Attorneys arguing cases before the Court have 30 minutes to present their legal arguments, a rule that is strictly enforced. A flashing white light signals when the attorney has but five minutes remaining; when the light turns red, time has elapsed and the attorney must stop immediately at that time—even in midsentence. Although attorneys often prepare for weeks, or even months, for their appearance before the Supreme Court, there is no guarantee that they will be able to present all of their arguments. The members of the Court may interrupt at any time with probing questions that can befuddle a lawyer who is not on top of his or her game. An attorney cannot possibly anticipate all the questions the justices may ask, but the experienced ones are able to use these questions to emphasize the points they want to make. Chief Justice Roberts has become quite vocal and hard-edged during oral arguments and in a 2009 session ridiculed a lawyer's argument saying, "That's like the old elephant whistle. You know, I have this whistle to keep away the elephants. Well there are no elephants, so it must work."[27]

Late on Wednesday afternoons after hearing oral arguments, and all day on Fridays when the Court is sitting, the justices meet in conference to decide the cases just argued. Since 1836, the justices have begun the conference session with a round of handshaking. It serves as a subtle reminder that they remain colleagues even though they may soon be engaged in a heated exchange of views. The associate justice with the least seniority acts as both official stenographer and doorkeeper.

By tradition, the chief justice presides over the conference and has the task of allowing adequate discussion, while at the same time moving the Court efficiently through its docket of cases. The chief justice speaks first, followed by the eight associate justices in order of seniority. At one time, justices tried to change

The Supreme Court decided the outcome of the Bush-Gore 2000 presidential election when it did not allow a recount of the contested Florida ballots.

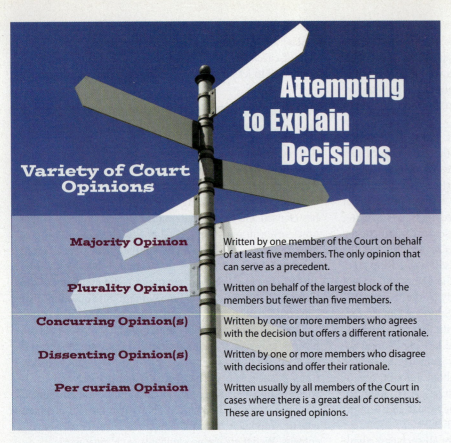

Attempting to Explain Decisions

Variety of Court Opinions

Majority Opinion	Written by one member of the Court on behalf of at least five members. The only opinion that can serve as a precedent.
Plurality Opinion	Written on behalf of the largest block of the members but fewer than five members.
Concurring Opinion(s)	Written by one or more members who agrees with the decision but offers a different rationale.
Dissenting Opinion(s)	Written by one or more members who disagree with decisions and offer their rationale.
Per curiam Opinion	Written usually by all members of the Court in cases where there is a great deal of consensus. These are unsigned opinions.

the minds of others with their comments, but the purpose of the conference session is now just to discover consensus.[28] The individual justices vote at the same time they discuss the case. At this point, however, the individual votes are still tentative and subject to change. The Court will not deliver a final vote until the completion of the next stage of the process.

Explaining Decisions

After the members of the Court cast their initial votes concerning a case **decision**, their next task is to explain their votes by writing **opinions**. Whereas the decision indicates which litigant the Court supports and by how large a margin, the opinion explains the reasons behind the decision. Only one justice writes the opinion for the Court, but other justices have the option of writing additional opinions. The chief justice decides who will write the opinion if he or she is in the majority on the initial vote in a case. If not, the most senior associate justice in the majority assigns the task.

When John Marshall was chief justice of the Supreme Court, the Court's decision was most often explained in just one opinion. Today, the members of

decision The indication of which litigant the court supports and by how large a margin.

opinions The written arguments explaining the reasons behind a decision.

majority opinion An opinion written by a justice who represents a majority of the court.

concurring opinion An opinion written by one or more of the justices who agree with the decision but for different reasons than those stated in the majority opinion.

the Court are more likely to be fragmented in their reasoning as well as in their votes. As a result, four different types of opinions may accompany any particular decision. A **majority opinion** is written by one member of the Court on behalf of at least five members of the Court; the reasoning in the opinion can serve as a precedent for future cases. A **concurring opinion** is one written by a justice who agrees with the decision, but offers a different rationale for the Court's finding. A **plurality opinion** is one that is written on behalf of the largest bloc of the justices, but less than a majority, who agree on the reasons supporting the court's decision. A plurality opinion does not serve as a precedent for future cases. Finally, a **dissenting opinion** is one that is written by one or more justices who disagree with the case decision and the opinion of the majority or plurality of the Court. Occasionally, the Court will submit a **per curiam opinion** to explain its reasoning in a case. These are unsigned opinions that represent the view of the Court in a case where there is a great deal of consensus or in a case where time is a critical factor. The Court issued a per curiam opinion in the case of *Bush v. Gore* (2000). Justices may dissent from such opinions but rarely do so.

The combination of opinions that finally accompanies the decision in a particular case is the result of negotiations that begin after one of the jurists in the majority receives the assignment to write the Court's opinion. According to political scientist David O'Brien, "Writing opinions is the justice's most difficult and time-consuming task."[29] Since the original conference vote is not final, a dissenting opinion occasionally becomes the majority opinion, and vice versa. In 1971, for instance, the Court voted 5 to 3 in conference to deny famous boxer Muhammad Ali's conscientious objector claim for refusing induction into the Army. After two months of negotiation, however, the Court ruled for Ali.[30] Ultimately, the bargaining ends, the final votes are recorded in a conference meeting, and the opinions are printed and made public.

Implementing Decisions

Once the Supreme Court has reached its final decision in a case, the decision has to be implemented. Implementation consists of how judicial decisions are enforced on the parties to the lawsuit, as well as how and whether the decisions are translated into general public policies.

With respect to the litigants, if the Supreme Court affirms a lower court decision, the lower court then enforces its original decision. If the Supreme Court reverses the lower court ruling, the original decision is void. Often, the Supreme Court remands a case—sends it back to the court that originally heard it—with instructions to retry it under proceedings consistent with the Court's opinion. After the Supreme Court ruling in *Miranda v. Arizona* (see Chapter 4), the trial court retried Miranda, but the prosecution was not allowed to use his confession. Even so, the lower court once again found the defendant guilty.

Turning Supreme Court decisions into general public policy is a more difficult process. The Court alone cannot enforce its decisions; it must depend on other public officials who may not always desire to cooperate to do so. When upset with a Supreme Court ruling, President Andrew Jackson is reported to have said, "John Marshall has made his decision; now let him enforce it." In other words, implementation is not an automatic process.

Two political scientists have written that the implementation of a Supreme Court decision depends on several elements.[31] First, there is the *interpreting population,* made up largely of judges and lawyers, who must correctly understand and reflect the intent of the decision in subsequent decisions. Lower judges usually follow the rulings of the Supreme Court, but sometimes they circumvent rulings to pursue their own policy preferences.[32] The federal district court judges in the South, for example, circumvented the *Brown v. Board of Education* decision (see Chapter 5) for years.[33] The second element in the process is the *implementing population*, such as school administrators who implement prayer in school decisions or police departments that implement search and seizure decisions. Finally, a *consumer population* must be aware of these new rights if they are to exercise them. Suspects who are about to be interrogated are the consumers of the *Miranda* decision, and women who want abortions are the consumers of the *Roe v. Wade* decision. The Supreme Court must hope that other actors will respect its moral authority and legal expertise enough to implement its policies. The Court can help itself, however, by writing clear opinions.

Understanding Decisions

Scholars today look to a variety of nonlegal factors to understand Supreme Court decisions. Some of these factors are external to the individual justices and comprise the political environment, such as Congress, the president, and public opinion. Other factors, including ideology, perception of their role, and the ability to negotiate with colleagues on the bench, originate with the individual justices.

External Factors When making decisions, the Supreme Court is aware of the many checks the Constitution provides Congress over the behavior of the Court. If Congress is unhappy with a Supreme Court decision, it can propose a constitutional amendment to overturn the decision. The Eleventh, Fourteenth, Sixteenth, and Twenty-Sixth Amendments were all passed in response to congressional unhappiness with a Court decision. Congress can also threaten to modify the Court's appellate jurisdiction. If Congress believes the Court has interpreted one of their laws or their legislative intent erroneously, Congress can rewrite the law. In 1993, for example, Congress enacted the Religious Freedom Restoration Act because members believed a Court decision was too restrictive of religious liberty.[34] The Rehnquist Court responded, however, by declaring the law unconstitutional.[35] At other times, the Court clearly responds to congressional wishes, such as when it began to declare New Deal legislation constitutional. Congress can also express its displeasure with Court decisions by withholding funds necessary for implementation of a decision and by careful Senate scrutiny of future Court nominees.

Presidents exercise control over the Supreme Court by filling vacancies on the Court with nominees who share their beliefs. As chief executive, the president also often plays a

> **plurality opinion** An opinion that is written on behalf of the largest bloc of the justices, representing less than a majority, who agree on the reasons supporting the court's decision.
>
> **dissenting opinion** An opinion written by one or more justices who disagree with a decision.
>
> **per curiam opinion** An unsigned opinion of the Supreme Court that usually signals a high degree of consensus.

President Lyndon B. Johnson nominated the first African American justice Thurgood Marshall, to the U.S. Supreme Court.

key role in implementing Supreme Court decisions that have broad policy ramifications. If President Eisenhower had not called out the troops to enforce school integration in Little Rock, Arkansas, the implementation of *Brown v. Board of Education* (1954) might have been hopelessly stalled. Presidents also appoint the solicitor general, who has an important relationship with the Court. The solicitor general and staff argue cases before the Court when the national government is a party as well as submit friend of the court briefs to influence decisions. Occasionally, they are asked their procedural position on a case as they were in the extraordinary rendition case discussed below.

Since the American public does not directly elect Supreme Court justices, the justices do not have to worry about constantly analyzing public opinion polls or running for reelection. This does not mean, however, that public opinion has no effect on the Court's behavior. After all, the justices work and live among the rest of us, and social trends influence their attitudes as well. Since popularly elected officials must nominate and approve Supreme Court justices, the justices' views usually reflect those of the majority of Americans. Justices who have been on the Court for a long time may reflect political views that are no longer in vogue, but even they know that a decision at odds with public opinion will produce a backlash and even resistance to obeying the law. There are even times when the Court clearly follows public opinion in making decisions. In its 2002 ruling that executing mentally retarded criminals constitutes cruel and unusual punishment, the Court noted "powerful evidence that today our society views mentally retarded offenders as categorically less culpable than the average criminal."[36]

Internal Factors Supreme Court justices do not magically rid themselves of all their attitudes and political biases so that they can function as neutral judges. In fact, the president chooses nominees—and the Senate confirms them—largely on doctrinal qualifications. Therefore, it is reasonable to assume that justices often follow their own policy preferences when making legal decisions. Justices with a liberal ideology typically support civil liberties and civil rights claims, back the government in economic regulation cases, and vote for national regulation in federalism cases. Conservatives, of course, cast votes in the opposite direction. Knowledge of the justices' ideology can lead to accurate predictions of their voting patterns. For instance, conservative justices Antonin Scalia and Clarence Thomas vote together much of the time, in opposition to liberal justices Ruth Bader Ginsburg and Stephen Breyer. Not all cases, however, can be analyzed neatly on a liberal versus conservative basis.

Other studies emphasize that a single justice can accomplish little because a majority of justices must reach the same conclusion to render a decision, and a majority must agree on a single opinion in order to set a precedent. Therefore, a single justice must work strategically in order to advance his or her goals.[37] Such strategic behavior manifests itself in the number of times justices change their votes and revise their opinions. Studies have shown that between the initial vote in conference and the official announcement of the decision, at least one vote switch occurs more than 50 percent of the time.[38] Also, in almost every case, some justice will revise an opinion to please his or her colleagues.[39] It is not unusual for a justice to revise an opinion ten times in order to hold the original majority.

Individual justices also hold their own views as to the proper role of a good judge and of the Court. Some justices subscribe to a philosophy of **judicial activism**, arguing that the Court should make public policy and vigorously review the policies of the other branches. Others, convinced that the Court should not become involved in questioning the operations and policies of the elected branches unless absolutely necessary, believe in **judicial restraint**.

Hot or Not?

Is it appropriate for Supreme Court justices to make policy?

judicial activism The belief that the Supreme Court should make policy and vigorously review the policies of other branches.

judicial restraint The belief that the Supreme Court should not become involved in questioning the operations and policies of the elected branches unless absolutely necessary.

SUPREME COURT SELECTION

One hundred and eleven individuals have served on the Supreme Court. Most have been wealthy, white males between the ages of 41 and 60, with Protestant backgrounds. Although the Constitution is silent with regard to qualifications, all have been lawyers and many were federal judges, were state judges, or had their own legal practice just prior to nomination. Seven had served as attorney general, and several others had held other high executive offices such as secretary of state. Eight had served in Congress; three had been state governors. Their number has even included a former president, William Howard Taft. Let's now examine the process by which these men and (a few) women have risen to the most powerful court in the land.

Nomination

Unlike with other appointments, presidents are intimately involved in the selection of Supreme Court nominees. The retirement or death of a sitting justice gives the president a chance to make a lasting impact on the direction of U.S. legal and political practices. The president fills openings for associate justices from a wide pool of candidates, as we will discuss shortly. When the chief justice position becomes vacant, however, the president may select the new chief justice from among the sitting associate justices. In most cases, however, presidents have chosen someone from outside the Court to fill the position. Only 3 of the 17 chief justices came from among sitting associate justices. When a president chooses a sitting associate justice to be the new chief justice, an opening is created for a new associate justice.

Presidents play the major role in selecting Supreme Court nominees, although other individuals and groups also influence the selection process. More than half of all nominees have been personal friends of the president, which suggests that presidential advisors play a lesser role in shaping the president's choice. Interest groups close to

the administration may participate privately in the selection process, or at least receive consideration of their views. Conservative interest groups and columnists, for example, sank the nomination of Harriet Miers, whom President Bush originally selected to replace Sandra Day O'Connor, claiming that Miers was not conservative enough. The American Bar Association (ABA) plays a unique role in the nomination process by assigning nominees a rating of "well qualified," "qualified," or "not qualified." These ratings signal to the public the ABA's assessment of a nominee's legal qualifications. The Reagan administration did not work with the ABA in choosing its nominees, and George W. Bush announced early in his presidency that he would use the more conservative Federalist Society to investigate his nominees to the federal bench. Obama has not continued this practice.

To further ensure that damaging information regarding a candidate does not surface and affect the credibil-

Did You Know?

... William Howard Taft was both the twenty-seventh president of the United States and the ninth chief justice of the United States Supreme Court. No other individual has occupied both positions. He was also the first president to be buried in the National Cemetery in Arlington, Virginia, and the first to get stuck in the White House bathtub. It became necessary to have an oversized tub brought to the White House to accommodate Taft, who at 6'2" weighed over 300 pounds.

United States Supreme Court Chief Justices

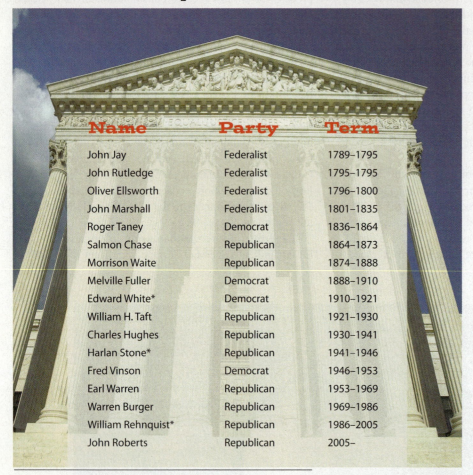

Name	Party	Term
John Jay	Federalist	1789–1795
John Rutledge	Federalist	1795–1795
Oliver Ellsworth	Federalist	1796–1800
John Marshall	Federalist	1801–1835
Roger Taney	Democrat	1836–1864
Salmon Chase	Republican	1864–1873
Morrison Waite	Republican	1874–1888
Melville Fuller	Democrat	1888–1910
Edward White*	Democrat	1910–1921
William H. Taft	Republican	1921–1930
Charles Hughes	Republican	1930–1941
Harlan Stone*	Republican	1941–1946
Fred Vinson	Democrat	1946–1953
Earl Warren	Republican	1953–1969
Warren Burger	Republican	1969–1986
William Rehnquist*	Republican	1986–2005
John Roberts	Republican	2005–

*Appointed chief justice while serving as an associate justice.

ity of the president who makes the nomination, the FBI has played an increasingly important role in the selection process. Candidates who pass an initial screening process fill out questionnaires that include information about their personal lives. FBI agents thoroughly examine the potential nominee's life to make sure there are no skeletons in the closet. The examinations, however, do not always turn up every potentially damaging fact about a nominee. The Reagan administration, for instance, withdrew the nomination of Douglas Ginsburg when the media verified that he had smoked marijuana as a youth and as a member of the Harvard University law faculty.

Nomination Criteria

Political scientists disagree about which criteria presidents use when choosing a Supreme Court nominee. Some argue that the relatively high caliber of appointments over time demonstrates that presidents rely primarily on merit and do not want to be embarrassed by choosing unqualified nominees.[40] Others stress that the politics inherent in the selection process outweighs any concern for merit.[41] Herbert Hoover's nomination of Benjamin Cardozo in 1932 shows that the truth lies somewhere between these extremes. Cardozo, a Democrat, was the chief judge of the New York Court of Appeals and author of the universally praised book *The Nature of the Judicial Process*. He was "a man widely regarded as one of America's most brilliant jurists," who enjoyed great support from the legal community and the U.S. Senate.[42] The Republican Hoover drew considerable praise when he crossed party lines to nominate Cardozo. Although it was a merit selection, it was also a political maneuver by the president. At the time, Hoover's administration was struggling to respond to the Great Depression, and he may have seen Cardozo's nomination as a way to restore some luster to his presidency.

There is a high degree of consensus among political scientists, however, on some basic selection criteria. First, the president wants a justice who is capable of doing the work on the Court and working with his or her colleagues. President Woodrow Wilson was chagrined by the fact that one of his nominees, James C. McReynolds, turned out to be one of the most obnoxious individuals ever to serve on the Court. Chief Justice Taft described McReynolds as "selfish to the last degree, . . . fuller of prejudice than any man I have ever known, . . . one who delights in making others uncomfortable. He has no sense of duty. He is a continual grouch."[43] Presidents also desire predictability, the assurance that nominees will share the president's views on

President Herbert Hoover, shown here, was praised for his nomination of Benjamin Cardozo to the Supreme Court.

public policy. In this way, presidents can leave their mark on national policy long after leaving the White House. Since the Supreme Court consists of members who are not elected, it is important that the institution be representative of the people it serves. Scholars believe that citizens will accord a diverse Court greater legitimacy than if "it were dominated by a few rich, old, white Protestant males from the Northeast educated at the Ivy League schools and still effectively wearing the old school tie."[44] By increasing the representativeness of the Court, the

similar to those that will reach the Supreme Court; therefore, they have established a record on those cases that the president can evaluate, and they have opinions that can be analyzed.

Presidents generally have an accurate sense of how a nominee will perform on the Court, but not all their predictions are correct. President Dwight Eisenhower was disappointed with liberal decisions by two of his appointees, Democrat William Brennan and particularly Republican Earl Warren. When asked if he had made any

CHIEF JUSTICE TAFT described McReynolds as "selfish to the last degree, . . . fuller of prejudice than any man I have ever known, . . . one who delights in making others uncomfortable. He has no sense of duty. He is a continual grouch."

president also seeks to win political support and dispense political rewards through the nomination process.

Professional Qualifications Presidents look to professional qualifications to determine whether candidates possess the characteristics necessary to perform the tasks of a Supreme Court justice. These qualifications include not only evidence of an eminent public or private career but also a reputation of high moral character that provides the basis for any valid professional qualifications. Recent Supreme Court appointments would indicate that presidents choose their nominees from some of the nation's most prominent law schools and that they view appellate judicial experience as a vital qualification for service. All of the current justices are former federal appeals court judges. Nominees who fall short on professional qualifications may fail Senate confirmation. If they are approved and then serve poorly on the Court, they can be an embarrassment to the appointing president.

Doctrinal Qualifications Presidents seek nominees who share their views about policy. Since the common law tradition leaves the judge with a great deal of discretion to interpret policy, having sympathetic justices on the Court gives the president an advantage in making and implementing policy. As a result, recent presidents have attempted to increase the doctrinal predictability of candidates by nominating appellate judges. Appellate judges, particularly federal ones, hear cases

mistakes as president, Eisenhower replied, "Yes, two, and they are both sitting on the Supreme Court."[45] More recently, Justices O'Connor, Kennedy, and Souter have not been as conservative as Presidents Ronald Reagan and George H. W. Bush may have hoped. Today the Court has

The Supreme Court

Judge/ Appointing President	Prior Judicial Experience	Law School	Political Party	Senate Vote
Antonia Scalia **Reagan**	U.S. Court of Appeals	Harvard	R	98–0
Anthony Kennedy **Reagan**	U.S. Court of Appeals	Harvard	R	97–0
Clarence Thomas **G. H. W. Bush**	U.S. Court of Appeals	Yale	R	52–48
Ruth Bader Ginsburg **Clinton**	U.S. Court of Appeals	Columbia	D	96–3
Stephen Breyer **Clinton**	U.S. Court of Appeals	Harvard	D	87–9
John Roberts **G. W. Bush**	U.S. Court of Appeals	Harvard	R	78–22
Samuel Alito **G. W. Bush**	U.S. Court of Appeals	Yale	R	58–42
Sonia Sotomayor **Obama**	U.S. Distirct Court and U.S. Court of Appeals	Yale	D	68–31
Elena Kagan **Obama**	Solicitor General	Harvard	D	63–37

In 1981, Sandra Day O'Connor became the first woman to serve on the Supreme Court.

a liberal bloc consisting of Justices Ginsburg, Breyer, Sotomayor, and Kagan and a conservative bloc of Justices Roberts, Scalia, Kennedy, Thomas, and Alito. Sometimes Kennedy becomes a "swing vote" who supports the liberal bloc.

Representational Qualifications Representational qualifications are attributes that link a nominee to significant portions of the American public—political party, age, religion, race, and gender. Presidents almost always choose justices from within their own political party. It provides them opportunities not only to alter the partisan balance on the Court but also to reward leading lawyers and politicians of their own party. Presidents have crossed partisan lines only 13 times in selecting the 110 successful nominees to the Court.

Presidents typically choose nominees who are old enough to have gained some prominence, but also young enough to serve an extended time on the bench. The last four nominees, Roberts, Alito, Sotomayor, and Kagan were 50, 55, 55, and 50, respectively. Most members of the Supreme Court have been Protestants, but a tradition began

in the late nineteenth century to have at least one "Catholic seat" on the Court. The tradition has held since that time, except for the period between 1949 and 1956.[46] Today, Justices Kennedy, Scalia, Thomas, Roberts, Alito, and Sotomayor are Catholics. In 1916, Justice Louis Brandeis became the first Jewish member of the Supreme Court. He was followed on the Court by other Jewish justices, including Cardozo, Felix Frankfurter, Arthur Goldberg, and Abe Fortas. Current Jewish members of the Court include Ruth Bader Ginsburg, Stephen Breyer, and Elena Kagan.

Until the presidency of Lyndon Johnson, all Supreme Court Justices had been white. In 1967, Johnson appointed the famous NAACP lawyer Thurgood Marshall to the bench. Johnson's nomination of Marshall was not only an acknowledgment that Marshall had been successful as an advocate in getting the Supreme Court to change civil rights policy (see Chapter 5) but also a political reward to the African American community that was becoming a solid supporter of the Democratic Party in national elections. When Marshall retired from the bench in 1991, President Bush filled the vacancy with another African American, albeit one with a far more conservative philosophy, Clarence Thomas. In 2009, Justice Sotomayor became the first Hispanic American to ever serve on the august tribunal.

By the 1970s, interest groups were calling for female representation on the Supreme Court. The number of women graduating from law school and serving on federal and state courts was growing, producing a sufficient pool of qualified women from which to choose a Supreme Court nominee. Facing serious opposition among female voters, presidential candidate Ronald Reagan promised that if he was elected, his first appointment to the Supreme Court would be a woman. He fulfilled his campaign promise by selecting Sandra Day O'Connor. Clinton appointee Ruth Bader Ginsburg became the second woman to serve on the bench of the nation's highest court and now Sonia Sotomayor and Elena Kagan are the third and fourth.

Senate Confirmation

As we have discussed, the Senate exercises an advice and consent role with respect to presidential nominees. Although presidents do not have to ask the Senate for advice on Supreme Court nominees, these nominees must receive Senate confirmation by a majority vote. A sitting justice nominated to be the new chief justice must also undergo Senate confirmation to assume his or her new position.

Confirmation is not an automatic process. During the nineteenth century, more than 25 percent of Supreme Court nominees failed to receive Senate confirmation. Since that time, the number of unsuccessful nominations has declined. One political scientist attributes this decline to two factors.[47] First, presidents are now aware that the

Senate exercises close scrutiny over the process, so they are more inclined to choose nominees who are likely to win confirmation. Second, senators today generally begin the confirmation process with a presumption that the nominee is qualified.

Several factors may weaken the presumption of confirmation, such as strong and widespread opposition to the nominee's views on legal issues. Confirmation is also less likely when the president's party is not in control of the Senate. Confirmation chances are slimmer for nominees chosen near the end of a president's term. In such a situation, senators from the opposition party may desire to keep the vacancy open until after the next election in case their candidate captures the White House. The confirmation process also tends to be more contentious if the Court is split along conservative and liberal grounds and the newest member could tilt the ideological balance.

After the president announces a nomination to the Supreme Court, the Senate Judiciary Committee asks the nominee to complete a questionnaire that probes the candidate's work history, judicial philosophy, speeches, media interviews, articles and books, and judicial opinions if the candidate has served as an appellate judge. The committee also contacts potential witnesses to testify concerning the nominee's fitness to serve on the Supreme Court. At this point in the process, interest groups become mobilized for or against a candidacy. When President Reagan announced the nomination of Robert Bork, "more than twenty groups and dozens of individual experts . . . abandoned their families and summer vacations to prepare in-depth analyses and reports that addressed their specific individual and institutional concerns."[48] These groups ran television commercials against the Bork nomination. Spokespersons for 86 different interest groups testified before the Senate Judiciary Committee during the Bork confirmation hearings, helping to sink his confirmation.[49]

In 1939, Felix Frankfurter set a precedent by appearing in person before the committee and answering questions pertaining to his qualifications. All subsequent nominees have followed the tradition except one: Sherman Minton, a U.S. senator from Indiana. The 1981 nomination of the first woman to the Supreme Court, Sandra Day O'Connor, drew the interest of the television networks; since that time, all the hearings have been televised. Following the hearings, the Judiciary Committee makes a recommendation to the full Senate on the question of whether the nominee should be confirmed. Most recent nominees have won overwhelming approval from the Senate, including unanimous votes for O'Connor, Stevens, Scalia, and Kennedy. By contrast, Clarence Thomas was confirmed by a 52-48 vote, the closest in over a century.

LOWER COURT SELECTION

Congress established the same process for the selection of lower federal court judges as the Constitution set for Supreme Court justices. Traditionally, presidents have been less involved in these selections because of the geographical decentralization of these courts and their lesser importance. Beginning with Ronald Reagan, however, presidents have been more directly involved in the process. The White House has become particularly interested in selections to the various federal courts of appeal. They realize that these courts handle very important issues—and that these judgeships have become stepping-stones to seats on the Supreme Court.

senatorial courtesy In the selection of lower federal court judges, deference shown to home-state senators who are of the same party as the president.

Presidents have the constraint of **senatorial courtesy** when naming lower court judges, particularly district court judges. Under this tradition, the Senate defers to the wishes of the senators from the home state of the judicial

Since the 1981 nomination of Sandra Day O'Connor to the Supreme Court, all Supreme Court nomination hearings have been televised, stimulating greater public interest in the process.

Today the Court decides cases that affect the personal lives of citizens, including those with specific challenges that make access to public facilities difficult.

nominee, particularly if they are members of the president's party. The senator or senators have almost a veto power because the full Senate can deny confirmation as a courtesy to the one or two senators of the president's party from the state of the nominee.

Although home-state senators still have a veto power, their support of a candidate no longer guarantees an easy confirmation. "This change seems to derive partly from a general decline in senators' deference to each other and partly from the growing recognition that lower-court judgeships are important."[50] This trend is particularly clear at the court of appeals level. In 1997, Republican senators held up Bill Clinton's appointment of Sonia Sotomayor to a federal appeals court for over a year, believing that as a Hispanic American appellate judge, she would be a formidable candidate for the Supreme Court. In 2005, the minority Democrats in the Senate held up 17 of President Bush's nominees by threatening filibusters. Their actions were supposedly in response to Republican actions against a similar number of the judicial nominees of President Clinton. After the Senate majority leader threatened to change the rules on cloture votes for filibusters on judicial nominees, seven moderates from each party got together and reached a compromise. They agreed not to change the filibuster rules in exchange for allowing most of the Bush nominees to face a vote. The Senate confirmed many of these nominees, but the trend toward subjecting lower court appointments to greater scrutiny continues.

CIVIC ENGAGEMENT AND THE JUDICIARY

Today, individuals and particularly interest groups actively use the courts to shape public policy. In today's political environment, lawsuits provide interest groups with an easier means of achieving their goals than elections. In the 1950s and 1960s, liberal groups used the courts to achieve expanded civil liberties, civil rights, and environmental protections. By the 1980s, conservative groups were using litigation to further the interests of crime victims, private property owners resisting government regulation, and plaintiffs claiming "reverse discrimination" in affirmative action cases.[51]

The expanding role of the courts in making public policy has been the product of decisions made by both Congress and the Supreme Court. In 1988, Congress passed the Act to Improve the Administration of Justice, which gives the Supreme Court almost complete discretion in choosing its agenda. The act allows the Court to choose cases with the greatest public policy implications, as measured by the number of *amicus curiae* briefs submitted to the justices. Title II of the 1964 Civil Rights Act also contributed to the expansion of judicial policymaking by designating plaintiffs who filed suits under the statute as "private attorneys general." The act defined their actions as contributions to the enforcement of federal law and made plaintiffs eligible to collect attorneys' fees if they prevailed at trial.[52] This practice, known as fee-shifting, expanded under the 1976 Civil Rights Attorney's Fee Award Act that allowed for the recovery of attorneys' fees for actions brought under all civil rights laws enacted since 1876.

Other legislation that has expanded access to the courts to address political and social issues includes the 1990 Americans with Disabilities Act, which opened the path for extensive litigation by interest groups supporting the rights of people with disabilities, and the 1991 Civil Rights Act, which gave the victims of gender bias access to the federal courts. A number of regulatory statutes passed by Congress in the 1970s also allowed public interest groups to challenge the decisions of executive agencies in consumer fraud and environment cases. The Equal Access to Justice Act in 1980 gave business groups the same access to challenge government regulations.

Supreme Court decisions also have expanded the role of the courts in making public policy. We have seen that the Court relaxed the rules governing justiciability by allowing taxpayers to have standing. It has modified the Rules of Civil Procedure to facilitate class action suits, which permit a court to combine the claims of many individuals by treating them as a class during a lawsuit.[53] Court rulings, however, have limited class action suits brought by advocates for immigrants against the Immigration and Naturalization Service and by Legal Services lawyers on behalf of poor persons. For others, the class action suit remains an important political weapon.[54]

The Court has all but abandoned three of the four parts of the political question test, ruling it always has a duty to rule on the constitutionality of political decisions of the president or Congress if there are manageable judicial standards.[55] The Court also effectively has dropped the doctrine under which federal courts decline to hear cases not yet resolved by state courts. As a result, "Stretching the legal concept of justiciability has broadened the range of issues subject to judicial settlement and allowed a wider range of litigants access to the courts."[56]

The expanded role of courts in this era, which emphasizes personal rights, presents questions of propriety. Do the courts permit groups with narrow interests to affect national policy without having to create broader coalitions of support? Does litigation allow for a full consideration of the range of alternative views? Does policymaking by judges, who are not elected, circumvent democracy? The answers to these questions are complex and require a consideration of just how democratic the other branches of government are today. We know that accommodating the participation of interest groups in submitting *amicus curiae* briefs has allowed the Court to view issues in ways similar to the other branches. They provide the Court with a great deal of factual material, focus its attention on the broader interests involved, allow the Court to better assess the probable consequences of its actions, and illuminate the unwillingness of the other branches to deal with certain political issues.[57]

Summary

1. What is the nature of the judicial process?

- Judges have considerable discretion in deciding issues contained in real cases, but they are limited by the rules of jurisprudence and justiciability as to which cases they can hear.
- Federal judges exercise their power in the judicial process in district courts, courts of appeal, specialized courts, and the U.S. Supreme Court.
- With its use of judicial review, the Supreme Court has evolved from its early days into a court with great power that has at times angered presidents and Congress.
- Today the Court's role in the judicial process emphasizes personal rights in its constitutional law cases.

2. How are Supreme Court justices selected?

- Supreme Court justices are appointed by the president and confirmed by the Senate for terms of good behavior, which is the equivalent of a life term because no justice has been both impeached by the House and removed from office by the Senate.
- In making nominations, presidents consider a variety of professional, doctrinal, and representational qualifications.
- Confirmation by the Senate is not assured, but the likelihood is greater if the president's party has a majority in the Senate and the nomination is not made in the last year of a president's term.
- Today, nominees appear before the Senate Judiciary Committee in person to answer questions, and the hearings are televised.

3. What is the nature of Supreme Court decision making?

- The Supreme Court follows the Rule of Four in making agenda decisions.
- After hearing cases during oral argument, the justices take an initial vote during the conference. Votes can be changed after the justices read each other's opinions, and it takes a majority vote to decide a case.
- Opinions are written to explain the votes of the justices, and they are often the results of negotiation because of the fluidity of the votes until the final pronouncements are made.
- The Court must depend on others to implement its decisions, but it can aid implementers by writing clear opinions.
- In making decisions, justices are motivated not only by the law but also by external factors, such as Congress, the president, and public opinion, and internal factors, such as personal attitudes, strategic behavior, and conceptions of their judicial role.

National Journal

Do Gender And Race Mean Greater Empathy?

Supreme Court Justice Sonia Sotomayor has repeatedly said that female and minority judges should, over time, issue more compassionate and caring courtroom decisions than white males, but a review of two decades' worth of legal and scientific literature shows that gender and race may not have a significant influence on verdicts. In fact, research finds little difference in decisions made by men and women, even though those decisions can be reached in different ways by each gender.

Judge Sotomayor has over the years consistently presented her view that gender and race certainly could, and probably should, affect the way judges make decisions, if only because women and minorities are likely to have had different experiences than their white male counterparts. In a 2001 speech she said, "Whether born from experience or inherent physiological or cultural differences . . . our gender and national origins may and will make a difference in our judging."

Since the 1970s, feminist legal scholars have made the same point, although most also acknowledge that the scarcity of female and minority judges at the federal level has until recently hindered attempts to test the notion. With some research now suggesting that race and gender have little effect on judicial decision-making, scholars on the left have instead tended to emphasize the political imperatives when advocating for more female and minority judges.

"You really can't see a clear gender effect" in the studies, Judith Resnik, a feminist writer and the Arthur Liman professor of law at Yale Law School, acknowledged. But the "political legitimacy" of the courts requires that the bench include judges from a variety of backgrounds, she said. "It's a mechanism for saying, this is everybody's court, not just for one group, such as those who are both white and male."

Sotomayor's conservative critics generally denounce the arguments that gender and race should influence courtroom outcomes. Those on the right say that advocates on the left merely want to free judges from curbs embodied in the Constitution, says activist Roger Clegg. The liberals' approach, he said, "does not accept the conservative definition of what a judge's job is: to interpret and apply legal texts in a dispassionate way."

Several decades of feminist writing, on the other hand, contend that it is very unlikely that any judge can be completely dispassionate about any case, and that it may be unrealistic to try.

The first wave of influential arguments for the appointment of more women to the bench formed in the 1970s. As more women entered the legal profession, and as feminism gained ground, some legal scholars focused on the need to ensure the courts' equal treatment of men and women, and to eliminate discrimination in the legal system. This first wave of feminist argument is personified by Justice Ruth Bader Ginsburg, who was voted onto the Court in 1993 after a career of advocating for equality between men and women, sometimes as an American Civil Liberties Union litigator and often in the face of openly sexist judges and colleagues.

A second wave of arguments soon gained force, emphasizing the importance and value of the differences between men and women, and between whites and minorities—differences that advocates said would lead to different and perhaps better decisions as women and minorities integrated the courts. Sotomayor, whose parents were from Puerto Rico, played a role in the second wave. She graduated from Princeton University in 1976 and Yale Law School in 1979 and later described herself as an "affirmative-action baby." She said in a 1996 speech at Princeton's Third World Center, "I began a lifelong commitment to identifying myself as a Latina, taking pride in being Hispanic, and in recognizing my obligation to help my community reach its fullest potential in this society."

In the 2001 Berkeley speech, Sotomayor echoed the work of law professor Robin West, who argued that women's thinking is deeply shaped by their physiology, including their ability to give birth. Gilligan and West both came out of the "difference school" of feminists that emerged in the 1980s.

Resnik represents a more recent third wave of thinking that differing cultural and personal experiences—not factors inherent only to women—could, or would, lead male and female judges to make different decisions.

Sotomayor has only summarized these evolving feminist philosophies in public. But she has cited them far more often and more favorably than rival, older notions that judges should dispassionately apply the law regardless of their individual inclinations or biases. In the 2001 speech, for example, Sotomayor said, "I wonder whether by ignoring our differences as women or men of color we do a disservice both to the law and society."

In most of her public statements, however, Sotomayor gives a nod to the goal shared by many judges to rise above their own experiences and feelings to reach fair verdicts. Her 2001 speech includes this passage: "I can and do aspire to be greater than the sum total of my experiences . . . [and] to judge when those opinions, sympathies, and prejudices are appropriate."

As for the science, the evidence is modest that gender and race shape judicial decisions. A pending peer-reviewed article by political scientist Christina Boyd concludes, "The presence of women in the federal appellate judiciary rarely has an appreciable empirical effect on judicial outcomes. Rarely, though, is not never."

The research drew from a database of 1,275 Appeals Court cases decided between 1985 and 2002. Boyd compared decisions made by male and female judges sharing comparable ideologies and histories—conservatives and liberals alike. Examining cases in 13 categories of law, she found that only in sex-discrimination cases did a judge's gender make a difference. "For these disputes, the probability of a judge deciding in favor of a party alleging discrimination decreases by about 10 percentage points when the judge is a male."

Gender also made a small difference in the so-called panel effect, Boyd found. When a female judge sits on a panel of Appellate Court judges deciding a case, "the men are significantly more likely to rule in favor" of a plaintiff alleging discrimination. Because many federal appeals cases are closely divided, and often are decided by three-judge panels, that 10 percent shift, she said, could flip the results in as many as 30 percent of sex-discrimination cases.

According to Boyd's analysis, the presence of female judges made no statistical difference in cases of capital punishment, federalism, sexual harassment, government property seizures, and racial discrimination. The data showed minimal gender-based differences in decisions related to

> "I wonder whether by ignoring our differences as women or men of color we do a disservice both to the law and society."
> —Justice Sonia Sotomayor

abortion, the environment, business contracts, affirmative action, and campaign finance, although Boyd noted that there are too few female judges to make reliable estimates in these categories.

Laboratory scientists have tried but failed to detect significant gender differences in decision making. "The folk belief is that women are more empathetic, but the behavioral data doesn't really support that," said Claus Lamm, a Zurich-based scientist who uses magnetic resonance imaging to track brain activity in men and women in controlled experiments. Although MRIs reveal that women and men use different portions of their brains to respond to crises, men's and women's actions are very similar. The subjects' individual inclinations had more influence on their actions than their gender did, Lamm concluded, and those personal views can be influenced by social rewards.

There might be something to the effects of race on judgment, however. A study published in 2005 by Joan Chiao, a psychologist at Northwestern University, concluded that

people within particular cultural or racial groups can more accurately recognize emotional expressions such as anger in the faces of other people within their group than outsiders can. That emotional recognition skill can be useful for trial judges, who listen to defendants and witnesses, but it is probably less relevant for Appeals Court judges, who read briefs and weigh attorneys' arguments.

A June 2009 study in The Journal of Neuroscience similarly indicates that the brain's empathy response is more easily triggered among members of the same racial group than across racial lines. White and Asian participants announced the same degree of empathy when a member of either racial group was shown experiencing pain, but an analysis of their brain functions showed that Asians reacted more strongly for other Asians, and whites reacted more for other whites. Racial empathy, then, may in fact play a role in the courts.

In the past few months, long after many pundits had cited her as a likely nominee to the Court but before she was nominated, Sotomayor also dialed back her emphasis on race and gender. "I hope that it does not take a grand historical event like the presidential election of a person of color to remind us that the differences we project onto others and which so often alienate us from each other are superficial and not terribly meaningful," she told an audience at an April 17 event organized by the Black, Latino, Asian Pacific American Law Alumni Association in New York City. "The other day at an event, I reminded people that we have different faces, but the same physical heart beats in all of us."

For Discussion:

■ Is total impartiality, regardless of a judge's race, gender, or background, an achievable goal? Do you think judges are capable of putting aside their identities to decide cases? More important, should they?

■ Do you agree with the science that indicates race may play a part in determining empathies?

■ Discuss some important decisions in the history of the federal court system that might be better understood through the lens of the judges' backgrounds.

15

THIS G M FACIL
CLOSED

PUBLIC

RESPONDING TO CITIZENS

TALES FROM TWO CITIES ▌Kevin Corkhill recalls the work ethic that inspired generations of auto workers even as he ponders his next moves now that General Motors closed the Janesville, Wisconsin, plant where he worked for years. "My grandfather worked here, and my father worked here. The one thing my father told me is you work hard to make things better for the next generation, but now I worry we won't be able to do that anymore."[1]

Corkhill's story was repeated thousands of times over the past few years as manufacturing plants across the nation were shuttered, two auto giants filed for bankruptcy, and the nation settled into a long and painful recession. Toward the end of 2009, the unemployment rate rose to nearly 10 percent nationwide, but some towns like Janesville were closer to 13 percent. Other industrial towns with ties to the auto industry like Detroit suffered near Depression-era unemployment rates of 18 percent and higher.

A thousand miles away, Carlos Araya, a worker with a very different background from Corkhill's, was facing similar problems. Once a high-flying crude oil trader on the floor of the New York Mercantile Exchange, Araya lost his job in the wake of the financial crisis that wiped out tens of thousands of financial services jobs in ➥

POLICY

As You READ >>

- What is public policy, how is it made, and how can we explain policy outcomes?
- What is domestic policy and what are some of the problems it addresses?
- How is economic policy made and implemented?

Manhattan. Once a customer at the Palm Restaurant where he dined on fine food and wine, Mr. Araya now seats customers there. He has seen his annual salary plunge from $200,000 to $25,000.[2]

Stories like these have become all too familiar in the past few years. Millions of Americans are feeling economic pain and wondering how an economy that was booming just a few years ago could come crashing down so quickly. Many actors played a role in creating the economic crisis. American auto companies failed to heed warnings about the need for more fuel-efficient cars and were unable to reduce costs of production to keep their industry competitive in the new global economy. American financial institutions took huge risks by granting mortgages to homebuyers with poor credit, betting that ever-increasing home prices would guarantee returns on debt they repackaged and sold to others. And American consumers, convinced that home prices and incomes would continue to rise, took on far more debt than was prudent.

The confluence of these forces caused investors to lose confidence in financial institutions that were underwriting American prosperity, and a financial tsunami ensued. Credit tightened; home sales dipped; consumers stopped buying cars; auto sales fell; workers were laid off; banks failed; stock prices plunged; many investors—particularly retirees—lost their life savings. Policymakers who had loosened the lending rules that contributed to the crisis were caught off guard and quickly began improvising to slow the downward economic spiral. The Federal Reserve (discussed later in this chapter) made aggressive interest rate cuts to keep credit flowing; Congress approved a $700 billion bailout for some of the largest financial institutions; President Obama shepherded passage of a $787 billion stimulus package to stem job losses; General Motors and Chrysler were given billions in government loans to keep them afloat; the U.S. government became a major—though reluctant—shareholder in both auto companies and financial institutions.

Taken together, these actions may help stabilize credit markets and avoided economic meltdown. But unemployment remains stubbornly high and job prospects for Kevin Corkhill, Carlos Araya, and millions of Americans like them continue to be uncertain at best. Stories like theirs demonstrate several valuable lessons about public policy in America. First, public policies arise in response to the tangible problems of real individuals—people like Kevin and Carlos. Second, social and economic problems that begin in one sector often spill over into others and

Carlos Araya at the Palm Restaurant in New York.

eventually affect nearly every American. We live in an interdependent world where the fate of a GM worker in Wisconsin and a Wall Street trader in New York are inextricably linked. Finally, when government decides it must take action, it must balance the interests of a wide variety of players, some with a much larger stake in the outcome than others, and some of whom exert more political clout than others. Let's take a look at how public policy is made. ❖

THE NATURE AND SCOPE OF PUBLIC POLICY

Public policy pervades our lives; it is impossible to go through the day without being affected by programs issuing from federal, state, and local governments. If you go to a university, even a private one, you may participate in student loan programs, Pell grants, and work-study opportunities that pay at least the federally mandated minimum wage. If you attend a public university, the state bears the largest share of the cost of your education, and a host of state laws and programs affect everything on campus from curriculum to traffic safety. When you shower, you use water regulated by a host of federal, state, and local laws. The wastewater from your shower is treated by local governmental authorities following federal guidelines. In return for these services, you pay taxes to all of these governmental units.

Simply put, **public policy** is anything the government chooses to do or not to do.[3] This can include tangible actions, such as providing student grants or imposing taxes,

Crises such as a terrorist assault on our nation require immediate action as well as long-range planning.
....

as well as symbolic gestures, such as creating a legal holiday to commemorate the birthday of Martin Luther King, Jr. Governments assert policy even when they fail to act. For example, the Senate's failure to ratify the Kyoto Protocol, which was signed by 192 other nations in order to control greenhouse gases, communicated the U.S. government's decision to pursue unilateral strategies for addressing the issue.

POLICYMAKING AND EVALUATION

A host of actors, including both government officials and private citizens, shape the policymaking process. Their options are limited by a number of factors, including the availability of resources and political control of the instruments of power (e.g., which party controls the Congress and the presidency). Tradition and public opinion serve as additional constraints. For example, even if it were possible to eliminate poverty by placing limits on how much property an individual could own, few Americans would agree to such a policy. It simply is not part of the American tradition, nor does it reflect the guiding ideology of either major political party. The process sometimes moves very slowly, at other times with great speed. With these caveats in mind, let us review the basic stages in the policymaking process.

> **public policy** Anything the government chooses to do or not to do.

Problem Recognition

The first step in policymaking is identifying and defining the problem as something the government can and should do something about. Some problems are easy to identify, such as the BP oil spill in the Gulf of Mexico that began with the explosion of the Deepwater Horizon rig. The threat to our coastal waters and shoreline was clear and immediate; the impact on fishing and tourism jobs was devastating. In other situations, we may only dimly or gradually perceive a problem and government's role in addressing it. For example, even though some scientists have long warned that greenhouse gas emissions caused by human activity are producing climate change, many lawmakers remained reluctant until recently to involve government in devising solutions.

Agenda Setting

After identifying a problem, we need to determine how important it is and how urgent it is for us to act. Problems such as a massive oil spill require immediate action as well as long-range planning to prevent further occurrences. Following the BP disaster, the government took immediate steps to clean coastal waters, but various government agencies also began exploring long-range plans to reduce the probability of future spills.

Unlike the spill, climate change is a more contentious issue for policymakers. Some lawmakers have doubts about its existence or about the role humans play in causing it. As a result, it has been difficult to get consensus about its importance as an agenda item and about what can or should be done about it. During the 111th Congress (2009–11), a group of determined House members managed to pass a major climate-change bill, but the Senate had more immediate policy goals, like reducing unemployment. As a result, the bill failed to become law.

Competing political actors often have different agendas as they jockey for national attention. The president commands the national spotlight when he speaks, but so do members of Congress and interest groups—all of whom can sound alarms about problems they want confronted; and states have their own priorities and solutions that may be at odds with the federal agenda.

Policy Formation

Once an item has been determined to be of significant importance for government action, the next step is to review possible solutions and select those most likely to be successful. Potential solutions come from a variety of sources, including lawmakers, scholars and think tanks, politicians, interest groups, and even average citizens who suggest ideas to lawmakers. In most cases, experts within government agencies present their own ideas to Congress and members of the executive branch.

Following the BP spill, the president proposed a moratorium on new offshore wells until their safety could be guaranteed. He also conducted talks with the oil giant about compensation for the spill. Members of Congress, particularly those from the Gulf region, offered their own solutions, many of them seeking to reverse the president's moratorium on new drilling. Both the president and Congress reviewed their options in preparation for action. State officials also acted to protect their beaches and sought additional compensation for their citizens and state coffers.

As policymakers sorted through proposals about paying for the Deepwater cleanup and how to avoid future recurrences, various government agencies such as the U.S. Coast Guard, the Environmental Protection Agency, the Interior Department, and others dispatched workers and volunteers to contain the spill and prevent its spread. Whereas there may have been debate and disagreement over how to handle the spill, there was no debate about the government's role or ability to do something about it. Necessity and public opinion demanded quick action on the part of government officials in the case of the Deepwater spill. However, on many policy fronts, debate over policy options continues for years, often until a crisis demands action or until consensus is reached about how best to address the problem.

Policy Adoption

Elected leaders are responsible for choosing which of the available policy options to adopt and how to put them into effect. At the federal level, this generally includes presidential actions and congressional lawmaking. After the immediate cleanup response by federal agencies, President Obama extended his moratorium on new deepwater wells, set up a commission to investigate the cause of the spill and future preventative measures, and worked with BP officials to set up a $20 billion fund to compensate victims and cover costs of cleanup. Congress offered a variety of legislative responses as well, including bills to eliminate caps on oil company liability for spills and to improve oversight of federal agencies that are supposed to protect wildlife and the environment.

Policy Implementation

As we discussed in Chapter 13, government bureaucracies usually carry out the task of executing policy. In carrying out policy directives in the BP disaster, the Department of Homeland Security played a lead role in coordinating the government's response by overseeing the activities of a host of other government agencies including the U.S. Coast Guard and the Environmental Protection Agency. Meanwhile, the president established by Executive Order the National Commission on the BP Deepwater Horizon Oil Spill and Offshore Drilling, requiring a final report by January 2011; appointed an independent body, the Gulf

Coast Claims Facility (GCCF), to receive and pay claims for compensation from the newly established BP fund; and ordered federal agencies to monitor and respond to potential public-health and environmental concerns in the Gulf region. Congress also held hearings about the lax oversight of agencies such as the now defunct Minerals Management Service, which regulated offshore drilling.

In implementing policies, officials must be sensitive to the effects policies may have on multiple constituencies. The Obama administration ran into opposition from energy company executives who believed the moratorium on new deepwater wells was an overreaction; environmentalists who believed the president should call for an outright ban on deep-sea wells; and state government officials who believed the federal response was too slow and cumbersome. Eventually, the president lifted the moratorium earlier than planned.

The courts play a role in the policy process as well. Once the GCCF began accepting requests for compensation from the BP fund, a lawsuit was filed in Louisiana claiming the agency was making misleading statements to claimants about their right to sue BP on their own for restitution. The GCCF was forced to revise its practices to conform to a court order.

Policy Evaluation

Ideally, once policies are in place, the government assesses their impact to determine their continued utility. Once again, bureaucracies play a vital role by collecting statistics and conducting studies to measure the progress of these policies. The president and Congress use this information to reauthorize programs and to make changes

The BP oil spill in the Gulf of Mexico necessitated quick action by the government to initiate cleanup as well as long term planning to avoid recurrences.

to fine-tune their impact. Political factors may be as important as objective measures of success in the decision to continue, change, or abandon a policy. Each policy has a constituency that supports it and individuals who benefit from its operation—whether or not it works as intended. Because all of these factors are difficult to balance, it is not surprising that most policymaking involves incremental rather than wholesale change.

In January 2011, the president's commission on the Deepwater spill issued its final report stating that the accident could have been averted and listing more than 50 pages of recommendations for industry and government to prevent future recurrences. Congress and administrative agencies continue to review these and periodically offer legislation to revise regulations and requirements.

Policies often have unintended consequences that are not always apparent at the time they are adopted. For example, the Deepwater commission found that splitting jurisdictional authority for matters such as granting drilling permits and selecting ecological sites for protection diminishes the kind of interagency cooperation that may have limited drilling in the affected area. Policymakers can minimize unintended consequences by carrying on conversations about proposed policies with constituencies and administrative agencies that may be impacted by the policy decision. As policies are evaluated and changes adopted, they continue to cycle through the policymaking process. Rarely does policymaking produce a finished product that escapes revisiting.

Explaining Policy Outcomes

Whether or not government adopts a policy depends largely on the costs the policy imposes and the benefits it confers. How the policy allocates costs and benefits plays a significant role in determining whether the policy is adopted, how well it is accepted, and how easily it can be

Types of Policy Outcomes

Benefits

	Widely Distributed	Concentrated
Widely Distributed	Social Security Defense Policy	Aid to Public Education Agriculture Subsidies
Concentrated	Air Pollution Controls Auto Fuel Economy	Tax Policy Telecommunications

Costs

Source: Adapted from James Q. Wilson, *Political Organizations* (Princeton NJ: Princeton University Press, 1995), 332–337.

altered. The figure above illustrates different ways to classify the allocation of costs and benefits, and it gives some examples of policies that fit each classification.[4]

Policies that allocate costs and distribute benefits widely are often easiest to sustain. The popularity of Social Security, despite questions about its long-term sustainability, provides an example. The costs of the program are widely distributed across millions of American workers, and most citizens will eventually receive its benefits. Conversely, when the costs of widespread benefits are borne by a relatively concentrated population, those who pay most of the bill will lobby intensely against it. For example, energy companies are generally unhappy when they are forced to meet strict pollution standards, even though disgruntled stockholders will be among the beneficiaries of cleaner air.

Policies with widely distributed costs but concentrated benefits receive strong support from individuals and groups that benefit from them but tend to raise little organized opposition because no one group or class pays the entire cost. For example, all taxpayers support public schools and colleges, even though the benefits go primarily to parents and children. When both costs and benefits are concentrated, narrow interests may clash and the government must mediate the resulting disputes. Conflicts of this sort often occur when Congress writes tax legislation. There is perhaps no other policy that draws the attention of so many interests, each petitioning for advantages benefiting its own members. Ski lodge owners who have lost income because of warm winter weather, military contractors who desire long-term tax deferrals for military contracts, and home builders and owners who want to protect federal tax write-offs for mortgage payments are all examples of the interests jockeying for favorable treatment when tax bills are written.

DOMESTIC POLICY

Domestic policy consists of government action (and inaction) that affects citizens within the United States. Each branch of the American government and many bureaucratic agencies at all levels are involved in formulating domestic policy, which includes a wide variety of initiatives such as police and environmental protection, public education, fair housing laws, income security programs, and antidiscrimination policies, to name but a few. However, in an era of globalization, the actions of other nations and those of international agencies may also have a strong impact on domestic policies, even though the levers that control their actions are further removed and often more difficult to access. We will examine more closely two areas of domestic policy that are sources of continuing controversy: environmental protection and antipoverty programs.

Protecting the Environment

Americans have long appreciated the beauty of the natural environment and sought to preserve its wilderness areas. President Theodore Roosevelt (1901–1909) was an early champion of government involvement in conservation, creating the country's first national parks and establishing the National Park Service to protect them. The rapid advance of industrialization in the twentieth century, however, produced enormous amounts of pollution and chemical toxins that threatened human health and wildlife. By

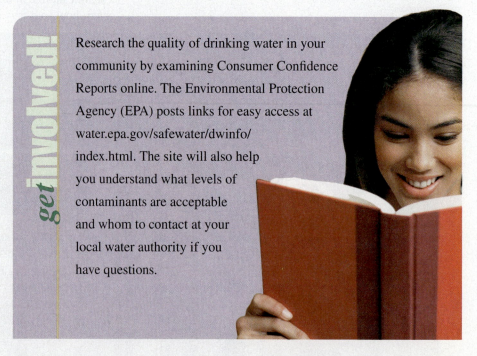

get involved!

Research the quality of drinking water in your community by examining Consumer Confidence Reports online. The Environmental Protection Agency (EPA) posts links for easy access at water.epa.gov/safewater/dwinfo/index.html. The site will also help you understand what levels of contaminants are acceptable and whom to contact at your local water authority if you have questions.

Did You Know?

the middle of the twentieth century, naturalists sounded the alarm about the damage pollution was doing to the environment. In her controversial 1962 book, *Silent Spring*, author and naturalist Rachel Carson alerted the nation to the dangers of pesticides and urged Americans to seek protection for our fragile ecosystem.

Government Responds By 1970, environmental activists had managed to elevate environmental protection to prominence in the political arena and claimed two major victories: the creation of the Environmental Protection Agency (EPA) and the passage of the Clean Air Act. The EPA's mission is to develop and enforce regulations to protect the nation's air, water, and soil. Today, it employs more than 18,000 individuals, including many scientists working at monitoring stations and labs across the nation. The Clean Air Act of 1970 gave the EPA the authority to identify major sources of pollution, to determine permissible levels of toxins that businesses can emit into the atmosphere, and to enforce regulations against polluters. The EPA also has been influential in requiring auto manufacturers to produce cleaner-burning engines and to increase automobile fuel efficiency. Congress enacted additional statutes to regulate pollution in waters and streams (Clean Water Act of 1972) and to protect various endangered species of wildlife

Hot or Not?

Should the government enact a carbon tax to protect the environment?

(Endangered Species Act of 1973). It also amended the Clean Air Act in 1977 and again in 1990 to deal with additional environmental threats, including acid rain and ozone depletion.

Since the federal government enacted these measures, the nation has witnessed a substantial reduction in pollution. According to its ongoing study of ambient air quality, the EPA reports that emissions of most major air pollutants have declined by 30 to nearly 80 percent since 1980. Emission of sulfur dioxide (SO_2), which has been linked to acid rain, has declined by 71 percent since 1980.[5] Many rivers and streams that once teemed with pollution—such as Cleveland's Cuyahoga River, which caught fire in 1969—have responded to cleanup efforts and again support wildlife. A number of once-endangered species, including the peregrine falcon, have returned to viability with help from recovery programs operated by the U.S. Fish and Wildlife Service.

cap and trade Market-based system of pollution control whereby individual businesses can buy and sell emission credits even while the total level of industry pollution is capped at some level.

These successes have generated a good deal of controversy. Environmental regulations concentrate the costs of cleanup on polluting industries, while distributing the benefits of cleaner air and water to everyone. As we discussed earlier, such policies tend to elicit resistance from those who bear the costs. Industries that paid millions of dollars to switch to cleaner-burning fuels, install scrubbers on smokestacks, and adopt more expensive means of discharging wastes often balked at the EPA's regulation and enforcement procedures.

To compel compliance with environmental regulations, the EPA initially employed the tactic of command and control—enforcing uniform rules through threat of fine or prosecution. The procedure became especially burdensome as our economy became more tied to global markets. The costs of complying with domestic clean-air standards put U.S. firms at a disadvantage against competitors from countries with lower environmental standards or none at all. In response to industry complaints, the EPA moved to a system of regulatory negotiation in which representatives from government and industry meet in an attempt to forge a consensus on tactics for cleaning the environment that are acceptable to all parties.

For some emissions like sulfur dioxide, regulatory negotiation has produced a market-based system of pollution credits, called **cap and trade**, in which companies can trade credits with one another for cash. Under this system, a facility that fails to meet certain pollution standards for SO_2 can purchase pollution "credits" from a facility whose emissions are below allowable levels. The EPA approves the transaction as long as the resulting exchange does not increase

the cap, or overall level of pollution for the industry as a whole. This more flexible approach gives lagging companies more time to bring their plants into compliance, while rewarding with cash those companies that already have achieved lower levels of pollution. Although industry insiders prefer this new approach, critics charge that the market-based trading of pollution credits undermines efforts to bring all polluters into uniform compliance. They also claim that the EPA does not set targets low enough to adequately address the rising threat posed by global warming. Some elements of command and control have been maintained, however. Since the mid-1970s, Congress has authorized executive agencies to set fuel-efficiency standards that have steadily risen. In 2009, President Obama set a standard of 35.5 miles per gallon for all new cars sold in the United States after 2016.

Environmental Protection in a Global Context

Policymakers have also been engaged in efforts to stem the tide of pollution on a worldwide scale to stave off the threat of global warming, thought to be a by-product of the use of fossil fuels. International treaties have met with varying degrees of success. Under the auspices of the United Nations, the 1992 Rio Treaty was negotiated;

The U.S. House passed a climate change bill in 2009 that would have promoted renewable forms of energy. Opposition in the Senate prevented its passage.

in it 154 nations pledged voluntarily to reduce the emission of greenhouse gases (carbon dioxide, methane, and several other industrial pollutants) in an effort to stem climate change. In 1997, industrialized nations negotiated a follow-up treaty, the Kyoto Protocol, which committed signatories to achieve reductions in greenhouse gases below 1990 levels by the year 2012. Hopes for Kyoto were dashed, however, when the United States, the largest user of fossil fuels per capita, failed to sign on, citing economic concerns and calling for voluntary guidelines instead. A new climate conference held in Copenhagen, Denmark, in December 2009 was the forum for a new round of negotiations aimed at producing enforceable limits on greenhouse gases to stem the potential for widespread natural disasters including regional flooding, drought, and the elevation in sea level along coastal areas. (See the Global Perspectives box.) The conference failed to achieve binding quotas on emissions but did result in pledges of financial support from industrialized nations to help developing countries mitigate the cost of new technology for cleaner energy.

Resistance to the scientific evidence of global warming seems to be weakening among policymakers. Although there continue to be serious debates about who should pay the costs for a greener planet, consensus is growing about the need to attack the problem. For the first time, the EPA has been given authority to regulate vehicle carbon dioxide emissions and has set a goal of reducing them by 900 mil-

Greenhouse Gas Polluters

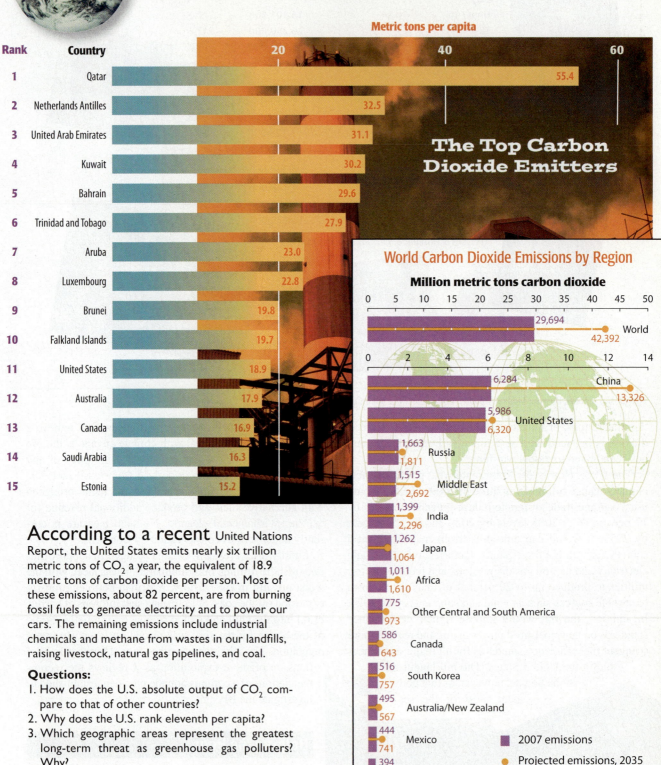

Metric tons per capita

Rank	Country	Metric tons per capita
1	Qatar	55.4
2	Netherlands Antilles	32.5
3	United Arab Emirates	31.1
4	Kuwait	30.2
5	Bahrain	29.6
6	Trinidad and Tobago	27.9
7	Aruba	23.0
8	Luxembourg	22.8
9	Brunei	19.8
10	Falkland Islands	19.7
11	United States	18.9
12	Australia	17.9
13	Canada	16.9
14	Saudi Arabia	16.3
15	Estonia	15.2

The Top Carbon Dioxide Emitters

World Carbon Dioxide Emissions by Region

Million metric tons carbon dioxide

Region	2007 emissions	Projected emissions, 2035
World	29,694	42,392
China	6,284	13,326
United States	5,986	6,320
Russia	1,663	1,811
Middle East	1,515	2,692
India	1,399	2,296
Japan	1,262	1,064
Africa	1,011	1,610
Other Central and South America	775	973
Canada	586	643
South Korea	516	757
Australia/New Zealand	495	567
Mexico	444	741
Brazil	394	761

■ 2007 emissions
● Projected emissions, 2035

According to a recent United Nations Report, the United States emits nearly six trillion metric tons of CO_2 a year, the equivalent of 18.9 metric tons of carbon dioxide per person. Most of these emissions, about 82 percent, are from burning fossil fuels to generate electricity and to power our cars. The remaining emissions include industrial chemicals and methane from wastes in our landfills, raising livestock, natural gas pipelines, and coal.

Questions:
1. How does the U.S. absolute output of CO_2 compare to that of other countries?
2. Why does the U.S. rank eleventh per capita?
3. Which geographic areas represent the greatest long-term threat as greenhouse gas polluters? Why?

Sources: Top figure: United Nations Millennium Development Goals Indicators. Accessed on June 4, 2011 at http://mdgs.un.org/unsd/mdg/Data.aspx. Bottom figure: U.S. Energy Information Administration. Accessed on June 4, 2011 at http://www.eia.gov/emeu/international/carbondioxide.html.

Who Are the Poor?

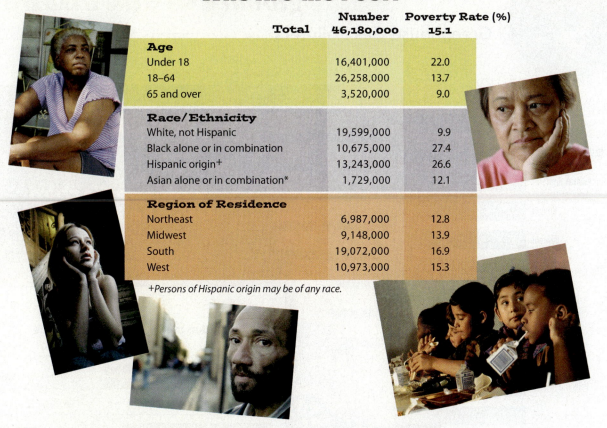

	Total	Number 46,180,000	Poverty Rate (%) 15.1
Age			
Under 18		16,401,000	22.0
18–64		26,258,000	13.7
65 and over		3,520,000	9.0
Race/Ethnicity			
White, not Hispanic		19,599,000	9.9
Black alone or in combination		10,675,000	27.4
Hispanic origin+		13,243,000	26.6
Asian alone or in combination*		1,729,000	12.1
Region of Residence			
Northeast		6,987,000	12.8
Midwest		9,148,000	13.9
South		19,072,000	16.9
West		10,973,000	15.3

+Persons of Hispanic origin may be of any race.

Source: U.S. Census Bureau, *Income, Poverty, and Health Insurance Coverage in the United States,* September 2010.

lion metric tons, or by about 30 percent, by 2016. Carbon dioxide is believed to pose a threat to human health and has been linked to global warming.

The U.S. House of Representatives passed a new climate-change bill midway through 2009. The bill would use a cap-and-trade system to reduce greenhouse gases by 17 percent from 2005 levels by 2020 and by 83 percent by 2050. It would cap emissions from major industrial sources, including power plants, factories, refineries, and electricity and natural gas distributors, and require electric utilities to produce up to 20 percent of their power from renewable sources such as wind and solar energy by 2020. In addition, the bill would impose tighter performance standards on new coal-fired power plants and require more stringent fuel efficiency standards for all major appliances sold in the United States. The bill languished in the Senate, however, as that body spent most of the ses-sion on other matters. Many environmentalists believe a more effective way to deal with climate change is the use of a carbon tax that would be added to the price of any product that is made with or derived from fossil fuel. The tax would both encourage purchases of items produced with alternative fuels and produce additional revenue for use in environmental cleanup. No such measure is currently under serious consideration by Congress.

Shortly after President Obama pledged to support limited offshore drilling, his administration was faced with the worst oil spill in U.S. history. A British Petroleum oil rig explosion off the coast of Louisiana sent millions of barrels of oil into the Gulf and defied stoppage for months. Some of the blame for the spill was placed on lax government regulation. The administration has issued tougher regulations on offshore exploration as it reviews the recommendations of a commission the president established to investigate the BP spill.

Helping the Poor

The "social safety net," designed to protect the health and welfare of American citizens, offers an example of

In 2010, more than 46 million Americans lived below the poverty threshold of $22,050 a year for a family of four.

The Escalating Share of Mandatory Spending

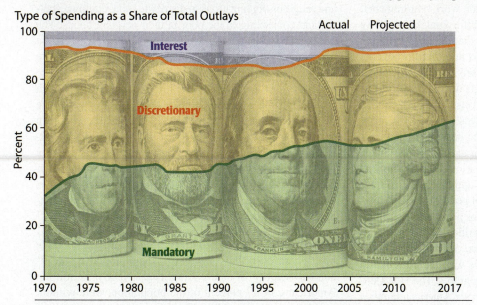

Type of Spending as a Share of Total Outlays

Actual   Projected

Interest

Discretionary

Mandatory

Percent (y-axis): 0, 20, 40, 60, 80, 100

1970 1975 1980 1985 1990 1995 2000 2005 2010 2017 (x-axis)

Source: Office of Management and Budget and the Congressional Budget Office.

the major causes of widespread poverty: unemployment, disability, and old age.

These programs have had considerable success in reducing poverty, especially among the elderly. Whereas the poverty level in the 1950s stood at about 30 percent, by the 1970s it had fallen to about 11 percent.[6] Since then, there have been marginal increases and declines based on a number of factors, including the amount of funds available for antipoverty programs and the state of the U.S. economy. In 2010, the official poverty rate was 15.1 percent, meaning that 46.2 million Americans were living below the income threshold of $22,050 for a family of four. This represented the third consecutive annual increase in the number of people in poverty and the highest rate since 1994.[7] The highest percentage of poverty occurs among children, minorities, and urban populations. Even so, in absolute numbers, there are more white adults between the ages of 18 and 64 living in poverty than any other single group.

The problem with social safety net programs is their burgeoning cost. These programs, known as **entitlements** because anyone who qualifies is entitled to receive benefits from them, account for approximately 50 percent of the federal budget. Their expenditure is mandatory because they represent a promise made to those who are eligible to receive benefits, and that proportion of the population grows as the country ages. On our current budget trajectory, this will leave little for discretionary programs in other areas the government seeks to pursue. As a result, the debate over entitlements such as Social Security is highly charged. Attempts to reform these popular programs present political obstacles for those who try to hold down costs. Budget battles in the last few years have skirted these problems without resolving them.

> **entitlements** Programs promising aid without time limit to anyone who qualifies.
>
> **welfare** Term characterizing the wide variety of social programs developed during the New Deal to help the poor, unemployed, disabled, and elderly.

a dramatic change in government policy over time. Prior to the turn of the twentieth century, few laws protected American workers, and private charitable organizations provided virtually all relief to the poor. The dangerous conditions in early twentieth-century factories gave rise to the first laws against child labor, laws improving sanitation, and laws favorable to the formation of labor unions as a means to increase wages. All of these initiatives, first enacted for the most part by the states, played a part in relieving poverty among urban populations.

The widespread unemployment and financial panic triggered by the Great Depression of the 1930s forced the federal government to take a more central role in alleviating suffering. Many programs now basic to American society, such as unemployment compensation and Social Security, emerged as part of the massive Social Security Act of 1935. Unemployment compensation, financed through a combination of employer contributions and federal and state funding, provides temporary and partial wage replacement for those who have been involuntarily laid off from their jobs. Another provision of the act, known as the Supplemental Security Income program (SSI), provides supplemental income to those who are blind, aged, or disabled. The major provision of the act, the federal Old-Age and Survivors Insurance Trust Fund (currently known as Social Security), provided retirement income to the elderly, financed by employer and employee contributions. In 1965, the government added health-care coverage for the elderly through a program known as Medicare, financed again through a combination of employer and employee contributions. This was followed shortly thereafter by a companion program for the poor called Medicaid. The government designed these programs to attack

Welfare Reform The biggest changes in antipoverty policy have come in the form of public assistance programs—generally known as **welfare**. From the New Deal until the mid-1990s, the principal program for poor families was Aid to Families with Dependent Children (AFDC). This entitlement program provided payments to families with children who either had no income or earned below the annually adjusted standard poverty level established by the Bureau of Labor. Responding to complaints that AFDC generated welfare dependency and thwarted self-sufficiency, Congress passed a reform measure in 1996 that ended welfare's status as an entitlement. Under the new program, Temporary Assistance for Needy Families (TANF), the federal government provides block grants (see Chapter 3) to the states, which decide work requirements, payment levels, and time limits within guidelines set by Congress. These guidelines specify that the state must cap continuous cash benefits at two years and lifetime benefits at five years. In 1997, Congress passed amendments to the program to ensure that cash payments under TANF did not go below previous AFDC benefit levels.

Scholars debate the overall success of welfare reform. One study shows that those who fared best after welfare reform found additional government programs—food stamps, job counseling, child care, and various state-sponsored medical programs for children—to supplement their TANF income.[8] As states struggle to control poverty, they are having difficulty in sustaining funding for programs, especially medical programs, that have proved critical to the success of welfare reform. State officials are also concerned about the growing number of working families who are poor but do not qualify for many government programs. The U.S. Census Bureau reports that almost one in six American families has at least one working member living in poverty. Many of the workers in these families are the most vulnerable to changes in the workforce generated by recession and the outsourcing of jobs associated with globalization.

Unlike Social Security, where both costs and benefits are widely dispersed, programs for the poor provide concentrated benefits that are secured only through well-organized pressure. But the poor lack the political clout to advance their programs. They are not as active politically as are the elderly. Although a variety of interest groups such as the Children's Defense Fund exist to speak for the poor, interests that are more vocal and active than America's poor dominate lobbying for government funds.

The lack of affordable health care is a major contributor to economic insecurity among Americans today.

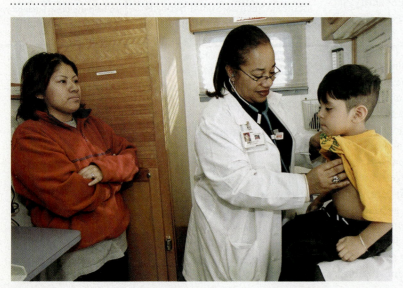

Religious groups, which have historically sought to help the poor, became partners with the government in administering antipoverty programs under George W. Bush's faith-based initiative, which provided federal funds to churches and religious organizations to distribute food, clothing, shelter, and counseling to the poor in their neighborhoods. The program came under attack by critics who complained that the partnership blurred the lines between church and state by permitting religious groups to proselytize and to ignore antidiscrimination laws in their hiring practices.[9] Although Barack Obama expressed similar concerns as a candidate on the campaign trail, once elected, he established his own White House Office of Faith-based and Neighborhood Partnerships. Instead of banning discriminatory practices by faith-based partners outright, he promised to monitor their practices to ensure that services paid for with federal government funds are provided in a manner consistent with fundamental constitutional principles and guarantees.[10]

Health Care and Poverty In recent years, rising health-care costs have become a major threat to the financial security of many Americans. Nearly 52 million Americans, or 17 percent of the population, were without health insurance in 2008. This represents an increase of almost 13 million uninsured people since the year 2007, which marked the beginning of the longest recession since World War II. More than 80 percent of the uninsured come from working families—almost 70 percent from families with one or more full-time workers and 11 percent from families with part-time workers.[12] These individuals often do not qualify for Medicaid but cannot afford to buy their own health insurance. The outsourcing of manufacturing and some service jobs contributes to the problem, as businesses that once provided health-care coverage either reduce or cancel this benefit in order to compete with foreign companies that do not. In most other industrialized nations, government provides universal coverage, thus freeing businesses from shouldering the costs themselves. The recession has made matters much worse, adding an estimated 2.4 million workers to the uninsured.[13] Congress eased the burden on low-income families with children by passing an expansion of the Children's Health Insurance Program that enables states to cover more than four million uninsured children by 2013, while continuing coverage for seven million youngsters. The bill increased tobacco taxes to offset the increase in spending, estimated at more than $32 billion over four and a half years.[14]

After a highly contentious, yearlong public debate marked by raucous town hall meetings, Congress passed landmark health-care legislation in March 2010. The bill guarantees access to health care for 30 million previously uninsured Americans. It requires that all individuals obtain coverage either by employers or by purchas-

The poor are especially vulnerable when disasters hit. They rely on government programs for assistance.

ing it themselves. In order to assist individuals in buying insurance, each state is to set up a health-care exchange where coverage and rates can be compared. The government will provide financial assistance to those who cannot afford the premiums and for small business that will be required to cover their employees. Many of these provisions are phased in over 10 years, but some began almost immediately. For example, young people are now allowed to remain on their parents' insurance until the age of 26, and insurance companies can no longer deny benefits to those with preexisting conditions. The bill is estimated to cost about $938 billion over 10 years, but it is expected to reduce the federal deficit by about $138 billion through cost savings over the same period.

Many uncertainties remain, however. First, more than 30 states have announced plans to challenge the law in courts—especially the individual mandate. Second, even supporters of the legislation recognize that the bill does little to enforce cost containment. If health-care costs continue to skyrocket, the law will be a further drain on the economy and increase the nation's debt.

ECONOMIC POLICY

The federal government has played a role in economic activity since its inception, collecting taxes, funding the construction of roads and canals, and granting licenses to companies, all in the name of economic development. The Great Depression, however, triggered the most extensive expansion of government activity into the economic realm.

Many factors contributed to the Great Depression. Increases in productivity outpaced wages, leading to a sur-

plus of goods many Americans could not afford. Restrictive international trade practices worsened this situation, as overseas sales by U.S. firms plummeted. Investors overspeculated in the booming stock market of the 1920s, and investors who lost money stopped supplying capital for business expansion. Laid-off workers defaulted on mortgages and cut back on purchases, further depressing business activity and investor confidence. More than a quarter of the labor force was out of work. Banks began to fail as depositors demanded their savings and banks were unable to collect on outstanding loans fast enough to provide liquidity. Food riots were not uncommon, and lines of men, women, and children waiting for help at soup kitchens stretched for blocks.

Franklin Roosevelt's New Deal attempted to prop up the failing economy, reassure financial markets, and provide hope for the legions of unemployed. Although scholars debate the overall economic effectiveness of these policies, they agree that the New Deal marked a significant change in the nature of federal intervention in the economy. Under Roosevelt, the national government took the direct hand in promoting, directing, and regulating economic activity that it maintains today. Some of the same factors that led to the Great Depression contributed to the recent economic recession, although the recession was not nearly as deep, and some of the tools developed in the New Deal kept the recession from becoming even worse.

The recession that began in 2007 was triggered by multiple factors. For one, many Americans had become hooked on easy credit. Abetted by low interest rates and creative financial instruments, Americans bought more than they could afford. Financial institutions extended credit—especially in the form of home mortgages—to many who simply could not afford it, believing that losses could be prevented by repackaging mortgages and selling them to other financial institutions in chunks certified as secure by Wall Street ratings agencies. Many of these new banking practices escaped government regulators. When home sales began to lag, home buyers began to default and financial institutions were unable to recoup their losses, producing a crisis in confidence among banks that bought and sold the repackaged debt. In this environment, banks became wary of lending—even to other banks—and credit began to evaporate. With less credit, Americans cut back their spending and businesses were forced to lay off workers. Particularly hard hit were auto companies that carried the additional burden of paying for health care and pensions for retired workers as well as for their current workforce, something foreign competitors did not face. These factors cascaded, and the financial system began to unravel amid rumors of potential failure of Wall Street behemoths like Bear Stearns and Lehman Brothers. When these and other financial giants, deemed "too big to fail," saw their stock values plummet and faced bankruptcy, a number of federal agencies moved in to prevent a global banking failure.

In attacking the recession, the government relied on a number of tools which were developed in the wake of the Great Depression and are now well developed. For example, since 1933 depositors have been protected against bank failures by the Federal Deposit Insurance Corporation (FDIC). The insurance limit was recently raised and expanded to $250,000 for a variety of accounts. However, policymakers also found it necessary to improvise in ways that will inform how we deal with such crises in the future.

Fiscal Policy

Fiscal policy consists of the use of the government's taxing and spending authority to influence the national economy. By virtue of its sheer size, the government's fiscal policies can dramatically affect the direction of the economy. Government regulations, such as those that ensure the quality of food and drugs and protect workers, also affect economic activity.

Tools for Fiscal Policy Fiscal policy is made by the president, who proposes a yearly budget for the U.S. government, and by Congress, which authorizes taxing and spending through a process discussed in Chapter 11. The adjacent figure shows the fiscal year 2011 budget figures President Obama sent to Congress, illustrating the sources of expected revenue and where the money is to be spent.

Much of the thinking about the goals and effects of fiscal policy was outlined early in the twentieth century by British economist John Maynard Keynes (1883–1946). Keynes argued that fiscal policy can be used as a discretionary tool to moderate cycles of inflation and unemployment, known as the business cycle. By varying the amount of taxes they levy or spending they authorize, Keynes asserted, governments can control overall economic demand. For example, government can respond to **recessions**—periods of high unemployment and reduced demand—in one of two ways. It can either buy more goods and services itself, thereby putting income into the hands of workers who will, in turn, increase their own spending, or decrease taxes so consumers can keep and spend more of their own money. Either way, demand will rise, absorbing excess production and raising economic activity. To combat **inflation**, a rise in prices that occurs when the demand for goods and services outstrips the supply, government must slow aggregate demand. It can do so either by cutting back on its own spending and reducing the income it pumps into the economy or by raising the tax rate and depressing consumer spending.

fiscal policy Taxing and spending policies prescribed by Congress and the president.

recession Period of the business cycle characterized by high levels of unemployment.

inflation Economic condition in which the supply of money overwhelms the capacity to produce, creating rising prices.

supply-side economics Approach to economic policymaking focusing on lowering the barriers to production on the assumption that supplies at the right price will create their own demand.

Where the Money Comes from and Where It Goes

Federal Revenues by Source FY2011 (Estimated)

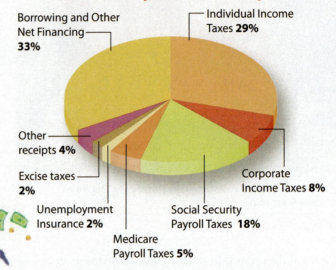

Total Federal Outlays FY2011 (Estimated)

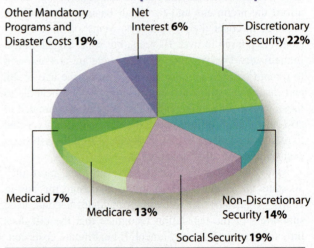

Source: Office of Management and Budget.

A different take on fiscal policy emerged in response to the unusual scenario of stagflation, simultaneously high unemployment and high inflation, produced by an oil crisis in the late 1970s. President Ronald Reagan's team of economists called for government to concentrate on factors that increase aggregate supply, an approach known as **supply-side economics**. Reagan's economists argued that if the goods and services people want are available at the right price, consumers will buy them without the need for direct government intervention. Under this theory, the government's main economic role should consist of keeping prices low by reducing regulations that increase the costs of production and by keeping taxes low so as to increase consumer spending on goods and services. Some

WOULD YOU LIKE A RECEIPT FOR YOUR TAXES?

Americans frequently complain about high taxes and call upon the government to cut spending. Often, the areas they target for cutting, like foreign aid, contribute very little to the national debt, while the spending they support, such as Social Security, Medicare, and defense, are the real cost drivers. It may be that we have a difficult job fathoming the costs of programs when they are listed in billions of dollars. Some members of Congress have proposed giving each taxpayer a receipt for their yearly taxes so they can better understand how their money is spent. To the right is an example.

supply-side supporters estimate, for example, that federal regulations regarding safety and fuel efficiency add about $3,000 to the price of a new car.[15] A reduction in regulation, they claim, will reduce prices and create incentives for consumers to buy more products. When this happens, businesses will produce more and employ more people. Supply-siders also believe that high taxes act as a disincentive for workers, who will forgo increases in income that would put them in a higher tax bracket. Thus, reducing taxes also encourages people to work more, boosting productivity.

Supply-side economics has a checkered track record. After a severe recession in the early 1980s, the country experienced a period in which both inflation and unemployment declined. Despite reduced tax revenues, government spending continued to climb under Reagan, resulting in historically high federal deficits. When Bill Clinton took office in January 1993, he raised taxes. By the end of his second term, the nation had undergone a dramatic economic expansion, and the federal government was running a surplus. The election of President Bush in 2000 marked a return to supply-side thinking with passage of one of the largest tax cuts in history. Once again, however, the government failed to match tax cuts with reductions in federal spending, largely because of expenditures related to the war on terror and the war in Iraq. A return to the deficits ensued. The banking crisis of 2008 added to the deficit problem. By mid-2008, it became apparent that the banking system was in critical condition. President Bush's treasury secretary, Henry Paulson, and Federal Reserve Chairman Ben Bernanke urged immediate passage of the Troubled Asset Relief Program (TARP) to provide an infusion of up to $700 billion to help stabilize the banking system. The funds were to be used to provide capital so banks would continue to lend while they worked off losses tied to bad mortgages and associated financial instruments. In return, the federal government would receive partial ownership in the banks in the form of stocks that could be sold back at some future time. Congress reluctantly obliged, and the money was spread across some of the largest financial institutions deemed to be "too big to fail." By mid-2010, many of these institutions had returned to profitability and returned the money they had received. Nevertheless, the program is still expected to cost the government more than $100 billion in unrecoverable losses.[16]

Household Income		$50,000.00
Income/FICA Taxes Paid		$6,883.00

You paid

Social Security		$1,110.96
National Defense		$1,107.39
Overseas combat operations	$250.46	
Medicare		$703.93
Net interest on the federal debt		$654.61
Low-income assistance programs		$595.24
Housing assistance	$118.52	
Food stamps and other food programs	$152.84	
Other federal health programs		$573.32
National Institutes of Health and other health research and training programs	$56.84	
Food, drug, consumer safety, and other health-related regulatory activities	$7.65	
Unemployment benefits		$299.14
Veterans' benefits and services		$191.94
Education		$183.59
K–12 and vocational education	$129.48	
Higher education	$31.49	
Job training and assistance	$16.77	
Highway, mass transit, and railroad funding		$126.32
Federal employee retirement and disability benefits		$103.87
Justice and law enforcement funding, including the FBI, federal courts, and federal prisons		$95.65
Foreign aid		$63.32
National parks and other land, water, and natural resources funding		$61.80
Science and technology research and advancement		$58.44
NASA	$33.27	
Air transportation, including the Federal Aviation Administration		$38.48
Farm subsidies		$36.98
Alternate energy funding, energy regulation, and the Strategic Petroleum Reserve		$32.95
Disaster relief and insurance, including the Federal Emergency Management Administration		$28.75
Diplomacy and embassies		$25.39
EPA and pollution control programs		$19.97
IRS and Treasury operations		$19.63
Coast Guard and maritime programs		$18.03
Community Development Block Grants		$17.05
U.S. Congress and legislative branch activities		$7.49
U.S. Postal Service		$1.80
Executive Office of the President		$0.99
All other net federal spending		$7.09

The total federal debt (as of January 1, 2011):	$14,025,215,218,709.00
Amount of debt per legal U.S. resident:	$45,411.00
Amount of additional federal borrowing per legal U.S. resident in 2010:	$5,559.00

Source: Congressman Jim Cooper. Accessed on June 5, 2011 at http://cooper.house.gov/index.php?option=com_content&task=view&id=479&Itemid=73.

Ronald Reagan rejected the economic policies that characterized Democratic presidents since the New Deal and adopted a new economic approach, supply-side economics.

Entering office during the twin crises of a deepening recession and a near credit collapse, President Obama assembled an economic team drawn from the worlds of government, high finance, and academia to rebuild the economy. This team worked with the Federal Reserve Chairman, Ben Bernanke, to stabilize financial institutions, to pump capital into banks to spur lending, and to encourage mortgage providers to renegotiate terms with borrowers who could not pay. They infused money into Chrysler and General Motors on the condition that they reorganize and become more efficient. And they helped design a $787 billion stimulus plan to stem the loss of jobs. Since then, many of the loans to banks have been repaid, and the auto companies are returning to profitability. Technically, the recession brought on by the financial crisis has ended.

Nevertheless, unemployment remains painfully high while political attention has turned to combating growing government debt. While each of these programs on their own generated controversy, together they inspired concern over the size of future deficits and sparked protests around the country.

gross domestic product (GDP) A measure of the value of all goods and services produced in the United States.

Deficits When the government spends more than it takes in, it finances the deficit by selling U.S. Treasury bonds to financial institutions, individuals, and even foreign governments. Purchasers see these bonds as a good investment, since they pay competitive interest rates and are backed by the full faith and credit of the U.S. government. As we saw in our earlier discussion, deficits may be acceptable and appropriate in times of economic recession as a way of stimulating economic activity, but deficits have become an almost omnipresent feature of the American economy. Are deficits good, are they bad, or don't they make a difference?

Whether a deficit is a weight on the nation's economy depends on several factors: the deficit's size, its sustainability, its impact on economic investment, and the faith of its creditors. The Office of Management and Budget forecasts the budget deficit for fiscal 2011 to be about $1.6 trillion, three times the deficit recorded in 2008. This is a mind-boggling amount of money, but most economists

Total Deficit or Surplus, 1969–2019

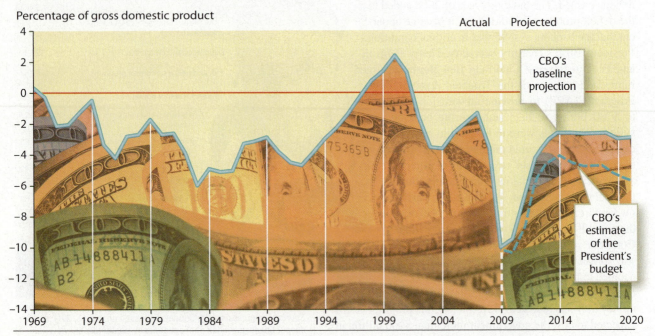

Percentage of gross domestic product

Actual   Projected

CBO's baseline projection

CBO's estimate of the President's budget

Source: Congressional Budget Office.

Timothy Geithner, former New York Federal Reserve President, was one of the architects of President Obama's economic recovery policies.

occur until the long-term debt is brought under control.

Monetary Policy

Government can also regulate economic activity by controlling the availability of money. Like any other commodity, money has a price that goes up when the supply is scarce and goes down when supplies are plentiful. That price is the interest rate that lenders charge to those who want to borrow money. When the supply of money is plentiful, interest rates fall, encouraging consumers to borrow more. Conversely, when the money supply is tight, interest rates rise, discouraging borrowers from taking out more debt.

By varying the money supply, government can alleviate the impact of recession or inflation. When more money is available in the form of inexpensive loans, the economy will expand. An expanding economy should put unemployed workers back into the active labor force. Similarly, when businesses are incapable of producing enough goods and services to meet demand, making loans more expensive is one way to get consumers to reduce spending and relieve inflationary pressures.

evaluate its size against the overall productive capacity of the American economy as measured by the **gross domestic product** (GDP), the value of all goods and services produced in the United States. As a percentage of GDP, the current deficit is about 9 percent, the largest since World War II. Even though the recession is also the worst since the same period in history, a prolonged debt this size is worrisome. President Obama has acknowledged as much, promising to cut waste and raise revenues to the level where the deficit will be halved by the end of his first term. Of course, unless economic growth allows GDP to increase substantially, even a deficit of 6 or 7 percent is well above the previous 40-year average of 2.4 percent.

The debt must also be measured against rising costs in mandatory spending for programs like Medicare, Medicaid, and Social Security, which are expected to continue rising in the foreseeable future as the population ages. In light of such trends, we will have to cut programs, raise taxes, and borrow more from others. When the government borrows, it must pay interest to its creditors. Some economists argue that government borrowing diverts investment from private businesses and slows economic growth. Others worry that more than half of the creditors buying U.S. securities are foreign investors, an increase of about 20 percent since the 1970s. Should world events or global financial markets take a turn for the worse, we might not be able to attract these investors and might not be able to pay for the things their money finances.

The one thing economists of all stripes can agree on is that the United States must come to grips with its long-term debt in the coming years. The number of elderly for whom Social Security and Medicare costs will increase will burgeon, placing a heavy burden on younger workers. Each year, Congress must raise the debt ceiling to allow more borrowing to pay our bills. In 2011, Congress balked at raising the ceiling until substantial cuts were made in government programs. Conflicts like these are likely to re-

Making Monetary Policy A quasi-independent agency called the Federal Reserve, or simply the Fed, controls the supply of money. President Woodrow Wilson and Congress created the Fed in 1913 to regulate the money supply and establish confidence in the nation's banking system. A seven-member Board of Governors, appointed by the president and confirmed by the Senate, oversees the Fed. Governors serve 14-year terms, and appointments are staggered so that no one president will be able to control all appointments. This procedure somewhat removes the board from politically motivated policymaking. The Chair of the Federal Reserve is selected to serve a four-year term by the President of the United States, with Senate confirmation, from among sitting Governors. Ben Bernanke, appointed by George W. Bush in 2006, was nominated by

Did You Know

. . . That after the 1929 Wall Street crash, the Fed bore major responsibility for turning a large market "correction" into a prolonged, long-lasting depression? Following what was then considered economic orthodoxy, the Fed raised interest rates and tightened the money supply. Modern economic theory and policymaking would dictate the opposite responses.

President Obama to a second term beginning in 2010.

The Fed consists of 12 regional banks, each run by a board of nine directors. All nationally chartered banks must belong to the Federal Reserve System; state-chartered banks may join if they wish. Member banks in each region elect six of the directors; the Board of Governors appoints the other three. Member banks buy stock in the Fed and pay for its operation. In return, they receive various benefits for joining, including the privilege of borrowing from the Fed member banks at attractive rates. The Fed also provides check-clearing services, processing the millions of checks consumers and businesses use in their daily financial transactions. The Fed acts essentially as a kind of credit union in which member banks hold shares. The Fed is also the U.S. government's bank, maintaining accounts and providing services for the Treasury Department. The regional Reserve Banks work with the Board of Governors to establish and implement **monetary policy** and are responsible for supervising the operation of member banks.

monetary policy Control of economic growth through management of the money supply by the Federal Reserve.

reserve requirement ratio The amount of money the Fed requires banks to keep on hand to meet their liabilities. Its size helps determine how much banks can lend.

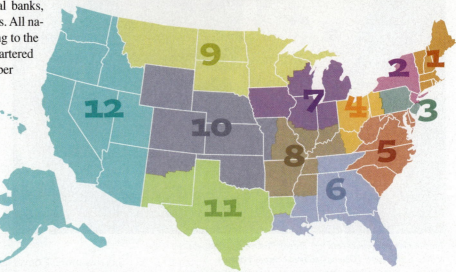

Twelve Regions Served by Fed Banks

Source: Federal Reserve Bank.

The chairperson of the Fed frequently appears before budget-writing committees in Congress. Members of that body look to the chairperson for informal advice about fiscal policy. They also use the voluminous data on economic conditions collected by regional banks to solicit predictions from the chairperson about the course of the economy. Financial institutions closely follow the chairperson's pronouncements for possible clues about the economy's direction. Some in Congress sometimes try to prod the chairperson into making public statements about the economy that will enhance their prospects for reelection in the months leading up to election day.[17] Although unelected officials who do not answer to the public make monetary policy, they can come under intense scrutiny and criticism by elected officials when Fed policies seem to be at odds with the economic welfare of the nation.

Tools for Making Monetary Policy The Fed uses several tools to affect changes in monetary policy: the reserve requirement ratio, the discount rate, open market operations, and the federal funds rate. The **reserve requirement ratio** is the amount of money the Fed requires banks to keep on hand to meet their liabilities. Even a small change in this requirement can dramatically affect the amount of money a bank can lend to its borrowing customers. An increase in the requirement limits the money available to borrowers; a decrease expands the supply of money. The Fed has been working recently to increase the reserve requirements in order to ensure enough liquidity to cover bad loans. The **discount rate** is the interest rate the Fed charges to its members on a short-term basis to cover shortfalls in their reserves. A change in the rate can alter the amount of money banks make available to borrowers. Faced with concerns about the potential economic fallout from defaults in risky mortgages made by some lenders, the Fed repeatedly cut rates in late 2007 and early 2008 in an attempt to stem a drop in investor confidence. The Fed also agreed to in-

Ben Bernanke, chairman of the Federal Reserve, was forced to improvise as well as rely on proven economic tools in dealing with the recent recession and financial crisis.

vestigate regulations it could impose on home mortgage lenders to improve home loan practices.

Through its **open market operations**, the Fed buys and sells government securities or bonds in the marketplace. When the Fed sells bonds, it issues a certificate to the purchaser and takes currency out of circulation equal to the amount of the bonds. This reduces the amount of money available to make loans or to buy goods and services in the marketplace. As a result, selling bonds is a good tool for fighting inflation. Individuals and member banks buy these securities because they yield competitive rates of interest and because, being backed by the U.S. government, they are extremely safe. When the economy is slumping, the Fed will offer to buy back securities, often at a premium—that is, above their face value. This encourages investors to trade in their certificates for cash, which they can then use for making loans and for marketplace transactions. Buying bonds should result in an expanded money supply and serve as an economic stimulus. The Fed employs open market operations more than any other tool because this approach has a more subtle impact on financial markets. The Federal Open Market Committee (FOMC), a 12-member body consisting of some permanent and some rotating members from the Fed's 12 regional branches, makes open market decisions eight times a year. The FMOC can also adjust the rate at which member banks lend each other money to cover short-term needs, the federal funds rate. Changes in this rate, or the discount rate, generally affect consumer loans for things like automobiles and credit card purchases.

For several reasons, the Fed generally is more successful fighting inflation than recession. First, it is easier to curtail spending by drying up the money supply than it is to encourage spending simply by placing more money in circulation. There is no guarantee that consumers will spend the newly available money, especially if they are still recovering from an economic setback. Second, since the Fed is primarily responsive to member banks, it worries more often about inflation than recession because of the impact inflation has on the banking community. Although people borrow less during recessions, banks are still able to make money by collecting on existing loans. However, inflation reduces the value of money over time, which means that borrowers are repaying banks with money that is worth less than it was when the bank lent it.

The financial crisis of the last few years has forced the Fed to be very active in using the tools at its disposal and to invent new tools to stabilize the credit markets. When home sales began to dip in 2007 and 2008, many of the banks that were supplying new types of mortgages to homeowners began to fail. These mortgages were known as subprime loans. Banks that issued them charged borrowers lower initial interest rates that would increase in future years on the theory that the value of these homes would continue to rise. Often, these loans would finance more than the house was worth, and some banks did not verify the incomes of the borrowers. These banks also counted on their ability to sell the mortgages in whole or in part to other financial institutions and thus limit their own liability.

The end of the housing boom meant that banks that had participated in backing these mortgages were stuck with debt they could no longer unload. This led to a spate of bank failures, particularly in some western and southern states where home prices had risen precipitously in previous years. When banks fail, the Fed moves in either to run them or sell them to other banks. Fortunately, depositors who keep their money in Fed-backed banks are insured up to $250,000. This insurance is paid for by member banks and is a legacy of the New Deal.

During the recent financial crisis, Fed chairman Bernanke demonstrated an important feature of policymaking: policymakers sometimes find it necessary to act boldly when a crisis hits, even if there is little precedent. A student of the Great Depression in his graduate studies and scholarly writings, Bernanke wanted to ensure that credit problems stemming from financial failures did not dry up needed capital and cripple economic growth. As a result, he worked diligently behind the scenes to orchestrate the sale of some large financial players—as a result, he worked diligently behind the scenes to orchestrate the sale of large financial players facing bankruptcy, to distribute TARP money to bail out troubled banks, and to inject credit into markets to stave off collapse. Finally, he engaged in what is known as **quantitative easing**, a procedure by which the Fed floods the markets with additional reserves it creates in an effort to spur financial activity when low interest rates alone are not enough. These actions helped stabilize markets but some economists warn they risk inflation.

discount rate Interest rate at which member banks can borrow money from the Federal Reserve.

open market operations The buying and selling of government securities by the Federal Reserve with the intention of altering the nation's money supply.

quantitative easing Additions to the money supply by the Fed to increase financial activity when interest rates are already close to zero.

protectionism Policy of using taxes and tariffs to limit the kinds and amounts of foreign goods entering the nation.

Global Economic Policy

Despite the immense size and productivity of the U.S. economy, the global economy increasingly affects American prosperity. American consumers have become accustomed to enjoying products made throughout the world. You probably enjoy playing video games on a device made in Japan, wear clothing made in Indonesia, and drive cars whose parts were made in Mexico, if not cars entirely constructed in a foreign nation. This has led to a large trade deficit; America spends far more on foreign goods and services than people in other countries spend on U.S. goods and services.

One potential response to world competition is **protectionism**, the use of taxes and tariffs to protect domestic production by limiting the products we buy from other nations. Protectionist policies, however, can lead to retaliation as foreign countries build walls to limit the importation of American goods. Some economists believe tariff policies lead inevitably to recessions and even depressions. Another response is to develop **free trade** policies that remove barriers to international trade and increase the flow of products across borders. Ideally, this should increase productivity and income for all trading partners, as each comes to rely on a steady stream of goods and services produced by the nations that can offer them most efficiently at competitive prices.

Free trade arguments motivated passage of major trade policies such as the 1994 **North American Free Trade Agreement** (NAFTA), supported by Democrats and Republicans alike. NAFTA created the world's largest free-trade zone by removing most trade barriers among the United States, Canada, and Mexico. However, it also generated intense opposition among certain groups. Organized labor in the United States opposes those free-trade treaties, which it believes displace low-skilled American workers by outsourcing jobs to countries with lower wages.

free trade The idea that commerce should flow between countries without government restrictions.

North American Free Trade Agreement A 1994 trade agreement eliminating trade barriers among the United States, Canada, and Mexico.

Several international bodies have emerged to coordinate world economic policy and to regulate trade. One of these is the G20, a group of world leaders from the 20 largest developed and developing economies. The group met several times in recent years to deal with the effects of the world financial crises. In September 2009, they met in Pittsburgh, Pennsylvania, to discuss regulating financial practices and compensation for banking executives. Another important world body is the World Trade Organization (WTO). A successor to the General Agreement on Tariffs and Trade, or GATT, a trade negotiating and coordinating body created in the wake of World War II, the WTO has become the principal world body responsible for negotiating trading agreements, monitoring compliance, and adjudicating trade disputes among 153 member nations. The WTO's top-level decision-making body is the Ministerial Conference, which meets at least once every two years. Decisions are made by the entire membership, typically by consensus. The United States fields a team of negotiators that works with the WTO and with individual trading partners through the Office of the United States Trade Representative, whose chief administrator is appointed by the president with Senate confirmation. Another important global financial agency is the International Monetary Fund (IMF), whose 187 member nations make loans and help promote economic growth in developing nations.

The WTO has been the focus of much protest by workers and environmentalists from around the world. Recent WTO meetings have been greeted by thousands of demonstrators and even by violence. Protesters believe that global organizations like the WTO remove important decisions from the hands of the citizens in democratic nations and turn them over to bureaucrats more interested in advancing the interests of multinational corporations than those of workers or environmentalists. Free trade advocates respond by pointing out that democratic institutions are not being subverted by WTO decisions. Trade representatives are responsible to the president and the Congress, who are ultimately accountable to the American electorate. Nevertheless, debate about the role of global institutions is likely to continue as the uneven effects of trade rules are felt by various interests throughout the world.

Meetings of the World Trade Organization have been the focus of much protest by workers and environmentalists unhappy with the trade policies the WTO has adopted.

CIVIC ENGAGEMENT AND PUBLIC POLICY TODAY

Opportunities to influence policy abound. Some of you may choose to run for elective office and firmly imprint your views on policies that are adopted. Others may work for government agencies that shape the ways policies are implemented. Some will enter professions like journalism, where you will serve as opinion leaders favoring or opposing government policies. Even if you choose none of these public paths, your continued participation as a voter and citizen will nevertheless ensure that you have an impact. Recall from our discussion in Chapter 7 that in the long run, policies tend to respond to major currents in public opinion.[18]

We have also seen repeatedly that our system of federalism provides multiple arenas for citizen activism. In recent years, state and local governments have taken the lead in forging environmental and health-care policies when the federal government was paralyzed by gridlock. These levels of government provide opportunities for citizens to communicate directly with lawmakers who are often their neighbors. They provide opportunities for neighbors to come together themselves to explore solutions to community problems.

The recession has spurred numerous responses by community activists to assist those who have lost their jobs and those in danger of losing their homes. Thousands have donated and volunteered their time to food pantries hard-pressed to keep up with the demand in areas suffering from high unemployment. Volunteers.org, an online service that matches volunteers with opportunities, has reported a sharp increase in visitors. Big Brothers Big Sisters of Philadelphia has seen a 25 percent increase in inquiries from potential mentors since the recession began.[19] Many of the newly unemployed have found volunteering to be a productive use of the time not spent looking for jobs themselves. Nonprofit agencies "have marveled at the sudden flood of bankers, advertising copywriters, marketing managers, accountants, and other professionals eager to lend their formidable but dormant skills. The Financial Clinic, which counsels the working poor on economic matters, recently dispatched an MIT-educated ex–Wall Street type to help people in Chinatown prepare their tax returns."[20]

Community leaders in Boston brought endangered homeowners together with representatives from five mortgage companies to try to restructure loans that were in danger of defaulting. Workshops were offered on home ownership and maintaining good credit, and residents were provided with access to foreclosure prevention counselors.[21] Across the country, volunteer organizations have teamed up to help homeowners renegotiate loans with lenders and to provide emergency services to those whose homes have been foreclosed. Local governments are listening—and lending a hand.

If we are to solve the many policy problems we reviewed in this chapter, we will need to bring even more citizens into the political process. Community organizations, churches, labor groups, and other mobilizing agents are already hard at work implementing innovative ideas to make this happen in hundreds of communities nationwide. A number of online forums where citizens can share experiences, gain policy expertise, and explore ideas for expanding citizen participation also exist.[22] Until our discussion is enriched by participants from all sectors of the political community, the true promise of citizenship for all will be unfulfilled. The good news is that there is no shortage of ideas and energy among Americans already hard at work to make this happen.

Summary

1. **What is public policy, how is it made, and how can we explain policy outcomes?**
- Public policy is anything the government chooses to do or not to do.
- The policy process includes problem recognition, agenda setting, policy formation, policy implementation, and policy evaluation.
- Policy outcomes can be explained by considering the distribution of costs and benefits to various groups affected by the policies.
- Both costs and benefits can be either widely distributed or concentrated.

2. **What is domestic policy and what are some of the problems it addresses?**
- Domestic policy consists of government action (and inaction) that affects citizens within the United States.
- Each branch of the American government and many bureaucratic agencies at all levels are involved in formulating domestic policy.
- Climate change, energy production, and pollution of our air, land, and water are all growing and controversial areas that domestic policymakers must address. Some agencies

such as the Department of Energy and the Environmental Protection Agency specialize in dealing with these problems.
- Poverty and the rising costs of Social Security and health care are domestic policy areas that have resisted easy solutions because they are expensive and affect many diverse interests.

3. **How is economic policy made and implemented?**
- The major tools of economic policy are fiscal and monetary policy.
- Fiscal policy consists of the use of the government's taxing and spending power to influence the nation's economy.
- Fiscal policy is made by the president and Congress through their taxing and spending decisions.
- Monetary policy uses changes in the supply of money to influence the nation's economy.
- The Federal Reserve uses the tools of the reserve requirement ratio, the discount rate, the federal funds rate, and open market operations to direct monetary policy.
- American economic policy is also affected by global economic policies that often divides political leaders into positions of protectionism versus free trade.

National Journal

Is Stability A Realistic Goal?

In many ways, Congress' major 2010 financial reform bill resembles other landmark pieces of legislation. Like health care reform, it tackles a pernicious side effect of America's free-market economy and treats it with a typically light touch by offering a package of incentives and disincentives for businesses and consumers. Instead of forcing banks to become smaller, the bill encourages them to do so. Instead of banning the kinds of home loans that contributed to the housing crisis, the legislation sets up a consumer protection agency that will rely mainly on disclosure to prompt Americans to make smarter financial decisions.

In at least one way, though, the financial reform plan represents a new approach. Grafted onto the largely familiar array of agencies that regulate banks is a council of top economic officials tasked with counteracting instability in the financial system before it becomes a critical threat. The council will look beyond individual institutions and practices to anticipate bubbles and spot potentially destabilizing financial innovations—such as the bonanzas that subprime lending and collateralized debt obligations seemed to be a few years ago.

The proposed Financial Stability Oversight Council, as the Senate legislation calls it, is an interagency group of nine people chaired by the Treasury secretary; it would include the chairman of the Federal Reserve Board, the heads of other financial agencies, and one or two other appointees. Some of its functions approximate the emergency powers that the Federal Reserve and Treasury have traditionally kept for themselves. But giving the council the job of foreseeing problems and acting to preserve stability in the nation's vast and complex financial system is an audacious undertaking, even for the U.S. government.

To put this commitment into perspective, consider the scope of the health care reform package enacted this year. Imagine for a moment that Washington had empowered a council to guarantee the stability of the U.S. health care system. If medical care, like credit, was scarce or too expensive, the council could intervene to make sure it was affordable and readily available, by acting wherever it chose to head off, say, shocking rate increases, or by guaranteeing medical care to everyone, with or without insurance. This sounds far-fetched because the epic health debate revealed that Americans are hardly eager to embrace government intervention to guarantee such ambitious outcomes.

Compared with many other countries, the U.S. government has tended to take a laissez-faire approach to regulating such essential services as transportation, electricity, and telecommunications. Washington does attempt to preserve the stability of agricultural supply and prices, with only mixed results. Most economists say that the current system of farm subsidies and price controls exists more to boost the farmers' income than to protect consumers.

But even these examples involve industries much smaller and simpler than the financial system, which extends beyond banks to include insurance, mortgage lending, and consumer credit—sectors that will remain relatively free of federal regulation, even after the regulatory reform package becomes law. The most comparable example of the government ambitiously trying to maintain the stability of markets was World War II and the extensive system of rationing and price controls that the Roosevelt administration used to prevent inflation, hoarding, and profiteering. That intervention was arguably successful, but a more recent iteration wasn't.

President Nixon imposed wage and price controls from 1971 to 1973 to combat inflation and escalating wage demands by labor unions. The move triggered runaway inflation, slow growth, food and commodity shortages, and an era of declining living standards. Economists consider the controls one of the most disastrous economic policy decisions ever by a U.S. president.

Oddly, the debate over financial reform hasn't focused much on the question of whether government can or should try to assume responsibility for stabilizing the financial system. Neither party in Congress has drawn attention to the goals of the systemic risk council or to the very notion that a government body would try to head off instability throughout the financial system before it causes a crisis.

In one form or another, the federal government has always taken emergency action to stem financial panics and other crises that threaten the economy, according to banking expert Liaquat Ahamed. Congress established the Federal Reserve Board in 1913 to coordinate emergency action, using the power to make emergency loans to counter bank runs and otherwise manipulate interest-rate policy to maintain liquidity in the banking system. Although the Fed and Treasury took actions during the recent crisis that were messy and in some ways unprecedented in size and scope, the interventions essentially followed past patterns, Ahamed says.

In Ahamed's view, the earliest days of the crisis made it clear that the United States had to do three things to minimize the risk of a plunge that could wreck the financial system. First, the government needed to bolster the capital reserves of banks, which had used holes in the accounting rules to evade reserve requirements; second, Washington needed to take on increased oversight to prevent excessive risk-taking and leveraging; and third, if the first two requirements weren't met, government would need a more streamlined and effective process to handle emergencies.

The first and final functions were already important government responsibilities, according to Ahamed, but the middle role—seeking to guarantee the stability of the financial system—is different. The Fed has been responsible for auditing many of the largest banks, and it has important duties to keep interests rates and inflation low and employment and the economy growing.

The Fed's responsibility for maintaining the overall stability of the financial system has been more ambiguous, especially in recent decades. Although regulators have stepped up its efforts to stabilize the financial system, "it is also true that the financial system is more complex" than a decade or two ago, Ahamed said.

The Federal Reserve has long had close relations with large bank holding companies such as Citigroup and Bank of America (where Fed examiners actually showed up for work every day). Until recently, though, Fed accountants were not as involved in the day-to-day operations of Wall Street banks—such as Bear Stearns, Goldman Sachs, and Lehman Brothers—that were some of the biggest customers for the Fed's Treasury bills. The chaos of the financial crisis revealed just how little attention the Fed paid to ensuring their stability and how limited were its powers to help them.

A hallmark of the era of Fed Chairman Alan Greenspan, from 1987 to 2006, was the Fed's unwillingness to serve as the kind of guarantor of financial stability envisioned in the plan for the Financial Stability Oversight Council. At the same moment that Long Term Capital Management's derivatives trades were souring, Greenspan was otherwise engaged in killing off an effort by Brooksley Born, then the chairwoman of the Commodities Futures Trading Commission, to regulate derivatives. At multiple

> "Neither party in Congress has drawn attention to the goals of the systemic risk council or to the very notion that a government body would try to head off instability throughout the financial system before it causes a crisis."

congressional hearings, Greenspan argued successfully that no oversight was needed—because the self-interest of big banks and investors would be more effective than any government agency in controlling risk and maintaining stability.

Since then, Greenspan has expressed wonderment at the failures of such market discipline during the financial crisis, but he has not admitted that he might have been mistaken about unregulated trading in derivatives. Ten years after his tidy and privately financed rescue of Long Term Capital Management, one type of unregulated derivative was at the center of the subprime mortgage meltdown, and a related derivative underlay the $182 billion bailout of AIG, which at last count is expected to cost taxpayers $50 billion.

Vincent Reinhart has low expectations for the systemic risk council and the rest of the regulatory overhaul because he thinks that Congress is aiming at the wrong target—preventing banks from becoming "too big to fail." Reinhart, a former director of the Fed's Division of Monetary Affairs, believes that in the 24 years since the government made major changes to the tax code, banks have exploited weaknesses in accounting rules. Banks' "splintering" of their balance sheets, he says, made it impossible for regulators to understand what was going on, for the mar-

ket to exercise the discipline that Greenspan was depending on, and even for managers of the banks to understand the risks that had accumulated.

Would the risk council use such countercyclical means to try to head off the next financial bubble? Goldstein thinks it is possible, but Reinhart is doubtful. When Greenspan issued his famous warning in late 1996 about "irrational exuberance" in the stock market, Reinhart said, no one wanted to listen. The market doubled in the next four years, until the dot-com crash, and Greenspan, according to his memoirs, concluded that even Fed chairmen are powerless to puncture a financial bubble.

No elected or appointed official would risk the political fallout from taking action against a possible bubble, Reinhart argues. At best, a lot of people will be poorer. At worst, he said, government officials risk destabilizing rather than stabilizing the situation.

If we are lucky, former investment banker Elliot says, the risk council's existence will be enough to deter excessive risk-taking. More likely though, Reinhart warns, it will take another crisis to move government to directly address the complexity of large banks that is at the root of systemic risk. "I fully expect it," he said.

For Discussion:

■ What do you think government's role should be in controlling risk in the markets? What are the advantages and liabilities of government intervention?

■ Is it possible for America to have an economy without large banks that risk becoming "too big to fail"? Why or why not?

■ Explain in your own words the steps Liaquat Ahamed believes the government needs to take to ward off crisis. Which steps do you think would be easy, and which would be more of a challenge?

16

FOREIGN AND DEFENSE

PROTECTING AMERICAN INTERESTS IN THE WORLD

REMOTE CONTROL WARFARE ■ Sam Nelson's morning appears unremarkable as he leaves home to drive to his day job about 40 miles away at Creech Air Force Base near Indian Springs, Nevada. Once there, he takes his position behind a cockpit of computer screens and prepares to do battle—with an enemy 7,500 miles away in Afghanistan.[1]

Sam is part of a new breed of air force pilot who have traded fighter jets for drones, remote-controlled aircraft that have become part of our mission in Iraq and Afghanistan since 9/11. The facility in Nevada where Sam works as an Air Force captain is only one of two locations used by the CIA to fly missions. The other is located at Langley Air Force Base just outside of Washington, D.C. At both locations, pilots work in teams, one controlling the aircraft and the weapons, the other handling visual surveillance controls. Both are in constant communication with commanders on the ground in the war zone.[2]

- What are the major goals of American foreign policy?
- Who are the principal actors in the foreign-policy-mak[ing] process?
- What are the tools that foreign-policy makers have at [their] disposal?

Air Force Major Bryan Callahan, a Creech facility veteran now stationed at Langley, described the experience of being a [drone] warrior to one reporter: "You get more attached than you would think from being in Nevada. . . . Killing someone with an [remotely piloted aircraft] is not different than with an F-16. We're well aware that if you push that button somebody can go away. [It's not a] game. You take it very seriously."[3]

In 2009, President Obama expanded the CIA's authority to conduct drone attacks over the Pakistani border where th[ey are] credited with killing dozens of senior Al Qaeda and Taliban figures. Drone surveillance was also crucial to the succes[sful mission to] kill Osama bin Laden. But drone attacks also kill civilians, incurring protests and animosity from many of the people w[e want] to protect. Pakistanis complain that the United States has violated sovereign air space with its attacks; and Afghan Pr[esident] Karzai, whose government we are supporting, has blamed drone attacks for numerous civilian deaths. Some human-rig[hts groups] have called for an end to drone strikes, saying that their use violates the conventional rules of warfare. Others have rai[sed concerns] about the morality of remote control warfare where fighters don't directly confront the horrors of the battlefield. Drone p[ilots reject this] characterization, one of them telling reporters: "You see a lot of detail. . . . We feel it, maybe not to the same degree as if w[e were] there, but it affects us. Part of the job is to try to identify body parts."[4]

The U.S. military and its NATO allies who rely on drone strikes to advance and protect their missions have begun [to develop] more-precise missiles for use on drones that can hit with less damage to noncombatants. President Obama has person[ally apologized] for unintended civilian casualties and has pl[edged to reduce them] in the future. Still, drones have proven effecti[ve at eliminating] enemy targets while protecting American lives[. Deciding how] and when to use weapons that advance Am[erican interests] without sacrificing our ideals is not a new pro[blem, but] it is one that is growing more complicated in [an age of] remote control warfare.

In this chapter, we will discuss the foreig[n policy dilem-] mas that the United States faces in an increas[ingly dangerous] world. We will examine the institutions charg[ed with assess-] ing risks and formulating policies to protec[t the American] homeland and provide security for U.S. intere[sts abroad.] Along the way, we will identify the role that [citizens] must play to protect the ideals we value. ◆◆

New technology has changed the way we wage warfa[re. It] is safer for the American military but can result in uni[ntended] and political fallout.

DEFENSE AND FOREIGN POLICY IN HISTORICAL PERSPECTIVE

The world has changed dramatically during your lifetime. Many of you were born about the time of the collapse of the Soviet Union in 1991, which marked the end of the Cold War. Many observers believed that a period of world peace would follow. A bloody war in the Balkans, bombing of the World Trade Center in 1993, attacks on U.S. embassies in Kenya and Tanzania in 1998, and most especially the events of September 11, 2001, shattered that dream and ushered in a period of increased global terrorism.

The requirements for defending the nation change dramatically depending on the source and the nature of the enemies it faces. Defense and foreign policies that promoted peace and security during the Cold War may not meet the challenges of the "age of terrorism." New policies must be developed. **Defense policy** generally involves strategic decisions about the scale and use of military force in national security. **Foreign policy** is broader: It deals with the whole array of military, diplomatic, economic, and security exchanges the United States has with foreign nations.

Finding a Place in the World

Alexis de Tocqueville noted that America's prosperity rested in part on its geographic isolation, its defensible borders, and the absence of passion for war:

> The Americans have no neighbors and consequently no great wars, financial crises, invasions, or conquests to fear; they need neither heavy taxes nor a numerous army, nor great generals; they have also hardly anything to fear from something else which is a greater scourge for democratic republics than all these others put together, namely, military glory.[5]

He went on to observe that the foreign policy of early American presidents took advantage of the country's relative isolation and was guided by a defensive posture that steered clear of entangling alliances.[6]

Despite George Washington's admonition in his farewell address to avoid embroilment in the affairs of other nations, it soon became clear that America could not isolate itself from the world, especially since much of the North American continent was still in the hands of European nations. Early on, presidents were called upon to deal with naval skirmishes that interfered with free trade and hostilities with Native Americans that were instigated or exacerbated by foreign powers. Americans soon began to develop an active foreign policy aimed at expanding American territorial frontiers at home and defending American commercial interests abroad against ambitious Europeans.[7]

By the time James Monroe became president in 1817, America's western frontier had already been pushed almost halfway across the continent. Faced with the dual threat of Russian incursions in the Pacific Northwest and European designs on reacquiring recently liberated countries in Central and South America, Monroe presented a new foreign policy to Congress on December 2, 1823. The Monroe Doctrine, as it came to be known, warned that the United States would consider any attempt by European powers to extend their systems to the Western hemisphere as a threat to the nation's peace and safety. In return for European restraint, the United States would refrain from interference in the internal affairs of Europe. In subsequent years, this doctrine—which was never enacted by Congress and had no status in international law—was expanded to ward off European powers and to justify U.S. expansion to the Pacific.

> **defense policy** Strategic decisions about the scale and use of military force for national security.
>
> **foreign policy** Strategies for dealing with foreign nations on a broad array of military, diplomatic, economic, and security issues.

In the second quarter of the nineteenth century, America supplemented its westward territorial expansion with international economic expansion. Diplomatic relations with the rest of the world continued to grow, along with American prestige; but the domestic fight over slavery consumed most of the nation's energy, and in 1861 the growing schism between slave states and free states led to the Civil War.

Becoming an International Power

When the Civil War ended, the United States once again turned its gaze outward. Unlike many European nations, America sought to achieve economic expansion without acquiring political outposts. By the turn of the twentieth century, it was becoming a world power, exercising military might to protect its interests in the Western hemisphere and expanding its influence in the South Pacific. America also began carving out a larger role for itself on the international stage. The Open Door Policy, initiated by John Hay, secretary of state in the administration of President William McKinley, declared that all nations trading with China should have equal privileges and also opposed China's partition by foreign powers.

In 1904, President Theodore Roosevelt issued his Roosevelt Corollary to the Monroe Doctrine, reasserting U.S.

> **Did You Know?**
>
> . . . That the Monroe Doctrine was actually the creation of Monroe's secretary of state, John Quincy Adams? Both Monroe and Adams were experienced diplomats, but Adams was the shrewder practitioner of international politics.

opposition to European intervention in this hemisphere but claiming America's right to intervene in the domestic affairs of its neighbors if they proved unable to maintain order and national sovereignty on their own. The corollary was used as a justification for U.S. intervention in a number of Caribbean countries, including Cuba, Haiti, and the Dominican Republic. The United States consolidated its dominance in the hemisphere with the opening of the Panama Canal in 1914.

Eventually, America was dragged into playing an even larger role. Despite President Woodrow Wilson's determination to keep the country out of World War I, the sinking of American merchant vessels by German submarines compelled America to join the fight. After the war, Wilson's efforts to prevent future wars by establishing the League of Nations, one of his Fourteen Points for international cooperation, failed to gain traction either at home or abroad, and the Treaty of Versailles he helped negotiate to end the war was not even ratified by the U.S. Senate.

During this period, the involvement of American citizens in executing foreign policy decisions expanded. The military draft was initiated in 1917 as a democratic response to the need for military personnel. Wealthy citizens could no longer buy their way out of military service as they could in earlier eras. A peacetime draft was instituted just before the United States entered World War II—a conflict that the country had tried to avoid. The Selective Training and Service Act of 1940 required all men between the ages of 21 and 35 to register with the Selective Service System and to remain available for service regardless of wealth or education. Deferments were available in the case of hardship, and those who opposed war on religious grounds were given the opportunity for alternate service.

Did You Know?

. . . That President Truman announced the "Truman Doctrine" to frighten Americans about the Soviet threat? Republican senator Arthur Vandenberg told Truman that Congress would not support committing the United States to a strong anti-Soviet policy unless he managed to "scare hell out of the American people." Truman made his statement to a joint session of Congress and achieved that aim.

Despite President Woodrow Wilson's determination to keep the country out of World War I, the sinking of American merchant vessels by German submarines compelled America to join the fight.

nuclear arsenals and could dispatch conventional military forces quickly anywhere in the world. In 1947, President Harry Truman issued the Truman Doctrine, declaring the intention of the United States to support free peoples who were resisting attempted subjugation by armed minorities or by outside pressures. This doctrine informed the U.S. policy of **containment**, which was used to justify U.S. military interventions in wars with perceived Soviet surrogates like North Vietnam.

Vietnam marked another change in citizen involvement in war. Deferments for those who could afford to go to college led to disenchantment with the way the Selective Service operated. In response, a draft lottery that limited deferment opportunities was initiated in 1969. In 1973, as the Vietnam War was winding down, the draft was replaced by a system of voluntary military enlistment. Today, the all-volunteer army includes a growing number of women, although they are barred from direct combat roles.

U.S. nuclear policy during the Cold War was informed by a principle of **mutually assured destruction** (MAD), which presumed that neither superpower would be the first to launch a nuclear attack if it understood that such an act would lead to its own certain destruction. The discomfort many Americans felt living under this threat was reflected in the popular culture of the 1960s. Movies such as *Dr.*

The Nuclear Age

After World War II, the United States and the Soviet Union were the world's preeminent powers; both possessed large

Military Costs of Major U.S. Wars

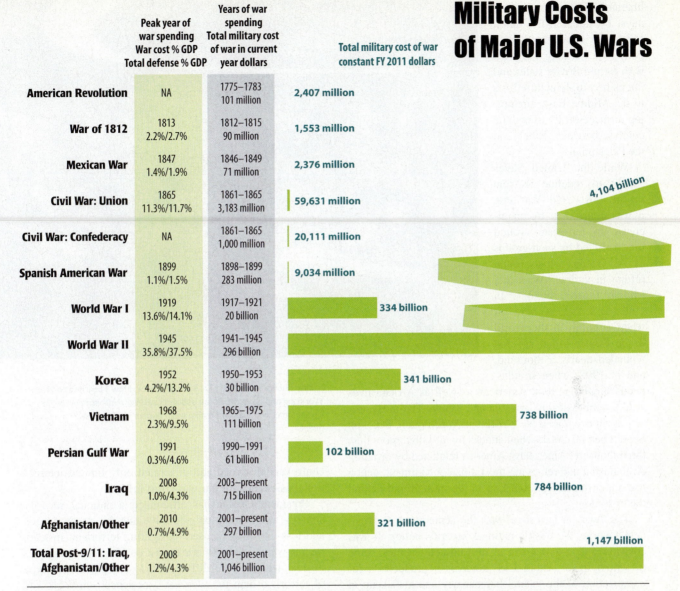

	Peak year of war spending War cost % GDP Total defense % GDP	Years of war spending Total military cost of war in current year dollars	Total military cost of war constant FY 2011 dollars
American Revolution	NA	1775–1783 101 million	2,407 million
War of 1812	1813 2.2%/2.7%	1812–1815 90 million	1,553 million
Mexican War	1847 1.4%/1.9%	1846–1849 71 million	2,376 million
Civil War: Union	1865 11.3%/11.7%	1861–1865 3,183 million	59,631 million
Civil War: Confederacy	NA	1861–1865 1,000 million	20,111 million
Spanish American War	1899 1.1%/1.5%	1898–1899 283 million	9,034 million
World War I	1919 13.6%/14.1%	1917–1921 20 billion	334 billion
World War II	1945 35.8%/37.5%	1941–1945 296 billion	4,104 billion
Korea	1952 4.2%/13.2%	1950–1953 30 billion	341 billion
Vietnam	1968 2.3%/9.5%	1965–1975 111 billion	738 billion
Persian Gulf War	1991 0.3%/4.6%	1990–1991 61 billion	102 billion
Iraq	2008 1.0%/4.3%	2003–present 715 billion	784 billion
Afghanistan/Other	2010 0.7%/4.9%	2001–present 297 billion	321 billion
Total Post-9/11: Iraq, Afghanistan/Other	2008 1.2%/4.3%	2001–present 1,046 billion	1,147 billion

Note: The current year dollar estimates are converted to constant prices using estimates of changes in the consumer price index for years prior to 1940 and using Office of Management and Budget and Department of Defense estimates of defense inflation for years thereafter. The CPI estimates used here are from a database maintained at Oregon State University. The database periodically updates figures for new official CPI estimates of the U.S. Department of Commerce.

Source: Stephen Daggett, "Cost of U.S. Major Wars," *CRS Report for Congress*, June 29, 2010.

Strangelove or: How I Learned to Stop Worrying and Love the Bomb poked fun at living in a world of permanent nuclear stalemate.

A period of **détente** opened in the 1970s when the United States and the Soviet Union attempted to ease tensions by undertaking a number of cooperative actions like signing treaties to limit the arms race. America also began discussions with other formerly hostile nations such as China. By the time of the Reagan administration, however, the fervor for détente had waned, and America commenced an arms buildup that the Soviets could not match. The Soviets' failure to keep pace with America, coupled with internal economic problems, contributed to the collapse of the Soviet empire in the early 1990s.

The Growing Threat of Terrorism

The breakup of the Soviet Union and the Soviet bloc ended the Cold War, but the role that the sole surviving superpower would play in this new era was uncertain. President George H. W. Bush helped bring former Soviet satellites into Western alliances like the North Atlantic Treaty Organization (NATO) at this time. He also asserted U.S. commitment to global stability by assembling a multinational coalition with the authorization of the United Nations to aid Kuwait after it was invaded by Iraq in 1990. Coalition forces

> **détente** Foreign policy begun in the Nixon administration stressing accommodation with rivals rather than conflict.

liberated Kuwait in just 42 days. President Bill Clinton continued President Bush's policy of building alliances with former Soviet states and intensified diplomatic efforts in the Middle East, attempting unsuccessfully to end the conflict between Israel and the Palestinians.

While the United States sought to redefine its role in the post–Cold War era, it was confronted by an increase in terrorism around the world led by such groups as Al Qaeda, which found refuge in various Asian and Middle Eastern nations. In 1993, U.S. targets were hit when a bomb in the World Trade Center killed six and wounded nearly a thousand, and in 1998, when simultaneous bombings took American as well as African lives at U.S. embassies in Tanzania and Kenya. The most serious assaults came in New York and Washington, D.C., on September 11, 2001, when attacks by air killed more than three thousand Americans. America retaliated by invading Afghanistan and removing the Taliban government, which had supported Osama bin Laden, the mastermind behind the operation.

The "war on terrorism" was the centerpiece of President George W. Bush's national security policy. It was envisioned as a global war against unseen enemies, some of whom travel within U.S. borders. It produced a reorganization of the federal bureaucracy and a shakeup in the nation's intelligence-gathering operations, as well as a change in official military policy from the use of force only to counter imminent threats to a doctrine of **preemption**. President Bush outlined this new approach shortly after the September 11 attacks when he called for the use of preemptive force to prevent hostile acts, even if it was uncertain where and when those acts would occur.[8] The new policy was implemented when America invaded Iraq over fears of an alleged buildup of weapons of mass destruction.

President Bush outlined the principal elements of his national security policy, sometimes referred to as the Bush Doctrine, in a speech on November 19, 2003. He said that the peace and security of free nations rests on three pillars: (1) working together to build strong and effective international institutions; (2) restraining aggression and evil by force; and (3) committing to the global expansion of democracy. Allying ourselves with democratic reformers, the president argued, was consistent not only with our own heritage but also with our security interests because "democratic governments do not shelter terrorist camps or attack their peaceful neighbors."[9] The policy was highly

Stanley Kubrick's 1964 film, Dr. Strangelove or: How I Learned to Stop Worrying and Love the Bomb, *spoofed Cold War relations between the United States and Russia at a time when nuclear warfare posed a very real threat.*

controversial abroad and generated only limited international assistance for our war effort in Iraq.

President Obama has articulated a national security strategy that is more collaborative than his predecessor's and less narrowly focused on fighting terrorism. Instead, he has warned that America must develop new strategies to deal with a more diffuse and less sophisticated type of terrorism than the type we experienced on 9/11. The president has also broadened national security threats to include stopping the spread of weapons of mass destruction, enhancing cybersecurity, combating global warming, and promoting economic security.

In meeting these threats, the president maintains that the United States can no longer afford to "go it alone"; instead, we must expand and extend global cooperation. Winning the war in Afghanistan remains a top priority, and the president has not ruled out the continuation of secret operations to stem the spread of Al Qaeda in Pakistan. He has stressed the importance of negotiation and dialogue in dealing with international threats and said a major goal of American foreign policy should be to promote universal human rights abroad, in part, by modeling them at home.

The president's record in meeting these goals has been mixed. He signed a significant treaty with Russia reducing the number of strategic warheads deployed by each side and permitting mutual inspections. He also scored a major national-security success with the mission that killed Osama bin Laden in May 2011. However, Afghanistan

Americans were targets of terrorist attacks well before the September 11, 2001, assault that triggered the U.S. war on terror. In 1993 a bomb in the World Trade Center for which Al Qaeda claimed responsibility took the lives of six and wounded nearly a thousand Americans.

remains volatile; and the president has not been very successful diplomatically in getting hostile nations such as Iran and North Korea to abandon their nuclear ambitions. Nevertheless, the president received support from world leaders for the collaborative style he embraced in contrast to his predecessor. It was partly in recognition of this new tone that he was awarded the Nobel Peace Prize during his first year in office.

DEFENDING U.S. INTERESTS IN A CONSTANTLY CHANGING WORLD

Foreign and defense policy experts often explain the positions they advocate in terms of protecting national interests. What are national interests? How do we determine what will best serve these interests? And how do we achieve our interests when other nations' interests may clash with ours? To answer these questions we must first address the sometimes conflicting nature of the interests that we seek to protect as well as the dynamics of nation-state interactions.

Defining National Interests

The most important foreign policy goal facing any nation is maintaining its own security in the face of potential threats. Security comes in many forms. First is physical security from attacks like those of September 11, 2001. Nations must ensure the protection of their citizens and the integrity of their borders. Second is secure access to the resources needed for economic well-being. For example, until new sources of energy are abundantly available, the economic integrity of the United States depends upon access to oil around the globe. Third is promotion of values that maintain domestic institutions and that contribute to a world environment supportive of those values. For example, one of the stated goals of U.S. foreign policy is to support fledgling democracies. Democracies, we believe, tend to favor negotiated solutions over the violent resolution of conflict. Taken together, this constellation of military, economic, and ideological concerns about security constitute a country's **national interests**.

preemption Doctrine espoused by President George W. Bush permitting U.S. use of force to prevent hostile acts by its enemies even if we are uncertain about the time and place of the enemy attack.

national interests The constellation of military, economic, and ideological concerns surrounding a nation's security.

It is easy to see how security interests may clash. For example, the United States often has tolerated and even supported dictatorial regimes such as those of the shah in Iran (1941–1979), who served as a reliable ally and militant anticommunist in the oil-rich Middle East. The Nixon administration helped overthrow the democratically elected president of Chile, Salvador Allende, whom it viewed as hostile to U.S. business interests.[10] In fashioning foreign policy we must weigh the relative importance of these different interests and understand how each contributes to our national security. It also requires that we understand how nations perceive the actions of others in a constantly changing world.

Understanding Nation-State Dynamics: Perspectives and Strategic Choices

Foreign policy is generally guided by the assumption that nations act in a world that is anarchic, that is, one that lacks a recognized arbiter with the authority to settle disputes. As a result, each nation is limited in the pursuit of its own interests only by the strength of its own resources and the countervailing power of other nations.[11] Each nation weighs the military power, resources, and goodwill at its disposal and assesses how best to advance its interests. These assessments are guided by both broad theoretical perspectives and analytical tools that help policymakers map strategic choices.

Perspectives Foreign policy **realism** is one of the most venerable and persistent perspectives used by foreign policy professionals, although it exists in a variety of shades. Realists, like Henry Kissinger, secretary of state under President Richard Nixon, believe that national interests can best be assured by a military that is strong enough to deter other nations. Although realists place a premium on the nation's ability to take coercive action when necessary, they realize that alliances and peace treaties may also serve our interests. Nevertheless, peace, they believe, only can be achieved through the maintenance of a strong defense as a credible deterrent.[12]

realism In foreign policy, the belief that national interests are best assured by a strong military that can act as a deterrent to other nations.

foreign policy liberalism In foreign policy, the belief that national interests are best secured by building alliances and making conflict more costly than cooperation.

idealism In foreign policy, the belief that American values such as democracy, freedom, and cultural diversity promote our national interests and should be emulated by other nations.

Foreign policy liberalism focuses on the potential for cooperation among nations in meeting common goals such as prosperity and peace. Franklin Roosevelt's efforts to build the United Nations as a vehicle for averting war and the Truman administration's Marshall Plan to rebuild war-torn Europe are examples of liberal commitment to internationalism and the proposition that a stable world order is necessary for nations to grow and prosper. Foreign policy liberals believe that our national interests are best secured by building alliances that strengthen the bonds among nations, making conflict more costly than cooperation.

Closely aligned to liberalism is foreign policy **idealism**, which emphasizes the promotion of American values such as democracy, freedom, and cultural diversity. Such promotion, idealists believe, will attract nations wishing to emulate our success and to gain our support. Often foreign aid is contingent upon the recipient's accepting these principles and making tangible efforts to institutionalize them. Idealists believe spreading our values allows us to influence the actions other nations take as long as they believe that we are truly guided by them ourselves.[13] U.S. foreign policy idealists of the twentieth century include former presidents Woodrow Wilson and Jimmy Carter.

Although some political leaders rely more heavily on one of these perspectives than others, most foreign policy decisions are guided by a combination of approaches. **Neoconservatism**, one of the more notable recent hybrids, blends aspects of realism with idealism. Neoconservatives seek the dual goals of enhancing American military might and spreading support for democratic values around the globe. Neoconservatives such as former deputy secretary of defense Paul Wolfowitz molded George W. Bush's Middle East policy, including his doctrine of preemptive war. By 2006, however, the prolonged nature of the Iraq war and the lack of success in fostering democratic institutions in the Islamic world led some intellectual founders of neoconservatism to rethink their support for this theory.[14] The Obama administration does not seem tied to any one theoretical perspective. It has emphasized dialogue and multilateral cooperation but has not shied away from the unilateral use of force when necessary (for example, the troop buildup in Afghanistan). It has sought to reestablish the image of the United States as a country committed to lofty goals and the rule of law by ordering the closure of the Guantanamo detention center and outlawing extreme forms of interrogation prohibited by the Geneva Conventions. Different nations pose different challenges, and one size does not appear to fit all. As the administration's foreign policy challenges continue to unfold, so too may its overall approach to solving them.

Neoconservatives such as former deputy secretary of defense Paul Wolfowitz molded George W. Bush's Middle East policy, including his doctrine of preemptive war.

Strategic Choices In pursuing foreign policy options, political leaders of various theoretical persuasions often employ complex mathematical tools, such as game theory, to guide their deliberations. **Game theory** is built on the assumption that states act rationally in their self-interest. In an environment that is filled with uncertainty, each state attempts to maximize gains and minimize losses in its dealings with others. In weighing decisions, state leaders must decide if they should act alone or in concert with others in trying to get as much power or resources as they want. In some situations, gains and losses are absolute: a gain for one nation means a total loss for another, as in the case of all-out war. In other cases, gains and losses may be shared with other nations, as in the case of security agreements where nations trade away their right to develop nuclear weapons in return for the promise of protection by stronger nations.

Game theory allows policymakers to work through various scenarios in an attempt to develop incentives and deterrents that can entice other "rational" actors to do as the policymakers wish. Incentives can include protection by another country's military, as in the case of South Korea, where the United States has maintained a presence since the end of the Korean War in 1953. They can also be financial, as in the case of direct foreign aid or the sharing of technology with developing nations that want to compete in international markets. Deterrents include the use of military force but also reduction in trade, boycotts, or the freezing of foreign assets in U.S. banks. Game theorists have developed sophisticated algorithms designed to predict how nations will respond to changes in world affairs.

MAKING FOREIGN POLICY

Foreign policy links diplomatic, intelligence, economic, and military operations into a coherent framework for achieving American goals in the world. As we saw in earlier chapters, the constitutional authority for making and conducting such policies is shared by Congress and the president. However, the executive branch is in charge of day-to-day operations, and its role in the formation and execution of foreign policy decisions has grown steadily.

The Primacy of the Executive Branch

Overseeing the operations of agencies dealing with foreign and defense policies has been a feature of executive branch power since President Washington. For the most part, Americans are highly deferential to the president in his capacity as foreign policy chief (see Chapter 12). However, Congress, interest groups, and public opinion can significantly limit the president's options. The president relies on a wide range of departments and agencies to provide guidance on national security.

National Security Council Established in 1947 by Congress and made part of White House operations in 1949, the National Security Council

> **neoconservatism** Perspective advocating military strength and the promotion of American values abroad.

> **game theory** Foreign policy tool that allows policymakers to predict how nation-states will act to promote their self-interest.

OBAMA'S NATIONAL SECURITY TEAM

NATIONAL SECURITY ADVISOR **Thomas E. Donilon** is President Obama's second National Security Advisor. Donilon worked as assistant secretary of state for public affairs and has served as the chief of staff to the Secretary of State during the Clinton administration. He was an advocate for early disengagement from Afghanistan.

SECRETARY OF STATE **Hillary Rodham Clinton** was elected to the U.S. Senate from New York in 2000 and ran as a U.S. presidential candidate in 2008. As first lady during the tenure of the 42nd president, Clinton acted as an international goodwill ambassador championing women's rights.

DEFENSE SECRETARY **Leon Panetta** served as Director of the Central Intelligence Agency for the Obama administration from 2009 until 2011 when he replaced retiring Robert Gates. Panetta served as Chief of Staff and Director of the Office of Management and Budget under President Clinton following his service in Congress from 1977 to 1993.

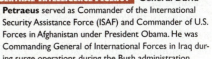

DIRECTOR OF NATIONAL INTELLIGENCE **Lt. Gen. James R. Clapper Jr.**, a retired Air Force lieutenant general and the Pentagon's top intelligence official, was appointed by President Obama in 2010 to replace Dennis Blair who resigned amid criticism for his handling of the attempted Christmas Day 2009 bombing of a Northwest Airlines jet. General Clapper served under George W. Bush as undersecretary of defense for intelligence.

DIRECTOR OF CENTRAL INTELLIGENCE AGENCY **General David Petraeus** served as Commander of the International Security Assistance Force (ISAF) and Commander of U.S. Forces in Afghanistan under President Obama. He was Commanding General of International Forces in Iraq during surge operations during the Bush administration.

SECRETARY OF HOMELAND SECURITY **Janet Napolitano** was appointed secretary midway through her second term as governor of the state of Arizona where she opened the first state counterterrorism center and spearheaded efforts in immigration reform. Previously, while serving as U.S. Attorney, she helped lead the domestic terrorism investigation into the Oklahoma City Bombing.

U.N. AMBASSADOR **Susan Rice** served as a Senior Advisor for National Security Affairs on the Obama for America Campaign. From 2002–2009, she was a Senior Fellow at the Brookings Institution where she focused on U.S. foreign policy, transnational security threats, weak states, global poverty, and development. From 1997 to 2001, Ambassador Rice was the U.S. Assistant Secretary of State for African Affairs.

U.S. Department of State

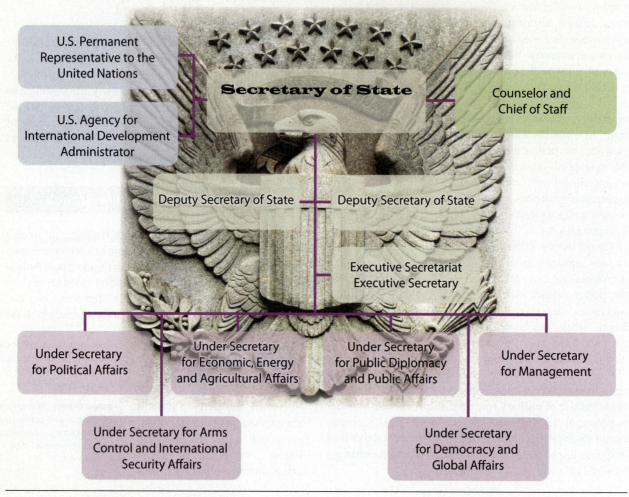

U.S. Permanent Representative to the United Nations

U.S. Agency for International Development Administrator

Secretary of State

Counselor and Chief of Staff

Deputy Secretary of State

Deputy Secretary of State

Executive Secretariat Executive Secretary

Under Secretary for Political Affairs

Under Secretary for Economic, Energy and Agricultural Affairs

Under Secretary for Public Diplomacy and Public Affairs

Under Secretary for Management

Under Secretary for Arms Control and International Security Affairs

Under Secretary for Democracy and Global Affairs

Source: Department of State.

(NSC) serves both to advise the president on defense and foreign policy matters and to coordinate the implementation of policy among various government agencies. By law and custom, membership includes the president; the vice president; the secretaries of state, defense, and the treasury; the chairman of the Joint Chiefs of Staff, who represents the military leaders of each branch of the armed forces; the director of national intelligence; and the national security advisor (NSA) to the president. Other agency heads may be invited to contribute to deliberations as needed. President Obama has added the secretaries of energy, homeland security, the attorney general, and the ambassador to the United Nations. The entire council rarely meets, so the NSA serves as the president's liaison with the other members; he also meets daily with the president to brief him regarding current challenges and the status of ongoing policies. The director of national intelligence also briefs the president daily. Obama is far more of a hands-on president than his predecessor on matters of national security. He was inti-

Foreign Service Corps of U.S. diplomats stationed around the world.

mately involved with the details of his troop buildup in Afghanistan, frequently chairing his regular meetings with the NSC,[15] and he was intimately involved in planning the details of the raid that killed Osama bin Laden.

Department of State The State Department is the chief diplomatic arm of the U.S. government. It is responsible for leading and coordinating U.S. representation abroad and for conveying U.S. foreign policy to foreign governments and international organizations. It operates abroad through diplomatic offices or embassies in approximately 180 countries and through mission offices that act as liaisons with international organizations such as the United Nations. Its staff negotiates agreements and treaties on issues ranging from trade to nuclear weapons. Domestically, it is in charge of issuing passports and visas to U.S. citizens traveling abroad and, with the Justice Department, for monitoring the issuance of visas granted to foreign visitors.

The secretary of state oversees the conduct of agency business by civil servants and the staffing of the **Foreign Service**, the diplomatic corps that represents U.S. inter-

ests abroad. Although top diplomats to foreign countries are political appointees, the experts who staff the embassies are drawn from Foreign Service professionals who undergo intensive training within the agency. Secretaries of state are often eager to reflect their agency's positions when they offer advice to the president. Whether or not their views make their way into policy depends on a number of factors, including their personal relationship with the president, consistency between their views and presidential priorities, and the strength of personalities with whom they must compete. In the days leading to the American invasion of Iraq, Colin Powell's views were often overlooked in favor of stronger voices within the White House, such as Vice President Cheney, and in the Department of Defense, such as Secretary Donald Rumsfeld. Although President Obama's secretary of state, Hillary Rodham Clinton, chided Obama for his lack of foreign policy experience during the 2008 presidential primary campaign, her views on most foreign policy issues do not seem to differ greatly from the president's. Clinton was granted considerable autonomy by the president in organizing the State Department and has played an active role in foreign policy decisions, including the troop buildup in Afghanistan.[16]

Department of Defense Like the departments of State and Treasury, the Department of Defense is as old as the Republic. However, it is constantly adapting to new technologies and strategies in carrying out its primary mission of maintaining combat readiness to defend the nation. It employs more than 650,000 civilians and 1.4 million active-duty service personnel. The secretary of defense reports to the president and sits atop a defense structure in which each branch of the armed services is represented by a military department responsible for training and equipping it and by the leadership offices for the army, navy, air force, and marines, which are responsible for strategic planning and coordination of military operations and are represented by the Joint Chiefs of Staff. The Joint Chiefs are the military leaders of the army, navy, air force, and marines; each is appointed by the president and confirmed by the Senate for nonrenewable four-year terms. The chairman of the Joint Chiefs is eligible for two renewable two-year terms. Reporting to the Joint Chiefs of Staff are leaders of command operations in various military theaters as well as officers in charge of special units.

U.S. Department of Defense

Secretary of Defense
Deputy Secretary of Defense

Chairman of the Joint Chiefs of Staff	Military Departments	Office of the Secretary of Defense	United Combatant Commands
Vice Chairman of the Joint Chiefs of Staff			

Source: Department of Defense.

Intelligence Community In response to intelligence failures regarding the existence of weapons of mass destruction in Iraq, Congress passed the Intelligence Reform and Terrorism Prevention Act of 2004, a key provision of which was the creation of the Office of the Director of National Intelligence, which is responsible for coordinating intelligence from a variety of domestic and foreign sources and reporting findings to the president. As titular head of the intelligence community, the director oversees and coordinates intelligence gathering from 16 agencies. This office is also responsible to the legislative branch that created it, and the director often reports to select intelligence committees in each house.

Perhaps the best-known member of the nation's intelligence community is the Central Intelligence Agency (CIA). The CIA grew out of the Office of Strategic Services (OSS), which was created by Franklin Roosevelt in 1942 to collect and manage strategic information during World War II. The National Security Act of 1947 gave rise to its current moniker and function in providing national security intelligence to senior U.S. policymakers. Headed by a director who is appointed by the president and confirmed by the Senate, the agency collects intelligence through human and electronic sources, evaluates it, and provides assessments of threats to the nation's security. Although some agents in the field perform hazardous duty by infiltrating terrorist organizations and spying on foreign governments, the bulk of CIA employees spend their time translating and analyzing foreign newspapers, checking websites, and evaluating aerial maps and photographs.

Intelligence that has a bearing on national security is also gathered by other agencies in the Department of Defense, including various branches of the military; by the Federal Bureau of Investigation (FBI) and the Drug Enforcement Administration (DEA), which are both part of the Justice Department; and by other bodies. According to the 9/11 Commission, which investigated the attacks on the World Trade Center and the Pentagon, the failure of the intelligence community to identify and track the perpetrators was due in part to the lack of intelligence sharing among these agencies.[17] Reorganization under the supervision of the Office of the Director of National Intelligence was meant to integrate foreign, military, and domestic intelligence in defense of the homeland and of U.S. interests abroad.

Some civil libertarians fear that the resulting amalgamation of information from domestic and foreign sources may lead to unwarranted spying on U.S. citizens. In fact, in 2002, President Bush signed a secret order authorizing the NSA to eavesdrop on U.S. citizens and foreign nationals in the United States, despite previous legal prohibitions against this practice. The aim of the program was to rapidly monitor the phone calls and other communications of people in the United States believed to have contact with suspected associates of Al Qaeda and other overseas terrorist groups. Techniques employed under the program included the use of data harvesting to monitor and sort through the e-mail, telephone calls, and other communications of hundreds, and perhaps thousands, of people. In 2007, the president signed into law the Protect America Act, which eased restrictions on surveillance of terrorist suspects when one or both parties are located overseas. As a result, communications that begin or end in a foreign country may be wiretapped.

In response to claims by critics that these laws gave the executive branch almost unchecked power to snoop on citizens, Congress and the president agreed to a new law in June 2008. The law strengthens the ability of intelligence officials to eavesdrop on foreign targets and allows them to conduct emergency wiretaps without court orders on American targets for a limited time if it is determined that important national security information would otherwise be lost. However, the law limits the use of such wiretaps to terrorism and espionage cases and calls for greater oversight, including advance approval by a secret court created under the Foreign Intelligence Surveillance Act of 1978. The **FISA court** is staffed by 11 judges appointed by the chief justice of the United States to serve seven-year terms. The 2008 legislation also included a controversial provision to extend immunity to telecommunication companies that had acceded to prior administration requests for information about their customers at a time when the transfer of such information

Member Agencies of the Intelligence Community

Central Intelligence Agency	National Security Agency
National Reconnaissance Office	Defense Intelligence Agency
Energy Intelligence (Department of Energy)	National Geospatial-Intelligence Agency
Department of Homeland Security Intelligence	Intelligence, Surveillance and Reconnaissance (Air Force)
Federal Bureau of Investigation (Justice Department)	Drug Enforcement Administration (Justice Department)
Bureau of Intelligence and Research	Office of Terrorism and Financial Intelligence (Treasury Department)
Marine Corps Intelligence	
Naval Intelligence	U.S. Coast Guard Intelligence
	Army Military Intelligence

Source: Carroll Publishing, Office of the Director of National Intelligence, Appendix C: Intelligence Primer from the Commission on the Intelligence Capabilities of the United States Regarding Weapons of Mass Destruction (March 2005). Accessed online at www.pbs.org/wbbh/pages/frontline///////darkside/etc/cia.html on September 6, 2008.

was not authorized. The Obama administration supported these same provisions when they were unsuccessfully challenged in court. The Obama administration also supported the extension of several surveillance provisions of the USA PATRIOT Act that expired in December 2009, including allowing investigators to use roving wiretaps to monitor suspects who may be trying to escape detection by switching cell phone numbers, and obtaining business records of national security targets. The USA PATRIOT Act was first passed in the wake of the September 11, 2001, terrorist attacks and has undergone congressional revision and reauthorization since then.

Other Executive Agencies In an era dominated by concerns about global terror and the global economy, virtually no executive agency is without some role in advancing U.S. foreign policy goals. The departments of Commerce and Treasury help expand peaceful trade; the Drug Enforcement Administration (DEA) attempts to interdict drug shipments; the departments of Energy, Defense, and Commerce all monitor the types of technology we transfer to potentially hostile nations; the Department

President Obama ordered the closure of the Guantanamo detention center, which had undermined world support for the Bush administration's war on terror. However, Obama had difficulty finding nations willing to accept detainees.

of Health and Human Services provides technical support to nations combating HIV/AIDS. All of these activities advance the national security goal of creating "a more secure and prosperous world that benefits the American people and the world community."[18]

During the Bush administration, Vice President Cheney exercised unprecedented power in foreign-policy making by creating additional ad hoc working groups that conducted their own reviews of intelligence and made input directly to the president. He worked closely with an inner circle of lawyers, including his chief of staff, David Addington, to formulate policies on torture and the detainment of enemy combatants.[19]

> **Foreign Intelligence Surveillance Act court (FISA court)** Secret court housed in the Justice Department and used to oversee requests by federal agencies for surveillance warrants based on suspected espionage or terrorism.

The current vice president, Joseph Biden, is included in most White House foreign policy discussions and has traveled the globe to deliver foreign policy statements on behalf of the Obama administration. He is also charged with building support for foreign policy proposals in Congress.[20] His role is far more circumscribed than that of his predecessor, however, and Biden himself has been critical of placing too much authority in the hands of any vice president.[21]

Congress's Role

Congress can play a key role in foreign and defense policy even if it is sometimes overshadowed by executive branch power. In Chapter 11, we learned that the Framers split authority for national security by authorizing the president to take immediate action to defend against attacks on U.S. interests but reserved to Congress the prerogative to declare war. We also learned that presidents have usually managed to secure authorization from Congress for waging war short of formal declarations. Nevertheless, Congress is not powerless to oppose presidential powers related to defense and security. Congress can cut off funding for war; it can reject presidential requests for authority to commence hostile activities; it can expand or reject presidential requests for foreign aid; and, by holding hearings on presidential policies and procedures, Congress can convey its own preferences. The House Permanent Select Committee on Intelligence and the Senate Select Committee on Intelligence receive briefings from the intelligence community, conduct oversight hearings, and authorize budgets for intelligence operations. In addition, the Senate can reject treaties with other nations. These checks on presidential authority are not merely hypothetical.

Congress has successfully reined in presidential authority on a number of occasions. Nevertheless, in times of international tension, support for presidential authority is sometimes difficult for congressional opponents to overcome. Such was the case in 2007, when a newly elected Democratic Congress repeatedly triedunsuccessfully to end the war in Iraq by rejecting President Bush's call for the infusion of more troops. In 2011, the House rebuked President Obama for not obtaining Congressional consent before committing resources to a military operation in Libya designed to protect the civilian population. However, they did not take any direct action to end our involvement in the NATO-led mission.

One of Congress's principal foreign policy functions is to provide funding for military, diplomatic, and foreign aid programs. The cost of being the world's only superpower is enormous. According to the Congressional Budget office, about 20 percent of the fiscal year 2009 federal budget (approximately $515 billion) was spent on national defense. This does not include additional appropriations of about $200 billion for the wars in Iraq and Afghanistan. Critics charge, however, that actual defense-related expenditures are much higher but are hidden because they are subsumed under other categories of spending.[22] For example, we continue to pay the costs of past military operations in the form of payments for veterans' benefits and interest on money borrowed to pay for past wars. The chart on the next page shows that these additional expenditures swell the defense portion of the budget to over 50 percent.

Congressional Actions Influencing War Termination

Year	Congressional action
1801	Amended treaty ending quasi-war with France, forced further negotiations
1919	Rejected Versailles Treaty that ended World War I
1919	Tie vote on resolution calling for withdrawal of U.S. troops intervening in Soviet Russia, prompting order for withdrawal within days
1923	Voted on resolution asking for immediate return of U.S. occupation troops from Germany, prompting withdrawal announcement within days
1970	Barred further military operations in Cambodia following U.S. withdrawal
1973	Forced U.S. air combat operations in Southeast Asia to end
1975	Rejected last-minute requests for aid to South Yemen
1993	Wrote into law Clinton administration promise to withdraw troops from Somalia

Source: Adapted from Charles A. Stevenson, *Congress At War: The Politics of Conflict since 1789* (Dulles, VA: Potomac Books, 2007), 68.

Other Actors

You will recall from Chapter 15 that the costs and benefits of national security are widely dispersed. As a result, policymakers receive advice from many segments of the political community. Both nonpartisan and partisan groups can play a significant advisory role. For example, the Council on Foreign Relations is a well-respected, nonpartisan body composed of scholars, corporate and government leaders, and other interested citizens who study foreign policy and try to influence its course through publications and meetings with policymakers. Think tanks with particular ideological perspectives also weigh in. The conservative Heritage Foundation and the more liberal-leaning Brookings Institution are among the most influential. Political movements sometimes spawn think tanks as incubators for new policies to advance their worldviews. The neoconservative movement created the Project for the New American Century.

When it comes to policies dealing with particular countries or specific weapons, national security policy often involves the concentrated costs and benefits that generate intense competition by groups with an immediate interest in their out-

Defense Expenditures FY 2009—Different Perspectives

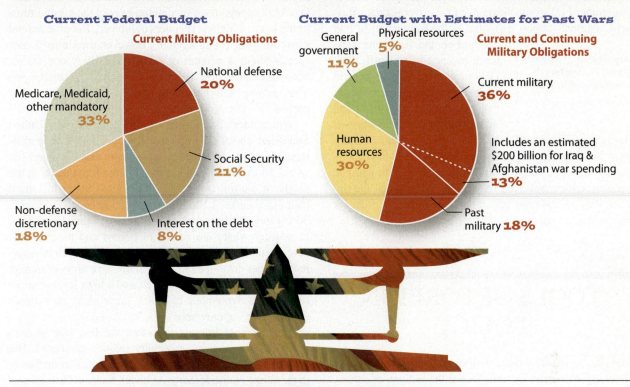

Current Federal Budget

Current Military Obligations

- National defense **20%**
- Medicare, Medicaid, other mandatory **33%**
- Social Security **21%**
- Non-defense discretionary **18%**
- Interest on the debt **8%**

Current Budget with Estimates for Past Wars

Current and Continuing Military Obligations

- General government **11%**
- Physical resources **5%**
- Current military **36%**
- Human resources **30%**
- Includes an estimated $200 billion for Iraq & Afghanistan war spending **13%**
- Past military **18%**

Source: (Left figure) Office of Management and Budget; (Right figure) War Resisters League.

comes. For example, political action committees, such as the powerful American Israel Public Affairs Committee, regularly donate millions of dollars to candidates who support the defense of Israel; whereas a number of smaller, vocal Muslim American groups espouse the cause of Islamic nations in the Middle East. Defense contractors are also active participants in foreign policy debates.

The Public's Role

Ultimately, foreign and defense policy is guided by the limits of public opinion. As we saw in Chapter 6, for the most part Americans display far less knowledge and interest in international and foreign affairs than in domestic policy matters. Nevertheless, they are quick to direct their attention to foreign policy issues when American interests are threatened. Some public opinion experts have employed the term *cognitive misers* in explaining the selective attention of Americans to foreign affairs and to the likelihood that they will employ mental shortcuts in fashioning opinions about foreign policy.[23] For example, phrases such as "soft on defense" or "war on terrorism" are useful for framing Americans' views about foreign policy options. Policymakers are well aware of how useful such phrases can be in building support for their policies.

Although Americans give their leaders wide latitude in making foreign and defense policy decisions, they will react when they feel policies are counterproductive. Americans gave President Bush strong support for the war in Afghanistan following the September 11, 2001, attacks, but

Although the Iraq war drew antiwar protests, their size and intensity is not as great as those directed against the Vietnam War at a time when young men were faced with a military draft.

support was more muted for the war in Iraq, which many Americans could not directly connect with the events of September 11. Despite the quick victory over Saddam Hussein, national support dwindled as the occupation in Iraq dragged on and insurgent resistance increased. By April 2008, Gallup reported that 63 percent of the American public believed that the war was a mistake; and dissatisfaction with the war was partly responsible for Barack Obama's presidential victory over his Republican rival, John McCain.[24] Policymakers do not slavishly follow polls when dealing with national security issues; however, they do understand that the options they pursue must attract popular support in order for the policies to succeed.

diplomacy The use of peaceful means to build support for common interests and to avoid warfare.

TOOLS OF FOREIGN POLICY

Nations, particularly those with significant resources, have a variety of means for influencing the actions of others. Military power is the bluntest weapon in any nation's foreign policy arsenal; and nuclear weaponry, for those who have it, inspires the most fear. However, nations also attempt to influence the actions of others through diplomacy, the promise of financial aid, and support from international organizations.

Military Power

You may have heard the saying that "War is the continuation of politics by other means." The author was the Prussian military historian and theorist Carl von Clausewitz (1780–1831), who was reflecting the realist position that

tial aggressors. The defense budget of the United States, however, dwarfs those of all other nations. In actual dollars, U.S. expenditures on defense exceed the expenditures of the next 14 highest spenders combined. Relative to total gross domestic product (GDP), however, the United States spends about 4 percent of GDP on military operations, about the same percentage as China. Some smaller nations, among them Israel and Jordan, spend more than 8.5 percent.[25]

Where does all of this money go? Currently, the United States has about 1.5 million active members of the military. Many are stationed at permanent bases around the world. More than 170,000 served in the Iraq theater at the height of the military surge. The United States has more than 7,500 tanks, 2,100 fighters, 235 bombers, 27 cruisers, 30 frigates, 49 destroyers, 80 submarines, and 12 carriers. In addition, there are scores of bombs and missiles and new weaponry—including an air defense system—currently under development. This impressive array of human and material resources has purchased a high level of security. But, as September 11, 2001, made clear, no nation's defenses are impenetrable.

Despite these impressive assets, the Iraq war strained some of our resources, especially military personnel. The war required more personnel and money than its architects in the White House foresaw. Although Saddam Hussein was toppled from power in a relatively short time, the insurgency that resulted from the subsequent U.S. occupation has proved long and deadly. Critics warn that President Obama's deployment of additional troops to Afghanistan has the potential to drag on and undermine support for his foreign policy.

Diplomacy

Diplomacy is the use of peaceful means to build support for common interests and to avoid warfare. It involves the use of incentives and deterrents in order to build alliances and support for a nation's policies. Often, diplomacy involves face-to-face discussion, as when the president or

THE COST of being the world's only superpower is enormous. . . . 20 percent of the national budget in 2009 (approximately $515 billion) was spent on national defense.

military power is a nation's most potent resource in furthering its interests. Military might is both an offensive weapon and a powerful deterrent. Enemies can be dissuaded from using military force if their opponent has clear military superiority. As a result, one of the most important jobs of a nation's leaders is to ensure that the nation has sufficient military power to dissuade others from attacking and to successfully defend the country if it is attacked.

Nations spend enormous sums on national defense. Even small nations with anemic economies find it necessary to spend significant sums in order to ward off poten-

the secretary of state meets with foreign leaders to bridge differences. Presidents have met regularly in recent years with Israeli and Palestinian leaders in an attempt to broker a lasting peace, as President Obama did during his first few months in office. Former Senate Majority Leader George Mitchell, named by President Obama as special envoy for the Middle East, resigned with little to show for his efforts after spending more than two years attempting to bring Palestinians and Israelis to the negotiating table. Sometimes, diplomacy involves working with other nations as intermediaries; for instance, the United States relied on

global **Perspectives**

Military Expenditures

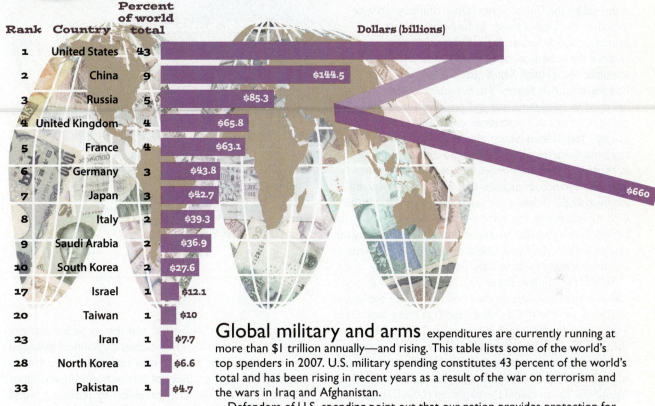

Rank	Country	Percent of world total	Dollars (billions)
1	United States	43	$660
2	China	9	$144.5
3	Russia	5	$85.3
4	United Kingdom	4	$65.8
5	France	4	$63.1
6	Germany	3	$43.8
7	Japan	3	$42.7
8	Italy	2	$39.3
9	Saudi Arabia	2	$36.9
10	South Korea	2	$27.6
17	Israel	1	$12.1
20	Taiwan	1	$10
23	Iran	1	$7.7
28	North Korea	1	$6.6
33	Pakistan	1	$4.7

Global military and arms expenditures are currently running at more than $1 trillion annually—and rising. This table lists some of the world's top spenders in 2007. U.S. military spending constitutes 43 percent of the world's total and has been rising in recent years as a result of the war on terrorism and the wars in Iraq and Afghanistan.

Defenders of U.S. spending point out that our nation provides protection for many other countries and contributes to global stability. Critics argue that our allies should pick up more of the tab for their own defense and that current levels of spending are unsustainable given the current level of debt.

1. As a percentage of U.S. military spending, how much do our European allies combined spend on military operations?
2. How might our allies respond if the U.S. cut back on military aid?
3. Why is Saudi Arabia's spending greater than Israel's?
4. What factors might account for China's rise to second place in military spending?

Notes: U.S. figure includes funding for wars and nuclear weapons. North Korea figure is estimate from U.S. State Department. Data from Congressional Research Service, Office of Management and Budget, International Institute for Strategic Studies, State Department. Figures for other countries are converted into U.S. dollars by various methods that attempt to capture market exchange rates. For additional methodological considerations, see source listed below.

Source: U.S. Defense Spending vs. Global Defense Spending, Center for Arms Control and Non-Proliferation, February 26, 2009.

China to broker a deal with the North Koreans to abandon the development of nuclear weapons (a matter that has not been resolved). Sometimes diplomacy involves the use of multinational coalitions to provide joint security. For example, the North Atlantic Treaty Organization (NATO), founded in 1949, seeks to provide mutual deterrence and defense against common enemies as well as to promote consultation, crisis management, and economic partnerships among member nations. Since the breakup of the former Soviet Union, NATO membership has expanded to include Estonia, Latvia, and Lithuania, as well as several formerly Communist nations that were part of the Soviet

sphere, among them the Czech Republic, Hungary, Poland, Bulgaria, Romania, Slovakia, and Slovenia.

Diplomacy, usually the domain of specialists in the Department of State, is a subtle weapon of foreign policy. Success depends on a number of factors, including the skillful deployment of rewards and punishments, the willingness of parties to negotiate, and domestic pressures faced by national leaders. Diplomats, like skilled chess players, must think several moves ahead, recognizing that any action they take will evoke a response for which they must be prepared.

Foreign Aid

As the richest nation in the world, the United States can make friends and influence the policies of other nations by making loans and grants available to them. Some of this money is designated as military aid; the recipient can use it to enhance its own internal security in ways approved by the United States. Often, military aid is returned to the United States to buy weaponry and armaments from American firms. Grants and loans may enhance the security of both donor and receiver. For example, the United States gives some Middle Eastern countries money for law enforcement designed to stem terrorism and provides funds to Latin American countries to curb drug trafficking. The United States also makes money available to developing countries to assist them in expanding their economies, particularly when cash infusions provide a measure of social stability for the impoverished. Assistance is given for humanitarian causes such as combating the spread of HIV/AIDS. Finally, the United States provides assistance to multinational organizations such as the United Nations and the World Bank to accomplish many of these same objectives.

In all, the United States provides assistance to about 150 countries and international bodies. Among the largest recipients in recent years have been Iraq and Israel. Since September 11, 2001, aid has increased for Afghanistan, Pakistan, Turkey, Jordan, and Indonesia, which are seen as key partners in the war on terrorism. These programs are administered by a variety of agencies including the U.S. Agency for International Development (USAID), the Treasury Department, the Department of Defense (DOD), and the State Department. The House International Relations Committee and the Senate Foreign Relations Committee have primary congressional responsibility for authorizing foreign aid programs, whereas the Appropriations Committee in each house appropriates the funds.[26]

Polls have shown that many Americans are not convinced of the effectiveness of aid programs; In fact, it is often difficult to prove that these funds achieve the desired ends. Nevertheless, ending these programs would limit the tools available to policymakers for achieving U.S. security goals and could push some nations into alliance with our enemies. Although the dollar amount of foreign aid has increased in recent years, after a long period of decline, it still constitutes less than 1 percent of the national budget. The United States is the largest international economic aid donor in absolute terms, but when aid is calculated as a percentage of gross national income it is the smallest contributor among the major donor governments.[27]

Working with International Organizations

The threats that our nation faces are not solely military in nature. We face economic threats in the form of oil-supply disruptions, public health threats in the form of medical

U.S. Economic Assistance to the World

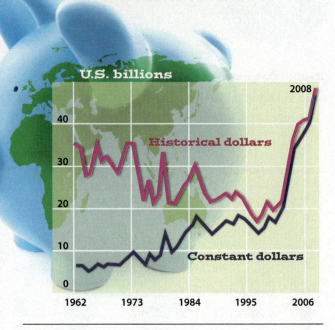

Source: USAID.

pandemics such as swine flu, and threats to the security of our friends and neighbors caused by political upheaval or rampant poverty. To cope with such threats, the United States works with a variety of international organizations to share information and resources, to influence world opinion, and to develop solutions to problems that cross national boundaries.

In coping with potential health crises, for example, the United States works closely with the World Health Organization (WHO), an arm of the United Nations. WHO monitors disease outbreaks, assesses the performance of health systems around the globe, serves as a repository for research on major diseases affecting the international community, and provides technical support to countries coping with medical emergencies. For example, it assists nations facing HIV/AIDS epidemics with programs for treatment and prevention as well as with help obtaining needed drugs and diagnostic supplies. In 2009, WHO declared the swine flu a pandemic because of its rapid spread across the globe. The declaration, the first in 41 years, sped vaccine production and spurred governments to take action to combat the disease.

Another international partner is the World Bank, which offers financial and technical assistance to developing countries. Composed of 187 member nations, the World Bank provides low-interest loans, interest-free credit, and grants to developing countries for education, health, infrastructure development, communications, and many other purposes. By tradition, the bank's president is a U.S. national and is nominated by the United States, the bank's largest shareholder.

The UN Security Council is charged with settling international disputes and authorizing military action. It is comprised of 10 rotating member nations and 5 permanent members: China, France, Russia, the United Kingdom, and the United States.

Diplomats in the State Department build support for American policy through bilateral discussions with individual nations and through multilateral organizations such as NATO. But it is also necessary at times to engage all nations in dialogue in order to avert war, broker solutions to international crises, or work cooperatively to address humanitarian needs. The United Nations (UN) provides a forum for such activities. Chartered in 1945, the United Nations was intended to promote international peace and security as well as to facilitate cooperation in solving international economic, social, cultural, and humanitarian problems. Critics are quick to point out that the structure of the body limits its effectiveness in maintaining world peace. The Security Council, which is charged with settling disputes and authorizing military action, comprises 10 rotating member nations and 5 permanent members: China, France, Russia, the United Kingdom, and the United States. Any permanent member nation can prevent action by exercising its veto power.

The United States has met with varying degrees of success in securing UN support for its foreign policy agenda. At the urging of the United States, the Security Council voted in August 1990 to condemn Iraq's invasion of Kuwait, and subsequently to use UN armed forces to oppose Iraq's occupation of its neighbor. U.S. commanders led multinational forces in the Persian Gulf War, which lasted six weeks and resulted in the Iraqi withdrawal from Kuwait. Subsequently, the UN agreed to monitor Iraq's compliance with a resolution requiring Iraq to eliminate its weapons of mass destruction. The United States and the UN also have cooperated in a number of peacekeeping operations, including a 1999 mission in Kosovo. In 2003, however, the United States was unable to persuade the UN to authorize a mission to disarm Iraq of the weapons of mass destruction it suspected Iraq of having. Although UN members supported the use of economic sanctions, Security Council members, including France, Russia, and Germany, questioned the reliability of intelligence estimates on WMD and declined to support a military invasion. Instead, the United States formed its own "coalition of the willing," including Great Britain, Australia, Italy, and many smaller nations, to topple the Iraqi regime. The UN has been more willing to consider sanctions against North Korea and Iran in order to stop their development of nuclear weapons. President Obama has signaled a willingness to work with the United Nations to reduce nuclear threats and to combat terrorism.

CONFRONTING THE FUTURE

From the end of World War II until the dismantling of the Berlin Wall in 1989, the world was dominated by two superpowers in a bipolar world. Each held the other in check with the threat of sufficient nuclear force to obliterate it. The superpowers often fought each other by proxy, taking up the cause of surrogates, as in Vietnam and in Afghanistan during the 1979 Soviet invasion, which pitted the various opposition groups known as mujahideen against the Red Army. Since the demise of the Soviet empire, nations have struggled to come to grips with the fact that there remains but one major superpower in a unipolar world.

That is not to say that the United States can automatically get its way. It continues to rely on its allies to advance its trade and security interests, and upon all countries to confront global threats such as terrorism.[28] And the rise of a unipolar world with the United States as its leader has not gone unchallenged. Russia's invasion of neighboring Georgia in 2008 was, in part, a statement by the Russians that they would not sit idly by while the United States expanded its influence into Russia's backyard. Few observers believed this would reopen the Cold War, but the invasion indicated Russia's willingness to aggressively defend its interests. Even some longtime allies have resisted U.S. attempts to "go it alone" in foreign policy. Nevertheless, the United States, as the world's leading power, must forge consensus in the coming years on a number of fronts, including continuing threats from terrorism and nuclear weaponry and the growing challenges stemming from regional conflicts and the rapid rise of China as an economic and military power.

The Terrorist Threat

The roots of terrorism are many and complex. They include, but are not limited to, extremist ideology, feelings of powerlessness, and lack of economic opportunity. The nature of the terrorist threat facing the United States today is linked to Islamic fundamentalism, which grew in response to the partition of Palestine and the establishment of Israel under UN General Assembly Resolution 181 in 1947. Palestinians who were displaced by the resolution were dealt another blow in 1967, when Israel's army preempted Egypt's call for an Arab invasion by capturing Arab territories in the Six-Day War. Unable to match the firepower of Israel and its Western allies, Islamic militants supporting the reclamation of Palestinian territories developed a sophisticated network of terrorist supporters in Muslim countries throughout the Middle East and South Asia. Often aided by state sponsors such as Iran and Syria, these militants spread terrorist techniques worldwide,

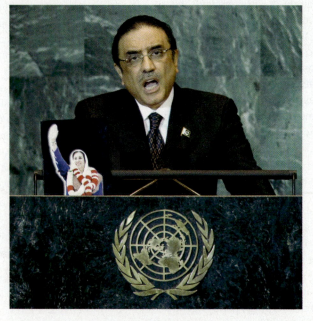

Pakistani President Asif Ali Zardari is a crucial player in America's effort to rout Al Qaeda from Afghanistan since many members of the terrorist group have found safe haven in his country.

organizing the attacks on Israeli athletes at the Munich Olympics in 1972; the bombing of Pan Am Flight 103 in 1988; the bombing of U.S. embassies in Kenya and Tanzania in 1998; the attack on the USS *Cole* in 2000; and, of course, the attacks on the World Trade Center and the Pentagon on September 11, 2001. Although the terrorist network comprises various distinct factions and movements, it is united by an animus for Israel and the Western nations supporting it.

Because terrorism is a tactic, not a nation, how does one defend against it? Until 2001, the United States had treated terrorism much like a criminal activity, protecting targets as best it could and prosecuting terrorists as criminals. For example, suspects were prosecuted and convicted in U.S. courts for their role in the 1993 World Trade Center bombing and the 1998 U.S. embassy bombings in Kenya and Tanzania. The trials produced significant evidence implicating Al Qaeda and Osama bin Laden in terrorist crimes. After September 11, 2001, American strategy changed. First, given the evidence that the attacks were directed by bin Laden and that he was being harbored by the Taliban regime in Afghanistan, the United States and a coalition of allies—with widespread international support—attacked that country, replacing the Taliban government with a new regime led by Hamid Karzai. However, there was less international support for the second phase of the American response, the invasion of Iraq.

The future of fighting terrorism remains cloudy. As noted, the Iraq war proved hugely unpopular with both world and American public opinion, especially after waves of sectarian violence resulted in thousands of American and Iraqi deaths. The violence was abetted by Syrians, Iranians, and Saudis who poured over the porous borders of Iraq to exploit the chaos and foment discontent with the American occupiers. The new government, installed with American help, lacked the cohesion necessary to get things done to enhance security and rebuild the country. Nevertheless, as the Bush administration came to an end, Iraqi prime minister Nouri al-Maliki was eager to negotiate an end to the American occupation, even while violence in Afghanistan was once again on the rise.

President Obama ended the U.S. combat mission in Iraq on August 31, 2010, but approximately 35,000 troops remain to provide security and training for the Iraqi military. Escalating violence in Afghanistan led Obama to send additional military forces there, and he

Faisal Shazhad, a Pakistani-born American citizen, pleaded guilty to attempting to set off a car bomb in New York's Times Square, saying that Islamic extremists would continue to attack the U.S.

renewed his call for international partners to assist in rooting out a resurgent Taliban. The successful raid on Abbottabad that killed Osama bin Laden, along with substantial progress in disrupting Al Qaeda outposts, led the president to call for a reduction of forces in August 2011, although a substantial number will remain until 2014. Meanwhile, diplomatic efforts have been stepped up to craft a political solution in which the Taliban renounce violence in return for a share in power.

Pakistan poses an equally daunting threat since Al Qaeda has increased its presence there. The raid on Osama bin Laden revealed that his mansion was located near a military school, raising questions about whether that country was harboring the 9/11 mastermind. The situation in Pakistan is particularly dangerous because Pakistan is a nuclear power, and world leaders worry about the possibility that terrorists might gain access to nuclear materials.

The Nuclear Threat

Since the end of the Cold War, the United States and Russia have destroyed a significant portion of the nuclear arsenals that they once maintained. Nevertheless, the United States still has more than four thousand operational weapons and an additional five thousand in stockpiles.[29] The U.S. arsenal is dwarfed, however, by the number of nuclear weapons that Russia maintains. It is estimated that Russia holds more than 5,500 operational nuclear weapons and warehouses more than 14,000 in stockpiles. Weapons once maintained in former territories were all to have been returned to Russia.

In 1991, the U.S. Congress passed the Cooperative Threat Reduction Act (CTR), pledging to help Russia dismantle and destroy some of its nuclear weapons and as-

sociated delivery systems. As part of this program, which originally stemmed from a request by Soviet president Mikhail Gorbachev, the United States has spent more than $400 million per year disarming nuclear weapons and facilities in Russia, Ukraine, Kazakhstan, and former Soviet satellites. President Obama and Russian president Dmitry Medvedev signed a new nuclear arms treaty in April 2010. It calls for about a 25 percent reduction in strategic warheads, provides for mutual inspections, and encourages members of the world's nuclear club to do the same. The strategic arms reduction (START) treaty was ratified by the Senate in December 2010.

Perhaps the most wide-ranging nuclear treaty was the 1968 Nuclear Non-Proliferation Treaty signed by the United States, the USSR, the United Kingdom, and 133 countries without nuclear weapons. This treaty, made permanent in May 1995, instituted measures to prevent countries without nuclear weapons from initiating weapons production. The treaty's success, however, has been mixed. Today, at least eight nations are part of the "nuclear club": the United States, Russia, the United Kingdom, France, China, India, Pakistan, and most likely Israel. South Africa has dismantled the nuclear arsenal that it once maintained. Some of the nuclear players are located in the most unstable regions of the world. India and Pakistan, for example, harbor long-standing grievances stemming from the partition of the subcontinent by Great Britain in 1947. They have fought sporadically, and recent terrorist bombings in India are suspected to have their roots in Pakistan. In addition, the current regime of Pakistan has been quite unstable in the face of Taliban violence in the region, raising substantial questions about the security of its nuclear arsenal. What is more, it is suspected that Iran is pursuing a nuclear weapons program. If true, this poses a direct threat to Israel, a nation that most experts believe maintains its own nuclear arsenal.

North Korea, long believed to be developing a nuclear weapon, dismantled one of the cooling towers at a nuclear plant where plutonium was processed. In response, in June 2008, President Bush announced his intention to remove North Korea from the list of state sponsors of terrorism and lift some long-standing economic sanctions once the information it has submitted can be verified. More recently, however, North Korea has test-fired missiles capable of carrying nuclear warheads and threatened to bring its plans to create a nuclear weapon to fruition, triggering renewed efforts by the world community to isolate the country.

Concerns over Iran's nuclear ambitions are also on the rise. Despite unified Western opposition to Iran's continued development of fissile material (which it claims it will use for energy production), attempts to secure access to inspect nuclear sites have been stymied by a leader, Mah-

Perhaps even more disconcerting than the prospect of unstable nations obtaining nuclear weaponry is the threat of non-nation-state actors, such as extremist groups, gaining access to nuclear material. Although security experts believe extremist groups would not be able to develop a nuclear bomb—let alone the means of delivering one—they could mix radioactive material with other explosive agents in a "dirty bomb" should they be able to obtain the raw materials. The U.S. Nuclear Regulatory Commission has determined that although the explosive impact of a "dirty bomb" would not be much greater than that of a conventional bomb, such an explosion could create widespread panic, contaminate property, and necessitate costly cleanup.[30]

moud Ahmadinejad, who has proclaimed commitment to the destruction of Israel. President Obama secured United Nations approval for increased sanctions against Iran and for a document denouncing the development of nuclear weapons by countries such as North Korea and Iran, committing the world body to negotiating a treaty banning the production of fissile material and urging nation-states that have not yet done so to ratify the Comprehensive Test Ban Treaty (CTBT) negotiated in 1996. He committed himself to getting the United States itself to sign on, something the U.S. Senate refused to do in 1999.

Since the Reagan administration, the United States has been developing a missile defense system that would potentially shield America and its allies from incoming nuclear missiles by exploding them in mid flight. The Bush administration proposed deploying components of the system in the former Soviet satellites of Poland and the Czech Republic. The Obama administration announced it would scrap the deployment of missile defenses in Eastern Europe and instead develop a more mobile and flexible system designed to shoot down short- and medium-range missiles likely to be delivered by rogue states with nuclear ambitions such as Iran.

Threats Posed by Regional Conflicts

As we have learned, the world system is anarchic in the sense that there is no designated umpire to settle regional conflicts. Still, nations today are connected by a vast array of economic, communication, and transportation networks, so that upheavals in one region are likely to have an impact elsewhere. A serious conflict in the Middle East is likely to disrupt oil supplies and send world markets reeling. An infectious disease outbreak in Africa or Asia can result in a pandemic that all nations must confront. Globalization has tied the fate of nations much more closely together than in the past. Regional problems that once might not have drawn close scrutiny by a major power can no longer be ignored.

Middle East Although the roots of Middle East tensions are numerous, complex, and not easily resolved, a solution to the continuing dispute over the establishment of a permanent Palestinian state might go a long way toward dif-

The Oslo Accords, signed by Palestinian leader Yasser Arafat and Israeli prime minister Yitzhak Rabin at a public ceremony at the White House in 1993, outlined a framework for future relations between the two parties.

fusing tension in the region. During the 1967 Six-Day War, which was spawned by border disputes, Israel captured the Golan Heights from Syria, the West Bank from Jordan, and the Gaza Strip and Sinai Peninsula from Egypt, displacing thousands of Palestinians. Despite efforts by the United Nations to arrange a trade of captured lands for a peace agreement, the Palestinian Liberation Organization (PLO), which claimed leadership of those displaced by the war, refused to drop its support for the destruction of Israel. Shortly thereafter, Israelis began building permanent settlements in the occupied regions, intensifying Palestinian resentment. Over the next few decades, American presidents made numerous attempts to broker agreements among regional leaders. One major breakthrough occurred in 1979 when President Jimmy Carter arranged a peace treaty between Egypt and Israel. A second major breakthrough occurred in 1993 with the signing of the 1993 Oslo Accords, in which the PLO recognized Israel's right to exist in exchange for the promise of Israeli withdrawal from unspecified territory in the West Bank and the Gaza Strip. Talks implementing the accords with the goal of creating a two-state solution—a secure Israel with official recognition by previously belligerent nations, and an independent Palestinian state—were intended to continue for a number of years until a final settlement was reached. Since then, Israel has ceded some local control to Palestinians in the occupied territories, but neither side has been willing to bring negotiations to a conclusion. Israel has complained about continuing Palestinian terrorism, and the Palestinians have complained about Israeli foot-dragging and settlement expansion in regions that were supposed to be returned to Palestinian control. President Obama has made repeated overtures to both Israeli and Palestinian leaders to reopen a peace initiative in the region with the express goal of achieving the two-state solution. Peace efforts were complicated in 2011 with the reconciliation of two rival Palestinian factions, one of which (HAMAS) is a sworn enemy of Israel.

Arab Spring

In December 2010, a Turkish man in Tunisia burned himself to death to protest his treatment by police, triggering a series of protests and revolutions in neighboring countries that have dramatically altered politics in this sensitive region of the world. Often sparked by an outpouring of youth and the use of social media to coordinate events, these demonstrations, sometimes referred to as the Arab Spring, have produced a change of leadership in nations that had seen decades of authoritarian rule. Tunisian President Zine El Abidine Ben Ali fled to Saudi Arabia and Hosni Mubarak resigned as Egyptian president after a reign of 30 years. Additional upheavals in Algeria, Jordan, Sudan, Oman, Yemen, Syria, Morocco, and Bahrain triggered a variety of concessions by political leaders struggling to stay ahead of the demonstrators.

While some of these changes took place with relatively little violence, this was not the case in all nations. For ex-

ample, in Libya and Syria entrenched leaders mounted substantial resistance. In Libya, Muammar Gaddafi waged warfare against his own people, triggering a civil war. In response to a potential bloodbath, NATO forces led an effort to protect the civilian population and provide humanitarian relief. President Obama pledged air support but would not commit ground forces.

The long-term impact of these revolutions is uncertain. While President Obama has lauded peaceful protest in the region as "prodemocracy movements," the direction of these popular upheavals is difficult to predict. Some observers warn that some of these nations may seek extremist leadership, further complicating peace efforts in the region.

Tahrir Square in Cairo was the site of prodemocracy demonstrations that toppled the nation's president, Hosni Mubarak, after a reign of 30 years.

Africa Africa has been riddled by civil wars pitting ethnic and tribal rivals against each other and resulting in displacement, starvation, and massive loss of life. Recent conflict in Darfur set Arab militia groups such as the Janjaweed, widely believed to be supported by the government of Sudan, against a variety of non-Arab rebel groups that claimed the government was ignoring their needs. Thus far the conflict has resulted in more than 400,000 deaths from violence and disease and the displacement of as many as 2.5 million. Like the ethnic conflict between Hutus and Tutsis in Rwanda years earlier, the carnage in Darfur has been called genocide by the U.S. government and many nongovernmental aid organizations. In 2006, a peace agreement was reached between Sudan and some rebel groups, and the United Nations sent a peacekeeping force to the region. However, Sudan has objected to the presence of peacekeepers, and there is continuing sporadic violence between various factions and tribes. Meanwhile, humanitarian groups have called for massive amounts of aid to help those who remain displaced and without food, shelter, and medical supplies. A referendum in early 2011 on self-determination for Southern Sudan led to the partitioning of the nation. In July 2011, South Sudan became the world's newest country.

Hot or Not?

Does the U.S. have a duty to intervene when genocide occurs anywhere in the world?

Other recent conflicts have involved Uganda (1987–present), Angola (1974–2002), Sierra Leone (1991–2002), Liberia (1999–2003), and the Democratic Republic of Congo (1998–2004) where more than four million people lost their lives. The lack of economic development, slow progress toward modernization, and the persistence of tribal and ethnic rivalries plague the region. Even once-stable nations like Kenya and Zimbabwe have experienced instability in recent years. Zimbabwe's president, Robert Mugabe, who helped bring independence to his country, led a regime that became increasingly repressive and corrupt. In 2008, he agreed to form a power-sharing government with his one-time rival, Morgan Tsvangirai, who was named the country's prime minister. The relationship has been rocky, however, and many nations are reluctant to provide needed economic aid for fear that the money will be misspent.

Events in Africa may not present an immediate threat to American national security, but widespread unrest and poverty breed extremism as well as disease. They present opportunities for terrorists to exploit tensions and build safe harbors for their ideologies of hatred. They serve as the breeding grounds for pandemics that can spread quickly to other regions. As a result, American policymakers cannot afford to ignore the challenges posed by events on this continent.

The Rise of China

The People's Republic of China will play an increasingly important role in world affairs in the coming decades. Despite its Communist government, China has adapted since the death of its founder, Mao Zedong, to a Western-style commercial economy, one that has been growing at over 9 percent per year in the recent past. At this rate, China will become the second-largest economy in the world by 2020, behind only the United States. Reasons for this growth include China's ability to keep costs of production low, to attract foreign capital, and to build huge trade surpluses with other nations that buy its relatively inexpensive products. In 2007 Americans spent more than $237 billion more on Chinese goods than the Chinese spent on U.S. products, and until the recent recession, the gap was growing by more than 25 percent per year.[31]

With the money that it receives, China is able to flex its military and economic muscles. China is now the second-largest military spender, behind only the United States. It has increased its military spending by double digits every year since 1993. Military analysts say that China is purchasing increasingly sophisticated weaponry. They note, for example, a recent successful test of an antisatellite missile, which destroyed a defunct Chinese weather satellite, and the deployment of a state-of-the-art jet fighter, the J-10, which Chinese and foreign experts have described as a breakthrough for the Chinese defense industry.[32]

China is also using its financial clout to finance U.S. debt. China is now second only to Japan as a foreign holder of U.S. securities. These securities include Treasury debt, U.S. agency debt, U.S. corporate debt, and U.S. equities. Given the United States' relatively low savings rate, the U.S. economy depends heavily on foreign capital inflows from countries with high savings rates, such as China, to help promote growth and to fund our federal budget deficit, as we discussed in Chapter 15.[33] China's rapid economic growth is also a growing concern for those worried about dwindling oil supplies and global warming.

The United States and China have maintained fairly cordial relations in recent years because of their reciprocal economic needs. Nevertheless, two flashpoints continue to dominate U.S.-China relations: Taiwan and China's record on human rights. China considers Taiwan, long an ally of the United States, as part of its territory, but it has not attempted to annex it. U.S. policy centers on maintaining good relations with both China and Taiwan and on easing tensions between them. With regard to human rights, many Americans remember the Chinese government's brutal clampdown on free expression after the student demonstrations in Tiananmen Square in 1989. More recently, human rights advocates have called attention to China's suppression of religious liberty in Tibet, which China claimed with much bloodshed after World War II.

For the most part, American diplomats seem content to lecture Chinese leaders on the importance of human rights without letting the subject interfere with other negotiations. President Bush refused to boycott the opening ceremony of the 2008 Olympic Games in Beijing, unlike some world leaders who wanted to protest China's human rights record. Bush claimed a boycott would only alienate the Chinese and threaten future cooperation. The Obama administration seems content to follow the same policy course with China.

CIVIC ENGAGEMENT AND FOREIGN POLICY TODAY

As we have seen, Americans appear to pay less attention to matters of foreign policy than to domestic policy, except during major crises or catastrophes such as the terrorist attacks of September 11, 2001. One reason for this relative inattention is that most Americans believe that there is little that they can do to make a difference in this arena. Of course, voters can voice their preferences at the polls. But, as we learned in earlier chapters, elections are blunt instruments that do not address the complexities of policymaking. Even when the voters register their disagreement with a policy, as they did in 2006 and 2008 when opposition to the Iraq war produced electoral change, altering course in foreign policy is not easily or quickly accomplished. Still, there are ways in which individual Americans can make a positive contribution to the lives of others and enhance the humanitarian reputation of the United States throughout the world.

nongovernmental organizations (NGOs) Nonprofit citizens' groups organized for a variety of charitable and humanitarian purposes on a local, national, or international level.

Each year, **nongovernmental organizations (NGOs)** send volunteers and money all over the world to feed the hungry, alleviate poverty, combat disease, educate the young, and provide expertise to help local populations build civil societies and the infrastructure needed to succeed in development. NGOs are nonprofit, voluntary citizens' groups organized on a local, national, or international level. On the international stage, NGOs perform a variety of service and humanitarian functions, bring citizen concerns to governments, advocate and monitor policies, and encourage political participation. Although some NGOs are partly funded by or housed within larger bodies such as the UN, for the most part governments do not play an active role in their governance or operation.

PORTRAIT OF AN ACTIVIST

Bill and Melinda Gates

What would you do with $56 billion? Bill Gates, founder and Chairman of Microsoft Corporation and his wife, Melinda, have decided on nothing less than changing the world. Their foundation, the Bill & Melinda Gates Foundation, sponsors numerous projects throughout the world to combat disease and promote economic development.

One program focuses on treating and curtailing the spread of malaria. Malaria is responsible for nearly one million deaths per year, 90 percent of which occur in Africa. Eighty-five percent of those who die are children under five years of age.

The foundation is pursuing the development of a vaccine that is safe and affordable by the year 2025. Current treatments are expensive, and parasites are becoming increasingly resistant to them. In the meantime, funding provides topical treatment to prevent the spread of the disease.

The foundation has similar programs aimed at combating HIV/AIDS, pneumonia, and tuberculosis. To find out how you can get involved, see their website at http://www.gatesfoundation.org/global-health/Pages/overview.aspx.

NGOs offer many and varied opportunities for Americans interested in working to help others in foreign lands. Some NGOs are well known, such as the American Red Cross and Save the Children. Many are associated with religious organizations, such as the Quakers. For instance, the American Friends Service Committee operates the Mexico Summer Project, which brings together youth from diverse communities for seven weeks to live with indigenous peoples in the Sierra Norte de Puebla, Mexico. The project aims to expand social justice and sustainable development in the region.

soft power The ability to persuade others without coercion.

Such opportunities not only provide direct help to those in need but also spread goodwill. This goodwill is part of **soft power**, the ability to shape the preferences of others without coercion.[34] Soft power is spread through the sharing of American values, customs, and culture. Through civic outreach, we foster cooperation and inspire others to share our concerns for fairness and just outcomes. We motivate others to want the same outcomes that we want. You can read about one such example in this chapter's "Portrait of an Activist."

Summary ⌄⌄

1. **What are the major goals of American foreign policy?**

- Foreign policy seeks to secure the nation's defense and to promote its economic and ideological interests.

- Defining a country's national interest involves making strategic choices about how best to use military, economic, and moral strength to keep the nation safe and secure.

- Foreign policy is guided by theoretical perspectives, such as realism, foreign policy liberalism, idealism, and neo-conservatism, and by analytic tools such as game theory.

2. **Who are the principal actors in the foreign-policy-making process?**

- The president plays the primary role in foreign-policy making through executive agencies that include the National Security Council, the Director of National Intelligence, the Department of State, and the Department of Defense.

Congress also plays a role through its appropriations and approval of international treaties by the Senate.

- Foreign-policy making can also involve interest groups, defense contractors, think tanks, nongovernmental organizations, and the general public, whose support is needed to sustain policies.

3. **What are the tools that foreign-policy makers have at their disposal?**

- Foreign-policy makers employ military powers, diplomacy, and foreign aid in advancing U.S. interests.

- They also seek to forge ties with other nations and with multinational organizations to achieve shared objectives.

- Foreign-policy makers will use these tools to confront such future challenges as the terrorist threat, the nuclear threat, regional conflicts, and the rise of China as a major economic and military power.

APPENDIX

★★

- ★ The Declaration of Independence
- ★ The Constitution of the United States of America (Annotated)
- ★ Federalist Paper No. 10 (James Madison)
- ★ Federalist Paper No. 51 (James Madison)

THE DECLARATION OF INDEPENDENCE

IN CONGRESS, JULY 4, 1776

The Unanimous Declaration of the Thirteen United States of America

When, in the course of human events, it becomes necessary for one people to dissolve the political bands which have connected them with another, and to assume, among the powers of the earth, the separate and equal station to which the laws of nature and of nature's God entitle them, a decent respect to the opinions of mankind requires that they should declare the causes which impel them to the separation.

We hold these truths to be self-evident, that all men are created equal; that they are endowed by their Creator with certain unalienable rights; that among these, are life, liberty, and the pursuit of happiness. That, to secure these rights, governments are instituted among men, deriving their just powers from the consent of the governed; that, whenever any form of government becomes destructive of these ends, it is the right of the people to alter or to abolish it, and to institute a new government, laying its foundation on such principles, and organizing its powers in such form, as to them shall seem most likely to effect their safety and happiness. Prudence, indeed, will dictate that governments long established, should not be changed for light and transient causes; and, accordingly, all experience hath shown, that mankind are more disposed to suffer, while evils are sufferable, than to right themselves by abolishing the forms to which they are accustomed. But, when a long train of abuses and usurpations, pursuing invariably the same object, evinces a design to reduce them under absolute despotism, it is their right, it is their duty, to throw off such government and to provide new guards for their future security. Such has been the patient sufferance of these colonies, and such is now the necessity which constrains them to alter their former systems of government. The history of the present King of Great Britain is a history of repeated injuries and usurpations, all having, in direct object, the establishment of an absolute tyranny over these States. To prove this, let facts be submitted to a candid world:

He has refused his assent to laws the most wholesome and necessary for the public good.

He has forbidden his governors to pass laws of immediate and pressing importance, unless suspended in their operation till his assent should be obtained; and, when so suspended, he has utterly neglected to attend to them.

He has refused to pass other laws for the accommodation of large districts of people, unless those people would relinquish the right of representation in the legislature; a right inestimable to them, and formidable to tyrants only.

He has called together legislative bodies at places unusual, uncomfortable, and distant from the depository of their public records, for the sole purpose of fatiguing them into compliance with his measures.

He has dissolved representative houses repeatedly for opposing, with manly firmness, his invasions on the rights of the people.

He has refused, for a long time after such dissolutions, to cause others to be elected; whereby the legislative powers, incapable of annihilation, have returned to the people at large for their exercise; the state remaining, in the meantime, exposed to all the danger of invasion from without, and convulsions within.

He has endeavored to prevent the population of these States; for that purpose, obstructing the laws for naturalization of foreigners, refusing to pass others to encourage their migration hither, and raising the conditions of new appropriations of lands.

He has obstructed the administration of justice, by refusing his assent to laws for establishing judiciary powers.

He has made judges dependent on his will alone, for the tenure of their offices, and the amount and payment of their salaries.

He has erected a multitude of new offices, and sent hither swarms of officers to harass our people, and eat out their substance.

He has kept among us, in time of peace, standing armies, without the consent of our legislatures.

He has affected to render the military independent of, and superior to, the civil power.

He has combined, with others, to subject us to a jurisdiction foreign to our Constitution, and unacknowledged by our laws; giving his assent to their acts of pretended legislation:

For quartering large bodies of armed troops among us:

For protecting them by a mock trial, from punishment, for any murders which they should commit on the inhabitants of these States:

For cutting off our trade with all parts of the world:

For imposing taxes on us without our consent:

For depriving us, in many cases, of the benefit of trial by jury:

For transporting us beyond seas to be tried for pretended offences:

For abolishing the free system of English laws in a neighboring province, establishing therein an arbitrary government, and enlarging its boundaries, so as to render it at once an example and fit instrument for introducing the same absolute rule into these colonies:

For taking away our charters, abolishing our most valuable laws, and altering, fundamentally, the powers of our governments:

For suspending our own legislatures, and declaring themselves invested with power to legislate for us in all cases whatsoever.

He has abdicated government here, by declaring us out of his protection, and waging war against us.

He has plundered our seas, ravaged our coasts, burnt our towns, and destroyed the lives of our people.

He is, at this time, transporting large armies of foreign mercenaries to complete the works of death, desolation, and tyranny, already begun, with circumstances of cruelty and perfidy scarcely paralleled in the most barbarous ages, and totally unworthy of the head of a civilized nation.

He has constrained our fellow citizens, taken captive on the high seas, to bear arms against their country, to become the executioners of their friends, and brethren, or to fall themselves by their hands.

He has excited domestic insurrections amongst us, and has endeavored to bring on the inhabitants of our frontiers, the merciless Indian savages, whose known rule of warfare is an undistinguished destruction of all ages, sexes, and conditions.

In every stage of these oppressions, we have petitioned for redress, in the most humble terms; our repeated petitions have been answered only by repeated injury. A prince, whose character is thus marked by every act which may define a tyrant, is unfit to be the ruler of a free people.

Nor have we been wanting in attention to our British brethren. We have warned them, from time to time, of attempts made by their legislature to extend an unwarrantable jurisdiction over us. We have reminded them of the circumstances of our emigration and settlement here. We have appealed to their native justice and magnanimity, and we have conjured them, by the ties of our common kindred, to disavow these usurpations, which would inevitably interrupt our connections and correspondence. They, too, have been deaf to the voice of justice and of consanguinity. We must, therefore, acquiesce in the necessity which denounces our separation, and hold them as we hold the rest of mankind, enemies in war, in peace, friends.

We, therefore, the representatives of the United States of America, in general Congress assembled, appealing to the Supreme Judge of the world for the rectitude of our intentions, do, in the name, and by the authority of the good people of these colonies, solemnly publish and declare, that these united colonies are, and of right ought to be, free and independent states: that they are absolved from all allegiance to the British Crown, and that all political connection between them and the state of Great Britain is, and ought to be, totally dissolved; and that, as free and independent states, they have full power to levy war, conclude peace, contract alliances, establish commerce, and to do all other acts and things which independent states may of right do. And, for the support of this declaration, with a firm reliance on the protection of Divine Providence, we mutually pledge to each other our lives, our fortunes, and our sacred honor.

The foregoing Declaration was, by order of Congress, engrossed, and signed by the following members:

JOHN HANCOCK

New Hampshire
Josiah Bartlett
William Whipple
Matthew Thornton

Massachusetts Bay
Samuel Adams
John Adams
Robert Treat Paine
Elbridge Gerry

Rhode Island
Stephen Hopkins
William Ellery

Connecticut
Roger Sherman
Samuel Huntington
William Williams
Oliver Wolcott

New York
William Floyd
Philip Livingston
Francis Lewis
Lewis Morris

New Jersey
Richard Stockton
John Witherspoon
Francis Hopkinson
John Hart
Abraham Clark

Pennsylvania
Robert Morris
Benjamin Rush
Benjamin Franklin
John Morton
George Clymer
James Smith

George Taylor
James Wilson
George Ross

Delaware
Caesar Rodney
George Reed
Thomas M'Kean

Maryland
Samuel Chase
William Paca
Thomas Stone
Charles Carroll,
   of Carrollton

Virginia
George Wythe
Richard Henry Lee
Thomas Jefferson

Benjamin Harrison
Thomas Nelson, Jr.
Francis Lightfoot Lee
Carter Braxton

North Carolina
William Hooper
Joseph Hewes
John Penn

South Carolina
Edward Rutledge
Thomas Heyward, Jr.
Thomas Lynch, Jr.
Arthur Middleton

Georgia
Button Gwinnett
Lyman Hall
George Walton

Resolved, That copies of the Declaration be sent to the several assemblies, conventions, and committees, or councils of safety, and to the several commanding officers of the continental troops; that it be proclaimed in each of the United States, at the head of the army.

THE CONSTITUTION OF THE UNITED STATES OF AMERICA[1]

We the People of the United States, in Order to form a more perfect Union, establish Justice, insure domestic Tranquility, provide for the common defence, promote the general Welfare, and secure the Blessings of Liberty to ourselves and our Posterity, do ordain and establish this CONSTITUTION for the United States of America.

>> See Chapter 1 for comparison of democratic form of government with other forms and reasons for civic engagement.

ARTICLE I

SECTION 1

All legislative Powers herein granted shall be vested in a Congress of the United States, which shall consist of a Senate and House of Representatives.

SECTION 2

The House of Representatives shall be composed of Members chosen every second Year by the People of the several States, and the Electors in each State shall have the Qualifications requisite for Electors of the most numerous Branch of the State Legislature.

No Person shall be a Representative who shall not have attained to the Age of twenty-five Years, and been seven Years a Citizen of the United States, and who shall not, when elected, be an Inhabitant of that State in which he shall be chosen.

[Representatives and direct Taxes[2] shall be apportioned among the several States which may be included within this Union, according to their respective Numbers, which shall be determined by adding to the whole Number of free Persons, including those bound to Service for a Term of Years, and excluding Indians not taxed, three fifths of all other Persons.][3] The actual Enumeration shall be made within three Years after the first Meeting of the Congress of the United States, and within every subsequent Term of ten Years, in such Manner as they shall by Law direct. The Number of Representatives shall not exceed one for every thirty Thousand, but each State shall have at Least one Representative; and until such enumeration shall be made, the State of New Hampshire shall be entitled to chuse three, Massachusetts eight, Rhode-Island and Providence Plantations one, Connecticut five, New York six, New Jersey four, Pennsylvania eight, Delaware one, Maryland six, Virginia ten, North Carolina five, South Carolina five, and Georgia three.

When vacancies happen in the Representation from any State, the Executive Authority thereof shall issue Writs of Election to fill such Vacancies.

The House of Representatives shall chuse their Speaker and other Officers; and shall have the sole Power of Impeachment.

>> The states set suffrage requirements subject to the 14th, 15th, 19th, 24th, and 26th Amendments.

>> The three-fifths compromise was made obsolete by the 13th and 14th Amendments.

SECTION 3

The Senate of the United States shall be composed of two Senators from each State, chosen by the Legislature thereof, for six Years; and each Senator shall have one Vote.

>> See Chapter 11 for differences between House of Representatives and the Senate.

[1.] This version, which follows the original Constitution in capitalization and spelling, was published by the United States Department of the Interior, Office of Education, in 1935.
[2.] Altered by the Sixteenth Amendment.
[3.] Negated by the Fourteenth Amendment.

>> This clause was modified by the 17th Amendment that provides for the direct election of senators.

Immediately after they shall be assembled in Consequence of the first Election, they shall be divided as equally as may be into three Classes. The Seats of the Senators of the first Class shall be vacated at the Expiration of the second Year, of the second Class at the Expiration of the fourth Year, and of the third Class at the Expiration of the sixth Year, so that one-third may be chosen every second Year; and if Vacancies happen by Resignation, or otherwise, during the Recess of the Legislature of any State, the Executive thereof may make temporary Appointments until the next Meeting of the Legislature, which shall then fill such Vacancies.

No Person shall be a Senator who shall not have attained to the Age of thirty Years, and been nine Years a Citizen of the United States, and who shall not, when elected, be an Inhabitant of that State for which he shall be chosen.

The Vice President of the United States shall be President of the Senate, but shall have no vote, unless they be equally divided.

The Senate shall chuse their other Officers, and also a President pro tempore, in the absence of the Vice President, or when he shall exercise the Office of President of the United States.

The Senate shall have the sole Power to try all Impeachments. When sitting for that purpose they shall be on Oath or Affirmation. When the President of the United States is tried, the Chief Justice shall preside: And no person shall be convicted without the Concurrence of two thirds of the Members present.

Judgment in Cases of Impeachment shall not extend further than to removal from Office, and disqualification to hold and enjoy any Office of honor, Trust, or Profit under the United States: but the Party convicted shall nevertheless be liable and subject to Indictment, Trial, Judgment and Punishment, according to Law.

SECTION 4

>> Congress based the Voting Rights Act of 1965 on this section to protect the right to vote. See Chapter 5.

The Times, Place and Manner of holding Elections for Senators and Representatives, shall be prescribed in each State by the Legislature thereof; but the Congress may at any time by Law make or alter such Regulations, except as to the Places of Chusing Senators.

>> The 20th Amendment has invalidated this paragraph.

The Congress shall assemble at least once in every Year, and such Meeting shall be on the first Monday in December, unless they shall by Law appoint a different Day.

SECTION 5

Each House shall be the Judge of the Elections, Returns and Qualifications of its own Members, and a Majority of each shall constitute a Quorum to do Business; but a smaller number may adjourn from day to day, and may be authorized to compel the Attendance of absent Members, in such Manner, and under such Penalties, as each House may provide.

Each House may determine the Rules of its Proceedings, punish its Members for disorderly Behaviour, and, with the Concurrence of two thirds, expel a Member.

Each House shall keep a Journal of its Proceedings, and from time to time publish the same, excepting such Parts as may in their Judgment require Secrecy; and the Yeas and Nays of the Members of either House on any question shall, at the Desire of one fifth of those Present, be entered on the Journal.

Neither House, during the Session of Congress, shall, without the Consent of the other, adjourn for more than three days, nor to any other Place than that in which the two Houses shall be sitting.

SECTION 6

The Senators and Representatives shall receive a Compensation for their Services, to be ascertained by Law, and paid out of the Treasury of the United States. They shall in all Cases, except Treason, Felony, and Breach of the Peace, be privileged from Arrest during their Attendance at the Session of their respective Houses, and in going to and returning from the same; and for any Speech or Debate in either House, they shall not be questioned in any other Place.

No Senator or Representative shall, during the Time for which he was elected, be appointed to any civil Office under the Authority of the United States, which shall have been created, or the Emoluments whereof shall have been increased, during such time; and no Person holding any Office under the United States shall be a Member of either House during his continuance in Office.

SECTION 7

All Bills for raising Revenue shall originate in the House of Representatives; but the Senate may propose or concur with Amendments as on other bills.

Every Bill which shall have passed the House of Representatives and the Senate, shall, before it becomes a Law, be presented to the President of the United States; if he approve he shall sign it, but if not he shall return it, with his Objections, to that House in which it shall have originated, who shall enter the Objections at large on their Journal, and proceed to reconsider it. If after such Reconsideration two thirds of that House shall agree to pass the bill, it shall be sent, together with the objections, to the other House, by which it shall likewise be reconsidered, and if approved by two thirds of that House, it shall become a Law. But in all such Cases the Votes of both Houses shall be determined by Yeas and Nays, and the Names of the Persons voting for and against the Bill shall be entered on the Journal of each House respectively. If any Bill shall not be returned by the President within ten Days (Sundays excepted) after it shall have been presented to him, the Same shall be a Law, in like Manner as if he had signed it, unless the Congress by their Adjournment prevent its Return, in which Case it shall not be a Law.

Every Order, Resolution, or Vote to which the Concurrence of the Senate and House of Representatives may be necessary (except on a question of Adjournment) shall be presented to the President of the United States; and before the Same shall take Effect, shall be approved by him, or being disapproved by him, shall be repassed by two thirds of the Senate and House of Representatives, according to the Rules and Limitations prescribed in the Case of a Bill.

SECTION 8

The Congress shall have Power To lay and collect Taxes, Duties, Imposts and Excises, to pay the Debts and provide for the common Defence and general Welfare of the United States; but all Duties, Imposts and Excises shall be uniform throughout the United States;

>> This general clause gives the national government the authority to pursue the domestic and foreign policies discussed in Chapters 15 and 16.

To borrow money on the credit of the United States;

To regulate Commerce with foreign Nations, and among the several States, and with the Indian Tribes;

To establish a uniform rule of Naturalization, and uniform Laws on the subject of Bankruptcies throughout the United States;

To coin Money, regulate the Value thereof, and of foreign Coin, and fix the Standard of Weights and Measures;

To provide for the Punishment of counterfeiting the Securities and current Coin of the United States;

To establish Post Offices and post Roads;

To promote the Progress of Science and useful Arts, by securing for limited Times to Authors and Inventors the exclusive Right to their respective Writings and Discoveries;

To constitute Tribunals inferior to the Supreme Court;

To define and punish Piracies and Felonies committed on the high Seas, and Offenses against the Law of Nations;

To declare War, grant Letters of Marque and Reprisal, and make Rules concerning Captures on Land and Water;

To raise and support Armies, but no Appropriation of Money to that Use shall be for a longer Term than two Years;

To provide and maintain a Navy;

To make Rules for the Government and Regulation of the land and naval forces;

To provide for calling forth the Militia to execute the Laws of the Union, suppress Insurrections and repel Invasions;

To provide for organizing, arming, and disciplining the Militia, and for governing such Part of them as may be employed in the Service of the United States, reserving to the States respectively, the Appointment of the Officers, and the Authority of training the Militia according to the discipline prescribed by Congress;

>> The listing of the enumerated powers of the national government serves as the basis of the extent of national power with respect to the states (Chapter 3), with respect to civil liberties (Chapter 4), and with respect to congressional and presidential powers (Chapters 11 and 12).

To exercise exclusive Legislation in all Cases whatsoever, over such District (not exceeding ten Miles square) as may, by Cession of particular States, and the acceptance of Congress, become the Seat of the Government of the United States, and to exercise like Authority over all Places purchased by the Consent of the Legislature of the State in which the Same shall be, for the Erection of Forts, Magazines, Arsenals, Dock-yards, and other needful Buildings;—And

>> This clause served as the basis of the Supreme Court's implied powers doctrine first espoused in *McCulloch v. Maryland*.

To make all Laws which shall be necessary and proper for carrying into Execution the foregoing Powers, and all other Powers vested by this Constitution in the Government of the United States, or in any Department or Officer thereof.

SECTION 9

The Migration or Importation of such Persons as any of the States now existing shall think proper to admit, shall not be prohibited by the Congress prior The Constitution of the United States of America to the Year one thousand eight hundred and eight, but a tax or duty may be imposed on such Importation, not exceeding ten dollars for each Person.

The privilege of the Writ of Habeas Corpus shall not be suspended, unless when in Cases of Rebellion or Invasion the public Safety may require it.

No bill of Attainder or ex post facto Law shall be passed.

>> These limitations on congressional power reveal a heritage of rights and liberties that existed before the addition of the Bill of Rights. See Chapter 4.

>> The poll tax was invalidated by the 24th Amendment.

No capitation, or other direct, Tax shall be laid unless in Proportion to the Census or Enumeration herein before directed to be taken.

No Tax or Duty shall be laid on Articles exported from any State.

No Preference shall be given by any Regulation of Commerce or Revenue to the Ports of one State over those of another: nor shall Vessels bound to, or from, one State, be obliged to enter, clear, or pay Duties in another.

No Money shall be drawn from the Treasury, but in Consequence of Appropriations made by Law; and a regular Statement and Account of the Receipts and Expenditures of all public Money shall be published from time to time.

No Title of Nobility shall be granted by the United States: And no Person holding any Office of Profit or Trust under them, shall, without the Consent of the Congress, accept of any present, Emolument, Office, or Title, of any kind whatever, from any King, Prince, or foreign State.

SECTION 10

No State shall enter into any Treaty, Alliance, or Confederation; grant Letters of Marque and Reprisal; coin Money; emit Bills of Credit; make any Thing but gold and silver Coin a Tender in Payment of Debts; pass any Bill of Attainder, ex post facto Law, or Law impairing the Obligation of Contracts; or grant any Title of Nobility.

No State shall, without the Consent of the Congress, lay any Imposts or Duties on Imports or Exports, except what may be absolutely necessary for executing its inspection Laws; and the net Produce of all Duties and Imposts, laid by any State on Imports or Exports, shall be for the use of the Treasury of the United States; and all such Laws shall be subject to the Revision and Control of the Congress.

No state shall, without the Consent of Congress, lay any duty of Tonnage, keep Troops, or Ships of War in time of Peace, enter into any Agreement or Compact with another State, or with a foreign Power, or engage in War, unless actually invaded, or in such imminent Danger as will not admit of delay.

ARTICLE II

SECTION 1

The executive Power shall be vested in a President of the United States of America. He shall hold his Office during the Term of four years, and, together with the Vice President, chosen for the same Term, be elected, as follows:

» Limits on a presidential term were added in the 20th Amendment.

Each State shall appoint, in such Manner as the Legislature thereof may direct, a Number of Electors, equal to the whole Number of Senators and Representatives to which the State may be entitled in the Congress: but no Senator or Representative, or Person holding an Office of Trust or Profit under the United States, shall be appointed an Elector.

[The Electors shall meet in their respective States, and vote by Ballot for two persons, of whom one at least shall not be an Inhabitant of the same State with themselves. And they shall make a List of all the Persons voted for, and of the Number of Votes for each; which List they shall sign and certify, and transmit sealed to the Seat of the Government of the United States, directed to the President of the Senate. The President of the Senate shall, in the Presence of the Senate and House of Representatives, open all the Certificates, and the Votes shall then be counted. The Person having the greatest Number of Votes shall be the President, if such Number be a Majority of the whole Number of Electors appointed; and if there be more than one who have such Majority, and have an equal Number of Votes, then the House of Representatives shall immediately chuse by Ballot one of them for President; and if no Person have a Majority, then from the five highest on the List the said House shall in like Manner chuse the President. But in chusing the President, the Votes shall be taken by States, the Representation from each State having one Vote; a quorum for this Purpose shall consist of a Member or Members from two-thirds of the States, and a Majority of all the States shall be necessary to a Choice. In every Case, after the Choice of the President, the Person having the greatest Number of Votes of the Electors shall be the Vice President. But if there should remain two or more who have equal votes, the Senate shall chuse from them by Ballot the Vice President.][4]

» This selection clause was modified by the 12th Amendment.

The Congress may determine the Time of chusing the Electors, and the Day on which they shall give their Votes; which Day shall be the same throughout the United States.

No person except a natural-born Citizen, or a Citizen of the United States, at the time of the Adoption of this Constitution, shall be eligible to the Office of President; neither shall any Person be eligible to that Office who shall not have attained to the Age of thirty-five years, and been fourteen Years a Resident within the United States.

In Case of the Removal of the President from Office, or of his Death, Resignation, or Inability to discharge the Powers and Duties of the said Office, the same shall devolve on the Vice President, and the Congress may by Law provide for the Case of Removal, Death, Resignation, or Inability, both of the President and Vice President, declaring what Officer shall then act as President, and such Officer shall act accordingly, until the disability be removed, or a President shall be elected.

» This disability and transfer of power clause was modified by the 25th Amendment.

The President shall, at stated Times, receive for his Services a Compensation, which shall neither be increased nor diminished during the Period for which he shall have been elected, and he shall not receive within that Period any other Emolument from the United States, or any of them.

Before he enter on the execution of his Office, he shall take the following Oath or Affirmation:—"I do solemnly swear (or affirm) that I will faithfully execute the Office of President of the United States, and will, to the best of my Ability, preserve, protect, and defend the Constitution of the United States."

[4] *Revised by the Twelfth Amendment.*

SECTION 2

The President shall be Commander in Chief of the Army and Navy of the United States, and of the Militia of the several States, when called into the actual Service of the United States; he may require the Opinion, in writing, of the principal Officer in each of the executive Departments, upon any subject relating to the Duties of their respective Offices, and he shall have Power to Grant Reprieves and Pardons for Offenses against the United States, except in Cases of Impeachment.

He shall have Power, by and with the Advice and Consent of the Senate, to make Treaties, provided two-thirds of the Senators present concur; and he shall nominate, and by and with the Advice and Consent of the Senate, shall appoint Ambassadors, other public Ministers and Consuls, Judges of the supreme Court, and all other Officers of the United States, whose Appointments are not herein otherwise provided for, and which shall be established by Law: but the Congress may by Law vest the Appointment of such inferior Officers, as they think proper, in the President alone, in the Courts of Law, or in the Heads of Departments.

The President shall have Power to fill up all Vacancies that may happen during the Recess of the Senate, by granting Commissions which shall expire at the End of their next Session.

SECTION 3

He shall from time to time give to the Congress Information of the State of the Union, and recommend to their Consideration such Measures as he shall judge necessary and expedient; he may, on extraordinary occasions, convene both Houses, or either of them, and in Case of Disagreement between them, with respect to the Time of Adjournment, he may adjourn them to such Time as he shall think proper; he shall receive Ambassadors and other public Ministers; he shall take care that the Laws be faithfully executed, and shall Commission all the Officers of the United States.

SECTION 4

The President, Vice President and all civil Officers of the United States, shall be removed from Office on Impeachment for, and Conviction of, Treason, Bribery, or other high Crimes and Misdemeanors.

ARTICLE III

SECTION 1

The judicial Power of the United States, shall be vested in one supreme Court, and in such inferior Courts as the Congress may from time to time ordain and establish. The Judges, both of the supreme and inferior Courts, shall hold their Offices during good Behaviour, and shall, at stated Times, receive for their Services, a Compensation, which shall not be diminished during their Continuance in Office.

SECTION 2

>> The power of judicial review is not mentioned among the Court's powers.

The judicial Power shall extend to all Cases, in Law and Equity, arising under this Constitution, the Laws of the United States, and Treaties made, or which shall be made, under their Authority;—to all Cases affecting ambassadors, other public ministers and consuls;—to all cases of admiralty and maritime Jurisdiction;—to Controversies to which the United States shall be a Party;—to Controversies between two or more states;—between a State and Citizens of another State;[5]—between Citizens of different

[5.] *Qualified by the Eleventh Amendment.*

States—between Citizens of the same State claiming Lands under Grants of different States, and between a State, or the Citizens thereof, and foreign States, Citizens, or Subjects.

In all Cases affecting Ambassadors, other public Ministers and Consuls, and those in which a State shall be Party, the supreme Court shall have original Jurisdiction. In all the other Cases before mentioned, the supreme Court shall have appellate Jurisdiction, both as to Law and Fact, with such Exceptions, and under such Regulations as the Congress shall make.

The trial of all Crimes, except in Cases of Impeachment, shall be by Jury; and such Trial shall be held in the State where the said Crimes shall have been committed; but when not committed within any State, the Trial shall be at such Place or Places as the Congress may by Law have directed.

SECTION 3

Treason against the United States, shall consist only in levying War against them, or in adhering to their Enemies, giving them Aid and Comfort. No Person shall be convicted of Treason unless on the Testimony of two Witnesses to the same overt Act, or on Confession in open Court.

The Congress shall have power to declare the Punishment of Treason, but no Attainder of Treason shall work Corruption of Blood, or Forfeiture except during the Life of the Person attainted.

ARTICLE IV

SECTION 1

Full Faith and Credit shall be given in each State to the public Acts, Records, and judicial Proceedings of every other State. And the Congress may by general Laws prescribe the Manner in which such Acts, Records and Proceedings shall be proved, and the Effect thereof.

>> Relations among the states are discussed in Chapter 17, State and Local Government, available on the *AM GOV* Online Learning Center.

SECTION 2

The Citizens of each State shall be entitled to all Privileges and Immunities of Citizens in the several States.

A Person charged in any State with Treason, Felony, or other Crime, who shall flee from Justice, and be found in another State, shall on demand of the executive Authority of the State from which he fled, be delivered up, to be removed to the State having Jurisdiction of the crime.

No Person held to Service or Labour in one State, under the Laws thereof, escaping into another, shall, in Consequence of any Law or Regulation therein, be discharged from such Service or Labour, but shall be delivered up on Claim of the Party to whom such Service or Labour may be due.

>> The 13th Amendment eliminated the fugitive slave clause.

SECTION 3

New States may be admitted by the Congress into this Union; but no new State shall be formed or erected within the Jurisdiction of any other State; nor any State be formed by the Junction of two or more States, or parts of States, without the Consent of the Legislatures of the States concerned as well as of the Congress.

The Congress shall have Power to dispose of and make all needful Rules and Regulations respecting the Territory or other Property belonging to the United States; and nothing in this Constitution shall be so construed as to Prejudice any Claims of the United States, or of any particular State.

SECTION 4

The United States shall guarantee to every State in this Union a Republican Form of Government, and shall protect each of them against Invasion; and on Application of the Legislature, or of the Executive (when the Legislature cannot be convened) against domestic Violence.

ARTICLE V

>> The Constitution may also be changed by informal means. See Chapter 2.

The Congress, whenever two-thirds of both Houses shall deem it necessary, shall propose Amendments to this Constitution, or, on the Application of the Legislatures of two-thirds of the several States, shall call a Convention for proposing Amendments, which, in either Case, shall be valid to all Intents and Purposes, as part of this Constitution, when ratified by the Legislatures of three-fourths of the several States, or by Conventions in three-fourths thereof, as the one or the other Mode of Ratification may be proposed by the Congress; Provided that no Amendment which may be made prior to the Year One thousand eight hundred and eight shall in any Manner affect the first and fourth Clauses in the Ninth Section of the first Article; and that no State, without its Consent, shall be deprived of its equal Suffrage in the Senate.

ARTICLE VI

All Debts contracted and Engagements entered into, before the Adoption of this Constitution, shall be as valid against the United States under this Constitution, as under the Confederation.

This Constitution, and the Laws of the United States which shall be made in Pursuance thereof; and all Treaties made, or which shall be made, under the Authority of the United States, shall be the supreme Law of the Land; and the Judges in every State shall be bound thereby, any Thing in the Constitution or Laws of any State to the Contrary notwithstanding.

The Senators and Representatives before mentioned, and the Members of the several State Legislatures, and all executive and judicial Officers, both of the United States and of the several States, shall be bound by Oath or Affirmation to support this Constitution; but no religious Tests shall ever be required as a qualification to any Office or public Trust under the United States.

ARTICLE VII

The Ratification of the Conventions of nine States shall be sufficient for the Establishment of this Constitution between the States so ratifying the same.

Done in Convention by the Unanimous Consent of the States present the Seventeenth Day of September in the Year of our Lord one thousand seven hundred and Eighty seven, and of the Independence of the United States of America the Twelfth. In Witness whereof We have hereunto subscribed our Names.[6]

George Washington
President and deputy from Virginia

New Hampshire
John Langdon
Nicholas Gilman

Massachusetts
Nathaniel Gorham
Rufus King

Connecticut
William Samuel Johnson
Roger Sherman

New York
Alexander Hamilton

New Jersey
William Livingston
David Brearley
William Paterson
Jonathan Dayton

[6.] *These are the full names of the signers, which in some cases are not the signatures on the document.*

Pennsylvania	John Dickinson	North Carolina
Benjamin Franklin	Richard Bassett	William Blount
Thomas Mifflin	Jacob Broom	Richard Dobbs Spaight
Robert Morris		Hugh Williamson
George Clymer	*Maryland*	
Thomas FitzSimmons	James McHenry	*South Carolina*
Jared Ingersoll	Daniel of St. Thomas	John Rutledge
James Wilson	Jenifer	Charles Cotesworth
Gouverneur Morris	Daniel Carroll	Pinckney
		Charles Pinckney
Delaware	*Virginia*	Pierce Butler
George Read	John Blair	
Gunning Bedford, Jr.	James Madison, Jr.	*Georgia*
		William Few
		Abraham Baldwin

Articles in Addition to, and Amendment of, the Constitution of the United States of America, Proposed by Congress, and Ratified by the Legislatures of the Several States, Pursuant to the Fifth Article of the Original Constitution[7]

AMENDMENT I

Congress shall make no law respecting an establishment of religion, or prohibiting the free exercise thereof; or abridging the freedom of speech, or of the press; or the right of the people peaceably to assemble, and to petition the Government for a redress of grievances.

>> The first nine amendments are the basis of citizens' civil liberties protections. See Chapter 4. The 1st Amendment, in particular, is the legal basis for political participation (see Chapter 7), and the role of interest groups (see Chapter 8), political parties (see Chapter 9), and the media (see Chapter 10).

AMENDMENT II

A well regulated Militia, being necessary to the security of a free State, the right of the people to keep and bear Arms shall not be infringed.

AMENDMENT III

No Soldier shall, in time of peace, be quartered in any house, without the consent of the Owner, nor in time of war, but in a manner to be prescribed by law.

AMENDMENT IV

The right of the people to be secure in their persons, houses, papers, and effects, against unreasonable searches and seizures, shall not be violated, and no Warrants shall issue, but upon probable cause, supported by Oath or affirmation, and particularly describing the place to be searched, and the persons or things to be seized.

AMENDMENT V

No person shall be held to answer for a capital or otherwise infamous crime, unless on a presentment or indictment of a Grand Jury, except in cases arising in the land or naval forces, or in the Militia, when in actual service in time of War or public danger; nor shall any person be subject for the same offence to be twice put in jeopardy of life or limb; nor shall be compelled in any criminal case to be a witness against himself, nor be deprived of life, liberty, or property, without due process of law; nor shall private property be taken for public use, without just compensation.

[7.] *This heading appears only in the joint resolution submitting the first ten amendments, which are collectively known as the Bill of Rights. They were ratified on December 15, 1791.*

AMENDMENT VI

In all criminal prosecutions, the accused shall enjoy the right to a speedy and public trial, by an impartial jury of the State and district wherein the crime shall have been committed, which district shall have been previously ascertained by law, and to be informed of the nature and cause of the accusation; to be confronted with the witnesses against him; to have compulsory process for obtaining witnesses in his favour, and to have the Assistance of Counsel for his defence.

AMENDMENT VII

In suits at common law, where the value in controversy shall exceed twenty dollars, the right of trial by jury shall be preserved, and no fact tried by a jury, shall be otherwise reexamined in any Court of the United States, than according to the rules of the common law.

AMENDMENT VIII

Excessive bail shall not be required, nor excessive fines imposed, nor cruel and unusual punishments inflicted.

AMENDMENT IX

The enumeration of the Constitution, of certain rights, shall not be construed to deny or disparage others retained by the people.

AMENDMENT X

The powers not delegated to the United States by the Constitution, nor prohibited by it to the States, are reserved to the States respectively, or to the people.

AMENDMENT XI [1795]

The Judicial power of the United States shall not be construed to extend to any suit in law or equity, commenced or prosecuted against one of the United States by Citizens of another State, or by Citizens or Subjects of any Foreign State.

AMENDMENT XII [1804]

The Electors shall meet in their respective States and vote by ballot for President and Vice-President, one of whom, at least, shall not be an inhabitant of the same State with themselves; they shall name in their ballots the person voted for as President, and in distinct ballots the person voted for as Vice-President, and they shall make distinct lists of all persons voted for as President, and of all persons voted for as Vice-President, and of the number of votes for each, which lists they shall sign and certify, and transmit sealed to the seat of the government of the United States, directed to the President of the Senate;—The President of the Senate shall, in the presence of the Senate and House of Representatives, open all the certificates and the votes shall then be counted;—The person having the greatest number of votes for President, shall be the President, if such number be a majority of the whole number of Electors appointed; and if no person have such majority, then from the persons having the highest numbers not exceeding three on the list of those voted for as President, the House of Representatives shall choose immediately, by ballot, the President. But in choosing the President, the votes shall be taken by states, the representation from each state having one vote; a quorum for this purpose shall consist of a member or members from two-thirds of the states, and a majority of all the states shall be necessary to a choice. And if the House of Representatives shall not choose a President whenever the right of choice shall devolve upon them, before the fourth day of March next following, then the Vice-President shall act as President, as in the case of the death or other constitutional disability of the President.—The person having the greatest number of votes as Vice-President, shall be the Vice-President, if such number be a majority of the whole number of Electors appointed, and if no person have a majority, then from the two highest numbers on the list, the Senate shall choose the Vice-President; a quorum for the purpose shall consist of two-thirds of the whole number of Senators, and majority of the whole number shall be necessary to a choice. But no person constitutionally ineligible to the office of President shall be eligible to that of Vice-President of the United States.

AMENDMENT XIII [1865]

SECTION 1

Neither slavery nor involuntary servitude, except as a punishment for crime whereof the party shall have been duly convicted, shall exist within the United States, or any place subject to their jurisdiction.

SECTION 2

Congress shall have power to enforce this article by appropriate legislation.

AMENDMENT XIV [1868]

SECTION 1

All persons born or naturalized in the United States, and subject to the jurisdiction thereof, are citizens of the United States and of the State wherein they reside. No State shall abridge the privileges or immunities of citizens of the United States; nor shall any State deprive any person of life, liberty, or property, without due process of law; nor deny to any person within its jurisdiction the equal protection of the laws.

>> The due process clause is the basis of the incorporation doctrine, Chapter 4, and the equal protection clause is the constitutional basis of equality cases, Chapter 5.

SECTION 2

Representatives shall be apportioned among the several States according to their respective numbers, counting the whole number of persons in each State, excluding Indians not taxed. But when the right to vote at any election for the choice of electors for President and Vice-President of the United States, Representatives in Congress, the Executive and Judicial officers of a State, or the members of the Legislature thereof, is denied to any of the male inhabitants of such State, being twenty-one years of age, and citizens of the United States, or in any way abridged, except for participation in rebellion, or other crime, the basis of representation therein shall be reduced in the proportion which the number of such male citizens shall bear to the whole number of male citizens twenty-one years of age in such State.

SECTION 3

No person shall be a Senator or Representative in Congress, or elector of President and Vice-President, or hold any office, civil or military, under the United States, or under any State, who, having previously taken an oath, as a member of Congress, or as an officer of the United States, or as a member of any State legislature, or as an executive or judicial officer of any State, to support the Constitution of the United States, shall have engaged in insurrection or rebellion against the same, or given aid or comfort to the enemies thereof. But Congress may by a vote of two-thirds of each House, remove such disability.

SECTION 4

The validity of the public debt of the United States, authorized by law, including debts incurred for payment of pensions and bounties for services in suppressing insurrection or rebellion, shall not be questioned. But neither the United States nor any State shall assume or pay any debts or obligation incurred in aid of insurrection or rebellion against the United States, or any claim for the loss or emancipation of any slave; but all such debts, obligations, and claims shall be held illegal and void.

SECTION 5

The Congress shall have the power to enforce, by appropriate legislation, the provisions of this article.

AMENDMENT XV [1870]

SECTION 1

The right of citizens of the United States to vote shall not be denied or abridged by the United States or by any State on account of race, color, or previous condition of servitude.

SECTION 2

The Congress shall have power to enforce this article by appropriate legislation.

AMENDMENT XVI [1913]

The Congress shall have power to lay and collect taxes on incomes, from whatever source derived, without apportionment among the several States, and without regard to any census or enumeration.

AMENDMENT XVII [1913]

The Senate of the United States shall be composed of two Senators from each State, elected by the people thereof, for six years; and each Senator shall have one vote. The electors in each State shall have the qualifications requisite for electors of the most numerous branch of the State legislatures.

When vacancies happen in the representation of any State in the Senate, the executive authority of such State shall issue writs of election to fill such vacancies: Provided, That the legislature of any State may empower the executive thereof to make temporary appointments until the people fill the vacancies by election as the legislature may direct.

This amendment shall not be so construed as to affect the election or term of any Senator chosen before it becomes valid as part of the Constitution.

AMENDMENT XVIII [1919]

SECTION 1

After one year from the ratification of this article the manufacture, sale, or transportation of intoxicating liquors within, the importation thereof into, or the exportation thereof from the United States and all territory subject to the jurisdiction thereof for beverage purposes is hereby prohibited.

SECTION 2

The Congress and the several States shall have concurrent power to enforce this article by appropriate legislation.

SECTION 3

This article shall be inoperative unless it shall have been ratified as an amendment to the Constitution by the legislatures of the several States, as provided in the Constitution, within seven years from the date of the submission hereof to the States by the Congress.

AMENDMENT XIX [1920]

The right of citizens of the United States to vote shall not be denied or abridged by the United States or by any State on account of sex.

Congress shall have power to enforce this article by appropriate legislation.

>> The amendment was the result of the second national Women's Movement.

AMENDMENT XX [1933]

SECTION 1

The terms of the President and Vice-President shall end at noon on the 20th day of January, and the terms of Senators and Representatives at noon on the 3d day of January, of the years in which such terms would have ended if this article had not been ratified; and the terms of their successors shall then begin.

SECTION 2

The Congress shall assemble at least once in every year, and such meeting shall begin at noon on the 3d day of January, unless they shall by law appoint a different day.

SECTION 3

If, at the time fixed for the beginning of the term of the President, the President elect shall have died, the Vice-President elect shall become President. If a President shall not have been chosen before the time fixed for the beginning of his term or if the President elect shall have failed to qualify, then the Vice-President elect shall act as President until a President shall have qualified; and the Congress may by law provide for the case wherein neither a President elect nor a Vice-President elect shall have qualified, declaring who shall then act as President, or the manner in which one who is to act shall be selected, and such person shall act accordingly until a President or Vice-President shall have qualified.

SECTION 4

The Congress may by law provide for the case of the death of any of the persons from whom the House of Representatives may choose a President whenever the right of choice shall have devolved upon them, and for the case of the death of any of the persons from whom the Senate may choose a Vice- President whenever the right of choice shall have devolved upon them.

SECTION 5

Sections 1 and 2 shall take effect on the 15th day of October following the ratification of this article.

SECTION 6

This article shall be inoperative unless it shall have been ratified as an amendment to the Constitution by the legislatures of three-fourths of the several States within seven years from the date of its submission.

AMENDMENT XXI [1933]

SECTION 1

The eighteenth article of amendment to the Constitution of the United States is hereby repealed.

SECTION 2

The transportation or importation into any State, Territory, or possession of the United States for delivery or use therein of intoxicating liquors, in violation of the laws thereof, is hereby prohibited.

SECTION 3

This article shall be inoperative unless it shall have been ratified as an amendment to the Constitution by conventions in the several States, as provided in the Constitution, within seven years from the date of the submission hereof to the States by the Congress.

AMENDMENT XXII [1951]

No person shall be elected to the office of the President more than twice, and no person who has held the office of President, or acted as President, for more than two years of a term to which some other person was elected President shall be elected to the office of the President more than once.

But this Article shall not apply to any person holding the office of President when this Article was proposed by the Congress, and shall not prevent any person who may be holding the office of President, or acting as President, during the term within which this Article becomes operative from holding the office of President or acting as President during the remainder of such term.

This article shall be inoperative unless it shall have been ratified as an amendment to the Constitution by the legislatures of three-fourths of the several states within seven years from the date of its submission to the states by the Congress.

AMENDMENT XXIII [1961]

SECTION 1

The District constituting the seat of Government of the United States shall appoint in such manner as the Congress may direct:

A number of electors of President and Vice-President equal to the whole number of Senators and Representatives in Congress to which the District would be entitled if it were a State, but in no event more than the least populous State; they shall be in addition to those appointed by the States, but they shall be considered, for the purposes of the election of President and Vice-President, to be electors appointed by a State; and they shall meet in the District and perform such duties as provided by the twelfth article of amendment.

SECTION 2

The Congress shall have power to enforce this article by appropriate legislation.

AMENDMENT XXIV [1964]

SECTION 1

The right of citizens of the United States to vote in any primary or other election for President or Vice President, for electors for President or Vice President, or for Senator or Representative in Congress, shall not be denied or abridged by the United States or any state by reason of failure to pay any poll tax or other tax.

SECTION 2

The Congress shall have the power to enforce this article by appropriate legislation.

AMENDMENT XXV [1967]

SECTION 1

In case of the removal of the President from office or of his death or resignation, the Vice President shall become President.

SECTION 2

Whenever there is a vacancy in the office of the Vice President, the President shall nominate a Vice President who shall take office upon confirmation by a majority vote of both Houses of Congress.

SECTION 3

Whenever the President transmits to the President Pro Tempore of the Senate and the Speaker of the House of Representatives his written declaration that he is unable to discharge the powers and duties of his office, and until he transmits to them a written declaration to the contrary, such powers and duties shall be discharged by the Vice President as Acting President.

SECTION 4

Whenever the Vice President and a majority of either the principal officers of the executive departments or of such other body as Congress may by law provide, transmit to the President Pro Tempore of the Senate and the Speaker of the House of Representatives their written declaration that the President is unable to discharge the powers and duties of his office, the Vice President shall immediately assume the powers and duties of the office as Acting President.

Thereafter, when the President transmits to the President Pro Tempore of the Senate and the Speaker of the House of Representatives his written declaration that no inability exists, he shall resume the powers and duties of his office unless the Vice President and a majority of either the principal officers of the executive departments or of such other body as Congress may by law provide, transmit within four days to the President Pro Tempore of the Senate and the Speaker of the House of Representatives their written declaration that the President is unable to discharge the powers and duties of his office. Thereupon Congress shall decide the issue, assembling within forty-eight hours for that purpose if not in session. If the Congress, within twenty-one days after receipt of the latter written declaration, or, if Congress is not in session, within twenty-one days after Congress is required to assemble, determines by two-thirds vote of both Houses that the President is unable to discharge the powers and duties of his office, the Vice President shall continue to discharge the same as Acting President; otherwise, the President shall resume the powers and duties of his office.

AMENDMENT XXVI [1971]

SECTION 1

The right of citizens of the United States, who are eighteen years of age or older, to vote shall not be denied or abridged by the United States or by any State on account of age.

SECTION 2

The Congress shall have the power to enforce this article by appropriate legislation.

AMENDMENT XXVII [1992]

No law varying the compensation for the service of Senators and Representatives shall take effect until an election of Representatives shall have intervened.

FEDERALIST PAPER NO. 10
(JAMES MADISON)

Among the numerous advantages promised by a well-constructed union, none deserves to be more accurately developed than its tendency to break and control the violence of faction. The friend of popular governments never finds himself so much alarmed for their character and fate as when he contemplates their propensity to this dangerous vice. He will not fail, therefore, to set a due value on any plan which, without violating the principles to which he is attached, provides a proper cure for it. The instability, injustice, and confusion introduced into the public councils have, in truth, been the mortal diseases under which popular governments have everywhere perished, as they continue to be the favorite and fruitful topics from which the adversaries to liberty derive their most specious declamations. The valuable improvements made by the American constitutions on the popular models, both ancient and modern, cannot certainly be too much admired; but it would be an unwarrantable partiality to contend that they have as effectually obviated the danger on this side, as was wished and expected. Complaints are everywhere heard from our most considerate and virtuous citizens, equally the friends of public and private faith and of public and personal liberty, that our governments are too unstable, that the public good is disregarded in the conflicts of rival parties, and that measures are too often decided, not according to the rules of justice and the rights of the minor party, but by the superior force of an interested and overbearing majority. However anxiously we may wish that these complaints had no foundation, the evidence of known facts will not permit us to deny that they are in some degree true. It will be found, indeed, on a candid review of our situation, that some of the distresses under which we labor have been erroneously charged on the operation of our governments; but it will be found, at the same time, that other causes will not alone account for many of our heaviest misfortunes; and, particularly, for that prevailing and increasing distrust of public engagements and alarm for private rights which are echoed from one end of the continent to the other. These must be chiefly, if not wholly, effects of the unsteadiness and injustice with which a factious spirit has tainted our public administration.

By a faction I understand a number of citizens, whether amounting to a majority or minority of the whole, who are united and actuated by some common impulse of passion, or of interest, adverse to the rights of other citizens, or to the permanent and aggregate interests of the community.

There are two methods of curing the mischiefs of faction: the one, by removing its causes; the other, by controlling its effects.

There are again two methods of removing the causes of faction: the one, by destroying the liberty which is essential to its existence; the other, by giving to every citizen the same opinions, the same passions, and the same interests.

It could never be more truly said than of the first remedy that it was worse than the disease. Liberty is to faction what air is to fire, an aliment without which it instantly expires. But it could not be a less folly to abolish liberty, which is essential to political life, because it nourishes faction than it would be to wish the annihilation of air, which is essential to animal life, because it imparts to fire its destructive agency.

The second expedient is as impracticable as the first would be unwise. As long as the reason of man continues fallible, and he is at liberty to exercise it, different opinions will be formed. As long as the connection subsists between his reason and his self-love, his opinions and his passions will have a reciprocal influence on each other; and the former will be objects to which the latter will attach themselves. The diversity in the faculties of men, from which the rights of property originate, is not less an insuperable obstacle to a uniformity of interest. The protection of these faculties is the first object of government. From the protection of different and unequal faculties of acquiring property, the possession of different degrees and kinds of property immediately results; and from the influence of these on the sentiments and views of the respective proprietors ensues a division of the society into different interests and parties.

The latent causes of faction are thus sown in the nature of man; and we see them everywhere brought into different degrees of activity, according to the different circumstances of civil society. A zeal for different opinions concerning religion, concerning government, and many other points, as well of speculation as of practice; an attachment to different leaders ambitiously contending for pre-eminence and power; or to persons of other descriptions whose fortunes have been interesting to the human passions, have, in turn, divided mankind into parties, inflamed them with mutual animosity, and rendered them much more disposed to vex and oppress each other than to co-operate for their common good. So strong is this propensity of mankind to fall into mutual animosities that where no substantial occasion presents itself the most frivolous and fanciful distinctions have been sufficient to kindle their unfriendly passions and excite their most violent conflicts. But the most common and durable source of factions has been the various and unequal distribution of property. Those who hold and those who are without property have ever formed distinct interests in society. Those who are creditors, and those who are debtors, fall under a like discrimination. A landed interest, a manufacturing interest, a mercantile interest, a moneyed interest, with many lesser interests, grow up of necessity in civilized nations, and divide them into different classes, actuated by different sentiments and views. The regulation of these various and interfering interests forms the principal task of modern legislation and involves the spirit of party and faction in the necessary and ordinary operations of government.

No man is allowed to be a judge in his own cause, because his interest would certainly bias his judgment, and, not improbably, corrupt his integrity. With equal, nay with greater reason, a body of men are unfit to be both judges and parties at the same time; yet what are many of the most important acts of legislation but so many judicial determinations, not indeed concerning the rights of single persons, but concerning the rights of large bodies of citizens? And what are the different classes of legislators but advocates and parties to the causes which they determine? Is a law proposed concerning private debts? It is a question to which the creditors are parties on one side and the debtors on the other. Justice ought to hold the balance between them. Yet the parties are, and must be, themselves the judges; and the most numerous party, or in other words, the most powerful faction must be expected to prevail. Shall domestic manufacturers be encouraged, and in what degree, by restrictions on foreign manufacturers? [These] are questions which would be differently decided by the landed and the manufacturing classes, and probably by neither with a sole regard to justice and the public good. The apportionment of taxes on the various descriptions of property is an act which seems to require the most exact impartiality; yet there is, perhaps, no legislative act in which greater opportunity and temptation are given to a predominant party to trample on the rules of justice. Every shilling with which they overburden the inferior number is a shilling saved to their own pockets.

It is in vain to say that enlightened statesmen will be able to adjust these clashing interests and render them all subservient to the public good. Enlightened statesmen will not always be at the helm. Nor, in many cases, can such an adjustment be made at all without taking into view indirect and remote considerations, which will rarely prevail over the immediate interest which one party may find in disregarding the rights of another or the good of the whole.

The inference to which we are brought is that the *causes* of faction cannot be removed and that relief is only to be sought in the means of controlling its *effects*.

If a faction consists of less than a majority, relief is supplied by the republican principle, which enables the majority to defeat its sinister views by regular vote. It may clog the administration, it may convulse the society; but it will be unable to execute and mask its violence under the forms of the Constitution. When a majority is included in a faction, the form of popular government, on the other hand, enables it to sacrifice to its ruling passion or interest both the public good and the rights of other citizens. To secure the public good and private rights against the danger of such a faction, and at the same time to preserve the spirit and the form of popular government, is then the great object to which our inquiries are directed. Let me add that it is the great desideratum by which alone this form of government can be rescued from the opprobrium under which it has so long labored and be recommended to the esteem and adoption of mankind.

By what means is this object attainable? Evidently by one of two only. Either the existence of the same passion or interest in a majority at the same time must be prevented, or the majority, having such coexistent passion or interest, must be rendered, by their number and local situation, unable to concert and carry into effect schemes of oppression. If the impulse and the opportunity be suffered to coincide, we well know that neither moral nor religious motives can be relied on as an adequate control. They are not found to be such on the injustice and violence of individuals, and lose their efficacy in proportion to the number combined together, that is, in proportion as their efficacy becomes needful.

From this view of the subject it may be concluded that a pure democracy, by which I mean a society consisting of a small number of citizens, who assemble and administer the government in person, can admit of no cure for the mischiefs of faction. A common passion or interest will, in almost every case, be felt by a majority of the whole, a communication and concert result from the form of government itself; and there is nothing to check the inducements to sacrifice the weaker party or an obnoxious individual. Hence it is that such democracies have ever been spectacles of turbulence and contention; have ever been found incompatible with personal security or the rights of property; and have in general been as short in their lives as they have been violent in their deaths. Theoretic politicians, who have patronized this species of government, have erroneously supposed that by reducing mankind to a perfect equality in their political rights, they would at the same time be perfectly equalized and assimilated in their possessions, their opinions, and their passions.

A republic, by which I mean a government in which the scheme of representation takes place, opens a different prospect and promises the cure for which we are seeking. Let us examine the points in which it varies from pure democracy, and we shall comprehend both the nature of the cure and the efficacy which it must derive from the Union.

The two great points of difference between a democracy and a republic are: first, the delegation of the government, in the latter, to a small number of citizens elected by the rest; secondly, the greater number of citizens and greater sphere of country over which the latter may be extended.

The effect of the first difference is, on the one hand, to refine and enlarge the public views by passing them through the medium of a chosen body of citizens, whose wisdom may best discern the true interest of their country and whose patriotism and love of justice will be least likely to sacrifice it to temporary or partial considerations. Under such a regulation it may well happen that the public voice, pronounced by the representatives of the people, will be more consonant to the public good than if pronounced by the people themselves, convened for the purpose. On the other hand, the effect may be inverted. Men of factious tempers, of local prejudices, or of sinister designs, may, by intrigue, by corruption, or by other means, first obtain the suffrages, and then betray the interests of the people. The question resulting is, whether small or extensive republics are most favorable to the election of proper guardians of the public weal; and it is clearly decided in favor of the latter by two obvious considerations.

In the first place it is to be remarked that however small the republic may be the representatives must be raised to a certain number in order to guard against the cabals of a few; and that however large it may be they must be limited to a certain number in order to guard against the confusion of a multitude. Hence, the number of representatives in the two cases not being in proportion to that of the constituents, and being proportionally greatest in the small republic, it follows that if the proportion of fit characters be not less in the large than in the small republic, the former will present a greater option, and consequently a greater probability of a fit choice.

In the next place, as each representative will be chosen by a greater number of citizens in the large than in the small republic, it will be more difficult for unworthy candidates to practice with success the vicious arts by which elections are too often carried; and the suffrages of the people being more free, will be more likely to center on men who possess the most attractive merit and the most diffusive and established characters.

It must be confessed that in this, as in most other cases, there is a mean, on both sides of which inconveniencies will be found to lie. By enlarging too much the number of electors, you render the representative too little acquainted with all their local circumstances and lesser interests; as by reducing it too much, you render him unduly attached to these, and too little fit to comprehend and pursue great and national objects. The federal Constitution forms a happy combination in this respect; the great and aggregate interests being referred to the national, the local and particular to the State legislatures.

The other point of difference is the greater number of citizens and extent of territory which may be brought within the compass of republican than of democratic government; and it is this circumstance principally which renders factious combinations less to be dreaded in the former than in the latter. The smaller the society, the fewer probably will be the distinct parties and interests composing it; the fewer the distinct parties and interests, the more frequently will a majority be found of the same party; and the smaller the number of individuals composing a majority, and the smaller the compass within which they are placed, the more easily will they concert and execute their plans of oppression. Extend the sphere and you take in a greater variety of parties and interests; you make it less probable that a majority of the whole will have a common motive to invade the rights of other citizens; or if such a common motive exists, it will be more difficult for all who feel it to discover their own strength and to act in unison with each other. Besides other impediments, it may be remarked that, where there is a consciousness of unjust or dishonorable purposes, communication is always checked by distrust in proportion to the number whose concurrence is necessary.

Hence, it clearly appears that the same advantage which a republic has over a democracy in controlling the effects of faction is enjoyed by a large over a small republic—is enjoyed by the Union over the States composing it. Does this advantage consist in the substitution of representatives whose enlightened views and virtuous sentiments render them superior to local prejudices and to schemes of injustice? It will not be denied that the representation of the Union will be most likely to possess these requisite endowments. Does it consist in the greater security afforded by a greater variety of parties, against the event of any one party being able to outnumber and oppress the rest? In an equal degree does the increased variety of parties comprised within the Union increase this security. Does it, in fine, consist in the greater obstacles opposed to the concert and accomplishment of the secret wishes of an unjust and interested majority? Here again the extent of the Union gives it the most palpable advantage.

The influence of factious leaders may kindle a flame within their particular States but will be unable to spread a general conflagration through the other States. A religious sect may degenerate into a political faction in a part of the Confederacy; but the variety of sects dispersed over the entire face of it must secure the national councils against any danger from that source. A rage for paper money, for an abolition of debts, for an equal division of property, or for any other improper or wicked project, will be less apt to pervade the whole body of the Union than a particular member of it, in the same proportion as such a malady is more likely to taint a particular county or district than an entire State.

In the extent and proper structure of the Union, therefore, we behold a republican remedy for the diseases most incident to republican government. And according to the degree of pleasure and pride we feel in being republicans ought to be our zeal in cherishing the spirit and supporting the character of Federalists.

FEDERALIST PAPER NO. 51
(JAMES MADISON)

To what expedient, then, shall we finally resort, for maintaining in practice the necessary partition of power among the several departments as laid down in the Constitution? The only answer that can be given is that as all these exterior provisions are found to be inadequate, the defect must be supplied, by so contriving the interior structure of the government as that its several constituent parts may, by their mutual relations, be the means of keeping each other in their proper places. Without presuming to undertake a full development of this important idea I will hazard a few general observations which may perhaps place it in a clearer light, and enable us to form a more correct judgment of the principles and structure of the government planned by the convention.

In order to lay a due foundation for that separate and distinct exercise of the different powers of government, which to a certain extent is admitted on all hands to be essential to the preservation of liberty, it is evident that each department should have a will of its own; and consequently should be so constituted that the members of each should have as little agency as possible in the appointment of the members of the others. Were this principle rigorously adhered to, it would require that all the appointments for the supreme executive, legislative, and judiciary magistracies should be drawn from the same fountain of authority, the people, through channels having no communication whatever with one another. Perhaps such a plan of constructing the several departments would be less difficult in practice than it may be in contemplation appear. Some difficulties, however, and some additional expense would attend the execution of it. Some deviations, therefore, from the principle must be admitted. In the constitution of the judiciary department in particular, it might be inexpedient to insist rigorously on the principle; first, because peculiar qualifications being essential in the members, the primary consideration ought to be to select that mode of choice which best secures these qualifications; second, because the permanent tenure by which the appointments are held in that department must soon destroy all sense of dependence on the authority conferring them.

It is equally evident that the members of each department should be as little dependent as possible on those of the others for the emoluments annexed to their offices. Were the executive magistrate, or the judges, not independent of the legislature in this particular, their independence in every other would be merely nominal.

But the great security against a gradual concentration of the several powers in the same department consists in giving to those who administer each department the necessary constitutional means and personal motives to resist encroachments of the others. The provision for defense must in this, as in all other cases, be made commensurate to the danger of attack. Ambition must be made to counteract ambition. The interest of the man must be connected with the constitutional rights of the place. It may be a reflection on human nature that such devices should be necessary to control the abuses of government. But what is government itself but the greatest of all reflections on human nature? If men were angels no government would be necessary. If angels were to govern men, neither external nor internal controls on government would be necessary. In framing a government which is to be administered by men over men, the great difficulty lies in this: you must first enable the government to control the governed; and in the next place oblige it to control itself. A dependence on the people is, no doubt, the primary control on the government; but experience has taught mankind the necessity of auxiliary precautions.

This policy of supplying, by opposite and rival interests, the defect of better motives, might be traced through the whole system of human affairs, private as well as public. We see it particularly displayed in all the subordinate distributions of power, where the constant aim is to divide and arrange the several offices in such a manner as that each may be a check on the other—that the private interest of every individual may be a sentinel over the public rights. These inventions of prudence cannot be less requisite in the distribution of the supreme powers of the State.

But it is not possible to give to each department an equal power of self-defense. In republican government, the legislative authority necessarily predominates. The remedy for this inconveniency is to divide the legislature into different branches; and to render them, by different modes of election and different principles of action, as little connected with each other as the nature of their common functions and their common dependence on the society will admit. It may even be necessary to guard against dangerous encroachments by still further precautions. As the weight of the legislative authority requires that it should be thus divided, the weakness of the executive may require, on the other hand, that it should be fortified. An absolute negative on the legislature appears, at first view, to be the natural defense with which the executive magistrate should be armed. But perhaps it would be neither altogether safe nor alone sufficient. On ordinary occasions it might not be exerted with the requisite firmness, and on extraordinary occasions it might be perfidiously abused. May not this defect of an absolute negative be supplied by some qualified connection between this weaker department and the weaker branch of the stronger department, by which the latter may be led to support the constitutional rights of the former, without being too much detached from the rights of its own department?

If the principles on which these observations are founded be just, as I persuade myself they are, and they be applied as a criterion to the several State constitutions, and to the federal Constitution, it will be found that if the latter does not perfectly correspond with them, the former are infinitely less able to bear such a test.

There are, moreover, two considerations particularly applicable to the federal system of America, which place that system in a very interesting point of view.

First. In a single republic, all the power surrendered by the people is submitted to the administration of a single government; and the usurpations are guarded against by a division of the government into distinct and separate departments. In the compound republic of America, the power surrendered by the people is first divided between two distinct governments, and then the portion allotted to each subdivided among distinct and separate departments. Hence a double security arises to the rights of the people. The different governments will control each other, at the same time that each will be controlled by itself.

Second. It is of great importance in a republic not only to guard the society against the oppression of its rulers, but to guard one part of the society against the injustice of the other part. Different interests necessarily exist in different classes of citizens. If a majority be united by a common interest, the rights of the minority will be insecure. There are but two methods of providing against this evil: the one by creating a will in the community independent of the majority—that is, of the society itself; the other, by comprehending in the society so many separate descriptions of citizens as will render an unjust combination of a majority of the whole very improbable, if not impracticable. The first method prevails in all governments possessing an hereditary or self-appointed authority. This, at best, is but a precarious security; because a power independent of the society may as well espouse the unjust views of the major as the rightful interests of the minor party, and may possibly be turned against both parties. The second method will be exemplified in the federal republic of the United States. Whilst all authority in it will be derived from and dependent on the society, the society itself will be broken into so many parts, interests and classes of citizens, that the rights of individuals, or of the minority, will be in little danger from interested combinations of the majority. In a free government the security for civil rights must be the same as that for religious rights. It consists in the one case in the multiplicity of interests, and in the other in the multiplicity of sects. The degree of security in both cases will depend on the number of interests and sects; and this may be presumed to depend on the extent of country and number of people comprehended under the same government. This view of the subject must particularly recommend a proper federal system to all the sincere and considerate friends of republican government, since it shows that in exact proportion as the territory of the Union may be formed into more circumscribed Confederacies, or States, oppressive combinations of a majority will be facilitated; the best security, under the republican forms, for the rights of every class of citizen, will be diminished; and consequently the stability and independence of some member of the government, the only other security, must be proportionally increased. Justice is the end of government. It is the end of civil society. It ever has been and ever will be pursued until it be obtained, or until liberty be lost in the pursuit. In a society under the forms of which the stronger faction can readily unite and oppress the weaker, anarchy may as truly be said to reign as in a state of nature, where the weaker individual is not secured against the violence of the stronger; and as, in the latter state, even the stronger individuals are prompted, by the uncertainty of their condition, to submit to a government which may protect the weak as well as themselves; so, in the former state, will the more powerful factions or parties be gradually induced, by a like motive, to wish for a government which will protect all parties, the weaker as well as the more powerful. It can be little doubted that if the State of Rhode Island was separated from the Confederacy and left to itself, the insecurity of rights under the popular form of government within such narrow limits would be displayed by such reiterated oppressions of factious majorities that some power altogether independent of the people would soon be called for by the voice of the very factions whose misrule had proved the necessity of it. In the extended republic of the United States, and among the great variety of interests, parties, and sects which it embraces, a coalition of a majority of the whole society could seldom take place on any other principles than those of justice and the general good; whilst there being thus less danger to a minor from the will of a major party, there must be less pretext, also, to provide for the security of the former, by introducing into the government a will not dependent on the latter, or, in other words, a will independent of the society itself. It is no less certain than it is important, notwithstanding the contrary opinions which have been entertained, that the larger the society, provided it lie within a practicable sphere, the more duly capable it will be of self-government. And happily for the republican cause, the practicable sphere may be carried to a very great extent by a judicious modification and mixture of the federal principle.

GLOSSARY

adversarial or attack journalism Form of interpretive journalism that adopts a hostile position toward government, politics, and political figures. (Ch. 10)

advocacy groups Groups organized around broad public goals but without local chapters and often without formal membership. (Ch. 8)

affirmative action Programs that attempt to provide members of disadvantaged groups enhanced opportunities to secure jobs, promotions, and admission to educational institutions. (Ch. 5).

amicus curiae brief Legal briefs filed by organized groups to influence the decision in a Supreme Court case. (Ch. 4)

Antifederalists Opponents of the ratification of the constitution. (Ch. 2)

appellate jurisdiction The power of a court to receive cases from trial courts for the purpose of reviewing whether the legal procedures were properly followed. (Ch. 14)

astroturf lobbying Using deceptive practices and lack of transparency to manufacture grassroots support for an issue important to a particular set of unidentified interests. (Ch. 8)

bad tendency test Free speech test that prohibits speech that could produce a bad outcome, such as violence, no matter how unlikely the possibility the speech could be the cause of such an outcome. (Ch. 4)

battleground state Competitive state where neither party holds an overwhelming edge. (Ch. 12)

benchmark survey A campaign poll that measures a candidate's strength at the time of entrance into the electoral race. (Ch. 6)

bicameral Composed of two houses. (Ch. 2)

Bill of Rights The freedoms listed in the first ten amendments to the U.S. Constitution. (Ch. 4)

blanket primary Election in which voters can choose from among potential nominees in both parties; currently outlawed by the U.S. Supreme Court. (Ch. 9)

block grants Federal programs that provide funds for broad categories of assistance such as health care or law enforcement. (Ch. 3)

bloggers Citizens who create online diaries and forums for the posting of opinions and personal viewpoints. (Ch. 10)

budget resolution Early step in budgeting process in which both houses of Congress set spending goals. (Ch. 11)

bureaucracy A complex system of organization and control that incorporates the principles of hierarchical authority, division of labor, and formalized rules. (Ch. 13)

bureaucrats The civilian employees of the national government who are responsible for implementing federal laws. (Ch. 13)

Bush Doctrine Foreign policy position advanced by George W. Bush asserting the U.S. government's right to authorize preemptive attacks against potential aggressors. (Ch. 12)

BUYcotting Using purchasing decisions to support the products and policies of businesses. (Ch. 7)

Cabinet Presidential appointees to the major administrative units of the executive branch. (Ch. 12)

cabinet departments The fifteen major administrative organizations within the federal bureaucracy that are responsible for major governmental functions such as defense, commerce, and homeland security. (Ch. 12)

cap and trade Market-based system of pollution control whereby individual businesses can buy and sell emission credits even while the total level of industry pollution is capped at some level. (Ch. 15)

casework Practice of finding solutions to constituent problems, usually involving government agencies. (Ch. 11)

categorical grants Federal programs that provide funds for specific programs such as flood assistance. (Ch. 3)

caucus Voter gatherings used to select party candidates to run in the general election. (Ch. 12)

checkbook democracy A term that expresses the notion that little is required of citizens beyond their cash. (Ch. 7)

chief of staff The official in charge of coordinating communication between the president and other staffers. (Ch. 12)

citizenship Status conferring rights and protections to members of the political community but, in return, requiring allegiance and involvement. (Ch. 1)

civic engagement Involvement in any activity aimed at influencing the collective well-being of the community. (Ch. 1)

civil liberties The personal freedoms of individuals that are protected from government intrusion. (Ch. 4)

civic life Participation in the collective life of the community. (Ch. 1)

civil rights Protection of historically disadvantaged groups from infringement of their equality rights by discriminatory action. (Ch. 5)

Civil Rights Act of 1964 Historic legislation that prohibited racial segregation in public accommodations and racial discrimination in employment, education, and voting. (Ch. 5)

civil rights movement The litigation and mobilization activities of African Americans in the second half of the twentieth century that led to a greater realization of equality for all disadvantaged groups. (Ch. 5)

civil service A merit-based system of employment and personnel management that replaced patronage. (Ch. 9)

civil service system The merit-based employment system that covers most white-collar and specialist positions in the federal government. (Ch. 13)

civil society The broad array of voluntary associations that bring citizens together to deal with community and social issues of common concern. (Ch. 1)

civil union Legal recognition by a state of a gay or lesbian relationship; allows gay and lesbian couples to receive the same state benefits as heterosexual married couples. (Ch. 5)

class action suit Lawsuit in which one or more persons sue on behalf of a larger set of people claiming the same injury. (Ch. 14)

clear and present danger test Free speech test that only prohibits speech that produces a clear and immediate danger. (Ch. 4)

closed primary Election in which voters can choose from potential nominees only within their own party. (Ch. 9)

cloture The procedure that ends a filibuster with sixty votes of the Senate. (Ch. 11)

coattails The effect a winning candidate at the top of the ticket has in bringing success to those lower on the ballot. (Ch. 12)

cohort The members of one's own generation. (Ch. 6)

collective goods Goods that are not owned privately but benefit all citizens equally, such as clean air. (Ch. 8)

committee chairs The leaders of congressional committees, usually members of the majority party with the most seniority on that committee. (Ch. 11)

Committee on Rules In the House of Representatives, the committee charged with determining rules for debate, amendment, and vote on bills brought to the floor. (Ch. 11)

comparable worth The notion that individuals performing different jobs that require the same amount of knowledge, effort, skill, responsibility, and working conditions should receive equal compensation; the proposal would elevate the pay structure of many jobs traditionally performed by women. (Ch. 5)

concurring opinion An opinion written by one or more of the justices who agree with the decision but for different reasons than those stated in the majority opinion. (Ch. 14)

concurrent powers Powers shared by both state and national governments. (Ch. 3)

conference committees Committees composed of members of the House and Senate charged to resolve differences between the House and Senate versions of the bill. (Ch. 11)

Congressional Budget Office Nonpartisan agency created by Congress to assist in the budget process. (Ch. 11)

Congressional caucuses Unofficial party or special interest groups formed by like-minded members of Congress to confer on issues of mutual concern. (Ch. 11)

congressional review Congressional action, requiring approval by both houses and the president, that can stop implementation of executive branch regulations. (Ch. 11)

conservatism Political philosophy that rests on belief in traditional institutions and a minimal role for government in economic activity. (Ch. 6)

constituents The citizens from a state or district that an elected official represents. (Ch. 11)

consumer activism The practice of making a political or social statement with one's buying power. (Ch. 7)

containment American policies designed to limit the expansion of Soviet power around the world during the Cold War. (Ch. 16)

continuing resolution Vehicle for funding government operations at the previous year's levels of support when a new budget is delayed. (Ch. 11)

cooperative federalism Federal-state relationship characteristic of the post-New Deal era that stressed state and federal partnership in addressing social problems. (Ch. 3)

creative federalism Federal-state relationship that sought to involve local populations and cities directly in addressing urban problems during the 1960s and 1970s. (Ch. 3)

critical elections Elections signaling realignments, often sweeping the opposition party into control of the presidency and Congress. (Ch. 9)

dealignment A falloff in electoral support for both major political parties. (Ch. 9)

decision The indication of which litigant the court supports and by how large a margin. (Ch. 14)

de facto segregation Segregation that occurs because of past economic and social conditions such as residential racial patterns. (Ch. 5)

defense policy Strategic decisions about the scale and use of military force for national security. (Ch. 16)

de jure segregation Segregation mandated by law or decreed by government officials. (Ch. 5)

delegated powers Powers ceded by Congress to the president. (Ch. 12)

delegate role Theory of representation stressing the lawmaker's role as a tribune of the people who reflects their views on issues of the day. (Ch. 11)

democracy Form of government in which the people rule either directly or through elected leaders. (Ch. 1)

détente Foreign policy begun in the Nixon administration stressing accommodation with rivals rather than conflict. (Ch. 16)

devolution A movement to grant states greater authority over the local operation of federal programs and local use of federal funds that gained momentum in the 1980s. (Ch. 3)

diplomacy The use of peaceful means to build support for common interests and to avoid warfare. (Ch. 16)

diplomatic recognition Presidential power to offer official privileges to foreign governments. (Ch. 12)

direct democracy Form of government in which decisions about public policy extends to the entire citizenry. (Ch. 1)

direction The attribute of an individual's opinion that indicates a preference for or against a particular issue. (Ch. 6)

direct mobilization Process by which citizens are contacted personally by candidate and party organizations to take part in political activities. (Ch. 7)

discharge petition Method for freeing legislation from a committee in the House that requires the signatures of 218 members. (Ch. 11)

discount rate   Interest rate at which member banks can borrow money from the Federal Reserve. (Ch. 15)

discretionary powers   Powers the president assumes, giving him greater authority and flexibility in performing the duties of office. (Ch. 12)

dissenting opinion   An opinion written by one or more justices who disagree with a decision. (Ch. 14)

divided government   Control of the White House by one party while the opposition party controls one or both houses of Congress. (Ch. 9)

dual court system   System under which U.S. citizens are subject to the jurisdiction of both national and state courts. (Ch. 14)

dual federalism   Approach to federal-state relationships that envisions each level of government as distinct and authoritative within its own sphere of action. (Ch. 3)

Duverger's Law   Principle that asserts single-member district elections lead to two-party systems. (Ch. 9)

earmarks   Funding for specific projects that are added by members of Congress to appropriation bills usually without oversight or public debate. (Ch. 11)

earned media   Media attention for which candidates do not pay; associated with major events like debates. (Ch. 9)

elastic clause   Provision of Article I of the Constitution authoring Congress to make those laws necessary and proper for carrying out the other laws it passes. (Ch. 2)

elector   Member of the Electoral College. (Ch. 12)

Electoral College   The assemblage of state electors constitutionally charged with electing the president. (Ch. 9)

elites   Individuals in a position of authority, often those with a higher level education than the population at large. (Ch. 6)

emergency powers   Wide-ranging powers a president may exercise during time of crisis, or those powers permitted the president by Congress for a limited time. (Ch. 12)

enemy combatant   Enemy fighter captured on the field of battle whether or not a member of an army. (Ch. 12)

entitlements   Programs promising aid without time limit to anyone who qualifies. (Ch. 15)

enumerated powers   Powers specifically allocated to the national government alone by the Constitution. (Ch. 3)

Equal Rights Amendment   The proposed constitutional amendment that would have prohibited national and state governments from denying equal rights on the basis of sex. (Ch. 5)

equal time rule   The rule that requires that all broadcasters provide airtime equally to all candidates if they choose to provide it to any. (Ch. 10)

establishment clause   The First Amendment prohibition against the government's establishment of a national religion. (Ch. 4)

exclusionary rule   The judicial barring of illegally seized evidence from a trial. (Ch. 4)

executive agreement   A pact that is made between the president and a foreign leader of a government and that does not require Senate approval. (Ch. 12)

Executive Office of the President   Close presidential advisors that include the White House staff, the national security advisor, the chief of staff, and members of various policy councils. (Ch. 12)

executive order   A decree with the force of law but not requiring legislative approval. (Ch. 12)

executive privilege   Presidential power to shield from scrutiny White House documents and conversations among presidential advisers. (Ch. 12)

exit poll   Interviews of voters as they leave the polling place. (Ch. 6)

express powers   Powers granted to the president by the Constitution. (Ch. 12)

external political efficacy   An individual's belief that his or her activities will influence what the government will do or who will win an election. (Ch. 7)

extraordinary rendition   The practice of secretly abducting terror suspects and transporting them to detention camps in undisclosed locations. (Ch. 12)

faction   Group—most often driven by economic motives—that places its own good above the good of the nation as a whole. (Ch. 2)

fairness doctrine   The law that formerly required broadcasters to present contrasting views on important public issues. (Ch. 10)

federalism   Power-sharing arrangement between the national and state governments in which some powers are granted to the national government alone, some powers are reserved to the states, some powers are held concurrently, and other powers are prohibited to either or both levels of government. (Ch. 3)

Federalists   Supporters of the Constitution and its strong central government. (Ch. 2)

federal mandates   Federal requirements imposed on state and local governments, often as a condition for receiving grants. (Ch. 3)

Federal Register   A publication of the federal government used to announce public notice of the time, place, and nature of the proceedings to be followed when new agency rules are proposed. (Ch. 13)

Fifteenth Amendment   Civil War amendment that extended suffrage to former male slaves. (Ch. 5)

filibuster   Senate practice of continuous debate often employed to stop pending legislative action. (Ch. 11)

fiscal policy   Taxing and spending policies prescribed by Congress and the president. (Ch. 15)

527 groups   Tax-exempt organizations set up by interest groups to engage in political activities. (Ch. 8)

focus groups   Small gatherings of individuals used to test ideas before marketing. (Ch. 6)

Foreign Intelligence Surveillance Act court (FISA court)   Secret court housed in the Justice Department and used to oversee requests by federal agencies for surveillance warrants based on suspected espionage or terrorism. (Ch. 16)

foreign policy   Strategies for dealing with foreign nations on a broad array of military, diplomatic, economic, and security issues. (Ch. 16)

foreign policy liberalism   In foreign policy, the belief that national interests are best secured by building alliances and making conflict more costly than cooperation. (Ch. 16)

Foreign Service   Corps of U.S. diplomats stationed around the world. (Ch. 16)

formula grants   Federal programs that use mathematical calculations or demographic factors to allocate funds to states or localities. (Ch. 3)

Fourteenth Amendment   Civil War amendment that provided all persons with the privileges and immunities of national citizenship; the guarantee of equal protection of the laws by any state; and the safeguard of due process to protect one's life, liberty, and property from state government interference. (Ch. 5)

franking privilege   Free postage for members of Congress to communicate with constituents. (Ch. 11)

free exercise clause   The First Amendment provision intended to protect the practice of one's religion free from government interference. (Ch. 4)

free riders   Those who enjoy the benefits from activities without paying the costs of participation. (Ch. 7)

free trade   The idea that commerce should flow between countries without government restrictions. (Ch. 15)

full faith and credit   Constitutional provision requiring each state to recognize legal transactions authorized in other states. (Ch. 3)

game theory   Foreign policy tool that allows policymakers to predict how nation states will act to promote their self interest. (Ch. 16)

gender gap   Systematic variation in political opinions that exists between males and females. (Ch. 6)

generational effects   The impact of events experienced by a generational cohort on the formation of common political orientations. (Ch. 6)

gerrymander   Practice of drawing congressional boundaries to the advantage of one party. (Ch. 11)

government   The body (or bodies) charged with making official policies for citizens. (Ch. 1)

grand jury   A grand jury assesses a prosecutor's evidence against a potential defendant to be sure it is sufficient to proceed to trial. (Ch. 4)

grassroots mobilization   The practice of organizing citizen support for a group's policy or candidate preferences. (Ch. 8)

Great Compromise   Agreement at the Constitutional Convention splitting the legislature into two bodies—one apportioned by population, the other assigning each state two members. (Ch. 2)

Gregg v. Georgia   The Supreme Court decision that upheld the death penalty in the United States. (Ch. 4)

Gross Domestic Product (GDP)   A measure of the value of all goods and services produced in the United States. (Ch. 15)

hard money   Campaign money received by candidates or parties that can be used for any purpose. (Ch. 9)

hate speech   Prejudicial and hostile statements toward another person's innate characteristics such as race and ethnicity. (Ch. 4)

hold   Action a senator may place on a bill requiring personal consultation before the matter can proceed. (Ch. 11)

homophobia   Irrational fear and hatred directed toward persons who are homosexuals. (Ch. 5)

honeymoon period   The period following an election when the public and Congress give the newly elected president the greatest latitude in decision making. (Ch. 12)

idealism   In foreign policy, the belief that American values such as democracy, freedom, and cultural diversity promote our national interests and should be emulated by other nations. (Ch. 16)

ideological parties   Minor parties organized around distinct ideological principles. (Ch. 9)

ideologue   One who thinks about politics almost exclusively through the prism of his or her ideological perspective. (Ch. 6)

Ideology   Ideas, values, and beliefs about how governments should operate. (Ch. 1)

Impeach   To bring formal charges against a federal official, including the president. (Ch. 11)

imperial presidency   Perspective advanced by some scholars in the 1970s warning about excessive concentration of power in the hands of the chief executive. (Ch. 12)

implied powers   Powers necessary to carry out constitutionally enumerated functions of government. (Ch. 3)

impoundment   Presidential refusal to expend funds appropriated by Congress. (Ch. 12)

incumbent   Current occupant of an office. (Ch. 11)

indirect mobilization   Process by which political leaders use networks of friends and acquaintances to activate political participation. (Ch. 7)

independent executive agency   A governmental unit with special responsibilities that is not part of any cabinet department. (Ch. 13)

independent regulatory agency   An agency existing outside the major departments that regulates a specific economic activity or interest. (Ch. 13)

Inflation   Economic condition in which the supply of money overwhelms our capacity to produce, creating rising prices. (Ch. 15)

informational support   The attribute of an individual's opinion that measures his or her amount of knowledge concerning the issue. (Ch. 6)

Initiative   Procedure that enables citizens to place proposals for laws and amendments directly on the ballot for voter approval. (Ch. 1)

inner cabinet   Term applied to leaders from the Departments of State, Defense, Treasury, and Justice with whom the president meets more frequently than other cabinet officials. (Ch. 12)

inside strategy   A plan of action for advancing one's policies by working directly with influential political insiders. (Ch. 8)

Intensity   The attribute of an individual's opinion that measures how strongly it is held. (Ch. 6)

interest group   Any formally organized association that seeks to influence public policy. (Ch. 8)

intergovernmental lobbies   Professional advocacy groups representing various state and local governing bodies. (Ch. 3)

intermediate scrutiny test   Equal protection test used by the Supreme Court that requires the government to prove that the use of classifications such as age, gender, or race is substantially related to an important government objective. (Ch. 5)

internal political efficacy   An individual's self-confidence in his or her ability to understand and participate in politics. (Ch. 7)

interstate compacts   Cooperative agreements made between states, subject to congressional approval, to address mutual problems. (Ch. 3)

iron triangle   A decision-making structure dominated by interest groups, congressional committees, and executive agency personnel who create policies that are mutually beneficial. (Ch. 8)

issue networks   Decision-making structure consisting of policy experts, including lobbyists, members of Congress, bureaucrats, and policy specialists from think tanks and universities. (Ch. 8)

Jim Crow laws   Legislation in the South that mandated racial segregation in public facilities such as restaurants and restrooms. (Ch. 5)

judicial activism   The belief that the Supreme Court should make policy and vigorously review the policies of other branches. (Ch. 14)

judicial restraint   The belief that the Supreme Court should not become involved in questioning the operations and policies of the elected branches unless absolutely necessary. (Ch. 14)

judicial review   The power of the United States Supreme Court to review the acts of other political institutions and declare them unconstitutional. (Ch. 2)

jurisdiction   The power of a court to hear and decide cases. (Ch. 14)

justiciability   The doctrine that excludes certain cases from judicial consideration because of the party bringing the lawsuit or the nature of the subject matter. (Ch. 14)

Korematsu v. United States   The 1944 Supreme Court decision that upheld the constitutionality of the U.S. government's internment of more than one hundred thousand Americans of Japanese descent during World War II. (Ch. 5)

leadership PACs   Political action committees set up by political leaders as a means to finance the campaigns of political allies whom they believe will reciprocate with support for their own political ambitions. (Ch. 8)

leading question   A question worded to suggest a particular answer desired by the pollster. (Ch. 6)

legislative referendum   Ballot measure aimed at securing voter approval for some legislative acts, such as changes to a state's constitution. (Ch. 1)

legislative veto   Device, declared unconstitutional in 1983, allowing Congress to rescind rules promulgated by an executive agency. (Ch. 11)

lemon test   The three-part test for establishment clause cases that a law must pass before it is declared constitutional; it must have a secular purpose; it must neither advance nor inhibit religion; and it must not cause excessive entanglement with religion. (Ch. 4)

libel   Written statements that are false and injure another's reputation. (Ch. 4)

liberal democracy   Ideology stressing individual rights and expressing faith in popular control of government. (Ch. 1)

liberalism   Political philosophy that combines a belief in personal freedoms with the belief that government should intervene in the economy to promote greater quality. (Ch. 6)

Libertarianism   Political philosophy that espouses strong support for individual liberty in both social and economic areas of life. (Ch. 6)

life cycle effects   The impact of age-related factors in the formation of political attitudes, opinions, and beliefs. (Ch. 6)

line item veto   Executive power to reject a portion of a bill, usually a budget appropriation. (Ch. 12)

line organization   An administrative organization that is directly accountable to the president. (Ch. 13)

litigious   Marked by a tendency to file lawsuits. (Ch. 14)

lobbying   Tactic for influencing public decisions for private purposes, usually employing personal contact with elected officials. (Ch. 8)

logrolling   The practice of trading votes to the mutual advantage of members. (Ch. 11)

majority leader   Leader of the majority party in each house, responsible for marshaling support for the party's agenda. (Ch. 11)

majority opinion   An opinion written by a justice who represents a majority of the court. (Ch. 14)

majority rule   The requirement that electoral majorities determine who is elected to office and that majorities in power determine our laws and how they are administered. (Ch. 1)

markup   Committee sessions in which members review contents of legislation line by line. (Ch. 11)

mass media   The total array of mass communication, including television, radio, newspapers, magazines, and the Internet. (Ch. 10)

merit system   The system that classifies federal civil service jobs into grades to which appointments are made on the basis of performance on competitive exams. (Ch. 13)

***Miller* test**   The current judicial test for obscenity cases that considers community standards, whether the material is patently offensive, and whether the material taken as a whole lacks serious literary, artistic, political, or scientific value. (Ch. 4)

minority leader   Leader of the minority party in each house, responsible for marshaling support for the party's agenda. (Ch. 11)

minority-majority district   District in which minority members are clustered together, producing a majority of minority voters in the district. (Ch. 11)

minority rights   Protections beyond the reach of majority control guaranteed to all citizens. (Ch. 1)

Miranda rights   The warning police must administer to suspects so that the latter will be aware of their right not to incriminate themselves. The rights include the right to remain silent, the right to know statements will be used against them, and the right to have an attorney for the interrogation. (Ch. 4)

mobilizing the grass tops   Mining databases for high-status community leaders for purposes of contacting legislators in key districts regarding sponsoring a group's position. (Ch. 8)

monetary policy   Control of economic growth through management of the money supply by the Federal Reserve. (Ch. 15)

mutually assured destruction   Arms policy followed by the superpowers during the Cold War, in which each side maintained an arsenal of nuclear weapons sufficient to destroy its enemy even after a first strike. (Ch. 16)

narrowcasting   Programming targeted to one small sector of the population, made possible by the emergence of cable television and the Internet. (Ch. 10)

national convention   Event held every four years by each political party to formally anoint its presidential candidate and to signal the initiation of the general election campaign. (Ch. 9)

national interests   The constellation of military, economic, and ideological concerns surrounding a nation's security. (Ch. 16)

negative or attack advertising   Advertising that attacks one's opponents, usually on the basis of issue stance or character. (Ch. 9)

neoconservatism   Perspective advocating military strength and the promotion of American values abroad. (Ch. 16)

New Deal coalition   Constellation of social groups that became the core base of support for the Democratic Party after the election of Franklin D. Roosevelt. (Ch. 9)

nominating convention   A meeting of state party delegates to select their presidential nominee. (Ch. 12)

nonattitudes   The generation of opinions by a poll that do not exist in reality. (Ch. 6)

nongovernmental organizations (NGOs)   Nonprofit citizens' groups organized for a variety of charitable and humanitarian purposes on a local, national, or international level. (Ch. 16)

North American Free Trade Agreement   A 1994 trade agreement eliminating trade barriers among the United States, Canada, and Mexico. (Ch. 15)

nullification   Doctrine that asserted the right of states to disregard federal actions with which they disagreed. (Ch. 3)

open market operations   The buying and selling of government securities by the Federal Reserve with the intention of altering the nation's money supply. (Ch. 15)

open primary   Election in which voters can choose from among potential nominees from their own party or those from the other major political party. (Ch. 9)

opinions   The written arguments explaining the reasons behind a decision. (Ch. 14)

opposition research   Practice of searching for events in candidates' records or personal lives that can be used to attack them during elections. (Ch. 9)

original jurisdiction   The power of a court to hear and decide a case first. (Ch. 14)

outside strategy   A plan of action for advancing one's policies by building popular support for one's cause. (Ch. 8)

oversight   Congressional authority to monitor the actions and budgets of executive agencies it creates. (Ch. 11)

paid media   Media access for which candidates or party must pay a fee; advertisements. (Ch. 9)

patronage   A practice of providing jobs in exchange for political loyalty. (Ch. 9)

per curiam opinion   An unsigned opinion of the Supreme Court that usually signals a high degree of consensus. (Ch. 14)

platform   Statement of political principles and campaign promises generated by each party at its national convention. (Ch. 9)

pluralism   View positing that various groups and coalitions constantly vie for government favor and the ability to exercise political power but none enjoys long-term dominance. (Ch. 1)

plurality   Having more votes than any other single candidate; may not constitute a majority. (Ch. 9)

plurality opinion   An opinion that is written on behalf of the largest bloc of the justices, representing less than a majority, who agree on the reasons supporting the court's decision. (Ch. 14)

pocket veto   Automatic veto achieved when a bill sits unsigned on a president's desk for ten days when Congress is out of session. (Ch. 11)

police powers   Authority states utilize to protect the health and welfare of their residents. (Ch. 3)

political action committees (PACs)   Organized financial arms of interest groups used to collect and distribute money to candidates for elective office. (Ch. 8)

political culture   The dominant values and beliefs of a political community. (Ch. 6)

political cynicism   The view that government officials look out mostly for themselves. (Ch. 6)

political disadvantage theory   View positing that groups are likely to seek remedies in courts if they do not succeed in the electoral process. (Ch. 8)

political efficacy   The belief that an individual's actions can have an impact on the political process. (Ch. 6)

political engagement   Psychological predisposition toward or interest in politics. (Ch. 7)

political entrepreneur   Individual who develops support for latent causes or projects that have not yet gained widespread popularity. (Ch. 8)

political ideology   A cohesive set of beliefs that form a general philosophy about the role of government. (Ch. 6)

political information   A measure of the amount of political knowledge an individual possesses concerning political issues, political figures, and the workings of the political system. (Ch. 7)

political interest   An attribute of political participants that measures one's concern for an election outcome and the positions of the candidates on the issues. (Ch. 7)

political machine   A strong party organization that maintained control by giving favors in return for votes. (Ch. 9)

political mobilization   Process whereby citizens are alerted to participatory opportunities and encouraged to become involved. (Ch. 7)

political movement   An organized constellation of groups seeking wide-ranging social change. (Ch. 8)

political participation   Taking part in activities like voting or running for office aimed at influencing the policies or leadership of government. (Ch. 1)

political party   Organization created for the purpose of winning elections and governing once in office. (Ch. 9)

political power   The ability to get things done by controlling or influencing the institutions of government. (Ch. 1)

political questions   Issues determined by the Supreme Court to be better resolved by Congress or the president. (Ch. 14)

political socialization   The process by which individuals come to adopt the attitudes, values, beliefs, and opinions of their political culture. (Ch. 6)

politico   Approach to representation in which the lawmaker alternates between trustee and delegate roles as he or she deems appropriate. (Ch. 11)

politics   The process by which we choose government officials and make decisions about public policy. (Ch. 1)

popular referendum   A device that allows citizens to approve or repeal measures already acted on by legislative bodies. (Ch. 1)

population   The people whose opinions are being estimated through interviews with samples of group members. (Ch. 6)

populist   Political philosophy expressing support for greater equality and for traditional social values. (Ch. 6)

pork barrel projects   Term applied to spending for pet projects of individual members of Congress. (Ch. 11)

precedent   A former case that was supported by a majority on an appellate court and provides guidance for the determination of a present case. (Ch. 14)

precinct   The geographic area served by a polling place and organized by local party units. (Ch. 9)

preemption   Doctrine espoused by President George W. Bush, permitting U.S. use of force to prevent hostile acts by its enemies even if we are uncertain about the time and place of the enemy attack. (Ch. 16)

presidential doctrine   Formal statement that outlines the goals and purposes of American foreign policy and the actions to take to advance these goals. (Ch. 12)

president pro tempore   The second-highest-ranking official in the U.S. Senate. (Ch. 11)

primary election   Election in which voters choose candidates to represent the political parties in the general election. (Ch. 9)

prior restraint   A practice that would allow the government to censor a publication before anyone could read or view it. (Ch. 4)

privileges and immunities   Constitutional phrase interpreted to refer to fundamental rights, such as freedom to make a living, and access to the political and legal processes of the state. (Ch. 3)

probability sampling   A sample design showing that each individual in the population has a known probability of being included in the sample. (Ch. 6)

probable cause   A practical and nontechnical calculation of probabilities that is the basis for securing search warrants. (Ch. 4)

program grants   Federal programs that provide funds for very narrow purposes and contain clear time frames for completion—e.g., construction of a portion of highway. (Ch. 3)

prohibited powers   Powers denied one or both levels of government. (Ch. 3)

proportional representation   System of representation in which seats for office are apportioned according to proportion of votes received by candidates or parties. (Ch. 9)

prospective voting   Voting choice made on the basis of anticipated results if the candidate of choice is elected. (Ch. 9)

protectionism   Policy of using taxes and tariffs to limit the kinds and amounts of foreign goods entering the nation. (Ch. 15)

public interest groups   Those advocating policies they believe promote the good of all Americans and not merely the economic or ideological interests of a few. (Ch. 8)

public opinion   Opinions held by private individuals that governments find it prudent to heed. (Ch. 6)

public policy   Anything the government chooses to do or not to do. (Ch. 15)

push poll   Campaign tactic that attacks an opponent while pretending to be a poll. (Ch. 6)

rallying around the flag   Sense of patriotism engendered by dramatic national events such as the September 11, 2001, terrorist attacks. (Ch. 12)

rational actor theory   The theory that choices are based on our individual assessment of costs and benefits. (Ch. 7)

rational basis test   Equal protection test used by the Supreme Court that requires a complainant to prove that the use of a classification such as age, gender, or race is not a reasonable means of achieving a legitimate government objective. (Ch. 5)

realignments   Periodic changes in party strength, composition, and direction. (Ch. 9)

realism   In foreign policy, the belief that national interests are best assured by a strong military that can act as a deterrent to other nations. (Ch. 16)

reapportionment   The periodic reallocation of 435 House seats among the states as population shifts from one region to another. (Ch. 11)

recall   Procedure whereby citizens can remove and replace a public official before the end of a term. (Ch. 1)

recess appointment   Political appointment made by the president when Congress is out of session. (Ch. 12)

recession   Period of the business cycle characterized by high levels of unemployment. (Ch. 15)

rescission   Cutback of funds for particular programs that requires Congressional approval. (Ch. 11)

reconciliation   Process of amending spending bills to meet budget targets. (Ch. 11)

redistricting   The practice of drawing congressional district boundaries to accord with population changes. (Ch. 11)

Regents of the University of California v. Bakke   The 1978 Supreme Court case that declared unconstitutional the use of racial quotas to achieve a diverse student body but allowed the use of race as one of many factors in admissions decisions. (Ch. 5)

representative democracy   Form of government in which popular decision making is restricted to electing or appointing the public officials who make public policy. (Ch. 1)

reserved powers   Powers constitutionally allocated to the states. (Ch. 3)

reserve requirement ratio   The amount of money the Fed requires banks to keep on hand to meet their liabilities. Its size helps determine how much banks can lend. (Ch. 15)

retail politics   Campaign style emphasizing close personal contact between candidate and voters. (Ch. 9)

retrospective voting   Voting on the basis of the candidate's or party's record in office. (Ch. 9)

revenue sharing   A grant program begun in 1972 and ended in 1987 that funneled money directly to states and local governments on the basis of formulas that combined population figures with levels of demonstrated need. (Ch. 3)

reverse discrimination   Argument that the use of race as a factor in affirmative action programs constitutes unconstitutional discrimination against the majority population. (Ch. 5)

revolving door   Term referring to the back-and-forth movement of individuals between government and interest group employment. (Ch. 8)

Roe v. Wade   The Supreme Court case that legalized abortions in the United States during the first two trimesters of a pregnancy. (Ch. 4)

rule making   The administrative process that creates rules that have the characteristics of a law. (Ch. 13)

Rule of Four   Requirement that a minimum of four justices must vote to review a lower court case by issuing a writ of certiorari. (Ch. 14)

ruling elite theory   View positing that wealthy and well-educated citizens exercise a disproportionate amount of influence over political decision making. (Ch. 1)

runoff election   Second election between top two vote-getters in a race that did not produce a majority winner. (Ch. 9)

safe district   Electoral district in which the candidate from the dominant party usually wins by 55 percent or more. (Ch. 11)

safe seats   Legislative districts that regularly remain in the hands of the same candidate or party. (Ch. 9)

salience   The attribute of an individual's opinion that indicates how central it is to her or his daily concerns. (Ch. 6)

sample   The individuals whose opinions are actually measured. (Ch. 6)

sampling error   The measure of the degree of accuracy of a poll based on the size of the sample. (Ch. 6)

scientific polls   Any poll using proper sampling designs. (Ch. 6)

selective incorporation   The process of applying some of the rights in the Bill of Rights to the states through the due process clause of the Fourteenth Amendment. (Ch. 4)

senatorial courtesy   In the selection of lower federal court judges, deference shown to home-state senators who are of the same party as the president. (Ch. 14)

seniority system   A system that rewards those with longer service with positions of leadership. (Ch. 11)

service learning programs   Agencies that help connect volunteers with organizations in need of help. (Ch. 1)

sexual harassment   The practice of awarding jobs or job benefits in exchange for sexual favors, or the creation of a hostile work or education environment by unwarranted sexual advances or sexual conversation. (Ch. 5)

signing statement(s)   Documents presidents append to legislation indicating their particular interpretation of its contents. (Ch. 11)

single-issue or -candidate parties   Minor parties arising in electoral response to important issues not addressed by major-party candidates or around a strong personality. (Ch. 9)

simple random sampling   Technique of drawing a sample for interview in which all members of the targeted population have the same probability of being selected for interview. (Ch. 6)

single member district   Electoral system in which the candidate receiving a plurality of votes wins the election to represent the district. (Ch. 9)

slander   Oral statements that are false and injure another's reputation. (Ch. 4)

social capital   Bonds of trust and reciprocity between citizens that form the glue that holds modern societies together. (Ch. 1)

social class The perceived combination of wealth, income, education, and occupation that contributes to one's status and power in society. (Ch. 1)

soft money Money that is outside the federal regulatory framework but raised and spent in a manner suggesting possible intent to affect federal elections. (Ch. 9)

soft power The ability to persuade others without coercion. (Ch. 16)

sound bites News programs' short video clips of politicians' statements. (Ch. 10)

Sovereign Independent. (Ch. 2)

Speaker of the House The most powerful leader of the House of Representatives. (Ch. 11)

spin A campaign's favorable interpretation of their campaign and unfavorable view of their opponent's activities. (Ch. 10)

spin doctors Political campaign operatives who interpret campaign events in the most favorable light to their candidate. (Ch. 10)

splinter parties Political parties that are formed as offshoots of major political parties, usually by dissenters. (Ch. 9)

spoils system The expansion of the patronage system to a level of corruption that placed political cronies into all levels of government. (Ch. 13)

stability The attribute of an individual's opinion that measures how consistently it is held. (Ch. 6)

standing Proof that a party has suffered harm or been threatened with harm by the circumstances surrounding a lawsuit. (Ch. 14)

strategy A group's overall plan for achieving its goals. (Ch. 8)

straw poll An unscientific survey of popular views. (Ch. 6)

strength of party identification The degree of loyalty that an individual feels toward a particular political party. (Ch. 7)

strict scrutiny test Equal protection test used by the Supreme Court that places the greatest burden of proof on the government to prove that classifications such as age, gender, or race are the least restrictive means to achieve a compelling government goal. (Ch. 5)

***Sullivan* rule** Standard requiring public officials and public figures in defamation suits to prove that allegedly libelous or slanderous statements are both false and made with malice. (Ch. 4)

superdelegates Democratic Party leaders and elected officials attending the party convention who may pledge support to a candidate prior to the convention. (Ch. 12)

supply-side economics Approach to economic policymaking focusing on lowering the barriers to production on the assumption that supplies at the right price will create their own demand. (Ch. 15)

supremacy clause Provision of Article VI stipulating that the federal government, in exercising any of the powers enumerated in the Constitution, must prevail over any conflicting or inconsistent state exercise of power. (Ch. 2)

symbolic speech Actions meant to convey a political message. (Ch. 4)

systematic sampling A sample design to ensure that each individual in the population has an equal chance of being chosen after the first name or number is chosen at random. (Ch. 6)

tactics Specific actions that groups take to implement strategies. (Ch. 8)

test case Practice by which a group deliberately brings a case to court in order to secure a judicial ruling on a constitutional issue. (Ch. 8)

third party Minor parties that run a slate of their own candidates in opposition to major-party organizations in an election. (Ch. 9)

Thirteenth Amendment Civil War amendment that specifically prohibited slavery in the United States. (Ch. 5)

tracking polls Campaign polls that measure candidates' relative strength on a daily basis. (Ch. 6)

trial heat survey A campaign poll that measures the popularity of competing candidates in a particular electoral race. (Ch. 6)

trustee Theory of representation stressing the lawmaker's own judgment in legislative decision making. (Ch. 11)

unicameral Single body legislature. (Ch. 2)

unfunded mandates Requirements imposed on state and local governments for which the federal government provides no funds for compliance. (Ch. 3)

unitary executive Theory stressing the importance of giving the president greater authority in foreign policy and in enforcing discipline over members of the executive bureaucracy. (Ch. 12)

unit rule Practice of awarding all of a state's electoral votes to the candidate who wins a plurality of the popular vote in presidential contents. (Ch. 12)

unpledged delegates Elected and appointed party leaders who are chosen as delegates to the national party conventions with the ability to cast their votes for any candidate regardless of primary election results. (Ch. 12)

voter fatigue A tendency to tire of the process of voting as a result of frequent elections. (Ch. 7)

Voting Rights Act of 1965 Federal legislation that outlawed literacy tests and empowered federal officials to enter southern states to register African American voters; the act dismantled the most significant barriers to African Americans' suffrage rights. (Ch. 5)

welfare Term characterizing the wide variety of social programs developed during the New Deal to help the poor, unemployed, disabled, and elderly. (Ch. 15)

Whips Assistant party leaders in each house whose jobs include ensuring that party members are present for floor votes and prepared to vote as the party prefers. (Ch. 11)

whistle-blowing The practice whereby individuals in the bureaucracy bring public attention to gross inefficiency or corruption in the government. (Ch. 13)

writ of certiorari Order issued by a superior court to one of inferior jurisdiction demanding the record of a particular case. (Ch. 14)

Chapter 1: Citizenship in Our Changing Democracy

1. David Weigel, "Outside the White House on V-OBL Day," posted Monday, May 02, 2011 3:37 AM, http://www.slate.com/blogs/weigel/2011/05/02/outside_the_white_house_on_v_obl_day.html.

2. Tamara Audi, Stu Woo, Alexandra Berzon, "Reaction To Bin Laden Death Rolls Across the Web-Dispatch," *Wall Street Journal online,* posted Monday May 2, 2011, 12:05 AM ET.

3. Weigel, op. cit.

4. Paul Taylor and Scott Keeter, eds. *Millennials: A Portrait of Generation Next,* Pew Research Center, February 2010.

5. Mark Hugo Lopez and Paul Taylor, *Dissecting the 2008 Electorate: Most Diverse in U.S. History,* Pew Research Center, April 30, 2009. Accessed on May 9, 2009 at http://pewresearch.org/assets/pdf/dissecting-2008-electorate.pdf. See also, The Center for Information and Research on Civic Learning and Engagement, "Young Voters in the 2008 Presidential Election: Fact Sheet," Updated December 19, 2008. Accessed on May 3, 2011 at http://www.civicyouth.org/PopUps/FactSheets/FS_08_exit_polls.pdf.

6. Peter Leyden and Ruy Teixeira, The Progressive Politics of the Millennial Generation. Paper presented for the New Politics Institute, June 21, 2007. Accessed on May 3, 2011 at http://www.newpolitics.net/node/360?full_report=1.

7. Taylor and Keeter, op. cit.

8. Center for Information and Research on Civic Learning and Engagement, *Young Voters in the 2010 Election. Updated November 17, 2010.* Accessed on April 9, 2011 at http://www.civicyouth.org/wp-content/uploads/2010/11/2010-Exit-Poll-FS-Nov-17-Update.pdf.

9. Frank Newport, "Trust in Legislative Branch Falls to Record-Low 36%," *Gallup Poll,* (September 24, 2010). Accessed on May 3, 2011 at http://www.gallup.com/poll/143225/Trust-Legislative-Branch-Falls-Record-Low.aspx

10. Robert D. Putnam, *Bowling Alone: The Collapse and Revival of American Community* (New York: Simon and Schuster, 2000).

11. See, for example, C. Everett Ladd, *The Ladd Report* (New York: Free Press, 1999).

12. See, for example, C. Wright Mills, *The Power Elite* (New York: Oxford University Press, 1956); Michael Parenti, *Democracy for the Few,* 7th ed. (Belmont, CA: Wadsworth Publishing, 2001); Gaetano Mosca, *The Ruling Class* (Boston: McGraw-Hill, 1959); see also Peter Bachrach, *The Theory of Democratic Elitism: A Critique* (Boston: Little-Brown, 1967).

13. Robert Dahl, *A Preface to Democratic Theory: How Does Popular Sovereignty Function in America?* (Chicago: University of Chicago Press, 1963).

14. See, for example, Jeffrey A. Winters and Benjamin I. Page, "Oligarchy in the United States?" *Perspectives on Politics* 7(4) 2009, 731–751. See also, American Political Science Association, "Task Force on Inequality and American Democracy," *Perspectives on Politics* 2(4)2004, 651–666 and Lawrence R. Jacobs and Theda Skocpol, eds. *Inequality and American Democracy: What We Know and What We Need to Learn* (New York: Russell Sage, 2005).

15. Joseph Losco and Leonard Williams, *Political Theory: Classic and Contemporary Readings,* vol. 2, 2d ed. (Los Angeles: Roxbury Press, 2003).

16. Report of the American Political Science Association's Standing Committee on Civic Education and Engagement, *Democracy at Risk: Renewing the Political Science of Citizenship* (Chicago: American Political Science Meeting, 2004), 69.

17. Michael Olander, Emily Hoban Kirby, and Krista Schmitt. Attitudes of Young People Towards Diversity: Fact Sheet of the Center for Information and Research on Civic Learning and Engagement. February, 2005.

18. Janny Scott and David Leonhardt, "Class in America: Shadowy Lines That Still Divide," *The New York Times,* May 15, 2005, 1.

19. Organization for Economic Cooperation and Development, *Growing Unequal? Income and Poverty Distribution in OECD Countries* (Paris: OECD Publishing, October 2008).

20. Study prepared for the *New York Times* by Susan Weber and Andrew Beveridge, reported in Scott and Leonhardt, 16.

21. Study by Thomas Hertz reported in "Ever Higher Society, Ever Harder to Ascend," *The Economist,* Dec. 29, 2004.

22. Jacob S. Hacker and Paul Pierson, *Winner-Take-All Politics: How Washington Made the Rich Richer-And Turned Its Back on the Middle Class* (New York: Simon & Schuster, 2010), p. 29.

23. Robert Scott and Adam Hersh, *Economic Snapshots* (Washington, DC: Economic Policy Institute, June 11, 2003).

24. Donald P. Green and Alan S. Gerber, *Get Out the Vote: How to Increase Voter Turnout,* 2d ed. (Washington, D.C.: Brookings Institution, 2008).

Chapter 2: The Constitution: The Foundation of Citizens' Rights

1. Jennifer Steinhauer, The Constitution Has Its Day (More or Less) in House. *The New York Times,* January 6, 2011. Accessed on April 9, 2011 at http://www.nytimes.com/2011/01/07/us/politics/07constitution.html.

2. Quoted in: Chris Good, Should Congress Have Read the WHOLE Constitution? Jesse Jackson, Jr. Makes the Case. *The Atlantic,* January 6, 2011. Accessed on April 9, 2011 at http://www.theatlantic.com/politics/archive/2011/01/should-congress-have-read-the-whole-constitution-jesse-jackson-jr-makes-the-case/68983/

3. Steinhauer, op cit.

4. Charles Beard, *An Economic Interpretation of the Constitution of the United States* (New York: Macmillan, 1913).

5. John P. Roche, "The Founding Fathers: A Reform Caucus in Action," *American Political Science Review 55* (1961): 816.

6. Congressional Quarterly, *Origins and Development of Congress,* 2d ed. (Washington, DC: Congressional Quarterly, 1982).

7. Ibid., 61.

8. Roche, 816.

9. James Madison, "Federalist 51," *The Federalist Papers,* Clinton Rossiter, ed. (New York: Mentor, 1961), 322.

10. Ibid., 323.

11. Joseph J. Keenan, *The Constitution of the United States: An Unfolding Story,* 2d ed. (Chicago: Dorsey Press, 1988), 27.

12. Patrick Henry, "Against the Federal Constitution: June 5, 1788," American Rhetorical Movements to 1900. Accessed online at http://www.wfu.edu on July 18, 2005.

13. James Madison, "Federalist 10," *The Federalist Papers,* Clinton Rossiter, ed. (New York: Mentor, 1961), 77–84.

14. Quoted in Keenan, 35.

15. Daniel Diller and Stephen H. Wirls, "Commander in Chief," in *Powers of the Presidency,* 2d ed. (Washington, DC: CQ Press, 1997), 165.

16. Alexander Hamilton, "Federalist 78," *The Federalist Papers,* Clinton Rossiter, ed. (New York: Mentor, 1961), 467.

17. *Roe v. Wade,* 410 U.S. 113 (1975).

18. Frederick Jackson Turner, *The Frontier in American History* (New York: Holt, 1920).

19. Pub. L. 108–447, *Consolidated Appropriations Act*, 2005.

Chapter 3: Federalism: Citizenship and the Dispersal of Power

1. Kelly Shannon, *Perry fires up anti-tax crowd,* Associated Press (April 15, 2009).

2. U.S. Census Bureau Government's Integrated Directory, accessed online at http:www.census.gov/compendia/statab/tables/09s0410.pdf. May 8, 2009.

3. James Madison, "Federalist 51," *The Federalist Papers,* Clinton Rossiter, ed. (New York: Mentor, 1961), 232.

4. Steven Macedo, Yvetee Alex-Assensoh, Jeffrey M. Berry, Michael Brintnall, David E. Campbell, Luis Ricardo Fraga, Archon Fung, William A. Galston, Christopher F. Karpowitz, Margaret Levi, Meira Levinson, Keena Lipsitz, Richard G. Niemi, Robert D. Putnam, Wendy M. Rahn, Rob Reich, Robert R. Rogers, Todd Swanstrom, and Katherine Cramer Walsh, *Democracy at Risk: How Political Choices Undermine Citizen Participation and What We Can Do About It* (Washington, DC: Brookings Institution, 2005), 68–73.

5. For an excellent discussion of the legacy of Jefferson's nullification movement and its contribution to factional strife leading to the Civil War, see Garry Wills, *A Necessary Evil: A History of American Distrust of Government* (New York: Simon and Schuster, 1999).

6. *McCulloch v. Maryland*, 4 Wheaton 316 (1819).

7. Ibid.

8. *Dred Scott v. Sandford,* 60 U.S. 393 (1857).

9. *Hammer v. Dagenhart*, 247 U.S. 251 (1918).

10. *U.S. v. E.C. Knight Co.,* 156 U.S. 1 (1895).

11. *Lochner v. U.S.,* 198 U.S. 25 (1905).

12. *Schechter Poultry Co. v. U.S.,* 295 U.S. 495 (1935).

13. *U.S. v. Butler,* 297 U.S. 1 (1936).

14. *Brown v. Board of Education of Topeka*, 347 U.S. 483 (1954).

15. *Roe v. Wade*, 401 U.S. 113 (1973).

16. See, for example, *Gideon v. Wainwright*, 372 U.S. 335 (1963).

17. *South Carolina v. Katzenbach*, 383 U.S. 301 (1966).

18. *United States v. Lopez,* 514 U.S. 549 (1995).

19. *Printz v. United States*, 521 U.S. 898 (1997).

20. *Kimel v. Florida Board of Regents*, 528 U.S. 62 (2000).

21. *Board of Trustees v. Garrett*, 531 U.S. 356 (2001).

22. Marcia Howard, executive director of Federal Funds Information for States, quoted in: Alan Greenblatt, "Federalism in the Age of Obama," State Legislatures, (July/August 2010), p. 28.

23. Donald Boyd, "2006 Rockefeller Institute Reports on State and Local Government Finances," Rockefeller Institute for Government, May 2006.

24. Ben Canada, *Federal Grants to State and Local Government: A Brief History* (Washington, DC: Congressional Research Service, 2003).

25. Ben Canada, "Federal Grants to State and Local Governments: Overview and Characteristics, RS 20669," *CRS Report for Congress* (Washington, DC: Congressional Research Service, November 22, 2002), 3.

26. The first block grant, the Partnership for Public Health, was created by Congress in 1966. See Canada, 11.

27. Canada, 4.

28. Canada, 13.

29. Carl Tubbesing, "Think Recovery," *State Legislatures* (April 2009), p. 32.

30. Kenneth Finegold, Laura Wherry, and Stephanie Schardin, "Block Grants: Historic Overview and Lessons Learned," *New Federalism: Issues and Options for States,* Series A, No. A-63 (Washington, DC: Brookings Institution, 2004). Accessed online at http://www.urban.org on Feb. 5, 2005.

31. Congressional Budget Office, *CBO's Activities Under the Unfunded Mandates Reform Act, 1996–2000* (Washington, DC, May 2001).

32. National Council of State Legislatures, *Mandate Monitor*, vol. 1, no. 1 (March 31, 2004). Accessed online at http://www.ncsl.org on February 9, 2005.

33. David C. Nice and Patricia Fredericksen, *The Politics of Intergovernmental Relations*, 2d ed. (Chicago: Nelson-Hall, 1995), 35.

34. See, for example, Paul E. Peterson, "Federalism, Economic Development, and Redistribution," in *Public Values and Private Power in American Politics,* J. David Greenstone, ed. (Chicago: University of Chicago Press, 1982). Also see Grant McConnell, *Private Power and American Democracy* (New York: Knopf, 1966).

35. *Garcia v. San Antonio Metropolitan Transit Authority,* 469 U.S. 528 (1985).

36. *New York v. United States,* 505 U.S. 144 (1992).

37. *Printz v. United States*, 521 U.S. 898 (1997).

38. *Gonzales v. Raich*, 545 U.S. 1 (2005).

39. *Alden v. Maine,* 527 U.S. 706 (1999).

40. *Kimel v. Florida Board of Regents,* 528 U.S. 62 (2000).

41. *Tennessee v. Lane,* 541 U.S. 509 (2004).

42. *District of Columbia v. Heller,* 554 U.S. (2008).

43. Nice and Fredericksen, 122.

44. Robin Minietta, "Southern Hospitality," *Online Newshour* (October 14, 1996). Accessed online at http://www.pbs.org on February 5, 2005.

45. *New State Ice v. Liebmann,* 285 U.S. 262 (1932).

46. Jack L. Walker, "The Diffusion of Innovations Among the American States," *American Political Science Review* 63, no. 3 (1969): 880–899. For somewhat differing analyses and a discussion of the methodological problems involved in measuring innovation and diffusion, see Virginia Gray, "Innovation in the States: A Diffusion Study," *American Political Science Review* 67 (1973): 1174–1185; Jack L. Walker, "Comment: Problems in Research on the Diffusion of Policy Innovation, *American Political Science Review* 67 (1973): 1186–1191; John L. Foster, "Regionalism and Innovation in the American States," *Journal of Politics* 40:1 (1978): 179–187; David C. Nice, *Policy Innovation in the States* (Ames: Iowa State University Press, 1994).

47. Michael Mintrom, "Policy Entrepreneurs and the Diffusion of Innovation," *American Journal of Political Science* 41 no. 3 (1977): 738–770.

48. Susan Welch and Kay Thompson, "The Impact of Federal Incentives on State Policy Innovation," *American Journal of Political Science* 24:4 (1980): 715–729.

49. Daniel J. Elazar, *Federalism: A View from the States*, 3d ed. (New York: HarperCollins, 1984).

50. Macedo, et al., 72.

51. Alexis de Tocqueville, trans. George Lawrence, by J. P. Mayer, *Democracy In America* (New York: HarperCollins, 1969), 164.

Chapter 4: Civil Liberties: Expanding Citizens' Rights

1. Brandi Grissom, "Texas Death Row Inmate Skinner Gets Stay," (*The Texas Tribune,* March 25, 2010.)

2. Liliana Segura, "With DNA Still Untested, Texas Prisoner Hank Skinner Scheduled to Die Tonight," accessed June 16, 2011 at http://

blogs.alternet.org/speakeasy/2010/03/24/with-dna-still-untested-texas-prisoner-hank-skinner-scheduled-to-die-tonight/

3. Daniel J. Elazar, "How Present Conceptions of Human Rights Shape the Protection of Rights in the United States," in Robert A. Licht, ed. *Old Rights and New* (Washington DC: AEI Press, 1993), 39.

4. Daniel A. Farber and Suzanna Sherry, *A History of the American Constitution* (St. Paul, MN: West Publishing Company, 1990), 221–222.

5. Alexander Hamilton, John Jay, and James Madison, *The Federalist Papers,* Benjamin F. Wright, ed. (New York: Metro Books, 1961), 535.

6. Of the two that were rejected, one provided for the state to add a representative to the House each time their population grew by thirty thousand and the other called for an intervening congressional election before any pay raise for members of Congress could take effect. The latter became the Twenty-seventh Amendment nearly two hundred years later.

7. *Barron v. Baltimore* (1833).

8. Highlighting supplied by the authors.

9. *Farber and Sherry,* 122–123.

10. Although the establishment clause is mentioned first in the First Amendment, the free exercise clause is dealt with first because its interpretation is easier for students to understand.

11. Letter quoted in *Reynolds v. United States* (1879).

12. *Cantwell v. Connecticut* (1940).

13. *Reynolds v. United States* (1879) and *Employment Division, Department of Human Resources of Oregon v. Smith* (1990).

14. *Sherbert v. Verner* (1963).

15. *Wisconsin v. Yoder* (1972).

16. *Goldman v. Weinberger* (1986).

17. *City of Boerne v. Flores* (1997).

18. The Pew Forum on Religion & Public Life, "Comparative Religion-U.S. Religion Landscape Study," 2008. 21. See Michael J. Malbin, *Religion and Politics: The Intentions of the Authors of the First Amendment* (Washington, DC: American Enterprise Institute, 1978).

19. See Michael J. Malbin, *Religion and Politics: The Intentions of the Authors of the First Amendment* (Washington, DC: American Enterprise Institute, 1978).

20. *Lemon v. Kurtzman* (1971).

21. *Walz v. Tax Commission of the City of New York* (1970).

22. *Epperson v. Arkansas* (1968).

23. *Edwards v. Aguillard* (1987).

24. *Widmar v. Vincent* (1981).

25. *Engle v. Vitale* (1962).

26. *School District of Abington Township v. Schempp* (1965).

27. Lee Epstein, Jeffrey A. Segal, Harold J. Spaeth, and Thomas G. Walker, *The Supreme Court Compendium: Data, Decisions, and Developments* (Washington, DC: Congressional Quarterly, 2003), Tables 8–23.

28. *Wallace v. Jaffree* (1985).

29. *Lee v. Weisman* (1992).

30. *Santa Fe Independent School District v. Doe* (2000).

31. The Pew Forum on Religion & Public Life, "Courts Not Silent On Moments of Silence," April 24, 2008, p. 4.

32. *Zobrest v. Catalina Foothills School District* (1993).

33. *Agostini v. Felton* (1997).

34. *Zelman v. Simmons-Harris* (2002).

35. *County of Allegheny v. A.C.L.U.* (1989).

36. *Lynch v. Donnelly* (1984).

37. *Van Orden v. Perry* (2005).

38. *McCreary County v. A.C.L.U. of Kentucky* (2005).

39. John Stuart Mill, *Essential Works of John Stuart Mill,* Max Lerner, ed. (New York: Bantam Books, 1961).

40. *Schenck v. United States* (1919).

41. *Whitney v. California* (1927).

42. *Gitlow v. New York* (1925).

43. *Brandenburg v. Ohio* (1969).

44. *Buckley v. Valeo* (1976).

45. *Virginia State Board of Pharmacy v. Virginia Citizens Consumer Council, Inc.* (1976).

46. *Bates v. State Bar of Arizona* (1977).

47. *United States v. O'Brien* (1968).

48. *Tinker v. Des Moines School District* (1969).

49. *Texas v. Johnson* (1989).

50. *United States v. Eichman* (1990).

51. *Jacobellis v. Ohio* (1964).

52. *Miller v. California* (1973).

53. Timothy C. Schiell, *Campus Hate Speech on Trial* (Lawrence, KS: University of Kansas Press, 1998), Chap. 1–3.

54. *Blackstone's Commentaries on the Laws of England,* vol. 4 (London, 1765–1769), 151–152.

55. *Smith v. Daily Mail Publishing Company* (1979).

56. *Nebraska Press Association v. Stuart* (1976).

57. *Miami Herald Publishing v. Tornillo* (1974).

58. *Branzburg v. Hayes* (1972).

59. *Houchins v. KQED* (1978).

60. *Wilson v. Layne* (1999).

61. *Gannett Company v. DePasquale* (1979).

62. *Edwards v. South Carolina* (1963).

63. *Cox v. Louisiana* (1965).

64. *Adderley v. Florida* (1966).

65. *Madsen v. Women's Health Center, Incorporated* (1994).

66. *Hill v. Colorado* (2000).

67. *NAACP v. Button* (1963).

68. *Board of Directors of Rotary International v. Rotary Club of Duarte* (1987).

69. *New York State Club Association v. City of New York* (1988).

70. *Hurley v. Irish-American Gay, Lesbian and Bisexual Group of Boston* (1995).

71. *Boy Scouts of America v. Dale* (2000).

72. Highlighting supplied by the authors.

73. *United States v. Miller* (1939).

74. *District of Columbia v. Heller* (2007).

75. The taking clause of the Fifth Amendment that guarantees a citizen the right to just compensation for property taken by the government is the only provision not related to the rights of the accused in the Fourth, Fifth, Sixth, and Eighth Amendments.

76. *Chimel v. California* (1969).

77. *United States v. Knights* (2001).

78. *Warden v. Hayden* (1967).

79. *Illinois v. Wardlow* (2000).

80. *Cupp v. Murphy* (1973).

81. Ibid.

82. *Ferguson v. City of Charleston* (2001).

83. *Hester v. United States* (1924).

84. *Florida v. Riley* (1988).

85. *Kyllo v. United States* (2001).

86. *City of Indianapolis v. Edmond* (2000).

87. *Weeks v. United States* (1914) and *Mapp v. Ohio* (1961).

88. *United States v. Leon* (1984).

89. *Dickerson v. United States* (2000).

90. *Powell v. Alabama* (1932).

91. *Gideon v. Wainwright* (1963).

92. *Argesinger v. Wainwright* (1972).

93. *Scott v. Illinois* (1979).

94. *Alabama v. Shelton* (2002).

95. *Strauder v. West Virginia* (1880) for African Americans and *Taylor v. Louisiana* (1975) for women.

96. *Batson v. Kentucky* (1986), *Georgia v. McCullum* (1992), and *J.E.B. v. Alabama ex rel. T.B.* (1994).

97. *Williams v. Florida* (1970).

98. *Johnson v. Louisiana* (1972) and *Apodaca v. Oregon* (1972).

99. *Furman v. Georgia* (1972).

100. *Gregg v. Georgia* (1976).

101. *Atkins v. Georgia* (2002).

102. *Roper v. Simmons* (2005).

103. *Baze v. Rees* (2007).

104. *Kennedy v. Louisiana* (2007).

105. *Griswold v. Connecticut* (1965).

106. By the time her case reached the Supreme Court, McCorvey had already given birth to the baby and put it up for adoption.

107. Charles S. Franklin and Liane Kosaki, "The Republican Schoolmaster: The Supreme Court, Public Opinion, and Abortion," *American Political Science Review* 83 (1989): 751–772.

108. *Akron, Ohio v. Akron Center for Reproductive Health* (1983).

109. *Webster v. Reproductive Health Services* (1989).

110. *Beal v. Doe* (1977) and *Harris v. McRae* (1980).

111. *Gonzales v. Carhart* (2006).

112. *Cruzan v. Director, Missouri Department of Health* (1990).

113. *Watchtower Bible and Tract Society v. Stratton* (2002).

114. Gregory A. Calderia and John R. Wright, "Organized Interests and Agenda Setting in the U.S. Supreme Court" *Political Science Review* 82 1109 (1988).

Chapter 5: Civil Rights: Toward a More Equal Citizenry

1. Lisa Belkin, "She Says She Was Rejected by a College for Being White. Is She Paranoid, Racist, or Right?" *Glamour* (November 1998): 2.

2. Ibid., 1.

3. Ibid., 2.

4. For an excellent discussion of the difference between civil liberties and civil rights, see John C. Domino, *Civil Rights and Liberties in the 21st Century,* 2d ed. (New York: Longman Publishers, 2003), 1–5.

5. *Dred Scott v. Sanford* (1857).

6. "Jim Crow" was the stereotypical name given to African Americans in a nineteenth-century minstrel song.

7. See C. Vann Woodward, "The Case of the Louisiana Traveler," in John A. Garraty, ed., *Quarrels That Shaped the Constitution* (New York: Harper & Row: 1987), 157–174.

8. The grandfather clause denied the right to vote to anyone whose grandfather did not vote before the Reconstruction period.

9. For an excellent discussion of the NAACP's strategy, see Richard Kluger, *Simple Justice* (New York: Vintage Books, 1975).

10. The decision in *Missouri ex. Rel. Gaines v. Canada* (1938) led to the group's success in *Sweatt v. Painter* (1950).

11. *McLaurin v. Oklahoma* (1950).

12. *Brown v. Board of Education II* (1955).

13. *Swann v. Charlotte-Mecklenberg County Schools* (1971).

14. *Missouri v. Jenkins* (1995).

15. Southern Democratic Senator Strom Thurmond conducted an eight-week filibuster to hold up the voting on the bill. It is the longest filibuster in the history of the United States.

16. *Heart of Atlanta Motel v. United States* (1964).

17. *San Antonio Independent School District v. Rodriguez* (1973).

18. *United Steelworkers of America v. Weber* (1979).

19. *United States v. Paradise* (1987).

20. *Local 28 of the Sheet Metal Workers v. EEOC* (1986) and *Johnson v. Transportation Agency of Santa Clara County, California* (1987).

21. *Aderand Constructors v. Pena* (1995).

22. *New York Times,* February 2, 2003.

23. *Meredith v. Jefferson County Board of Education* (2007) and *Parents Involved in Community Schools v. Seattle School District No. 1* (2004).

24. For a criticism of affirmative action programs, see John David Skrentny, *The Ironies of Affirmative Action: Politics, Culture, and American Justice in America* (Chicago: The University of Chicago Press, 1996).

25. Harry Holzer and David Newmark, "Assessing Affirmative Action," *Journal of Economic Literature* 38 (2000): 245–269.

26. Rennard Strickland, "Native Americans," in Kermit Hall, ed., *The Oxford Companion to the Supreme Court of the United States* (New York: Oxford University Press, 1992), 557.

27. Dee Brown, *Bury My Heart at Wounded Knee* (New York: Holt, Rinehart, and Winston, 1971).

28. Joanne Nagel, *American Indian Ethnic Renewal: Red Power and the Resurgence of Identity and Culture* (New York: Oxford University Press, 1996).

29. David Pfeiffer, "Understanding Disability Policy," *Policy Studies Journal* (1996): 157–174.

30. *Cedar Rapids v. Garret F.* (1998).

31. *Bregdon v. Abbot* (1998).

32. *Sutton v. United Air Lines* (1999), *Albertsons v. Kirkinburg* (1999), and *Murphy v. United Parcel Service* (1999).

33. *O'Connor v. Consolidated Coil Casterers Corp.* (1996).

34. *Massachusetts Board of Retirement v. Murgia* (1976).

35. *Reeves v. Sanderson* (2000).

36. *Kimel v. Florida Board of Regents* (2000).

37. *CBOCS v. Humphries* (2007).

38. See Diane Helene Miller, *Freedom to Differ: The Shaping of the Gay and Lesbian Struggle for Civil Rights* (New York: New York University Press, 1998).

39. *Romer v. Evans* (1996).

40. *Bowers v. Hardwick* (1986).

41. *Boy Scouts of America v. Dale* (2000).

42. *Baehr v. Lewin* (1993).

43. *Baker v. Vermont* (1999).

44. See Judith A. Baer, *Equality Under the Constitution: Reclaiming the Fourteenth Amendment* (Ithaca, NY: Cornell University Press, 1983), 44–47.

45. See Nancy E. Glen and Karen O'Connor, *Women, Politics, and American Society,* 2d ed. (Upper Saddle River, NJ: Prentice Hall, 1998).

46. *Minor v. Happersett* (1875).

47. Robert Putnam sees this as one of the positive aspects of the Progressive Era in *Bowling Alone* (New York: Simon and Schuster, 2000), Chap. 23.

48. See Glen and O'Connor, 6–10.

49. *Hoyt v. Florida* (1961).

50. *Orr v. Orr* (1979).

51. *Mississippi University for Women v. Hogan* (1982).

52. *JEB v. Alabama ex rel.* (1996).

53. *Michael M. v. Superior Court of Sonoma County* (1981).

54. *Rotsker v. Goldberg* (1981).

55. Sara M. Evans and Barbara J. Nelson, *Wage Justice: Comparable Worth and the Paradox of Technocratic Reform* (Chicago: The University of Chicago Press, 1989).

56. *Meritor Savings v. Vinson* (1986).

57. *Burlington Industries v. Ellerth* (1998).

58. Charles Black, *The People and the Court* (New York: Macmillan, 1960).

Chapter 6: Public Opinion

1. See, for example, Jeffrey M. Jones, "Obama's Approval Ratings More Polarized in Year 2 Than Year 1: Ranks as fourth-most-polarized year for a president since 1953," Gallup. Accessed on April 27, 2011 at http://www.gallup.com/poll/145937/Obama-Approval-Ratings-Polarized-Year-Year.aspx.

2. Pew Center for the People & the Press, "Independents Take Center Stage in Obama Era: Trends in Political Values and Core Attitudes: 1987-2009," Accessed on April 27, 2011 at http://people-press.org/2009/05/21/independents-take-center-stage-in-obama-era/.

3. See, for example, Morris P. Fiorina, Samuel J. Abrams, and J. C. Pope. *Culture War? The Myth of a Polarized America: Second Edition,* (New York: Pearson Longman, 2006). See also G. C. Jacobson, "Party Polarization in National Politics: The Electoral Connection," in J. R. Bond & R. Fleisher (Eds.), *Polarized politics,* Washington, D.C.: CQ Press, 2000, pp. 9-30.

4. See, for example, Alan I. Abramowitz and Kyle L. Saunders, "Ideological Realignment in the U.S. Electorate," *The Journal of Politics.* 60(3),1998, pp. 634-52.

5. See, for example, Dan Bernhardt, Stefan Krasa, and Mattias Polborn, ,"Political Polarization and the Electoral Effects of Media Bias," *Journal of Public Economics,* vol. 92(5-6), 2008, pages 1092-1104.

6. V.O. Key, Jr., *Public Opinion and American Democracy* (New York: Alfred Knopf, 1961), 14.

7. Gabriel Almond and Sidney Verba, *The Civic Culture: Political Attitudes and Democracy in Five Nations* (Princeton: Princeton University Press, 1963). See also a series of critiques of the political culture thesis in Gabriel Almond and Sidney Verba, eds., *The Civic Culture Revisited* (Newbury Park, CA: Sage, 1989).

8. Herbert McClosky and John Zaller, *The American Ethos: Public Attitudes Toward Capitalism and Democracy* (Cambridge: Harvard University Press, 1984).

9. Alexander Hamilton, *The Federalist Papers, No. 71,* Clinton Rossiter, ed. (New York: Mentor, 1961), 432.

10. Forrest McDonald, *The American Presidency: An Intellectual History* (Lawrence: University of Kansas Press, 1994), 216.

11. Michael Schudson, *The Good Citizen: A History of American Civic Life* (New York: Free Press, 1998), 121.

12. Tom W. Smith, "The First Straw? A Study of the Origin of Election Polls," *The Public Opinion Quarterly* 54 no. 1 (1990): 27.

13. Bernard Hennessey, *Public Opinion,* 4th ed. (Monterey, CA: Brooks/Cole, 1981), 43.

14. See Fred I. Greenstein, *Children and Politics* (New Haven: Yale University Press, 1965); Robert D. Hess and Judith V. Torney, *The Development of Political Attitudes in Children* (Chicago: Aldine, 1967); and David Easton, *Children in the Political System: Origins of Political Legitimacy* (New York: McGraw-Hill, 1969).

15. David O. Sears, "Political Socialization," in Fred I. Greenstein and Nelson Polsby, eds. *Micropolitical Theory* (Reading, MA: Addison-Wesley, 1975), 93–153.

16. Ibid., 119.

17. M. Kent Jennings and Richard G. Niemi, "The Persistence of Political Orientations: An Over Time Analysis of Two Generations," *British Journal of Political Science* 8, no. 3 (1978): 333–363.

18. Richard G. Niemi and Jane Junn, *Civic Education: What Makes Students Learn?* (New Haven: Yale, 1998).

19. Sidney Verba, Kay Lehman Schlozman, and Henry E. Brady, *Voice and Equality: Civic Voluntarism in American Politics* (Cambridge: Harvard University Press, 1995), 422–426.

20. M. Kent Jennings, "Political Knowledge Across Time and Generations," *Public Opinion Quarterly* 60 (Summer): 228–252.

21. Neil Howe and Reena Nadler. *Yes We Can: The Emergence of Millennials As a Political Generation.* (New America Foundation, Washington, D.C.), Feb 2009, p. 18. Accessed on April 29, 2011 at http://www.newamerica.net/files/nafmigration/Yes_We_Can.pdf.

22. Paul Allen Beck, "The Role of Agents in Political Socialization," in Stanley Allen Renshon, ed., *Handbook of Political Socialization* (New York: Free Press, 1977), 117.

23. Lake, Snell, Perry, and Associates and the Tarrance Group, Inc., "Short-Term Impacts, Long-Term Opportunities: The Political and Civic Engagement of Young Adults in America," *Analysis and Report for the Center for Information and Research in Civic Learning & Engagement, The Center for Democracy and Citizenship, the Partnership for Trust in Government, and the Council for Excellence in Government,* March 2002. Accessed online at http://www.youngcitizensurvey.org on March 7, 2004.

24. Ibid.

25. Barry A. Kosmin and Egon Mayer, *American Religious Identification Survey* (New York: Graduate Center of the City University of New York). Accessed online at http://www.gc.cuny.edu on March 7, 2004.

26. Verba, Schlozman, and Brady, 228–268.

27. Peter Hart and Associates, "Making a Difference, Not a Statement: College Students and Politics, Volunteering, and an Agenda for America," *Panetta Institute Survey,* April 2001. Accessed online at http://www.panettainstitute.org on March 7, 2004.

28. Lake, Snell, Perry, and Associates and the Tarrance Group, Inc.

29. Alfonso Damico, M. Margaret Conway, and Sandra Bowman Damico, "Patterns of Political Trust and Mistrust: Three Moments in the Lives of Democratic Citizens," *Polity* 32 (2000): 333–356.

30. See Paul Lazerfeld, Bernard Berelson, and Hazel Gaudet, *The People's Choice* (New York: Columbia University Press, 1948); Bernard Berelson, Paul Lazarfeld, and William McPhee, *Voting* (Chicago: University of Chicago Press, 1954)

31. See Doris Graber, *Processing the News* (New York: Longman, 1988).

32. *What Americans Know: 1989–2007, Public Knowledge of Current Affairs Little Changed By News and Information Revolutions* (Washington, DC: Pew Center for People and Press, April 15, 2007).

33. Franklin D. Gilliam, Jr. and Shanto Iyengar, "Prime Suspects: The Influence of Local Television News on the Viewing Public," *American Journal of Political Science* 44:3 (2000): 560–573.

34. 1994 National Election Study. Some contend that the wording of NES questions on affirmative action exaggerate the differences between the races. See Lee Sigelman and Susan Welch, *Black Americans' View of Racial Inequality—The Dream Deferred* (Cambridge, England: Cambridge University Press).

35. Barbara A. Bardes and Robert W. Oldendick, *Public Opinion: Measuring the American Mind,* 2d ed. (Belmont, CA: Wadsworth/ Thomson, 2003), 88.

36. Myriam Miedaian, *Boys Will Be Boys: The Link Between Masculinity and Violence* (New York: Doubleday, 1991).

37. Michael X. Delli-Carpini and Scott Keeter, *What Americans Know About Politics and Why It Matters* (New Haven: Yale University Press, 1996), 203–209.

38. Sidney Verba, Nancy Burns, and Kay Lehman Schlozman, "Knowing and Caring about Politics: Gender and Political Engagement," *The Journal of Politics* 59 (1997): 1055.

39. Gallup Organization, *Majority Still Extremely Proud to Be American*, July 3, 2006. Accessed online at http://www.galluppoll .com on September 5, 2007.

40. Daniel Elazar, *American Federalism: A View From the States,* 3d ed. (New York: Harper Collins, 1984).

41. Herbert Asher, *Polling and the Public: What Every Citizen Should Know,* 6th ed. (Washington, DC: Congressional Quarterly Press, 2004), 28.

42. *Newsweek*, "How Dumb Are We?" (March 20, 2011). Accessed on May 3, 2011 at http://www.newsweek.com/2011/03/20/ how-dumb-are-we.html.

43. Delli-Carpini, and Keeter, 238.

44. Gallup Survey, *Americans Know Little About European Union* (June 16, 2004).

45. Markus Prior, "Political Knowledge After September 11," *PS: Politics and Society* (September 2002), 523–529.

46. Seymour Martin Lipset and William Schneider, *The Confidence Gap: Business, Labor, and Government in the Public Mind* (New York: The Free Press, 1983), 43.

47. Center for Democracy and Citizen Council for Excellence in Government, "Banners from a Nationwide Survey of 1,000 15–25 Year Olds," November 17–24, 2003. Accessed online at http://www .youngcitizensurvey.org on March 30, 2004.

48. Recent empirical evidence has confirmed this assessment. See Luke Keele, "Social Capital and the Dynamics of Trust in Government," *American Journal of Political Science* 51:2 (2007): 241–254.

49. See Pippa Norris, ed., *Critical Citizens: Global Support for Democratic Governments* (New York: Oxford Press, 1999); Ronald Inglehart, *Modernization and Postmodernization* (Princeton: Princeton University Press, 1997); Stein Ringen, "Wealth and Decay: Norway Funds a Massive Political Self-Examination and Finds Trouble for All," *Times Literary Supplement* (February 13, 2004), 3–5.

50. Angus Campbell, Gerald Gurin, and Warren E. Miller, *The Voter Decides* (New York: Harper and Row, 1954), 187.

51. See Samuel Stouffer, *Communism, Conformity and Civil Liberties* (New York: Doubleday, 1955); Herbert McClosky, "Consensus and Ideology in American Politics," *American Political Science Review* 58 (1964): 361–382.

52. John E. Meuller, "Trends in Political Tolerance," Public *Opinion Quarterly* 52 (1988): 1–25; John L. Sullivan, James E. Pierson, and George E. Marcus, *Political Tolerance and American Democracy* (Chicago: University of Chicago Press, 1982).

53. See Carol Pateman, *Participation and Democratic Theory* (New York: Cambridge University Press, 1970); Benjamin R. Barber, *Strong Democracy: Participatory Politics for a New Age* (Berkeley: University of California Press, 1984); and Jack L. Walker, "A Critique of the Elitist Theory of Democracy," *American Political Science Review* 60, (1966): 285–295.

54. Pew Center for the People and the Press, *Evenly Divided, Increasingly Polarized: 2004 Political Landscape* (Washington, DC: Pew Research Center, 2003), Table T-6.

55. Gallup, *Civil Liberties.* Accessed online at http://www .galluppoll.com on February 10, 2006.

56. Alan D. Monroe, "Public Opinion and Ideology," in *The Handbook of Political Behavior,* vol. 4, Samuel L. Long, ed. (New York: Plenum, 1981), 155–196.

57. See, for example, Gallup Organization, *Many Americans Use Multiple Labels to Describe Their Ideology* (December 6, 2006). Accessed online at http://www.galluppoll.com on September 6, 2007.

58. American *National Election Studies, 2008.* Ann Arbor, MI: University of Michigan Center for Political Studies, May 2010.

59. Ibid.

60. John Halpin and Karl Agne, *State of American Political Ideology 2009: A National Study of Political Values and Beliefs,* Washington, DC: Center for American Progress, March 2009.

61. John Halpin and Karl Agne, *The Political Ideology of the Millenial Generation: A National Study of Political Values and Beliefs Among 18 to 29 Year Old Adults,* Washington, DC: Center for American Progress, May 2009.

62. Eileen Lorenzi McDonagh, "Constituency Influence on House Roll Call Votes in the Progressive Era, 1913–1915," *Legislative Studies Quarterly* XVIII:2 (May 1993), 185–210.

63. Benjamin I. Page and Robert Y. Shapiro, "Effects of Public Opinion on Policy," *The American Political Science Review* 77:1 (1983): 175–190.

64. See Alan D. Monroe, "Public Opinion and Public Policy, 1980–1993," *The Public Opinion Quarterly* 62:1 (1998): 6–28; Lawrence Jacobs and Robert Y. Shapiro, "Public Opinion, Institutions, and Policy Making," *PS: Political Science and Politics* 27:1 (1994): 9–17.

65. See, for example, John R. Hibbing and Elizabeth Theiss-Morse, *Stealth Democracy: Americans' Beliefs about How Government Should Work* (New York: Cambridge University Press, 2002).

66. Based on interview by Robin Gerrow, University of Texas at Austin Online Newsletter, 2003. Accessed at http://www.utexas.edu/ features/archive/2003/polling.html, May 22, 2008.

67. Benamin I. Page and Robert Y. Shapiro. *The Rational Public: Fifty Years of Trends in Americans' Policy Preferences* (Chicago: University of Chicago Press, 1992), 389.

Chapter 7: Political Participation: Equal Opportunities and Unequal Voices

1. Kathryn Gregory, "Glenville Elects State's Youngest Female Mayor," Sunday Gazette—Mail, Charleston, W.V., June 14, 2009. http://findarticles.com/p/. accessed March 28, 2010.

2. Ibid.

3. "Glenville Grad Serves as Youngest W.VA. Female Mayor," The Pioneer Connexion, Glenville State College, Fall 2009, pp. 1–2. http://www.glenville.wvnet.edu/pdfs/PionerConneXion_Fall09.pdf. (accessed March 28, 2010).

4. Sidney Verba, Kay Lehman Schlozman, and Henry E. Brady, *Voice and Equality: Civic Voluntarism in American Politics* (Cambridge: Harvard University Press, 1995), 115.

5. Alexis de Tocqueville, *Democracy in America,* trans. by George Lawrence and ed. by J. P. Mayer (New York: Perennial Classics, 1969), 520–521.

6. Verba, et al., 38.

7. This section roughly follows the "Civic Volunteerism Model" developed by Verba et al., 1995.

8. See Sidney Verba and Norman H. Nie, *Political Participation in America: Political Democracy and Social Equality* (New York: Harper & Row, 1972).

9. Steven J. Rosenstone and John Mark Hansen, *Mobilization, Participation and Democracy in America* (New York: Macmillan, 1993), 77.

10. Scott Keeter, Cliff Zukin, Molly Andolina, and Krista Jenkins, *The Civic and Political Health of the Nation: A Generational Portrait,* report prepared for the Center for Information and Research on Civic Learning and Engagement (September 19, 2002), 32.

11. Verba et al., 320–333.

12. Mark Hugo Lopez and Paul Taylor, *Dissecting the 2008 Electorate: Most Diverse in U.S. History,* Washington, DC: PEW Research Center (April 30, 2009).

13. Ibid., 255.

14. Frederick Solt, "Economic Inequality and Democratic Political Engagement," *American Journal of Political Science* 52 (January 2008): 48–60.

15. Verba et al., 345–348.

16. See Robert E. Lane, *Political Life: Why and How People Get Involved in Politics* (New York: Free Press, 1959).

17. These are Voting Age Population rates. Curtis Gans and Jon Hussey, "African-Americans, Anger, Fear and Youth Propel Turnout to Highest Level Since 1960," Center for the Study of the American Electorate, American University, Washington, D.C. (December 17, 2008).

18. Mark Hugo Lopez and Paul Taylor, *Dissecting the 2008 Electorate: Most Diverse in U.S. History,* Washington, DC: PEW Research Center (April 30, 2009).

19. Emily Hoban Kirby and Kei Kawashima-Ginsberg, *The Youth Vote in 2008 Factsheet,* Center for Research and Information on Civic Learning and Education, Tufts University, Medford, MA (April 2009).

20. Lake Snell Perry and Associates and the Tarrance Group, "Short-Term Impacts, Long-Term Opportunities: The Politics and Civic Engagement of Young Adults in America," report prepared for the Center for Information and Research on Civic Learning and Engagement, the Center for Democracy and Citizenship, the Partnership for Trust in Government, and the Council for Excellence in Government (March 2002), 31.

21. Stuart Comstock-Gay, Steven Carbo, and Regina Eaton, "Voters Win With Election Day Registration; Election Day Registration States Outpaced Others in Turnout by 7percent." Accessed on May 3, 2011 at http://www.demos.org/pubs/voterswin_09.pdf.

22. R. Michael Alverez and Jonathan Nagler, *Same Day Voter Registration in Maryland: Demos Briefing Paper,* (New York: Demos), Winter 2010. Accessed on May 3, 2011at http://www.demos.org/pubs/SDR_MD.pdf.

23. Michael McDonald, *United States Elections Project.* Accessed on May 13, 2009 at http://elections.gmu.edu/CPS_2008.html.

24. Francis Fox Piven and Richard A. Cloward, *Why Americans Don't Vote* (New York: Pantheon, 1989).

25. See discussion by Rosenstone and Hansen, 179–183.

26. See Samuel H. Barnes, Max Kaase, et al., *Political Action: Mass Participation in Five Western Democracies* (Beverly Hills: Sage, 1979), 541–542.

27. Verba et al., 115.

28. Pippa Norris, ed., *Critical Citizens: Global Support for Democratic Government* (New York: Oxford University Press, 1999).

29. Verba et al., 186–227.

30. See Theda Skocpol, *Diminished Democracy: From Membership to Management in American Civic Life* (Norman, OK: University of Oklahoma Press, 2004).

31. Keeter, et al., 20–22.

32. Stephen Shaffer, "Policy Differences Between Voters and Nonvoters in American Elections," *Western Political Quarterly* 35, no. 4 (1982), 496–510. Also see Verba, Schlozman, and Brady, 1995; Wolfinger and Rosenstone, 1980.

33. See also Stephen Earl Bennett and David Resnic, "The Implications of Nonvoting for Democracy in the United States," *American Journal of Political Science* 34, no. 3 (August 1990): 771–802.

34. Sidney Verba, "Would the Dream of Political Equality Turn Out to be a Nightmare?" *Perspectives on Politics* 1, no. 4 (2003): 671.

35. Solt, *AJPS,* 58.

36. Larry Bartels, "Economic Inequality and Political Representation." Revised Paper presented at the Woodrow Wilson School of Public and International Affairs, Princeton, N.J., August 2005. Accessed on May 3, 2011 at http://www.princeton.edu/~bartels/economic.pdf.

37. *Verba,* 675.

38. This conforms to the views of many writers, see Thomas R. Dye and Harmon Zeigler, *The Irony of Democracy* (Pacific Grove, California: Brooks/Cole), 1990; Seymour Martin Lipset, *Political Man* (Garden City, NY: Doubleday, 1963); and William Kornhauser, *The Politics of Mass Society* (Glencoe, IL: Free Press, 1959).

39. See Emily Hoban Kirby and Mark Hugo Lopez, *State Voter Registration and Election Day Laws,* paper prepared for the Center for Information and Research on Civic Learning and Engagement. Accessed online at http://www.civicyouth.org on June 24, 2006. Also see Raymond E. Wolfinger, Benjamin Highton, and Megan Mullin, "Mailed Ballots Might Increase Youth Vote," *Institute of Governmental Studies Public Affairs Report* 43, no. 4 (2002).

40. Martin Wattenberg, *Is Voting for Young People?* (New York: Pearson Education, 2007).

41. Macedo et al., 33.

42. Rosenstone and Hansen, 227.

Chapter 8: Interest Groups in America

1. calpirgstudents.org/mission.

2. The classic definition of an interest group offered by political scientist David Truman is "any group that, on the basis of one or more shared attitudes, makes certain claims upon other groups in the society for the establishment, maintenance, or enhancement of forms of behavior that are implied by the shared attitudes." David Truman, *The Governmental Process* (New York: Alfred Knopf, 1951), 33.

3. James Madison, *No. 10,* in Alexander Hamilton, James Madison, and John Jay*, Federalist Papers,* Clinton Rossiter, ed. (New York: New American Library, 1961), 78.

4. Sidney Verba, Kay Lehman Scholzman, and Henry E. Brady, *Voice and Equality: Civic Voluntarism in American Politics* (Cambridge, MA: Harvard University Press, 1995), 72–73. But see somewhat contradictory data from Steven J. Rosenstone and John Mark Hansen, *Mobilization, Participation, and Democracy in America* (New York: Macmillan, 1993), chap. 3. Skocpol (2003) argues that much of this activity is managed by Washington profes-

sionals. Theda Skocpol, *Diminished Democracy: From Membership to Management in American Civic Life* (Norman, OK: University of Oklahoma Press, 2003).

5. Arthur M. Schlesinger, "Biography of a Nation of Joiners," *The American Historical Review* 50 no. 1 (1944): 25.

6. Shirley J. Yee, *Black Women Abolitionists: A Study in Activism 1828–60* (Knoxville: University of Tennessee Press, 1992).

7. Matthew A. Crenson and Benjamin Ginsberg, *Downsizing Democracy* (Baltimore: The John Hopkins University Press, 2002), 107.

8. Robert D. Putnam, *Bowling Alone: The Collapse and Revival of American Community* (New York: Simon & Schuster, 2000), 80–92.

9. Michael Schudson, *The Good Citizen: A History of American Civic Life* (New York: Free Press, 1988), 245.

10. Michael Pertschuk, *Giant Killers* (New York: W. W. Norton, 1996).

11. Theda Skocpol, *Diminished Democracy.*

12. Kay Lehman Schlozman and John T. Tierney, *Organized Interests and American Democracy* (New York: Harper & Row, 1986), 66–68.

13. See, for example, Jack L. Walker, "The Origins and Maintenance of Interest Groups in America," *American Political Science Review* 77 (1983): 390–406.

14. Kay Lehman Schlozman, "What Accent the Heavenly Chorus? Political Equality and the American Pressure System," *Journal of Politics* 46 (1984): 1009.

15. Schlozman, 1022–1024.

16. Political scientist David Truman coined the term *latent interests* to refer to the ever-present possibility that new groups will arise at any time to meet yet unforeseen challenges. See Truman, 1951.

17. James Q. Wilson, *Political Organizations* (New York: Basic Books, 1973).

18. Rosenstone and Hansen, 1993.

19. Mancur Olson, *The Logic of Collective Action* (Cambridge, MA: Harvard University Press, 1965).

20. Jack L. Walker, *Mobilizing Interest Groups in America* (Ann Arbor: University of Michigan Press, 1991), 87–89. This result is confirmed by the research of Verba, Schlozman, and Brady.

21. Verba, Schlozman, and Brady, 121–127.

22. Jonathan D. Salant, "The Lobbying Game Today," *Extensions: A Journal of the Carl Albert Congressional Research and Studies Center* (2006): 19.

23. Ibid., 17.

24. See Clyde Wilcox, "The Dynamics of Lobbying the Hill," in Paul S. Herrnson, Ronald G. Shaiko, and Clyde Wilcox, eds., *The Interest Group Connection* (Chatham, NJ: Chatham House Publishers, 1998), 89–90.

25. Norman J. Ornstein and Shirley Elder, *Interest Groups, Lobbying and Policymaking* (Washington, DC: Congressional Quarterly Press, 1978), 77–78.

26. Ibid., 86–87.

27. See John E. Chubb, *Interest Groups and the Bureaucracy* (Stanford: Stanford University Press, 1983) for a good discussion of the relationship of interest groups and the bureaucracy in the energy policy field.

28. Schlozman and Tierney, 333.

29. For an excellent discussion of research into "capture theory," see James Q. Wilson, *The Politics of Regulation* (New York: Basic Books, 1980).

30. Robert H. Salisbury, John Heinz, Robert L. Nelson, and Edward O. Laumann, "Triangles, Networks, and Hollow Cores: The Complex Geometry of Washington Interest Representation," in Mark Petracca, ed., *Interest Group Politics* (Washington, DC: Congressional Quarterly Press, 1995), 131.

31. See Walker, 125.

32. William T. Gromley, Jr., "Interest Group Interventions in the Administrative Process: Conspirators and Co-Conspirators," in Paul S. Herrnson, Ronald G. Shaiko, and Clyde Wilcox, eds., *The Interest Group Connection* (Chatham, NJ: Chatham House Publishers, 1998), 213–223.

33. Center for Responsive Politics, Database, Accessed on May 6, 2011 at http://www.opensecrets.org/lobby/clientsum .php?id=D000019798&year=2009.

34. Frank R. Baumgartner, Jeffery M. Berry, Marie Hojnacki, David C. Kimball, and Beth L. Leech, *Lobbying and Policy Change: Who Wins, Who Loses, and Why* (Chicago: University of Chicago Press, 2009.

35. Quoted in Larry Makinson, *Speaking Freely: Washington Insiders Talk About Money in Politics* (Washington, DC: Center for Responsive Politics, 2003), 85.

36. Schlozman and Tierney, 221.

37. *McConnell v. Federal Election Commission* 540 U.S. 93 (2003) and *FEC v. Wisconsin Right to Life* 551 U.S. (2007).

38. Salant, 17.

39. Center for Responsive Politics. Accessed online at http://www .opensecrets.org.

40. For an analysis of the general reliability of this finding, see Thomas Brunell, "The Relationship Between Political Parties and Interest Groups: Explaining Patterns of PAC Contributions to Candidates for Congress," *Political Research Quarterly* 58 no. 4 (2005): 681–688.

41. Center for Responsive Politics. Accessed online at http://www .opensecrets.org on May 17, 2009.

42. Center for Responsive Politics, accessed on May 6, 2011 at http://www.opensecrets.org/pacs/list.php.

43. Center for Responsive Politics, accessed on May 6, 2011 at http://www.opensecrets.org/527s/index.php.

44. Center for Responsive Politics, accessed on May 6, 2011 at http://www.opensecrets.org/news/2011/05/citizens-united-decision-profoundly-affects-political-landscape.html.

45. Karen O'Connor, *Women's Organizations' Use of the Courts* (Lexington, MA: Lexington Books, 1980).

46. Stuart Scheingold, *The Politics of Rights* (New Haven: Yale University Press, 1974).

47. Karen O'Connor and Lee Epstein, "The Role of Interest Groups in Supreme Court Policymaking," in Robert Eyestone, ed., *Public Policy Formation* (Greenwich, CT: JAI Press, 1984) 63–81.

48. See Lucius J. Barker, "Third Parties in Litigation: A Systemic View of the Judicial Function," *Journal of Politics* 29 (1967): 41–69.

49. See Gregory A. Calderia and John R. Wright, "Organized Interests and Agenda Setting in the U.S. Supreme Court," *American Political Science Review* 82 (1988): 1109–1127.

50. James G. Gimpel, "Grassroots Organizations and Equilibrium Cycles in Group Mobilization and Access," in Paul S. Herrnson, Ronald G. Shaiko, and Clyde Wilcox, eds. *The Interest Group Connection* (Chatham, NJ: Chatham House Publishers, 1998), 100–115.

51. Emily Cadei, "Advocacy Groups Employ Web's Extended Reach," *CQ Weekly* (May 4, 2009), p. 1015.

52. Kenneth M. Goldstein, *Interest Groups, Lobbying, and Participation in America* (New York: Cambridge University Press, 1999), 62.

53. Gimpel, 104.

54. See Kevin Hula, "Rounding Up the Usual Suspects: Forging Interest Group Coalitions in Washington," in Allan J. Cigler and Burdett A. Loomis, eds., *Interest Group Politics* (Washington, DC: Congressional Quarterly Press, 1995), 239–258.

55. Verba, Schlozman, and Brady, 189–191.

56. Crenson and Ginsberg, 151.

57. Skocpol, *Diminished Democracy*.

58. Crenson and Ginsberg, 194.

59. E. E. Schattschneider, *The Semisovereign People* (New York: Holt, Rinehart, and Winston, 1960), 35.

Chapter 9: Parties and Political Campaigns: Citizens and the Electoral Process

1. Information about Keli Carender is taken from a profile about her in: Kate Zirnike, "Unlikely Activist Who Got to the Tea Party Early," *The New York Times,* February 27, 2010. http://www.nytimes.com/2010/02/28/us/politics/28keli.html on April 12, 2010 (accessed April 12, 2010).

2. Ibid.

3. See, for example, "Tea Party Could Hurt GOP in Congressional Races," Quinnipiac University, March 24, 2010, http://www.quinnipiac.edu/x1295.xml?ReleaseID=1436 (accessed April 11, 2010). See also, "Behind the Headlines: What's Driving the Tea Party Movement?" The Winston Group, April 1, 2010, http://winstongroup.net/2010/04/01/behind-the-headlines-whats-driving-the-tea-party-movement (accessed April 11, 2010).

4. Kate Zernike and Megan Thee-Brenan, "Poll finds Tea Party Backers Wealthier and More Educated, *New York Times,* April 14, 2010. Accessed on May 8, 2011 at http://www.nytimes.com/2010/04/15/us/politics/15poll.html.

5. *Ibid.*

6. Wayne, October 31, 2008.

7. Severson, April 16, 2008.

8. V.O. Key, Jr., *Politics, Parties, and Pressure Groups, 5th Ed.,* (New York: Crowell, 1964).

9. E.E. Schattsneider, *Party Government*, (New York: Holt, Rinehart and Winston, 1942).

10. Anthony Downs, *An Economic Theory of Democracy* (New York: Harper & Row, 1957), 25.

11. E. E. Schattschneider, "Intensity, Visibility, Direction, and Scope," *American Political Science Review* 51:4 (December 1957): 933–942.

12. See, for example, Morris Fiorina, "The Decline of Collective Responsibility in American Politics," *Daedalus* 109 (Summer 1980): 25–45. See also American Political Science Association, *Toward a More Responsible Two Party System* (New York: Rinehart, 1950).

13. Alexis de Tocqueville, 1848; *Democracy in America,* trans. George Lawrence, ed. J. P. Mayer). New York: Perennial Classics, 1969, 174.

14. Maurice Duverger, *Political Parties: Their Organization and Activity in the Modern State,* (New York: Wiley, 1954).

15. For a more thorough examination of other voting systems and their potential effects, see Joseph F. Zimmerman, "Alternative Voting Systems for Representative Democracy," *PS: Political Science and Politics* 27:4 (December 1994): 674–677.

16. Information available at The Reform Institute for Campaign and Election Issues, *Presidential Ballot Access,* http://reforminstitute.org/ (accessed September 7, 2007).

17. John H. Aldrich, *Why Parties? The Origins and Transformation of Political Parties in America* (Chicago: University of Chicago Press, 1995), 70–82.

18. Aldrich, 99.

19. See discussion in Frances Fox Piven and Richard A. Cloward, *Why Americans Don't Vote* (New York: Pantheon, 1989).

20. John C. Green, *The American Religious Landscape and Political Attitudes: A Baseline for 2004* (unpublished ms.).

21. See, for example, Susan J. Carroll, "Women's Autonomy and the Gender Gap: 1980 and 1982," in Carol M. Mueller, ed., *The Politics of the Gender Gap: The Social Construction of Political Influence* (Beverly Hills, CA: Sage Publications, 1988).

22. Jeffrey Jones, "GOP Losses Span Nearly All Demographic Groups," *Gallup Organization,* May 18, 2009. Accessed on May 20, 2009 at http://www.gallup.com/poll/118528/GOP-Losses-Span-Nearly-Demographic-Groups.aspx.

23. For a discussion of various factors associated with realignments, see Samuel Merrill III, Bernard Grofman, and Thomas L. Brunell, "Cycles in American National Electoral Politics: 1854–2006: Statistical Evidence and an Explanatory Model," *American Political Science Review* 102 (February 2008): 1–17.

24. V. O. Key, Jr., "A Theory of Critical Elections," *Journal of Politics* 17 (1955): 3–18; Walter Dean Burnham, *Critical Elections and the Mainsprings of American Politics* (New York: Norton, 1970); Paul Allen Beck, "A Socialization Theory of Partisan Realignment," in Richard Niemi, ed., *The Politics of Future Citizens* (San Francisco: Jossey-Bass, 1974).

25. A. James Reichley, "The Future of the American Two-Party System After 1996," in John C. Green and Daniel M. Shea, eds., *The State of the Parties: The Changing Role of Contemporary American Parties, 3rd Ed.* (Lanham, MD: Rowman and Littlefield, 1999), 10–27.

26. See, for example, David R. Mayhew, *Electoral Realignments: A Critique of an American Genre* (New Haven, CT: Yale University Press, 2002).

27. See, for example, Martin P. Wattenberg, *The Decline of American Political Parties, 1952–1996* (Cambridge, MA: Harvard University Press, 1998); Paul Allen Beck, "The Changing American Party Coalitions," in John C. Green and Daniel M. Shea, eds., *The State of the Parties: The Changing Role of Contemporary American Parties, 3rd Edition* (Lanham, MD: Rowman and Littlefield, 1999), 28–49.

28. Larry M. Bartels, "Partisanship and Voting Behavior, 1952–1996," *American Journal of Political Science* 44:1 (January 2000): 35–50. See also Michael Lewis-Beck, William G. Jacoby, Helmut Norpoth, and Herbert F. Weisberg, *The American Voter Revisited* (Ann Arbor: University of Michigan Press, 2008).

29. James Q. Wilson, *Political Organizations* (Princeton, NJ: Princeton University Press, 1995), xiii.

30. Thomas E. Mann, "A Collapse of the Campaign Finance Regime?" *The Forum* 6:1. Available at: http://www.bepress.com/forum/vol6/iss1/art1 (accessed June 1, 2008).

31. *Citizens United v. Federal Election Commission* (588U.S.__2010).

32. John F. Bibby, "Party Networks: National-State Integration, Allied Groups, and Issue Activists," in John C. Green and Daniel M. Shea, eds., *The State of the Parties: The Changing Role of Contemporary American Parties, 3d Edition* (Lanham, MD: Rowman and Littlefield, 1999), 69–85.

33. Center for Responsive Politics, http://www.opensecrets.org. Accessed on July 11, 2011.

34. Malcolm Jewell and David Olson, *American State Political Parties and Elections,* Rev. Ed. (Homewood, IL: Dorsey Press, 1982).

35. Third parties have been categorized in a number of ways. Key speaks of short-lived and doctrinal parties (Key, 1964). Orren lists principled, personalistic, and protest as third party types. See Gary R. Orren, "The Changing Styles of American Party Politics," in

Joel L. Fleishman, ed., *The Future of American Political Parties*, (Englewood Cliffs, NJ: Prentice Hall, 1982). Here, we employ the categories splinter, ideological, and issue candidate.

36. *Federal Election Commission v. Wisconsin Right to Life*, 551 U.S. (2007).

37. Center for Responsive Government, "Leadership PACs." Accessed on May 20, 2009 at http://www.opensecrets.org/pacs/industry.php?txt-Q03&cycle=2008.

38. Stephen R. Weissman and Kara D. Ryan, "Soft Money in the 2006 Election and the Outlook for 2008: The Changing Nonprofits Landscape," Report from the Campaign Finance Institute, 2007. At http://www.cfinst.org/books_reports/pdf/NP_SoftMoney_0608.pdf (accessed on June 1, 2008).

39. Clyde Wilcox, "Internet Fundraising in 2008: A New Model?" *The Forum*: 6 :1. Available at http://www.bepress.com/forum/vol6/iss1/art1 (accessed September 17, 2008); Also see Richard L. Hasen, "Political Equality, the Internet, and Campaign Finance Regulation, *The Forum*: Vol. 6 : Iss.1, Article 7. Available at http://www.bepress.com/forum/vol6/iss1/art1; (accessed June 1, 2008).

40. *California Democratic Party v. Jones* 530 U.S. 567 (2000).

41. Wattenberg, p. 35.

42. Thomas E. Patterson, *The Vanishing Voter: Public Involvement in an Age of Uncertainty* (New York: Knopf, 2002), 99–127.

43. Gina M. Garramone, Charles K. Atkin, Bruce E. Pinkleton, and Richard T. Cole, "Effects of Negative Political Advertising on the Political Process," *Journal of Broadcasting and the Electronic Media* 34 (1990): 299–311.

44. Stephen Ansolabehere and Shanto Iyenger, *Going Negative: How Political Advertisements Shrink and Polarize the Electorate* (New York: Free Press, 1995). But see Robert Jackson, Jeffrey J. Mondak, and Robert Huckfeldt, "Examining the Possible Corrosive Impact of Negative Advertising on Citizen's Attitudes toward Politics," *Political Research Quarterly* 62 (March 2009): 55–69. Jackson et al. find no evidence to support the claim that negative ads erode voter attitudes other than efficacy.

45. Steven E. Finkel and John G. Geer, "A Spot Check: Casting Doubt on the Demobilizing Effect of Attack Advertising," *American Journal of Political Science* 42:2 (April 1998): 573–595.

46. Patterson, 51.

47. Richard R. Beeman, "Deference, Republicanism, and the Emergence of Popular Politics in Eighteenth Century America," *William and Mary Quarterly* 49:3 (July 1992): 417.

48. Michael E. McGerr, *The Decline of Popular Politics: The American North, 1865–1928* (New York: Oxford University Press, 1986).

49. Lewis-Beck, et al., 2008.

50. Stephen A. Jesse, "Spatial Voting in the 2004 Presidential Election," *American Political Science Review* 103 (February 2009): 59–81.

51. Michael Tomz and Robert Van Houweling, "The Electoral Implications of Candidate Ambiguity," *American Political Science Review* 103 (February 2009): 83–98.

52. Patrick Lynch traces the impact of retrospective economic voting on presidential election outcomes back to 1872 in "Presidential Elections and the Economy 1872 to 1996: The Times They Are A 'Changing or The Song Remains the Same?" *Political Research Quarterly* 52:4 (December 1999): 825–844.

53. See, for example, Larry M. Bartels and John Zaller, "Presidential Vote Models: A Recount," *PS: Political Science and Politics* 34:1 (March 2001), 9–20 ; Michael Lewis-Beck and Charles Tien, "Modeling the Future: Lessons from the Gore Forecast," *PS: Political Science and Politics* 34:1 (March 2001), 21–24; James E. Campbell, "Assessments of the 2004 Vote Forecasts," *PS: Political Science and Politics* 38:1 (January 2005): 23–24.

54. James E. Campbell, "Assessments of the 2004 Vote Forecasts," *PS: Political Science and Politics* 38:1 (January 2005): 23–24.

55. Edison Media Research, AP/Network Exit Polls, Nov. 4, 2008.

56. Some studies contend that voters are more likely to vote for candidates who reflect their own demographic characteristics. See, for example, Eric Plutzer and John Zip, "Identity Politics, Partisanship, and Voting for Women Candidates," *Public Opinion Quarterly* 60:1 (Spring 1996): 30–57. See also, Jan E. Leighley and Arnold Vedlitz, "Race, Ethnicity and Political Participation: Competing Models and Contrasting Explanations," *Journal of Politics* 61:4 (November 1999): 1092–1114. For contrasting findings and explanations, see Richard Seltzer, Jody Newman, and Melissa Voorhees Leighton, *Sex as a Political Variable: Women as Candidates and Voters in U.S. Elections* (Boulder, CO: Lynne Reinner, 1997), esp. ch. 5; Monika McDermot, "Race and Gender Cues in Low Information Elections" *Political Research Quarterly* 51:4 (December 1998): 895–918.

57. Emily Hoban Kirby, Karlo Barrios Marcelo, Joshua Gillerman, and Samantha Linkins, *The Youth Vote in the 2008 Primaries and Caucuses* Center for Information & Research on Civic Learning & Engagement, June 2008.

58. Peter Slevin, "Obama Campaign Dispatching Thousands," *Washington Post*, June 13, 2008, A5.

59. Kevin Arceneaux and David W. Nickerson, "Who is Mobilized to Vote? A Re-Analysis of 11 Field Experiments." *American Journal of Political Science* 53 (January 2009): 1–16.

60. Wilcox.

Chapter 10: Media

1. Hugh Macleod and Annasofie Flamand, "Tortured and killed: Hamza al-Khateeb, age 13," *Al Jazeera,* May 31, 2011, http://english.aljazeera.net/indepth/features/2011/05/201153185927813389.html.

2. James Lee Phillips, "'Children's Friday' Full of Woe As Syrian Internet Shuts Down," *International Business Times,* June 6, 2011, http://www.ibtimes.com/articles/158214/20110606/children-s-friday-full-of-woe-as-syrian-internet-shuts-down.htm.

3. Steven J. Vaughan-Nichols, "Syria shuts down the Internet," *ZDNet,* June 3, 2011, http://www.zdnet.com/blog/networking/syria-shuts-down-the-internet/1127.

4. Frank Ahrens, "The accelerating decline of newspapers," *The Washington Post,* October 27, 2009, http://www.washingtonpost.com/wp-dyn/content/article/2009/10/26/AR2009102603272.html.

5. "The Internet's Broader Role in Campaign 2008," Pew Research Center Publications, January 11, 2008, http://pewresearch.org/pubs/689/the-internets-broader-role-in-campaign-2008.

6. Katherine Mangan, "Stop the Presses! Revamped Journalism Courses Attract Hordes of Students," *The Chronicle of Higher Education,* September 21, 2009, p. 4.

7. Brian Morelli, "Journalism Students Face Uncertain Future," *Iowa City Press-Citizen,* April 5, 2009, p.1.

8. Robert Zemsky, *Merchants, Farmers, and River Gods: An Essay on Eighteenth-Century American Politics* (Boston: Gambit, 1971), 59.

9. Frank Luther Mott, *American Journalism: A History 1690–1960* (New York: The Macmillan Company, 1962), 52.

10. Michael Schudson, *The Good Citizen* (New York: The Free Press, 1998), 40.

11. Culver H. Smith, *The Press, Politics, and Patronage* (Athens: University of Georgia Press, 1977), 52.

12. Walter Lippman, "Two Revolutions in the American Press," *Yale Law Review* 20 (1931): 433–441.

13. Mott, 539.

14. Paul H. Weaver, *News and The Culture of Lying* (New York: The Free Press, 1994), 35.

15. Schudson, 179.

16. George Jurgens, *Joseph Pulitzer and the New York World* (Princeton, NJ: Princeton University Press, 1966), 239.

17. Doris Graber, *Mass Media and American Politics*, 3d ed. (Washington, DC: CQ Press, 2002), 12.

18. Carnegie Corporation of New York, *Abandoning the News*. Accessed online at http://www.carnegie.org on September 24, 2005.

19. Aaron Smith and Lee Rainie, Pew Interest and American Life project, June 15, 2008.

20. Ibid., 1.

21. Aaron Smith, "The Internet's Role in Campaign 2008," Pew Internet and American Life Project, April 15, 2009.

22. Jonathan S. Morris and Peter L. Francia, *From Network News to Cable Commentary: The Evolution of Television Coverage of the Party Conventions,* paper presented at the State of the Parties Conference, University of Akron, October 5, 2005.

23. Richard Davis, *The Press and American Politics* (Upper Saddle River, NJ: Prentice Hall, 1996), 13.

24. Stephen Ansolabehere, Roy Behr, and Shanto Iyengar, *The Media Game: American Politics in the Television Age* (New York: Macmillan, 1993), 28–29.

25. Christina Holtz-Bacha and Lynda Lee Kaid, "A Comparative Perspective on Political Advertising," in Linda Lee Kaid and Christina Holz-Bacha, eds. *Political Advertising in Western Democracies* (Thousand Oaks, CA: Sage, 1995), 13.

26. See Robert McChesney, *Rich Media, Poor Democracy* (New York: New York Press, 1999).

27. *Near v. Minnesota* (1931).

28. *New York Times v. Sullivan* (1964).

29. Speech given by Robert McNeil at the University of South Dakota, Vermillion, SD, Wednesday, October 16, 1996. Cited in Jeremy Iggers, *Good News, Bad News* (Boulder, CO: Westview Press, 1998), 2.

30. James Fallows, *Breaking the News* (New York: Pantheon Books, 1996), chap. 3.

31. Ibid., 105.

32. S. Robert Lichter and Richard E. Noyes, *Good Intentions Make Bad News* (Lanham, MD: Rowman and Littlefield, 1995), 3.

33. Michael Schudson, *Discovering the News* (New York: Basic Books, 1973), 178–181.

34. "The Times and Iraq," *The New York Times*, May 26, 2004.

35. S. Robert Lichter, Stanley Rothman, and Linda S. Lichter, *The Media Elite* (Bethesda MD: Adler & Adler, 1986), 21–25.

36. Dave D'Alessio and Mike Allen, "Media Bias in Presidential Elections: A Meta-Analysis," *Journal of Communication* 50:4 (2000): 133–156.

37. See Graham Browning, "Too Close for Comfort?" *National Journal* (1992): 2243.

38. Media Research Center, "Slanted Morning TV Helps 2008 Democrats," November 7, 2007, 1.

39. Ibid., 2.

40. Thomas E. Patterson, *The Vanishing Voters Public Involvement in an Age of Uncertainty* (New York: Knopf, 2002), 57.

41. *Graber*, 248–249.

42. Alliance for Better Campaigns, "Political Ad Spending on Television Sets New Record" November 24, 2004. Accessed online at http://www.bettercampaigns.org on September 25, 2005.

43. Gina M. Garramone, Charles K. Atkin, Bruce E. Pinkleton, and Richard T. Cole, "Effects of Negative Political Advertising on the Political Process," *Journal of Broadcasting and the Electronic Media* 34 (1990): 299–311.

44. Stephen Ansolabehere and Shanto Iyengar, *Going Negative: How Political Advertisements Shrink and Polarize the Electorate* (New York: The Free Press, 1995).

45. Steven E. Finkle and John G. Geer, "A Spot Check: Casting Doubt on the Demobilizing Effect of Attack Advertising," *American Journal of Political Science* 42:2 (1998): 573–595.

46. Felicia R. Lee, "Survey of the Blogosphere Finds 12 Million Voices." June 20, 2006, 1.

47. Marketing VOX, "Top 10 U.S. Social Network and Blog-Site Rankings Issued for May," June 18, 2008, 1.

48. Howard Kurtz, "Blogging Without Warning," *Washington Post*, June 9, 2008, 1.

49. Staci D. Kramer, "CBS Scandal Highlights Tension Between Bloggers and News Media," USC *Annenberg Online Journalism Review,* October 10, 2004. Accessed online at http://ojr.org.

50. Thomas E. Patterson, *Out of Order* (New York: Vintage Books, 1993), 57.

51. Ibid., 116.

52. Fallows, 181.

53. See Roderick Hart, *Seducing America: How Television Charms the Modern Voter* (New York: Oxford University Press, 1995).

54. Larry Sabato, *Feeding Frenzy* (New York: The Free Press, 1991), 68.

55. See Kenneth T. Walsh, *Feeding the Beast* (New York: Random House, 1996) for an excellent treatment of the relationship between the president and the media.

56. Ibid., 23.

57. Ibid., 28.

58. Ibid., 77–78.

59. See Everette E. Dennis and Robert Snyder, eds., *Covering Congress* (New Brunswick: Transaction Publishers, 1998).

60. See John Hibbing and Elizabeth Theiss-Morse, *Congress as Public Enemy: Political Attitudes Toward American Political Institutions* (New York: Cambridge University Press, 1995).

61. Quoted in Stephen Macedo, et al., *Democracy at Risk: How Political Choices Undermine Citizen Participation and What We Can Do About It* (Washington, DC: Brookings Institution, 2005), 42.

62. See Pew Center for People and the Press, *America Lacks Background to Follow International News: Public's News Habits Little Changed by September 11* (Washington, DC: Pew Center for People and the Press, June 9, 2002).

63. See Joseph N. Capella and Kathleen Hall Jamieson, *Spiral of Cynicism: The Press and the Public Good* (New York: Oxford University Press, 1997).

64. Pew Center for the People and the Press, *Public Wants Neutrality and Strong Point of View: Strong Opposition to Media Cross Ownership Emerges* (Washington, DC: Pew Center for People and the Press, July 13, 2003), 5.

65. Macedo, et al., 42.

66. Ted Koppel, "And Now a Word for Our Demographic," *New York Times*, January 29, 2006, 2. Accessed online at http://selectnytimes.com.

67. Ibid.

68. News grazing is similar to the citizen scanning and monitoring views of news advanced by Michael Schudson, 1998, 311.

69. Pew Research Center for the People & the Press, "Key News Audiences Now Blend Online and Traditional Sources," August 17, 2008.

70. Pew Research Center for the People & the Press, "Today's Journalists Less Prominent," March 8, 2007.

71. Bill Moyer's Journal, PBS. April 27, 2007.

72. Pew Research Center for the People & the Press, "Public Knowledge of Current Affairs Little Changed by News and Information Revolutions: What Americans Know: 1989–2007." April 15, 2007.

73. Pew Research Center, "The Daily Show: Journalism, Satire, or Just Laughs?" May 8, 2008, 1.

74. Ibid., 2.

75. Ibid., 2.

Chapter 11: Congress: Doing the People's Business

1. This story is taken from: Julia Preston, "Illegal Immigrant Students Await Votes on Legal Status, *The New York Times,* December 8, 2010, p. A-18.

2. Julia Preston, "Immigration Vote Leaves Obama's Policy in Disarray," *The New York Times,* December 19, 2010, p. A-35.

3. Scott Wong and Shira Toeplitz, "DREAM Act dies in Senate," POLITICO.com, December 18, 2010 11:39 AM EDT. Accessed on May 14, 2011 at http://www.politico.com/news/stories/1210/46573.html.

4. Ibid.

5. Preston, Dec. 8.

6. Quoted in Congressional Quarterly, Inc., *Origins and Development of Congress,* 2d ed. (Washington, DC: Congressional Quarterly, 1982), 43.

7. Ibid., 219.

8. Lee Hamilton, *How Congress Works and Why You Should Care* (Bloomington, IN: Indiana University Press, 2004).

9. Center for Responsive Politics, *2010 Overview: Most Expensive Races.* Accessed on May 15, 2011 at http://www.opensecrets.org/overview/topraces.php?cycle=2010&Display=allcands.

10. Rep. Bill McCollum in Larry Makinson, *Speaking Freely: Washington Insiders Talk About Money in Politics,* 2 ed. (Washington, DC: Center for Responsive Politics, 2003), 36–37.

11. Dave Levinthal, Michael Beckel, and Evan Mackinder, "OpenSecrets.org's Top 10 Money-in-Politics Stories of 2010," posted December 31, 2010 11:15 AM. Accessed on May 17, 2011 at http://www.opensecrets.org/news/2010/12/the-top-10-money-in-politics-storie.html.

12. Center for Responsive Politics, *2010 Overview: Incumbent Advantage.* Accessed on May 15, 2011 at http://www.opensecrets.org/overview/incumbs.php.

13. Paul Herrnson, "Money and Motives: Spending in House Elections," in *Congress Reconsidered,* 6th ed., Lawrence C. Dodd and Bruce L. Oppenheimer, eds. (Washington, DC: Congressional Quarterly, 1997), 100–131.

14. *Baker v. Carr*, 369 U.S. 186 (1962); *Reynolds v. Sims*, 377 U.S. 533 (1964); *Westberry v. Sanders*, 376 U.S. 1 (1964). The facts of these cases are discussed in some detail in Chapter 5.

15. *League of United Latin American Citizens et al. v. Perry*, 548 U.S. (2006).

16. *Davis v. Bandemer*, 478 U.S., 109 (1986).

17. *Veith v. Jubelirer*, 541 U.S., 267 (2004).

18. *League of United Latin American Citizens et al v. Perry*, 548 U.S. (2006).

19. Andrew Gelman and Gary King, "Enhancing Democracy Through Legislative Redistricting," *American Political Science Review* 88 (1994): 541–559.

20. Alan Abramowitz, Brad Alexander, and Matthew Gunning, "Don't Blame Redistricting for Uncompetitive Elections," *PS: Politics and Society* 39 (2006): 87ff.

21. *Bartlett, Executive Director of North Carolina State Board of Elections, et al. v. Strickland et al.* Slip Opinion, March 9, 2009.

22. Public Policy Institute of California, "Voter Turnout in Majority Minority Districts," *Research Brief* 46 (June 2001).

23. See a full discussion of this matter in David Epstein and Sharyn O'Halloran, "Measuring the Electoral and Policy Impact of Majority-Minority Voting Districts," *American Journal of Political Science* 43:2 (1999): 367–395.

24. Richard Fenno, *Home Style: Members in their Districts* (Boston: Little Brown, 1978), 50ff.

25. Michael Losco, "Homestyle 2.0: House Members Online in the 21st Century," unpublished thesis, Georgetown University, May 2010.

26. Robert S. Erikson and Gerald C. Wright, "Voters, Candidates, and Issues in Congressional Elections," in Lawrence C. Dodd and Bruce L. Oppenheimer, eds., *Congress Reconsidered,* 6th ed. (Washington, DC: Congressional Quarterly, 1997), 143.

27. David R. Mayhew, *Congress: The Electoral Connection* (New Haven: Yale University Press, 1974).

28. Support for Congress varies greatly ranging from a low of 18 percent in mid-2007 to a high of 84 percent just after the 9/11 attacks. (Gallup Organization at www.gallup.com, various years.)

29. G. William Whitehurst, "Lobbies and Political Action Committees: A Congressman's Perspective," in Lou Frey, Jr. and Michael T. Hayes, eds., *Inside the House: Former Members Reveal How Congress Really Works* (Lanham, MD: University Press of America, 2001), 210.

30. Ibid., 222.

31. Representative Ernest Istook (R-OK), then chair of the appropriations subcommittee with jurisdiction over the IRS, told the *New York Times* that the provision had been inserted in the bill without his knowledge. See David E. Rosenbaum, "Panel Chief Denies Knowing about Item on Inspecting Tax Returns," *The New York Times*, November 23, 2004, 22A.

32. Barbara Sinclair, *The Transformation of the U.S. Senate* (Baltimore: Johns Hopkins University Press, 1989), 101.

33. Citizens Against Government Waste, "2009 Congressional 'Pig' Book Summary," accessed online at http://www.cagw.org/site/PageServer?pagename=reports_pigbook2009 on May 27, 2009.

34. Richard Rubin, "Party Unity: An Ever Thicker Dividing Line," *CQ Weekly Online* (January 11, 2010): 122–131, http://library.cqpress.com/cqweekly/weeklyreport111-000003276736 (accessed April 25, 2010).

35. Sarah Binder, Thomas E. Mann, and Molly Reynolds, "Is the Broken Branch on the Mend? An Early Report on the 110th Congress," paper presented at forum sponsored by the Brookings Institution, September 4, 2007.

36. Gallup Organization, *Congress Approval at Twelve-Year Low*, April 17, 2006. Accessed online at http://poll.gallup.com on August 2, 2006.

37. See, for example, David Mayhew, *Divided We Govern* (New Haven, CT: Yale University Press, 1991); Charles O. Jones, *The Presidency in a Separated System* (Washington, DC: Brookings Institution Press, 1994).

38. See, for example, James L. Sundquist, *Constitutional Reform and Effective Government, rev. ed.* (Washington, DC: Brookings Institution Press, 1992); Samuel Kernell, "Facing an Opposition

Congress: The President's Strategic Circumstance," in (Gary W. Cox and Samuel Kernell, eds.) The Politics of Divided Government (Boulder, CO: Westview Press, 1991).

39. George C. Edwards, III, Andrew Barrett, and Jeffrey Peake, "The Legislative Impact of Divided Government," *American Journal of Political Science* 41 (2), 1997 545–563.

40. Douglas B. Harris and Garrison Nelson, "Middlemen No More? Emergent Patterns in Congressional Leadership Selection," *PS: Political Science and Politics* 41 (January 2008), 49–55.

41. Lawrence A. Becker and Vincent G. Moscardelli, "Congressional Leadership on the Front Lines: Committee Chairs, Electoral Security, and Ideology, *PS: Political Science and Politics* 41 (January 2008), 77–82.

42. Robert S. Walker, "A Look at the Rules of the House," in Lou Frey, Jr. and Michael T. Hayes, eds., *Inside the House: Former Members Reveal How Congress Really Works* (Lanham, MD: University Press of America, 2001), 250.

43. *Origins and Development of Congress*, 261.

44. Hamilton, 55–56.

45. Barbara Sinclair, *Unorthodox Lawmaking: New Legislative Processes in the U.S. Congress* (Washington, DC: Congressional Quarterly Press, 1997).

46. Congressional Research Service, Report RL30172: *Instances of Use of United States Armed Forces Abroad, 1798–2001.*

47. This sentiment is traced to Roger Sherman. See *Origins and Development of Congress*, 62.

48. *Hamdan v. Rumsfeld*, 548 U.S. (2006).

49. Binder, Mann, and Reynolds, 15.

50. *Immigration and Naturalization Service v. Chadha*, 454 U.S. 812 (1983).

51. The War Powers Act includes a form of legislative veto.

52. Senate Historical Office, "Treaties." Online at http://www.senate.gov on July 30, 2006.

53. John R. Hibbing and Elizabeth Theiss-Morse, *Congress as Public Enemy* (Cambridge: Cambridge University Press, 1995).

54. Gallup Organization, *Congress Approval Rating Matches Historic Low*, August 21, 2007. Accessed online at http://www.galluppoll.com on September 11, 2007.

55. Thomas Mann and Norman Ornstein, *The Broken Branch: How Congress is Failing America and How to Get It Back on Track* (New York: Oxford University Press, 2006).

56. Jennifer Steinhauer, "Californians Compete for a Shot at Redistricting," *The New York Times,* March 4, 2010, p. A18.

57. Edward G. Carmines, Jessica C. Gerrity, and Michael W. Wagner, *How the American Public Views Congress: A Report Based on the Center on Congress at Indiana University's 2004 Public Opinion Survey* (Bloomington, IN: Indiana University Press, 2005).

58. Franklin D. Gilliam, Jr. "Influences on Voter Turnout for U.S. House Elections in Non-Presidential Election Years," *Legislative Studies Quarterly* 10:3 (1985): 339–351.

59. Steven E. Gottlieb, "Incumbents Rules," *The National Law Journal*, February 25, 2002, A21.

Chapter 12: The Presidency: Power and Paradox

1. Obama on bin Laden: The full "60 Minutes" Interview, *CBS News,* May 8, 2011. Accessed on May 31, 2011 at http://www.cbsnews.com/8301-504803_162-20060530-10391709.html.

2. Ibid.

3. Helen Kennedy, "Osama bin Laden dead: President Obama, advisors watched raid to kill Al Qaeda leader unfold live," *New York Daily News,* May 2, 2011. Accessed on May 31, 2011 at http:

//articles.nydailynews.com/2011-05-02/news/29523679_1 _president-obama-seal-team-al-qaeda-leader.

4. Harold F. Bass, Jr., "The President and Political Parties," in *The President, the Public, and the Parties* (Washington, DC: Congressional Quarterly Press, 1997), 33.

5. D. Robert Dahl, "Myth of the Presidential Mandate," *Political Science Quarterly* 105 (1990): 359.

6. Ibid., 360.

7. John Aldrich, "The Invisible Primary and Its Effect on Democratic Choice," *PS: Political Science and Politics* 42 (January 2009): 33–38.

8. But see Michael Lewis Beck and Peverill Squire, "Iowa: The Most Representative State?" *PS: Political Science and Politics* 42 (January 2009): 39–44. The authors claim that while the demographics of the state are not a microcosm of the nation as a whole, on many important social, political and economic indicators it ranks about the midpoint of many states.

9. Brian Knight and Nathan Schiff, "Momentum and Social Learning in Presidential Primaries," *Journal of Political Economy,* forthcoming.

10. Thomas E. Patterson, *The Vanishing Voter* (New York: Knopf, 2002), 169.

11. Darren Carlson, "Public Flunks Electoral College," Gallup Organization, November 2, 2004. Accessed online at http:www/galluppoll.com on March 16, 2007. For excellent discussions of some of the problems associated with the Electoral College as well as the pros and cons associated with various types of reform, see: *Harvard Law Review,* "Rethinking the Electoral College Debate: The Framers, Federalism, and One Person One Vote," 114 (8), 2001:2526–49.

12. Quoted in James Pfiffner, *The Modern Presidency* (New York: St. Martin's Press, 1994), 54.

13. William G. Howell, *Power Without Persuasion: The Politics of Direct Presidential Action* (Princeton: Princeton University Press, 2003), Chap. 1.

14. Sidney M. Milkis and Michael Nelson, *The American Presidents: Origins and Development, 1776–1993* (Washington, DC: CQ Press, 1994), 77.

15. Paul C. Light, *The President's Agenda: Domestic Policy Choice from Kennedy to Clinton* (Baltimore: Johns Hopkins Press, 1999), 230.

16. *Clinton v. City of New York* 524 U.S. 417 1998.

17. National Commission on Terrorist Attacks upon the United States, *The 9–11 Commission Report* (Washington, DC: United States Printing Office, 2004).

18. W. Craig Bledsoe, Christopher J. Bosso, and Mark J. Rozell, "Chief Executive," in *Powers of the Presidency*, 2d ed. (Washington, DC: CQ Press, 1997), 41.

19. Milkis and Nelson, 45.

20. Daniel Diller and Stephen H. Wirls, "Commander in Chief," in *Powers of the Presidency,* 2d ed. (Washington, DC: CQ Press, 1997), 165.

21. Abraham Lincoln, "Letter to Albert Hodges," in John Nicolay and John Hay, eds., *The Complete Works of Abraham Lincoln* (New York: Francis Tandy, 1891), 10–66.

22. *Boumediene v. Bush*, 553 U.S. ___ (2008).

23. Charlie Savage, "Obama's War on Terror May Resemble Bush's in Some Areas," *The New York Times,* February 17, 2009.

24. Jonathan Wilkenfeld, "Structural Challenges for American Foreign Policy in the Obama Administration," in *Obama in Office* (ed. by James A. Thurber), (Boulder, CO: Paradigm, 2011), pp. 227–242.

25. Daniel Diller and Stephen H. Wirls, "Chief Diplomat," in *Powers of the Presidency,* 2d ed. (Washington, DC: CQ Press, 1997), 140.

26. George Edwards, III, *At the Margins: Presidential Leadership in Congress* (New Haven: Yale University Press, 1989), 212.

27. Christopher J. Bosso, "Legislative Leader," in *Powers of the Presidency,* 2d ed. (Washington, DC: CQ Press, 1997), 86.

28. Samuel A. Alito, Jr., Office of Legal Counsel, U.S. Department of Justice, "Using Presidential Signing Statements to Make Fuller Use of the President's Constitutionally Assigned Role in the Process of Enacting Law," February 5, 1986, 1.

29. Jeremy D. Mayer and Lynn Kirby, "The Promise and Peril of Presidential Polling: Between Gallup's Dream and the Morris Nightmare," in Stephen J. Wayne, ed., *Is This Any Way to Run a Democratic Government?* (Washington, DC: Georgetown University Press, 2004), 103.

30. Lawrence R. Jacobs and Melinda S. Jackson, "Presidential Leadership and the Threat to Popular Sovereignty," in Michael A. Genovese and Matthew J. Streb, eds., *Polls and Politics: The Dilemmas of Democracy* (Albany, NY: State University of New York Press, 2004).

31. Presidents sometimes elevate additional advisers to cabinet status as well.

32. These were the sentiments of Richard Nixon, who was included in cabinet deliberations. Quoted in Pfiffner, 12.

33. Bradley Patterson, Jr., *The White House Staff: Inside the West Wing and Beyond* (Washington, DC: The Brookings Institution, 2000), 11.

34. Dan Froomkin, "White House Briefing." Accessed online at http://www.washingtonpost.com on September 17, 2004.

35. James P. Pfiffner, "Organizing the Obama White House," in *Obama in Office* (ed. by James A. Thurber), (Boulder, CO: Paradigm, 2011), p. 78.

36. B. Patterson, 62.

37. Karen M. Hult, "The Bush White House in Comparative Perspective," in Fred I. Greenstein, ed., *The George W. Bush Presidency: An Early Assessment* (Baltimore, MD: Johns Hopkins University Press, 2003), 64.

38. Pfiffner, p. 79.

39. Pfiffner, p. 76.

new 38 & 39

40. This model was advocated by advisers Clark Clifford and Richard Neustadt. See James Pfiffner, *The Strategic Presidency* (Chicago: Dorsey Press, 1988), 23–25.

41. Pfiffner, 67.

42. Gary Jacobson, *A Divider, Not a Uniter* (New York: Pearson, 2007), 74.

43. See, for example, Richard A. Clarke, *Against All Enemies: Inside America's War on Terror* (New York: Free Press, 2004); Paul O'Neill and Ron Suskind, *The Price of Loyalty: George W. Bush, the White House, and the Education of Paul O'Neill* (New York: Simon & Schuster, 2004). See also, account of interviews with cabinet members from the Bush White House in Bob Woodward, *Plan of Attack* (New York: Simon & Schuster, 2004).

44. James P. Pfiffner, "President George W. Bush and His War Cabinet," Paper presented at conference on *The Presidency, Congress, and the War on Terrorism*, University of Florida (February 7, 2003).

45. Stephen J. Wayne, "Obama's Personality and Performance," in *Obama in Office* (ed. by James A. Thurber), (Boulder, CO: Paradigm, 2011), p. 69-70.

46. See, for example, Edward Hargrove, "What Manner of Man?" in James David Barber, ed., *Choosing the President* (New York: Prentice-Hall, 1974). Also see Thomas E. Cronin and Michael A. Genovese, *The Paradoxes of the American Presidency* (New York: Oxford, 1998), 33–38.

47. James David Barber, *The Presidential Character*, rev. ed. (New York: Prentice-Hall, 1992).

48. Arthur M. Schlesinger, Jr., *The Imperial Presidency* (Boston: Houghton Mifflin, 1973).

49. See, for example, Steven G. Calabresi and Christopher S. Yoo, "The Unitary Executive During the Second Half-Century," *Harvard Journal of Public Policy* 668 (2003).

50. Richard Neustadt, *Presidential Power and the Modern Presidents: The Politics of Leadership from Roosevelt to Reagan* (New York: Free Press, 1991).

51. Quoted in Cronin and Genovese, 317.

52. Dan Eggan, "Cheney, Biden Spar in TV Appearance," *Washington Post,* December 22, 2008, A02.

53. Thomas S. Langston, *With Reverence and Contempt: How Americans Think About Their President* (Baltimore: Johns Hopkins University Press 1995), xi.

Chapter 13: Bureaucracy: Citizens as Owners and Consumers

1. Allison Damast, "Asking for Student Loan Forgiveness," *Business Week,* February 24, 2010.

2. Ibid.

3. The Biz Beat, "Student loan debt is now more than credit card debt," Accessed on May 12, 2011 at http://blogs.ajc.com/business-beat/2011/04/12/student-loan-debt-is-now-more-than-credit-card-debt/.

4. Joyce Appleby, "That's General Washington to You," *The New York Times Book Review,* February 14, 1993, 11.

5. Herbert Kaufman, *Red Tape: Its Origins, Uses, and Abuses* (Washington, DC: The Brookings Institution, 1977), 11.

6. See David A. Stockman, *The Triumph of Politics: How the Reagan Revolution Failed* (New York: Harper and Row, 1986).

7. Mosher, 57.

8. James D. Richardson, *Messages and Papers of the Presidents*, Volume II (Washington, DC: Bureau of National Literature and Art, 1903), 438.

9. Robert C. Caldwell, *James A. Garfield* (Hamden, CT: Archon Books, 1965).

10. Matthew A. Crenson and Benjamin Ginsberg, *Downsizing Democracy* (Baltimore: Johns Hopkins University Press, 2002), 86.

11. David Osborne and Ted Gaebler, *Reinventing Government: How the Entrepreneurial Spirit Is Transforming the Public Sector* (Reading, MA: Addison-Wesley, 1992).

12. Mark Green and John Berry, *The Challenge of Hidden Profits: Reducing Corporate Bureaucracy and Waste* (New York: William Morrow, 1985).

13. See an interview in Ralph P. Hummel, *The Bureaucratized Experience* (New York: St. Martin's Press, 1977), 23.

14. Gerald E. Caiden, "What Is Maladministration?" *Public Administration Review*, 51: 6 (1991): 486–493.

15. Alexander Hamilton, James Madison, and John Jay, *The Federalist*, Benjamin F. Wright, ed. (New York: Metro Books, 2002), 451.

16. Hugh Helco, *A Government of Strangers: Executive Politics in Washington* (Washington, DC: Brookings Institution, 1997).

17. Postal workers have their own organization but are not allowed to strike. There are other federal workers like federal air traffic controllers who also are not allowed to strike. Political appointees, unlike career civil servants, serve at the pleasure of the president.

18. Robert Lineberry, *American Public Policy: What Government Does and What Difference It Makes* (New York: Harper & Row, 1977).

19. Theodore Lowi, *The End of Liberalism*, (New York: W. W. Norton, 1969).

20. See Cornelius M. Kerwin, *Rulemaking: How Government Agencies Write Law And Make Public Policy* (Washington, DC: CQ Press, 1994).

21. Ibid., 162.

22. Ibid., 194.

23. Ibid., 196.

24. Kerwin, 170–171.

25. Ibid., 170.

26. Ibid., 170.

27. *Humphrey's Executor v. United States* (1935).

28. Donald D. Kettl, *Government by Proxy: (Mis)Managing Federal Programs* (Washington, DC: The CQ Press, 1998).

29. Paul C. Light, *The True Size of Government* (Washington, DC: Brookings Institution, 1999).

30. Ibid., 9.

31. B. Dan Wood and Richard W. Waterman, *Bureaucratic Dynamics: The Role of Bureaucracy in a Democracy* (Boulder: Westview Press, 1994), 105.

32. See Patricia W. Ingraham and David H. Rosenbloom, *The Promise and Paradox of Civil Service Reform* (Pittsburgh: University of Pittsburgh Press, 1992), 4.

33. Wood and Waterman, 104.

34. John Brehm and Scott Gatew, *Working, Shirking, and Sabotage: Bureaucratic Response to a Democratic Public* (Ann Arbor: University of Michigan Press, 1997).

35. James Q. Wilson, *Bureaucracy: What Government Agencies Do and Why They Do It* (New York: Basic Books, 1989), 236

36. *McGrain v. Daugherty* (1972).

37. Johanna Neuman, "FAA's 'Culture of Coziness' Targeted in Airline Safety Hearing," *Los Angeles Times*, April 4, 2008, 1.

38. See Clinton Rossiter, *The American Presidency* (New York: Harcourt, Brace, and World, 1960).

39. James G. March and Johan P. Olson, "Organizing Political Life: What Administrative Reorganization Tells Us About Government," *American Political Science Review* 77 (1983): 281–296.

40. Richard W. Waterman, *Presidential Influence and the Administrative State* (Knoxville: The University of Tennessee Press, 1989), 27.

41. Ibid., 30.

42. Gerald Ford, *A Time to Heal: The Autobiography of Gerald R. Ford* (New York: Harper & Row, 1979), 352.

43. Waterman, 37.

44. Ibid., 1–2.

Chapter 14: The Courts: Judicial Power in a Democratic Setting

1. Sean Gregory, "Why the Supreme Court Ruled for Westboro," *Time,* March 3, 2011, p. 1, http://www.time.com/time/nation/article/0,8599,2056613,00.html.

2. *Snyder v. Phelps (2011).*

3. Sean Gregory, *Time,* p.4

4. Oral argument in *Snyder v. Phelps,* page 10.

5. Edward D. Re, *Stare Decisis* (Washington, DC: Federal Judicial Center, 1975), 2.

6. See Charles Rembar, *The Judicial Process* (New York: Oxford University Press, 1968), 12.

7. *Flast v. Cohen* (1968).

8. Ibid.

9. *Colegrove v. Green* (1946).

10. *Baker v. Carr* (1962).

11. Jethro K. Lieberman, *The Litigious Society* (New York: Basic Books, 1983), viii.

12. See Christopher E. Smith, *Courts, Politics, and the Judicial Process*, 2d ed. (Chicago: Nelson Hall, 1997), 330.

13. Howard Abadinsky, *Law and Justice: An Introduction to the American Legal System* (Chicago: Nelson Hall, 1995), 55.

14. Article III, Section 1 of the Constitution.

15. Alexander Hamilton, John Jay, and James Madison, *The Federalist Papers*, Benjamin F. Wright, ed. (New York: Metro Books, 1961), 490–491.

16. Bernard Schwartz, *A History of the Supreme Court* (New York: Oxford University Press, 1993), 15.

17. The number of justices on the Supreme Court is set by Congress because no set number was specified in the Constitution.

18. *Ex parte McCardle* (1869).

19. All the justices today have four clerks (Justice Stevens only has three law clerks).

20. Quoted in H. W. Perry, *Deciding to Decide: Agenda Setting in the U.S. Supreme Court* (Cambridge, MA: Harvard University Press, 1992), 144.

21. Ibid., 222.

22. Ibid., 75.

23. See Lawrence Baum, *The Supreme Court*, 6th ed. (Washington, DC: CQ Press, 1998), 114.

24. Doris M. Provine, "Deciding What to Decide: How the Supreme Court Sets Its Agenda" *Judicature* 64, no. 7 (1981): 320.

25. See Lincoln Caplan, *The Tenth Justice: The Solicitor General and the Rule of Law* (New York: Vintage Books, 1987).

26. See Rebecca Mae Salokar, *The Solicitor General: The Politics of Law* (Philadelphia: Temple University Press, 1992), 3.

27. Jeffrey Toobin, "No More Mr. Nice Guy," *The New Yorker,* May 25, 2009, p. 2.

28. O'Brien, 294.

29. Ibid., 313.

30. Bob Woodward and Scott Armstrong, *The Brethren* (New York: Simon & Schuster, 1979), 136–139.

31. Charles A. Johnson and Bradley C. Canon, *Judicial Policies: Implementation and Impact,* 2d ed. (Washington, DC: Congressional Quarterly Press, 1999), Chap. 1.

32. See Richard L. Pacelle, Jr., and Lawrence Baum, "Supreme Court Authority in the Judiciary," *American Politics Quarterly* 20 (1992): 169–191.

33. J. W. Peltason, *Fifty-Eight Lonely Men: Southern Federal Judges and School Desegregation*, 2d ed. (Urbana: University of Illinois Press, 1971), 246.

34. *Employment Division, Department of Human Resources v. Smith* (1990).

35. *City of Boerne v. Flores* (1997).

36. *Atkins v. Virginia* (2002).

37. See Lee Epstein and Jack Knight, *The Choices Justices Make* (Washington, DC: CQ Press, 1998); Forest Maltzman, Paul J. Wahlbeck, and Jack Spriggs, *Crafting Law on the Supreme Court: The Collegial Game* (New York: Cambridge University Press, 2000); and Walter F. Murphy, *Elements of Judicial Strategy* (Chicago: University of Chicago Press, 1964).

38. Saul Brenner, "Fluidity on the Supreme Court, 1956–1967," *American Journal of Political Science* 90 (1996): 581.

39. Epstein and Knight, Chap. 3.

40. See Henry J. Abraham, *Justices and Presidents,* 2d ed. (New York: Oxford University Press, 1985).

41. See David O'Brien, *Storm Center* (New York: Norton, 1986).

42. Abraham, 191.

43. Alpheus T. Mason, *William Howard Taft: Chief Justice* (New York: Simon & Schuster, 1965), 215–216.

44. Philip Cooper and Howard Ball, *The United States Supreme Court: From the Inside Out* (Upper Saddle River, NJ: Prentice-Hall, 1996), 50.

45. Scigliano, 147–148.

46. Roger Taney was a Catholic who served on the Court from 1835 until 1864, but the tradition of a Catholic seat did not begin with him, because his replacement was not a Catholic.

47. Lawrence Baum, *American Courts*, 4th ed. (Boston: Houghton Mifflin, 1998), 106.

48. Michael Pertschuk and Wendy Schaetzel, *People Rising* (New York: Thunder's Mouth Press, 1989), 68.

49. See Karen O'Connor, "Lobbying the Justices for Justice," in Paul S. Herrnson, Ronald G. Shaido, and Clyde Wilcox, eds., *The Interest Group Connection* (Chatham, NJ: Chatham House, 1998), 273.

50. Baum, 112.

51. Lee Epstein, *Conservatives in Court* (Knoxville: University of Tennessee Press, 1985).

52. In *Newman v. Piggie Park Enterprises Inc.* (1968), the Supreme Court upheld the fee-splitting provision.

53. See Stephen C. Yeazell, *From Medieval Group Litigation to the Modern Class Action* (New Haven, CT: Yale University Press, 1987).

54. Samuel Issacharoff, "Goverance and Legitimacy in the Law of Class Actions," *Supreme Court Review* (1999): 337.

55. *Powell v. McCormack* (1969).

56. Matthew A. Crenson and Benjamin Ginsberg, *Downsizing Democracy: How America Sidelined Its Citizens and Privatized Its Public* (Baltimore: Johns Hopkins University Press, 2002), 154.

57. See Lucius J. Barker, "Third Parties in Litigation: A Systematic View of the Judicial Function," *The Journal of Politics,* 29, no. 1 (1967): 54–60.

Chapter 15: Public Policy: Responding to Citizens

1. Steven Greenhouse, "Ex GM Workers Try to Reboot Their Lives," *The New York Times,* February 13, 2009.

2. Mary Pilon, "From Ordering Steak and Lobster to Serving It," *Wall Street Journal,* June 1, 2009. Accessed on June 4, 2009 at http://online.wsj.com/article/SB124390425824574861.html.

3. Thomas R. Dye, *Understanding Public Policy,* 10th ed. (Upper Saddle River, NJ: Prentice-Hall, 2002), 1.

4. This section draws heavily on the work of James Q. Wilson whose typology is described. See James Q. Wilson, *Political Organizations* (Princeton, NJ: Princeton University Press, 1995), 332–337.

5. Environmental Protection Agency, "Air Trends." Accessed on June 5, 2009 at http://www.epa.gov/airtrends/.

6. Dye, 106.

7. U.S. Census Bureau, Income, Poverty, and Health Insurance Coverage in the United States, September 2011. Accessed on September 17, 2011 at http://www.census.gov/prod/2011pub/p60–239.pdf.

8. Urban Institute, *Assessing the New Federalism: Eight Years Later* (Washington, DC: Urban Institute, 2005).

9. Michael A. Fletcher, "Two Fronts in the War on Poverty: Bush Seeks More Aid for Church Groups; Others Face Uncertainty," *Washington Post*, May 17, 2005, A01.

10. Amendments to Executive Order 13199, issued on February 5, 2009. http://www.whitehouse.gov/the_press_office/Amendmentsto-ExecutiveOrder13199andEstablishmentofthePresidentsAdvisory-CouncilforFaith-BasedandNeighborhoodPartnerships/.

11. Mark Holmes, Thomas C. Ricketts, and Jennifer King. "Updating Uninsured Estimates for Current Economic Conditions: State Specific Estimates," Cecil G. Sheps Center for Health Services Research and North Carolina Institute of Medicine (March 2009).

12. Kaiser Family Foundation, *Health Coverage, and the Uninsured: Profile of the Uninsured*. Accessed online at http://www.kff.org on September 14, 2007.

13. Center for American Progress, "More Americans Losing Health Insurance Every Day Analysis of Health Coverage Losses During the Recession." Accessed on June 6, 2009 at http://www.american-progress.org/issues/2009/05/insurance_loss.html.

14. Robert Pear, "Senate Approve Children's Health Bill," *The New York Times,* January 29, 2009.

15. Stephen Moore, ed., *Restoring the Dream: The Bold New Plan by House Republicans* (Washington, DC: Times Books, 1995), 156.

16. Office of the Special Inspector General for the Troubled Asset Relief Program, Quarterly Report to Congress, April 20, 2010, http://www.sigtarp.gov/reports/congress/2010/April2010_Quarterly_Report_to_Congress.pdf. (accessed May 12, 2010).

17. Dye, 152.

18. Benjamin I. Page and Robert Y. Shapiro, *The Rational Public* (Chicago: University of Chicago Press, 1992).

19. Julie Bosman, "From the Ranks of Jobless, A Flood of Volunteers," *The New York Times,* March 15, 2009.

20. Ibid.

21. Katie Zezima, "In Boston, Residents Seek Face to Face Advice to Avoid Foreclosure," *New York Times,* March 30, 2008.

22. See, for example, The Center for Deliberative Democracy at Stanford University (accessed online at http://cdd.stanford.edu on May 25, 2005); the Deliberative Democracy Consortium (accessed online at http://www.deliberative-democracy.net on May 25, 2005); the Center for Deliberative Polling at the University of Texas Austin (accessed online at http://www.la.utexas.edu/research/delpol/cdpindex.html on May 25, 2005).

Chapter 16: Foreign and Defense Policy: Protecting American Interests in the World

1. David Zucchino, "Drone Pilots Have a Front-Row Seat on War, From Half a World Away." *Los Angeles Times,* February 21, 2010, accessed at http://articles.latimes.com/2010/feb/21/world/la-fg-drone-crews21–2010feb21 on May 13, 2010.

2. Marc Pitzke, "How Drone Pilots Wage War," *Spiegel Online,* March 12, 2010. Accessed at http://www.spiegel.de/international/world/0,1518,682420,00.html on May 13, 2010.

3. Ibid.

4. Zucchino, op. cit.

5. Alexis de Tocqueville, *Democracy in America,* trans. George Lawrence, ed. J. P. Mayer (New York: Harper and Row, 1969), 278.

6. Ibid., 227.

7. H. William Brands, *The United States in the World: A History of American Foreign Policy,* vol. 1 (Boston: Houghton Mifflin, 1994), 110.

8. George W. Bush, "President Bush Delivers Graduation Speech at West Point," White House website, http://www.whitehouse.gov/news/releases/2002/06/20020601-3.html (accessed April 29, 2005).

9. George W. Bush, "Remarks by the President at Whitehall Palace," White House website, http://www.whitehouse.gov/news/releases/2003/11/20031119-1.html (accessed May 17, 2005).

10. The Kissinger Telcons: Kissinger Telcons on Chile, National Security Archive Electronic Briefing Book No. 123, edited by Peter Kornbluh, posted May 26, 2004. This particular dialogue can be found at TELCON: September 16, 1973, 11:50 a.m. Kissinger Talking to Nixon. Accessed online November 26, 2006.

11. See, for example, Robert J. Lieber, *No Common Power: Understanding International Relations* (Boston: Scott Foresman, 1988).

12. See, for example, the excellent discussion of the school of realism in Bruce W. Jentleson, *American Foreign Policy: The Dynamics of Choice in the 21st Century,* 2d ed. (New York: W. W. Norton, 2004).

13. See, for example, Joseph Nye, *The Power to Lead: Soft, Hard, and Smart* (New York: Oxford University Press, 2008).

14. Francis Fukuyama, "After Neoconservatism," *The New York Times*, February 19, 2006.

15. James P. Pfiffner, "Organizing the Obama White House," in *Obama in Office* (ed. by James A. Thurber), (Boulder, CO: Paradigm, 2011), p. 79.

16. Ibid.

17. *National Commission on Terrorist Attacks, The 9/11 Commission Report: Final Report of the Commission on Terrorist Attacks upon the United States* (New York: W. W. Norton, 2004).

18. U.S. Department of State, *Mission Statement*, online at http://www.state.gov/m/rm/rls/dosstrat/2004/23503.htm (accessed May 1, 2005).

19. Jane Mayer, *The Dark Side: The Inside Story of How the War on Terror Turned into a War on American Ideals* (New York: Doubleday, 2008).

20. Nicole Gaudiano, "Kidding Aside, Biden Plays Key Role for Administration," *Gannett Content online,* April 27, 2009. Accessed on June 11, 2009 at http://gns.gannettonline.com/apps/pbcs.dll/article?AID=/20090427/OBAMA100DAYS/90424004.

21. Brian Knowlton, "Biden and Cheney Clash on Role of No. 2," *The Caucus, The New York Times,* December 21, 2008. Accessed June 11, 2009 at http://thecaucus.blogs.nytimes.com/2008/12/21/with-biden-and-cheney-clashing-views-of-a-job/.

22. See, for example, Robert Higgs, "The Trillion-Dollar Defense Budget Is Already Here," The Independent Institute, online at http://www.independent.org/newsroom/article.asp?id=1941 (accessed January 26, 2008). See also War Resisters League, "Where Your Income Tax Money Really Goes," online at http://www.warresisters.org/piechart.htm (accessed January 26, 2008).

23. Ole R. Holsti, *Public Opinion and American Foreign Policy,* rev. ed. (Ann Arbor: University of Michigan Press, 2007), 55.

24. Gallup Organization, "Gallup's Pulse of Democracy: The War in Iraq," April 18–20, 2008, survey, online at http://www.gallup.com/poll/1633/Iraq.aspx (accessed July 6, 2008).

25. CIA World Factbook, online at https://www.cia.gov/library/publications/the-world-factbook/ (accessed January 27, 2008).

26. Curt Tarnoff and Larry Nowels, *Foreign Aid: An Introductory Overview of U.S. Programs and Policies* (Washington, DC: Congressional Research Service, April 15, 2004).

27. Ibid.

28. Joseph S. Nye, *Soft Power: The Means to Success in World Politics* (New York: Public Affairs, 2004), 4.

29. The Nuclear Information Project, Status of World Nuclear Forces, online at http://www.nukestrat.com/nukestatus.htm (accessed February 6, 2008).

30. United States Nuclear Regulatory Commission, *Fact Sheet on Dirty Bombs*, online at http://www.nrc.gov/reading-rm/doc-collections/fact-sheets/dirty-bombs.html (accessed February 9, 2008).

31. U.S. Census Bureau, *Foreign Trade Statistics*, online at http://www.census.gov/foreign-trade/balance/c5700.html#2007 (accessed February 9, 2008).

32. David Lague, "Beijing Increases Defense Spending," *International Herald Tribune*, March 4, 2007.

33. Wayne M. Morrison and Marc Labonte, "China's Holdings of U.S. Securities: Implications for the U.S. Economy," *Congressional Research Service Report for Congress*, January 9, 2008.

34. Nye, *Soft Power,* 5–11.

CREDITS

FIGURES/TEXT

Chapter 1 p. 3 (figure) Reprinted with the permission of the School of Public Policy, University of Maryland. p. 6 Reprinted with the permission of World Economic Forum USA. p. 8 Copyright © 2005 by The Gallup Organization. Reprinted with permission.

Chapter 2 p. 26 Reprinted with the permission of the School of Public Policy, University of Maryland. p. 30 Copyright © 1988 by Dorsey Press. Reprinted with the permission of Cengage Learning. Fax 800 730-2215.

Chapter 3 p. 59 Copyright © 2002 by The Urban Institute. Reprinted with permission.

Chapter 4 p. 69 (both figures) Copyright © 2006. Reprinted with the permission of the McCormick Tribune Freedom Museum, www.freedommuseum.us. p. 71 Copyright © The Pew Forum on Religion & Public Life. Reprinted with permission. p. 72 Copyright © The Pew Forum on Religion & Public Life. Reprinted with permission. p. 72 Copyright © The Pew Forum on Religion & Public Life. Reprinted with permission. p. 73 Copyright © The Pew Forum on Religion & Public Life. Reprinted with permission. p. 76 Copyright © 2006. Reprinted with the permission of the McCormick Tribune Freedom Museum, www.freedommuseum.us. p. 85 Copyright © Death Penalty Information Center. Reprinted with permission. p. 86 Copyright © Death Penalty Information Center. Reprinted with permission. p. 90 W. Cukier and V. Sidel, The Global Gun Epidemic: From Saturday Night Specials to AK 47s (New York: Praeger, 2006).

Chapter 5 p. 97 (map) From Alan Brinkley, American History. Copyright © 2013. Used by permission of McGraw-Hill, Inc. p. 104 The New York Times/CBS News Poll. p. 105 Pew Hispanic Center tabulations of 2010 American Community Survey. p. 108 Reprinted with the permission of Dr. Dennis O'Neil, Palomar College. p. 109 Pew Hispanic Center tabulations of 2010 American Community Survey. p. 111 Courtesy Pew Research Center. p. 113 Reprinted with the permission of the Human Rights Campaign, www.hrc.org. p. 114 ABC News/Washington Post Poll (March 10–13, 2011). p. 117 Reprinted with the permission of the School of Public Policy, University of Maryland. p. 118 Institute for Women's Policy Research.

Chapter 6 p. 131 Reprinted with the permission of The Pew Research Center for the People and the Press. p. 134 Reprinted with the permission of The Pew Research Center for the People and the Press. p. 138 Reprinted with the permission of The Pew Research Center for the People and the Press. p. 139 Copyright © 2008 by The Gallup Organization. Reprinted with permission. p. 140 Copyright © 2010 by American National Election Studies. Reprinted with permission, www.electionstudies.org. p. 140 Copyright © 2004 by American National Election Studies. Reprinted with permission, www.electionstudies.org. p. 141 From Robert S. Erikson and Kent L. Tedin, American Public Opinion, Sixth Edition. Copyright © 2003. Reprinted with the permission of Pearson Education, Inc. p. 144 Courtesy Center for American Progress, 2009. p. 144 Copyright © by The Gallup Organization. Reprinted with permission.

Chapter 7 p. 157 Copyright © 2009 by American National Election Studies. Reprinted with permission, www.electionstudies.org. p. 160 Reprinted with the permission of The Pew Research Center

INDEX

Sherman, Roger, 24

signing statements, **290**

Silent Spring (Carson), 185, 383

Silver, Nate, 172

simple random sampling, **136**

single issue or candidate, **216**

single-member district, **204**

Six-Day War, 323, 420

Skinner, Hank, 65–67

Skinner v. Switzer, 66, 87

slander, **78**

slavery, 24–25, 97–98

Smith v. City of Jackson, Mississippi, 112

SNCC. *See* Student Nonviolent Coordinating Committee

Snyder, Matthew, 353

social capital, **3**

social class, **9**, 11

Social Security, 9, 144, 387

soft money, **211**

soft power, **427**

Sotomayor, Sonia, 38, 122–123, 370, 372, 374–375

sound bites, **244**

Southern Christian Leadership Conference (SCLC), 102

sovereign, **22**

Speaker of the House, **281**

spin, **244**

spin doctors, **244**

splinter parties, **215**

spoils system, **332**

Springer, Jerry, 137–138

stability, **135**

stagflation, 390

standing, **359**

Stanton, Elizabeth Cady, 115

Starr, Kenneth, 38

START. *See* strategic arms reduction treaty

state secrets privilege, **323**

States' Rights Party, 207

Steele, Michael, 210

Steinberg, Saul, 324

Stewart, Jon, 256

Stewart, Potter, 77

Stockman, David, 321

Stonewall Riots, 113

Stowe, Harriet Beecher, 109

strategic arms reduction treaty (START), 421

strategy, **184**

straw polls, **128**

strength of party identification, **158**

strict scrutiny test, **106**

student loans, 329–330

Student Nonviolent Coordinating Committee (SNCC), 102–103

student PRIGs, 175–176

Sullivan rule, **78**

Sumner, Charles, 264

superdelegates, **303**

supply-side economics, **390–391**

supremacy clause, **28**

Supreme Court, 252, 356

   decision making by, 361–366

   selection to, 366–371

Susman, Louis, 316

symbolic speech, **76–77**

systematic sampling, **136**

T

tactics, **184**

Taft, William Howard, 366–369

Talan, Scott, 1

Taliban, 402, 421

Taney, Roger B., 47, 98, 361

TANF. *See* Temporary Assistance to Needy Families

TARP. *See* Troubled Asset Relief Program

Tauzin, Billy, 186

Tea Party, 17–18, 148–149, 172–173, 201–202, 215

Temporary Assistance to Needy Families (TANF), 388

Tenth Amendment, 31, 41, 47, 49, 57

terrorism, 405–406, 420

test case, **89**

third parties, **215**, 216*f*

Thirteenth Amendment, 36, 47, **98**

Thomas, Clarence, 252, 366, 370

three-fifths compromise, 24

Thurmond, Strom, 284

Tilden, Samuel, 99

Tocqueville, Alexis de, 61, 154, 177, 203, 403

traditionalistic political culture, 134

Treaty of Paris, 22

Treaty of Versailles, 291, 404

trial by jury, 85

Troubled Asset Relief Program (TARP), 172, 391

Truman Doctrine, 313

Trump, Donald, 104

trustee, **271**

Tsvangirai, Morgan, 424

Twelfth Amendment, 32, 299, 305

Twenty-second Amendment, 299–300

Twenty-seventh Amendment, 32

Twenty-sixth Amendment, 226, 365

U

UN General Assembly Resolution 181, 420

Uncle Tom's Cabin (Stowe), 109

unfunded mandates, **55**

Unfunded Mandates Reform Act, 55

unicameral, **24**

unit rule, **305**

unitary executive, **323**

unpledged delegates, **303**

U.S. Agency for International Development (USAID), 418

U.S. Nuclear Regulatory Commission, 422

U.S. v. E. C. Knight Co., 47–48

V

Van Buren, Martin, 206

VAP. *See* Voting-Age Population

Vaughan-Nichols, Steven J., 231

VEP. *See* Voter-Eligible Population

Verba, Sidney, 169

vice president, 323–324

Vietnam War, 77, 112, 250, 287

voluntarism, 7, 132, 165

voting, 12, 111*f,* 155, 160–164, 169*f,* **224**

   African Americans and, 100

   women and, 35

voter fatigue, **163**

Voter-Eligible Population (VEP), 162

Voting Rights Act of 1965, **103**

Voting-Age Population (VAP), 162

W

Walker, Jack L., 59, 183

Walker, Robert S., 284

Walker, Scott, 53

Wallace, George, 215

Wal-Mart Stores, Inc. v. Dukes, 119

Walsh-Healey Act, 48

war, 33, 287–288. *See also specific wars*

Portrait of the Millennial Generation

83% sleep with a cell phone by the bed

75% have a profile on a social networking site

61% say their generation has a unique and distinctive identity

24% of these say it's because of their use of technology

38% have a tattoo

23% have a piercing in some place other than an earlobe

40% identify as moderates

29% identify as liberals

28% identify as conservatives

55% say their generation is more racially tolerant than their elders'

75% agree that "you can't be too careful" when dealing with people

25% are unaffiliated with any religion

15% say being successful is one of the most important things in life

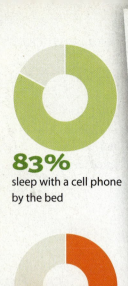

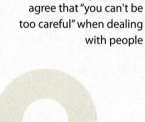

Source: Pew Research Center, *Millennials: Confident, Connected, Open to Change*. February 2010.
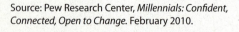